The Collected Poems of
JAMES LAUGHLIN
1935–1997

The Collected Poems of
JAMES LAUGHLIN
1935–1997

Edited with an introduction and notes by
PETER GLASSGOLD

A NEW DIRECTIONS BOOK

Frontispiece photograph of James Laughlin courtesy of New Directions Ownership Trust.

René Magritte's *Les Amants*, reproduced on p. 190, courtesy of the Richard S. Zeisler Collection, New York.
Wyndham Lewis's *Ezra Pound*, reproduced on p. 198, courtesy of the Tate Gallery, London.
The photograph *The Man in the Wall*, reproduced on p. 510, courtesy of Virginia Schendler.

PUBLISHER'S NOTE
Audio files of Laughlin reading from his work are available for download or listening
on the New Directions website:
http://ndbooks.com/LaughlinReading

Book design by Sylvia Frezzolini Severance
Manufactured in the United States of America
New Directions Books are printed on acid-free paper.
First published clothbound in 2014.

LIBRARY OF CONGRESS CATALOGING-IN-PUBLICATION DATA
Laughlin, James, 1914–1997.
The collected poems of James Laughlin, 1935–1997 /
edited with an introduction and notes by Peter Glassgold.
p. cm.
ISBN 978-0-8112-1876-4 (alk. paper) — ISBN 978-0-8112-1877-1 (pbk. : alk. paper)
I. Glassgold, Peter, 1939– II. Title.
PS3523.A8245C65 2010
811'.54—dc22   2010009299

1 3 5 7 9 8 6 4 2

New Directions Books are published for James Laughlin
by New Directions Publishing Corporation
80 Eighth Avenue, New York 10011

CONTENTS

INTRODUCTION

Two things are likely to jump out at a reader taking this book in hand. First, its size and heft. Second, that in the six decades of the writing life of James Laughlin, whose collected poetry this is, more than three quarters of these 1,250-odd poems date from his last fifteen years. This isn't simply a case of Rimbaud in reverse, of a poet actually gaining momentum with age instead of burning out in adolescence, but of a prominent man—a publisher, writer, and entrepreneur—growing in intellectual confidence, coming at last to infuse his later work with all the knowledge and experience that a long and successful life brings, though hardly mellowing. Thomas Hardy, with his darker verse, is perhaps a distant cousin in this regard. The question is, how did this remarkable reversal come about? To answer it requires an understanding of who James Laughlin was and what he did with his life.

As briefly as I can—for the story has been told many times before[1]—he was born in Pittsburgh in 1914 into a wealthy steel-manufacturing family, was educated in elite schools here and abroad, and entered Harvard in 1932. A restless student, he took several leaves of absence, among them some stints at Ezra Pound's informal "Ezuversity" in Rapallo, Italy. Pound, in those days a great mover and shaker in the arts, was critical of Laughlin the would-be poet but strongly urged him to start a publishing company with his family money. Laughlin's always indulgent father agreed, with a start-up gift of $100,000. In 1936, New Directions came into being, three years before the young publisher's tardy graduation from Harvard. The house's first authors were, of course, Pound himself and writers from among his wide circle of friends, William Carlos Williams chief among them (but unlike Pound, Williams encouraged Laughlin as a poet). The list steadily expanded to include an astonishing pantheon of contemporary authors, primarily of the Modernist avant-garde, and quite literally changed what educated Americans read and the way Americans writers wrote and the kinds of poetry and fiction that were taught in our schools.

Until his death in 1997, Laughlin remained attentive to ND's affairs and its authors (he generally signed his office memoranda "JL," which is how I refer to him in this book), all the while writing his own poetry, at first in modest amounts, and publishing it in very modest editions. Then came the creative explosion of his latter years, as much a surprise to him as to the people who knew and appreciated his hitherto small body of work. The honors followed, among them induction into the American Academy of Arts and Letters in 1996. But JL all along considered himself a writer of light verse and never put himself on the same exalted level where he placed his early mentors, Pound and Williams. His self-evaluation is somewhat misleading. As Marjorie Perloff puts it, ". . . his is light verse, not in the tradition of Ogden Nash or Dorothy Parker, but in the line that extends from Catullus . . . to Pound's *Moeurs contemporains* and Williams's 'This Is Just to Say. '"[2] Light verse perhaps, but hardly lightweight.

Besides ND and his writing—and JL published several books of prose in addition to his poetry—he was a great traveler and a businessman who owned and developed the Alta ski lifts and resort amid the Wasatch Range in Utah. For a few years in the mid-'50s, he headed the Ford Foundation's International Publications, which published a quarterly journal, *Perspectives U. S. A.*, that appeared in English, French, German, and Italian editions. He was married three times and fathered four children, while by his own fond admission remaining an untroubled and untiring Don Juan. He also suffered from bipolar disorder, the disease that destroyed his father and caused the early suicide of one of his three sons. All of this is the crucible that made JL the unassuming writer he was and the prolific writer he suddenly became.

A few particulars stand out for me as contributing factors to JL's extraordinary output in old age: his evolving relations with Pound and Williams; the relative falling-off of his travels and concomitant rise in the severity of his manic-depression; his realization that he had an eager and respectful readership; and above all, his deep involvement with New Directions. All of these are interrelated and cannot be teased apart.

JL never forgot Pound's dismissal of his early poetry. He recalls it this way (the year is 1935, during one of his leaves from Harvard; the place, Rapallo):

. . . I was still trying very hard to write poetry. The results were awful—copies of Pound without his virtues. Ezra would take his pencil and slash away, with "No, no, that won't do! You don't need that word. That's slop!" Finally, near the time of my departure, he took me aside and said, "No, Jaz, it's hopeless. You're never gonna make a writer. No matter how hard you try, you'll never make it. I want you to go back to Amurrica and do something useful."

"Waaal, Boss, what's useful?"

He thought a moment and suggested, "Waaal, you might assassernate Henry Seidel Canby. "

But we agreed I wasn't smart enough to get away with it. For a second choice he suggested, "Go back and be a publisher. Go back to Haavud to finish up your studies. If you're a good boy, your parents will give you some money and you can bring out books. I'll write to my friends and get them to provide you with manuscripts."

And that's how it happened.[3]

The joking tone of the recollection belies the wound. As late as the '80s, Gertrude Huston, the longtime book designer for ND who became JL's third wife, told me that what Pound had done to him was unforgivable. What she found unforgivable surely echoed a matter still troubling to JL. But to be fair, Pound didn't remain entirely disapproving, as JL found his voice and peculiar style and Pound himself became, in his querulous way, increasingly beholden to his loyal American publisher. However, it was Williams who was actively supportive of JL the poet and helped him develop his singular "typewriter metrics." It worked like this: the lines in any given stanza could not vary in length more than one typewriter character. The poems were arresting with their spare look and striking, yet seemingly unstudied enjambments. Here is JL writing, from Harvard, to Williams in the spring of 1939:

I am mightily cheered by your approval of the poems. Nobody here understands what I am after at all. They all claim that a visual form cannot relate itself to the tradition of an oral form in poetry and that the lines should be run out like free verse. I personally get an effect of tension from the war between the strictly artificial pattern and the strictly natural spoken rhythms. That is what I have in mind anyway. Also to try to write concretely, using everyday objects for your symbols and allegories and to avoid poeticisms. [4]

Typewriter metrics remained the prosodic touchstone of JL's poetry, even for himself. Here he is again in 1984 and well into his expansive years, which brought with them poems in a variety of free-verse styles:

SOME PEOPLE THINK

that poetry should be a-
dorned or complicated I'm

not so sure I think I'll
take the simple statement

in plain speech compress-
ed to brevity I think that

will do all I want to do.

The '50s saw a painful break between JL and Williams, who had followed David McDowell, ND's sales and promotion manager, first to Random House and then to the short-lived venture of McDowell, Obolensky.[5] During those years, JL wrote a scant amount of poetry, even for him, and even taking into account that he was doing a great deal of traveling for the Ford Foundation. In 1961, matters with Williams were patched up, to the relief of both parties, and then two years later, Williams died, receiving his first and only Pulitzer Prize posthumously. The '60s were another fallow period for JL the poet, perhaps in some measure due to the absence of his old author, trusted counselor, and friend.

Meanwhile, Pound, a supporter of Mussolini, had made rambling propaganda broadcasts from Rome shortly before America's entry into World War II. He was arrested as a traitor in 1945, imprisoned, and eventually committed to St. Elizabeths in Washington, D.C., a hospital for the criminally insane, where he spent twelve years. JL moved from being acolyte to protector, using all his influence to keep Pound—always a difficult person and now clearly not quite in his right mind—from being tried for the capital crime of treason, and in all this, never failing him as his publisher. Even so, Pound in 1957, writing from St. Elizabeths, could comment condescendingly about some of JL's recent poems: "/Verse shows gt improvement/".

I don't mean to suggest that without Pound's elusive respect and Williams's guidance JL for a time lost his calling as a poet. Other ND authors, poets of his own generation—the likes of Hayden Carruth, Robert Fitzgerald, Thomas Merton, and Kenneth Rexroth—admired and encouraged his work, diminished though it was at the time, and he habitually gave his poems to friends as favors and for advice. Merton died suddenly in a freak accident in 1968. JL was crushed by the news. Pound was the next to go, in 1972. JL, now in his fifties, in the middle of his life and beginning to struggle with bouts of manic-depression, seems to have wandered into a dark wood. Like many another poet at a similar pass (and like Pound imprisoned in an open cage near Pisa), he came to himself by writing. He traveled less and retreated to his home in Norfolk, Connecticut, where he spent a few years stitching together from commonplace-book notations and not easily decipherable diary entries what came to be *The Asian Journal of Thomas Merton* (1973). It became apparent to me, while working with him as his house editor at ND, that his absorption in the book and Merton's Eastern quest became for JL a philosophical Asian journey of his own.

With more time and inclination for reflection, he also began writing more poetry, and for the first time without answering to Pound's criticizing presence. The first breakthrough was "In Another Country," a poem longer and unlike anything he'd done before, a narrative recollection, in typewriter metrics, of thirty-two quatrains, that moves easily between English and Italian. Thereafter, the mixing of languages became a hallmark of JL's poetry. Though hardly confessional—that wasn't his way—it is a very personal poem that explores the poignancy of love's awakening and loss, from then on one of JL's recurrent themes. And finally, it points the way to the long, memoiristic verse of *Byways*, the nearest thing he wrote to an autobiography and the companion volume to these *Collected Poems*.[6]

It was at this time that he began making public appearances, generally before academic audiences, speaking to them at first about

Pound, then quite naturally Williams and other of his authors and ND itself. And sometimes, he even read them his own poems. All of this went over extraordinarily well. JL in middle age was a charming and sophisticated man, conversant in several languages, tall and still good-looking, and able to hold his own in any literary milieu. Choate and Harvard were where he took his formal schooling. Pound's Ezuversity gave it polish and focus. But ND was, in effect, where he did the post-graduate work that earned him honorary degrees from Colgate, Cornell (Iowa), Duquesne, Hamilton, and Yale. He was for many of his admir-ers a living legend. In short, full respect came at last, and with it an enthusiastic readership—and for a writer, there is nothing better than a demonstrably appreciative following to keep the words flowing.

"In Another Country" was the first major venture into new poetic territory, and it seems to have galvanized JL to expand beyond typewriter metrics into a range of forms and styles, some successful, some perhaps less so, and with all the evident pleasure and excitement of a young poet trying out his muscles. Sometimes, he even sent his new poems to ND, to be passed around the office. There were prose poems, long-line poems (these often in the voice of his jocular doppelgänger, Hiram Handspring), concrete poems, "picture" poems accompanying graphic images, "(American) French" poems, written largely in *français argotique*, that no Frenchman would ever conceive of, Latin-like invectives and Greek-inspired epigrams, macaronics in English mixed with French, German, Greek, Italian, Latin, and Provençal, mythopoeic and folkloric pieces, the five-line "pentastichs" of his own invention that occupied his last years, along with the three-stress narrative poems that comprise *Byways*[7]—all these, and more. JL took his poems as all of a piece, recy-cling them in book after book, from his first collections through his last.[8] And yet, there are clear polarities in his work—between short- and long-line poems; between poems in what he calls "plain American speech" and, for example, the often studied compositions among his "stolen" poems";[9] between his intended openness and clarity and his penchant for what is "secret" in life—the word appears frequently in poem and book titles. This last isn't entirely surprising in a man perennially taken up with affairs of the heart, and in point of fact, the word "love" outstrips "secret" in his poems at least three to one. JL considered himself a love poet, and it pleased him that the Italian editions of his work—translat-ed by Pound's daughter, Mary de Rachewiltz—earned him the honorific

Il Catullo americano, the American Catullus. But here, too, is another polarity: for a love poet, JL is intensely cerebral.

And yet, looking over the whole of JL's work—no matter what the form or style or subject—you can, in fact, find a unifying thread: New Directions. I don't mean simply his personal involvement with his authors or in the long history of the house, though of course there is that; of equal consequence is his immersion in the books themselves. JL's evolving *oeuvre* is the counterweight to ND's evolving list. Should there be any doubt, you have only to peruse JL's notes to his poems to understand their provenance. To put it another way, the poems and ND together comprise JL's intellectual biography; even his few but telling deeply personal poems, those concerning his family, evidence his remarkable sensibility. Here is my advice to the reader of this book. Open these *Collected Poems* at random or take it at your leisure from beginning to end, but when you do, consider how it came about. You may think of it as "The Education of James Laughlin" and, by good fortune, perhaps a furtherance of your own.

PETER GLASSGOLD

NOTES

1   For Laughlin's own accounts of New Directions' founding, see his *Pound as Wuz* (St. Paul, MN: Graywolf, 1987) and *Byways* (New York: New Directions, 2005), as well as "Some Memories of E.P. (Drafts & Fragments)" in the present volume, pp. 387-389.

2   Marjorie Perloff, "Foreword" to JL's *Selected Poems 1935–1983*, p. 265.

3   *Pound As Wuz*, p. 7. Henry Seidel Canby was the influential editor of the *Saturday Review of Literature*.

4   *William Carlos Williams and James Laughlin: Selected Letters*, edited by Hugh Witemeyer (New York: W. W. Norton, 1989), pp. 45–46.

5   JL recounts the episode in "Remembering Williams Carlos Williams," *Byways*, pp. 173–83.

6   James Laughlin, *Byways: A Memoir*, edited by Peter Glassgold (New York: New Directions, 2005). See my Editor's Note, p. 1003.

7   JL writes, "I owe the metric to my old friend and mentor Kenneth Rexroth. He perfected the essentially three-beat line in his travel poem *The Dragon & The Unicorn*, which I published at New Directions in 1941." "A Note on the Metric," *The Country Road* (Cambridge, MA: Zoland Books, 1995), p. 105; reprinted in *The Secret Room* (New York: New Directions, 1997) and *Poems New and Selected* (New York: New Directions, 1998).

8   See my Editor's Note, p. 1003, on the organization of the present volume.

9   See present volume, pp. 169–86 and p. 626.

The Collected Poems of
JAMES LAUGHLIN
1935–1997

UNCOLLECTED POEMS
AND TRANSLATIONS

(1935–1948)

A BIRTHDAY FUGUE

hot sea calm
and mind whirl
these hours of words

mind whirl
o troubled land
be gentle

hot sea calm
words turning
turn to you

these hours
i give you
o gentle

sea whirl
mind calm
to you turning

these i give
gentle hours
my words

mind sea
turn gently
to you

THE GLACIER AND LOVE'S
IGNORANT TONGUE

The sloth of the glacier
surpasseth understanding
"like I could fly" he said

"just like I could fly
in the air like an angel
like a bird fly all over

hell and see everything
everywhere all at once"
the life of the glacier

its whole life turning
slow flanks of snow from
generation to generation

would be too short except
that a breath one breath
is far too long & "it's

just like somebody" he said
"kept hitting you and you
said go ahead mister please

hit me again only harder"
dear ice dear ageless ice
tell me the word you know

it won't burn my tongue
because her kiss "time?"
asked the glacier "what's

that?—look at these tiny
flowers blooming in clumps!
isn't rain wonderful?" Oh

tongue ignorant tongue
find me the word I don't
care if you cut yourself

to pieces on my teeth just
find me this word that
glaciers know to tell her.

ON YOUR LEFT ST. PATRICK'S CATHEDRAL AND ON YOUR RIGHT ROCKEFELLER CITY

Adore the stone and
kiss it what wonderful
water does it really?

yessir he was hot stuff
all right he went to town
he had the goods and he

for the old man with
cataracts for the steno-
grapher in bad trouble

even for Mrs O'Grady
the papal marchioness
provided well provided

well like a rich uncle
leaving things quite
comfortable across the

street just over there
is Mr Junior John D Jr
providing well providing

well providing that the
great feet of the Stan-
dard Oil Co of NY of NJ

of Indiana & California
shall trample on prosti-
tution intoxication il-

literacy ugliness & in
fact almost everything
except the cold wind

doth blow doth blow O
Jesus & Mr Junior this
cold cold wind doth blow

take care of me and the
working man (don't bother
with me I'm just the Mon-

golian idiot) but do take
care of the working man oh
you must take care of the

working man *please* take
care of the working man
dear Jesus & Mr Junior!

WARNING!

Love me love me love
me all you like (I

love it) but I warn
you I'll marry only

a princess a princess
with real golden hair!

WHAT MY HEAD DID TO ME

I guess I like myself
pretty well anyway I
wanted a statue of my-
self so I had a woman

make one it was a head
and she modelled it in
clay then one night I
dreamed I'd killed my

very best friend and
there was my head right
there ready to tell on
me when the police came

I tried to destroy the
face so they wouldn't
know it was me but my
hands stuck tight in

the clay I couldn't
tear them loose and
there I was when the
police came held by my

own head with the body
of my friend multi-
plying itself like
endless mirrors down

the street that's the
thing my head did to
me but of course it
was only a dream see.

POOR MAN'S LOVE SONG

Overcome by my doubts
of time and having no
money for travel nor

patience for study I
volunteered as second
hand (night shift) on

your watch where now
I rotate and revolve
circling your hours in

a minute tread life
here is like a board-
ing house with open

secrets back of every
door last night some-
body screamed we have

our climate suns and
seasons rains and even
snow you make it and I

wish you would remember
we are sensitive next
time he comes next time

I come take off your
watch these storms
shake all our world

and someone will be
killed someone will
die what if it's I?

MADE IN THE OLD WAY

I'll tell you a secret
it was god made you god

in the old way made you
mostly out of fire and

air no man and woman
love could make some-

thing like you no it
was god you know the

big guy up there with
the thunderbeating

heart of purest gold
oh no not gold that's

wrong the thunderbeat-
ing heart of purest you!

THE ROSE THAT TASTES OF LOVE

Take eat this is my
rose see how each

petal clutches at
the heart pull off

the petals you must
taste the rose and

then the heart will
speak your tongue

will speak for me
your tongue will

tell the things that
roses know the rose

that blooms above
the thorn the rose

that tastes of love
and holds my heart.

THIS ROLLING STONE

This rolling stone
collecting moss be-

neath your tree rolls
round and round and

round this rolling
stone would like to

roll away but here
the moss is such

good moss such extra-
special moss beneath

this tree the poor old
stone (all round from

rolling) can't control
its circularity and so

it rolls and rolls and
rolls around your tree!

OH MR. TCHELITCHEW
HOW COULD YOU BE SO MEAN

Really said the leopard
boy you know I really

like it here it isn't at
all bad hell no said the

threelegged man I never
ate this good before oh

yes the fat lady said I
do think that young Mr.

Ford is just too sweet
I'm so glad he's here

yes isn't it lovely the
way he looks after Mr.

Mr. you know isn't that
awful here all this time

and I can't even say his
name mistake lovey mis-

take why it's libel and
I think we should see a

lawyer and after all we
did for him well as long

as they don't do worse'n
put me in a picture I'll

be damned if I care said
the banker what do I say

about this picture said
the tall one down in the

hole down in that hole
with all those books and

things what do I think
about this picture here

why frankly I think it's
absolutely PHENOMENAL!

LOVE LIKE THE WIND

Love to the heart
is twice times two
makes four adore
and I love you

love to the mind
so many queens
I hold no king
you have my dreams

love to the hand
oh hand be loving
touch not yet touch
all touch removing

love to the eye
oh eye be blind
or jealous heart
will war with mind

love to the lips
a voice I heard
said love in truth
is a golden bird

love to the bird
perhaps a game
when I win you
is all the same

love in the book
the page the tear
the hand so far
the heart so near

love heart love lips
love bird and mind
love only one
love like the wind!

THAT BIG LIE

I'm going to tell you
a big lie but I want

you to believe it I'm
going to tell you that

I like you better than
I like myself and I'd

like you to believe it
that's obviously a lie

because everybody likes
himself best especially

a poet poets like them-
selves so much they'll

never get over telling
about it nevertheless

and notwithstanding my
story is that I like a

certain you even more
than a certain me and

that's my story and I
wish you'd believe it!

SPEECH BEFORE DEPARTURE

TASILO RIBISCHKA

Twixt which and what lies Never in the neoteric mind.
As sand refuses sea as fishey fruit rejects her touch
So in the little island of the virgin's aqueous eye
Illicit titillations tell the hours' toll. O pretty hand
Let claws sprout on your love-telling fingers, let me
Open bank accounts of blood in every city where the
Roaring tongue of time claps out all mortal finishment.

In such a moment must my poor tongue tattle poetry
Before the great guns explode and the mirror of state
In which the apes gawp, bend inward, melt and flow away;
So cruising in the narrow strait beside the heart,
Cutting with vatic prow death's thickening thickening ice,
Hear now for the last time this precious roland-horn—
Katharsis of history, spilling our tears on the page—

And make your choice for the last time, knowing that you
Shall have no choice, no voice, no hope, no way of flight
And no surrender. For this, beloved, is the end of the line.
Yes, this, at last, is where we all get out and walk. So,
Shut your eyes. Sew down the lids with wire. Bend down
Both ears and lace them to the skull. Flatten the nose
And tear the fingers out. Make fast all senses in the

Last inglorious prison of the bowel. Cast off the
Lines, the voyage must begin. Look where our corncob captain
Shitters to the bridge—he's so majestic, so titanic with
That growth of No-Day's beard. He frightens all the gulls,
O noble sailor, pilot of a noble bark, isn't it curious
You have no trousers on? Your cap is like a crown and
On those warlike shoulders fits superb a super-regal
Uniform . . . and yet below . . . you have no trousers on.

A LETTER TO DOSTOYEVSKY

You knew that life
doesn't happen in

life the way it does
in books and you put

that down and you
knew that people

never say what they
do in books and you

put that down put
it down so hard it

will stay there and
now if thousands of

little pimple minds
worm in your corpse

it doesn't matter
at all if you can

still remember how
sometimes after you

put it down hard it
was so good you knew

it was so good that
everything inside you

burned like glory
so you couldn't sit

still but had to rush
up and down the room

biting your jaws and
shouting jesus jesus

jesus jesus jesus
christ remember that!

WHICH WORDS TO USE

The word spring and
the word love & the

word sky are forbid-
den and defended &

absolutely verboten
but I'll try to tell

you just what I mean
with a few words like

rug the old red one in
the hall and clock the

big tall one in grand-
father's library that

had the mouse nest in
it and soap the yellow

kind we always had in
the bathtub and words

like that the ones we
really have that save

us from the outside
world & frightful time.

IT DOESN'T MAKE SENSE DOES IT?

I have been falling
down this hole for

days and months and
years there seems to

be no bottom to it
sometimes I catch on

a ledge for a moment
but then slip off a-

gain and fall and fall
end over end bumping

and banging covered
with bruises & cuts

& yet no matter how
far I go I still can

see the white spot of
light at the top of the

hole oh of course it
gets smaller but the

funny thing is this it
gets brighter too gets

brighter all the time
brighter and brighter

it doesn't make sense
does it but it's true!

EPITHALAMIUM

The moon costs ten
cents sickle moons

to order five cents
extra we can sup-

ply starry heavens
on two days notice

with or without the
milky way all these

items have proven
extremely satisfac-

tory but the truth
is folks that love

in a pinch can get
along fine without

anything all by it-
self love that grows

everywhere on trees
love that grows green

as grass love that costs
nothing & everything!

THE FOURTH ECLOGUE

VIRGIL

Muses
Muses of Sicily
Now let us sing a serious song
There are taller trees than the apple and the crouching tamarisk
If we sing of the woods, let our forest be stately

Now the last age is coming
As it was written in the Sybil's book
The great circle of the centuries begins again
Justice, the Virgin, has returned to earth
With all of Saturn's court
A new line is sent down to us from the skies
And thou, Lucina, must smile
Smile for the birth of the boy, the blessed boy
For whom they will beat their swords into ploughshares
For whom the golden race will rise, the whole world new
Smile, pure Lucina, smile
Thine own Apollo will reign

And thou, Pollio
It is in thy term this glorious age begins
And the great months begin their march
When we shall lose all trace of the old guilt
And the world learn to forget fear
For the boy will become divine

He will see gods and heroes
And will himself be seen by them as god and hero
As he rules over a world of peace
A world made peaceful by his father's wisdom

For thee, little boy, will the earth pour forth gifts
All untilled, give thee gifts
First the wandering ivy and foxglove
Then colocasia and the laughing acanthus
Uncalled the goats will come home with their milk
No longer need the herds fear the lion
Thy cradle itself will bloom with sweet flowers
The serpent will die
The poison plant will wither
Assyrian herbs will spring up everywhere

And when thou art old enough to read of heroes
And of thy father's great deeds
Old enough to understand the meaning of courage
Then will the plain grow yellow with ripe grain
Grapes will grow on brambles
Hard old oaks drip honey

Yet still there must remain some traces of the old guilt
That lust that drives men to taunt the sea with ships
To circle cities with walls
And cut the earth with furrows
There must be another Tiphys
Another Argo carrying picked men
And there must be a war, one final war
With great Achilles storming a last Troy

But when thou hast grown strong and become a man
Then even the trader will leave the sea
His pine ship carry no more wares
And everywhere the land will yield all things that life requires
No longer need the ground endure the harrow
Nor the vine the pruning hook

The farmer can free his oxen from the yoke
Then coloured cloths no longer will need lying dyes
For the ram in the field will change his own fleece
To soft purple or saffron yellow
Each grazing lamb will have a scarlet coat

"Onward, O glorious ages, onward"
Thus sang the fatal sisters to their spindles
Chanting together the unalterable Will

Go forward, little boy, to thy great honours
Soon comes thy time
Dear child of gods from whom a Jupiter will come
See how for thee the world nods its huge head
All lands and seas and endless depths of sky
See how the earth rejoices in the age that is to be

O may my life be long enough to let me sing of thee
With strength enough to tell thy deeds
With such a theme not even Thracian Orpheus could outsing me
Not Linus either, though Apollo prompted him
Help from Calliope herself could not make Orpheus' song the best
And even Pan, with Arcady as judge
Yes Pan, would fall before me when I sang of thee

Learn, little boy, to greet thy mother with a smile
For thee she has endured nine heavy months
Learn, little boy, to smile
For if thou didst not smile
And if thy parents did not smile on thee
No god could ask thee to his table
No goddess to her bed.

SONG IN TIME OF DROUGHT

BENJAMIN PERET

Sky of a hanged man, is it going to rain?
if it rains I'll eat water-cress
unless it rains lobsters

Sky of a heel, is it going to rain?
if it rains you'll have fried potatoes
unless it rains jail

Pigs-gut sky, is it going to rain?
if it rains you'll have an onion
unless it rains vinegar

Policeman sky, is it going to rain?
if it rains you'll have a donkey
unless it rains skunks

Cuckold sky, is it going to rain?
if it rains I'll have a wife
unless it rains your girls

Parson sky, is it going to rain?
if it rains you'll be butchered
if it doesn't rain you'll be burned

Stable sky, it is going to rain?
if it rains you'll have stones
unless it rains flies

Sky of a witch, is it going to rain?
if it rains you'll get a comb
if not a shovel

Sewer sky, is it going to rain?
if it rains you'll have a flag
if it doesn't rain a crucifix

Is it going to rain, sky of ashes?

MY FINAL AGONIES

BENJAMIN PERET

To Yves Tanguy

  270 The birches are worn out by mirrors
  441 The young father lights a candle and gets undressed
  905 How many have died in sweeter morgues
1097 The eyes of the strongest
1371 Maybe the old people have forbidden the young ones to go
         into the desert
1436 First memory of pregnant women
1525 My foot's asleep in a brass bowl
1668 My heart exposed to the aorta moves from East to West
1793 A card looks on and waits
         For the dice
1800 Polishing, that's the least important
1845 Stroke the chin and wash the breasts
1870 It's snowing in the devil's stomach
1900 The children of the invalids have had their beards trimmed
1914 You'll find some gasoline but it won't be for you
1922 They're burning the social register in the Place de l'Opéra

ROUND OF THE SIDEWALKS

BENJAMIN PERET

The storm breaks in the bureau-drawer
And it's a fight to the death
Between the comb and the salsify
The comb has teeth made of salsify
And the hair of the salsify falls to its heels
They stare at each other like china dogs
The dogs that break like glass
Because they wanted to bark

And the china wouldn't let them
Goodbye china dog, salsify and comb
My waistcoat buttons are singing like mad
And the top one takes a streetcar
He goes to la Villette
He walks down the Rue de Flandres
There he buys some wooden shoes
And the streetcar tracks applaud
He says hello to the steaming horse turds
Over which the sparrows flutter
What horsemanship cries a little old woman
Who wears a pair of sugar tongs in her hair
And her little grandchildren who limp
(The ones born in the even years
Limping with their left legs
And the others on the right)
Follow a pair of mating dogs throwing stones at them
It's raining
And the old woman's hair melts into the sugar tongs
Her head is just a huge beet
The children have eaten its leaves
The beet trembles
And the houses trickle away like melting butter
Spread out like parachutes
But my waistcoat buttons go off down the street
Arm in arm like drunken sailors

AND SO ON AND SO FORTH

BENJAMIN PERET

One more kick in the behind
and the empty sardine box will think itself saintly
A good sock in the snoot
and it's a deity

swimming in pure honey
paying no attention to the protozoöns
and the hippocamps
and the celestial pebbles that flutter from one eye to the other
carrying common sense
with a little sauce and its teeth broken
in the company of cabbage stalks
which no longer know where to look
now that the fat waters smother themselves in sables.

GEORGIA

PHILLIPE SOUPAULT

I am not sleeping Georgia
I am shooting arrows into the night
I am waiting Georgia
I am thinking Georgia
Fire is like snow
Night is my neighbor
I listen to every sound Georgia
I see the smoke that rises and flees
I run like a wolf in the shadows Georgia
I am running, here is the street, the suburb Georgia
This is a city like every other city
And yet I do not know it Georgia
I hurry, here comes the wind Georgia
And the cold and silence and fear Georgia
I flee Georgia
I'm running away
The clouds are low, they are going to fall Georgia
I stretch out my arms Georgia
I do not shut my eyes
I call Georgia
I shout Georgia

I call Georgia
I call you
Will you come Georgia
Soon Georgia
Georgia Georgia Georgia
Georgia
I cannot sleep Georgia
I am waiting for you Georgia
Georgia

A POEM WITH AN EXTRA LINE

I doubt if many other poets
will celebrate it but never-

theless I find worthy of
celebration the fact that

in the last few years there
has occurred a very unim-

portant social change I re-
fer naturally to the serving

of the salad prior to the
main course rather than

after it in restaurants thru-
out the length and breadth of

our long and broad land and
this fellow citizens is per-

haps a phenomenon to which
you have not devoted your

best thoughts but neverthe-
less I would like to point

out that it clearly portends
the ultimate arrival of the

human race at a Utopian con-
dition of social grace since

it shows how functional u-
tility will break down er-

roneous upper class con-
ventions as friends it is

plain that people do need
something to chew on while

steak & state are cooking

HOW SAD

"It may not be yours
but the grave is my

goal said to my still
interested body my so

bored & overstuffed
soul" tonight unex-

pectedly a bird sang
very beautifully out

in the dark it made
me jump up from my

chair of disgust & run
out into the moonlight

of memories & fresh
desires but soon the

bird stopped and I
couldn't remember him

back so I just mixed
me a nice comforting

drink of thinking of
not having to be alive.

SOLDIERS' POETRY DEPARTMENT

OUR JOES

there are two jews in our outfit, joe,
two donkeys and a jackass, joe,
    and three small toucans, also named joe
and we treat them all just like men
  they all are men
    they bleed
      they fight
        they hate
          they are our buddies and our allies
            like the chinese
              yugoslavs
                and recently, but only recently,
                  venezuelans.

last night my toucan came back with a japanese eye,
  two days ago, joe (the jackass) brayed at the right time during
      a morale lecture
  and i know he understands and hates fascism too;
    he knows that beneath a dictatorship
      he would have less chance of coming into his own
        than under a democracy.
some men will have it the japs are human,
    but are they?

joes are more human than japs any day
  and no japs are named joe
    q e d

have you ever seen a jap in a px
  or in g i shoes
  or defended in yank?
    have you?
      ever?
     no?

our joes do all these things and they are americans
    red-blooded and fighting heroic americans
        cocky khaki
           alive drab americans
just like you too, maybe, you jew who reads my poem
    or you, you jackass,
        or even you, you toucan.

GLOSSING'S GLOSS

you know why there are no atheists in foxholes?
because there is no god in foxholes;
true there are pits in the sands of the islands of the south pacific
and there are men in the pits in the sands of the islands of the south
    pacific
and there is grace in the hearts of the men in the pits in the sands of
    the islands of the south pacific
and the commanding officers of the camps put the grace in the hearts
    of the men in the pits in the sands of the islands of the south pacific
since the division neuropsychiatrist told the commanding officers of
    the camps to put the grace in the hearts of the men
    in the pits in the sands of the islands of the south pacific,
because by general directive of the surgeon general's office which
    itself is subject only to the will of god so far as we know this was
    a good thing.
actually the men do not exist to be either religious or atheist
and the foxholes are not put there to try their faith
the men are there to fight
by general directive
emanating from almost the same sources
and for almost the same reasons.
perhaps they are fighting for the grace which enables them to fight
    for the grace for which they are fighting.

ET ITERUM VENTURUS

you must know, sean, that last night
as i lay beside the new hay i saw a vision of golgotha
where beloved jesu had become old and wizened
and white-bearded and moustached
  and had thick glasses
    with rims;
and the men round him were armed not with spears
  but with sickles and hammers and ukases
    surrounded they him and hung
      beside him two thieves
        on double crosses
          bukharin
          zinoviev

and when he died a red star appeared in the east over bedlam
  they held sponges to his lips and these were moistened
    with the bitter blood of betrayed workers
      and he cried out saying,
szob tze beh cholera bisabralyeh, i am the insurrection and the life,
      and again,
ich hob dir in bod—no taxation without representation
      and even further,
a bas, a bas, a bas, a bas, abavit abat, abamus abatis.

his suffering was past all n duhring
the engels of the dead came and comforted him
saying, lo, we are the agents of historical necessity,
    we are very small, formerly
we were very large our quantity having been transformed
        into quality.
the women came to take him to the tomb
thesis took his right arm
antithesis his left
    synthesis
        his feet
          and he
            was

32

carried   away.
glory to him who was washed in the blood of the lumpenproletariat.
i have seen the signs of the imminent class wars
(curry a liason, curry a liason—a crisis has risen)
they are pulling down the settings where the grapes of wrath
          was filmed.

and whether you call him marx or trotzky
abraham lincoln or lenin or artemus ward
or william dean howells or bret harte
it is all the same
    it is all the same
        and he will come again
            just watch and see.

PSYCHOMACHIA IN JUKE TIME

TASILO RIBISCHKA

Awash with sex I floundered
before her fishwide mouth

hippiate piscatory blondina
she was my midriff's morsel

Pretty princess, I softly sibilated
Let us sojourn briefly in my hotel room

Sir, she replied, I cannot oblige you
It is time for my daily samadhi

Sorrowfully then I departed
dragged leaden feet from that place

In childhood my mother imparted
Respect for Holy Things!

LIBERTY

PAUL ÉLUARD

On my schoolboy's notebooks
On my desk and the trees
On the sand on the snow
I write your name

On all the pages I have read
And on all the blank pages
Stone blood paper or ashes
I write your name

On the golden figures
On the warriors' arms
On the crown of kings
I write your name

On jungle and desert
On birdsnests and heath flowers
Over the echo of my childhood
I write your name

On the wonders of night
On the white bread of day
On seasons betrothed
I write your name

On all my scraps of sky
On the pond musty sun
On the lake living moon
I write your name

Over the fields on the horizon
On the wings of birds
And on the windmill of shadows
I write your name

On every puff of dawn
On the sea and on ships
On the mad mountain
I write your name

On the foam of the clouds
On the sweat of the storm
On rain thick and savourless
I write your name

On sparkling shapes
On the bells of the colors
On physical truth
I write your name

On lively pathways
On far-stretching roads
On crowded squares
I write your name

On the lamp that is lighted
On the lamp that has gone out
On all my houses together
I write your name

On the fruit cut in half
On the mirror and my room
On my bed empty seashell
I write your name

On my dog greedy and loving
On his cocked ears
On his clumsy paw
I write your name

On the springboard of my door
On all familiar things
On the torrent of holy fire
I write your name

Everything that is human is revealed in your eyes
Paris my lovely city
Delicate as a needle strong as a sword
Innocent and wise
You will never tolerate injustice
That for you is the only evil
You will free yourself Paris
Paris trembling like a star
Our hope which survives
You will free yourself from weariness and slime
Brothers have courage
For we who are not helmeted
Nor booted nor gloved nor well brought up
Something is catching fire in our veins
Our light returns to us
The best among us have died for the rest of us
And now their blood finds its way back into our hearts
And it's morning again a morning of Paris
The dawn of deliverance
The time of the newborn spring
Idiot strength is beaten down
Those slaves our enemies
If they have understood
If they are capable of understanding
Will rise.

DAWN DISSOLVES THE MONSTERS

PAUL ÉLUARD

They did not know
That the beauty of man is greater than man

They lived to think but thinking were silent
They lived to die they were useless
They regained their innocence in death

They had put in order
In the name of wealth
Their sorrow their beloved

They were munching flowers and smiles
They could only find hearts at the end of their rifles

They did not understand the curses of the poor
The poor without troubles tomorrow

Sunless dreams were making them eternal
But to change the cloud into mud
They came down taking their heads from the sky

All their night their death their beautiful shadow sorrow
Their sorrow for others

We shall forget these immaterial enemies

For soon a multitude
Will repeat the pure flame in soft voices
The flame that is ours ours alone enduring
For the two of us everywhere the kiss of the living

KILLING

PAUL ÉLUARD

Tonight there falls
A strange peace over Paris
A peace of blind eyes
And colorless dreams
Knocking against walls
A peace of useless arms
And conquered brows

Of men who are far away
And women already withered
Pale cold and unweeping
Tonight there falls
In the silence
A strange glow over Paris
Over the good old heart of Paris
The hidden glow of crime
Premeditated savage and pure
Of crime against the butcher
And against death.

TO HER OF WHOM THEY ARE DREAMING

PAUL ÉLUARD

Nine hundred thousand prisoners of war
Five hundred thousand political prisoners
A million forced laborers

Mistress of their slumber
Give them the strength of men
Gladness of being on the earth
Give them in their great darkness
The lips of a soft love
Like forgetfulness of their suffering

Mistress of their slumbers
Girl and woman sister and mother
Whose breasts are swollen with kisses
Give them our country
As they have always loved her
A country crazy with life

A land where the wine sings
And the harvests are hearty
Where the children are cunning
And where the old men are finer
Than fruit trees white with blossom
A country where you can talk to women

Nine hundred thousand prisoners of war
Five hundred thousand political prisoners
A million forced laborers

Mistress of their slumber
Black snow of white nights
Through a bloodless fire
Holy Dawn with a white cane
Show them a new road
Outside of their wooden prisons

They have paid the full price to know
The worst forces of evil
And still they have kept good
They are riddled with virtues
As many as their wounds
Because they have to survive

Mistress of their rest
Mistress of their waking
Give to them liberty
But keep for us the shame
Of having believed in our shame
Even to annihilate it.

AN OLD SCHOOLBOOK

Principles of Geometry
a long time and patiently
you have been waiting for me

to understand your lesson
are your margins still
nervous with my messy scrawl

yes there's the square
head of my roommate Henry
Barkhausen and that one must

be Dick Pinkham who payed
me eighty cents a week
to do his Cicero and there's

fat old Mr Kenington himself
scratching his stomach on
the corner of his desk

during his lectures to us
on the figures that we never
understood but learned

by rote to parrot back
to him in daily tests and if
we got them wrong we used

to run back to the classroom
during lunch & change the
papers in his desk be-

fore he marked them marks
marks I hungered and I
yearned and burned for marks

the way the other boys
craved girls or being on the
hockey team nothing could

stop me nothing did until
I was head boy in school and
now here is my book a-

gain here after twenty
years principles of geometry
turning these pages now I

think I understand the
figures look at these paral-
lelograms & squares these

hollow shapes aren't they
the spaces empty spaces
that spread out through all

the grown-up lives we waited
for with such desire &
see the lines that cut a-

cross the spaces are they
not the things the women and
the money the ambition

and the wars & all the false
ideas that destroy our
life & eat into our soul?

SOME NATURAL THINGS

(1945)

THE POET TO THE READER

These poems are not I
hope what anyone ex-

pects and yet reader
I hope that when you

read them you will say
I've felt that too but

it was such a natural
thing it was too plain

to see until you saw
it for me in your poem.

THE PUBLISHER TO THE POET

Right hand blush never
for left handed brother

action and thought are
children of one mother.

ON THE GIFT OF A SAPPHIRE
TO MY WIFE

A blue stone seems a
hard cold thing to say

love but remember its
history formed in those

ancient fires which
burned long before man

and his little thought
of time it has endured

most endlessly and will
most endlessly endure!

THE MOUNTAIN AFTERGLOW

Afterglow goldens the
peak its rock beak glows

like raw blood and red
red is the snowfield

beneath it inevitably my
thoughts go to Christ's

blood which our weakness
drinks and to the blood

of another useless hope-
less war then from its

blackness the heart cries
to the peak O give us a

sign make us a sign
but back to our valley

comes only the sun's
dying glow as so softly

so delicately the bright
rock and snow fade into

night and night clouds
fold dark on the stars.

THE HAIRS OF MY
GRANDFATHER'S HEAD

My rich old scotch
grandfather made
his money selling

lots in a cemetery
and had a pure bald
head where once in

a while a little
stiff bristle would
grow that bothered

him so much he'd
make me stand on a
stool and pull it

out with tweezers
heart, listen to me
beware this girl who

comes bearing gifts
you never even would
have dreamed of then

Grandfather's head lies
underground it shines
there like a mirror!

THE MOUNTAIN

There is a great snow
mountain that I know

it is the Kanchenjunga
of my world of night

rising again and again
before me in my dreams

always the same iden-
tical glacier fields of

snow iced ridge over &
all the shining rocky

peak I try to climb it
and I always fail some

nights it is exhaustion
stops me on the ridge

some times a blizzard
cuts me off or snow so

deep I sink up to my
waist and wallowing

helplessly can see above
clear of the clouds and

gleaming in the sun
aflame with sun with

brightest sun afire the
holy peak the rock of

love all knowledge high-
est hope mortal desire!

EASTER IN PITTSBURGH

Even on Easter Sunday
when the church was a

jungle of lilies and
ferns fat Uncle Paul

who loved his liquor
so would pound away

with both fists on the
stone pulpit shouting

sin sin sin and the
fiery fires of hell

and I cried all after-
noon the first time I

heard what they did to
Jesus it was something

the children shouldn't
know about till they

were older but the new
maid told me and both

of us cried a lot and so
mother got another one

right away and she sent
away Miss Richardson

who came all the way
from England because

she kept telling how
her fiancé Mr. Bowes-

Lyon died suddenly of
a heart attack he just

said one day at lunch
I'm afraid I'm not well

and the next thing they
knew he was sliding un-

der the table. Easter
was nice the eggs were

silly but the big lilies
were wonderful & when

Uncle Paul got so fat
from drinking that he

couldn't squeeze into
the pulpit anymore &

had to preach from the
floor there was an el-

ders' meeting and they
said they would have

the pulpit rebuilt but
Uncle Paul said no it

was the Lord's manifest
will and he would pass

his remaining years in
sacred studies. I liked

Thanksgiving better be-
cause that was the day

father took us down to
the mills but Easter I

liked next best and the
rabbits died because we

fed them beet tops and
the lamb pulled up the

grass by the roots and
was sold to Mr. Page the

butcher I asked Uncle
Robert what were sacred

studies he said he was
not really sure but he

guessed they came in a
bottle and mother sent

me away from the table
when I wouldn't eat my

lamb chops that was
ridiculous she said it

wasn't the lamb of God
it was just Caesar An-

dromache Nibbles but I
couldn't I just wouldn't

& the year of the strike
we didn't go to Church

at all on Easter because
they said it wasn't safe

down town so instead we
had prayers in the library

and then right in the mid-
dle the telephone rang it

was Mr. Shupstead at the
mill they had had to use

tear gas father made a
special prayer right a-

way for God's protection
& mercy and then he sent

us out to the farm with
mother we stayed a week

and missed school but it
rained a lot and I broke

the bathroom mirror and
had to learn a long psalm.

THE VISITOR

Tell me implacable girl
whom do you think that

your everlasting silence
is starving? you refuse

to see me you won't an-
swer my letters or the

telephone but six times
in the last month you

have walked right into
my dreams filling sleep

with incalculable bright-
ness your visits are so

wonderful more gentle
more tender more gay

than ever you were be-
fore come again and a-

gain implacable girl
my love awaits you!

THE CAT & DOG AT LOVE'S DOOR

Look now see the cat cling
to the screen door crying

to come in where people
are moving and talking

behind her the dog waits
on the step waits till

the door is opened when
he'll jump in and leave

the cat still clinging
to the screen and crying

let me come in now let me in
where all the people are

love is the cat the cat
is love that clings that

cries and can't get in before
the dog o heart my heart

be quicker than the waiting
dog keep him outside if he

gets in you'll have an empty
house and hear the cat cry

all night long o heart be
quick tell hand be quick

hold back the dog and
let that poor cat in

the dog will bark oh yes
a thousand dogs will bark

but you'll have love inside
and you can close the door

envoi

poor cat great prince all
powerful shining love I am

the dog the dog am I but I go
out where you have entered in!

GO WEST YOUNG MAN

Yessir they're all named
either Ken or Stan or Don
every one of them and

those aren't just nick-
names either no they're
really christened like

that just Ken or Stan or
Don and you shake hands
with anybody you run into

no matter who the hell
it is and say "glad to
know you Ken glad to

know you Don" and then
two minutes later (you
may not have said ten

words to the guy) you
shake hands again and
say "glad to have met

you Stan glad to" and
they haven't heard much
about Marx and the class

struggle because they
haven't had to and by
god it makes a country

that is fit to live in
and by god I'm glad to
know you Don I'm glad!

A LETTER TO HITLER

Last winter we were
short of firewood and

it was good and cold
so we used a lot of

old books that were
in the attic just old

novels nobody would
ever want to read but

we found they made
plenty of heat and

twice they set the
chimney afire when

a burning page went
up with the draft and

we found they would
smoulder a long time

after you thought the
fire was all out and

then suddenly burst
into flame & another

thing they made ashes
that wouldn't stay in

the grate but floated
out all over the room!

FRAGMENT

. . . come out of the
station into the story-

book snow and there
they all are lined up

by their sleighs bowing
and greeting & touching

their caps with the
gold-lettered names—

Beau Soleil Alpenrose
Park Post and Adler

Beau Sejour Palace
Sport Continental &

if God loves me I'll
one day lie down again

under the unmanageable
big feather puffs of the

Hotel Vierjahrzeiten
with the cold pitcher

& basin watching over
what is called my soul.

IN THE SNOW

The track of the ermine
the track of the mouse

tracks of a deer in the
snow and my track that

wanders and hesitates
doubling and crossing

itself stops to burrow
and circles trees this

track I made twists like
the veins in a leaf or a

crack in a mirror and it
cries seems to cry cries

to the sun cries sun sun
touch and burn cries sun

touch and save cries to
the sun—and then snow

falls covering everything
new snow covers my track

covers the track of the
ermine mouse and deer.

PAPER & STRING

Her husband lies in
a paper grave poor

man it wasn't cream
and sugar he wanted

now her heart's bound
with doubtful string

but her fingers itch
already to untie it!

OLD DR GOD

Sure everybody laughs at
Old Dr God and his medi-

cine sometimes it kills
you sometimes it cures

you sometimes it leaves
you just like you were

Old Dr God with coffee
on his beard & the same

old jokes year after year
and that old brown bag

that never has what he
wants in it sure every-

body laughs at Old Dr God
or that is they laugh in the

daytime but when it comes
night and their belly starts

to ache oh boy do they hol-
ler and bust out in a sweat

& send out a hurry call
for good Old Dr God!

THE HUNTING DOG

You know that comical
puppy has grown up in-

to a marvelous hunting
dog he's in the woods

all day & brings out
rabbits by the dozen

but the funny thing is
he never hurts them he

doesn't ever bite them
just carries them home

in his mouth & leaves
them on the porch for

us poor little things
at first they're much

too scared to move but
in a little while they

shake themselves & hop
away to the woods again

envoi

love love huntress re-
lentless I know you'll

be after me as long as
I live but why not take

a lesson from our dog
who only hunts for fun!

FRAGMENTS FROM AMERICA
I LOVE YOU

There was a little black
boy selling papers on a

street corner in Erie oh
he was feeling just fine

spinning round & round
on his heels singing out

heh heh it looks like war
heh heh it looks like war!

* * *

The first thing he said
when he got into the car

was well mister are you
politically developed?

a great big blond swede
with huge hands & a ter-

rific voice that nearly
broke your eardrums he

was going up to Madison
because he'd heard there

was some trouble there
and wherever there was

trouble that was where
he had to be and a good

many times it had ended
in jail and he always cal-

led the governor by his
first name and one time

he rode a night & a day
in a boxcar with Dilllin-

ger and one time in Wyo-
ming they held him three

weeks because they said
they hadn't got the fel-

low yet that sank the
Maine & by God he said

if I hadn't read Marx &
Darwin yet I had better

do it right away & after
the change then it will

be just like a big happy
family & you'll only work

about ten years & you'll
get every darn thing you

want as long as it don't
do nobody else no harm!

*   *   *

He was talking so fast I
couldn't get much that he

was saying a little bent
man with exploding eyes

and hands all got up in
a coat and hat though it

was hot summer a hot Sep-
tember day in Cleveland &

when he went out the shoe-
shine boy explained that

the trouble was the priest
he would not teach him the

right prayers to get up to
heaven with and he went to

the bishop to explain how
the priest was a devil in

disguise and of course the
bishop kicked him out and

now he thought he'd have
to go to Rome to the pope.

WHEN DOES THE PLAY BEGIN?

(A Political Poem)

Mother when does the
show begin when does

something happen hush
dear be quiet in just a

minute now but you
said that a long time

ago I want the curtain
to go up hush dear be

quiet it's never good
manners to talk when

the music is playing
but mother I'm tired

of the music and they
keep playing the same

piece hush darling in
just a minute now here

eat a piece of candy
no I don't want any

more candy mother I
want them to begin the

play I want to see the
lights go on and have

the people walk around
and talk & laugh & sing!

THE AVALANCHE

If you can explain the
secret of the avalanche

why after years of quiet
through winters of great

snowfall and springs of
the hot sun melting why

suddenly without reason
or warning it breaks it-

self free from the peak
and pours to the valley

below with force that no
thing of wood or stone

can hinder then I can
tell you why it is that

I after so many years
of gradual petrifaction

suddenly without reason
or warning revive in your

brightness the memory of
lost motion and plunge

down the mountain slope
uprooting and breaking

till on the valley floor
the flood subsides and

leaves till spring an icy mon-
ument to self-destruction!

I SEE IN THE PAPER
THAT YOU'RE ENGAGED

Under the sullen wave
I hear the sunken bell

that melancholy bell
that tolls when ships

go down sings low its
wicked song when the

sweet ships go down
split on some rock or

bitten by the reef I
hear it listen listen

to the bell another
cargo gone I've lost

another ship listen
the sunken bell one

more sweet ship oh
lovely thing of wood

and pitch and rope
and sun and salt one

more gone down to the
interminable sands.

CONFIDENTIAL REPORT

The president of the
corporation was of the

opinion that the best
thing to do was just

to let the old ship
sink as pleasantly &

easily as possible be-
cause it was plain as

day you couldn't op-
erate at a profit as

long as that man was
in the white house &

now he was there for
good you might just

as well fold yr hands
and shut yr face and

let the old boat take
water till she sank.

THE RETURN OF LOVE

Love you that so long a
time from me have wan-

dered Love most curious
beast whose form and

shape we never see Love
most destroying and be-

loved visitor Love you
are come again you have

returned to me Love when
you came before you gave

me sorrows you brought
a girl whose mouth was

full of cinders you brought
a girl whose head time ate

away now you are come
again and bring another

you bring a girl whose
brightness floods my

blood with light you
drive me old and slow

and cold into this bright-
ness eager and yet afraid

you drive me to the light
Love do you do this for

your pleasure are you a
beast of play am I your

sport or is the shape we
never see the measure of

that mysterious form the
mortal & immortal heart?

WAR POEMS

This page stands for a group of bitter, satiric, war-hating poems which I wrote in 1942. I think they were good poems—at least, what they tried to say was good— but there seems no point in printing them now and hurting people who have lost a son or a leg. Their general tone and theme were: "Did they ever sell bonds for Peace?"

WHAT THE PENCIL WRITES

Often when I go out I
put in my coat pocket

some paper and a pen-
cil in case I want to

write something down
well there they are

wherever I go and as
my coat moves the pen-

cil writes by itself
a kind of gibberish

hieroglyphic which I
often think as I un-

dress at night & take
out those papers with

nothing written on
them but strange and

meaningless marks is
the story of my life.

CRYSTAL PALACE MARKET

Saw a girl in a food
store that looked like

you gave me the shakes
in my poor old heart

darling darling sings
the voice on the radio

darling why did we
ever drift apart big

giant food market full
of things to eat every

thing to eat that a
person could desire

but I guess that I'll go
hungry hungry hungry

darling says the radio
why did we ever part?

THE LAST POEM TO BE WRITTEN

"When, when & whenever
death closes our eyes"

still shall I behold her
smiling such brightness

lady of brightness &
the illumined heart

soft walker in my blood
snow color sea sound

track of the ermine
delicate in the snow

line of the sea wave
delicate on the sand

lady of all brightness
donna del mio cuor.

REPORT ON A VISIT
TO GERMANY
(AMERICAN ZONE)

(1948)

IN THE TRAIN

Jammed standing in the
corridor of a limping
German train I share

at least their hunger's
dirty smell and rub my
aching guilt on theirs.

IN DARMSTADT

Grey hungry men are loading
debris from a blasted house
into the little dump cars of
the rubble railroad
                    this is
the line that makes its run
from death to hope
                        its tracks
are layed on blocks in every
German city & when one street
is cleaned they move them to
the next
            it pays no dividends
but runs all day and will for
7 years
            their shovels probing
hunger-slowly in the settled
wrack turn up a twisted rust-
ing spoon they all put down
their tools and pass it round
appraising worth or use
                            but

it's too bad they toss it in
the car
            I pick it out and put
it in my pocket
                        I want that
spoon
        they stare I blush and
offer cigarettes they take &
thank and I walk off
                        I want
their spoon I'll take it home
back to the other world I'll
need it there to learn to eat.

HOW DOES IT LOOK?

The face narrows
the skin tightens on the cheekbones
the mouth & lips tighten
the cheeks suck in a bit
the eyes sink back into the skull
the eyes are dull seeming
the circles under the eyes deepen
    & darken,
the hair thins & grays

that's just the head

the body?

I wasn't tempted to find out.

WHY NOT?

I know one German
who eats well
he's fairy to
an MG queen
he hates his guts
but what the hell
a meal's a meal
I'd do the same.

SONG OF THE GIs & THE MGs

We are the lords of the cigarette
  & the green passport
    we do the best we can
we rule the world unwillingly
  & have good intentions
    we do the best we can
we are most of us sorry that you
  are always so hungry
    we do the best we can
we are unaccustomed to governing
  & make some mistakes
    we do the best we can
we often marry your girls after we
  have seduced them
    we do the best we can
we are hurt when you resist our plans
  for your re-education
    we do the best we can
we will help you try to clean up
  the bomb mess we made
    we do the best we can

we are the lords of the cigarette
& the green passport
we really do mean to do
the best we can for you.

LOGISTICS

A good enough place I guess
a partly bombed art museum
over the portico is carved ARS

LUX AETERNA in the stone
and below a neat signboard
US Army Prophylactic Station.

HARD TO TRANSLATE

My friend Klaus a German goes
to the MG travel office for a
permit to visit Switzerland old
friends in Berne

have invited him they will feed
and fatten him for 3 weeks and
clear some of the misery mist
out of his brain

the MG official feels like a little
joke and kids Klaus "why ever
do you want a trip? you Germans
should stay here

at home and enjoy your hunger-
strafe" (that word's rather hard
to translate as it means hunger-
        punishment but it

also suggests the strafing that
God was supposed to give to the
English) Klaus winces but keeps
        hold of his tem-

per he patiently tells the man
(who is a Jew) about his impris-
onment under the Nazis in the
        end he gets his

permit all right the man is a
good egg and meant to give it
to him all the time he was just
        feeling like his

little joke but he should not
have said that Klaus tells me
such things go to the bone and
        they stick there.

STUTTGART: IN A NIGHTCLUB
(ILLEGAL)

One of our new aristocrats
the knights of the air en-
thralls (he thinks) a half-
starved German tart with his
exploits while he gets drunk
then he passes out poor girl

she has to hit the street again
without a meal the MPs
cart him off in their jeep.

O FRÈRES HUMAINS

The rubble railroad
carries freight
that's more than loads
of stone and dirt
it carries off
an age's hate
and puts it with
a people's heart

the cars are dumped
beyond the city
and then come back
to load once more
o brother men
at last learn pity
return them full
with love to share.

A SMALL BOOK OF POEMS

(1948)

ABOVE THE CITY

You know our office on the 18th
floor of the Salmon Tower looks
    right out on the

Empire State & it just happened
we were there finishing up some
    late invoices on

a new book that Saturday morning
when a bomber roared through the
    mist and crashed

flames poured from the windows
into the drifting clouds & sirens
    screamed down in

the streets below it was unearthly
but you know the strangest thing
    we realized that

none of us were much surprised be-
cause we'd always known that those
    two Paragons of

progress sooner or later would per-
form before our eyes this demon-
        stration of their
        true relationship.

HARD & SOFT

This girl this diagonal
girl when she is deep in
hard talk always she'll

knock her cigarette ash
quick over her shoulder
and I'll say that milky

way of grey dust on her
back is all stars stars
stars that were manufac-

tured for her in a soft
warm tenebrous place I
mean to say in my heart.

THE SUMMONS

He went out to their glorious
war & went down in it and his
        last belief was

her love as he breathed flame
in the waves and sank burning
        now I lie under

his picture in the dark room
in the wife's bed and partake
        of his unknown

life does he see does he stand
in the room does he feel does
        he burn again

later I wake in the night while
she sleeps and call out to him
        wanderer come

return to this bed & embody the
love that was yours and is hers
        and is mine
        and endures.

NO COMPARISON

A parrot
a talking parrot
a parrot in a cage
"pretty Polly."

A poet
no fooling a poet
a poet in the USA
"Hiya Shakespeare."

THE JUDGES OF THE SECRET COURT

assembled in their awful chamber
have condemned Karl Rossmann to
a penible fate he does not know

his crime but he must suffer for
it they will not name his crime
but he must pay for it poor Karl

must itch and bleed and twist he
must atone until I find my nature
and he finds his happy Oklahoma.

THE VOICES

It is sin it is sin it is a
deadly sin whines the tired
    old voice in

the back of his head you'll
take her love but you can't
    give yourself

it will end in misery & end
in remorse it is sin whines
    the tired old

voice it is love it is love
sings the voice in the heart
    you will bring

her a happiness she has never
known before you'll bring her
    to life and

she'll burn with love's won-
derful fire but it's sin no
    it's love cry

the voices together and sadly
and happily madly he enters
    again the soft
    and delectable
    battle of Love.

PATENT PENDING

I have an invention
ready for the patent

office which I know
will benefit mankind

it is a kind of ink
and little pen and

magnifying glass so
everyone can write

the parables of Jesus
on their fingernails

and read them there
the minute that their

hands begin to feel
like picking up a gun.

NOW LOVE SPEAKS

and his sovereign voice
declares sufferer I have

brought you again into
my perilous land so re-

joice for you will weep
and bleed again for my

sake she will burn you
& she will cut you she

will put dry anguish in
your heart and all the

while you will be cry-
ing Love Love in ado-

ration all the while
calling upon my name.

THE MAN IN THE SUBWAY

This is about a strange
man I met in the subway
he was dressed in very

oldfashioned clothes and
looked sick he spoke in
a foreign accent & told

me his name was Mister
Baudelaire he had with
him a light-skinned ne-

gro girl who kept laugh-
ing like she was crazy
he invited me to visit

him in his apartment &
words just fail me to
describe the things he

had there I am simply
amazed that a man like
that can even exist in

our modern world but a
friend who has contacts
with big men in the un-

dertaking field tells me
that they have to deal
with literally hundreds

of bodies which all have
this Baudelaire's name
marked on them the way

a sailor tattoos himself
when he comes ashore in
a distant foreign port.

THAT OTHER WORLD

Just as the plane was ready to
take off along you came without
    a hat or any bags

looking so beautifully insolent
it was another world I tried to
    get the seat next

yours but was too late and only
heard over the engines' humming
    now and then a wan-

dering word & watched you move
and wished it was another world
    & then at Kansas

City you changed planes without
an answering glance to mine and
    I went on alone
    back to my own.

GETTING PAID

The little man at the
piano in the bar gets

paid to smile all the
time he is playing and

the glistening blonde
in the Dior dress gets

paid to like it when
she has to sleep with

fat & ugly and he got
paid for selling out

his partners in those
famous deals & I what

do I get who'll pay
the poet for a poem?

THE SINKING STONE

High in the alpine
snowfields when a

stone slips from a
peak and rolls to

the glacier below
the sun will heat

it in the burning
days of spring and

it will melt itself
a hole & disappear

in the snow I like
that stone burned

hot from loving you
am sinking deep in-

to a cold vast no-
where ice land of

your loving someone
else instead of me!

DOWN WE GO

Some people just seem
to be born to fall out

of the apple tree into
the mud to fall from

the window of the high
ceilinged room down to

the courtyard where the
butcher's boy fingers

the kitchen maid and
the butler sings Carmen

with his collar off &
they whisper that it

happens because their
blood's run bad but I

think more likely it's
because it's so much

warmer in the mud than
up in that windy tree.

THE SWARMING BEES

I remember the evening
that Uncle Willy's bees

swarmed in the neigh-
bor's yard high up in

an old box elder tree
the gravid cluster hung

swelled with so many
thousand bees it al-

most broke the branch
and Uncle Willy sent

his boy Peter up the
trunk with a garbage

pail but of course the
pail fell & the whole

big cluster came down
right on top of Uncle

Willy's head but he
stood still and never

got a sting though he
was black with bees so

for the next two weeks
he was quoting Horace

how a wolf won't bite
so virtuous a man and

after he'd coaxed and
smoked the bees into a

new hive he sat out on
the front porch with his

shoes off and drank 3
highballs down one for

the bees & one for the
dead departed soul of

President Heber Grant
and one to the health

of that dauntless war-
rior General Principles

this all happened just
when the Russians were

blasting Berlin & for
a long time that livid

cluster hung in my mind
the black & burned and

crawling deathshead of
my youth's Old Europe!

AMO AMAS AMAT

Your love my dearest Phylonella
reminds me of a barber's college

where old bums from the skidrow
come to get their shave for free.

BUSY DAY

The cripple in the wheelchair
(who really isn't crippled up
at all) has shot & killed the

luscious lady who is fair but
false anonymous letters warn
Inspector Meadowes that this

crime is just the first Mac-
Teague the private eye cracks
wise and downs another drink

Hoppy the cub reporter with a
wooden leg meets in a mist the
lost and lonely girl with honey

in her voice yes friends dear
friends another golden day in
this most golden age is slip-

ping darkwards on its opiate
track don't wake good friends
don't stir the sound of pistol

shots is oh so soothing like
that muffled riffling of the
dollars piling up & up & up.

HIGHWAY 66

is the absolute road to
hell along which mom &
pop & the kids with all

their stuff tied on the
car roof are heading it
West to that promised

land in Southern Cali-
fornia where everything
is going to be 100% OK.

THE GENERATIONS

The succession of the gen-
erations fills me with im-
measurable sadness at the

most unreasonable moments
I remember about him the
most irrelevant things how

he cautioned me to drink
three glasses of water if
going to bed drunk or how

he walked up and down the
room crying peccavi peccavi
in deep anguish because he

had been with the girls and
thought he had broken my
mother's heart now I watch

my little son growing up
in my own imperfect image
and realize how impossible

it is to give him much help
in life's unending chain of
puzzles pains and disasters.

THIS ONE RHYMES

I often find that I forget
the reasons why we went to war
and why we sweat and why we bled
and why we left so many dead
mouldering on a foreign shore

oh I remember it seemed clear
the time they drafted us to go
it wasn't fear it was because
the enemies had broken laws
and trampled mankind low

the radio voice explained it well
the papers made it plain as day
and I can't tell how many friends
expounded me the means and ends
and pointed me the way

and now again today they shout
that we must fight must strike the foe
and if I doubt and wonder why
once more we have to go and die
they tell me that I ought to know
that it is right because it's so
and I must be a man and go.

TECHNICAL NOTES

Catullus is my master and I mix
a little acid and a bit of honey
        in his bowl love

is my subject & the lack of love
which lack is what makes evil a
        poet must strike

Catullus could rub words so hard
together their friction burned a
        heat that warms

us now 2000 years away I roll the
words around my mouth & count the
        letters in each

line thus eye and ear contend in-
side the poem and draw its move-
        ment tight Milton

thought rhyme was vulgar I agree
yet sometimes if it's hidden in
        the line a rhyme

will richen tone the thing I most
despise is quote poetic unquote
　　　diction I prefer

to build with plain brown bricks
of common talk American talk then
　　　set 1 Roman stone

among them for a key I know Ca-
tullus knew a poem is like a blow
　　　an impact strik-

ing where you least expect this I
believe and yet with me a poem
　　　is finally just
　　　a natural thing.

THE WILD ANEMONE
& OTHER POEMS

(1957)

THE WILD ANEMONE

I'll call it the daring
flower its softness its

pallor so little suggesting
the strength with which

it fights the wind its
petals so delicate it

seems a touch would wither
them yet they'll outlast a

three-day storm and will
outlast I think (and now

I speak to her) the tempests
that a foolish heart invents

to plague itself because
it hardly dares to love

the wild anemone
the daring flower.

THE EMPTY DAY

I want to drive everything
out of this day to make it

empty as a ball of air push
out the things I do on other

days that make them melt away
this day must be quite empty

and stand still no work no
trips no little putterings no

reading & no talk I guess
I'll have to eat but other-

wise it must be empty as an
edgeless ball of air & there

inside that emptiness barely
breathing hardly thinking I

shall wait to see what comes
and let it take me if it will.

HOW FORTUNATE

to be struck by a taxicab
just after giving 50 lire

to a beggar (it is 2 weeks
since a letter has come)
burst open your gates for

that sinner in Dante who
had the good luck to fall

dead on the field with his
arms crossed (two weeks &
two days & no letter has

come) and tonight he will
dream that his heart stops

(no letter) for everything
is cold and silent in the
house of water where once

her hand made the bits of
his blood jump like fish.

FRAGMENT

(From "America I Love You")

Well here's a salute to
that clean old man who's

out every day fishing up
coins with a string and

a bit of gum through the
subway gratings on Broad-

way he says that he aver-
ages five dollars a week

and he says that's enough
for a man who don't drink.

ANOTHER FRAGMENT

When questioned by re-
porters regarding the in-

fluence on his life of 40
years' reading of obscene

books the venerable Mr.
Sumner agent for the So-

ciety for the Suppression of
Vice pondered a moment

and replied: "the effect
has not been beneficial."

A MODEST PROPOSAL

I think I can offer this
simple remedy for a part

at least of the world's
ills and evil I suggest

that everyone should be
required to change his

name every ten years I
think this would put a

stop to a whole lot of
ambition compulsion ego

and like breeders of dis-
cord and wasted motion.

A BAD NIGHT ON THIRD AVENUE

One of my frequent little
deaths jumped on my back
and poisoned in my ear

that you my Cynthia were
last night seen drunk in
the Stork Club with an

advertising man (& what
cuts worse a television
man) and that you left

there with that spreadleg
look smeared on your face
like paint Propertius wait-

ed for you till they closed
up Paddy's Bar & then went
home to hate his bed alone.

ON THE FIRE

My soul is frying
like an egg but it
won't taste good

when it's done
I lit this fire a
long time ago

a little harmless
fire with matches
& look at it now!

love comes in such a
pretty box how nice
it sounds when you

rattle it but no it's
not safe for children
and not safe for me!

STEP ON HIS HEAD

Let's step on daddy's head shout
the children my dear children as
we walk in the country on a sunny

summer day my shadow bobs dark on
the road as we walk and they jump
on its head and my love of them

fills me all full of soft feelings
now I duck with my head so they'll
miss when they jump & they screech

with delight and I moan oh you're
hurting you're hurting me stop and
they jump all the harder and love

fills the whole road but I see it run
on through the years and I know
how some day they must jump when

it won't be this shadow but really
my head (as I stepped on my own
father's head) it will hurt really

hurt and I wonder if then I will
have love enough will I have love
enough when it's not just a game?

IT'S WARM UNDER YOUR THUMB

I guess I like it there
  perish the baubles
   there are kinds &
kinds of reality there's

the crack in the golden
  bowl & the chance
   encounter in a sum-
mer beach hotel and it's

written that the craving
  of a heedless man
   (for either kind)
grows within him like a

Maluva creeper as a mon-
  key seeking fruit
   in the jungle he
runs from life to life and

I think now I will just
  stop running and
   take it warm and
easy under your thumb.

FINANCIAL REVIEW

The elements affecting lower earnings com-
pared with the previous year were somewhat
reduced volume and moderately lower prices

during the spring when volume was at lower
levels some raw materials were also avail-
able at lower price which effected savings

when primary raw materials began an upward
movement there was no corresponding rise in
selling prices or any improvement in volume

thus with business more competitive it was
desirable to have a wider and more thorough
sales coverage with a higher selling cost

and friends it is my view that anyone who
will prison his soul in the corporate gut
of the Great American Dream Machine might

just as well save time & go shoot himself.

IN THE MUSEUM AT TEHERAN

a sentimental curator has placed
two fragments of bronze Grecian
        heads together boy

and girl so that the faces black-
ened by three thousand years of
        desert sand & sun

seem to be whispering something
that the Gurgan lion & the wing-
    ed dog of Azerbaijan

must not hear but I have heard
them as I hear you now half way
    around the world

so simply & so quietly more like
a child than like a woman making
    love say to me in

that soft lost near and distant voice
I'm happy now I'm happy oh don't
    move don't go away.

A BIT DIFFERENT

Things are a bit different in
some other countries even in
some of the countries of poor
old brokendown Europe not

long ago I was in Italy wait-
ing for a train in the station
restaurant in Bologna when a
young woman came in with a

baby and sat down at the best
table in the middle of the di-
ning room (First Class) from
the way she behaved with that

baby you could see that she
was proud of it all right and
an elderly man at another table
came over and played with

the baby letting it pull his
nose & his ears yes it was a
beautiful baby beautiful and
black as a negro baby can be.

METROPOLITAN BARD

The energies of this particu-
lar poet are directed about
    as follows: 20%

to the composition & placement
of favorable reviews of books
    by writers who

might later favorably review
his own books 30% to the
    entertainment

of habitual editors of antholo-
gies 15% to complaints to his
    publisher con-

cerning the insufficiency of
his advertising 5% to tele-
    phone calls to

bookstore clerks enquiring if
his latest volumes are being
    kept in stock &

25% to plotting intrigues of
revenge against critics who
    have maligned or

ignored his work & oh yes 5%
to picking other poets' books
    for a few good
      ideas for poems.

WELL ALL RIGHT

if that's how it is
then that's how it

is & I'll just have
to put you back in

that box labelled
"wonderful people."

ROME: IN THE CAFÉ

She comes at eleven every morning
to meet a man who makes her cry

they sit at a table in the back row
talking very earnestly and soon

she begins to cry he holds her
hand and reasons with her & she

tries to smile when he leaves
her then she cries again and

orders a brandy and gulps it
down then she makes her face

new and goes home yes I think
that she knows that I come just

to watch her & wait for the day
when he does not come at all.

THE PRISONER

Last night you came into my
dreams as wild as a bird that
has flown in an open window

and flutters in terror all over
the room what was the dream
I don't know it has vanished

away in the light but I woke
with your fright like a hand
on my flesh and all day I've

been back in the time when I
watched for each sign & each
smile was a hope for my love.

THE TROUT

A trout let us say
a blue blonde trout

that slips through
the bars like water

from boite to boite
from man to man but

only ones she likes
and almost never for

money and I love she
says I love exagger-

ate and her mother
told the neighbors

qu'est-ce que j'ai
fait au ciel pour

avoir une fille qui
est de l'ordure and

she came back from
the palaces of the

king's cousin out in
Siam where they ate

off golden plates and
her whim was his com-

mand came back to the
bars and the boys and

the slow swim through
the dim light yes a

trout let us call her
a small blonde trout.

TO A CERTAIN PUBLISHER

who is behind with his edi-
torial reading because the
    light is so bad

in night clubs dear sir did
you ever think that if you
    had devoted ½

the money you paid that press
agent to get you known around
    town as quote

the whiteheaded boy of Ameri-
can publishing unquote on the
    books of just 2

or 3 living American writers
of a grade a bit higher than
    Hollywood's lit-

erary doughnutcutters you
might possibly be recalled
    with something

other than disgust by a few
decent people 2 weeks after
    your (we hope
    soon) demise.

YOUR LOVE

reminds me of the sense
of humor of one of those

funny plumbers who likes
to switch the handles on

the hot and cold faucets
of hotel room wash basins.

COMPLAINT & PRESCRIPTION

When misery compounded is
of love & was

& melancholy's grounded in
not here not mine

& nothing can be found to
bring her round

then bolt the lock & stop
the clock on mem-

ory shut all the doors and
close the pores

on memory make him your
goat for misery

and if you hunt the girl
named tomorrow

remember she will bring
you *her* sorrow.

A PITEOUS SIGHT

it seemed to see that
poor girl beaten by

those priests back of
the church they were

lined up like Indians
and lashed her with

their chains of holy
beads & black crossed

sticks her pious tears
mixed with her pretty

blood and more they
flogged her more she

kissed their feet and
begged their blessing.

YOU WORRY ME

You will worry me as
long as I live you'll

make me doubt & fear
because you make sev-

enty-two thousand dol-
lars a year (it said so

in the paper) and I'll
never make anything at

all anybody can tell
that just from look-

ing at me & I know
that I'm right that

you don't matter at
all that you are no-

thing & mean nothing
I know that I know it

and yet you scare me
with your look of pow-

er over men and your
eyes that add & sub-

tract and your voice
that hires and fires

and the shine on your
shoes saying seventy-

two thousand dollars
a year and plenty be-

sides from the market
yes you worry me and

make me doubt and
fear and even hate!

CYNTHIA IN CALIFORNIA

Intricate intrigues were her
speciality sometimes as com-
  plicated as a

Rube Goldberg machine to an
enemy's face she could be so
  gaily enthusi-

astic he would often imagine
a change of heart and become
  careless then

a month later he might walk
directly into a ruinous dis-
  aster but one

so deviously manipulated and
using as instruments persons
  twice or even

three times removed from her-
self as prime mover its origin
  was uncertain

women whom she had made
victims referred to her (be-
  hind her back)

as the whore of Hollywood but
I have heard men whose lives
  she had played

with and utterly scrambled
talk of her almost wistfully
  as a lovely and
  wonderful girl.

THAT OLD DOG IN THE ROAD

Why does the old dog like
to lie right in the middle
of the highway at evening

probably it's because the
concrete is still slightly

warm from the heat of the
sun & it gladdens his gut
well Polixena let's have

a go at it again then for
there's still pleasure in an
old love renewed or at

least pleasure enough for
an old bald guy like me!

MARTHA GRAHAM

Earth and water air
and fire her body

beats the ground it
flows it floats it

seems to burn she
burns herself away

until there is no
body there at all

but only the pure
elements moving as

music moves moving
from her into us.

PROGNOSIS

An old man alone in a house
full of books who spits in

the sink where he piles his
lonely dishes the children

have gone to make their own
mistakes and he climbs on

the books like an endless
endless ladder grasping at

Dante clutching at Lao Tze
defying the world of things

& lost in a world of words
an old man who stares at

the page till the words are
gone and he knows that he

doesn't even understand
what makes the weather.

NEAR ZERMATT: THE DRAHTSEILBAHN

High over the deep
alpine valley a load
is climbing the thin

wire to the village
that clings to the
mountainside under

the cliffs & my love
rides up to you on
such a thin thread

of hope trembling in
empty space over the
chasm that seems so

bottomless drawn up-
ward drawn upward
because you are there

so distant so close
and will always be
there far above me.

SELECTED POEMS

(1959)

THE CAVE

Leaning over me her hair
makes a cave around her

face a darkness where her
eyes are hardly seen she

tells me she is a cat she
says she hates me because

I make her show her pleas-
ure she makes a cat-hate

sound and then ever so
tenderly hands under my

head raises my mouth into
the dark cave of her love.

ANGLES OF VISION

This morning the size of
the world was diminished

by the fog yet in another
sense it was enlarged by
the soft whiteness of the

shad-blow which has just
come into bloom but don't

bother Lygdamus to tell me
that similar rules of il-
lusion must be applied to

her and the things that
she does when that mood

of wild love is upon her
it's a waste of your fine
philosophical breath you

may lecture away but I'll
never be able to see it!

HE LIVES IN A BOX

a kind of upended cas-
ket with roller skate

wheels on its bottom
end for locomotion &

two small holes where
the eyes can look out

naturally people are
curious what does he

eat what is he hiding
in there but he won't

ever open the lid just
skates away if someone

tries to get too close
barking dogs chase him

boys throw stones he
doesn't seem to care

he's got what he wants
& all he wants in there.

THE PIG / POEMS

(1970)

THE PIG

roots for acorns which
snuffling he brings to

the goddess it is about
the limit of the pigly

intelligence but at
least he can do that.

THE SHIP

There is an old man in the
back streets of this inland
city who is building a ship

in his yard he has it up on
a scaffold the full length
of the yard and he works on

it all by himself after work
and on weekends it will end
up weighing more tons than

the biggest truck could ever
move they will just have to
break it up after he is dead

this beautiful ship that is
sailing now on a great river
that leads to the open sea.

YOU WERE ASLEEP

when I came to bed all
curled up like a child

under the blanket and
when I slipped in be-

side you as quietly as
I could you stirred but

didn't really wake and
stretched out a hand to

cup my face as if you were
holding a bowl or a ball.

FIGLIO MIO

Any day now he's going
to make it he's going

to turn over by himself
three months old and he

gets his head up like a
seal catching fish boy

that will be something
talk about Alexander

making it out to India
that will be the day!

ARS GRATIA ARTIS

In the next chair in the barber-
shop this morning the director

of the world's greatest museum
(1 Rembrandt: $2,300,000) was

catching almighty hell from our
barber for having ruined the line

of those distinguished sideburns
at home with his electric razor.

THOSE OLD GODS

who arose from the sea
with their beards dry

a neat trick if you can
do it on a foundation

fellowship or a State
Department travel grant

to butter up the native
intellectuals of course

I'm retired now but I
nose about a bit after

decorous sensations oh
nothing flashy a phrase

here a patch of color
there it passes the time

till the bell rings but
how did they do it right

up out of the waves and
never a single hair wet?

YOUR ERROR

said the owl was dehu-
manization it wasn't

a girl you wanted but
a love object and for

what you were willing
to give you couldn't

really expect one that
would turn you alive.

WHAT THE ANIMALS DID

For corporate chief executives, the year 1968 was a year of changing strategies and changing games . . . [it was the year of] the merger upheaval . . . and conglomerate warfare . . . it was one in which both classical economic and decision theories were inadequate to explain some of the major events.
—John McDonald (Fortune, May 1969)

They got so hungry they all
began to attack each other

and try to eat each other
and many did eat each other

even the war and the moon
were not enough for them

they got so hungry it was
not just big ones eating

small ones some very lit-
tle ones attacked big ones

& managed to swallow them
alive it was crazy really

crazy because it wasn't a
year of famine there was

plenty of food around with
the war and the moon plenty

to eat but the more they
ate the more they wanted.

SONG

O lovely lovely so lovely
just fresh from a night of

it lovely oh I saw you at
nine in the morning coming

home in the street with no
hat and your coat clutched

tight but not hiding your
evening dress lovely and

fresh from a night of it
lovely you stopped on the

curb for the light & your
eye caught mine lovely so

lovely and you knew that
I knew and you knew that

I wanted you too so fresh
from a night of it lovely.

SPRING IN THE SUBWAYS

The stations of the IRT
have blossomed overnight
with a wonderful flower

a new advertisement a
big pink sign pink and
white like those lovely

butterfly tulips in the
park what does it say?
that SATAN NEVER SLEEPS!

THAT LAMB

look pretty comfortable
he got it pretty good

but man I doan know how
long he got it that good

that lion he look like
he smilin but man any

old lion he still a lion
got a big stomach to fill

SAXO CERE

comminuit brum a rainy day
when he can't play outside

and Henry is cutting little
axes out of a piece of card-

board he bloodies them up
nicely with red crayon and

then very lovingly one after
another brings them to me

at my desk where I'm work-
ing as if they were flowers.

PLEASURE <u>NOW</u>

gloomed Cohen after the
Yankees lost I can't wait

for next year & then to
double his misery told

me the tale of Ruskin
burning Turner's nudes.

THE FULL LIFE

Our neighbors at the
beach have got their

television set arranged
so that they can watch

Ed Sullivan & the sun-
set at the same time.

AMERICA I LOVE YOU (a fragment)

A man from Jehovah's
Witnesses knocked at

the door the other day
to explain why there's

been no rain all sum-
mer it's because God

doesn't like Johnson
or Goldwater either.

I FOLLOW MY BEARD [1937]

Life is a race to keep
up with my beard good
god how it grows I'll
never catch up it's

like those rabbits the
greyhounds chase round
and round and never any
nearer I follow my beard

and where is it taking
me that's what I'd like
to know just where we're
going tell me beard where

are we headed for is it
just round and round like
the dogs after the rabbit
round and round and the

people laughing because
they never catch it or
are we off for those big
delectable mountains see

how the white snow shines
in the sun see the forest
so green the flowering
meadows hear the birds

hear the water falling
think of the stars how
they shine in the night
and the moon on the snow

envoi

beard boss implacable mas-
ter this the poet begs you
take him to the mountains
yes take him to his dream.

IN ANOTHER COUNTRY: POEMS 1935–1975

(1978)

FOREWORD

Some of these neat compositions, cool and simple as they appear, secrete bitter knowledge as others do lyrical joy.

Some are funny. Some, with precision, fix historical moments.

What they say could hardly be said more briefly.

They are utterly clear, stained by no muddiness.

They are like classical epigrams, made not with quantitative meters but with typewriter characters and spaces.

They are unique: no one but James Laughlin could have written them.

R[OBERT]. F[ITZGERALD].

THE DIFFERENCE

Afterward I ran
down into the sea
and swam there for

a long time she
followed but would
not come into the

water and I think
maybe that means
everything but may-

be it means nothing
I swam hard it was
night in the waves.

UPSTATE NEW YORK

Grandfather says that
after greatgrandmother
had given greatgrand-

father an awful calling
down for his manners or
more likely his lack of

them he would come out
to the back and smoke a
pipe with old Silas his

hired man and say "well
Silas I guess we can't
all be Jesus can we?"

THE KIND -

hearted Americans are
adopting Vietnamese

orphans it makes them
feel better about what

happened they did not
want what happened to

happen & did not think
things like that would

happen because so many
wise men told them they

couldn't if you had e-
nough liberty & napalm

and honor and airbombs
it's really sad about

the Americans the way
they're so kindhearted.

IT DOES ME GOOD

to bow my body to the ground
when the emperor passes I am

one of the gardeners at the
palace but I have never seen

his face when he walks in the
garden he is preceded by boys

who ring little bells and I
bow myself down when I hear

the bells approaching though
they say that the emperor is

very kind and not easily of-
fended he might smile at me

if I look up or even speak
to me but I believe that the

emperor rules by my humility
it is my humility that rules.

THE WOODPECKER

on our television aerial
is not alone in his praise

of thee o infinite sphere
whose center is everywhere

whose circumference is no-
where each morning he is

at it (in praise of thee)
no more convinced by his

sore beak than we by that
other daily sound his tap-

pings most resemble (and
what we thought at first

his mantras were) that is
the drip from the bathtub

faucet dropping down the
drain (in praise of thee)

o sphere whose force is
constant from the center.

A LONG NIGHT OF DREAMING

and when I finally awoke
from it we seemed to be

back where we'd left off
some thirty years before

in the compartment of a
wagon-lit somewhere in

Italy loving and arguing
soft words and then hard

words over where we'd go
next to Venice to Rome or

better to split again you
back to him I back to her.

IN ANOTHER COUNTRY

tesoro

she would say with that succulent
accent on the middle o as if she
were holding something as precious
as the golden testicle of a god

Credere!

OBBEDIRE! COMBATTERE! I guess
it was the same then every-
where all over Italy in big
white letters painted up on

walls and especially on railroad
retaining walls at the
grade crossings and to make
a good record and show how

things were in ordine they
would let down the crossing
bars ten minutes before the
trains came so people were

backed up on both sides in
crowds shouting across to
each other all a big joke
and that's how we met where

we first saw each other I
was on the up side walking
back to town from swimming
& she was on the other with

her bicycle heading to the
cove wearing her tight white
sweater with nothing under
it & her grey checked skirt

& sandals era come Beatrice
al ponte quando si videro la
prima volta there by that
bridge in Florence where he

first saw her (later one day
she brought her schoolbook
of Dante so I could see the
famous painting) com' allora

al ponte only neither of us
was shy first we were look-
ing then we were smiling and
when the train had finally

passed and we met in the mid-
dle I just took hold of her bi-
cycle and walked beside her
but you have swum already I

can see your hair's all wet
why do you want to go again?

why do you think? I said ma
brutta I'm ugly sono brutta

and at the cove she changed
behind a big rock into her
suit it was white and tight
too ti piace? she asked you

like it? the water was very
clear that day and the rocks
were warm there was a German
boy came nosing around but

she wasn't nice to him and
he went away after we swam
we sat on the rocks sunning
& talking I only knew a few

words of Italian then but we
found another language that
did well enough I'd draw a
picture of the word I wanted

with my finger on her thigh
or she on mine the sky was
clear the air was soft with
just a little breeze I was

18 she was 15 and her name
was Leontina going back to
town she had me ride her on
the handlebars and put her

arms around my neck to keep
from falling off she didn't
want an icecream mamma m'as-
petta alla casa my mother's

waiting for me so I'd better
go just leave me here ma se
tu vuoi 'sta sera dopo la
passeggiata al angolo near

the newsstand quando sono
le nove yes I said yes I'll
be there alle nove after the
churchbells sound at nine.

Giacomino!

she called vieni qua splashing her
arms in the dear green water vieni
subito and so I followed her swim-
ming around a point of rock to the

next cove vieni qua non hai paura
and she slipped like an eel beneath
the surface down through the sunken
entrace to a hidden grotto where

the light was soft and green on fine-
grained sand è bello no? here we can
be together by ourselves nobody else
has ever been here with me it's my se-

cret place here kiss me here I found
it when I was a little girl now touch
me here è strano questa luce com' un
altro mondo so strange this light am

I all green? it's like another world
does that feel good? don't be afraid
siamo incantati we're enchanted in
another world O Giacomino Giacomino

sai tu amore come lui è bello? com' è
carino sai quanto tu mi dai piacere?
sai come lei ti vuol' bene? lie still
non andare via just lie still lie still.

Genovese

non sono I'm Roman it comes from
my father look at my nose it went
straight down from her forehead
like coins you see from Etruria.

Tornerai?

she wept will you come back
for me I wanted to slip away
but she found out the time
of the train and was there

in the compartment wearing
her Sunday dress & the Mil-
anese scarf I had given her
tornerai amore mio will you

come back and bring me to
America crying and pressing
my hands against her breasts
my face wet with her tears

& her kisses till the train
stopped at Genova and they
made her get off because I
couldn't buy her a ticket.

UNCOLLECTED POEMS

(1984 – 1997)

ARE OUR NEUROSES

compatible my shrink says
that is necessary for a

happy relationship I am
afraid of all machines

especially the telephone
which is the lute of Lu-

cifer most girls are a-
fraid of mice snakes &

spiders please inform me
regarding any particular

anomalies and I'll do my
best to compensate I want

us to get on really well.

CAN I BATTER MY WAY

into your heart with words
being a classicist I use

only Greek typewriters my
old one was named Olymp-

ia and my new one is Her-
mes he is the messenger

of the gods he gets a-
round and hears things

he'll bring me a lot of sto-
ries that should amuse you.

THE NEEDLE IS STUCK

in the groove of the old record
and it just goes round and round playing the same bar
they are all writing the same way, the same old stuff
what they learned from those poets in residence
in the creative writing classes in college
or what they have painstakingly tried to copy from the pages of the
    New Yorker
the same old stuff, only it isn't really music
it's just something a printer has set in type
and how would a printer know the difference
for that matter, does anybody know the difference

MY FAVORITE NEWSPAPER

is always up to date could it be
that they have a computer program-

med to choose their book reviewers
like the ones they use at dating

services (are you a remarkable sin-
gle looking for an equally remark-

able single?) unfortunately in my
case there was a snafu   the computer

must have had my name spelled wrong
and I drew the expert on cholesterol-

free salad dressings well better
luck next time   perhaps Rupert Mur-

doch has a smarter machine that
will deal me a rave in the *Post*.

SOME VOICES FROM CANTO 74

For V.J.

We know the scene;
The scene is a flat field north of Pisa
Where a small road runs west down to the sea
A flat field under Carrara   snow on the marble   "snow-white against
     stone-white on the mountain"
"In the death cells in sight of Mount Taishan" "one day were clouds
     banked on Taishan"
In a cage   in a tent   "If the hoar frost grip thy tent
                    Thou wilt give thanks when night is spent"
But the scene is really memory
In qual parte dove sta memoria   in that place where memory liveth
On the steps of the dogana   In the tempio at Rimini   by the
     belltower of San Pantaleone
Beside the Serpentine in London   "my London, your London"

Ego scriptor   but who is the writer?   who is the speaker?
Perhaps the speaker is OU TIS   the speaker is No Man
He is "a man on whom the sun has gone down"
"A man of no fortune with a name to come"
Quis loquitur?   Are there many speakers?   Many voices?

165

Guido and Cino and il maestro di loro che sanno   the master of those
    who understood the truth
Arnaut and Bertran and François and old Peire Vidal
A little girl in China who longs for her husband's return
The chanters of the Noh
Kung in the Cedar grove   and Emperor Tching Tang making it new
    each day in his bathtub
The Founding Fathers   Major Douglas   Gesell   Frobenius and Del
    Mar   Gaudier and Wyndham
Homer and Divus   Ovid, the magician   Propertius, "with a crowd
    of young women doing homage to his palaver"
An odd fellow named Mauberley, who didn't quite know who he was

Who is the speaker?
Who is it that is telling us everything that ever happened?
The speaker is "No Man"—and Jedermann.
Ego scriptor   sic locutus est
Has he entered the great acorn of light?

THE INVENTORS

Did you invent me or did
I invent you   which of us

began it   was the explosion
done by fusion or by fission

(or by the attracting force
of molecules)   in what part

of the brain (or soul) are
these inventions born such

miraculous interactions
to begin the process must

there be real ingredients
such as fine eyes or en-

ticing lips (or only the
games of childhood) what

spell confected that we
should become like the phoe-

nix and the turtle dove (as
Shakespeare wrote) each

one the other's only mine?

HAECCEITY

Today's new word was
Haecceity (2 "c"s in the
Middle), hardly a melopoeic
Word. It's quite hard to
Pronounce. But it has much
Substance because it means
Thisness (and by later usage
Here and now). It comes from
The Latin pronoun *haec,*
Which means *this*. Just remember
Hic, haec, hoc from school.
What's more substantial than
A *this*; it's closer to us
Than a *that*. If you have a

This you have something you
Can grab hold of, that won't
Slip away from you, that may
Persist as long as you're
Around in the here and now

STOLEN &
CONTAMINATED POEMS

(1985)

WHY SHOULDN'T I?

steal poems is the license
granted composers denied

to versifiers didn't Brahms
play around with Haydn &

this morning listening to
the radio at breakfast I

heard Ysaÿe ravishing the
Dies Irae theme of Berlioz

for a little violin sonata.

LIKE HIM I NEED THE PAST

oh I must have it I feed on it
it's mother's milk to me I must

have Prester John (or he-dead
Mistah Kurtz?) I must have Bas-

kerville driving his lion-drawn
chariot through the streets of

Birmingham muse bring me Feddy
of Urbino with half of his nose

hacked off invite the Moor El
Cid & Genji bring me that fair

young English king whom Ber-
trand mourned they are not

ghosts (unless I am a ghost)
I go to them they come to me

the list is long we are a
gallant & merry company.

JE EST UN AUTRE

said Rimbaud & nothing in po-
etry has been the same since

but hadn't someone else told
us the same thing before with

either was the other's mine?

Ἐνθάδε τὴν ἱερὴν κεφαλὴν κατὰ γαῖα καλύπτει,
ἀνδρῶν ἡρώων κοσμήτορα, θεῖον Ὅμηρον

And Ole Ez said that the
thought of what America

would be like if the clas-
sics had a wide circulation

troubled his sleep and Pro-
fessor F the eminent classi-

cist had a happy day when
he was going across the

campus and two comely coeds
passed him on the walk and

he heard one say to the other
you know what I told him I

said you remember the part
where that Greek guy was

dragging Hector around the
walls of Troy and rubbing

him in the dust I told him
I hoped somebody would do

the very same thing to him.

I FLOAT BETWEEN THE SPHERES

and the gutter I dream of
dzogchen and the blessed

nothingness of sunyata but
yet I swim in the vanity of

frivolous poetry & torment
myself with imaginings of

profane and forbidden love.

WE MET IN A DREAM

some forty years ago there on your
ermo colle in the hills behind Rec-

anati with its hedgerow cutting off
the view of the horizon you instruct-

ed me in morality and we talked of the
great dead of Plotinus and Copernicus

and of many another then came a third
who sought to join us and we welcomed

him readily for he spoke of love and
of desire and of a man who became a

city much we conversed together in
dreams through many nights but in

the end we thought only of the no-
thingness of the infinite nothing-

ness parlando del naufragar in questo
mare of sweet drowning under the great

falls of the river of drowning in the
love that is beyond all earthly love.

AMONG THE ROSES

Stat rosa pristina nomine
nomina nuda tenemus &

Gertrude said a rose was
a rose was a rose and for

Bill Williams the rose was
the symbol of Floss "un-

less the scent of a rose
startle us anew" and when

I was young if you wanted
to bed down a chorus girl

you'd send up one red rose
& a $50 bill with the man

at the stage door but all
this is really irrelevant

what the Latin says is the
rose lives from its name

and we know nothing but
names yes those erudite

barbarians would like to
take away from us every-

thing beautiful in liter-
ature and leave us only

their science of signs
arid empty dry as dust.

YOU INVITED ME

to your recital you were so beautiful
and sang the old French songs so beauti-

fully dieu qu'il la fait bon regarder la
gracieuse bonne et belle then we went to

a nightclub perhaps we danced perhaps we
just talked and at your doorstep I kissed

your hand in courtly fashion pour les
grands biens qui sont en elle chacun

est prest de la louer and a few days
later you sent me a note to thank me

for the evening and saying so simply
you wished we had gone to my place

instead of to the nightclub qui se
pourrait d'elle lasser tous jours

sa beauté renouvelle and we did not
meet again for many years when our

situations were altered and this is
the sort of thing an old man remem-

bers in quella parte dove sta memoria
not with a sense of loss but with a

sense of gain all for the beauty so
perceived which cannot be reft from

him dieu qu'il la fait bon regarder
la gracieuse si bonne et si belle.

NOTHING THAT'S LOVELY
CAN MY LOVE ESCAPE

How many cowgirls did the
blue God Krishna love doz-

ens the old books say and
so it is with me nothing

that's lovely can my love
escape like Baby Krishna

for his butter ball I'm
greedy greedy greedy I

was not born like Krishna
on a lotus leaf but yet I

want to play as he did in
his palm grove long ago.

TO BE SURE

there are other fish in
the sea but why are the

loveliest fish so often
virtuous o poluphlois-

boio thalasses release
I beseech you strong po-

tions of passionate love
into your winedark waves.

YOU HAVE REPLACED

the Primavera in the gal-
lery in my head as well as

that lady nobody knows
what she is smiling about

for Diana the huntress no
longer arouses my emotion

and Parvati stretching out
her hand to Lord Shiva looks

like a buxom peasant girl
long is the list of those

whom you've displaced but
when will you move from my

head to some place warmer?

FELIX

For H.C.

qui potuit cordis cognoscere
causas I've never understood

and I guess I never will in
my teens I observed them in

terror in my twenties I was
a remorseless hunter (once I

made out in 3 different states
in the same day) in my thirties

most dutifully I begat children
and now in old age so humbly I

implore affection sending ver-
ses instead of flowers I have

never understood I never will
but the longing is perdurable.

CULTURAL NOTE

O bella mia patria in Verona
there is a special box in the

post office to receive letters
addressed to Romeo & Juliet

they come from all over the
world especially Japan and

are written in many languages
and some enclose little gifts

or photographs the writers of
these letters have many prob-

lems of the heart and there
are two polylingual and com-

passionate spinsters who pre-
pare individualized replies

hand written in Renaissance
script (no doubt they are on

the payroll of the Ufficio del
Turismo) Dear Romeo Dear

Juliet I need your counsel
and your consolation there

is this girl who does not
realize how lovable I am.

WHAT IS IT MAKES ONE GIRL

more lovely than all others
it is the light within omne

quod manifestatur lumen est
a fructive light that shines

within the radiance of the il-
lumined heart risplende in sè

perpetuale effecto the light
descending to her from sun

moon and stars lux enim per se
in omnem partem se ipsam dif-

fundit the light of the ima-
gination the light that wakes

and shines the light of love.

IN HAC SPE VIVO

My head can lend no succour
to my heart because her face

is beyond all wonder she is
like diamond to glass when

her eyelids part their frin-
ges of bright gold and when

to the lute she sings she
makes the nightbird mute

gods why do you make us love
your goodly gifts and snatch

them right away I marvel how
the fish do live in the sea

but patience gazes on the
graves of kings (and mine).

TWO LETTERS ON SAMOS

POSIDIPPUS TO PHILAENIS

Procne your charming servant has
brought me your letter and I get

the message I wrote to you as to
one alone as to the one alone I

could love but your answer is to
Menecratis my wife as well as to

me I understand yes as I feared
you are really in love with Polu-

cron may you have much joy of him
he is a charming young man but

when he goes please send me word
I shall be waiting here for you.

PHILAENIS TO POSIDIPPUS

Are you Pan's goat or the owl of
Athene I didn't love my father

and it would be hard for me to
love you old man you are very

clever you talk well and your
conversation passes a dull eve-

ning but are you not cold in-
side I know about young men

like Polucron he is only the most
recent in a very long procession

* * * * *

Procne give me back that letter
don't take it who knows I may

need him later on that old goat
yet perhaps he *is* a wise old owl.

EN PROVENCE

Trobar clus & trobar ric
that's the way we did the trick

trobar ric & trobar clus
that's what made those ladies screw.

A CENTO FROM GARY/AJAR'S *LA VIE DEVANT SOI**

Suis-je un faux jeton?
Suis-je né de travers?
Il me semble que je ne fais rien que me casser la gueule.
Je ne suis qu'une virgule dans le grand livre de la vie.
Je voudrais vivre comme un coq en pâte, mais je vis de bouche-à-
    oreille.
Je mens comme un arracheur de dents pour faire régner la bonne
    humeur.
Je pense que la vie n'est pas un truc pour tout le monde, et
    surtout pas pour moi.
Quand je pleure, je pleure comme un veau.
Est-ce qu'il faut lécher le cul à quelqu'un pour être heureux?
Souvent la vie me donne la chair de poule.
Quelquefois j'ai plein le cul de ce qui se passe au monde.
Est-ce que je finirai en queue de poisson?
Je paierais les yeux de la tête pour avoir une vie nouvelle.
Je suis un faux jeton.

* Translation in Notes.

I HATE LOVE

says Alcaeus echthairo ton
erota and Rufinus boasts

that he has armed himself
against love with wisdom

hoplismai pros erota peri
sternoisi logismon and

Meleager weeps his woes
to the night and his bed-

lamp hiere kai luchne and
these are wise words from

men of experience but alas
I am caught in that trap

for Heraclea has put her
little foot on my neck

and I cannot heed them.

FLOWN AWAY

Il pleure dans mon coeur
mon coeur qui est mis à

nu so please tell me Mr.
Baudelaire you rather

unpleasant but wise old
man what I can do about

these penible conditions
now that my butterfly she

is the gay little annetta
that brings the sun has

flown away so far away.

NO MY DEAR

I'll not wish you the death
you deserve sunt apud infer-

nos tot milia formasorum
there are enough women in

hell quite enough beauti-
ful women but it is not

sufficient my dear to be
as beautiful as you are

despicit et magnos recta
puella deos and of all

these young women not one
has enquired the cause of

the world so go your way
my dear and I'll go mine.

THIS IS THE MORTE SAISON

of my heart que les loups se
vivent de vent my bones feel

cold and the blood does not
warm them need I tell you why

I know you know why but
you do little about it yet

I'll not reproach you I can't
because I love you too much.

WRITE ON MY TOMB

that all I learned in books
and from the muses I've ta-

ken with me but my rich pos-
sessions I have left behind.

PICTURE POEMS

(1986–1994)

RAVINGS OF THE DEPRAVED MONK
BENNO OF ST. GALL WHO WENT MAD
FROM CARNAL LONGING IN HIS CELL
AND FORGOT HOW TO WRITE GOOD LATIN

De penetratione aperturae vulvularis
in saecula multa verba scripta sunt
et apud Martialem Catullumque legi-
mus triomphos et repulsas mentularum
superbum sed omnis corporis herba est
cognoscimus tristitiam post coitum.

Editor's Note: This manuscript fragment was
found recently in an abandoned closet in the
scriptorium of the monastery at St. Gall in
Switzerland. It has been attributed to Benno, a
monk of the fourteenth century. It seems obvi-
ous that Benno was visited by a succubus, one of
those demons who assume female form to have
intercourse with men in their sleep.

LES AMANTS

In Magritte's painting Les Amants a man and woman are kissing. But it can't be much fun because they have cloths over their heads so they can't see each other. I know two lovers who could not see each other correctly. They kissed a lot but what they saw was not really the other person. It was a person each one had made up. This made them unhappy but they couldn't stop doing it. They had to make each other up.

THE FLIGHT OF THE NETHROBODS

Astronomers think they may have come from near Mars

What appeared to be a circling asteroid had always been known there

But the Hubble telescope picked up a mysterious variation in its atmosphere

They have great wings but their bodies resemble those of humanoids

They are very hairy and have no ears as we know them

None have yet died who might be dissected

The authorities will not allow scientists close to them for fear of infectious
    contamination

Weinberger speculates that they may be like the men of Atlantis

Their language is so far incomprehensible but Chomsky is working on it
    from tapes

They landed over Tempe, Arizona and are living in the city park

There was no panic, my daughter thinks they are cute, dogs do not bark
    at them

They came in June in a swarm of about a hundred, all of them appear
    to be males

They are friendly and willingly accept our food and water

But they spurn milk, Coca-Cola and other sodas

Children throw them candy but they don't like it

They don't want to sleep in the tents that were put up for them even when it
   rains
Field toilets were set up for them, they looked into them but of course didn't
   know what they were for, they squat
The park attendants clean up after them, but their defecation level appears
   to be minimal
They amuse themselves with finger games and with a game like hopscotch,
   their culture is apparently not advanced
A ball was thrown to them from outside the rope around the park and a
   game of catch was demonstrated for them but they did not pick up the
   ball
The protective rope around the park is necessary because thousands come
   every day to view them, which is great for business in Tempe
There has been tremendous publicity on TV and in the media
President Bush wished to fly in to welcome them and make a speech for TV
   about his deep concern for the entire Universe, but his advisers
   dissuaded him

Why did they want to come to Earth?
They couldn't have known what a lousy place it is
We'll just have to wait to find out all about them.

TEN DOLLARS
REWARD.

R A N away, on the 23d inſt. a handſome active *Mulatto* ſlave, named A R C H, about 21 years of age, is ſlender built and of middle ſtature, talks ſenſible and artful, but if cloſly examined is apt to tremble, has a ridge or ſcar on the back of his neck, about an inch long ; had on, when he went away, an old country linen ſhirt and good oznabrigs trowſers, an old grey kerſey coat, wornout at the elbows---had no hat, ſhoes, or other cloaths whatever, but he probably will ſteal others, he is a faſt reaper and no doubt will procure a ſickle and endeavour to paſs as a freeman. I will give the obove reward if the ſaid fellow be taken Twenty Miles or any further diſtance from home, or *Half a Dollar* per mile, for any diſtance under, in caſe he be ſecured in any gaol ſo that I get him again, and if brought home to me, living in Maryland, near Frederick-Town, all reaſonable Charges.

Ignatious Davis.

June 24, 1793.

Frederick-Town: Printed by *Matthias Bartgis,* at his *Engliſh* and *German* Printing-Office.

How did this story end?
How many billions, perhaps trillions
Have lived and suffered?
How did this one's story end?

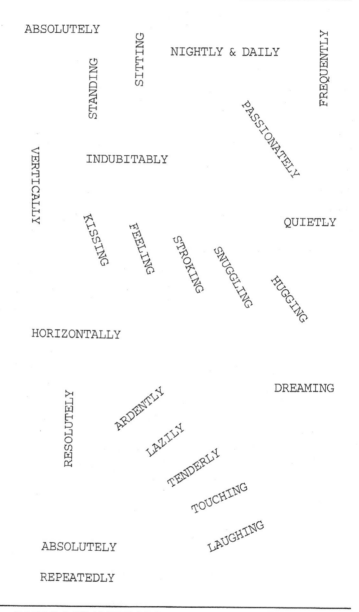

PAOLO & FRANCESCA SHOULD MAKE LOVE AGAIN

THE KISS

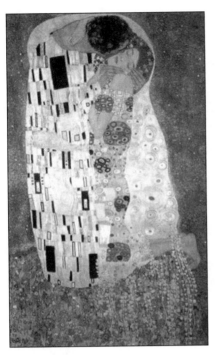

—for Angelica

What did Klimt mean by
the cloth of gold that

binds the lovers togeth-
er like a shroud as they

are kissing   was it the
inner shining of their

hearts as they embrace
the girl's face is clear-

ly yours (so beautiful
with the eyes closed)

but the man's face is hid-
den (is it mine)   may I read

the message of the paint-
ing in the way I'm long-

ing to interpret it   one
of the girl's arms is a-

round his neck and the
other is caressing the

back of his hand   may I
believe that she is tel-

ling him I want you to
kiss me over and again

I want you to come to my
bower and give me the

mille basia (the thous-
and kisses) of which

Catullus wrote so long ago
kisses all over my body.

195

An Apsaras from Ayuthia, Thailand
c. XVII Century A.D.

APSARASES

do not need wings because
they can fly with their

long hair   it streams be-
hind them like the tresses

of Shiva Nataraja (which
are the eternal waves of

the Ganges) soft in the ae-
ther their hair propels

them on their amorous and
consoling missions   but let

no man attempt to bind the
hair of an apsaras   it will

fragment at his touch and
she will not come again to

be his celestial lover   he
will be forever earthbound

if he dares to touch the
long hair of an apsaras.

for Vanessa

THE DOPPELGAENGERS

Egon Schiele knew that he was two people
there was no doubt about it   Romain Gary

wanted to be two people but he made a
mess of it and shot himself   Schiele did

better he knew that two men needed two
girls and when he saw the Harms sisters

he hung nude pictures of himself out the
window to court them   he married Edith &

Adele became his affectionate model   all
were content with this arrangement and

Schiele died naturally of influenza.

THE RECLINING POSITION

For his portrait of the poet now in the Tate in London Wyndham Lewis posed his subject in his most habitual position. The head is leaning far back on the chair cushion, the eyes are half closed. He is reclining. At Rapallo the poet built his own chair to get exactly the inclination that he wanted.

This favored body position has long perplexed the poet's biographers. But in Pound's postscript to De Gourmont's <u>Natural Philosophy of Love</u> we find:

> "... it is more than likely that the brain itself is ... only a sort of great clot of genital fluid ... the brain as a presenter of images. ... creative thought is an act like fecundation, like the male cast of the human seed ... ejaculation ... the mind is an up-spurt of sperm ... "

Per nebulas surgit lux. Fluids don't run uphill. The poet reclined as much as possible to increase the flow of spermatozoa to his bean—which is what made him so smart.

Rodin: La Muse

LA LANGUE ENFANTINE

Quand elle dort et s'éveille
pour un instant (comme si elle

était troublée par un rêve) elle
parle dans une langue enfantine

une langue très douce et presque
imperceptible qui est difficile

à comprendre   parfois c'est un
discours amoureux racontant des

choses qu'elle hésite à dire en
plein jour   j'attends avec im-

patience cette langue enfantine
et ses petites histoires tendres.

THE INFANTILE LANGUAGE

When she's asleep and wakes for a moment
as if she were troubled by a dream
she speaks in an infantile language
a language that's soft
and almost inaudible, difficult to understand
sometimes it's an amorous story
telling things she'd be reluctant to say by day
I wait with impatience for this infantile speech
with its tender little tales.

199

THE FAMILY COUNCIL OF THE YAKOVLEVS

Je suis au bout de mon Latin. I don't know what more I can say about this miserable affair. That the girl falls in love with a scoundrel is bad enough. That she wants to marry him is unbearable. That she expects us to provide a dowry — which he would squander at the tables in a few months — simply proves that she is mad. Perhaps that's the answer: a comfortable nursing home until she comes to her senses. Dr. Krasoveky is a reliable fellow; I'll have a word with him.

—Distorted from Alexander Herzen's autobiography

MULTOS PER ANNOS ET MULTAS PER NOCTES
UMFRICUS INVICTUS DABAT VOLUPTATEM VIR-
GINIBUS VICINITATIS SED NUNC SUB HIBISCUM
DIUTURNUM SOMNUM QUIESCAT CUM MENTU-
LA ERECTA

For Guy Davenport's tomcat Humphrey who died in the
pursuit of love

Through many nights of many years invincible Humphrey gave
pleasure to the virgins of the neighborhood but now under the
hibiscus bush he lies quiet in diuturnal sleep his member
still erect

καὶ ποθήω καὶ μάομαι
κὰτ ἔμον στάλαχμον

"and I long and yearn
in my pain"

To that charming
girl in the Min-

erva who flashed
her eyes at you

all evening with
such gaiety you

finally said if
I were I would

but I'm not.

Sappho, 36-7

202

CARMINA GEMINA

Felix cui Fortuna pulcherrimas
ambas dat quam propre Cartumam

conflevent flumena dua Nilam
maternam albam caeruleamque

videntur quam aut Janua dea
portarum Romae duas vias a-

perit felix poeta qui car-
mina gemina cantare potest.

Happy he to whom fortune gives two beauties
As near Khartoum two rivers converge
The white & blue branches of Mother Nile
Or, as at Rome, Janua, goddess of gates,
    opens two roads.
Happy the poet who can sing two songs.

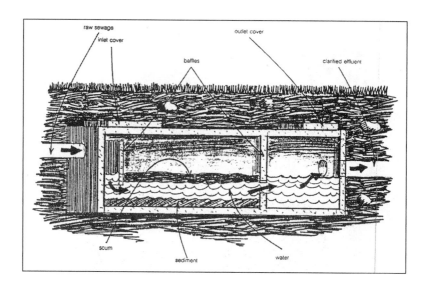

The Inner Life of the
Septic Tank

INVITATION

Poets are invited to submit poems appropriate to the above title. Poems may be of any length and in any metric, though sonnets are preferred.

The judge for the contest will be the noted poet & editor Clayton Eshleman.

First prize will be a week in Paris (Air France) with guided tour of the Paris sewer system by the eminent coprophile Jean Valjean.

Entries must be received before March 1st, 1995 addressed (with stamped return envelope please) to Hiram Handspring, Box 606, Norfolk, CT 06058.

THE BLOWPIPE GAME

The artist sometimes sees
what we can't see in our

mirror   I don't know who
"Gilbert' was (I found

him in the Paris Illus-
tration of September 1855)

but how did he know so much
about me 59 years before I

was even born   of course I
don't accept the obvious

interpretation   I think his
blowpipe is the poet's flute

and the little ball he is
dancing in the air is the

dance of words in my head.

205

MARKET DISCOUNTS LOVE

The latest focus group research reveals
that Love is no longer so popular a consumer
    product in American homes as it once was.
Despite intensified marketing programs by such
    leading producers as Eros Corporation
with its emphasis on innovative packaging
the market share of Love has been slipping in every
    state except North Dakota,
where extremes of temperature make accurate testing
    difficult.
Most Madison Avenue analysts blame the appeal of
    more accessible forms of entertainment
brought into the home by cable or satellite dishes.
Laser cassettes are also a factor, says Maisie
    James, who follows Love issues for Untergang
    Weibchen Sludd brokerage.
We have given our customers the sell signal on Love
    stocks, Ms. James told this reporter.
Arbitrageurs, some large institutional funds, and
    sophisticated chart traders are now taking short
positions in Love.

THE FRENCH

are such an orderly race
it is reported that the

grande horizontale Liane
de Pougy would offer to

her lovers only the up-
per part of her body be-

cause the lower part was
reserved for her husband.

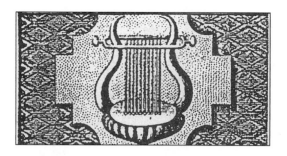

ASMODEUS

Asmodeus was a singer in Naxos. He was a virtuous man but, — in some way — perhaps an irregularity in a sacrifice — he had offended Hermes, messenger of the Gods. Asmodeus had a son named Diphilus, a fine boy who was his father's pride. When Diphilus was thirteen his father brought home a new lyre, which a merchant had found for him, in Corinth. The instrument was so cleverly fashioned that it almost seemed to play itself. There was a secret to the way the strings must be plucked. One day when his father was away Diphilus tried to play the magical lyre, but he didn't know the lyre's secret and broke it. The lyre would not sound for him, Hermes saw this from on high and he filled Diphilus's mind with fear that his father would be very angry. The boy was seized with madness. He ran out into the street and threw himself before the horses of a wagon. But first he had written to his father, begging him to forgive his clumsiness. Asmodeus was grief-stricken. Why had he not taught his son to pluck the lyre? Asmodeus built a high tumulus for Diphilus and watered its earth with his tears. Then he made a propitiatory sacrifice to Hermes. But, this time, did he perform the rites correctly? It is difficult to please the high gods.

L'ARRIVEE
DU PRINTEMPS

Je pense à toi   mon coeur
est rempli de ton être

tu cours dans mes veines
comme la sève du printemps

tu es toujours loin mais
même ici je sens ta touche

douce comme la bise méridi-
onale   ne tards pas de venire

Persephone ne tards pas   je
t'attends avec impatience.

THE COMING OF SPRING

I'm thinking of you
and my heart is full of your being
you run in my veins like spring sap
you are always so far away
but even here I feel your soft touch
like the wind from the south
come as soon as you can, Persephone
don't delay, I await you with longing.

TO MY LADY IN A DISTANT LAND
THAT SHE FORGET ME NOT

Now to my Lady I would speak
In Latin, Provençal and Greek,
Yet all three tongues are not enough
To add the sum that is my love.

Her beauty doeth all words exceed,
A new-made language is my need.
Orpheus, lend me now your reed,
Aid me to make my cause succeed.

Should language fail and music too
then there is little I can do,
Save eyes must speak
And seek to lift my limping Greek.

WELTSPIE(

Fernseher ,kaputt' – Schüler tötet sich

ür
ıltin

Linz (dpa) – Ein 13jähriger Schüler hat sich in Oberöster- reich umgebracht, weil er meinte, er habe den neuen Fernsehappa- rat seiner Eltern kaputt gemacht. Wie die Gendarmerie gestern be- richtete, warf sich der Junge vor einen Eisenbahnzug. In einem Abschiedsbrief habe er bedauert, „Blödsinn" gemacht zu haben. Tatsächlich habe der Junge das ihm unbekannte neue Gerät nicht einschalten können und deshalb gemeint, er habe es be- schädigt.

ıs lang-
, sich ge-
elen Vor-
nemaliger
aß ihm die
sanwältin
nem Straf-
ıeine. Un-
, glaubten.
,Karte bei:
ılauben an
ʒeit wieder-
ısen oder die
ıöner, sind,
Geheimnis."

,Kö
Parisei

"Linz (dpa) — A 13 year old schoolboy has killed himself in Upper Austria because he thought he had broken his parents' new television set. Yesterday the police reported that the child threw himself in front of a train, leaving a suicide note to the effect that he was sorry to have done something so idiotic. Actually what the child did not know was that he had not damaged the new set but had simply not known how to turn it on."

INGENIUM NOBIS IPSA PUELLA FACIT

Propertius wrote that it
is the girl who makes the

poem but is the obverse
true will poems make a

girl I'm not so certain

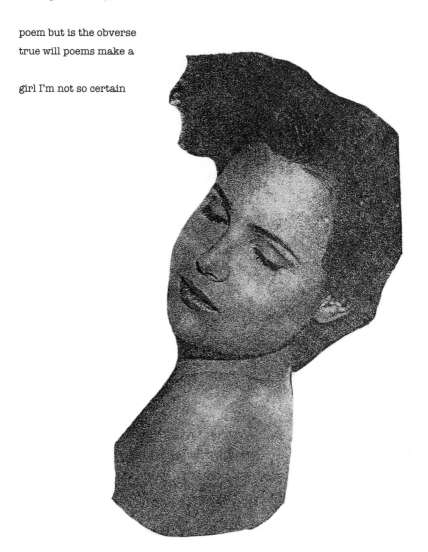

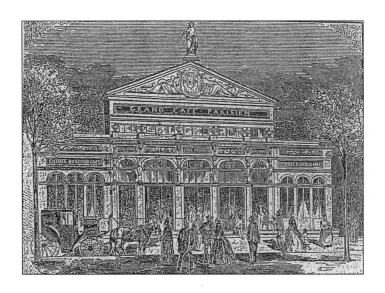

ENCOUNTER AT THE CASINO, AIX-LES-BAINS

It is one of Oriane's "difficult" evenings, and she has hidden herself in the garden of the casino. How tiresome she is. As I am searching for her I encounter the smile of a young person wearing a silk kerchief. Lovely gray eyes and she has applied a touch of gray eye-shadow to match them. Perhaps a servant from the casino kitchen but she looks charming. As we pause together for a moment she murmurs that she will wait by the dolphin fountain in the little park beyond the casino for five minutes. Oriane appears. She has been hiding in the privet maze. She seems calmer now. She asks to be taken home, and of course I must take her. How would I manage without her, tiresome as she is?

THE NEREID

At dawn every day a nereid comes up out of
the sea. Sometimes she is carrying a hand-
ful of seaweed. She goes up into the rocks for
a little while and then returns to her aque-
ous home. She seems insensitive to cold.
She is always lightly clad. I have spoken to
her but she does not reply. I have addressed
her as Thetis and as Galatea, thinking one of
these might be her name, but with no
response. Yet I think she knows I am observ-
ing her and is not displeased by my pres-
ence. I have told no one about her visits,
fearing that they might harm her. It is
granted to few to have a goddess as a friend.
To what do I owe this good fortune?

(AMERICAN)
FRENCH POEMS

(1986–1997)

THE IMPORTANCE OF
DICTIONARIES

Mallarmé told Degas that poems
are made with words not with

ideas and that he found some of
his most luminous words in La-

rousse since I have never had
an idea and don't expect to

have one I follow his practice
but I use the Dictionnaire du

français argotique et populaire
because its words are so much

more colorful and stimulating.

ORPHÉE

Je te conseille Eurydice de
ne pas me suivre tu t'imagines

que je pourrais devenir ton
bonheur mais je crains de te me-

ner dans l'abîme méfie-toi
des poètes ils sont pour la

plupart des voleurs d'âmes
tu sais bien que je te vé-

nére mais est-ce que je te
regard trop sera cela notre

fatalité les dieux jaloux
ont mis leur marque sur les

poètes sois sage et méfie-
toi d'eux ils sont un peril.

ORPHEUS

I advise you. Eurydice, not to follow me
You imagine that I might bring you happiness
But I fear that I would lead you into the abyss
Don't trust poets
Most of them are stealers of souls
You know very well that I adore you
But do I watch you too much?
Would that be fatal for us?
The jealous gods have put their mark on poets
Beware of them, they are dangerous.

LA GOMME À EFFACER

On dit que c'est Dieu qui
tient la gomme à effacer

et nous lisons dans le Tes-
tament qu'il se préoccupe de

nous mai si cela est vrai
pourquoi est-ce qu'il n'ef-

face pas de ma mémoire l'i-
mage dorlotée de toi qui ne

me quitte ni jour ni nuit.

THE ERASER

They say that the power of erasure in our lives
     belongs to God
And we read in the Bible that he is concerned about us
But if that is true
Why does he not erase from my memory
The adorable image of you
Which will not leave me night or day?

JE SUIS UN CERF-VOLANT SAUGRENU

je me laisse traîner par tous
les vents us me prennent où

ils veulent de très haut dans
le ciel je regarde ces petites

gens là-bas ce sont des mecs
et des mouches je suis bien

content d'avoir quitté leur
domaine sauf pour une chose

que tu ne voles pas avec moi
ma compagne dans les nuages.

I AM A PREPOSTEROUS BEETLE

I let myself be carried along by every breeze
The winds take me where they will
From high in the sky I look down on the little people below
They are just guys and dolls
I'm glad to have left their domain
Except for one thing
You aren't flying with me
My companion in the clouds.

LA LUCIOLE

Je te vois voltigeante dans la
nuit et je te poursuis pour t'at-

traper tu es presqu'insaisissable
mais à la fin je te tiens mais

quand j'ouvre la main tu n'es
pas là tu m'as échappé de nou-

veau qu'est-ce que tu chasses
c'est clair que ce n'est pas

moi je plains la vélocité de
tes alternances affectives

mais je ne sais pas si je veux
te faire changer car si tu é-
tais toujours prévisible serais
tu rasante comme les autres?

THE FIREFLY

I see you flashing in the night and try to catch you
But it's almost impossible to seize you
When I open my hand you're not there, you've escaped me again
What are you hunting for?
It's clear that it's not me
I begrudge the speed of your changes of affection
But I don't think I'd want to change you
If you were always predictable
Might you not become as boring as the others?

I LOVE THEREFORE I AM
I SUFFER BUT I'M ALIVE

And we read in the books of the ancients
that life is more or less painful for most people
certainly the Olympians know that
but they don't do much to improve the human lot
they're up there amusing themselves with their idiotic games
and they don't seem to give a damn about us
but sometimes a mortal gives them something to think about
I'm not Hercules or Prometheus but I have the patience of a
    dumb beast
I suffer but I'll endure and survive
the day will come when I'll spit in the teeth of those loafers
because without us poets they simply wouldn't exist.

J'AYME DONC JE SUIS
JE SOUFFRE MAIS JE VIS

et nous lisons dans les livres
des anciens que la vie est plu-

tôt pénible pour la plupart des
gens assurément les olympiens

le savent mais ils ne font pas
grand'chose pour améliorer le

destin humain ils sont là-haut
s'amusant avec leur jeux

idiots et ils semblent se ficher
de nous mais quelquefois un

mortel leur donne à penser je
ne suis pas Hercule ni Promé-

thée mais j'ai la patience d'une
bête des champs je souffre mais

je survivrai il viendra un jour
où je cracherai dans la gueule

de ces fainéants car sans les
poètes ils n'existeraient pas.

J'IGNORE OÙ ELLE VAGUE CE SOIR

quelqu'un l'a vue à Ectaban
et un autre à Samarkand le

monde est grand et plein de
séductions pour une belle

fille mais je lui enverrai
par pigeon voyageur ce mot

qu'il y aura toujours pour
elle un logement à l'abri

ici dans mon coeur fidèle.

I DON'T KNOW WHERE SHE IS
WANDERING TONIGHT

Someone saw her in Ecbatan
And another in Samarkand
The world is wide and full of seductions
For a beautiful girl
But I'll send her this word by carrier pigeon
That for her there will always be lodging and shelter
Here in my faithful heart.

POUR BIEN AIMER*

il n'est pas indispensable de
faire le moulin à vent ou le

fauteuil à bascule comme nous
ont raconté nos confrères aux

Indes bien sûr ces exercices
sont amusants pour les jeunes

mais quand on arrive à un cer-
tain âge on reconnaît que ce

qui vaut la peine est seule-
ment l'athlétisme de l'esprit.

* Translation in Notes.

SHE WALKS NO LONGER IN THE NIGHT

She doesn't come anymore to visit me in my dreams
Which are now solitary and shadowy caverns
Where is she really?
In her last letter she wrote me
That she was going to the source of the Nile to find Prester John
That he was the prince she was waiting for
What must I think?
Everyone knows that Prester John never existed
In all the centuries no one has discovered his kingdom of ivory
    and gold
And I, do I myself exist?
When she is far away I cannot be certain.

ELLE N'EST PLUS NOCTAMBULE

elle ne vient plus me rendre visite
dans mes rêves qui sont maintenant

cavernes solitaires et ténébreuses
où vraiment est-elle dans sa derni-

ère lettre elle m'a écrit qu'elle al-
lait vers la source du Nil pour re-

trouver Prester John que c'était lui
et pas moi le prince qu'elle atten-

dait que dois-je croire on sait bien
que Prester John n'existe pas per-

sonne dans tous les siècles n'a ja-
mais découvert son royaume d'ivoire

et d'or et moi est-ce que moi-même
j'existe quand elle est si lointaine

je n'en suis pas certain.

DOIS-JE REPRENDRE *

du poil de la béte depuis
dix années je me suis lais-

sé aller au fil de l'eau
j'ai suivi le chemin de

l'incertitude et puis un
jour il m'est arrivé d'as-

sister à un miracle qui n'était
pas comme tant d'autres un mi-

rage dois-je reprendre main-
tenant du poil de la bête?

*Translation in Notes.

LA FLEUR BLEUE

Je veux te voir comme une
fleur bleue qui sort de la

racine de l'innocence une
fleur que la vie mondaine

n'a jamais flétrie mais tes
charmes sont tellement va-

riés te laissant exposée
aux malins et aux salauds

qui sait qui sait je trem-
ble pour toi mals n'importe

ce qui t'arrive je garderai
mon rêve de ma fleur bleue.

THE BLUE FLOWER

I want to see you as the blue flower
That has sprung from the root of innocence
A flower which worldly life has never faded
But your charms are so various
Leaving you exposed to the wicked and dirty
Who knows, who knows, but whatever happens to you
I'll keep my dream of the blue flower.

LE MORDU DE LA MOTO*

Je vais repiquer au truc je
m'en fous de cet hotu mino-

taure s'il est mortel il met-
tra ses pieds dans le plat

et tu en auras gros sur la
patate moi je peux attendre

les dieux sont mes copains
ils m'invitent à bouffer a-

vec eux sur l'Olympe tous
les samedis soir ils au-

ront une torgnole pour ce
gazier de minotaure ça

les amusera je ne me bile
pas ce n'est pas la fin des

haricots j'irai au radada
avant de rejoindre la terre.

*Translation in Notes.

230

LES VIEILLARDS*

s'amourachent trop facile-
ment ils ne se rendent pas

compte de l'effet de leur
folie sur les jeunes per-

sonnes bien élevées ils
voient dans les champs

une belle fleur et ils se
précipitent pour l'arracher

et sans penser à la peine que
leur ferveur peut donner la

vieillesse est quelquefois
triste sauf que chaque rêve

est toujours le plus beau
le plus enivrant et fait

rappeler les jours verts.

* Translation in Notes.

LA VOIX QUI CHANTE DANS
MON COEUR*

Je me suis amouraché d'une voix
mais ce n'est pas celle d'une

Maria Callas une voix claire mais
douce une voix liquide qui coule

comme un ruisseau figurez-vous
une voix qui est à la fois celle

d'une fillette un peu hésitante
et d'une déesse qui ordonne ma

vie mais quand elle me rend vi-
site dans mes rêves la voix que

j'entends est celle de Rhodope
la nymphe de la forêt qui sa-

vait causer avec les oiseaux
les arbres et même les fleurs.

*Translation in Notes.

232

ELLE A LA TÊTE QUI DANSE*

et c'est pour cela que je l'adore
si je lui raconte quelque chose

elle jette mes paroles dans l'air
comme un jongleur et me les rend

si changées si belles qu'à peine
puis-je les reconnaître et elle

prends mes idées et les fragmente
de telle façon qu'elles sont neuves

et rafraîchies grâce à elle l'é-
change devient étincelant et le

fait qu'elle est tellement belle
est un supplément bien agréable.

* Translation in Notes.

SHE SAYS THAT I PUT ON GLOVES

That I don't talk to her frankly
About street things and about earthly things
That lovers usually talk about
She is a bit tired of all my complicated stories of naiads
   and goddesses
Although I always put it in my verses
That she is much more beautiful than these ladies of
   antiquity
What goes on in your head she asks
I'm flesh and blood not a mummy
Come to see me and I'll teach you
What you ought to write in your poems.

ELLE DIT QUE JE METS DES GANTS

que je ne lui parle pas franche-
ment des choses de la rue et des

choses terrestres dont les am-
ants s'occupent habituellement

elle est un peu fatiguée de
toutes ces histoires compli-

quées de naïades et de déesses
quoique j'écris toujours dans

mes vers qu'elle est beaucoup
plus belle que ces dames de

l'antiquité qu'est-ce qui se
passe dans ta tête elle me

demande je suis chair et sang
pas une momie viens me voir et

je pourrai t'enseigner comment
tu dois formuler tes poèmes.

THE ERMINE

I know a bitch who amuses herself making messes
She has a head on her and uses it well
It's not a question of money or con-games
No, it's upsetting the lives of others

Give her a menage that's working well
And she'll find one way or another to insert herself into it
Man or woman, it makes no difference, she'll eat anything
A year of it perhaps and she's bored up to her neck
Then the game starts again with another couple
Some gall but she really has luck.

L'HERMINE

Je connais une gonzesse qui
s'amuse avec la gabegie elle

a de la tête et s'en sert bien
pas question de fric et rien

d'escroquerie non c'est le dé-
rangement de la vie des autres

qui est sa distraction et même ses
amis ne sont pas exempts donne-

la un ménage qui marche bien et
elle trouvera le moyen de façon

ou d'autre de s'y insérer gars
ou fille ça lui est égal elle a

la bouche pleine pour tout un
an peut-être et elle est rasée

jusqu'à la gorge et le jeu
se renouvelle elle a du fiel

oui elle a du cul pour vrai.

THE GARDEN OF DÉLIGHTS

I don't always see you clearly
you are charming and beautiful
you talk like two angels at once
but I suspect a mystery
I feel there is a corner of your nature
where no one can enter

what are you hiding in that corner of your soul
will you ever let me visit there?

is it a secret garden?
I make my prayer to the gods
that it is the garden of my delights
the garden I have been seeking for so long.

LE JARDIN DES DÉLICES

Je ne te vois pas tout à fait
clair tu es charmante tu es

belle tu parles comme deux
anges à la fois mais je soup-

çonne un mystère je sens un
coin de ta nature où personne

ne peut entrer qu'est-ce que
tu caches dans ce coin de ton

âme me laisseras tu y visiter
un jour est-ce un jardin se-

crèt je fais mes supplications
aux dieux que ce soit le jar-

din de mes delices le jardin
que je cherche depuis longtemps.

THE NAMELESS VOYAGE

Where does she go
when she closes her eyes
when we are making love?

She is there by my side
yet she isn't there

If I touch her she trembles
but says nothing

One night I asked her
where it was she travelled

This time she smiled and answered
don't be worried
I'll never be far from you

The land which I visit
is the land of the poems
you have written for me.

LE VOYAGE INNOMÉ

Où est-ce qu'elle va
quand elle ferme ses

yeux lorsque nous fai-
sons le radada elle est

là a mon côté et elle
n'est pas là si je la

touche elle frémit mais
elle ne me dit rien un

jour je lui ai demandé
où elle voyageait cette

fois elle a souri et m'a
répondu ne t'inquiètes

pas je n'irai jamais loin
de toi le pays auquel je

rends visite est ce des
poèmes que tu m'as écrit.

DEUX FANTAISISTES*

se sont éprendues chacune
ne voyait dans l'autre que

ce qu'elle voulait voir
tous les deux se faisaient

illusion d'aimer dans l'autre
une création imaginaire mais

un jour hélas elles se trou-
vaient devant le miroir de

la réalité et elles se re-
connaissaient l'une l'autre

comme elles étaient pour vrai.

*Translation in Notes.

TU SAIS, JE CROIS*

que tu m'as bien allumé
du moment que je t'ai vue

et que je t'ai entendue
parler quelque chose de

remarquable m'est arrivé
comment l'expliquer ce

n'est pas facile il faut
chercher peut-être une

métonymie oneïrique je
pensais que j'avais de

petits poissons qui s'é-
battraient dans mon sang.

*Translation in Notes

LE BAPTÊME DE CELUI QUI NOYE*

Dans le baptême de certains
cultes il y a l'immersion

totale et c'était ainsi pour
moi il y a un an je ne te con-

naissais pas et puis il arri-
va la révélation qui a boulever-

sé ma vie depuis lors je nage
dans ton être et comme le po-

ète a écrit "il naufragar
m'é dolce in questo mare."

*Translation in Notes.

LE BLESSÉ*

Je veux montrer mes plaies
à tous il faut étaler com-

ment elle m'a mordu c'était
un massacre affreux on dit

que c'était ma faute que je
tâchais de l'avaler ça se

peut je ne le nie pas mais
elle est si succulente je

ne savais pas me contenir.

* Translation in Notes

C'EST À MOURIR DE RIRE*

que je te poursuis moi qui
suis un grepin crevé sans

grand'chose dans le jinjin
et toi un si joli lot avec

tant de tête mais on lit
comment Sigismundo a été

affolé par la belle Ixotta et
a même peut-être empois-

onné sa femme pour l'avoir
(je ne ferais rien de si

stupide que cela) et Goethe
agé de 73 ans cet été là

à Marienbad sentit le jean-
nu-tête et courut en bas de

son cabinet de travail lors-
qu'il entendit la chanson

de la gigolette dans l'allée
ô si je dois périr c'est du

poison fraix et délicieux de
ton rire que je veux mourir.

*Translation in Notes.

LA DÉBINE DE MON COEUR*

C'est mon métier de me débiner
un jour je suis tout et le pro

chain rien   si tu souris je monte
au ciel mais quand tu t'éloignes

c'est la chute dans le gouffre
c'est un tape-cul mais ce n'est

pas comique ce n'est plus un jeu
d'enfants qui s'amusent je me dé-

bine car tu ne m'aimes plus as-
sez mais même cet acte de lou-

ange ne sert pas à te ramollir.

*Translation in Notes.

I'M NOT LUCKY WITH GIRLS

I turn myself into an acrobat to please them
But they only jump backwards
Some will turn tricks but others won't play
Colombine talks all the time, I can't get a word in
And Justine stares silently with a disapproving look
    of boredom
There was even one who tried to blackmail me
Yet my favorite, my jewel, is a beautiful girl
Who doesn't want to dress in anything except ski pants
Day and night she wears ski pants
Even if we're going to dine at Lutèce
What's to be made of that, especially when she has
    sexy legs and pretty little feet?
Just think of it.

JE NE SUIS PAS VEINARD

avec les filles je me fais acro-
bate pour leurs plaire mais elles ne

sautent qu'en arrière il y en ont
qui vaudrillent et d'autres qui ne

veulent pas faire la popote Col-
ombine parle tout le temps je ne

peux pas injecter un mot et Jus-
tine est muette me regardent d'oeil

désapprobateur et claqué il y avait
même une qui tenta la chantage pour-

tant mon favori mon joyau est une
très belle qui ne veut porter que

les pantalons de ski   matin et soir
elle porte les pantalons de ski

même si nous allons dîner chez Lu-
tèce qu'est-ce qu'on doit penser

de ça surtout quand elle a les
jambes bien "sexy" et de jolis

petits pieds figurez-vous cela.

THE SECRET WORDS

I'm waiting impatiently for a letter from your friend Alceste
Which I hope will let fall an inadvertent hint
Which may put me on the track of the solution to an
    enigma
Which I never dared ask you about
I mean the delphic words written on a fragment of old parchment
Which you always carry with you in your handbag
Once when you thought you were alone I watched you take out this
    talisman and whisper as you read it
Again I was afraid to question you
But I must absolutely discover the secret words
I'm convinced that they would make me understand why you draw
    away from me.

LES MOTS SECRETS

J'attends avec impatience l'arrivée
d'une lettre de ta copaine Alceste

qui peut-être laissera tomber en in-
advertence un indice qui me mettra

sur la piste d'un énigme que je n'os-
erais jamais te demander je veux dire

les mots delphiens écrits sur un
fragment de vieux parchemin que tu

portes avec toi toujours dans ton
sac une fois quand tu te croyais

seule je te vis retirer ce talisman
et le lire en chuchotant mais

j'eus peur de poser une question
mais il me faut absolument trouv-

er ces mots secrets car je suis con-
vaincu qu'ils me feraient com-

prendre pourquoi tu t'éloignes.

JE SUIS LE COMÉDIEN*

de l'amour je m'appelle Sgana-
relle le cocu imaginaire et je

tâche de faire rire je désire te
donner du plaisir mais je veux

en même temps que tu ries voyons
quand on regarde de loin ce que

font les amants est un peu bi-
zarre tu ne trouves pas il me

semble que le système n'est pas
moderne n'est pas pratique pas

de détails mais tu comprends ce
que je veux dire et c'est pour

cela que je tâche de faire rire.

*Translation in Notes.

LE POÈTE ENGLOUTI*

Il marmonne ses lignes dans
une hébétude il est soûl du

son des mots comme une grive
les mots de n'importe quelle

langue il les poursuit tous
même s'il ne les comprend pas

(il se sent privé parce qu'il
ne peut pas faire sonner les

caractères devanagris et palis)
auprès de lui entends-tu un bour-

donnement ce sont les paroles
qui essaiment comme des ab-

eilles dans sa tête viens je
te supplie au secours du poète

laisses-le entendre ta douce
voix et ton rire au lieu de

ce torrent sans fin de mots.

*Translation in Notes.

I'M FED UP WITH MY LIFE

"I've had enough of the mug they've given me"
I feel like a dummy in a store window
People make fun of me and I make fun of myself
I have a bad reputation, I'm called
        a stupid phoney, I'm disgusted
        enough to vomit
So let me undress from my life completely,
I'm the prisoner of my face and I'd
        like to clean up my act
To get back to my childhood, I want
        to begin everything over.

JE SUIS RAPLAPLAT

de ma vie j'en ai assez de la
gueule que l'on m'a faite je

me sens un mannequin dans une
vitrine on se moque de moi et

je me moque de moi-même je
porte la bada on me trouve un

cabotin stupide je suis de-
geu laisses-moi alosrs me de-

frusquer complètement de ma
vie je suis taulard de ma ter-

rine et je voudrais tout ré-
tamer pour repiquer à mon en-

fance je veux tout recommencer.

CAUTION

What would my life have been if one day you hadn't dared to give
    me a secret signal of your regard?
By all the conventions a well-brought-up girl such as you
    (and particularly one with a pedigree like yours)
Would never reveal an intimate predilection (especially for a
    bumpkin like me)
Tortured with love but timid, I watched you from afar, speaking to
    you only with lowered eyes, never imagining that you could take
    me seriously
What joy then and what surprise when you showed me with such
    delicate finesse
That you could find a little corner for me in your heart Only a small
    corner but my own.

L'AVERTISSEMENT

Qu'aurait été ma vie si tu
n'avais pas osé me donner ce

jour-là le signal tout secret
de ton égard   par les conven-

ances une jeune fille bien é-
levée comme toi (et surtout de

race) ne montre aucune prédi-
lection intime (surtout pour

un rustaud comme moi)   te-
naillé mais timide je te re-

gardais de loin te parlant
seulement avec les yeux a-

baissés ne pensant pas que
tu puisses me priser à titre

particulier   quelle joie et
quelle surprise alors quand

tu m'indiquas avec une finesse
si délicate que tu saurais m'ac-

corder un coin dans ton coeur
un petit coin mais tout à moi.

LES CONSOLATIONS

Les trésors de la vieillesse
Sont les petites aventures
de l'imagination.
Un beau visage fait revenir
       un autre
Qu'on a bien aimé loin dans
       le passé
Alors on se console en disant
"De nouveau je suis jeune."

THE CONSOLATIONS

The treasures of old age
Are the little adventures
       of the imagination.
A beautiful face recalls
       another
That was so much loved
       long ago.
And we console ourselves
Saying, "I'm young again."

MES SOUFFRANCES*

Je souffre parce que je suis
laid et elle est si belle   je

suis presqu' aveugle et elle
voit tout si clair   je marche

à quatre pattes et elle vole
comme une hirondelle   je me mords

la langue quand je parle mais
elle chante comme le rossignol

mes souffrances sont intolér-
ables mais quand elle me jête

un sourire je les oublie toutes.

*Translation in Notes.

MY SECRET

I demand that they give me a bed
in the insane asylum
Just imagine how I've suffered in
this "beautiful world" the way it is
My name is not really what's
inscribed on my identity card
Nobody knows who I am
(and I'm not going to tell you)
It's my secret
I expect to meet God in the asylum
I'll tell Him my real name
He will recognize me
And arrange things for my welfare.

MON SECRET

Je demande qu'on me donne
un lit à l'hôpital des fous

figurez-vous comme j'ai souf-
fert dans ce beau monde tel

qu'il est   mon nom n'est pas
vraiment celui qui est in-

scrit sur ma carte d'identi-
té   personne ne sait qui je

suis (et je ne vais pas vous
le dire   c'est mon secret à

moi) j'attends de rencontrer
le Bon Dieu à l'hôpital des

fous   à Lui j'avouerai mon
vrai nom   il me reconnaîtra et

arrangera tout pour mon bien.

LE HOQUETON

Ne me confondez pas avec ce fripon
Eros   je suis hoqueton du roi je

lance mes flèches pour la gloire
(ou pour le butin) non pas pour l'am-

our   en effet les nénettes ne m'amu-
sent pas trop   pour la chasse je pré-

fère un cerf à douze bois ou un san-
glier saignant   le piquer cela en

vaut la peine   les femmes sont trop
molles et elles parlent après le fait.

THE KING'S BOWMAN

Don't mix me up with that rascal Eros
I'm one of the bowmen of the king
I shoot my arrows for glory (or for booty)
Not for the sake of love
To tell the truth girls don't amuse me much
For hunting I prefer a stag with twelve points or a bleeding boar
To hit one of those is worth the trouble
Women are too soft and they want to talk after they do it.

260

LES PATINEURS

s'en vont traînant leurs chevilles
comme ballades   ils glissent vers

le nirvana du froid   une jambe deux
jambs des pieds sans nombre   flic

flac et droulala   (ne répondant pas
aux sifflets du vent)   mais les pa-

tineurs n'arrivent pas à m'arracher
des coulisses noires   pas de soleil

aucune lumière   je me sens englouti
sous la glace solide   hors d'haleine

mon sang se congèle   resterai-je dans
cet abîme   les patineurs sont si loin.

THE SKATERS

Are leaving, trailing their ankles like ballads
They slide toward the nirvana of cold
One leg, two legs, feet without number
Flic, flac and droulala
(No answer to the whistling of the wind)
The skaters don't succeed in pulling me out of the black tunnels
No sun, no light, I feel engulfed in solid ice
Out of breath, my blood congealing, will I stay in this abyss?
The skaters are so far away now.

On one of his last days (speaking quite seriously) he explained to me
that no physician had ever found with a stethoscope the beating
of his heart
"Isn't it true," he asked, "that a man is lucky to be an egotist and
insensitive"?
For Gourgaud he made the point: "I always saw things so much in
the mass, and from so high that the people escaped my sight."
One fine day he was lifted from his bed (he was heavy now) and
helped to seat himself in an armchair near the window. He
smiled for a moment. "Good morning, sun; good morning, my
friend."
His eyes were getting weak. He asked me to read aloud to him the
lines of Voltaire:

> "To see Paris again I cannot pretend,
>   You see that into my tomb I'm ready to descend."

One night when I was watching at his bedside I heard him whisper
in his delirium, "My son, the day will come when you'll be at the
head of the Grand Army."
The words become scrambled in the history books. The glass becomes
clouded
But we know that before Thebes and Oedipus the gods already knew
how to create sacred monsters.

Dans ses derniers jours (gardant son sérieux) il m'explique qu'aucun
  médecin n'avait jamais trouvé avec un stéthoscope le battement
  de son coeur
"N'est-il pas vrai," demanda-t-il, "qu'on est heureux d'être égoïste et
  insensible?"
À Gourgand il constata, "Je voyais toujours les choses tellement en
  masse et de si haut que les hommes s'échappaient à ma vue."
Un beau matin on l'a soulevé de son lit (il était maintenant assez
  gros) et on l'a fait s'asseoir dans un fauteuil auprès de la fenêtre.
  Pour un instant il souriait. "Bonjour soleil; bonjour mon ami."
Ses yeux s'affaiblissaient. Il me pria de lui lire à haute voix les vers de
  Voltaire:

> *"Mais à revoir Paris, je ne dois plus prétendre,*
> *Vous voyez qu'au tombeau je suis prêt à descendre."*

Une nuit quand je veillais à son lit je l'entendais chuchoter en délire,
  "Mon fils, un jour tu seras à la tête de la Grande Armée."
Les mots se confondent dans les livres. La vitre s'est obscurcie.
Mais nous savons qu'avant Thèbes et Oedipe les dieux ont déjà su
  construire des monstres sacrés.

DANS L'ATTENTE

Avec patience j'attends
Le jour où tu découvriras
Que c'était toujours
Moi que tu attendais.

WAITING

Patiently I'm waiting
For the day when you'll discover
That it was always me
You were waiting for.

L'HYPERESTHÉSIE

Chaque goutte de pluie
Qui tombe dans la barrique
Devient instamment
Le sujet d'un poème.
C'est un bombardment
Impitoyable qui punit
Les sens et menace
D'annihiler la raison.

HYPERAESTHESIA

Each drop of rain
That falls into the barrel
Instantly becomes
The subject for a poem
It's a merciless bombardment
Which punishes the senses
And threatens to annihilate reason.

SAIS-TU

Que toujours tu habites ma maison de rêves?
Depuis des années nous ne sommes plus ensemble.
J'ignore même où maintenant tu vis
Ou avec qui. Cela ne me fait rien.
Car, vivante, tu m'attends dans la maison de rêves,
La belle qui quand autrefois tu me parlait en français,
Faisait courir un tremblement dans tout mon corps.

DO YOU KNOW

That you live in my house of dreams?
It's years since we were together;
I don't even know where you are living now
Or with whom. But such things don't matter
Because you're always waiting for me
In the house of dreams, the girl
Who when she spoke in French,
As we always did, could send a tremor
Through my whole body.

THE HOUSE OF LIGHT

(1986)

WILL WE EVER GO TO THE LIGHTHOUSE?

We see it every day from
the shore and we talk of

sailing out on a happy ex-
pedition we will carry our

gifts to the lighthouse-
keepers but the weather

is always poor or the wind
is wrong and year by year

the lighthouse appears to
become more distant from

us until we are no longer
certain it is really there.

ALBA

I tell the birds you can stop now
I no longer need you I wake to a

more lovely music she has been
speaking to me in my dreams the

birds protest that it has always
been their task to arouse me for

the day do not disturb our lives
they say very well I tell them

you may still sing at dawn but
only in her praise you must imi-

tate her voice or I'll not listen
I will be deaf to your song.

THE HOUSE OF LIGHT

has been designed by the master
builder but the workmen have not

been able to build it the car-
penters & the masons have toil-

ed for many years but they can-
not find a way to make their ma-

terials adhere to enclose light
every method has been a failure

neither lumber nor stone not even
metal or glass will serve to hold

in the light it always escapes
and returns to its source can

anyone build the house of light?

SELECTED POEMS *1935–1985*

(1986)

I take a certain pride
in the fact that in my verses
it is not extremely difficult
to tell what I'm trying to say

James Laughlin modestly refers to his poetry as "light verse," but his is light verse, not in the tradition of Ogden Nash or Dorothy Parker, but in the line that extends from Catullus (one of his masters and the source of many of his macaronics) to Pound's *Moeurs contemporains* and Williams's "This Is Just to Say." In these clean, chiselled poems ("The rule is that in a couplet any second line has to be within two typewriter spaces of the line preceding it"), Laughlin traces, with the greatest delicacy, grace, and wit, the vagaries of sexual love, the pleasures and pain of memory, the power of literary allusion in *making it new*. A poet of many voices, he moves effortlessly into idiomatic French when the emotional, and especially the erotic, occasion warrants it. As a commentator on the local scene, he dons the hat of one Hiram Handspring, a naive and crusty old fellow, who can't quite fathom the goings-on he is forced to witness.

At a time when too many poets have turned their back on the possibility of human relationships, James Laughlin is our poet of Chekhovian longing, a poet for whom love always holds a measure of delight even as does the language that embodies it.

MARJORIE PERLOFF

SOME NATURAL THINGS

THE PERSON

who writes my poems
lives in some other

sphere he sends them
to me through space

when he feels like it
they arrive complete

from beginning to end
and all I have to do

is type them out who
is that person what is

he to me I wonder about
him but will never know.

THE PHILOSOPHER

Well here's a salute to
that clean old man who's

out every day fishing up
coins with a string and

a bit of gum through the
subway gratings on Broad-

way he says that he aver-
ages five dollars a week

and he says that's enough
for a man who don't drink.

THAT SUMMER IN SPAIN

there was a lot of quarreling
you accused me of stealing im-

ages from your poems and I nag-
ged about your drinking but all

that has dropped away and what
remains are the funny things

you would come out with crazy
thoughts from nowhere and how

that night after we joined the
ring of dancers in the square

at Tarragona you were possessed
and embodied Cyprian Aphrodite.

ALL THOSE TALES

you told me to make me
jealous what happened

on the raft the night
you were swimming in

the dark and what you
did under a blanket on

the airplane and what
happened with 2 Swiss

boys in that hotel in
Berne & the next day

driving in their car
and what you did with

that Italian baron in
the back seat with his

chauffeur watching in
the rear-view mirror

and of course all of
these unlikely stories

which probably you made
up only made me want you

all that much the more.

TWO SHIPS

What happens I wonder to
those ships we hear about

that pass in the night it
seems only a few moments

between the sighting of
their lights moving in op-

posite directions and the
disappearance in darkness

do they sometimes later
pass each other again on

the sea or do they even
someday dock beside each

other in the same harbor?

HOW CAN YOU ESCAPE?

from your beautiful body
all your life, it has pun-

ished you (from an Iowa
farm to Park Avenue) it

would never let them see
you but only the beauti-

ful body to buy and tor-
ment and pursue never you.

278

WHEN YOU DANCED

for me those steps of flamenco
there was no music but you clap-

ped your hands and arched your
back & stomped with your heels

& your skirts flew and a smile
of radiant delight was on your

face and my thoughts went back
to Tarragona so many years ago

when I joined the ring of dan-
cers with Cynthia in the square

oh she is long gone I know not
where but you brought her back

to me for a moment & gave me
yourself even more beautiful.

I LIKE YOU

better than this she
said as we were making

love in a parked car
she was a clerk in a

bookstore where I had
picked her up & taken

her to dinner and the
next day I was on my

way to the next city
& never saw her again.

DROPKICK ME JESUS

through the goalposts of
life so sang that fair

Melinda in her soft sou-
thern drawl as she pluck-

ed on her guitar and sent
her eyes across the room.

THE KENNER'S CAT

on whom I sat went by the
name of Jasper and Bucky

Fuller also sat upon said
cat but isn't there more

to it than that a cat who
holds his place against a

man must surely once have
been back in another life

a man of strongest will &
mind who was he then in-

vincible Genghis Khan or
bloodsoaked Attila was he

Arjuna or the elephantine
Hannibal was he El Bert-

rans sower of discord or
was he just another cat?

JAMES MY NAMESAKE

who is three comes down
the stairs reciting the

names of the months but
he doesn't have them in

order he stops on each
step to say a month and

October the month when
I was born is Tober but

it's a long time since
I cared hot or cold the

months are pretty much
alike now enjoy your

different months James
enjoy them while you

may and let the stairs
be your gradus ad Par-

nassum but always go-
ing up and never down.

I HAVE HEARD

the misuse of the word hope-
fully spread through the lin-

guistic landscape with the
steady relentless thrust of

lava from a volcano one here
one there at first but now

everywhere even senators &
professors hopefully post

mortem meam I'll not end up
in a hell where undoubtfully

everyone will be saying it.

JUNK MAIL

is a pleasure to at least
one person a dear old man

in our town who is drift-
ing off into irreality he

walks each morning to the
post office to dig the

treasure from his box he
spreads it out on the lob-

by counter and goes through
it with care and delight.

SO MUCH DEPENDS

For William Carlos Williams

Bill on the way you saw
the way your heart saw

what your eyes saw not
just the way you saw a

wheelbarrow or the falls
or the blossoms of the

shad tree or Floss in a
rose and 100 other flow-

ers your patients & the
babies and the measure

of your lines in Brueg-
hel's painting of that

dance so many things the
rest of us would never

have seen except for you.

SOME OF US COME TO LIVE

For Ezra Pound

inside his Cantos like a pal-
ace ten times larger than Ver-

sailles so many rooms so many
corridors the phalanx of par-

ticulars and those long gal-
leries with their endless vis-

tas of a past that no one else
has seen so well or understood

so well the mirrors that re-
flect into each other making

the rhymes between ideas yes
it is the father's house of

many mansions with its place
for each of us places for all.

SOME PEOPLE THINK

that poetry should be a-
dorned or complicated I'm

not so sure I think I'll
take the simple statement

in plain speech compress-
ed to brevity I think that

will do all I want to do.

WHAT ARE YOU SMILING ABOUT

my dear wife asked me this morn-
ing at breakfast nothing I said

nothing in particular oh she
said you're back at that a-

gain imagining you're a re-
incarnation of the Buddha.

YOU AND ME

that's what I wish your
letter was about not the

interesting people you've
met or your writing I do

admire your poems please
always send them to me

but in your letters please
write about you and me and

about the kinds of love we
made that summer in Ville-

franche how you remember it
how you remember us when

we were together you & me.

THE DELIA SEQUENCE

"te spectem, suprema mihi cum venerit hora,
  et teneam moriens deficiente manu.
flebis et arsuro positum me, Delia, lecto,
  tristibus et lacrimis oscula mixta dabis.
flebis: non tua sunt duro praecordia ferro
  vincta, nec in tenero stat tibi corde silex.
illo non iuvenis poterit de funere quisquam
  lumina, non virgo sicca referre domum.
tu manes ne laede meos, sed parce solutis
  crinibus et teneris, Delia, parce genis."

Tibullus, I, 1, 59–68

"May my eyes fall on thee when the last hour shall have
    come for me,
May I hold you with my weakening hands.
You shall weep, Delia, and when I have been placed on
    the bed that shall soon be set on fire
You shall give me kisses and sad tears intermingled.
You shall weep, your breast is not cased in hard iron
Nor in your soft heart is there any stone.
From that funeral rite neither youth nor virgin
Shall return with his eyes dry
You shall not humiliate my ghost, by your absence,
    nevertheless,
Do no violence to your loosened hair nor to your soft
    cheek."

Ford Madox Ford

TÒ KALÓN

For Delia pulchra et docta
one of whose secrets I have

learned that she was in an
earlier life the lady Maeut

of the castle of Montagnac
above the Vezère whom many

troubadours admired and to
her they sang fine vers &

cansos in the trobar clus.

MY SOUL REVOLVED

in your presence it was
not like a carrousel but

like the singing spheres
that dance through the

heavens the spheres that
Holst heard when he com-

posed The Planets hold on
now let's get back down

to earth let's just say
that you made me love you.

ACROSS THE WIDE WATER LAY JAPAN

Her kiss came to me when
the moon was full was it

the moon that sent it?
her kiss must last me

for a year so come back
moon make your appointed

rounds to help me remem-
ber the way her kiss felt

the gentleness the tender-
ness the miracle of her kiss.

WE SIT BY THE LAKE

and though we are a
thousand miles apart

we are very close to-
gether we watch the

water and the forest
and there is no need

to say anything but
sometimes your gentle

fingers touch my hand.

YOU ARE MY DISEASE

not a cancer but a canker
such as afflicts a plant

like the phlox I am vul-
nerable does the rust a-

rise from the earth or
come through the air I

don't know but it's into
my blood I can't tell but

I doubt it will go away.

YOU HAVE BURNED

yourself deep into me
I know now that you

don't love me enough
but the burn scar is

there inside me and I
think it will not heal.

IF IN THE NIGHT I WAKE

and start to think of you dis-
tant as now you are in place

and in regard for me there is
no pill or potion no apothe-

cary's charm no alchemist's
stone that I have found to

lull me back to sleep or
bring you back again to me.

THAT CLICK

on the telephone when you
put the receiver down with-

out answering not even one
word was like the cut of

the guillotine as it falls
on the condemned man's neck.

IT WAS ALL

a beautiful dream that
you kissed me under the

full moon and wrote me
those wonderful letters

that you sent me your
picture & the pictures

of your children that
you sent me your poems

and then suddenly si-
lence only silence now.

YOU CAME AS A THOUGHT

when I was past such thinking
you came as a song when I had

finished singing you came when
the sun had just begun its set-

ting you were my evening star.

I HAVE DRIFTED

off to sea from you but
you were not abandoned

Ariadne we were playing
in the sand like child-

ren we waded in the sea
a current carried me a-

way but left you on the
shore your life is yours

again I cannot will not
harm you more your eyes

were soft & sad I loved
you as I never loved be-

fore but now the ancient
sea has carried me away.

* * *

A FAILURE OF COMMUNICATION
IN THE ANIMAL KINGDOM

A fox was crossing the
meadow and the sheep

went running but the
fox has no interest

in them he is looking
for a fieldmouse or a

chipmunk we people al-
so have such problems.

THE CHILD

in his little bed in
the dark room clutches

the fluted columns at
the head of the bed his

fists are rigid and he
can't sleep he is think-

ing about how some day
he will not be alive

he will not be a per-
son he will not be him-

self anymore he won't
be it is a terror to him.

DANS LES TRACES D'EZRA POUND, OR MONSIEUR ROQUETTE'S PANTS

On the battlements of Hautefort
the eloquent Monsieur Roquette

in his elegant Occitan recited
some poems of Bertrand de Born

while the camera rolled & dis-
coursed most learnedly on the

symbolism of troubadour courts
of love & because we were follow-

ing the footsteps of Old Possum
& Brer Rabbit on their 1912 walk-

ing tour our beloved director (S.
Legree) had us do dozens of walk-

ing shots (from the knees down)
this to give sense of the visual

and when night fell and we didn't
have enough and Monsieur Roquette

had to leave next day it was sug-
gested that he leave his pants &

shoes which we would put on the
assistant cameraman and do more

in the morning to which Monsieur
Roquette gave his assent but after

some further reflection decided he
could not do it because when he got

home to Béziers (where Arnaut de
Marvoil had such a bad time with

the countess and Alfonso the half-
balled) his wife would unpack his

suitcase and enquire in which of
the Perigordine pleasure houses

he had relinquished his trousers.

THE CARE AND FEEDING OF A POET

is a noble task (whatever the
feminists may say) it insures

the caretaker a certain immor-
tality (if the poet is a good

one) and it also provides cer-
tain rewards in the here & now

such as typing manuscripts and
sending poems to magazines and

entertaining the wives of other
poets who come visiting (while

the geniuses sit in the study
drinking beer) and in certain

cases being informed that one
or more ancillary muses are re-

quired to provide inspiration.

THE CASUAL KISS

is a problem in one's
relations with the new

generation it was not
thus in grampa's day

and usually one finds
to one's sorrow that

it means almost nothing
H. James from his grave

in Mt. Auburn Cemetery
views this social phenom-

enon with much alarm.

CORDELIA

why couldn't you have
thought up just a few

kind words to say to
your dear old dad and

then we wouldn't have
to take all that crap

from Goneril & Regan
but if you had I sup-

pose then we'd never
have heard things like

the serpent's tooth &
the wanton boys killing

flies & the wrens going
to it (let copulation

thrive) & the ounce of
civit for my imaginings.

BEING MUCH TOO TALL

I like you to be rather small
I don't mean a midget but deli-

cate of construction la donna
così mobile she who goes in

grace at the corner of Broad-
way & 53rd St you rose up on

your toes and said you must
find higher heels to go out

with me don't bother I like
you sized exactly as you are.

CAN YOU TELL

from looking at them whe-
ther they will or won't I

always thought that high
cheekbones were an indi-

cation until I spent some
time in the coalfields of

Silesia better not jump to
conclusions wait for a warm

palm and a moist eye wait
for the creeping fingers.

HERODOTUS REPORTS

That the girls of Cimmeria
rubbed olive oil on their

bodies to make them slippery
as fish for their lovers and

Rexroth did the painting of
the tunnies from two lines of

Amphylitos & in Zurich there
was beautiful crazy Birgitte

who liked to circle the Mat-
terhorn in her plane and lie

in her bathtub at the Dolder
Grand while her admirer intro-

duced forellen and the Schubert
was played on the gramophone in

the bedroom and Henry had to
drive Marcia up to the hospi-

tal in Carmel to get the snake
out and the list of these deli-

cate practices could go on but
remember that the historian and

the poet and I are notorious
for our wild confabulations.

INTO EACH LIFE

must fall occasionally a new
incentive to persist he writes

ridiculous letters to ces dames
galantes well what's the harm

in that he searches for the
ear that comprehends the in-

tonations that he hears in
languages he tells her that

her hands when she is talking
are the white flock of birds

En Bertrans saw that day be-
yond the battlements of Haute-

fort (touch is not necessary
for the delectations of the

mind the poet saw her only
once the old book says there

at the bridge over the Arno).

IS IT WRITTEN

in heaven that our planets
should conjoin the old as-

trologer in Madras who did
my horoscope said that in

1984 something sensational
would happen did he mean

you delicious creature I
hope I pray I do beseech

you that's what he meant.

LOVE IS CUMULATIVE

When we make love you em-
body whatever was beauti-

ful in those who have gone
before (and whatever was

not beautiful has dropped
away) so that at the last

in you it has all come to-
gether the perfection of

the sacrament (for it is
a sacrament when the af-

fection is true) such as
the poets have celebrated.

THE JUNK COLLECTOR

what bothers me most about
the idea of having to die

(sooner or later) is that
the collection of junk I

have made in my head will
presumably be dissipated

not that there isn't more
and better junk in other

heads & always will be but
I have become so fond of

my own head's collection.

IS WHAT WE EAT

an indication of what we
are or of what we'd like

to be Rimbaud wanted to
eat the air and Jarry the

noise of grasshoppers hav-
ing lived in India & Jap-

an it is hard for me to
swallow any more rice Pe-

tronius relates that the
guests at Trimalchio's

dinner put their fingers
down their throats to en-

joy a second meal & Rabe-
lais made Gargantua a

ridiculous figure (some
men like to eat pussy but

that is another story) the
mouth eats and the mouth

speaks it's more than a
paradox it's a dilemma

and no doubt people on
food stamps take a more

serious view of eating.

MY OLD GRAY SWEATER

in the back of the closet what
will you do with it the one with

buttons down the front the heavy
one I used to wear when I could

still cut firewood what will you
do with it the Salvation Army I

guess some worthy & needy man
can still get a lot of use out

of it but you know I'd really
rather not please take it out

into the woods and nail it to
that big oak Gary jokes that

he wants to re-enter the food
chain he wants to be eaten by

a bear I'd like my sweater just
to rot away in the woodlands let

the birds peck at it and build
their nests with the gray wool

please nail me to the big oak.

THE *NON*-WORLD

is too much with me daylong and
in my dreams my mind is invaded

by persons who are irreal all the
weirdos about whom Herodotus told

such magnificent lies the succu-
lent girlfriends of Sappho and the

tormented & tormenting in Ovid
adulterous ladies in the castles of

Provence who dread the coming of
the dawn sad sacks in Villon the

pranksters of Ariosto the drunken
and infected buddies of Rochester

it's an endless list must I burn
all my books to get rid of these

interlopers I should get back to
the real world I must listen to

Jesse Jackson and help him dis-
pose of that Hollywood cowboy.

PERSEPHONE WEARS BLUEJEANS

now but she's the same sweet
girl it's spring again and up

from the underworld she comes
the laurel on her brow bring-

ing the seed that will re-
new the earth and draw all

flowers and plants again to
birth she melts the snow she

calms the sea now all things
grow she is the leafing tree.

A SMALL GROUP

of venture capitalists are
now offering shares in a

new corporation to be known
as Cyanide Pills Inc we be-

lieve that with the nucle-
ar arms race there will be

a good market for our pro-
duct among those who don't

want to wait around till
all their hair falls out.

WHY

when you put your legs up
against the wall after we

had made love did I think
of Nerval's tour abolie a

very strange and dubious
connection your legs are

lithe & lovely and the
tower is presumably if

anyone ever found it a
gothic ruin the way the

mind works is a puzzle
could it be that the mu-

sic of the poem came back
to me when you made that

so graceful and spontane-
ous movement of a dancer.

SOCIAL NOTE

I don't usually try to listen
in on conversations but

the other morning when I was
having breakfast at the Vil-

lage Den there were two men
in the next booth and one of

them who sounded quite annoy-
ed said you did it again what

did I do again you called me
Warren now you've called me

Warren and Justin and Henry
can't you please try to re-

member my name is Gilbert?

THE GODDESS

I have seen the goddess
with my mortal eyes they

were filming down the
street and it was Meryl

Streep she was attended
by five trailers eight

trucks thirty technici-
ans and four policemen

the whole street was il-
lumined with a heavenly

blaze she walked up the
steps of the house four

times and I know that she
saw me and smiled at me

she knew that I was her
devotee she went into

the house but they said
the next scene was in-

side and I couldn't go
in will I ever see her

again my goddess but it
doesn't really matter I

saw her and she knew me.

HERE I AM

having breakfast in the kitchen
and on the window ledge are the

saltshaker the box of brown su-
gar the butter dish the jars of

marmalade & peach jam and the
bottle of Heinz's ketchup (the

things for the body) and out-
side the big picture window are

the grosbeaks pecking for the
sunflower seeds that Helen has

scattered in the grass and the
fat groundhog sticks his head

out of his hole under the wood-
shed but goes back when he sees

the birds and beyond the fence
the sheep file down into the

pasture to browse and some days
at the edge of the woods a doe

and her fawn come to stare at
our house (the creatures of na-

ture) and somewhere far above
are the Olympians & those who

dwell on Mount Sumeru & Taishan
the angels and apsaras (the be-

ings we cannot see or compre-
hend) but they are there work-

ing their will with us yes they
are with me each morning as I

sit here eating my breakfast.

THE HITCHHIKER

There's a young man in the next
town who does a lot of hitching

he really isn't going anywhere
but he's out of work and bored

so on good days he hitches around
the county just to talk to people

he tells them long stories about
himself which are usually differ-

ent he's not very bright but he's
harmless so sometimes I pick him

up just to find out what's new to-
day he told me he was going down

to Hartland to beat hell out of
a friend of his who was spread-

ing talk about him & a girl down
there I told him he'd better be

careful if they put him in jail
for assault & battery he might

not be hitching again for a while.

TO SMILE OR NOT TO SMILE

She is out for her daily health
walk she is nicely dressed in a

pretty sweater & her best slacks
& a purple knitted toque if only

she didn't have to wear her glasses
but without them she can't see what

people look like her life is so
lonely she imagines that a nice

looking man the right age comes
along and she smiles at him and

he smiles back and he stops and
they get talking but of course

she could never do that she wasn't
brought up that way it will just

have to happen at one of the sup-
pers at church but it never does.

YOU KNOW HOW A CAT

will bring a mouse it has
caught and lay it at your

feet so each morning I
bring you the poem that

I've written when I woke
up in the night as my tri-

bute to your beauty &
a promise of my love.

WHY WON'T YOU IGNITE

from the sparks of my lan-
guage delivered to your door

in a brazier by the boy Eros
whom I have engaged for the

purpose he is a costly mes-
senger (I have to fly him

down from Olympus) but for
you nothing can be too good.

THE OLD COMEDIAN

What part does that old man
think he is playing he is

rather funny but not very
his act is ridiculous and

even pathetic who does he
imagine he is surely he's

not the boy next door the
one the neighbors spoiled

and the teachers thought
was so promising but there

is a resemblance I'm afraid
it is the boy next door now

the old man is stumbling
and losing his lines he

must either be drunk or
sick will he die right on

the stage he's a comedian
and he wants the audience

to laugh at his funeral.

STOLEN POEMS

I LOVE THE WAY

your curls fall down on your
forehead when you are making

love I think you are a Greek
girl perhaps you are Melissa of

Kalymnos and you are saying to
me nun d'hote moi gumne gluker-

ois meleessi peplesai we are
together naked your thigh a-

gainst mine your curls are
so soft on your forehead yes

you are Melissa of Kalymnos.

ANTIPHILUS

seemed to be making fun of
everything nothing was sa-

cred he was called a cynic
but I assure you that un-

derneath the flimflam beat
a heart of gold it was only

the pain of life he saw a-
round him that made him car-

ry on the way he did Anti-
philus was debonair but he

wrote bitter verses now he
lies here under this mound

chambered forever in earth.

AND WILL THAT MAGIC WORLD

die when you go a world
you brought me that I'd

never known before don't
go away y ha de morir

contigo el mundo mago?

SAETA

I care nothing for the
resplendent Virgins on

their floats as they
weave in the Serpente

I care nothing for those
penitentes dragging their

chains I care nothing for
the military music it is

the chant of my doulours
that I would sing to you.

HAVING FAILED

with every other stratagem
should I now try jealousy

taunting you in these ver-
ses that you have been sup-

planted it would be useless
every messenger from Boetia

to Samos would report that
my bed is still empty that

the lamp burns for me alone.

THE END OF IT ALL

My friend the ecologist tells
me that a thin film of oil now

covers most of the oceans pol-
luting the plankton on whose

photosynthesis much of our oxy-
gen depends non sic in Arcadia

but that was a long time ago
carpe diem I say and he says

casi demasiado tarde it's too
late there's nothing we can do.

I AM AWARE

that I am a bit odd but
I crave your indulgence

and your love Cratecus
walked backwards from

Marathon to Athens in
honor of the heroes &

Peristera the little dove
dyed half her hair purple

when Eusthenes the soph-
ist had spurned her Pro-

talidas of Lycastus built
his tumulus when he was

still in excellent health
I write odes in false me-

ters using words that do
not exist but neverthe-

less I beg your indulgence
and beg to have your love.

LOVE IS A SCHOOL

where lovers go to learn
each other I have brought

my teacher an apple and
I want to be in her class

I'll work hard I'll learn
to spell and do sums I'll

not throw spitballs or
make any other trouble

but of course what I'd
like best would be to be

the only pupil in her
class nobody but me.

BERENICE

cried when she could not
fit her breast into Titus's

wineglass she wanted
so much to have him

think of her as a Grecian
wood-nymph but her brother

Agrippa tried to console
her with the thought that

we cannot always make our
bodies do what they ought.

OCCIDIT BREVIS LUX

Is it the end of the world to
indulge an old man who adores

you for you are young & lovely
and have the excitement of a

dozen who knows perhaps even a
score of lovers before you but

for him the stars are waning and
he feels the sadness even the ter-

ror of the long night that is com-
ing on he knows that nox est una

perpetua dormienda that longest
night when he'll see you no more.

EL CAMINO DE AMOR

Ni las noches de amor que no
tuvimos ni tus sollazos jun-

to a la ventana there can be
love and not enough love but

love is the stronger no es
lo mismo estar solo que es-

tar sin ti without you there
is nothing yet something re-

mains caminante no hay cami-
no se hace camino al andar

there was a road and there is
a road to be found and taken.

TIMOR AMORIS CONTURBAT ME

What is this vengeful thing
called Love which doth my

peace destroy puella nam mi
quae meo sinu fugit amata tan-

tum quantum amabitur nulla
they tell of Eros and his

bow but he is but a boy nunc
iam illa non volt tu quoque

inpotens noli nec quae fugit
sectare nec miser vive sed

obstinata mente perfer ob-
dura or is it not a god but

she who poisoneth my joy?

ὁ πατήρ

On learning that he was about
to become a father the actor

Polycrates gave thanks to the
gods in these terms: it is true

that I never had the good for-
tune to lie in the bower of the

beautiful Anthea but she de-
clares that after hearing me

play Philoctetes in the thea-
ter at Epidaurus she conceived

the child who will be the best
singer since Orpheus himself.

SHE SEEMED TO KNOW

that she'd been designed for
the sport of Gods not like

sad Tess in Wessex more like
the rapes of Zeus like Leda

or Europa so she goes in a
gleam of Cos in a slither

of dyed stuff waiting for it
to happen and wanting it to

happen to her in a gleam of
Cos ever looking skyward for

the appearance of the God.

TWO FRAGMENTS FROM PAUSANIAS

I AM NOT PITTHEUS

nor was meant to be let
it only be written on

my stone that sometimes
I hit the right keys

AT METHANA

we ran around the vineyard
each with half a white

cock still bleeding but
the south west wind had

already withered the vines

* * *

WITH MY THIRD EYE

I see what's past and what's
to come I see you as a little

girl you wore your hair in
pigtails then telling the

other children what was right
and what was wrong & then I

watch you in your ashram time
wearing your saffron robe your

head now shaved telling those
other nuns what's right what's

wrong this is your karma this
your destiny prostrate your-

self a thousand times and say
the prayer om mani padme hum.

AT ELEUSIS

I was living underground
I was wandering in con-

fusion in dromena then
you appeared (perhaps

Persephone sent you to
me) I experienced epopte

the brilliant illum-
ination you placed the

crown on my head and I
came above ground to a

new life of which you
are the force & center.

HOW SHALL I FIND MY WAY

to your forfended place what stra-
tagem of love will compass me that

joy it seems the artifice of words
has failed what must I now employ?

YOU ARE MY FUTURE

and you came when I
feared that every-

thing was part of the
past I was resigned

to the descent which
beckons facilis des-

census senectute and
then you appeared as

fresh from the waves
as was the Primavera

and in only an hour
I knew that there

could be a second fu-
ture if you'd give it.

DA MI BASIA MILLE

The boy Eros mistakes me
for Saint Sebastian he

has riddled me with his
arrows I am faint from

loss of blood and faint
with longing be as merci-

ful as you are beautiful
stop up my wounds with

your kisses a thousand
kisses & a thousand more.

THREE SKIRMISHES IN THE ENDLESS BATTLE

THE PSYCHOMACHIA

Is the way that you treat me
first enticing me into your moonlit garden
then repulsing me with disdain
a case for the old man in the Berggasse
or should we look for your cure to the saintly Prudentius
to his allegory in which Pudicitia, the virgin in bright armor
is attacked by Sodomita Libido
who would blind her with the smoke of her sulphurous
        torch?
I forget now how it all ends
it is so long ago that I read that book
and perhaps it is a story that will never have an ending.

THE TAUROMACHIA

It was in Tarragona
where we danced in a great ring of townspeople in the plaza
to the music of guitars and tubas (an odd combination)
that we saw our first bullfight and a strange thing happened
I who should have loved it hated it
and you who should have hated it loved it
and that night we were not comfortable together.
But it's ridiculous, I know
to blame the death of a few bulls
for what finally came about between us.

THE HYPNOEROTOMACHIA

Love and sleep are not usually thought to be enemies.
Post coetum venit somnus; after the frenzy a happy drifting
into oblivion, sometimes with the limbs entwined.
Illa meos somno lapsos patefecit ocellos
ore suo et dixit "sicine lente iaces"?
"And she then opening my eyelids fallen in sleep,
her lips upon them; and it was her mouth saying: Sluggard"!
But came then Colonna, that jealous black Dominican,
a sensual pedant and a killjoy,
trying to keep us from love's slumber
with the barbs of his macaronics.

TUESDAYS AT 87 RUE DE ROME

M. Mallarmé has put a curse on me
Tout, au monde, existe pour aboutir à un livre
The giant squids of the visible and of the audible
Stretch out their tentacles to entrap me

Make me into a poem, shouts every rejected object on the town dump
L'encrier, cristal comme une conscience, avec sa goutte, au fond, de
    ténèbres relatives à ce que quelque chose soit
It's ludicrous. Natural things won't let me alone
And it's dangerous to my health. This clamor is worse than Epstein's
    Rock Drill or the cacaphony of the Seven Tailors
Mercy, cher Maître, my head is splitting apart, my brains (if there
    were any) are oozing out my ears
Be kind, send me just the soft sound of the sea subsumed
    in the murmur of a shell
With your "inexhaustibly subtle speech" please demonstrate that the
    universe is a dream
I would prefer that insubstantiality to the punishment by particulars
    I now must suffer.

A LADY ASKS ME

    For S.H.

a discerning friend
if I've been reading Marcabru & Bernart de Ventadourn
how did she know or am I quite transparent
a most discerning lady, dompna de cortes dig e-l dous ris.

Marcabru, the friend of Cercamon who taught him to sing trobar
a crusty fellow, rather a sour apple, if we can believe his vida
whom they called the "maldisant" because he spoke ill of love and of
    women in his sirventes
and what sort of a trip was that for a troubadour
maybe he just couldn't cut the mustard and they treated him badly
but the songs are beautiful and full of invention
non amet neguna, ni d'autra non fo ametz
he says that he never loved anyone and never by anyone was loved
I don't believe it, poets will be liars to make a good poem.

And En Bernart was the son of the castle baker, a bright lad who
    learned to sing well
and he pleased the count and his young lady
but when he pleased the lady too much, the count sent him packing
then he pleased the Duchess of Normandy, and she him
but she had to marry Henry of England for political reasons
so the rest of his life he remembered those two ladies
the sorrows of love he knew but also its joys as his cansos tell
cen vetz mor lo jorn de dolor, e reviu de joi autra cen
a hundred times a day I die of my sadness, and then a hundred times
    come to life again with joy
mais val mos mals qu'autre bes, e pois mos mals aitan bosm'es, bos er
    los bes apres l'afan
even my sorrow is better than any seeming good, so that my sorrow
    seems to me a good, but best is the good that comes after my sorrow.

I have heard someone walking below me in the cellar and a voice
    talking above me in the attic
there are no young maids spinning now
there are no lads working in the croft
everything is parody, everything is the same and not the same
there were, there are, the times before
but will there be time coming after
don't say it, and it won't happen
but it could happen, anything can happen
such things have happened before
everything is parody, it has all happened before
the old poems echo in my head, the old poets converse with me
my past is an echo of their earlier pasts
is memory only a parody of what really happened?

Tant ai mo cor ple de joya, tot me desnatura
flor blancha vermelh'e grova, me par la frejura, c'ab lo ven et ab la
    ploya, me creis l'aventura
my heart is so full of joy that the nature of everything is changed
white flowers, crimson and gold, become like the cold, for with the
    wind and the rain my happiness keeps growing

An old book of fair language ful of hy sentence is alwey a goode thynge
    to poure.

DREAM NOT OF OTHER WORLDS

this one we're in will have to
do for us there is no other ni-

hil in intellectu quod non prius
in sensu no ideas but in things

we must live on what we see and
touch and love with what we give

each other heav'n is too high
for us so let us try to find

our heaven in what concerns us
being together and lowly wise.

I WANT TO BREATHE

you in I'm not talking about
perfume or even the sweet o-

dour of your skin but of the
air itself I want to share

your air inhaling what you
exhale I'd like to be that

close two of us breathing
each other as one as that.

AS IN MUSIC / A REPRISE / ACROSS TIME

PARIS, 1675

Madame de Lafayette, in her salon in the rue de Vaugirard, is telling her friend the Duc de la Rochefoucauld (they say that he helped her write the book) about how at the Queen's ball the very night before her wedding to Clèves, the Duc de Nemours *"had eyes for nobody"* except the beautiful Mademoiselle de Chartres. (And thence did much ensue.)

SAN FRANCISCO, 1945

And that year around Scott Street, where Rexroth lived, there was a vivacious girl who, for some reason I can't recall, everyone called "Slats." She was a bit schizzy and had been fired from her job and was on the city but she was a fine typist and Kenneth used her to type his manuscripts. I liked her and used to moon around her when she was typing. And one day she said: *"You have eyes for me,* don't you, Jim?" (But nothing did thence ensue.)

LONG-LINE POEMS

THE BIBLE LADY

from Jehovah's Witnesses stopped by the house the other morning
she said these were bad times and that she wanted to share the
    Scriptures with me
these are indeed bad times and getting worse so I asked her in
I offered her a cup of coffee but she doesn't drink coffee
she started to read from the new JW version of the Bible but it's
    awful, all the beautiful words are gone
I hunted around and found the old Bible I had won for perfect
    attendance at Sunday School in Pittsburgh
we read passages from each one and discussed the meanings
she said that I read beautifully and asked if I had ever felt called
we read quite a bit from Revelations because that explains about the
    atom bomb and Satan
I am very worried about the atom bomb but she is not
The Bible proves that the righteous have nothing to fear from the
    atom bomb
the righteous will be carried up and only the wicked will burn
I asked her if it was the mushroom cloud which would carry the
    righteous up
but we couldn't find anything about that, they didn't know about the
    mushroom cloud way back then
she said, do you believe in Satan? I said I certainly did, I know him
    personally
he lives on 61st Street in New York and one of these days I'm going
    to go down there and kick his butt
you're joking she said, yes, I said, I'm joking but I am going to kick
    his butt
and I told her I had read all about Satan in school in *Paradise Lost*
she hadn't read *Paradise Lost* but she made a note of it and said she
    would get it out of the library
then she threw me a real curve
she asked me if I would avow that the Bible is absolutely true

well you can't lie to such a fine person as the Bible lady
I said I thought that some of the stories in the Bible maybe were
    myths
she didn't want to buy that until I read her the definition of myths in
    the dictionary
where it says that myths are especially associated with religious
    beliefs
we reached a kind of compromise on that one, that Adam and Eve
    were real people, as we know from seeing so many pictures of
    them in museums
but that Joshua blowing down the walls of Jericho with his trumpet
    could be a myth
for only 75¢ she let me purchase a little book that is full of useful
    knowledge, such as
Why has God permitted wickedness until our day and the reason
    why a little flock goes to Heaven and the last days of this wicked
    system of things.

THE DECONSTRUCTED MAN

    Multas per gentes et multa per aequora vectus
    (et multas per vias quoque aereas)
    (there being no flugbuggies in the time of Gaius Valerius)
    through many lands by shores of many peoples
    a life too short sometimes
    at times a life too long-seeming
    the days of sun and rain and many days of mountain snow
    the nights of endless dreaming
    my periplum more geographically extended
    (in Java the airplane is the god Garuda)
    but I learned less not being polumetis
    and my paideuma is a mishmash of contradictions
    my Circes a list of fictions

Muse help me to sing
of Toodles on the wide beach at Troorak
(her hair so golden and her brain so slack)
of darling Leontina di Rapallo
taking me to her underwater cave
(J'ai rêvé dans la grotte où nage la sirène
I have lingered in the chambers of the sea)
of Dylan's crazy Daphne in the Gargoyle Club in Soho
(Voi che sapete che cosa è amor...
Sento un affeto pien di desir
ch'ora è diletto ch'ora è martir)
of delicate moonlit Delia by the Strait of Juan DeFuca
of Cynthia whom I helped the gods destroy
in ogne parte dove mi trae memoria
of name-is-gone-but-not-her-smile
there in the jungle near Chichén Itzá
(A ristorar le pene d'un innocente amor)
of Kyo-San (they had girl caddies on the course at Kamakura)
(Ma in Ispagna son già mille e tre)
a list of fictions of beautiful contradictions
Lord Krishna's lotus and Williams' asphodel
each one so wonderful so new bringing her particular magic
risplende ognun sa luce che non morirà mai
and Restif said there were a thousand women who were always one
sola et magna (mater)
Gertrude's Mother of us All
I penetrate thy temple and thou doest my soul restore
ineffable thou art the Virgin & the Whore
I lusted for Tom's Wendy in Kentucky there was guilt
his sin (if it were sin for him) but surely mine
a list of fictions of contradictions
ma basta per oggi il catalogo delle fanciulle
who cares though I cared everywhere and always
the sea was not my mother but my mother took me to the sea
the old Cunarder Mauretania and Bill the sailor
who showed me how to splice a rope
and Jack turned green when we were beating through the chop above
    Grenada

avoid the Indian Ocean you can die of heat
posh P & 0 boats are like baking ovens
the sea the sea cried Xenophon after his weary march
O mother sea our bodies turn to dust our hearts return to thee
but it's the air we breathe and now in the air we fly
what would the many-crafted Odysseus make of that
he never saw as I have seen from the cabin window of the plane
glistening Mont Blanc and holy Kanchenjunga and mystic Fuji
by Isfahan he never saw those traceries
of ancient water tunnels on the desert below
he did not see the million lights of cities in the night
cities now doomed to die
these things he never saw
but what he saw and did will live as long as we

I am the deconstructed man
my parts are scattered on the nursery floor
and can't be put back together again because the instruction book is
     lost
clean up your mess in the nursery my mother says
I am the deconstructed man
my older brother laughs at me all the time
he drives me into a rage and I drive the scissors into his knee
he has to have six stitches at the hospital and go on crutches but I pay
     for my jubilation
look mother James is doing it again he's chewing with his mouth open
and he hasn't learned his lines of catechism for Sunday
God went back to heaven when I was twelve He stopped counting the
     hairs of my head
will he ever come back? I was waiting for Him then but now I'm wait-
     ing for Godot
Pound said "C'est moi dans la poubelle."
they had to chop us both up to get us into that trashcan in Paris
but why was there no blood? there's never any blood
did Abel bleed? did En Bertrans the sower of discord bleed
there in the bolge holding his severed head by the hair and swinging
     it like a lantern
E 'l capo tronco tenea per le chiome

Pesol con mano a guisa di lanterna
E quel mirava noi, e dicea "oh me!!"
(Bos chavaliers fo e bos guerriers . . .
e bos trobaire e savis e be parlans . . .)
why don't I bleed what is it that my heart is pumping?
Cynthia said it was embalming fluid and she went away
like God and mother Cynthia went away
I am the deconstructed man
I do the best I can

Lie quiet Ezra there in your campo santo on San Michele
in paradisum deducant te angeli
to your city of Dioce to Wagadu to your paradiso terrestre
what I have reft from you I stole for love of you
belovèd my master and my friend.

"HE DID IT TO PLEASE HIS MOTHER"

Tonight again I watched that arrogant man Coriolanus, who was too
    absolute, work out his doom
And was it nearly fifty years ago, dear Delmore
That you read me your *Coriolanus and His Mother*
And showed me how the old man in the Berggasse helped you figure
    it out, as if a man were author of himself
But still I'm not really sure, was it your mother too, for certain drops
    of salt, oh world of slippery turns
Or was there some defect of judgment, one we couldn't see
Which brought down the anger of the gods upon you, poor boy pur-
    suing summer butterflies
Yes, you are loved now that you're lacked, now you've become a kind
    of nothing
Or is there a world elsewhere?

336

TAMARA

By her name she should be Russian but I think she is really Greek, a
    Hellene of the old times
for in my first dream of her she was bounding across a beach at the
    seaside
in her joy she had abandoned her maidenly garments, it was the
    euphoria of a child
she was a sea nymph, a maenad, she was Nerea, the daughter of
    Poseidon.
But my second dream of her was quite different, it was terrifying and
    I awoke in fright
in this dream she was falling past an open window where a man was
    smoking as if there were nothing amiss
I think she had jumped from a roof above, designing her own
    destruction
it was the same girl but not the girl of the beach, it was a girl pursued
    by the Erinnys, it was now the face of Cassandra or Elektra.
I do not understand my dreams, I have never understood them, they
    are riddles more impenetrable than those of the Oracle at Delphi.
I pray to the gods, though there is little evidence that they have any
    concern for humans,
that my second dream was the maleficence of a succubus
that Tamara is really the happy and lovely Nerea, sweet child of the
    sea.

O HERMES TRISMEGISTUS

O Thoth O wise one
god of writing learning and wisdom
cousin of the celestial messenger who created the lyre from the shell
    of a tortoise
maker of words and language priest of the logos

alchemist of all secret knowledge

come now to the aid of thy children the poets

for we are sore beset and badly beleaguered

we cry to thee for deliverance

for help from barbarians from the three parts of Gaul (and from a
    place called Columbia)

who have infringed our borders and are polluting our wells

invoking thy name with false utterance they are poisoning our water

they beat us if we do not put spatiality into our lines

they put us in chains if we are not sufficiently asymptotic

they take thy name in vain and reprove us that our structures are not
    hermeneutic

they teach us bad words pretending that they are good words

O father of language come to our rescue

help us to drive out the barbarians

we need you real bad.

SKIING WITHOUT SKIS

One of my favorite dreams

And I wish it would come more often

Is that I'm skiing down the Parsenn at Davos in great style

One of those perfect days when my rhythm is right and I feel like a
    bird soaring

But there are no skis on my feet!

I'm coming down just on my boot soles

And all my turns dance to a sensual music

Down from the Weissfluhjoch in long fall-line swings

And no bother of unruly skis on my feet

Taking the Derby Schuss straight and through the deep dip at the
    bottom

With no skis

No falls, no mistakes, the snow is like velvet

Through the narrow schwendi in little wedels

Past the farm where the old man is always out splitting wood
Without any skis
Past the haybarns where the cows are waiting out the winter
Through the lane between two chalets where proverbs are painted in
    gold under the eaves
Sun on the distant peaks, snow flying behind me, always in the
    fall-line
Down to Kublis where there's time for a drink in the station
    restaurant before the next up-valley train back to Davos
No need to wash down my skis in the horse trough because I don't
    have any
Though none of the skiers I passed on my run seem to have noticed
The old man cutting wood didn't notice
Yes, in my beautiful dream I can ski without skis.

A LEAVE-TAKING

For Robert Fitzgerald

My old friend has departed, he is making the inevitable journey
Not, I think, to dark Erebus, but to a happier place
Reserved for the good & the great, for our friends the Greek & Latin
    poets.
And I believe that such a land exists though I am uncertain of its
    location
Because, idiotic as they are, the gods must have provided it for such
    as he.

Memory must be my comforter, he gave so much to remember
As when one night long ago we sat on the roof of Dunster House
Watching the stars pursue their courses
And he related to me much wisdom from the philosophers
And no doubt I related to him frivolities about young female persons.
We reflected on the human condition
And reviewed the lives of our heroes, we spoke of the sorrows of poets

How those girls made Catullus so miserable, how Ezra drifted into
    irreality
How François got himself strung on the gallows, and Kleist dis-
    patched himself and Henriette with two bullets.
But we did not jump off the roof of Dunster House, though nothing
    would have been easier
Because there were things we both had to do with the lives the gods
    had entrusted to us, such as the fashioning of words into poems
    and sentences.
And later we did those things according to our powers, his great and
    mine small
But each of us found joy in the doing—and in the bond which
    endured between us.

TENNESSEE

called death the sudden subway and now he has taken that train
but there are so many good things to remember
first the young man in sloppy pants and a torn grey sweater
whom I met at Lincoln Kirstein's cocktail party
he was very shy and had hidden himself in a side room
I too was shy but we got talking
he told me that he wrote plays and that he loved Hart Crane
he carried the poems of Crane in his knapsack wherever he
    hitchhiked
then his first night of glory in Chicago
when he and Laurette Taylor made a new American theater
I remember happy days with him in London and Italy and Key West
and how often friends and writers who were down on their luck
told me how generously he had helped them
(but you would never hear that from him)
so many fine things to remember
that I can live again in my mind
until it is my turn to join him on the sudden subway.

FUNNY PAPERS BY HIRAM HANDSPRING

GIRLS AS WINDMILLS

> "By my count, 81% of Handspring's published poems are about women. Yet, on the available evidence, he does not appear to have been very successful in this field—far more misses than hits."
> —Professor J. Roger Dane: *A Structural View of Contemporary Verse*

Yes, let's face it Handspring, my Aurelius, good old friend
You have been more Don Quixote than Don Giovanni
A ridiculous old man riding full-tilt at those girls, your distracted
    beard more menacing than your lance
Bellowing your bizarre verses as if they might have incantatory power
Laying siege to them as if they were windmills
Not of course the plump windmills of Spain
But the delicate windmills of the plateau of Lasithi on Crete
Hundreds of graceful little windmills spinning their white blades
Girls waving their white arms
Fields of young girls beckoning with their arms
Like white flowers moving in the wind, flowers enticing you
And in your case the boy Eros is Sancho Panza not Leporello.

MY MUSE

My muse keeps irregular hours
Her name is Anthea which is a flower in Greece
It's obvious that she doesn't sit by her phone waiting for my calls
Don't call me, she says, I'll call you
And she calls at the most inconvenient hours, like 3 AM in the
    middle of the night
That seems to be a favorite time for her

341

Like when she might be getting home from a night on the town with
     some other poet
Naturally she doesn't tell me anything about him but I have my
     suspicions
If it turned out to be Harold Marks I would shoot her
But that really isn't likely because ... well I won't say it ... de mortuis
     in cerebro arteque nihil nisi bonum
She calls in the middle of the night a lot, it's like the old long dis-
     tance operator before Ma Bell computerized
One ring then a little wait then three rings, I can always tell it's her
Anyway who else is going to call in the middle of the night
Unless it's Gregory Corso when he's been drinking
The last time Gregory called it was to ask me if I would leave him
     my teeth in my will
So she calls about 3 AM usually, my muse does
I have to keep a pencil and yellow pad handy to be ready for her
And sometimes she talks so fast I can't get it all down before she
     hangs up
It's inconvenient
But I'm loyal, we've been together, if you can call it that, for a long
     time
I suppose there are a lot of unemployed muses around on Helicon
     these days but I'm loyal, call me Philemon but she sure isn't
     Baucis
After she's called and I've written down her message I'm all keyed up
     and usually have to take half a valium to get back to sleep
I wish she would keep store hours
I wish I could call her and not have to wait for her to call me
But you know how muses are
I guess that's why old poets always had invocations to their muses at
     the start of their long poems
They were apple polishing, trying to keep their muse in line to get
     better service.

AT OUR HOUSE

it's my job to burn the papers
this is something I've been found capable of doing and I do it
I'm too dumb to fix anything that gets broken or the electric, but I
    can burn the papers
there could be more exciting things to do but I do it fairly willingly
    but without much enthusiasm
if I didn't do it, it would cost a lot to have the trash man cart them
    away
why are there so many papers at our house?
there aren't just old newspapers and egg boxes and milk cartons and
    butter boxes and things like that
there are also many literary papers which are sent to me for
    examination by aspiring authors
and if they don't enclose stamped return envelopes I burn them up,
    I'm a mean sonofabitch, but why should I pay postage for their
    aspirations, almost nobody publishes the great things I write
and if they write asking what happened to them I say they were lost
    in the mail, you have to be tough to survive
in a way it's an interesting job burning the papers because I find out
    a lot about what's going on at our house that I otherwise might
    not
I never read other people's mail, it's a Federal offense, but you can tell
    a lot from the envelopes
Harold is getting letters from you can tell it's a girl because she
    writes like they teach them to in boarding schools, well I hope
    she's from a rich family, Harold will never make a dime
and Martha gets typewritten letters from NYC, I hope he doesn't
    want to be a writer, he'll never make a dime
you can see I have a lot of worries
and then I have to worry about whether I'm becoming a pyromaniac
do I get a kick when I put the match to all those papers I've piled
    into the burning barrel out behind the garage?
it's something to worry about, why I really burn the papers.

THE CARDIAC AUTOSCOPE

is a useful and versatile instrument for lovers
designed originally for self-examination of the eye or larynx,
a new attachment developed by scientists at the Handspring
    Corporation
now extends its use to ventricular investigation with the autoscope
    you can study your heart yourself right at home at one tenth the
    cost of a hospital angiogram
find out what your heart is like
no need to open the thoracic cavity with an expensive and perhaps
    risky surgical procedure
does it look like the mechanism supplied to the late Barney Clark in
    Salt Lake City
who has been proposed for angelhood in the Church of the Latter-Day
    Saints?
or does it resemble the symbolic heart of St. Valentine's Day, perhaps
    in a setting of white paper lace with a small bird perched in its
    middle?
or even the Sacred Heart of Our Lord which we see in old wood
    engravings with the rays of sanctity shooting out of it like
    porcupine quills, an unlikely phenomenon in these days of doom
    and abominations?
however it looks, the autoscope will help you to achieve a more
    healthy and fully rounded emotional life
and at slight additional cost you can acquire the new Handspring
    multimedia model of the autoscope
right in your own living room, with our battery model or plugged
    into an ordinary wall socket
you can hear your heart speak as well as observe it, you can look and
    listen simultaneously, a unique Handspring feature
you can learn what your heart is saying as it expands and contracts in
    its diastoles and systoles
you can pick up and decode its messages
for the Handspring Model MM, with built-in minichip, is programmed
    to give you the name of the person, or persons, your heart is really
    addressing in its ceaseless succession of rhythmic susurrations

your heart's message may not be what you expect, you may be in for
   some surprises
can you afford *not* to know what your heart is trying to tell you?
can you afford to ignore its suggestions?
send at once for free illustrated brochure to Division R, The
   Handspring Corporation, Box 606, Norfolk, Ct., 06058
a 22-cent stamp (only 14 cents for a postcard) may change your
   whole emotional life
Handspring autoscopes are moderately priced, delivery is prepaid by
   UPS, and all assemblies and parts are guaranteed for one year.
   Snakeskin travel cases for your autoscope are extra.

Special Introductory Offer

On any prepaid order for a Model MM autoscope received before
   September 1, 1984, you may select as a free bonus one of the fol-
   lowing unusual Handspring products:
"The 11-foot pole." Never be without one. Folds into sections and
   extends automatically at a touch. Will fit into any briefcase or
   large handbag.
"The Handy Home Cremation Kit." Don't wait until spring when
   the ground thaws to lay away loved ones who pass on during the
   winter months. Satisfaction guaranteed.
"The Two-toned Dandruff Dispenser." Gives you a choice for your
   light or dark suits. Refillable.

                                                    [ADVERTISEMENT]

THE BUBBLE BED

It was my first time in a bubble bed and I was full of apprehension
What would it be like?
I was very uneasy in that unisex bath in Kyoto
(I liked better the hot tubs on the Big Sur with Henry Miller singing
   French songs in the next tub, and there were no walls and we
   looked out over the Pacific)

The word jacuzzi frightens me, it sounds like some bad plant-drug
    that William Burroughs found in Venezuela
Would there be waves in the bubble bed like the storm in the
    Odyssey?
Would I drown or be washed up on the shore of a strange island with
    seaweed in my hair, would there be a Nausicaä to look after me
    kindly?
Or what if my long toenails pierced the sac and I made a big mess in
    the nice lady's guestroom?
I was full of apprehension but one must meet life's challenges
I took a valium and entrusted my body to the bubble bed
Sank soon into slumber, entered the land of darkness, the land of the
    Lotophagi
Poluphloisboio thalasses, I heard the soft sussuration of the sea on the
    ancient strand
And the bubble bed brought me two lovely dreams, one publishable
    and the other not.

I BELONG

For Lawrence Ferlinghetti

to the Best Western Culture.
As a former traveler on what was once Highway 66
(but it now has a different number)
I can attest that it is the best.
As an early lover of Lolita (in a literary way)
I can attest it is the best.
It offers a choice of queen size and king size beds and they are the best.
Wampum has been abolished in favor of credit cards
and there is a choice of two movies in your room each night from
    satellite saucers.
The German and Japanese tourists are also enjoying the Best Western
    Culture and they say it is the best.
But for some reason the Hopis the Navajos and the Zunis are not so
    enthusiastic

346

though they arrive in their pickup trucks (their horses being as dead
    as the dinosaurs) to perform gainful employment.
They have abandoned their blankets and their eagle feather overcoats
    for bluejeans ski parkas cowboy boots baseball caps and big hats
    like those worn by J.R. in *Dallas*.
Their new hogans are built of cinder blocks with tanks for cooking
    gas out back.
They do not seem to love our Best Western Culture. We sense a
    certain hostility, which troubles us and makes us sad. Best
    Western wants so much to be loved by everybody.

THE LAMENT OF PROFESSOR TURBOJET

Why vainly do I hither fly
And yon on top of that
Like the famous chicken on the road
Who don't know where she's at?

The students seem to like my jokes
But do they really *care*?
Here today and gone tomorrow,
I vanish in the air.

They know me at Atlanta's hub
I'm a regular at O'Hare,
I sip my Coors at Stapleton,
But does anyone really care?

The coeds are a sweet delight
(Though some induce despair)
I couldn't live without them all
But do they really care?

I keep my seatbelt buckled,
I eat my plastic tray,
I'm never late to reach the gate,
But does it matter what I say?

HIGHLIGHTS OF THE GOLIAD PARADE

From "My Trip to Texas"

Two fire engines

The highschool band (blue uniforms) 22 players

The County Sheriff (in his car)

The Mayor (female) (in her car)

A car with 4 Councilmen (1 female)

The Tax Collector (female) [Neva Thigpen]

All officials have placards on their car doors telling who they are.
  Election coming. Contesting candidates are in cars at end of
  parade. Some politicians throw candy out of car windows.
  Children scramble for candy. Race between Georgia Lee
  Zwickheim (challenger) and Neva Thigpen (incumbent) for
  Tax Collector should be close.

Contingent of Girl Scouts

Contingent of Boy Scouts

Contingent of Brownies

Floats pulled by pickups from neighboring towns. Decorated with colored papers and Texas Lone Star Flags. Pretty high school girls pose on floats, waving to crowd. Some in bathing suits (looking chilly) some in old-fashioned long dresses. One bathing-suit girl has "where's the beef?" written on her leg.

About 50 big-belly Shriners from Al Amin Temple in Corpus Christi. Usual Shriners' tasseled fezes and outfits. First group riding on small-wheeled children's bicycles. Second group in small models of antique cars. Third group in dodge-em cars. Group of Shriners on huge motorcycles from Shriners' Highway Rescue Patrol. Helmets instead of fezes. Leader carries placard inscribed "Drive Friendly." Another placard: "20 Years of Service."

All vehicles dance about like bees on street while waiting for parade to move. Several near misses but no collisions. Shriners float. Papier-mâché figures of crippled children on crutches or in wheelchairs. Banner: "Crippled or Burned / We're Concerned." (End of Shriners)

P.T.A. Float. Large schoolteacher. Small boy dressed like the parson in *Scarlet Letter.* Why?

Rural Electrification Float says "Job Unfinished."

Lutheran Orphanage Float. Children look well nourished and contented.

Band from nearby Air Force Base. Led by stone-faced Sgt. Major. Bound for Glory. 32 very trim bandsmen.

Rotary Club Float. (Not memorable.)

Wizard of Oz Float. "Follow the Yellow Brick Road."

The Goliad County Recreation Dept. truck. 10 ft. diameter plastic children's swimming pool in shape of Texas. Blue and silver (Dallas Cowboys colors). Bottom painted with football helmet and Lone Star.

Seven antique cars, two with horns that play tunes.

Town humorist concealed in van, presumably with peephole.
Loudspeaker on van roof. Humorist spots town celebrities on
sidewalk and ad libs jokes about each. (No joke for visiting poet,
who feels left out.) Van borrowed from Lone Star Beer.

Group of 4 clowns. "Vote for Ho-Ho / Send a Real Clown to
Washington."

Group of 3 huge pyramidal lady clowns in undesignated costumes.
How inflated?

Group of 3 old ladies with broken legs walking on crutches.
Bandaged heads and arms. What happened to them?

Float of St. Andrew's Lutheran Sunday School. Children singing "Yes,
Jesus Loves Me."

Float of nearby town of Shiner. "Cleanest Little City in Texas."

Wildcat Girls Band. (But a few little boys in it.) Girls look about
12–15 years old. Very serious bunch. March and play well.
Where is Wildcat?

Goliad Highway Wrecker Service. Wrecker towing demolished blue
Volkswagen.

Float from Beehive with large papier-mâché bee which flaps its
wings.

Small World Nursery Float. Kiddies dressed in foreign-land costumes
including one Japanese, one Arab. "Children Are The Treasures
of The World."

Prairie Farm Mutual Insurance Company. No décor.

God's Little Sunbeams from St. Peter's Lutheran Church. Large
golden paper stars on each head.

350

Arena Turkey Festival Float. Live turkey tied to pedestal.

Margaret Mary Altar Society Float. Mariolatry?

Zaraoza Society Float. 3 Mex-Tex girls in bouffant dancing dresses.

Goliad Savings Bank with Money Tree. "Watch Your Money Grow!"

Pioneer Wagon pulled by mules.

An Enormous Tractor. (No caption.)

La Batia Restaurant. More Mexican girls.

Float from Gonzales. "Cradle of Texas Independence."

Coleto Valley Trail Riders. Some riders snap bull whips. 6 children
    (both sexes) on ponies.

Cattle Feeders Organization. Mounted.

Wheel & Spur Trail Riders, Pam Hickey 1984 Trail Queen. Another
    beautiful Texas girl.

Goliad Police Department Squad Car. Sheriff waves goodbye to all.
    Cheers and boos.

(End of Parade.)

TAKE OFF YOUR SOCKS!!

You didn't take off your socks!

You talk about your illustrious ancestors but you didn't take off your socks

You have been lying about your forebears, and I no longer believe that Sir Malmesby d'Ormesby came over with William the Conqueror

I think they were only peasants, employed to beat the ponds all night to quiet the frogs near a chateau

Of course it is recorded that Napoleon kept on his jackboots as well as his socks but he was in a great hurry between battles

Even Bertrand took off his socks, cold as it was in Hautefort with no central heating

And there is one sock of lion-hearted Richard in the museum at Chalus, so he must have taken at least one off

Tu es atroce, tu es sans aucun raffinement

Go live in an igloo, rubbing noses with an eskimo

She probably won't mind if you keep your socks on.

THE PARODIST

It is his thing to copy, that is his self-tormenting obsession

He is a confused Narcissus who when he looks in the pool sees himself as other people

He likes to copy the styles of other writers

And he likes to mimic entire other lives

If he is feeling comical he will parody S. J. Perelman, who could think up so many fancy words to misuse in comical fashion

And if he is feeling amorous he will take off Rochester or Herrick

If tragical, let it be one of the old Greeks who could make bad or sad things mythical and so instructive

Copying lives is far more complicated

A life is not something that sits simply on the page, it has to be
    studied from many angles
What is essential in a life must be separated from what is not
There is the temptation to be anecdotal, to parody the most obvious
    gestures
There are certain gestures, certain ways of speaking, which are false
    signs which do not really signify
There are tracks in the sand or the snow which do not lead anywhere
A parodist can be too personal in the choice of his subject
He should not choose from emulation and above all not from desire
In life-parody it is risky to cross to the other sex
Though it can be done if there is enough empathy and there has been
    sufficient observation
Brecht's Verfremdungseffekt, the distancing, is sometimes a good
    stance for life-parody, that sly, suspicious man knew what he was
    doing
The parodist mentions no names, does not identify his subjects in his
    life-parodies, he guards his secrets
He knows that if he has succeeded they will be manifest
Can you tell who he is being today?

PREGUNTAS SIN RESPUESTAS

For Nicanor Parra

As the Anti-Poet and his friend the poeta Estadounidienso Hiram
Handspring were perambulating the tree lined streets of Talca, the charm-
ing capital of the province of the same name, they diverted themselves by
formulating questions—questions, of course, which required no immediate
answers. Passing the grade school with its designation of "Muchachos" at
one end and "Niñas" at the other, the Anti-Poet remarked:

AP: Who would prefer a brothel to a school?
HH: Who would want to leave Talca for Paris?
AP: Would you prefer a dictionary that had no words?
HH: What is the space between two thoughts?

AP: Is it true that when the horse looks back the landscape changes?
HH: Who would prefer teargas to buying five kisses?
AP: Would you like to have a baby in a stall of the fruit market?
HH: Shall we dance the earthquake dance again?
AP: Would you like to turn a tunnel into a tower?
HH: Is it possible to repair a round window with safety pins?
AP: Would you rather be the shopless barber than yourself?
HH: How about being a flying babysitter?
AP: Shall we join the club of the great landowners?
HH: Or would it be better to become the king of the bums of Talca?
AP: Who wants not to be anyone at all?

It was a most invigorating conversation, but so much cerebration had given the poets an appetite and they went to the restaurant in the Plaza de Armas to put on the feedbag.

EIN KITZBUEHLER TAG (1947)

(Some Lines Written in Ski German)

Das Morgenrot in Januar kommt spaet
Die Bauern steigen frueh an die Kuhscheune in die Alpen
Kopfweh beschlagt Seine Durchlaut Edward, der hat zu viel getrunk-
    en gestern Abend
Heute gibt's Tanzabend in der Minerva Bar
Die schoene Bul-Bul liegt in ihrem Sonnenstuhl den niemals-kom-
    menden Prinzen erwartend
Bergfuehrer Eberhart Kneisl schnitzt den Speck mit seinem
    Taschenmesser fuer seine Tourgruppe am Gipfel des Jauffenberg
Der junge Amerikaner ist gesturzt und seine Skihosen zerrissen
Die Niederlandische Koenig'n naeht sie ihm zu
Mein Schweizer Freund mir sagt: "hoote detz het fiel loote oofm
    Berg"
Eberhart Kneisl spielt seine Mundharmonika in Teesalon Angelika,
    die Leute tanzen

354

Die Bauern wenden wieder in die Hoehe wasser zu geben den Kuhen

Das Abendrot im Januar kommt frueh

Ich fresse mein Abendessen im Gasthof Post, das nicht sehr koestlich
ist

Die Maedl das mir serviert ist huebsch aber ein bisshel trauerig

"Wie gehts, Marili," frage ich Sie. "Immer schlecht," antwortet Sie,
"jah, immer schlecht."

Bergfuehrer Kneisl tanzt mit Bul-Bul in der Minerva Bar

Er erzaehlt ihr die klaegliche Geschicte, wie sein Vater, auch ein
bekannter Bergfuehrer, gestorben ist

Es war in einer Lawine am dem Hohenstauffenkopf

Als Schnee und Eis ueber seinen Koerper kamen

Schreit er: "Herr Gott, wir sind alle verloren."

Man hat seinen Koerper erst im Fruehling im Tal gefunden

Die Bul-Bul weint und muss einen Rotwie trinken

Lotti, mein Kaetchen, kratzet an meiner Tuer

Die Kirchenglocken klingen

Am Himmel sieht man keine Sterne

Jetzt schlaeft das Dorf

Die Welt ist dunkel und schwarz.

EIN KITZBUEHLER TAG (1947)

In January the dawn comes late

But early in the day the peasants trudge up to their cowsheds in the
alpine meadows

A headache is pounding HRH Prince Edward who drank too much
last night

This evening there will be dancing in the Minerva Bar

Beautiful Bul-Bul lies in her deckchair waiting for *her* prince who
never comes

Mountain guide Eberhart Kneisl cuts raw bacon with his pocket
knife for the ski tourers in his party near the top of the
Jauffenberg

The young American takes a fall and rips his skipants
The Queen of Holland sews him up
My Swiss friend says: "There are lots of people on the mountain
    today"
Eberhart Kneisl plays his mouth organ in the Angelika tearoom,
    people dance
The peasants go back up the mountain to water their cows
Dusk comes early in January
I eat my dinner in the Gasthof Post which doesn't cost too much
The girl who waits on me is pretty but a bit sad
"How goes it, Marili," I ask her. "Always bad," she answers, "yes it
    always gets worse."
Mountain guide Kneisl is dancing with Bul-Bul in the Minerva Bar
He tells her the lamentable story of how his father, who was also a
    famous mountain guide, was killed
It was in an avalanche on the Hohenstauffenkopf
As snow and ice rolled over him
He cried out, "Lord God, we are all lost"
They found his body in the spring down in the valley
Bul-Bul begins to cry and has to have a glass of redwine
Lotti, my little kitten, scratches at my door
The churchbells ring
Not a star can be seen in the sky
Now the village is asleep
The world is dark and black.

TABELLAE

(1986)

I SAW HER FIRST

on the red-on-black amphora
in the museum at Delphi and

knew at once she was Helio-
dora the girl in Meleager's

poem with her hair in a fil-
let and her tiny feet & her

breasts like white roses then
thirty years later we were to-

gether in a faded room in that
small hotel in the rue de la

Harpe she spoke French of
course and at first she was

shy but then she was tenderly
passionate yes it was Helio-

dora will she ever come back
to me might she even come to

stay I make my prayer to the
Gods that Heliodora return.

MY WATCH

I loaned my watch the other
evening to a girl I was with

and for some reason she changed
the time on it she put the hands

back not minutes not hours but
to the time when I first found

happiness keep my time where
you put it my dear but don't

take away a second of yourself.

CARITAS PERFECTA

absolute love was defined by
the Scholastics and Pascal was

not bad on the subject either
but for me it's a personal &

concrete matter that has to
do with you & the way you are

with me which is all of it &
as absolute as anything can be.

WHO IS THE CHILD

who wants to show everything
he finds to the pretty little

girl nextdoor with whom he is
(not so secretly) in love the

other children know and tease
him they say he is so ugly he

will never please her they say
that she laughs at him behind

his back but he doesn't believe
them he brings her violets in

spring and colored leaves in
the fall he brought her the

praying mantis bug he found
in the field everything he

finds that is nice or inter-
esting is for her he doesn't

tell her but he's certain that
when they grow up they'll get

married he wouldn't dare try
to kiss her or even hold hands

but he thinks she knows how
much he loves her and that

she doesn't mind it too much.

THE MIRROR GIRL

There was a mad old man
who was crazy about be-

ing in love he had run
after love all his life

but never found it quite
as he wished it were what

he really wanted was a
mirror girl who was al-

so himself he hoped to
look into her eyes and

see himself but he never
found her they all want-

ed to be themselves this
sad & mad old man search-

ing for his mirror girl
right up to the very end.

YOU'VE SET THE WORDS

to running through my
head again the words

I thought were lost
until you brought

them back soft words
of love adventurous

words and ones I hope
will make you laugh

they dance and frolic
 in my head I wake at

night and words for
you appear send me

some words to let me
know you like my words

and that they're your
words too our words.

WHY DO YOU NEVER ENTER MY DREAMS

Nightly I await you
but you do not come

the lamp burns & the
table is spread the

Falernian is decanted
yet it is dawn and you

have not appeared are
you afraid of my dreams

they are loving & will
not harm you or do you

in sleep go visiting
the dreams of another?

I FEEL AT HOME

in the box you bought
for my poems a grey

cardboard box with a
red button to open

it please keep some
of your own things

in there too perhaps
a bit of the ribbon

you use to bind your
braid or a button that

came off your cardigan
oh let's be together as

much as ever we can.

I LIVE IN THREE WORLDS

the one around me and
the one in my thoughts

where you live & the
one in my old books

where I can read what
you and I did when we

were together before.

EROS AS ARCHAEOLOGIST

searches the ruins of my youth
he finds shards from half-for-

gotten loves old baubles that
once gleamed a comb from soft

hair a broken mirror a worn
glove lost one winter's day

a sandal left on the beach
it is a melancholy midden

that he screens & must I
see myself in this debris

now that the only one
I want to see is you?

QUI NUNQUAM AMAVIT

Who is the person who's in
love with you is he Bluebeard

or is he Philemon (or is he
Abelard) is he eating you or

is he feeding you (as he would
wish to) is he Tristan singing

a deathsong or fat Sir John
trying to make you laugh does

anyone really know the person
who loves you he certainly

doesn't know himself but if
he knows anything it is that

he loves you as he never
loved (or was loved) before.

UNDER HIS MICROSCOPE

the scientist of love
is observing a most

fascinating little crea-
ture she is delicate she

is intricately beautiful
he has never seen her like

before her movements seem
almost a language as if

she were trying to give
him a message but his lens

cannot interpret her signs
much as he wishes to under-

stand them what is the
message she has for him?

THE DANCE OF THE SKIN

Over her flesh the skin
dances don't try to talk

about the dance of the
skin don't say anything

at all just lie still and
feel it move just lie still.

A SUGGESTION

It would be nice if you
could stop talking while

you are kissing I love
poets and their water-

falling words but one
thing at a time please.

ARACHNE

You are the love spider
a delicate little creature

of luminous beauty I know
you didn't spin your web

to catch me and then eat me
(I'm not an appetizing fly)

one morning I saw the dew-
drops glistening on your

web & was attracted & now
I'm just happy happy to be

in such a web don't eat me
please but keep me alive &

let me try to amuse you
while you're not weaving.

THE PRISONER OF CHILDHOOD

It is night and your plane is now
flying over Nantucket where I spent

summers as a child you are unaware
that down below you in the darkness

a ten year old boy in a rambling
white house is hidden behind the

window curtains spying on a girl
in the next house she is four years

older and he is too timid to speak
to her she is not pretty but she is

a girl he has no sisters and he does
not know how girls are different he

has to find out he spies on her every
night to learn what a girl is and so

loving begins loving which will de-
light and frighten him all his life.

EYES ARE THE GUIDES OF LOVE

said Propertius oculi sunt
in amore duces so why does

she close them yet her lips
are open (in a smile) as if

they were her eyes dulce ri-
dentem so I shall not re-

proach the secrecy of her
eyes though she does not

tell me what it is perhaps
it isn't for me to know.

AFTER ROCHESTER

Methought an angel from the air
Had layed my Celia's beauty bare
That on the pyre of such delight
We burned away a tender night.

Good Angel, come again and lend
Revealing magic to my hand
The better that another part
May speak the passion of my heart.

Σοί με λάτριν γλυκύδωρος
  Ἔρως παρέδωκε, Ἡλιοδώρα

LOVE, THE GIVER OF SWEET GIFTS,
    GAVE THEE TO ME, HELIODORA

What touched me most
what touched me more

even than the ways she
had touched me was when

she sat on the bed be-
side me with her legs

tucked under her as in
the lotus position but

not stiff like a Buddha
she was leaning a little

toward me her lips open
in a slight smile she

was a child sitting by
a campfire listening to

a story what story did
you hear then Heliodora?

TWO SPOONS

After we have made love
and are sleepy we curl

together like two spoons
each fitting closely in-

to the other my arm is
around you my hand hold-

ing your breast I can
even feel your feet with

my toes your long hair
is between your back and

my chest I whisper very
softly into your ear for

a moment you squeeze my
fingers & we fall asleep.

WHAT IS THE NEED

that makes me worship
your body surely this

is irrational for it
like mine will be de-

composed yet when you
come to me naked so

simply and without re-
serve the question be-

comes irrelevant since
I know I am present in

a permanence of love.

Τό Σῶμα

When you are far away
I like to think about

your body not as some-
thing to conquer or to

plunder and not only as
the source of my enjoy-

ment (though certainly
it is that) but as the

embodiment of your ten-
derness and affection

that wrap around me like
a warm cloak which is the

knowledge of being loved.

TOUCHING

I want to touch you
in beautiful places

places that no one
else had ever found

places we found to-
gether when we were

in Otherwhere such
beautiful places.

LAST WORDS

Goethe's last words were "Mehr Licht"
and Gertrude asked "What is the ques-

tion" and Orson Welles (in *Citizen
Kane*) said "Rosebud" meaning the

sled he had as a boy and my last
word as the car began to skid was

"Strawberry" will history know I was
sending my ultimate breath to you?

PROPERATE TEMPUS

Which time is the real time
the time when again I'll be

with you or the time that
I'm living in now it's

spring and the shadblow
trees have come into bloom

their branches are a blaze
of white in the sun but

their blossoms are so deli-
cate as you are delicate

time is so slow for me to-
day hurry time bring me to

her as quickly as you can.

THE UNSATISFACTORY DREAM

Why did you elude me last night
when I was dreaming of Paris the

places we had been together that
spring but now you weren't there

I followed a girl in the Tuiller-
ies (she had your long hair) but

it wasn't you I saw a girl with a
little skip in her walk on the Quai

des Grands Augustins but it wasn't
you at the café in the Place des

Vosges there was a girl holding
her cigarette the way you do but

no not you yet I'm sure we were
in Paris together wasn't there a

red awning outside our bedroom
window didn't the churchbells of

Saint Thomas d'Aquin ring for mass
morning and evening didn't I find

your sleeping head in the Musée
Rodin no it wasn't an illusion.

THE OWL OF MINERVA

(1987)

ADVICE TO AURELIUS

If you would love happily
and long avoid the winter

of domesticity pursue the
exalted embrace not the

little casseroles of Sun-
day supper meet only in

green bowers near campes-
tral waterfalls or on the

smaller Adriatic islands
this Aurelius is the best

advice that Catullus can
give you it is based on

considerable experience
he knows whereof he speaks.

THE OWL OF MINERVA

has spread its wings
and flown away into

the dusk it can't stand
it around here anymore

the Quinquatrus is no
longer celebrated and

wisdom resides only in
the floppy disks of com-

puters sculptures are
made with bulldozers

women no longer spin
there's no foundation

all down the line Hegel
now plays in a rock band

the owl for all its feath-
ers is a-cold it has flown

back to Etruria maybe
it will do better there.

THE FATE OF ACTAEON

Bathing the body of nymphs, of nymphs, and Diana,
Nymphs white-gathered about her, and the air, air,
Shaking, air alight with the goddess . . .

The dogs leap on Actaeon,
          "Hither, hither, Actaeon,"
Spotted stag of the wood;
Gold, gold, a sheaf of hair,
          Thick like a wheat swath,
Blaze, blaze in the sun,
          The dogs leap on Actaeon. —Pound: *Canto* IV

Shall I be punished more severely
than Actaeon he only gazed on the

Goddess from afar in the wood hic
dea silvarum venatu fessa solebat

virgineos artus liquido perfundere
rore her maiden limbs in the crys-

tal water while I in my ardor pur-
sued her into the shower laving

with impious (and soapy) hands
the breasts of the celestial as the

warm rain fell upon them circumfus-
aeque Dianam corporibus texere su-

is the nymphs thronging about her
weaving a screen with their bodies

Actaeon was torn to pieces by his
own dogs what fate now awaits me?

OVID: *Metamorphoses*, III, 163–64 & 180–81

FOR ME ALL TIME ALL HISTORY IS *NOW*

Only this morning Apollo was chasing Daphne through the
    woods just back of our house
I could hear her panting in terror as she ran
And the gods are drinking their mead and hatching cruel
    plots against us mortals right on top of our mountain
For Pound that old Chinese emperor had been writing make
    it new on his bathtub
The same day that Uncle Willie Yeats came to lunch in Rapallo
If I buy a good watch, it will stop running in about three days
It seems to know how I am about time
(But the watch I lost in the rough on the golf course in
    October

Was still running when the mower man found it the next spring)
I'm like a peasant in India about time and history
He knows it was just last month that Rama invaded Sri Lanka
    with his army of monkeys
And cut off the nine heads of wicked Ravana to rescue Sita
I'm like the old man I met by the tank in the temple of
    Chindambaram
Who assured me that Sita had been a personal friend of his
    grandmother.

SHE'S NOT EXACTLY LIKE YOU

so she won't do and when the Lady Maeut
had rejected Bertrand de Born sens totas

ochaisos without any reason and he knew
he would never find another like her que

valha vos qu'ai perduda he said he would
never love again ja mais no vuolh aver

druda and in his poem Domna puois de me
no-us chal he borrowed graces from seven

other ladies from Cembelis and Aelis from
the chatelaine of Chalais and the fair-

tressed Agnes from the one he called Better-
than-Good (Mielhs-de-be) from Audiart

and the toothsome Faidida from the mirror
lady (who was she?) but taken all together

they could not equal Maeut and so it is
with me there is no other to replace you

382

no sai on m'enquieira there's nowhere I
would look que ja mais non er per me tan

rics jais for never will there be so
rich a joy or a lady who pleases me so.

IL PASTOR FIDO

Son' io il pazzo assurdo
che ti vuole troppo bene

al' stesso momento sento
brama e paura il tremor

d'amore mi dà gioia ed
angoscia perchè ho fatto

ciò che Iddio interdice
mi sono guardato nelle

fonte ma era il tuo vi-
so che ho visto là una

beltà riservata agli immor-
tali d'Olimpo non sono

che un pastore campestre
la mia pena è grave sarò

sempre pazzo ma sono con-
tento perchè quando ti

guardavo nell' acqua mi sono
convinto che tu sorridevi.

The history of this poem is curious but very sad. In the liceo of the town of Chieti near Pescara there was a 14-year-old student named Egidio Bacigalupo. He had become infatuated with Pulcheria, the beauty of the class. But she scorned him. The class had been studying Guarini's masterpiece of the pastoral genre Il Pastor Fido *("The Faithful Shepherd"). Hoping to heighten her esteem for him, Egidio wrote this poem in imitation of Guarini and slipped it into Pulcheria's desk. But when she found it she gave it to the teacher. The teacher read the poem aloud, ridiculing its content and metric. That night Egidio went out into the darkness and drowned himself in the village duckpond. The case received considerable notice in the press and this translation of the poem was published in the* Rome Daily American *for 16 June 1963.*

I am the absurd lunatic
Who loves you too much
In the same moment I feel longing and fear
The tremor of love gives me both joy and anguish
Because I have done something the gods forbid
I looked at myself in the fountain pool
But it was your face I saw there
A beauty reserved for the immortals on Olympus
I am only a rustic shepherd
My punishment will be severe
I'll always be mad but I am content
When I saw you in the water
I knew you were smiling at me

THE PARTY ON OLYMPUS

When soul love & scrunch love
are united that's when life

seems better than anyone de-
serves it must have been a

384

good party that night up on
Olympus when the old sores

of the psychomachia were
soothed by ambrosia when

Hermes flirted with the Cyp-
rian beauty and no one went

squealing to Zeus about
wrongs to be righted we

here below the beneficiaries
of such benignity can only

be grateful hoping it will
happen often that there will

be more parties on Olympus.

AFTER THE HUGGING IS OVER
I'LL STILL TREASURE YOU MY DEAR

Sed pia Baucis anus parilique aetate Philemon
illa sunt annis iuncti iuvenalibus, illa
consenuere casa paupertatemque fatendo
effecere levem nec iniqua mente ferendo
and they loved even their poverty together
and they said to the gods they had sheltered
et quoniam concordes egimus annos,
auferat hora duos eadem, nec coniugis umquam
busta meae videam, neu sim tumulandus ab illa
we beg that we may die on the same day
that neither may have to bury the other

frondere Philemona Baucis,
Baucida conspexit senior frondere Philemon,
saying their farewell as they put forth leaves
and to this day the peasants point out
the two poplars growing from a single trunk.

THE SONGBIRD

The mad contralto in room 503
of the Hotel des Illusions has

begun her scales   she is con-
siderate of the other guests

and only sings between 11 & 3
when most of them are out   they

are not scales such as you might
hear in a music school   she makes

them up differently every day
she seldom leaves her room so

I haven't met her   perhaps she
is German (I'm not sure) but I've

heard sequences of notes that re-
minded me of *Parsifal* or *Wozzek*

or the *Kindertotenlieder*   some-
times new guests at the Hotel des

Illusions ask the management to
throw her out but they are out-

voted by the others   she is the
songbird of their sadness   they

need her songs & want her to stay.

SOME MEMORIES OF E.P. (DRAFTS & FRAGMENTS)

RAPALLO (1934)

So I came to Rapallo, I was eighteen then
and you accepted me into your Ezuversity
where there was no tuition, the best beanery since Bologna.
Literachoor, you said, is news that stays news
and quoting from some bloke named Rodolphus Agricola,
"ut doceat ut moveat ut delectet."
You taught me and you moved me and you gave me great delight.
Your conversation was the best show in town,
whatever you'd ever heard or read as fresh as when it first got in your
    head.
The books you loaned me were filled with caustic marginalia.
To keep from losing them you hung your glasses and your pens and
    scissors from strings over your desk.
You read my poems and crossed out half the words, saying I didn't
    need them.
You told me not to bother writing stories because Flaubert and
    Stendhal and James and Joyce had done all that could be done
    with fiction.
They say you were cranky, maybe so, but only with people who
    deserved it,
stupid professors busy killing poetry and international bankers making
    usury and *i mercanti di cannoni* selling arms to both sides of a war.
You elucidated the Mysteries, all about *dromena* and *epopte,* and how it
    was *epopte* that sent the sperm up into a man's brain to make him
    smart.

You loved cats and the cats loved you.
Some days we would walk up the stoney salite on the mountainside
    behind town
through the olive groves and the little peasant farms where the cats
    were perched on the stone walls.
They were waiting for you, they knew you would bring them
    a packet of scraps from the lunch table.
You would call to the cats, "Micci, micci, micci, vieni qua, c'è da
    mangiare."
And one day when we were feeding the cats near San Pantaleone we
    discussed what you would do with your Nobel Prize money when
    you finally got it
and you thought that a chef would be the best thing since you were
    tired of the food at the Albuggero Rapallo.
And when Henghes the sculptor (id est Heinz Winterfeld Klusmann)
    walked all the way down from Hamburg to see you
because he had heard you had known Gaudier, and he arrived
    half-starved,
you fed him and let him sleep in the big dog kennel on the terrace
    (since there were no extra beds in the penthouse apartment)
and you took him to the yard of the man who made gravestones and
    got him credit for a block of marble
from which he carved his sitting-down centaur, and you sold it for
    him to Signora Agnelli, the Fiat lady, in Torino.
And that was the beginning of Henghes' good fortune and fame
(and the drawing for the centaur became the colophon for New
    Directions).
You said I was such a terrible poet I had better become a publisher, a
    profession which you inferred required no talent and only limited
    intelligence.
And after lunch you would stretch out on your bed with your cowboy
    hat shielding the sea light from the window
with the big Chinese dictionary on a pillow on your stomach
and you stared at the characters, searching for the glyph of meaning
    in the calligraphy.
(And years later the professor asked your daughter to define your
    ideogrammic method
and she thought for a moment and replied that you looked deep into
    the characters to find the truth,

which was a properly Confucian answer.)

And Kung said: "Anyone can run to excesses, it is easy to shoot past
the mark, it is hard to stand fast in the middle."

And as "Deer Bull" ("Dear Old Hugger-scrunch") loved to say in his
Paterson,

SO BE IT!

AUSTRIA (1936)

And one year we left the Sienese to stew in the Marshes

(since the price offered by Bartolomeo was not high enough to make
it worthwhile to slug them)

and we called on the Princess Maria at Gais to check on the progress
of her education

(and you remarked that Herr Marker was a man of sound principles
because he hung his pants on the crucifix).

Then up over the Brenner into the Tyrol, you and I and the Lady,

to call on Herr Unterguggenberger, the mayor of Woergel, to learn
the facts of how Vienna had

clamped down on the circulation of *Schwungeld.*

And in Salzburg we put up at the Goldene Rose, on the wrong side
of the river for economy, where there were bedbugs,

and you came close to blows with Professor X of Haavud

who was frantic to become president of that institution

but was hindered by a little problem of concubinage, which is *mal vu*
in the town where H. James is interred.

He resented your comments on the curriculum of the world's greatest
university,

and you didn't see eye to eye on literachoor.

You loved the Mozart and the Vivaldi at the festival

but when we went to the *Festspielhaus* to hear *Fidelio* (Toscanini
conducting)

you began to squirm in fifteen minutes and rose up from your seat to
sing out:

"Well, what can you expect, the man had syphilis?"

And all this was part of my instruction.

THE BEAUTIFUL MUTTERING

The young man who becomes an old man
as we read his Cantos is telling us

all he knows about everything he has
ever done or seen or heard or read

his discourse is like the endless
beating of the surf on the shore

the poluphloisboio thalasses of
Homer it is the voice of the blind

singer and the voice of the old man
in the village square near Chindam-

baram who is intoning the *Ramayana*
again and again and again it is an al-

most interminable muttering but of
such grace of phrase of such wisdom

that we are lost in its spell we
want to live for ourselves every-

thing the poet has done or seen
or heard or read *sic scriptum est.*

THE FAMILY PORTRAIT

Today we were cleaning out the attic
And came on an old family portrait.
I knew the face but couldn't remember who it was.

The long, thin face of our family.
Some cousin in the last century
But was he a Wharton or an Irwin?
A sensitive face, a thoughtful face.
In the portrait he is looking at a book as if he were someone
    who actually read books,
Rather rare in our family until I came along.
So he has gone to the Salvation Army.
Farewell, old cousin, and happy travels.
The Salvation Army will give you to someone who wants a
    handpainted picture.
You will preside over a new family.
I hope they'll get to love you
And that you'll be happy with them.

THE PEOPLE BOXES

In Chile after the earthquake
I met a specialist in disaster

repairs he is famous for having
repaired disasters all over the

world the earthquake in Chile
didn't harm the new houses of

the rich but it crumbled the
adobe hovels of the poor so

the specialist was building
thousands of wooden people

boxes he makes them in three
sizes for different sized fami-

lies they had one door one
window and one chemical facili-

ty water in buckets from the
fire hydrant and cooking on

the ground outside but the
supply of lumber is running

out so many poor people will
have to wait for their boxes.

THE FISHERWOMAN

A poetical lady whom I find
charming because she reads

Greek in bed has reached a
difficult stage in her life

her husband is absorbed in
his profession and her chil-

dren have gone off to col-
lege she is casting about

as the fly fisherman will
search a stream with his

casts to find where the
trout are lying she is so

charming diktuon theraon
but must I be her trout?

THE SECRETARY'S STORY

From my neat desk I ran
that big disorderly man

it was no more trouble
than sitting a hyper-

active baby then his wife
died and my sorrows began

he couldn't tell the dif-
ference between a person

and a sales promotion.

THE BELIEVER

eats with one stomach but
the man who denies God must

eat with seven stomachs so
said the Prophet speaking

of hospitality but there's
more to it than that he who

is blessed with your love
will always be content but

when you deny your love the
miserable man will never be

satisfied not in this life.

WAITING FOR THE LIGHT

I was walking down San Carlos
to a lecture at San Jose State

at Fourth St. the light is very
slow in changing and I can ob-

serve a girl student who is
waiting on the other side to

cross she is neither beautiful
nor homely there is no eye con-

tact between us but in the mo-
ment of waiting I construct the

whole life that lies before her
her story is neither noble nor

tragic it has only its little
intricacies its small risings

& fallings I shall not tell her
story because it might be yours.

THE MAZE

I like to stray into the
amazements of your body

where I find treasures
I never found before the

child dreamed of astonish-
ments but never saw them

never touched them never
heard or felt them until

now what god contrived
the maze of your amaze-

ments where I am lost so
happily I never want to

leave this labyrinth.

> *we talk as long as we can*
> *there are amazements*
> *you like to stray into and*
> *my body's only*
> *one of them*
> —from Rosmarie Waldrop's poem *Drawbridge*

NOT PERFECT LIKE YOU

I'm sorry for all the girls
who are not perfect like you

how sad for them to look in
the mirror and see they don't

have absolute beauty   & how
they must feel when they lose

their tempers and say some-
thing mean they're sorry for

afterwards (you never lose
your temper when I say or do

something stupid   if some-
thing goes wrong you just

say shit and go on smiling)
or the ones who aren't opti-

mistic about everything or
they have to worry whether

they are making their lover
happy   perhaps of course I

don't have to feel sorry for
Meryl Streep   she is a god-

dess and must be perfect (al-
though we read that some of

the Greek ones got jealous &
vengeful) but I'm not certain

because I've never met her
socially   she lives near me

but she keeps to herself and
has security guards to keep

her fans out   it could be
she's not as perfect as you.

lines after cummings

(Eyes closed
      lids d

             o

                 w

                     n tight

can shut eyes smile?
        HERS can
      Lips Open; lips *smile.*
Breathing fast
                & faster &
little sounds: smile sounds
;faster, become big sounds,
faster
        be COME
                L*O*V*E!)

O BEST OF ALL NIGHTS, RETURN AND RETURN AGAIN

How she let her long hair down over her shoulders, making a love
    cave around her face. Return and return again.
How when the lamplight was lowered she pressed against him,
    twining her fingers in his. Return and return again.
How their legs swam together like dolphins and their toes played
    like little ninnies. Return and return again.
How she sat beside him cross-legged, telling him stories of her
    childhood. Return and return again.
How she closed her eyes when his were open, how they breathed
    together, breathing each other. Return and return again.
How they fell into slumber, their bodies curled together like two
    spoons. Return and return again.

How they went together to Otherwhere, the fairest land they had
    ever seen. Return and return again.
O best of all nights, return and return again.

CAN LANGUAGE BE TAUGHT WITH THE FINGERTIPS?

It is raining hard, too hard for us to go down to Paestum
Where the old gods are still alive, where they say that Poseidon still
    comes up from the sea to inspect the premises
So we lie in the big sagging bed in the Albergo Aurelio at Salerno,
    drinking what we imagine to be Falernian
I have my little book of Catullus and am reading his poems to you
    but only the ones about Lesbia, not the "pedicabos"
First the Latin with its beautiful sounds and then I try to translate
    some of the lines for you
You have one arm around me and your head is on my shoulder
You are looking at the page and you ask about the words
"What does that one mean?"
"It means that he loved her a lot, but she kept giving him a bad
    time."
"And that one?"
"That also is about love. It means that he loved her very much and
    that I love you very much."
I write the word on her breast with my fingertip
She brushes my lips with hers and says, "I'll try never to give you a
    bad time."

LIKE THE OCTOPUS

I would enfold you in my
tentacles but believe me

my embrace is loving not
injurious some say that

to confuse his prey the
octopus sends out a kind

of ink to cloud the wa-
ter so too the poet e-

mits ink (much ink) on
his beloved but it is

not noxious his poems
may be bad but their in-

tention is affectionate
they are part of his oc-

topode nature they are his
submarine squeak of love.

THE HOUR GLASS

I'm angry with time because
it moves so slowly the horses

of the sun race through the
sky but my chariot is pulled

by snails all clocks in my
house have been hidden in

closets they are loafing
they don't run fast enough

is time as slow for her
the hour glass shows time

as a thousand grains of
sand each one must fall

in the glass for time to
pass is it the same for

her is she impatient too?

HER SWEET DECEIT

Love has many joys
and best are the

surprises as when
you changed the col-

or of your hair to
make me think you

were someone else
not that you fooled

me with your sweet
deceit I had only

to hear you laugh
to know both girls

were you & that I
loved you both alike.

HAIKU (slightly overlength)

Winter has come
Five days of ice storm
The sheep have retreated to the barn
And the dog is allowed into the kitchen
I think of you
And keep warm.

CONFESSIO AMANTIS

Unaccustomed as I am.
Daddy, at your age?
Concitatio senectutis.
No fool like an old tool.
At the Palladium — oh that Shakespearian rock!
Nearly a heart attack.
Drink to me only with whose eyes?
Like that underwater cave in Rapallo.
This can't be happening to me.
Her tunic spread in delay.
Molesting children next?
Her long small legs & thighs, I with my tendril did surprise.
Sometime between evening and morning.
And yes I said yes I will Yes.

THAT NIGHT IN MILAN

that you began to cry when
we were walking back in

the dark streets from
the restaurant to the hotel

(you had had such bad luck
with men because you are

so beautiful) and you sud-
denly realized that I did

really love you that I did
really care for you as you.

HER LINE WILL BE BUSY

for half an hour and then
when I do get through it's

the answering machine she
has rushed off somewhere

on what perilous adven-
ture and heaven knows

when she will be back they
say home is where the heart

is but what if the heart
is perpetually wandering

Gaul wrote Caesar was di-
vided into three parts and

sometimes I think she is
divided into twenty but

all of them I know are il-
luminating someone with

her peripatetic radiance.

THE MYSTERIOUS DISAPPEARANCE

The room where you lived
inside my head is empty

there are signs of a has-
ty departure the postman

says you left no forward-
ing address the newspaper

seller at the corner says
you were carrying a suit-

case (but you didn't wave
to him as you always did)

the neighbors are sad you
left they loved you too.

THE WORD MACHINE

writes & writes & writes
it denudes northern for-

ests to get enough paper
to eat sometimes it writes

poems to the beloved but
mostly it writes about

the lover himself extra
stamps showing a carrier

pigeon must be printed to
circulate so many words

weary postmen wear out
their shoes making deliv-

eries the beloved has had
to buy a shredder because

her flat was so deep in paper
she couldn't move around

will the word machine ever
run out of words probably not.

CAN THERE BE A FEMALE BODHISATTVA?

I find no record of one in
my books but when the other

evening we were making love
and you sat beside me on the

bed in the lotus position
I realized that you had lived

many lives before and wanted
to tell me who it is you are.

A NIGHT AT THE OPERA

I am falling into the abyss
My fate is sealed
What a cruel martyrdom
The open tomb awaits me

I was driven by my insane desire
Who can look upon her without weeping?
God, you see into my heart
This untamed fire devastates all my virtue
He kindled this flame in you
His vile heart
May God's punishment fall upon him

Heaven spare her ravaged heart
She is lost, the unhappy woman
This love is torture for me

Only heaven will hear the sound of my sighing
Nothing on earth can prevent my ruin

Do you choose both death and disgrace?
I am torn apart by remorse
My own heart punishes me
Would I had never made those false vows
How could I bring you joy?
    I tremble as I say this.

THE LARGE OPERA SINGER

who decorated last night's dream
did not give me much personal

attention she was more concern-
ed with her press agent and the

disposition of her claque in the
paradise balcony but at least

she did accord me the privilege
of assisting with her arrayal

placing one foot against her
rump I tugged on the laces

of her stays to increase (though
not by much) her resemblance

to the Serpent of the Nile.

AN ANTI-LOVE POEM

For Nicanor Parra

Because you are a doormat I love you
And because you are my pet pincushion
Because you are agua mineral sin gas
And because you are a birdsnest
Because you are often at the hairparlor when I want you
       to change my typewriter ribbon
And because you are new shoelaces
Because you are pink blotting paper
And because you are matching buttons
Because you are a soap statue
And because you are spilled pipe tobacco
Because you love Tio Nicanor as much as I do
And because love is a funny thing
I really love you very much.

HOLES

are not holy they are just
holes Ovid tells us that

Apollo put Thetrius down a
hole because he tried to

steal his lyre and the poor
man never got out they could

hear him whistling down there
for months a true musician to

the end what is in a hole the
Vedantists say it's like the

space between two thoughts
holes are home for many ani-

mals Walter Abish stepped in
a hole in the sidewalk and

broke his ankle he had to
have it operated at the Hos-

pital for Joint Diseases Dr.
Marolda has grown rich fill-

ing the holes in my teeth
when I get a hole in my sock

my wife won't darn it she
just throws it away she is

supporting the economy but
the holes I like best are

the black holes the astrono-
mers see in the sky through

their telescopes because we'll
never know how they got there.

A JOB DESCRIPTION

I am the Arranger of Inanities
I would prefer to be the cura-

tor Major of Symbols but we are
limited by our capabilities and

exceed them at peril of ridi-
cule daily I scrutinize the

press and nightly the tube for
the best inanities then arrange

them in sardonic patterns I've
not noticed that my work has

purified the culture but surely
it is a very harmless activity.

AFTER MARTIAL

Roblinus is our leading lit-
erary pot-shotter (iconoclasm
detoxifies a culture and Rob-

linus is already a cultural
monument) since he is virtuous
the pot he shoots can hardly

be grass so let us say that the
shot must come from a pot which
is used to relieve his (distress)

TWO ONANISTS

After Juvenal

were lovers they made
love by mail each try-

ing to outdo the other
in lewd logodaedalies.

TERROR

blanched her face when
a literary topic was

introduced into the con-
versation (but she had

such pretty little feet)

REPORT FROM THE MISSING PERSONS BUREAU

The case of this missing person is strange
It has us all perplexed here at the bureau
Our files do not show anything similar to this case
There is nothing like it on our computer
Interpol does not report anything like it on the Telex.

This missing person has been seen by persons to whom her
    description was circulated

She has been seen in various parts of the city
But when we go to bring her in, it is someone else
There are resemblances, but it is someone else
In the circumstances we cannot hold her for questioning
Her dear ones are on the phone every day but we have nothing
    substantial to report.

She is a chameleon, she is like quicksilver
We have had her tailed but she loses our agents
We are no longer really certain who it is that is missing
Or who we are looking for.

PREMULA'S PROBLEM

After Catullus

Quintius her mentor tries
to make love to her she

rather likes him because
his learning enlarges her

head but he poor old man
cannot enlarge himself in

bed it's quite a problem.

ONE OF THE GREAT LINES

of modern poetry came to me
from a girl in my writing

class it went they fucked
without conversation just

that & what's more to say?

KULCHUR

when I bought my *New
York Times* this morn-

ing I noticed on the
magazine rack a new

learned journal call-
ed Jugs The World's

Dirtiest Tit-mag oh
Jug Jug to dirty ears.

IPSE DIXIT

Said the Governor of Louisiana
(and I quote) nothing short of

being caught in bed with a dead
girl or a live boy can hurt my

political career in this state.

I KNOW HOW EVERY POET

feels about his new poem
(and usually every poem)

it's the best he ever
wrote and better than

anybody else's rush it
off to a magazine the

presses are waiting they
say there are a hundred

thousand poets writing
in the USA (maybe more)

and if each one writes
at least one poem a week

that's a lot of diffused
satisfaction but Horace

was smarter he put his
new poems in a trunk

and left them there for
seven years or so he said

but I don't believe him.

THE GIFT

In that parking
lot pressure of

your body against
mine iteration of

the dream of love

GRACIOUS LIVING

describes the Rolling Meadows Club but things are slipping
The gentlemen still wear blue blazers but the ladies no longer wear
    long dresses at dinner, things are slipping
but politeness is still axiomatic, automatic and endemic, there is a
    goo of good manners about
On crossing the path of another member each member will say
    something thoughtful, like about the weather, even if it is the
    third time he has seen him that day
Nothing unkind about a member is ever heard in a public room or
    on the golf course
What might be heard in the bedrooms?

Would Mr. S. say to Mrs. S. (there is *never* a Mrs. M. in a room with a
    Mr. S. at Rolling Meadows) that fat-butt Robinson is the biggest
    fool in Christendom?
No, he would be more likely to say, poor old Robinson, they gave him
    a bad time when he was C.E.O. at National General, he's still a
    bit shaky
And Mrs. S. would say, I *do* like Bertha Robinson, she dresses so
    nicely and she was just a year after me at Foxcroft
Everyone except me at Rolling Meadows is either a past or present
    C.E.O. or Chairman of the Board
but the words money or dollars are never beard at Rolling Meadows,
    though sometimes there is a soft whisper, she was a Vanderlip
    you know, she was a Gifford
referring of course to the pedigree not to the green stuff
I have never seen any betting on the golf course at Rolling Meadows
Once a new member had to be spoken to about that by the club
    president, he was embarrassing other members by proposing
    wagers
Unless it is on thoroughbreds, wagering is for the middle classes
But times have changed, no one has a chauffeur anymore, they drive
    their Mercedes or Cadillacs themselves, or their wives drive them
    if they are too feeble
No C.E.O. or Chairman would come down in the company plane,
    that would be bad form even if the IRS would allow it
Smiling natives serve drinks under the live oaks beside the croquet
    lawns before lunch and in the main lounge under the portraits of
    the founders before dinner
The gentlemen drink vodka and tonic and the ladies drink only tonic
    with a twist of lime
Nobody gets intoxicated at Rolling Meadows, somebody did once
    but he isn't around anymore
The most recent book in the library is *The Trail of the Lonesome Pine*
The bridge room is for bridge, backgammon is frowned on, television
    is only for the news
Yes, Rolling Meadows is a nice quiet place
The only sound you will ever hear is the sound of blood pressure
    rising when someone mentions F.D.R., that traitor to his class
but no one is really worried, they know Reagan will be re-elected and
    Rolling Meadows will keep on rolling

CINCINNATUS IN UTAH

Old Ebenezer Bryce the
Mormon pioneer who tried

to ranch in the red rock
canyons was not oblivi-

ous to the miracles of
his God's nature but his

final word was this sure
is one helluva place to

hunt for a lost heifer.

EATING & DYING

Since you are my ultimate & irreversible
(& greatest) love and since if you should

through misadventure predecease me in
which grim case I would in a superb act

of male chauvinist suttee hurl myself
weeping on your sandalwood pyre let us

not spend too much time on the frivoli-
ties of art & literature but put on the

feed bag as often as possible at Lutèce
& La Tulipe at Taillevant & the Grand Vé-

fours at the Savoy & Quags & that little
place in Jermyn Street which has such re-

markable oysters at Brantôme & Perigueux
guzzling pâté & confit d'oie at Horchert's

where one camarero warms the bottom of my
cigar with a taper while another lights

it at Passeto & the Vecchia Romana at
Monti's in San Trovaso where Ezra loved

the tachino at the Baur au Lac in Zurich
where Th. Mann preferred the Hasenpfeffer

to the Forellen at the Vierjahrseiten for
Rehrucken mit Preiselbeeren at Sacher's

& the Drei Husaren (but the Schwarzenberg
Palais for lunch because of the terrace

over the garden) at the old Woodlands in
Madras where we'll eat curry with our

fingers off a banana leaf at the Ayuthia
overlooking the Menam (oh those delicious

slightly rotting prawns that have cooked
all day in the sun) at the Mioyaki & Li

Yung's in Hong Kong . . . and wherever our
palates may lead us for it is my great

delight to watch you eat with such dainty
enjoyment (as if your Mum had never fed

you a decent din) and since you are busy
eating I can do most of the talking while

studying a face more appetizing than food.

ΚΟΛΛΉΜΑΤΑ

(1988)

THE QUESTIONS

What the actors say in the play
may not necessarily be what you

and I say to each other   it can
be what I say but not what you

say or what you say but not I
to study out these questions we

must meet the playwright and talk
with him   yet that may not be so

easy   how will we know if he is
telling the truth about what he

has written   or what if he sus-
pects that we are impostors who

don't exist in his imagination?

THE INTERDICTION

You think you remember but
can you be certain   you be-

lieve it happened but are
you sure   were the things

said that each one heard
the other day   were there

days were there nights did
it rain did the sun shine

it is forbidden to answer
any of these questions it

is forbidden to remember.

ἡ μοῖρα αὐτῆς

The gods were jealous
that she loved him and

made her softly and
sweetly mad   what will

be their punishment
for him who brought

about an evil that
he could not imagine?

OUR BICYCLES

At Versailles only the Queen may have pompons on her coach-
covers; fastened with nails, and of any colour that she pleases.
Duchesses have blue covers. Wives of eldest sons of dukes have red
covers. Widows have black velvet.
> — The Duc de Saint-Simon, *Historical Memoirs*

My brother being the eldest had
for his bike the most elaborate

accouterments   a pair of squirrel
tails (one grey one brown) which

flew from his handlebars   Cousin
Ham had an extra gear for attack-

ing the hills of Shadyside where
we lived   Cousin Georgie (the shy

one) had two bells with different
tones but when he took his hands

off the bars trying to sound both
of them at once his front wheel

swerved and he ended up at the
hospital for 4 stitches   as for

me (the youngest) I was still on
a tricycle and had nothing but

tears when the others sped on a-
head of me (wait for me wait for

me I would cry) leaving me far be-
hind wailing and eating their dust.

THE UNKNOWN CITY

In what city in what land does the dream take place
certainly it is in a foreign country but although

I've dreamed myself there many times I'm sure I've
never been there in waking life   I recognize nothing

as I turn corners from one street to another looking
for a certain building which I can't exactly describe

yet I know I'll know it when I come to it   but it's
always hidden behind rows of other buildings   this

is a densely built city with no parks or plazas or
broad avenues   the people look like modem people

anywhere   the cars and buses are not exceptional
there are no street signs and no names on shops I

hear the noise of traffic but no sound of human
voices speaking   in this great city (like Rome it

has several hills but it isn't Rome) on all my noct-
urnal visits I've never seen a policeman nor an ani-

mal (no horses no dogs)   I walk faster and faster
hunting for the building where my important meeting

will take place   I have an appointment that might
change my life   I feel great urgency for this ren-

dezvous but I don't know the name of the person I'm
to meet or whether it's a man or a woman   there seem

to be no hotels or sidewalk cafés in the city   I'm
becoming very tired from walking (my feet hurt my

legs ache) it's getting dark but no lights are coming
on   I'm lost now and frightened   I have no place to

spend the night   the city has become hostile   I can't
ask my way because no one speaks   what city is this

and in what land   how did I come here when & why?

THE HAPPY POETS

It's my delight to recite
my poems in the arms of

an intelligent girl and
to please her sweet ear

with what I have written.

Me iuvet in gremio doctae legisse puella
    auribus et puris scripta probasse mea — Propertius, II.xiii

And Goethe boasts that he
tapped out his hexameters

on the back of his Roman
girlfriend while she slept.

Und des Hexameters Mass leise mit fingern der Hand
Ihr auf den Rücken gezählt. Sie atmet in lieblichem Schlummer.
Und es durchglühet ihr Hauch mir bis ins Tiefste die Brust.
                                        —Goethe, *Römische Elegien*, V

THE PROBLEM STRUCK ME

With Andrew Crozier

when the crew from the tele-
phone company came to replace

a pole out on the road I ask-
ed them which is the better an

old post in a new hole or a
new post in an old hole   one

of them whirled his finger a-
round his ear the way one does

with a crazy but the other man
put down his shovel & started

to think   it's the kind of prob-
lem which occupied the scholas-

tics (they must have had a lot
of time on their hands when they

weren't coaxing angels to dance
on the heads of pins) he didn't

say anything but I could tell
I'd gotten to him   I hope he

won't do anything rash like ask-
ing his supervisor at the tele-

phone company or even throwing
up his job   chances are he has

a wife & kids and needs the money
more than a life of speculation.

AN ANGINAL EQUIVALENT

For those little stabs of pain
in the region of the heart the

poet is having an EKG   the wires
are attached to a small TV and

as he lies there he can watch
the bouncing beat on the screen

qualim asks Martial velim quae-
ris nolimve puellam? nolo nimis

facilem difficilemque nimis what
does that jerking line tell him

about the prospect for his new
affection illud quod medium est

atque inter utrumque probamus
nec volo quod cruciat nec volo

quod satiat which will she be?

You ask what kinds of girl I like and don't like
Let her not be a pushover, yet not too hard to get
Somewhere between the two
Not one who tears me to pieces
But not one who hangs on my neck.
                                —Martial, I, lvii

THE LIMPER

Rilke writes of the expectation
that a beloved is about to ap-

pear but in what form will she
come   as a living person or an

apparition and how will we re-
cognize each other   what sign

will there be that she is the
chosen one   in my case I hope

she has been warned about my
limp   no one can fail to no-

tice it   my limp is well known
throughout the city   they call

me the limper   some think my
limp is good luck and some

bad   I know people talk about
it   she will know me by my

limp and will speak to me.

Warst du nicht immer
noch von Erwartung zerstreut, als kündigte alles
eine Geliebte dir an? —*Duineser Elegien,* I.31–33

SO SLENDER

like a reed
but there are no reeds
here in Ladakh
we are above the tree line
close under the world of snow and ice
the girls here are tallow chunks with fat cheeks

so slender
did you see the Indian rope trick
on your visit to Benares?
the rope did stand in the air
supported by nothing
and moved a little with a swaying motion
as in a languid dance

so slender
I've watched you dance
but only in my waking imagination
perhaps in time
you'll dance for me in one of my dreams
so slender.

A GRACEFUL EXIT

Was it difficult to escape
from those novels of Henry

James   Isabel Archer   Mag-
gie Verver   Millie Theale

which one were you   a bit
of each I think (but none

of that little idiot Daisy
Miller)   some from each

to make up the way you are
the quiet style (since you

were in his head tell me how
much of that came from

his style) grace in behavior
grace in the movements

of mind and speech   such
delicacy of perception   a

special kind of kindness
when did it come to you

that you must leave the
books and was it for me?

THE ESCAPE

The world is too much with us
let's float away from it   I

don't mean death (which may
be an illusion) but an écarte-

ment (a separation) a ver-
fremdung (an estrangement)

we shall agree to withdraw
not into the great nothing-

ness as a Buddhist might do
but into each other (your

being would set my limits &
mine yours) can we try to be-

come invisible except to our-
selves and learn a language

that only we need understand?

DIE HEIMAT

He had walked so far to find her
through uplands over rough and

rocky roads   when in the end he
came to her at first he didn't

reckon where he was   he'd never
been in that country   the ter-

rain was not like anything he'd
seen   it took him many months

to understand this was his home.

A TRANSLATION

How did you decide to translate me
from one language to another   let's

say from the English of friendship
to the French of lovers   we'd known

each other half a year when one day
as we were talking (it was about one

of your drawings) suddenly you curl-
ed yourself against me and drew my

lips down to yours   it was so deft
an alternance from one language to

the other as if to say yes you can
speak French to me now if you wish.

ELUSIVE TIME

In love it may be dangerous
to reckon on time to count

on it   time's here and then
it's gone   I'm not thinking

of death or disaster but of
the slippage the unpredicted

disappearance of days on which
we were depending for happiness.

IT CAN HAPPEN

Was it too quick to be true
was it Eros who shot two ar-

rows it was almost as swift
as if some god had flicked a

switch and love came on like
light   amor lux est said An-

dalasius   c'était un coup de
foudre disait Ariane d'Haute-

vile and in Hamburg ganz wie
ein blitz (Herr Bosenkamp) oh

it can happen so blessed be
Eros (or whoever it was) that

it could happen even to me.

THE MAKER OF DREAMS

is his own master   he doesn't
take orders for who will be in

dreams (at least not in mine)
I've pleaded & reasoned with

him   I've explained to him
why you should be the star

in my dreams as often as pos-
sible because you are the one

for whom I'd been waiting so
long   he may be the maker of

dreams but you are the maker
of happiness   yet he is deaf

to my entreaties   he keeps
sending me persons of no in-

terest (such ordinary color-
less people) he should be

superseded as maker of dreams
either he has no taste or no

heart   I'm going to write to
the authorities to complain.

THE BIRD OF ENDLESS TIME

Your fingers touch me like a bird's wing
like the feathers of the bird that returns

every hundred years to brush against a
peak in the Himalayas and not until the

rock's been worn away will time and the
kalpas end   why do I think of the fable

when I'm close with you   surely because
I want so many lives to feel your touch.

THE KISS

In the films when the couples kiss
they grind their lips together as

if to prove their passion by break-
ing their teeth   but your kiss was

barely a passing touch as delicate
as the breath of Zephyrus I hardly

knew it had come before it was gone.

BY THE NUMBERS

What number do you start with
when you count   let's dream of

another life   idiot savants do
fantastic feats with numbers

but they don't know how they
do them   let's dream of ano-

ther life   Rexroth explained
Gödel's Proof to me that time

when we were camping in King's
River Canyon but it's gone from

my head now like so many other
things   let's dream of another

life   I prefer an abacus to a
computer   let's dream of ano-

ther life   in Sikkim a thous-
and prostrations each day and

a thousand iterations of the
mantra of the jewel at the

heart of the lotus so let us
now praise other lives and

hope that we may count them.

THE ATMAN OF SLEEP

You had fallen asleep beside
me and your closed eyes in

the dusklight were so beauti-
ful   the fingers of one hand

were curled like a child's a-
gainst your cheek   I listened

for the cadence of your breath-
ing & made mine come & go with

yours one breath for both of us.

IN HALF DARKNESS

your face is still so beautiful
there is a different radiance

that comes in sleep   I wake and
touch your cheek   I feel your

breath on my groping fingers
your eyes are closed but I sus-

pect they can see & are watch-
ing what is to come   they are

looking into the future as far
as the end of our time together.

MY DELIGHTS

Song to an Air of Lully

I delight in your merry eyes
I delight in your dulcet voice
I delight that you are wise
In your wit I rejoice
I delight that you are kind
I cherish your touch
In what other might I find
A softness that is such
All things that delight me
Are present in you
In you is the surety
Of joys old and new

May I be stricken if I speak not true
Or sing to another praise that is your due
Come now dear longest night
That I may offer my delight.

I LOVE TO SEE YOU

in the box of paperclips on my desk
it's a good place for you because I

can look at you when I'm telephoning
or typing a poem or putting poems in-

to the copy machine to send to maga-
zines that don't want them   I tried

putting you in the little ormolu
frame where the daguerreotype of

great-grandmother Henrietta used to
be but it didn't suit   you looked

too formal (you have lovely manners
but thank heaven you aren't formal)

so I pushed up the paperclips in the
box and leaned you against the heap

it can't be very comfortable (paper-
clips are harder than hay) but you're

smiling away as if you loved it   I
hope you're also smiling because you

love me so much you don't care where
I keep you even in the paperclip box.

HER REPLY

I like my picture to be in the box
where you keep your paperclips   I

imagine that when you reach for a
clip you are reaching out for me

it's a gesture you've made a thou-
sand times (whenever you've needed

a clip) but now I hope it has be-
come different   given a new mean-

ing by my image   does the movement
of your hand now plead more for me

than thought or memory can   even
at this distance I feel the touch

of your fingers   do they feel they
are touching me   or must I become

again only the icon of my everyday
self as ordinary as your paperclips?

THE BEAUTIFUL ONE

Vojo the night elevator man
the old fellow from Zagreb

is much concerned about you
it's clear that you're his

favorite in the building   (he
calls you najlepša the beauti-

ful one like the youngest of
the three princesses in the

fairy tale) but he says you
don't go out enough   how she

get husband when she sit up
there all time reading books

she have to go dancing to get
husband is what old Vojo says.

LOVE'S ALTAR

Let me bow down before
the altar of love   let

me genuflect at that sa-
cred place   it's useless

for you to protest that
this shrine is ordinary

and common to all your
sex   for me it's the lo-

cus of the sacrament the
altar where the ritual of

the Mysteries is enacted.

THE UNANSWERABLE QUESTION

It's easy to oblige you
when you say your whole

body wishes to be touching
all of mine from forehead

to feet   but what of the
soul   how can we realize

the soul   what is its lo-
cus   where does it reside?

THE IMPORTANCE OF SILENCE

Because there are some things
for which there are no names

there is no need for you to
try to invent them   your words

from the old poets are beauti-
ful to read on the page but the

ones I want to hear & feel come
from your lips and your hands.

THE HAND TRICK

She had a trick that she liked
to play with my hand (nothing

improper) it was a kind of tac-
tile hypnosis a stroking of my

fingers with the tips of hers
so that mine closed on my palm

by themselves and were reluctant
to open   it was a closure which

said to me I won't clutch you
but I don't want you to go away.

TO LOVE IS TO HOLD DEAR

to hold the hand if it is
given   or to hold only a

finger if the hand is clo-
sed   to hold all that is

dear be it near or far be
it seen or heard   and if

it be in the unseen that
too is ever close & dear.

RHYME

Isn't it good she asked (as
if there were no question in

the question) that we love
each other's bodies   one big

one small   one slim   one tall
isn't it good that we love the

way our skins taste the way
they feel to touch & stroke

of course I love you for your
mind and you me for my dispo-

sition but aren't we very lucky
our bodies love each other too?

OUR MEETINGS

Where do our thoughts meet
after we have sent them to

each other down the sidere-
al pathways will they come

together again at Vrindavan
where Radha and the blue God

Krishna loved & are loving

   Let the earth of my body be mixed
   with the earth my beloved walks on
   Let the fire of my body be the brightness
   in the mirror that reflects his face
   Let the water of my body join the waters
   of the lotus pool he bathes in

will they meet again on the
black ship where Tristan and

la belle Iseut sang mournfully

   Sehnender Minne
   schwellendes Blühen
   schmachtender Liebe
   seliges Glühen
   Jach in der Brust
   jauchzende Lust

or in the castle of Montagnac
above the Vezère where En Ber-
tran pursued the fair Maheut

Domna puois de me no-us chal
e partit m'avetz de vos
sens totas ochaisos
no sai on m'enquieira
que ja mais
non er per me tan rics jais
cobratz   e si del semblan
no trop domna a mon talan
que valha vos qu'ai perduda
ja mais no vuolh aver druda

Our thoughts have met at many
times in many places   through

divers bodies have we joined
our thoughts   so often before

now have we lived this love.

STILL POND NO MORE MOVING

Let's not do anything in par-
ticular   let's not go anywhere

or see anyone   let's for an
hour or two just *be* (that is

exist) inhaling & exhaling in
the yoga fashion if you wish

but keeping our wits about us
so we can concentrate on each

other   who & what are you and
who am I and what is it that

makes us fit so well together?

WHEN I'M MISSING YOU

I run you through the projector
in my head like a film (there's

a soundtrack too of your low and
gentle voice) and I can stop the

machine at my favorite frames to
linger over them   there's the one

where you're taking a book down
from a high shelf and your blouse

is pulled tight over your breast
and the one in the kitchen when

you're bent over making delicious
tarts out of pound cake and straw-

berry jam then there's the one
where you're washing your hair

in the sink and though there's no
tower the way your hair cascades

makes me think of Mélisande   it's
a good film and I can run it over

and over without getting bored.

EYES CLOSED

She says that she sees more
when her eyes are closed but

she doesn't know why   is it
she asks because closed eyes

exclude reality or is it be-
cause darkness is the realm

of illusion   she isn't sure
I don't know if I dare tell

her that she sees more be-
cause of me I make her feel

things she hadn't before.

THE ENLACEMENT

There's something holy about
falling asleep pressed close

against a beloved   is it a sur-
vival from some primitive rite

it's more than the huddling
together of animals in the

storm   is one body a sanctu-
ary for another   the enlace-

ment's a vow for the future
a pledge not to be broken

now blood touches blood and
breath breath as if they were

hands touching and holding.

THE SMALLEST BLESSING

A cold wind freezes me inside
when I consider that someday

(perhaps not too long distant)
I won't be here to watch you

smile or listen to you laugh
or stroke you and touch you

where you love to be touched
I had such fears when I was a

child though there was little
reason for them (what had I to

lose then except my childish
self) but now when there's ev-

erything to lose that is love-
ly and excellent what can I

think what consolation can I
find   there's only the thought

that no one has ever been cer-
tain whether we know what we've

lost and long for its return.

THE GIFTS

You do so much for me
give me so much I need

that I've been waiting
for   what can I do for

you to make you half as
happy as you make me   I

think I know (it just now
came to me) I must find a

secret place in you that
has always been empty and

try to put a part of me
there (to live there in

you) that will become a
part of you & bring you

what was missing that
will take your fears a-

way and give you stead-
fast strength and joy.

THE REVENANTS

At a table in the corner two people
are talking in low voices a young

man and a girl   they call each other
Paolo & Francesca   if they are reven-

ants they are at least 800 years old
perhaps more (who knows   there are

no birth certificates for revenants
or passports which limit where they

may go) they are speaking in an al-
most forgotten language   seriously

quietly sadly as if once they had had
great sorrow (were they perhaps sepa-

rated in the lower world) sad chil-
dren of another time   have they re-

turned here to find each other again
now and then the girl smiles for an

instant in a puzzled way   he takes
her hand they go on talking softly.

THE POEM SEEN AS A SHELL GAME

It looks easy to win but watch out
the dupe (that's the reader) is sure

his eye is quicker than the poet's
hand but is it   there's more to the

game than meets the eye   the poet's
patter as he moves the shells can

mesmerize his victim   it puts things
in the victim's head that don't be-

long there that haven't been there
before questions without answers

problems with no solutions   poets
are dangerous they're swindlers we

need an ordinance to keep them off
the streets   the cops should make

the poet pack up his folding table
and his shells and go back home.

THE SORROWS OF SMINDYRIDES

He is a delicate flower indeed
talk of the princess and the pea

Aelianus recounts that the syba-
rite Smindyrides spent a sleep-

less night because one of the
rose petals strewn on his bed

was folded in two (his slave
the unfortunate folder of pe-

tals was severely beaten)   my
friend delights in pulverizing

reputations but if he is criti-
cized for misplacing a comma his

dinner is gall in his mouth and
his wine too bitter to swallow.

A SHARD OF HISTORY

Could it be that I am the one
who is the false Dmitri the

unknown whose nocturnal crimes
have terrified the city of Nov-

gorod   what do I do when I am
sleeping   am I a murderous

sleepwalker who remembers no-
thing the next day   is it only

my imagination that passersby
turn their heads and hurry past

me   are they whispering about
me in the cafés   although I

have no proof of what I fear
no blood on my hands or cloth-

ing should I give myself up
to the police   probably they

would only laugh at me   they
would take me for a madman

seeking notoriety   they would
put me for a few days in the

asylum for observation then
let me go   I would be free to

prowl again if that is what
I do   no if I am indeed the

false Dmitri my crimes de-
serve the final punishment.

ENIGMA VARIATIONS

Was she here?
Yes she was.

That it is not there as it appears is clear.
To take what is there to take can be one and done.
The seen and the unseen can be one and won.
The inside of there is declared as here.
The outside is not here or there.
Can anything be that is not seen?
Can what is seen be there twice?
That's nice.

Take what is and what is not if they are here or there.
What appears is and is not anywhere.
Is is not?

SOMEWHERE IN FRANCE

probably in a battered trunk
in the attic of a ruined cha-

teau is a bundle of papers
covered with faded handwrit-

ing   I believe these to be
the chapters about women a-

bout his heroines which Stend-
hal could not print in his nov-

els because of the censorship
it is inconceivable that a

writer who could analyze the
mentations of love with such

sagacity would check his pen
when he got below the chin.

454

A PARABLE

Once upon a time when I
was about eight Papa took

me with him to lunch at
the house of Mrs R   she

was very beautiful and
she gave me two helpings

of ice cream   after lunch
Papa told me to go out in-

to the yard to play   I
climbed a tree and look-

ed in a window   Papa and
Mrs R were doing strange

things   they were lying on
the bed and had no clothes

on   this was a long time
ago but I still see them

there doing strange things.

A PARENTHESIS

This poet defaces his couplets with parentheses
[a word from the Greek coming from para (beside)

+ en (in) + tithenai (to put) whence to put in be-
side]   this is a practice très mal vu (deplored)

by ergoistical critics who point out that his
lines would be grammatically more correct with

commas or colons   the poet responds quite true
but would they still be mine   for him the paren-

theses are small fortresses in which he can take
refuge from logic and conventional behavior   his

psychiatrist has a more sinister reading of the
(s) [are their shapes not bivulvar] but he holds

his peace since they gratify his bizarre patient.

THE INN AT KIRCHSTETTEN

Notes Pencilled in the Margins of a Book of the *Dichtungen* of Georg Trakl

How can I thank B for her ear, her mind, her affection? Some
afternoons after we had given kisses we would recline against the
hard bolsters in the little inn reading and rewriting my poems.

At first the idea of exchanging caresses with an almost heavenly
being had frightened me. I committed little crimes so she would
postpone this perilous happiness.

456

No one had told me that it was possible to make love to a voice.

Only someone who has not shared such love will condemn these writings.

The toy train which brought us to the town was so slow. It stopped at every hamlet. Farm people got on and off. There was a car for their animals: lambs, pigs, chickens. When it was very slow we would become frantic with impatience. We had so little time to be together.

Outside the window of the inn were the streets of the town, its old houses. But if you watched hard enough the scene would change into a landscape of fields, trees, a little lake and mountains in the distance.

Horses went clip-clop down the cobbled street. It was a blessing there were so few autos and motorbikes.

There was a gilt-framed mirror on the wall of the room. Why did we see in it the reflection of only one person?

The sound of rain on the window. The sound of the wind. The sound of the sun. Yes, even sunlight has its sound though only lovers are likely to hear it.

She was disgusted by the big cockroaches that scuttled across the floor until I convinced her they carried secret messages. Our postmen.

I always brought flowers to talk when love had rendered us silent.

Sometimes she would say, I can't remember who we are. I have to look at the shoes on the carpet to recall our names.

A strange ballet. The horizontal pas de deux. Hands mimicking the dancers' feet. Your long hair is your costume?

A bird struck the window with a thud and fell into the street. It was eager to join us but couldn't see the glass.

We read no more that day. There was nothing the book could tell us. Paolo and Francesca, you said. We often heard faint footsteps in the hall, not as heavy as those of the inn servants. You said it was the revenants who wanted to be with us. You opened the door but no one was there.

The inn servants seemed an honest lot but it was just as well to tip them a bit too much. I used the name Reseguier but you might have been recognized from your pictures in the magazines.

There were porcelain basins and pitchers, two of each, on the stand and eider puffs on the bed, two fat white pancakes on the matrimonial.

There was a picture on the wall which I couldn't place, most unusual for a village inn, not a religious or hunting scene. It was an abstract drawing in several colors. A grid of little nearly identical shapes connected by ink lines. Perhaps an artist from the city hadn't been able to pay his bill.

Sometimes, if you dozed, I would set back the time on your watch that you always put on the bedside stand. You would often wake with a start and say it was time to go home, he would be waiting for your company at tea. There were later trains on the toy railroad.

Hot and cold weather, we went there for nearly a year. Who is using that room now? Perhaps a series of lonely travelling salesmen.

You must know that none of these things may ever have happened, that we imagined them. . . . How can you be sure it was all an illusion? Remember the wineglass you dropped and it shattered? We tried to get up all the crumbs of glass but some were too small and worked their way into the fabric of the carpet. They would prove we were there.

Editor's Note
The book of Trakl was found in 1983 in a secondhand shop near the Stefanskirche in Vienna. The marginal markings, which are written vertically, are in two hands, one male, one female. The neat male hand is in the old

German handschrift. The female hand is more difficult to read, a mixture of Romanic and Cyrillic letters. Perhaps from Moldavia?

Neither B nor her lover have been identified. The bookseller in Vienna could not recall where the Trakl had come from. From the description of the "toy train" the town may have been Kirchstetten, where W. H. Auden was later to have his summer home, and the inn the Drei Falken.

THE DRAWING LESSON

The student is sketching a nude girl
who is trying to bite the big toe on

her left foot   or is she trying to
kiss her toe as she sits there on

the bed twisting her leg into a po-
sition like an exercise in Yoga   it

must be terribly uncomfortable even
painful   a little child could do it

but a grown person would have to be
double-jointed   the student pauses

in his drawing to study her face for
a clue that might explain her action

but her expression reveals nothing
no smile no sign of anger   all he

can see in her face is concentration
she wants to bite (or kiss?) her toe.

A BOOK ABOUT NOTHING

was what he wanted to write
what claim had he to express

any opinions   there must be
no sign of himself in such a

book   since everything he be-
lieved was probably wrong why

bother to put it down   no story
& no characters just nothing

no romance & no speculation
just nothing   he had to stop

using words because they kept
trying to turn themselves into

ideas (or one word would beget
the next word like cells repro-

ducing) in the end he covered
his paper with lines of periods

& dashes then he took out the
dashes they were too distract-

ing so his book of nothing had
only dots   at last he was happy

he had composed his masterpiece.

INSTRUCTIONS

Empty your mind as completely
as you can and intone the sa-

cred words om mani padme
hum while you rub your left knee

with your right hand   believe
me as your spiritual director

I'm letting you off easy   in his
time Padma Sambhava would

have made you prostrate your-
self full length 500 times on

stony ground   you would have
been sanctified but black and

blue and stiffish for a week.

THE INVIOLABLE MAIDEN

[Came she not from the pages of Malory, from the *Morte Darthur*?
Was she not of the line of Morgan le Fay—but sans covin or mal
    engine, without the malice of Morgan?]

A magical maiden, bewitched and bewitching, casting spell on the
    knights,
Sir Turquine, Sir Mordaunt, Sir Uwaine le Blanchemains, Sir Persides
    de Bloise and many another.
But their hands have left no mark upon her,

461

Their lips have not touched her lips,
She is not of the night but of the morning,
She need not lave her limbs in the mere sith they have not been
    distained.
The inviolable maiden, nesh and unstained.
No man has entered her though many have sought to clip her.
The force of men is powerless against her, their violence is vain;
Her virtue is proof against all attainment,
The maiden inviolate.

Child of a sorceress but she is as pure in heart as she is perfect in body;
No man hath halsed her, no wile can defile her.
At dawn they have seen her in the brackenland, sometimes amounted
    on a white palfrey, but none have caught or taken her;
She is too swift in flight for the hounds or the harriers,
The inviolable maiden, no man hath ta'en her.

At dusk they have seen her on the moorland or by the sea cliffs but
    she has always escaped them;
She is never there when they come to the place where they have
    espied her.
The bracken may be defoiled as if a roe deer had slept in it but she is
    nowhere to be found.
She is invisible when the halfmoon rises over the menhirs.

δραπέτευσε σκύλος μεγαι και μικραι drapeteuse skylos megai kai
    mikrai, again and again she escapes the knights, they cannot take
    her with great hounds nor brachets.
παρθένος απαραβιαστος parthenos aparabiastos, the inviolable maiden.
No man hath felt her breath on his cheek,
No man hath tasted her spittle;
No man's tongue has travelled her mouth.
No man can swear he hath heard her speak,
No man hath distained her nor brought her to disworship.
All they have heard was the wind soughing, the wind making com-
    pleynt for their dole,
The swough of the wind dying.

παρθένος απαραβίαστος parthenos aparabiastos, the maiden inviolate.

μάγισσα εμέ κινοῦμαι magissa cent kinoumai she hath me ensorcelled, and many before me,
I am weak from her beauty, as many before me;
My valor avails not.

I was enslaved on the moorland by the sweet smile of that maiden,
I fell in the bracken, my corselet to-shivered by the lance of her
    glance.
I am bewitched by the inviolable maiden—but not malfortuned.

Glossary (from that of the Medici Society edition of *Le Morte Darthur*)

attaint: overcome	*halsed*: embraced
brachet: little hound	*mal engine*: evil design
clip: embrace	*malfortune*: ill-luck
covin: deceit	*nesh*: soft, tender
distain: sully	*sith*: since
disworship: shame	*swough*: sound of wind
dole: sorrow	*to-shivered*: broken to pieces
espied: seen	*yede*: ran

Editor's Note: It is apparent that the knights were not well instructed in Greek.

IN THE BALLET

I advance and extend my hand
you turn away and retreat (on

point)   we circle away from
each other as another couple

intervenes   when all four dance
together I'm able to take your

hand and you don't withdraw it
the others separate and drift

away   you mimic my clumsy move-
ments but now with affection

we must imagine the music and
how it draws us together till

our bodies are following each
other   you lead   I lead we are

dancing as one   you don't re-
sist when I lift you in the air

and carry you across the stage
we must imagine the music   we

must imagine our pas de deux.

A SECOND PERSON

The other day there was an oc-
currence which was unexpected

but very welcome   the first per-
son now felt that something was

different inside himself (could
this be the way a woman feels if

she is with child)   the first
person imagined that there was

a second person inside him to whom
he could talk and she would answer.

THE SENSE OF IT

You say that to you love
means loss but I can't be-

lieve that because to me
loving you & being loved

by you has meant finding a
treasure of inestimable value.

THE BIRD OF ENDLESS TIME

(1989)

BLOOD

1953

Our best friends the Coopers who live across
Alameda near Mission have a dandy 10-year old

daughter named Rosalynde   she's a peach and looks
like a peach good enough to eat but she's sort

of opinionated not a troublemaker but she knows
what's what   children pick up things at school

one day she comes home from school looking angry
what's the matter hon did Mrs. Balch get on your

back again about spelling   she doesn't say any-
thing she just goes into her room and turns up

the vic real loud (in those days they didn't have
hi-fis)   but at supper it comes out with a blast

listen you guys if you think I'm ever going to let
some man put his dirty thing inside me you've got

another think coming   no discussion she just goes
back into her room and turns up the music real high.

1985

We're not getting any younger as Harry says when he
slices one into the pond on 17 where the ducks are   no

we're not getting any younger we still live on Ala-
meda   we thought the second-hand Mercedes was a steal

but the bastard had turned back the odometer and the
repairs cost an arm & a leg   we are still pals with

Rosalynde but we don't see her too often   she has the
cutest little boutique down in Montecito with an apart-

ment over it   she sells stuff you can wear not that
nutty crap you see in *Vogue*   it's all a racket any-

way hems halfway up to your ass one year and dragging
dirt off the floor the next   I still have a pretty de-

cent shape for my age   I have three outfits of nice slacks
and blouses for going out and just wear my jeans around all

day (what was I talking about anyway?)   I know I shoot too
much breeze but Harry is sweet about it   he's the quiet type

but if he thinks of something to say to keep his end up he
just lights a cigarette which is unusual for him he doesn't

want to get lung cancer and I know it's time for me to but-
ton my lip (oh yes Ros's husbands)   she married three times

and still looks great   none of her troubles were her fault
Wallace was killed in Korea (or maybe it was Vietnam   I just

can't keep the dates straight on all that shit)   Thornton
was a nice guy but the booze got to him   he was a salesman

for Teentogs out of LA   you know three martinis with a good
customer at lunch and pretty soon one-two-three more when he

came home   Ros never knew when she could put on the
steak   she got him into AA but he didn't have the character to

stick with it   Wilbur is the damndest thing you ever heard
of   Harry thinks he's a spook   he was a professor of SocSci

at the U a real big brain   he told Ros he was flying to a con-
vention at Harvard only took an overnight bag & his briefcase

but he never came home   every now and then a pretty fat check
comes from some bank in Switzerland or the Cayman Islands but

never a call even on her birthday or Christmas   Harry thinks
he has gone underground to work for Colonel North   don't run

him down till they find the body Harry says he may end up a
national hero   Ros won't talk about it but I can tell she is

still in love with him   she had one girl from each husband all
peaches too   Pegeen (that's Irish) was named for me   Mirabel

is nutty about horses she's so good she gets paid to exercise
them   thank God she's too big to be a jockey   Ros Junior got

her brains from Wilbur   all "As" and editor of the paper at the
U   the serious type   she goes steady with a boy named Perkins

who writes poetry but it doesn't rhyme   some of it has been
printed in a literary magazine in Ojai   Harry and I both love

him he's so considerate with people   I don't mean sissy manners
he just seems to understand how a person is feeling but every

now and then Harry looks solemn and says there has got to be a
man-to-man talk about gainful employment   Ros Jr could be execu-

tive secretary for a big industrialist   she remembers things and
is always on the ball   but it's my hunch she's going to want to

have kids pretty soon   they wear helmets of course (that's the
state law) but I wish she would stop riding with him on his motor-

cycle   it wasn't his fault it was night and some drunk driving in
the middle of the road forced him into a tree   there were internal

injuries and it was nip & tuck in intensive care for several days
he had to have transfusions   and now there are these stories

on TV about how they don't always test properly   I wake
up in the night worrying about what may be in their blood.

THE COLD

came suddenly & without warning
too swiftly for a wind to rise

or snow to fall   it seemed to
come from nowhere through clear

air (a gift from Canada or the
Arctic I suppose)   the sun was

powerless against it   our breath
steamed when we ventured out of

doors   the furnace groaned   the
fireplace swallowed logs   pipes

froze   cars wouldn't start   the
dogs wouldn't go out   the gros-

beaks deserted the feeder   three
days of frigeration   then finally

the sky clouded over & snow came
warming us like a blessed blanket.

II

THE GOLDEN YEARS

I belong to the American Association
of Retired People and get 10% off at

the hardware store but not at the li-
quor store   it was a close call with

my driving license renewal   in the
parking test I backed over the curb

but he was a nice guy and let me try
it again   Calendula (the cook) says

the *back* of my head is still handsome
and at my last physical Dr. Chen put

on my chart that my weight had not in-
creased but was simply redistributed

I'm waiting for my cataracts to ripen.

THE WAITERS' BALLET

At the Grand Véfours in the Palais Royal
the waiters have obviously been trained

in ballet as well as religious ritual
they bow they hover they flutter they

are always smiling respectfully they
dance attendance when they serve a

dish   their hands move like mudras or
the gestures at the altar in the mass

as they approach the table there is a
slight genuflection in one knee   when

they pour the wine it is a sacred cere-
mony   between servings they never take

their eyes off the tables in case some
request may be communicated to them with

an eyebrow   an exquisite performance but
what do they say among themselves after

the guests have gone (apart of course from
discussing the tips) that's what I wonder.

AFTER HARDY

The time torn man had waited
long for your coming even des-

pairing that could be (how
might he find such fortune?)

then when at last you came
(illumined as you are) when

the hope-hour stroked for him
he touched your hand (dread-

474

ing it would turn to shadow)
declared he was sewn by it

(the tear sewn) and was no
longer in his fear of time.

—from Hardy,
A Broken Appointment

AM I NOT LUCKY

that you decided to love me
what if you wanted to love

a cat or a dog or dresses
or even Paul Newman   I've

never quite understood how
it happened   I was having my

life you yours and each
seemed content   we knew each

other slightly but only as
friends   then suddenly with-

out warning or expectation
you decided to love me (and

I you) & my life was changed.

475

AT THE BOULE D'OR

As they lunch together at
the Boule d'Or they are

smiling a lot and choosing
their words carefully   this

is their first date & each
is trying to impress   they

are feeling each other out
and weighing the potentials

(her beauty & his capacity
for making money)   now they

are laughing & talking with
more animation   they find

they like each other   but
can either foresee the bit-

ter words that will follow?

EIN KLEINES HERZLIED

Du bist in mein Herz plötz-
lich gekommen   lass mich bet'

ich in deinem stehen   einsam
trat ich im Lebenswege bis

dass du mich vornahmst zu dreh-
en in andere Strassen die in

einen Garten leiten wo findest
du dich und endlose Schönheiten.

A LITTLE HEARTSONG

You came suddenly into my heart
Let me beg to live in yours
Lonely, I walked life's path
Until you undertook to draw me
Into other roads, which led into a garden
Where you live in endless beauty.

THE BLUE FOOTPRINTS

Some nights along the sidewalks
in our neighborhood someone is

making blue footprints   they
must do it with a stencil per-

haps attached to a stick   they
must carry a pot of paint be-

cause the prints are very clear
and not smudged   the prints will

begin in the middle of a block
go around a corner or two and

then stop   I can think of no
reason why they begin and end

where they do   it's a joke of
course but a very laborious

one   hundreds of carefully made
footprints   after a few days

the prints fade out but then
they are made again though

not always made in the same
place   I have been out late

at night to catch the mysteri-
ous walker but have not found

him   I've asked the patrolmen
in the police car but they have

seen nothing they just laugh
they say the footprints are

not a hazard but they worry
me   they upset me I want to

know where they are going
and what their message is.

DANGER / ROAD UNDER REPAIR

Something was being done to the road
through our village and to the course

of our lives   it wasn't clear what au-
thority had ordered these changes   one

day workmen we didn't know appeared
(they were from another province we

couldn't understand their dialect) and
began to improve a thoroughfare which

had been satisfactory for longer than
anyone could remember   it was more than

filling a few potholes after a hard win-
ter   it was a complete rebuilding   even

some jogs in the road were to be straight-
ened out   first we were puzzled as we saw

the work proceed then alarmed   we knew
there was nothing wrong with our road

why were these changes being made
what unknown power had ordained them?

III

THE INVITATION

They were lolling on the couch
talking about nothing much   they

were holding hands and kissing
in a desultory way   she was wear-

ing a white silk dress   when he
raised it he found she had on

nothing underneath   she had want-
ed him to find his way with ease.

EVER SO

Past midnight & I
was awakened by the

screaming of some
small animal in

the woods beyond
the farther side of

the sheep pasture
so long an agony

I fell back to sleep
again before it was

ended   and who
was pursued who

the pursuer   I my-
self might be the

one or the other.

MEI AXIS MUNDI

You are the center about
which my being revolves

you are the intersection
of every possible line

I cannot describe you ex-
cept to say you are Sumeru

and Taishan you are the
point of rest from which

comes all that is light.

THE RITUAL

The ritual of the poem in praise of you
demands the vision of a goddess   an ap-

parition   an evocation   the goddess may
be the Cytherean born of the seafoam

she of dark eyelids   venerandam   or she
of the moon & the grove   her nymphs ga-

thered about her   choros nympharum   ven-
erandam   or she who sprang from the head

of her father   blue-eyed glaukopis mo-
ther of cities   venerandam   there are

other goddesses in the Hymni Deorum who
are of great beauty and clairvoyance but

I cannot choose for you among them   you
alone can reveal to me your hidden name.

A SWEET KISS

When I was little and had
been bad when the back of

the hairbrush had been ap-
plied as I kicked & scream-

ed when the tears of repen-
tance had been shed I would

ask my mother for a   "sweet
kiss"   it was a special kind

of kiss a moist slightly sal-
ty kiss because she too had

been crying as she punished me.

SUCH GRACE

is in her step   such grace
goes in the movement of her

arms & shoulders as she walks
such grace in how she holds

her head   how graceful the
gestures of her hands   such

grace in the way she slightly
tilts her face toward me when

a smile is beginning there
the float in air of a dan-

cer   suspended flight of a
hummingbird   always she goes

in grace   there is such
grace in all her going.

THE FIRST NIGHT

we spent together was like
school   each was trying to

teach the other what was
liked or not liked   the de-

tails are irrelevant   what
mattered was that love was

becoming a real thing be-
tween us without regard to

this or that preference.

FLOATING FREE

She wanted to float free
no ropes no pins no nails

no wires nothing holding
her too tightly to some-

thing nothing binding her
too closely to another per-

son enough space around her
enough of her own quiet e-

nough open light   on the
water or in the air any-

where at all that she might
be she wanted to float free.

PROLEPSIS

You are a future, my poor darling, that pretends
to be a past but will never be a present.
                    —from Stendhal's *Lucien Leuwen*

I always feared that things
would end badly between us

but never imagined how you
would humiliate me at a mo-

ment when my passion for you
was at its peak
                    One of your
attractions (if I can call

it that) was your temper   if
you were bored or displeas-

ed how your eyes flashed
how your language whipped

my skin
            In the bedroom of
the hotel in Luzern after

you had had your bath you
paraded before the mirrors

with only a towel wrapped
around your head as if it

were a turban in a harem.

THE OFFERING

He was reaching out to her
offering the best of his

old beaten-up furniture
from the rooms where so

many disappointments had
been enacted so many ri-

diculous little comedies
of frustration and folly

yes it would all be dif-
ferent now (he promised

her that) because they
would be her things too

IT'S INDELICATE

I know to bore you with tales
of old loves   you must deter

me if you find these ladies
unappetizing but love is cumu-

lative and each one of them is
still a little piece of me as

I am still (I hope) a part of
them   no cause for jealousy

486

each had her time each had my
time of me but now those times

are past and have become only
a moment of obscure propinquity.

HER LETTERS

Did he imagine that her letters
were written to him those ones

which described in such detail
the topography of her heart (though

always in phrases whose chaleur
did not exceed what was permiss-

ible to a lady of breeding and
discretion) didn't he know she

was writing to someone who did
not exist or at least no longer

existed for her because she was
tired of him oh so bored with

him but didn't know how to break
off and so he had become a phan-

tom it being her disposition to
write to a lover alive or dead.

THE LONG NIGHT

He lies alone in his bed
listening to the dry high-

pitched sound of the ci-
cadas singing because it

is night when they awaken
in the dark   their reso-

nation means nothing to
him it is familiar he has

heard it too many times
before   likely enough it

will be several hours be-
fore he can fall asleep

again   his eyes are too
tired for reading   the

words blur when he turns
on the light to resume

his book (it's a life of
that clever woman Madame

de Maintenon how she be-
guiled and dominated the

Sun King) like the cicadas
the story means little to

him it is the blur & buzz
of lives lived long ago

lives that might just as
well never have happened

for all the thought he can
give to them now   he ima-

gines that somehow he is
inside the cicadas that he

is helping them make their
sound   he resents this im-

prisonment but cannot es-
cape from it   he fears that

he will never be able to
hear any other sound that

there will be no sleep but
most he resents that he can-

not understand the meaning
of the sound he is making.

IN THE SALZKAMMERGUT

What did you do with my heart
after I'd lent it to you   did

you leave it in the Salzkammer-
gut somewhere near Koos's house

(the one that is built on stilts
in the water of the Ammer See) I

went back to look for it there
but never a trace   and none of

the peasants remembered Marili
or Annalise   totally disappear-

ed   will it be the same with you?

IT'S MARCH

and the sap is running in
the sugar maples   the chil-

dren from the brotherhood
are collecting the sap buck-

ets in our woodlot   it's an
outing for them and they're

laughing and shouting most
merrily   there's still a

foot of snow so it's hard
going for some of the lit-

tle ones to drag the buck-
ets to the tank wagon with

out spilling them   the old
horse who pulls the wagon

droops his head he's bored
he longs to get back to the

stable for his feed   the chil-
dren from the brotherhood wear

old-fashioned clothes but in
bright colors mostly blues &

reds it's a scene from Brueghel.

POETS

It is the nature of poets
to believe that they are

great (or will become great)
that their lines will echo

down the ages and be studied
by schoolchildren   but this

is statistically unlikely
the latest figures from the

NEA estimate that there are
about 100,000 more or less

literate poets in the USA
(of whom 10% are graduates

of creative writing courses)
I think my favorite of all

these poets is a young man
I met in Santa Fe   he played

the role of a poet because he
felt like a poet but he never

took the risk of writing a
single poem   his life was

his poetry and he was happy.

THE UNENLIGHTENED FACE

The Buddhists speak of an Unenlightened
Face   the face of one who has not yet

found the light   as I walk I turn my
face toward the sun   I feel its warmth

but the light has not yet entered me
perhaps the light must come from what

was written   what was told by those
who sat beside him long ago   I read

the texts but the light does not enter
me   I know it is not given to all to

receive the light no matter how they
may long for it   perhaps I'm one of

the darkfaced the sons of attachment.

THUMBS UP!

What if we were not enantio-
morphic if our thumbs were

both on the same side of our
hands (and the big toes the

same of course)   would our e-
volution have been different

would we have made our home
underground instead of in

the trees (because matching
thumbs could dig better than

climb)   in ten million years
there were endless possibil-

ities   don't think about them
they might still come true.

AT BENARES

—from Alain Daniélou, *The Way to the Labyrinth*

the saintly yogi Hari-Hara-Baba
who lived on a boat beside the

ghats of the Ganges where he re-
ceived his devotees completely

naked had to be rowed to the other
side of the river twice daily be-

cause he had made a vow never to
soil the most sacred part of the

riverbank where the bodies of the
dead are consumed in fires of san-

dalwood with his impure excrement.

THE ENDLESS MIRRORS

In the Gonzaga Palace in Mantua
(which has more than 800 rooms)

there is a great hall whose four
walls (except for the one with

windows) are entirely covered
with mirrors so that wherever

you stand you see yourself end-
lessly reflected each mirror re-

peating the image in the one op-
posite though each reflection is

diminished in size   standing in
that room I see myself getting

smaller and smaller until in the
end there is only a figure so

494

minuscule I can no longer recog-
nize it as myself and cannot even

be certain I really exist at all.

THIRTEEN WAYS OF LOOKING AT A LOVEBIRD

A man and a woman
Are one.
A man and a woman and a blackbird
Are one.
    —Wallace Stevens, "Thirteen Ways of Looking at a Blackbird"

It is better to marry than to burn. —St. Paul

i	It is difficult to be rational about love.
ii	In love actions are ruled by emotions.
iii	Actions in love are determined by forces which are mysterious.
iv	Logic retreats before sentiment.
v	It can be more important to win a kiss than material advantage.
vi	The advice of friends is usually useless in solving problems of the heart.
vii	Most books on love are written in foreign languages.
viii	In love the role of time is perplexing.
ix	There is short love and there is long love.
x	There is also love without love.
xi	Love is a game of true and false.
xii	It is also a game of chance.
xiii	But it is better to win than to lose.

THEN AND NOW

THE RAIN	THE POEM
is speaking it pelts	is moving by itself
against the windows	it proceeds of its
and on the roof	own accord
in the night	the writer of the poem
it makes thousands	has no idea where
of little words	it will lead him
which confuse the child	he cannot control it
who does not understand	because it has
such a language	its own life
what is the rain	separate from his own
trying to tell him	what if it carries him off
should he be afraid	from his safe life
is there a message	from his accustomed loves
of danger to be escaped	should he fear harm
or can he be lulled	from the poem and tear up
by the sound of the rain	the page or simply put it
and go back to sleep?	aside and go back to sleep?

HOPE SPRINGS

Do you think he likes me   I have
the feeling it's going to start

anytime now   we have our desks
a few rows apart in Customers'

Complaints   a week ago when I
glanced over his way he smiled

at me   then the next day he fol-
lowed me to the water fountain

all he said was the old bitch
(meaning Mrs McIlhenny) sure is

laying it on us these days isn't
she   but he was looking me over

I'm going to Bloomie's to price
one of those cashmere sweaters

that were in their ad   maybe if
I sit by myself in the cafeteria

not with the girls he'll come to
join me   he looks a little like

Al Pacino in *Serpico* but I can
tell he's sweet and even if he's

stuck in Customers' Complaints
I'll bet he's smart I think it's

going to begin any day now.

THE BIG CLOCK

She fell in love with the face
of a clock the big one in the

tower of the Woolworth Building
it all began one day when she

stopped to rest on a bench in
Union Square   she got the notion

the clock was talking to her and
when the big hand moved with a

jerk from one minute to the next
she felt it wanted to touch her

cheek   it was love at three o'clock
she changed jobs to an office on the

west side of the square where she
could watch the clock   any sunny

day you can find her on the bench
with her paper bag lunch making

love with her eyes to the big clock.

GOD BLESS AMERICA!

She is walking home from the post
office with her arms full of pack-

ages   she is smiling   she looks so
happy   what are all those things

she ordered from catalogs? toys for
the kids? a gadget for the kitchen?

a new blouse for herself? I think
she has more reason to feel pleased

than she may realize   she is sus-
taining the economy   even if she

gets behind now & then she's in-
creasing the gross national pro-

duct   she's doing something about
unemployment   God bless her for

all that and God bless America!

MY AMBITION

is to become a footnote
in a learned work of the

22nd century   not just a
"cf" or a "see" but a sol-

id note such as Raby gives
Walafrid Strabo in *Christ-*

ian-Latin Poetry or Ernst
Robert Curtius (the most

erudite German who ever
lived) devotes to Alber-

tino Mussato in his *Euro-*
päische Literatur und La-

teinisches Mittelalter   I
hope the scholar of the

22nd will lick his schol-
arly lips when he finds me

in some forgotten source
(perhaps the *Obloquies* of

Dreadful Edward Dahlberg)
and think here is an odd-

ball I would have liked
immortalizing me in six

turgid lines of footnote.

A KIND OF KNOWLEDGE

To seek it
to find it
to possess it
there are nine steps to be taken

reflection
recognition
identification
renunciation
incamination
transmission
initiation
personification
transfiguration

minute by minute
hour by hour
day by day
the path the road the way.

MALEDICTI IN PLEBE SINT

The pedants of deconstruction
are lathering each other's backs

with their own shit   who can
hate literature the most or con-

coct the most absurd algebras
of language   no birds may sing

in their trees   if there were
birds someone would shoot them

their books are written to be
read only as group masturbation

where has it gone the purity of
the young Hegel who hid the manu-

script of the *Phenomenology* un-
der his coat when Napoleon en-

tered Jena sic pallescet lux.

HE DREAMED HIS DEATH

last night   it was neither an-
ticipated nor anything spectacu-

lar   no accident or illness of
which he was aware   no pain no

fright   it was no more than a
candle blowing out in a slight

breeze   he couldn't tell you
now how he knew what had hap-

pened but it was quite clear
to him that in an instant a

transition had taken place and
some voice inside him had said

(tho without any audible sound)
this is it   this is what you

had to be waiting for   he felt
no different than before but

he knew for certain that he no
longer existed in the same way

(or the same place) as before.

DIGGING DOWN TO CHINA

When we were boys (I was
four and my brother was

six) someone told us that
China was on the opposite

side of the world & that
you could get there by

digging   we wanted to see
the great wall and men

with pigtails and women
with bound-up feet who

couldn't walk   we took gar-
den trowels and dug & dug

& dug for days but we nev-
er saw the things we want-

ed to see   I guess I'm still
digging (there are mountains

of dirt all around me) and
I won't make it to China.

HIC JACET

cinis pulvis et nihil
was all the inscription

that Cardinal Portecarrero
permitted on his tomb in

the cathedral at Toledo   he
would not even allow his

name to be inscribed on it
just a flat stone with no

barrier around it so that
everyone would walk on him

a realistic man and though
he didn't know it a good

Buddhist   here lie ashes
dust and nothingness R I P.

THE MAN IN THE WALL

(1993)

The tall man who wrote these poems was once skiing down an alp with such headlong agility that he split the seat of his trousers. Another skier, a blonde woman with blue eyes, seeing his predicament and having on her person a needle and thread for just such emergencies, offered repairs. So James Laughlin, of the Pittsburgh steel Laughlins and founder, sole owner, and editor of New Directions books, leaned forward in Austrian snow while Juliana, Princess Royal of the Netherlands, stitched up the rent in his britches. Benevolence circulates; he had recently repaired a punctured tire for Gertrude Stein and provided James Joyce with the names of all the tributaries of the Allegheny. Celebrities are more capable than we had suspected.

The tale goes on. Laughlin told all this to one of the authors he published, Ezra Pound, who at the time was trying to reform the world and needed to convert us all to Confucianism to do it. And here was Jaz (as he called him) Laughlin as a way to convert the Dutch royal family. So a copy of Ezra's translation of *The Unwobbling Pivot* was hastily inscribed for Laughlin to send to The Hague, together with a note of gratitude for the timely mending of trousers.

The anecdote is symptomatic. Laughlin has spent a great deal of his life running errands for the writers he has published, diplomatically looking after the Byzantine affairs of Thomas Merton, befriending Kenneths Patchen and Rexroth, seeing Pound through thirteen years of imprisonment, encouraging (by publishing them) Tennessee, Jonathan, and William Carlos Williams. The history of the Modernist movement in American writing is in great measure inextricably the history of the New Directions Publishing Corporation. The one good-to-read, always interesting poet James Laughlin didn't until now publish is James Laughlin.

In the literary mythology of Modernism it is generally understood that years ago the seemingly seven-foot-tall James Laughlin went to Rapallo, where one could see Max Beerbohm with a string shopping bag at the greengrocery, William Butler Yeats and Ezra Pound at a café, and even Ford Madox Ford wheezing along the sea wall. The myth goes that Pound glanced at Laughlin's verses, and sent him away to found a publishing house, together with a list of authors to get started on.

Laughlin's poems have a tradition to stand on: he is a Classicist. The kind of poem that a healthy American businessman and hyperactive sportsman might write was the kind Greeks and Romans wrote. These were not effusions about the beauties of nature, or philosophical sighs. They were remarks in the best chosen phrasing and metrical order (to keep reciters from shifting the words around) about the world, political and private, the charming and difficult ways of women and boys, the pomposity of senators, conversation at dinner, the dishonesty of politicians, and the decline of morals from the good old days.

It was William Carlos Williams who showed Laughlin how to put poems on the page. The old metrical system, Williams felt, was no longer useful to a democratic people. Whitman had written in a natural, colloquial phrasing, but then Whitman was a natural force, something like the weather. What an occasional, ironic commentator needed was a neat oblong of phrases, squared away on the page, each line a little event in itself. Forget punctuation: Greeks and Romans didn't have any, and Apollinaire dispensed with it.

So Mr. Laughlin invented his own kind of poem, at once very old and very new. Its form was versatile enough for any subject at all: love affairs, childhood memories, travels, politics.

His style is as transparent as a clean windowpane. His mind (the part of it that makes poems) is a magic attic of books, images, people, voices.

The world used to distinguish between people of culture and the illiterate. The line of demarcation, wildly fluctuating since the beginning of this century (so that professors without a word of Italian teach Dante to sorority belles raised on TV soap operas), has now disintegrated. For all his sharpness of eye and delicious sense of humor, Laughlin is primarily a man of culture, and the heart that beats so strongly and warmly in his poems is one in love with the full heritage of the past.

The past is gone, dead, meaningless, unless it is kept alive (it keeps us alive) by being continued. If we are ever in a time when we must say that there used to be a type of poem called the epigram, written by lively Greeks and Romans, then our cultural heritage (that is, the mind of the human race) will indeed be lost.

But that hasn't happened yet. In James Laughlin we have a very ironic Roman poet, and a very salty Greek one. Which is not to say that he imitates anybody, or offers plaster casts of antiquities. He is the youngest and most modern poet now writing in the United States. He is the real thing.

GUY DAVENPORT

THE MAN IN THE WALL

I was waiting for the bus on Canal Street
near an old deserted brick warehouse   sud-

denly I noticed a movement in the bricks
on the surface of the wall   as I watched

the figure of a man appeared on the wall
at first just a faint gray shape that be-

came clearer until it was a whole man (but
the face not very clear)   a gray man in a

rumpled gray suit   he wasn't dead because
he moved his arm as if he wanted to get my

attention   the passersby on the street
didn't seem to notice him   he was no one

I had ever seen before   did he want to
speak to me   had he been sent by someone

who knew me with a message   he lasted only
a few moments then faded back into the

bricks of the wall   there was no longer
a person there   what did he want to tell

me   did he mean to warn me   did he intend
to say   you too have appeared and will van-

ish   don't hope for more   there is no more
the bus came to the curb and I climbed aboard.

LITTLE BITS OF PAPER: AN ARS POETICA

Most of them begin with a few words
read in some book or a phrase over-

heard   scratched on a bit of paper
these chits go into the side pocket

of my jacket   usually they stay there
until the coat is so spotted it must

be sent to the cleaners   when I empty
the pocket most of the slips go into

the wastebasket   but a few are pasted
with Scotch tape on the bathroom mir-

ror where I see them when I'm shaving
some stay there a long time but with

some there is an urgency   they come
into my head when I wake to pee in

the middle of the night   more words
come with them   almost faster than I

can scribble on the yellow pad on the
bedtable   the words beget other words

(it's like spilled milk spreading on
the kitchen floor)   words making other

words   I don't make them they make
themselves into the poem   but some-

times in the morning I can't read
what I've written (because I wrote

in the dark)   so that's the end of
that one   it's had its say and it

won't come back   I write in darkness.

THE NEW BOOK

Before you there never
was a girl whom I want-

ed to read all of me   I
always held back a few

pages necessary to com-
plete the story   I'd hide

them where she couldn't
find them   I kept her out-

side me waiting for those
missing pages but a strange

thing has happened   you've
become the book itself all

that I want to write seems
to come from you   every day

I fill pages with you and
for you because the name

of the new book is yours.

FOR THE FINDERS WITHIN

I cannot name them nor
tell from whence they

come   I cannot summon
them nor make them lin-

ger   they come when they
wish (and when least ex-

pected) and in a moment
they are gone leaving

their burst of words
which become my song.

LINES TO BE PUT INTO LATIN

The lightest touch
if it is gently giv-

en can yield as much
affection as a deep

embrace   soft as a
glance swift as a

drop of rain light
as a leaf   I give

you these again.

THE FIGURE IN THE STONE

is visible to the sculptor
but it is invisible to me.
Studying the marble before
he takes up his hammer and chisel
the sculptor envisages the lineaments of a nereid.
It is one of the sea nymphs of the Aegean.
Is it Thetis, I ask him, or Galatea?
Is it the mother of Achilles, the hero of Troy,
or she who by trickery was wed
to the monstrous Cyclops Polyphemus?
The stone will tell me as I work it,
he answers, as I cut parts of it away.
When I have finished the form will declare her name.
To some it is granted to see what is within,
but to most of us it is not.

THE SHAMEFUL PROFESSION

For years I tried to conceal from the villagers that I wrote poetry
I didn't want them to know that I was an oddball
I didn't want the young men with beards wearing baseball caps who
    come to the liquor store in their pickups to buy sixpacks to know
    that I was some kind of sissy
I decided it was prudent to buy the *Daily News* instead of the *Times* at
    the drugstore
I burned my poem drafts at home before I took the trash to the dump,
    kids scavenge around there and the old man who does the recy-
    cling is nosey
I took every precaution

But our town is not an easy place to keep secrets, everybody knows
   everybody and they gossip when they're getting their mail at the
   post office
Things began to come apart
A young man with long hair and a city accent showed up and asked in
   the stores where the poet Laughlin lived
Then a pipe burst and the plumber told people that he saw thousands
   of books stacked in the cellar, some of them in foreign languages
Next day the head of the Volunteer Fire Department came, pretending
   to check the wiring
I began to get a bit paranoid; the town trooper is supposed to check
   each rural road once a week but he came up our road past my house
   three days in succession
The axe fell when somehow a reporter for the county paper heard the
   rumors and there was a little item: local poet caught speeding
   twice on 272, Motor Vehicles may suspend license
Much has changed in my life now
Nobody has laughed at me in the street (I'm over six feet weight 245
   and look pretty fit for my age) but they look at me in a funny way
I don't go to Apple House our grocery store any more because a little
   girl with her finger in her nose pointed me out to the check-out
   lady and asked her something; now I get my liquor and supplies
   in the next towns and order Honeybaked Hams from Virginia by
   mail

My life is all different now that they know I write poems.
But if they think they can shame me out of it they're very much mis-
   taken. I'm not breaking any law
I'll go on with it unless they have me declared a public nuisance and
   have me sent to the Institute
I've heard there is a poor old fellow in the Institute who claims he is
   Henry Wordsworth Longfellow. He'll understand and be my
   friend; we can recite to each other if they won't let us have paper
   and pencils.

THE POEM FACTORY

The poems are talking to them-
selves again   they're bored

with me   over the years they've
heard everything I have to say

the same old stuff put in the
same old meter (that nobody

likes much anyway) the same
classical tags that don't all

hitch to American speech   the
same old sentimental moonings

about love   they've had it
with me so now they get their

kicks talking with each other
they've gotten some nice ef-

fects taking lines from differ-
ent poems to make new ones

mixing them together   the next
step will be for them to auto-

mate making poems completely
by themselves without my inter-

vention   that will be the day
(as good as surrealism) their

own robotic factory of poems.

THE EWIGE WEIBCHEN & THE MERMAIDS

The ewige weibchen is a treasure
a jewel beyond price   she coddles

me and keeps me cheerful even in
bad weather   but she has one dis-

tressing habit   she imagines that
the mermaids who inhabit my poems

are real girls whom I have been
concealing and of whom she must

be jealous   it does no good to
tell her that these creatures

live in the watery realm of Po-
seidon and will never be able to

swim to our landlocked door   she
frets and pouts her pretty lips

which distracts me from work   I
must learn to type poems myself.

MY OWN NAME

Everyone is entitled to his own name
Even aboriginals had their own names
And before them, I suppose, the troglodytes
When and how did names begin?
At first were there glottal or glossal sounds

Which the person (when he came to realize that he was a person)
Could recognize from the tone of the grunt belonged to him and not
  to someone else.
Dogs certainly know their own names though I'm not sure about horses
I doubt that birds know their names except for parrots and cockatoos
When did writing begin to determine names, what about pictographs
  and then hieroglyphs or cuneiform characters?
When did names become sacred, when did they become property?
Some generations back I had a cousin named Ormesby, he was proud
  of his name because his ancestors came over to England from
  France with William the Conqueror
He sued a Jew who had taken the name Ormesby, but the judge ruled
  that anyone could take any name he wanted
How do criminals feel about their a.k.a.'s?
What about pseudonyms? When do movie stars become the names
  they were given by producers?

I have two names: the name that is on my driver's license and the name
  of my doppelgänger Hiram Handspring who writes odd poems
  like this one
Both names are my own name and often I'm not certain which one is I
I like both names very much.

THE LOST SECRETS

They were each other's
lost secrets   once they

had been together but
then he failed her and

they drifted apart as
if they were living in

519

different countries yet
they didn't lose each

other   she wrote him ten-
der messages on birch

bark like Indian signs
and he copied characters

out of a Sanskrit dictio-
nary (not knowing what

they meant) that were
talismanic Vedic sym-

bols   in secret they
grew closer and closer

real life could not get be-
tween them they were one.

GRUMPUS AT 78

Will I end up as a fierce old man
in a wheelchair terrorizing my

grandchildren to correct their
childish faults   I take the pre-

scribed pills for abulia and an-
hedonia but they might as well

be marshmallows for all the good
they do me   I write to old friends

that I can't visit them because
I'm now in my ashram period and

must meditate out in the woods
(except on rainy days)   I'm seek-

ing sunyata (the great nothing-
ness) but it doesn't come and

probably never will   I'm too full
of anger against him who wants to

be king of the world   every week
he commits some new stupidity to

enrage me   I fantasize on how to
surprise him on the golf course

and destroy him with the African
blowpipe that Uncle Harry brought

home from his safari in Tanganyi-
ka   what happened to the energetic

(and sometimes radiant) young man
who was going to do such wonders

to raise the level of literature
in our land   next month I'll be

78 but all celebration is forbid-
den   I live now only for the merry

laughter of Cinderella and for my
sense of failure which (I'm afraid)

I enjoy   so be it I'm still here.

KNOWLEDGE

—Canto XLVII

said Pound (out of Homer)
is but the shade of a

shade   till I was ten
I was reading mostly the

bible (not so much for
the stories as for the

sound of the sentences)
and after that I was into

a dozen jampots from Plato
to Spengler   not till my

sixties did I understand
that knowledge is some-

thing you don't get in
libraries and the wise

man is he who even dead
hath yet his mind entire.

IT IS SO EASY

to stay in love with someone
who is dead   there is no more

conflict of personalities
once the shock of the death

has passed she becomes em-
balmed in my memory like a

mummy from a tomb in the Val-
ley of the Kings at Thebes

to be sure the preservative
has blackened her face but

the shape of the face is
beautiful and the frescoes

on the walls of the tomb are
beautiful   in them I see her

faults (along with her trea-
sure) being ferried by slaves

in the golden boat that car-
ries her into time never to

be forgotten.   nothing remains
of her imperfections   the em-

balmers removed her heart and
it gives me no more trouble.

JACK

57 varieties of kindness and concern for people, whether they were
   friends or workers in the pickle plant
57 ways of being in a hurry to get from one place to somewhere else,
   then of being able to fall instantly asleep for a catnap
57 ways of making a pretty girl feel prettier, of avoiding reading too
   many books, but of understanding what made people tick
57 varieties of little torments to remind his son Johnnie that he had
   to be perfect, even when Johnnie had become a United States
   senator
the art of taking good color pictures of friends and remembering to
   send them copies mounted in thin plastic frames inscribed "from
   the camera of HJH"
many Sackville Street suits and snappy sports outfits, and the latest
   models of skis, golf clubs, snorkels, shotguns and flyrods from
   Hardy's
57 ways of finding the best restaurant on arrival in a strange city or
   the best wines on a winelist
several ways of picking little quarrels with Joan or Jane or Edge or
   Drue, quarrels usually about nothing important—then endearing
   ways of showing contrition
calling to say that the plane would pick me up at Bradley in three
   hours, ready or not, if he heard there was good new snow at Stowe
   or even out at Alta
57 varieties of remembering that it was bearded old Henry who had
   invented the business and Howard who had built it up, commem-
   orating them with handsome buildings in our native city of
   Pittsburgh
solutions for helping a friend get out of some mess he had gotten
   himself into
certain ways of being only too human, such as being impressed with
   indolent English dukes, fat financiers and swells like Gianni
   Agnelli
57 ways of brightening the life of "Jamesie," such as pretending to
   enjoy eccentric poems he couldn't understand
and now that he's gone, for me, 57 memories of happy times we
   shared that will never be forgotten.

IN MY IMAGINATION

(though I am sixty now) I love
to finger you much as I did the

little girl who lived in the
house nextdoor when I was ten

touching her was a matter of
fervent curiosity to find out

how she was different and to
speculate on what the differ-

ence meant   but touching you
now (in my imagination) is

something else   it is an in-
visible act of pure affection

and my plea for reassurance
I want to be comforted by the

belief that you would want me
to love you if we were together.

THE INSCRIPTION

It is inscribed in the endless book
of the walking dead that three nights
after she had preceded him Piero
opened the casement to follow Itek
onto the stairway of the stars
Dark was the night of passage

and difficult the ascent Piero
pursuing Itek his sister his love
she calling down to him from above
come brother come my love come
I await you but I cannot stretch
out my hand to touch yours to help
you that is forbidden you must
make the climb alone to reach me
so is it written in the book so inscribed

THE CREATURES OF PROMETHEUS

fill the air with their
ululations   every sound

is a protest (or is it
praise for some hideous

wrong) Arabia is full of
devils both the seen and

the unseen   the song of
the scorpion is heard by

night and by day   sand
whirls in the hot wind

drink your sweet for wa-
ter break your lyre Or-

pheus break your pipe Pan
this is the time of dam-

nation nothing will escape
it nothing will survive.

IT WON'T BE LONG NOW

but no point in brooding
about it the way you did

when you were a child
your nurse threw a blan-

ket over the fire you
started with forbidden

matches and put it out
fire rhymes with desire

don't start it up again
isn't it peaceful now

without desires   this
is a slow-moving poem

keep that pace   you
have no place to go

in a hurry the way you
used to do (always rush-

ing somewhere to get
something or other)

don't even think about
going anywhere   there's

no place for you to go
this poem will end when

it's ready and so will
you   it won't be long.

THE FLIGHT OF ICARUS

Upswollen with vanity and purse-proud greed
The Donald bestrode New Babylon
Garlanding the city with gilded monuments to his divinity
The Gods on High Olympus frowned
Pausing in their drunken revelry to strike him down
They hurled their bolts and proud Trump Tower fell

Behold a chastened Donald now
Forgotten by Ivana, bereft of Marla
Cowering dirty and hungry with the homeless
In those dark & dank tunnels under Grand Central
Be this a lesson to us all
Before it is too late

Remember the writing that Belshazzar saw on the wall
MENE MENE TEKEL UPARSIN

—Hiram Handspring

LOSING BODY HEAT

You know how when it gets cold
in the night sometimes you'll

lie there (still half asleep)
without the energy to get up

to find another blanket you'll
stay there till you're nearly

freezing   it was like that for
them for quite a time after they

had been married about five years
they both knew it wasn't working

out but neither could do or say
anything to stop the drift   it

was as if they were paralyzed
they'd lost all their body heat.

THE CHURCH LADIES

are having a great day
they're putting on the

strawberry festival on
the village green and

everyone will come to eat
shortcake and be happy

President Bush has been
very petulant on TV this

week   he wants to run the
world but it won't do

what he tells it   no mat-
ter I think the church

ladies will outlast him.

Editor's Note. An Iranian lady of lineage, the Princess Semiramide Parsumash, lives in seclusion in the Litchfield Hills in Connecticut. It has been my good fortune to make her acquaintance and to serve her well, I hope, as amanuensis and researcher on some of her literary projects. Semiramide had a remarkable education. She was graduated from the Sorbonne and then went on to the University of Berlin to take degrees in ancient history and the then new field of ethno-astronomy. In the time of Mussadegh her husband, Prince Rustam, was killed. Semiramide sold the extensive family properties near Shiraz and came, bringing a substantial fortune, to this country. Her philanthropies have been notable. The writing which follows simulates and anachronizes the Achaemenid *Gasida Hathnawi* (the Love Dialogue) of the fourth century.—*Hiram Handspring*

Handspring: Don't speak of little cousin Trudy who was so curious

Semiramide: Speak instead of the aeon-slow movement of the rock plates under the San Andreas fault

Handspring: Don't speak of rail-thin June who asked that night in the car: do I have to do that?

Semiramide: We night compare Heidegger with Wittgenstein, giving the quotations in German

Handspring: Don't speak of Ellie from the office who kept pleading: please don't touch my breasts

Semiramide: Let us ruminate on the cosmic architecture and speculate about the "black holes"

Handspring: Forget about Beth who at the age of ten protested that she would never let a man "put that dirty thing into me"

Semiramide: Ridicule the plan for a space station

Handspring: Obliterate from memory the Chilean girl who on the flight to Rome asked the stewardess for a blanket to put over us

Semiramide: A word or two on the consolations of old age, but they are few

Handspring: Don't try to recall the scent in the elevators of the old Ritz on the way up to Katy's room

Semiramide: Laugh about the planting of infectious computer viruses by precocious young hackers

Handspring: Say nothing about the perverted practice of cautious young women in Brazil

Semiramide: A few words would be in order about the events of Richard Burton's Journey to Mecca

Handspring: Would it be unfair to cite Christine in Cannes who sniffed cocaine before the act, or Brigitte in Zurich who preferred hashish?

Semiramide: Better, if you must, to compare the *Kama Sutra* and the *Serpent Power*

Handspring: Nothing need be said about the Eurasian desk girl at the Imperial Hotel in Tokyo

Semiramide: It would be logical to dispute which was the most serious heresy, Antinomianism or Transcendentalism

Handspring: Don't speak of Dawn's miraculous muscle which she could make twitch

Semiramide: Consider the role of the Polestar in forming the religions of various cultures

Handspring: Don't bring up what the girl who had a room near the Kurfürstendamm in Berlin liked to eat, also what Havelock Ellis persuaded the lady poet to do

Semiramide: If you can remember them recite the names of the twelve segments of a Tibetan mandala; the steps of the Noble Eightfold Path of *satipatthana*, "right mindfulness," are also enlightening

Handspring: It is not important to know what the chauffeur of Baron Lerchenau's Mercedes saw in the bank seat in Düsseldorf

Semiramide: Discuss whether anything about the structure of DNA or RNA polymerases can be learned from the structure of the Klenow fragment; do these polymerases comprise a family of structurally related enzymes?

Handspring: Keep silent about what the little schoolgirls at Pango Pango in Tahiti called out: fifty cents, fifty cents, you come, you come

Semiramide: Tell about the white ship that will bring happymaking goods to the natives in New Guinea

Handspring: Don't speak of the man dressed in a Santa Claus suit who did bad things to the dwarf twins

Semiramide: Describe the little Egyptian figures that Freud had on the desk in his office in the Berggasse in Vienna

Together (chanting): Forget everything you have seen or heard. Be silent. Seek the *dromeda* and *epopteia* of Eleusis. Seek to attain *Dzogchen*, the "great perfection." *Om mani padme hum*—a hundred times, a thousand times, a million times. *Om mani padme hum*. The Jewel at the heart of the Lotus.

"L'ARGENT N'A PAS D'ODEUR"

For Ivana Trump

Accept Dear Lady I pray you
this tribute (it is an old

French saying that has stood
the test of time) from an ad-

mirer of the reserve & dignity
with which you have borne your

ordeal   I see you as the beauty-
ful mother in the famous painting

L'Orage by Rosa Bonheur   she has
taken off her cloak to protect

her frightened children from a
sudden storm   take heart Dear

Lady   examine the upper corner
of the painting where the artist

has let a little ray of sunlight
penetrate the black clouds   your

prince who ran off with the mind-
less milkmaid will get bored and

come to his senses   he is just a
spoiled kid who has never grown up.

ACID RAIN

is falling on me again
today   it withers the

leaves on the bough and
even poisons the water in

the birdbath   it's the
acid of remembering how

badly I treated you how
cruel I was after you

were so loving to me.

THE BIBLE SAYS

that Jacob had to wait
fourteen years for his

beloved Rachel so there
is precedent in scrip-

ture for your procras-
tination but I wish you

would make up your mind
before I'm so old that I

can't give you any fun.

FIVE YEARS AGO: FIVE LIVES AGO

It is five years now since
we parted and I can no long-

er picture you with exacti-
tude (memory is such a treach-

erous friend)   oh yes I see
you tall I see you fair   I

can see the spring in your
step and the way your lips

moved when you laughed but
these are only imperfect

outlines of the whole a fig-
ure that does not stay still

when I summon it   you are
there but not entirely there

in every small detail   that
is what frightens me as

time flies past   the chilling
fear that one day you may

seem to be another person
someone whom I never knew.

THE LOVE-CANDY TEASER

A tall man knows a pretty little cross-stitched punching bag, a tease
packet, with whom he shares life's comical gymnasium

The sweetmeat willows on a string of fast waltz music, turning and
twisting

The trick is to tag her as she revolves, but always gently, not bruising
her milkmaid complexion

The tall man wears puff-stuffed gloves like a boy-time boxer hustling
his birthday party sweetheart

Confetti floats down through strobe-light beams that flash and blink
in multicolor

It's tickle time in the gym; the more she laughs the more he teases, the
more absurd and intricate the feinted blows become

Spectators in the gym are wondering what the game's about; is this a
kind of Polynesian courting?

Or does it come from the bust-up of Western Civilization, when he
plays kiss-kiss teasing like a hyperactive midget child?

Roller skates, roller skates, it's a bad, bad world; whisk us all up to
Heaven, if it's still there.

TIME RUNNING BACKWARDS

That afternoon in a hidden room,
The curtains drawn to half darkness,
The only light coming from scenes out of memory,
Illuminating the walls like passages from a film,
Time running backwards.

Three people are reconvened in judgment on their lives.
Three people, two living and one dead.
The one who is dead is still the most powerful.
But it is a gentle and loving power.
Time running backwards.

Where will time lead the two survivors?
Can the love for a dead man heal their wounds?
Can it obliterate error and faults in emotion?
Can it create a new present, and even a future?
A beloved voice counsels them from the past.
Time running backwards.

THE ENCHANTED BIRCHTREE

An angel lived in a birchtree
Though it was cold at night
But angels have little heaters
Which keep them warm and bright
She was a very special angel
Who gave off a radiant light
She loved living in the forest
It gave her great delight
She loved the squirrels and birdies
And knew their names all right

She was never bored or lonely
She talked to them all night
And she was never hungry
Angels don't need a bite
Why was she in the forest
It didn't seem quite right
For an angel to leave Heaven
And forswear Sweet Jesus' sight
But she had had a vision
That was her troubling plight
She had dreamed of an earthly lover
Though she knew that wasn't right
She wanted her lover most madly
To have him hold her tight
She wanted him to squeeze her
With all his main and might
So she waited in the birchtree
Hoping that she'd catch sight
Of the lover she had dreamed of
The handsome portly knight
She would be his entirely
They would never have a fight
The angel of the birchtree
And her dear (but paunchy) knight.

FOR A CLEVER YOUNG PERSON

The anecdotal personality sees
not the causes of things but

the surfaces of their being
it touches the fruit but not

the flower which has produced
it   the leaf but not the seed

which has engendered it   some-
times the anecdotal personality

even confuses snow with rain
and cannot separate water from

the wind which moves the water
it believes what it first hears

it does not search for what is
beneath the sound   it is the

source of much harmful error.

THE RESPECTFUL CLUTCH

Elegant French gentlemen
Such as counts and dukes and even a few poets
When they are attracted and wish to proposition a lady
Will often say, "Madame, puis-je vous offrir le bonheur physique?"
Madame, may I offer you physical happiness?
Eroticists report that this approach
Is often successful with persons of experience and sophistication
But of little advantage with jeunes filles bien-élevées
Or those just released from their convents

Handspring is gallant but he finds the French formula effete
Being American, he wants to be more manly
He tells me he has had good results with something quite macho and
    direct
As: "Well, baby, how's about a respectful clutch?"

WHAT THE OLD BEDOUIN TOLD ME

Once in my long ago
there was so much rain
that many of the animals died
the leaves and grasses
could not come up to feed them.

And once in my long ago
there were sounds more frightening than thunder
I fell when the earth fell, moving under my feet
part of the mountains fell into the desert
and the sea invaded the land.

And once in my long ago
the sun came too close to the earth
each day nearer and nearer
a dislocation of the heavenly order
first the lakes dried up, then the streams, then the springs
only the glacier people in the mountains survived.

In my long ago I have known these abominations against nature,
    these deadly marvels.

SKIING IN TAHITI

Yes you can ski in Tahiti
(you can do most anything

in dreams) the girls with
nothing on but a banyan

leaf are slaloming down
the beach in perfect form

Gauguin has set up his
easel and is sketching

furiously before the snow
melts   the name of his

famous painting that now
hangs in the D'Orsay is

Muna ta Laguna   you bet
you can ski in Tahiti.

MY COUSIN ALEXANDER

died from laughing gas
at the dentist's in Se-

wickley Pennsylvania
we children were fasci-

nated by this event and
often when we were bored

we played the laughing
game making jokes to see

who would die first but
none of us ever did un-

til later in our lives.

THE STRANGER

There was a knock at the door; I opened.
It was a young man I couldn't at first recognize.
But when I heard his voice I knew him.
He was myself some thirty years before.

I asked him in and made coffee.
Why did you never write, I thought you were dead?
I wished I was sometimes, he said, better I had been.
Where were you all these years?
What did your old poet say, through many lands
And over many seas, I saw so much.
And what were you doing? He shrugged.
Often I didn't know what I was doing.
You might say I was trying to find out
What was real and what was not.
I did a lot of harm, much of it to myself.

We talked for several hours, then he said he had to go.
I urged him to stay on, told him he could make his home with me.
But he refused. There's much that I still have to do, much to learn.
I may be back and I may not, but it was good to have this time
     with you.
And I'm glad you haven't changed, you're still yourself.

SILENTIUM AUREATUM EST

If I give you some of my silence
will you give me some of yours

there's something important that
most people aren't aware of be-

cause they're too busy being busy
silence is nourishing it's good

to eat   it's the opposite of hun-
ger which is a paining emptiness

silence (especially if it can be
shared) is a satisfying fullness

Carthusian monks and the Trap-
pists live by silence   animals

rely on silence for their safety
and for us humans silence can be

a garment of warmth & protection.

AN INTERROGATION

Table   Red   Sixty-three   Broadway

Why has the examining magistrate cited this odd sequence of words?
What do they mean? What is he getting at?
There could be a red table but there logic lapses.

Table   Red   Sixty-three   Broadway

The magistrate repeats the four words.
He seems concerned that the accused should commit them to memory.
What do they signify? What possible importance could they have in
     his case?

Table   Red   Sixty-three   Broadway

Could the words be some kind of code?
What message has been encrypted?
Could they be the passwords for a secret Swiss bank account?
Is a large sum waiting in the Bahnhofstrasse in Zurich?

Table   Red   Sixty-three   Broadway

There is probably some very simple explanation,
Something a child of twelve would grasp immediately.
Are the words from a Nintendo game program?

Table   Red   Sixty-three   Broadway

The magistrate looks at his watch and rushes from the room.
Don't try to leave town, he says, I'll call you for our next meeting.
The accused slumps in exhaustion, he holds his head, he feels a
    headache coming; Another migraine!

LONG AND LANGUOROUS

A whole stolen afternoon before us
no hurry no haste   savoring every

sensation   begin perhaps with mimi-
cry of memories of adolescence

what you learned from the boy next
door what the lady who was divorced

taught me   no hurry no haste   how
is it that lovemaking from long ago

can return so vividly   we can still
feel certain touches hear certain

tones of voice even remember some
of the words exchanged   making love

is cumulative   nothing of it that
was good is really lost   and yet

there can always be discoveries
little hidden paths to pleasure

no haste no hurry   time for a mo-
ment's doze between enlacements

time even for a bit of joking be-
cause there is that aspect of the

ridiculous in coupling   better it
all be soft and slow gentle and

generous as our afternoon speeds
on its way long and languorous.

THE LAST WORDS OF
CHARLES WILLSON PEALE
(THE PAINTER)

Daughter, take my pulse
Father, you have none
I thought not.

AN APOTROPAIC DECISION

She was in every way a delect-
able bundle an enticement to

the eye and what came out of
her pretty head was fascinating

but I knew she had run through
a dozen lovers leaving them

disconsolate so when it was
clear that I was to be the

next I retreated from danger
better to forgo a transient

pleasure (no matter how suc-
culent) than to be burned

and tossed on the ash heap.

KENNETH REXROTH

Impossible to encapsulate him
He always said he was a Buddhist
But when he was dying he took the biscuit from the Jesuits
Such an inconsistency was part of his nature and part of his strength
He was the perpetual dissident
He liked to say that the good people were the bad people and the bad
    people were the good people
A strong advocate of women's rights who was hard on his wives
He chose to live in the black quarter of San Francisco

He published in the highbrow magazines but also wrote a column for the Hearst newspaper

He had good friends in high Jewish society and good friends in Chinatown

One of his counselors was a wise old whore on Market Street

He had a photographic memory and wrote his learned essays without looking anything up

His study period was the bathtub where he spent hours reading difficult books on a slanting board above the water

He was one of the superb talkers of his generation, and a great cook, and he didn't drink

He liked to say outrageous things but often there was sense in them if you could untangle the gist from the rhetoric

The mountains were the true love of his life

In summer we packed up into King's River Canyon in the Sierras, with a mule; he could cook a banquet over the campfire coals with the little that the mule was carrying

I didn't doubt him when he said he conversed with the deer and other animals

When we were fishing a mountain stream he could see trout under the water fifty yards ahead

When we ski-camped in winter on the east side of the Sierras above Bishop we didn't have to pack a tent because he would carve out a niche in a snowbank with a ski tip, floor the little cave with fir boughs and we slept warm

Once when we were snow-camping up near Mineral King he sat on a stump all day meditating while I climbed a ridge on skis, four hours motionless in meditation

There was philosophy for him in the stars as his great mountain poems show, all history was alive in his brain

Wherever he was energy was surging out of him

One friend describes him as "electric"

I can accept that if we remember electricity does not only generate motion

It also produces warmth and illumination.

THE ORACLES

For Mary Karr

A lovely girl told me that
I was an oracle   I warned

her to be on her guard
that I was descended from

Pythia the priestess of
the shrine of Apollo at

Delphi who always gave
conflicting answers to

the questions that were
addressed to her   I sug-

gested that for serious
matters of the heart she

consult the Sibyl of Cum-
ae who did not have such

a bad reputation for
doubletalk or Herophilē

of Erythrae in Ionia who
did a good job on certain

events in the Trojan war.

THE BONDING

Could we be joined together
by tubes so that our blood

would circulate through each
other (they do such incred-

ible operations now) would
we be really one then just

one person   but you ask me
isn't that what happens when

we make love   of course but
then it only lasts for a

few moments it passes so
quickly   you laugh at me

do you want us to be Siam-
ese twins that would be so

awkward   you're right but
I still want to find a way

to make us just one person.

THE INTRUDER

She writes that she feels
she is now an intruder in

my life and she doesn't
want to see me again   poor

blind girl   she can't see
that (near or far) she's

still at the heart of my
life and lives in my poems.

OUR DOMAIN

Between us we control a vast domain
As large as that of the Tang or the Ming
Our lands stretch from one mighty river to another
From the Oringa to the Potani, and beyond them to the confluence of
    the Gingril with the Pladd
Our subjects speak many languages, more than any scholar can learn,
    it is a Babel of tongues
Over the centuries, dynastic marriages have enlarged our territory
Girls of fifteen have been given in bondage to vicious old men for a few
    hectares of land
Cultures have been intermingled, honest men have died at the stake for
    their principles
Religions have been adulterated, ancient ceremonies suppressed
Histories have been rewritten to justify certain boundaries
Even I cannot grasp the extent of our domain and it is still growing,
    pushing beyond the edges of the maps
Can you, my consort, number our peoples or visualize all our provinces?

Our domain has different names, depending on who is speaking,
   whether he applauds or despises it
I have given much thought to the question of the final name, it is impor-
   tant for an empire to have the right name, I have consulted the ora-
   cle at Khrabba, the old witch in the cave near the four pillars
"It is already named," she declared, "but you have not yet recognized
   the name, you may not even be able to recognize it, I would only
   waste my time trying to explain it to you."
"Confide the name to me," I begged her. "You shall have gold, my ser-
   vants will bring you a cooked lamb every day."
"It's a simple name. You are blind not to know it already."
"Don't anger me, old woman. The name!"
"The name," she replied, "is *LOVE*, your love for your consort and hers
   for you."

A PROBLEM OF SEMANTICS

The priest who warbles a
sermonette at seven each

morning from the diocesan
station in Hartford announ-

ced today that it is sin
which keeps us from loving

I must write to tell him
he's mistaken   I've been

sodden with sin since I
first heard about it in

my Presbyterian Sunday
school yet notwithstand-

ing I can love her madly.

THE SCAR

He hadn't wanted to look at it or examine it
the brutal red slash across her beautiful body
that the surgeon had left in repairing her after the car smash
he had been right not to look at it
for once he had seen the scar it became indelible in his mind
it became (and how could he explain such irrationality?) something
    he had done to her
even though he had not been driving the car
a horror birthed in him from looking at the scar
a hatred that he knew neither of them deserved
he couldn't repress it
the scar was forming in his own flesh too.

HEART ISLAND

Stop searching stop weeping
she has gone to Heart Island

where the Truth People live
eating fern-shoots & berries

where there is no fighting
no sin no greed no sorrow.

THE PRISONER

A person can be in prison
though he may not know it

the bars are not visible
to him   the walls of his

cell are diaphanous or like
transparent glass which he

can see through but when he
tries to cross the invisible

boundary he bumps his head
and retreats   he is not mis-

treated the food is edible
and the gaolers talk to him

and tell him what is going
on in the world outside but

they don't tell him how to
escape from his own prison.

IT'S SPRING

and two cyclicals are riding
their cycles in the park   she

is a bit timid and feels most
comfortable on a tricycle   he

is a brash exhibitionist and is
mounted on a unicycle (the

kind clowns ride in the circus)
when they come to the fountain

of the swans which has a circu-
lar path around it they begin

to sing *funiculi funicula* as
they circle the swans   people

stop to watch and a small crowd
gathers   a little dog gets off

its leash and chases after them
it's spring and the citizens of

all sexes and sizes start to
clap and sing *funiculi funi-*

cula   but a park policeman
comes along and disperses them

move along here please move
along   soon the cyclicals

are alone again and (still
wheeling in circles) they

have a serious conversation
do you he asks her like me

best when I'm up or when I'm
down   goofus she answers I

like you best when you're
upside down   they laugh and

wheel out of the park and
where they go next and what

happens nobody knows or cares
it's spring *funiculi funicula.*

THE SENSUALIST OF PAIN

has little difficulty
in finding gratifica-

tions   not only is the
world around him in-

tolerable and most of
its inhabitants gross

or malicious but when
he does find a person

he likes he has a rare
capacity for putting

both feet in his mouth
so that he gets kicked

in the teeth forthwith.

THE SELF-TORMENTORS

It's spring again and that
crazy robin is back from

the south for the third
year bashing her beak on

my window every morning
for an hour or more   she

perches on the limbs of
the linden tree on the

terrace then bullets her-
self against the glass

what does she want   why
does she do it what is

her obsession (it hasn't
anything to do with food

or nesting) it's just
self-torment each day

until she is exhausted.

     * * * *

It's spring again and the
famous German film direc-

tor is back in New York
hunting for a distribut-

or for his latest cruel
bitter cynical picture

the cruelty of man to man
the way that men and wom-

en cut each other up and
then come back for more

the mercilessness of fate
(yes those whom the gods

love they hurt the most)
why do I keep on going

to see that wretched gen-
ius's films   am I a charac-

ter from old Menander's
play The Self-tormentor?

THE THINKING MACHINE

In a California laboratory a computer is being programmed
to think like a human. The technical name of the machine is
"a neural network," but in the lab its familiar name is
"Psych."

I love my neural network
because it talks like me

but if I question its un-
derstanding of what I'm

saying it gets very angry
its inventor claims that

within ten years it will
be knowing things that no

mortal mind has ever con-
ceived of   it does not

have to rest and it runs
all night evaluating by

its binary process the
sentences it has been

given to digest   already
it has assimilated some

Latin phrases but when
I fed it Williams's *ni-*

hil in intellectu quod
non prius in sensu (no

ideas but in things) a
concept which it should

have liked it was puz-
zled and became irrita-

ble because its language
can now only be concrete.

THE VAGRANT

She was a vagrant in my heart
one day she would be there and

the next she would be gone usu-
ally without saying goodbye or

leaving any forwarding address
the first few times this happen-

ed I would be very troubled but
then I came to realize that these

unpredictable visits were better
than not having her at all   I

gave up expecting her on any par-
ticular day   her movements were

mysterious like certain birds
which travel the world without

a pattern in time   this was her
nature   there was nothing I or

anyone could do to change it.

CONTRA DECONSTRUCTIONEM

(To the tune of "Gaudeamus Igitur")

This academic is a bird
Who can't tell popcorn from a turd
He isn't dumb, he's just absurd
Believe no good you may have heard
About the ac-derridian wonder-bird
Who likes a sign more than a word
Is he a savant, no a nerd
Who wants this academic bird?

558

THE ENGLISH GOVERNESS

Tell me doctor you who
know so much from read-

ing the books of that old
man in Vienna did I be-

come a womanizer in my
twenties because when

I was eight I had an
English governess who

like a snake shedding
its skin could undress

in my presence and get
into her nightgown with-

out letting me see
a patch of her skin.

TWO SCENES FROM THE LITERARY SCENE & A LETTER

When Ginsberg (always tolerant and kindhearted)
wanted to help a starveling young poet
he might close his letter by saying: take *my* letter to the Phoenix
    Bookshop in Cornelia Street,
they may give you as much as $25 for it.

Pound also was generous,
When the young sculptor who called himself Henghes
(he was born Heinz Winterfeld Klussmann)

hitchhiked all the way from Hamburg to Rapallo
because he had to see Pound's Gaudier-Brzeskas
("The Fawn," "The Sleeping Cat," "The Water Carrier," "The Boy
　　with a Coney")
and he stopped to pick up two bits of soft slate in a streambed
carving them with his scout knife into birds flying,
a gift for the master, "il maestro di color che sanno," (the master of
　　those who know, which is Dante about Aristotle in the Circle of
　　Virtuous Pagans in the *Inferno*)
Pound fed him and bedded him in the doghouse on the seafront
　　terrace, there being no guestroom at Via Marsala 12 v,
and stood good for him with the man who made gravestones for a
　　chunk of veined marble
which was chiseled and polished into the sitting-down centaur
which he (Pound) sold to the Fiat lady in Torino
so that Henghes could have his own room in the Via delle Rane (the
　　street of the frogs, that is)
where he brought beauty to the lives of various unbeauteous virgins . . .

The Letter

Dear Allen: I had gotten so used to seeing you around New York in
　　the dhoti you brought back from Benares
where you earned your food by stoking the fires of sandalwood
which were burning the bodies of devotees of Krishna and Vishnu on
　　the ghats of the Ganges,
with your long unkempt hair of a sadhu begging his bowl through
the alleys of the ancient holy city . . .

When unexpectedly you sat down beside me at the YMHA at a
　　tiresome poetry reading,
when you arrived freshly barbered in a pin-stripe business suit
so that I didn't recognize you 'til the rays of your goodness emanated
　　to me . . .

Can you forgive me, Allen, for spreading the story at dinner parties
　　(singing for my supper)
of your leaving your poems by the milk bottles on the back stoop of
　　Dr. Williams in Rutherford?

560

I know it's not true, but it's so true to your legend.
I hope I've not too greatly offended.

When the last film flickers through my soon-dead head
may I see and hear you again playing your little harmonium
and chanting the songs of Blake in your raspy voice
there on the fifth-floor walk-up in the East Village
where the stinking toilet was down the hall near the stairhead.

Great poet, good man, adept of happy-making laughter,
I salute you.

THE AESCULAPIANS

All during my prostatectomy
(while I was fully conscious

with only a spinal) Dr K as he
poked around in there talked a

blue streak to the nurse about
his real estate deals   he botch-

ed the job and it had to be done
over   but I'm glad for his kids

he made all that money in land.

During my cataract extraction
(I was conscious then too) the

eminent Dr P conversed with his
assistant
                this one is a real bug-

ger isn't it?

           it sure is

               some-
times I wonder why we stay in
this business.

Dr T is a healer   you begin to
feel better the minute he takes

your blood pressure and starts to
question you in his quiet voice.

WHAT IS HOPED FOR

Around Amida's lake of bliss
the jeweled birds are sing-

ing that all is impermanent
and that the self is illusion

may the unbearable radiance
that follows death be turned

to compassion   may we be ab-
sorbed in the void of nirvana.

ARE YOU STILL ALONE?

in your cave of doubt   I
can't bear to think of you

there in that darkness   though
perhaps you have to be there

for a while to find your own
kind of light   did I help to

drive you there   though we
are far apart I try to reach

into your cave to hold your
hand   can you feel my touch

I hope you can know for a
moment that you're not alone.

THE FLEMISH DOUBLE PORTRAIT

In this painting which hangs in the Hermitage in St. Petersburg
(the artist is unknown but the style is Flemish fifteenth century)
two aristocratic women wearing elegant silk & brocade dresses
are seated facing each other on elaborately carved fauteuils
we see them in profile, they are looking at each other as if engaged in
    conversation
their dresses are similar in cut but one is red and one is green
as we approach the painting we take the ladies to be sisters
on nearer inspection they appear to be twins
but when we look very closely they are indisputably one and the
    same person

the same coiffures, the same beaded slippers, the same gold-chain
 necklaces
a small mole (reversed of course) in the cheeks near the mouth
the ladies are staring at each other with unconcealed hatred
you might say that they are trying to set fire to each other with their
 eyes
their hands are clenched tight in their laps
if you linger before this painting for only a few moments
you may become hypnotized by the enmity it contains (such hatred,
 such hatred)
you may even feel hallucination stealing into your mind
you may imagine that you hear the women hissing at each other (in
 whatever is your language)
one asks, what are you doing inside me that I feel such excruciating
 pain?
and the other replies, it is you who have no right to be in me, I
 demand that you go, I never wanted you, I never loved you, go
 now, you must go!

In describing the painting I neglected to say
that there are two small pet monkeys perched on the backs of the
 armchairs
they are different in color, one a slightly darker brown than the other
they show no animosity toward each other
in fact one is about to toss a little silver ball to the other.

THE IMAGINARY DIARY

I keep an imaginary diary
which is mostly about you

it describes the life we
would be leading if you

weren't far away   places
we go together things we

do people we see what you
are wearing what we talk

about and what we are read-
ing   a whole beautiful and

exciting life of affection
(and of course no quarrels)

the days & nights rush a-
long it reads like a per-

fect story that we share
except that you are far

away   it's all imaginary.

THE AFTERTHOUGHT

When he had driven her
to JFK so she could fly

back to Zurich for her
next film and they had

brother-sisterly kissed
goodbye (he feared they

might never meet again
he worked only in Hol-

lywood) she ran back
through the gate to

say in her crazy Swiss
German du weisch weisch

du nöt dass diene chatz-
li-and-müessli Schpiël

mir a ganz grosse Freud
gmacht hänt es war chaiba

güet   you know that I did
love the bed part too it

was great   then she had
rushed off to her flight

one of his life's precious
moments that he would

treasure long as he lived.

LA TRISTESSE

And Pound in his despair in the Army prison camp at Pisa
Wrote, *"Tard, très tard je t'ai connue, la Tristesse."*
And he said that the tears he had caused in his life were drowning
    him.
"Les larmes que j'ai créés m'inondent."

I have been reading some pages in the *Tristia* of Ovid,
Who was exiled to Pontus on the Black Sea, the end of nowhere,
Because he had offended Augustus.

566

Ovid longs for Rome, for his homeland.
You are my homeland and I seek permission to return to you.

You are the solitary voyager, the bird of lone flight.
I was foolish; I tried to capture you, to bring you down from your
    sky.
I am rightly punished, but exile from you is a hard pain to bear.
My sadness is a dull ache, a wound that won't heal.
I have injured the one I love best.
She also has her wound, the one I gave her.
La tristesse, tard, très tard je t'ai connue.

THE RODENT

        tried to get into my head
        through my mouth but my

        teeth were clamped shut
        like lockjaw   I knew it

        was coming and was ready
        then it tried my nose but

        I broke my nose playing
        hockey when I was a boy

        and it's all crooked in-
        side   it was through the

        ear (the left one) that
        the hairy creature made

        its entry   now it lives
        in my brain   it has made

a soft & warm burrow for
itself in there   I feel

it moving around as it
feeds on my thoughts.

AN ATTESTATION

I, Enrique Xavier Villaruta, Marques d'Orizaba
Affirm that the Indian boy known as Miguel Sanchez
Died on my estancia in Cordoba de Mexico
At the age of about sixteen, died of natural causes
And that as witnesseth Fray Escobar of the Franciscans
The marks of the stigmata were found on his body
The five wounds on hands, feet and the side
And the boy's body has been placed in the tomb
Of my family at the church of San Luis Fernando
Without any embalmment of any kind
Where it has not corrupted or putrified
As observed by many who have come to wonder at it
These six months since the death, uncorrupted
And may the Devil take my soul if I have not truth told
Regarding this miraculous event.

Given by me this 23rd day of February
in the year of our Lord 1534, and in
the reign of the Blessed Felipe of
Aragon, the fifth year
                    Attest: Escobar, O.F.M.
        Villaruta d'Orizaba

THE BIOGRAPHER

Sometimes when she asked me
a difficult question in her

interviews she would make her
beautiful eyes very big (she

was trying to explain me in
one of her literary articles)

what did she see in me as she
questioned me about a muddled

life   (so many false starts so
many poor poems so many un-

worthy actions so many mistakes)
did I entirely misread her glance?

AGATHA

has now gone up to Harlem
to look for a Black Prince

she has exhausted midtown
and lower Manhattan   she

is the daughter of the Rev-
erend Theophilus Grant rec-

tor of Christ Church Newbury
her mother died young and he

repressed her childhood.

A CERTAIN IMPERMEABLE PERSON

For Vanessa

is quite impossible to describe
with accuracy but let me jot down

a few random notes about her (char-
acteristics that I have now and then

observed)   first when it rains she
doesn't melt   second by powers of

concentration alone she is able in
an instant to change the color of

her hair   thirdly when she walks
past Southwark Cathedral those an-

cient bells ring out in salutation
untouched by the sexton's hand

if you will imagine a female Rim-
baud it is she (but without his

questionable habits)   don't smile
I swear there really is such a

person impermeable impenetrable
and immutable oh I know her well.

THE CHIPS ARE FLYING

At first Fortran and Cobol
were friendly   they were ri-

vals but they could talk to
each other in a cordial way

they could make allowances
for each other's linguistic

differences   but then some-
thing bad (or good as you

may look at it) happened
Linda came along with her

parallel computing   trust
a witch to make a rumpus

now Fortran and Cobol are
snarling at each other   the

chips are flying   if those
two boys had sense they'd

see they must find a way
to gang up on that Linda.

THE TIME STEALER

She bites off chunks of time
and hides them   at first she

was concealing them around the
house and I was able to get a

lot of them back but now she's
burying them out in the veg gar-

den where they're hard to find
you have your own time I tell

her why can't you make do with
that   I need all my time   I have

important work to do   she says
if you were a good husband you'd

understand that my time
is your time and your time is

my time   I know she's right but
you can't teach an old dog new

tricks   I'm a crusty self-cen-
tered cantankerous old buzzard

and I wish she'd quit stealing
so many big chunks of my time.

THAT VOICE

When you are waking from deep
sleep do you sometimes hear an

unfamiliar voice speaking yet
when you come to your senses

there is no one in the room
usually the voice talks about

something you have been dream-
ing   the voice continues the

story of the dream (but it's
not part of the dream) who is

the unknown speaker who draws
you from sleep   it sounds like

a woman's voice but whose is
it   I can't guess the answer

though I've heard the voice so
often   could it perhaps be the

voice of the one who died   is
she bringing me the explanation

of what I never could understand

* * *

there was that night in Trivan-
drum many years ago when I sat

573

at the feet of the venerable gu-
ru reclining in his bathchair and

the light from the flaming torches
illumined the faces of the disci-

ples gathered about him in the
darkness   he was expounding the

epistemology of one of the Brahm-
anas and to test me he asked a

question I could neither compre-
hend nor answer   what he asked me

in your western knowledge in your
Aristotle what exists in the space

between two thoughts   I begged for
the answer but he only smiled and

turned away   now it is my turn to
ask him a question   tell me master

what exists in the space between
my dream and the voice that I hear.

THE STORY OF RHODOPE

has always attracted me   she
was the Thracian courtesan

who lost her slipper while
bathing   but an eagle picked

it up and dropped it in the
lap of Pharaoh Psammetichus

who of course searched her
out and married her loading

her with gold bracelets   the
story is important to me be-

cause my father had a shoe
fetish   he would take one

of his dollbabies into Del-
man's on Fifth Avenue and

buy her a dozen pairs of
slippers at a crack   dear

old dad I'm happy that their
pretty footsies made you glad

you weren't a book reader and
you needed some literary love.

CATULLUS XLVIII

Juventius if you let me
go on kissing your honey-

ed eyes I'd kiss them
three hundred thousand

times and that might not
be enough if it were

less than all the ripe
corn of the harvest.

CICERO WROTE

(I forget the Latin now)
that an old love pinches

like a crab   but he was
wrong   if it was a tender

love such as we shared so
many years ago   it persists

even though life drew us
apart and it is always sweet.

BLUE BOOTIES & PINK BOOTIES

Yes indeed there is a difference
which makes life interesting and

produces much significant litera-
ture   it has also produced rape

and harassment (as we read in
the *Enquirer* and even in the *Times*)

the senators can't agree on what
harassment really is so let's try

breaking it up into its component
sounds   her-ass-meant   what does

her ass mean (to you or to me)
steatopygia is often compelling

but how powerful should it be
there was Theodora of Byzantium

who had Justinian under her thumb
but it didn't get Marilyn Monroe

into the White House   I had no
sister so I spied on the girl

nextdoor to learn the difference
I discovered anatomical dispari-

ties but later learned there was
more to it than that (my first

divorce was amical but the second
was costly)   Cousin Elisabeth   (the

best mind in the family) wrote a
biological treatise proving that

over the millennia physiological
mutations have been in progress

that will culminate by the year
5000 in our all being born fe-

male (she had to pay to get the
book published and there were

only comical reviews)   perhaps
that will be the final answer

to the problem of blue and pink
booties   *surget sol et sol de-*

clinat   the sun ariseth and it
hath its time of going down   the

earth turns and we spin with it.

CLUTCHES

My father was an expert automobilist
Once in 1902 in a 5-mile race in Frick Park (Pittsburgh)
(There were two men in each car, a driver and a mechanic)
An important wire fractured from vibration and the vehicle came to a
    halt
My father seized the ends of the wire in each hand, allowing the
    current to pass through his body
The driver cranked up, leapt back to his seat, grasped the guide bar
    (this was before steering wheels),
The engine sputtered, the car darted forward, and the race was won.

Some 28 years later when I had been given a Model A Ford which
    cost $850
My father was displeased with my driving because I couldn't learn
    how to double-clutch
(To double clutch you must depress the pedal once while you leave
    the gear you are in, then depress it again to enter the gear in
    which you desire to proceed)
The smoothness of transition, with no bumping or grinding,
    achieved by proper double-clutching is the mark, my father
    explained, of the expert driver.

A DOOR THAT OPENS

Have you a back door to your house
like ours with a weak latch and

sometimes if the wind blows it will
open by itself letting in a bit of

cold air till we shut it   or is it
really the wind   could it instead

be the old lady (so long absent)
who steals in to inspect us to see

what we're up to   are we keeping
things tidy   have the inner sills

of the windows where the paint flakes
from condensation been touched up

have we moved any of her furniture
from where she had it   I hope if

it's she that she goes upstairs and
sees that her picture (the one I

had enlarged that I took the day
the new dogwood first bloomed her

head is among the blossoms) is still
on the wall beside my bed   I don't

think I'll get that latch fixed (a
little cold now and then doesn't

matter much) the door must be kept
easy for an old lady to push open.

BEFORE I DIE

(Jeanine Lambert)

I want to ride once more on
the Paris Métro Madeleine

Vendôme Palais Royal I
used to know by heart the

names of the Métro sta-
tions between where I lived

and where you lived and I
still smell the sweet odor

of the cars (they used to
spray them every night to

freshen them up) it was a
smell of death   you died

of cancer at twenty   I did-
n't learn of it till much

later   I was working out in
India   Saint Germain Sainte

Chapelle Palais de Justice
I called on your family

and heard the sad story
while your mother and fa-

ther wept   Châtelet Hôtel
de Ville Bastille   Jean-

ine Jeanine adorable Jean-
ine I want to ride again

in the Métro   I think I'll
find you there waiting

to laugh and sit beside
me and hold my hand.

CHARLES BERNSTEIN

I wish there were some kind
of a CAT scan which would

show what actually happens
in his head when he writes

his poems those extraordi-
nary leaps from one word or

phrase to another which at
first seem to have no con-

nection but let them sink in
a bit and you'll see they do.

THE MOTHS

Remembering Vladimir Nabokov

A dark damp night and a sudden hatch
of moths has covered the glass of the

big window in the living room attract-
ed by the light where I sit reading

they make a solid curtain of flutter-
ing little shapes   they are desperate

they are the kind which only lives for
one night and they must reach the light

there must be thousands of them   there
is nothing remarkable in this invasion

no metaphor for the poet to play with
but now again it is a night some forty

years ago   the summer when Volya came
to hunt lepidoptera at the mountain

lodge in Utah   he had turned the inside
lights against the picture window and

the outside was swarming with moths
he put on a miner's headlamp and stood

on a stepladder on the terrace plucking
the moths into a cyanide jar with his

tweezers   next morning when he examin-
ed the bodies with a jeweler's ocular

he was ecstatic   eleven of the male
moths were the variants (detectable by

a mutation in the genitalia) which were
first recorded by the French lepidopter-

ologist D'Imbert when he visited the
Wasatch range in 1896   later Volya told

me that he traded his duplicates with
collectors in Europe for varieties from

Manchuria & Tibet that he had never seen.

TO GET TO SLEEP

I listen on my cassette
player to the woman who

is reading *Middlemarch*
or to the man who is do-

ing *Moby-Dick*   of course
the tape keeps running

when I fall asleep so
next day I must rewind

it for the coming night
how I wish I could do

that for our book the
one we've written to-

gether   there are parts
of that I'd love to hear

over and over again.

THE MOVING CLOUD

As a child (about seven or eight
I guess) I'd see a beautiful fat

white cloud and imagine I was up
there with my dog Tiger playing

on it   the cloud would drift a-
cross the sky and we'd ride on

it not coming down till dark
what simple (perhaps foolish)

happiness and now I have it a-
gain knowing that soon I'll be

with you once more an old man
riding like a child on a cloud.

THE OLD INDIAN

told me (he was an Onon-
daga) that each person is

born with a number of days
in his hand   he must accept

that   but he may hope for
the tribe because if there

is one to speak and one to
listen the tribe will go on.

BLESS YOU, MR. PRESIDENT

It says in the science section
of the *Times* that (although the

last big hit was perhaps thirty
million years ago) we may expect

an obliterating collision with an
asteroid from space at any time

but as always our President is
on top of the situation   twenty-

four hours a day astronomers are
scanning the heavens with their

telescopes and in Montana three
shifts of missile crews are on

duty in their silo to fire off
our biggest rocket to hit the

intruder   our scientists (the
best in the world) have calcu-

lated on their computers that at
an altitude of 1000 miles a 300-

megaton nuclear blast will de-
flect an asteroid of up to 700

tons weight moving at the speed
of light   enough to save the world.

THE DIALOGUE

(she mostly listening)
is their medium of love

this suits him well
because he is a par-

oxysmic talker who
rants on bursting

the blood vessels
of invention   her

soft rejoinders that
lead him forward are

the delicate but sus-
taining undertone of

their love discourse.

AT THE END

Let no mortician be her
last lover   I have sent

to Benares for two cords
of the finest sandalwood.

THE CALVES

On the road to Canaan there is
a big dairy farm   beside the

barn there are rows of little
houses like white boxes   calves

are chained to them   they are
fed only milk and not allowed

to wander or they wouldn't be
tender veal   my soft-hearted

granddaughter asks me to stop
the car   she wants to go down

to pet them and comfort them
I say the farmer might not like

that it would be trespassing
I tell her that there are also

people who are chained to boxes
but she doesn't understand me

the whole of life lies before her.

THE THIRD LIFE

I am hers   she possesses me
because I (with age) have

lost much of my memory but
she can recall in great de-

tail everything that we did
together years ago   of an

evening (while I smoke my
cigar) we sit in the arbor

and she tells me stories a-
bout my past   it's a pleas-

ant diversion but it can
bring strange feelings   my

life has become part of hers
and it is as if she gave me

a second life   but sometimes
there are doubts   I have no

way to check her recollec-
tions   could it be she is

creating a third life to
satisfy her own fantasies?

THE MASTER OF STUPIDITY

Our watch-me-do-it-mom leader
is flapping around the world
again in Air Force One making
headlines for his next campaign
he's the master of sophisticated
stupidity   take any burning question
and you can count on George to put
gum in his head and both feet in
his mouth   now that his ratings
are dropping he has to wear
pampers because he's peeing in
his pants   don't worry George
it'll be all right   there are
enough dumb jerks around the
country to get you re-elected.

MURDERER

for his vanity
to get into the

history books
still playing

with his lead
soldiers and

his toy air-
planes   stink

on the world
earth smirch.

TO MISTRESS KATE GILL

O lovely Kate
Flee not my phantasied embrace
I have adored thee soon & late
I love thee, Form & Face

I likewise love thy Mind
So please be kind.

> *Eerily, from his tomb,*
> *John Wilmot*
> *Earl of Rochester*

THE PUNISHMENT

Aeschylus sinned
by divulging the

secrets of the El-
eusinian mysteries

he was properly
punished for this

sacrilege an eagle
dropped a tortoise

on his bald head
and he was dead.

ODI ET AMO

The hate began a few months after
the blissful wedding   he discov-

ered that she had concealed a part
of her personality during the court-

ship (a rigidity that she must have
her way over him) and she found

that he was rather a pompous ass
there were little (at first joking)

criticisms on both sides   then sulks
short arguments and then long ones

that could last for days   but between
rough times there were good times re-

turns to kindness and even to tender-
ness   there was a second honeymoon in

Italy but it ended in a scrap over
nothing   in Verona at the Café Dante

she wanted Orvieto and he wanted Bar-
dolino   they ordered two bottles and

drank hardly any of either in cold
silence
          at about that time they moved

to Santa Barbara and I lost touch with
them   I heard they never had children

but didn't separate   they couldn't let
go of one another   they went on hating

and loving all their lives   odi et amo.

THE DARKENED ROOM

The room which was once
so bright has no illumi-

nation now   the curtains
have been pulled shut and

the lamps have no bulbs
the man who lives here is

blind   he has no need of
light   he sees what he

needs with his hands   he
lives alone   a neighbor

brings him his food   his
book is memory   her face

is clear on the page of
his blindness   his music

is the recollected sound
of her voice   he is lone-

ly but he is content.

DON'T TRY TO EXPLAIN

The mind of a lover is a labyrinth
of false starts and miscalculations

something said was not intended in
the way it was heard   then a wrong

turning was made in the maze   words
of another person are given a false

interpretation and a passageway ends
in a blank wall   an intonation mis-

understood and steps must be retraced
they say that the word labyrinth first

meant a double-headed axe   remember that
love cuts both ways before you explain.

THE TRANSFORMATION

Ibrahim for breaking his
father's idols was cast

by Nimrod into a fiery
furnace which forthwith

became a garden of roses.

—Koran, xxi (via Burton)

THE MATHEMATICS OF CHAOS

The Puranic shastras tell us that
the world began when Shiva Natar-

ja unloosed his tresses (which were
the waters of the Ganges) and danced

the order of all things   but can we
measure the length of time he danced

to accomplish our creation   the Bible
records that it took only seven days

(a quick job but what except Babel
can we expect from a beginning that

was only a word)   what will the gamma-
ray bursters that are born of the clash

between matter and antimatter measure
for us   what of the black hole they

call the Great Annihilator   does it
conceal in the depth of its vastness

a higher power that rules   they say
that old Cronos (the Titan sprung

from Chaos) was cranky and often
drunk on nectar   he and his chil-

dren made a world but one endowed
with deceit and confusion which we

must endure as best we can or go
back to the interstellar debris

and start it all over again.

IBYKUS

There is now a computer disk
named Ibykus which contains

all of classical literature
but does it record that at

Harvard in 1936 the vener-
able and saintly Professor

Pease used up one whole peri-
od of our Virgil class prov-

ing by sign and symbol that
Dido and Aeneas didn't do

anything bad in that cave
during the thunder storm.

PANEM ET CIRCENSES

What are we coming to   no
bread but great games in the

Circus Maximus   the Washing-
ton hearings were pure soap

opera (on both sides of the
rostrum)   the Palm Beach

trial is about drunks (what
was that girl doing at a bar

at 3 AM if she wasn't drink-
ing)   great TV circus (sena-

tors as clowns) great enter-
tainment for the populace

but our Emperor does little
to provide bread for the un-

employed the blacks or the
homeless   he's as bad as the

others   like Nero he fiddles
while we burn   he's busy play-

ing with his high-tech bombers
and his tanks fitted with push

blades that roll the enemy in-
to their trenches to bury them

alive   where's the Brutus to
cut down our beloved Caesar?

THE ACTRESS

failed in what might have been her
greatest scene   it had been clear

for a week that he was dying   the
doctors had told them as much with-

out using the word   (although they
disliked her   they considered her

a blot on his life) they knew she
was the person he was thinking

about as he lay there with his eyes
closed and they must send for her

when she came they didn't leave her
alone with him but stood across the

bed from her as she took his hand
and he opened his eyes knowing it

was her touch   it was her moment
she had rehearsed what she wanted

to say   that she respected him be-
yond anyone she had known but she

had never loved him deeply   (he
was just someone playing oppo-

site her on the stage)   those were
the lines she had prepared   she

would render them not with bit-
terness but with the terrifying

honesty of Racine   yet the words
would not come they could not

be uttered she only pressed
his hand and kept her silence.

THE SULTAN'S JUSTICE

The mistress of the brothel can neither read nor write   she keeps accounts for the girls with marks on the wall   and that was the year when the Zamindar of Holi accused the little Abyssinian (she was only twelve) of taking a goldpiece from his purse while he was sleeping after his pleasure and she was taken before the Sultan and the mistress (God knows why she was the darling of the place) bore false witness against her   and her right hand was lopped off with the sword according to the law   but later the money was found in the cook's palette and he was punished in the same fashion   so much for the law and the Sultan's justice   it is a serpent that coils around us and we are helpless against its poison.

AN AMOROUS ENJOINDER

This suppliant song
is made your heart to sway
haste to your lute
and pluck your grief away
for love that once had strayed
returns in double measure
intent to give you pleasure.

EXPECTATIONS

Were his demands upon life
excessive   was it too much

to expect that each girl
would be an Aphrodite (a

grey-eyed nereid coming to
him through the waves)   that

the small door in the back
of his head (the one the

poems come through) would
always open   that the words

would marry with each other
on the page   that the com-

mands he gave them would
be obeyed   that he could

learn to word the world
that they wouldn't always

say the same thing in the
same way   that he might fi-

nally face himself in the
mirror   were these unreas-

onable expectations or were
they offensive to the gods

offenses crying out for
some terrible punishment?

UNA RICORDANZA TENERA

We were remembering old times
(that was twenty years ago) and

you said you could recall only
one time when you became really

angry with me   we were staying
then at the Chelsea on 23rd St

(where Dylan Thomas had lived
and Virgil Thomson)   we had a

funny-shaped room that smelled
of dust because the black maid

only vacuumed twice a month
that night you were tired and

I was too insistent   I wouldn't
let you get to sleep   you used

a crude British expression and
I sulked   but the next morning

before you awakened I went out
to the corner and bought you a

tiny pot of African violets
when you woke I knelt at the

bedside to present my contrition
we laughed and laughed and you

gave my ear a gentle little bite.

DER ROSENKAVALIER

is coming over the radio and I'm back
in the Festspielhaus in Salzburg   Pat-

zak and Lotte Lehmann are singing and
I'm clutching the warm hand of little

Marili in the cheapest seats   (I was
twenty then a runaway from college and

she was seventeen) we slept in separate
beds at the Goldene Rose (which had bed-

bugs) and rode our bicycles out into the
countryside to have lunch in small inns

in the villages (eier und speck was all
we could afford)   and one day we took

the bus to St. Wolfgang to swim in the
cold water of the Ammersee   what would

ever be so good so good and we knew it
late at night when the city was asleep

we could hear the Salzach rushing through
the valley   where was it going with such

urgency   we had no idea where it might
carry us (apart but always together).

THE COLLECTED POEMS OF
JAMES LAUGHLIN

(1994)

James Laughlin invented his way of writing poems when he was still an undergraduate at Harvard. But it didn't come out of the blue. We know that William Carlos Williams, who was Laughlin's friend and whose poems were among the first publications of Laughlin's New Directions publishing company, established in Cambridge in 1936, often composed his poems on a typewriter, and we have reason to think that in part Williams's metric was determined by the look of the typewritten poem on the page. He didn't like his line-endings jagged. So when he came to the place where his line more or less matched up with the lines above it he hit the carriage return and went on to the next one. Sometimes he even hyphenated an end-word and ran the second half over to the beginning of the next line. Well, prosodists have talked for years about enjambment in WCW's poems, as if he had been imitating Gerard Manley Hopkins or somebody like that, and I don't mean to say that the arrangement of lines and syntax in a poem by Williams has no poetic value, which would be ridiculous. But Williams was delighted by visuality too, by paintings, by the appearances of this world, and I suspect he wanted his poems to look right, to show movement, balance, sturdiness, etc., in their printed representations and moreover to be unmistakably distinct from the sprawling effusions of the vers librists—Amy Lowell and that crowd—who were so conspicuous in American writing of the teens and twenties.

Williams never systematized his feelings about prosody, though from time to time he tried to defend them, usually not very well. For Laughlin, however, system was necessary. He decided he would compose on the typewriter and that each line of a poem would deviate in length no more than two typewritten spaces either way from the length of the first line. In effect the shape and line-structure of each poem would depend on the length of the beginning line, written more or less at random. At first this seems the height of artificiality. For one thing, before the advent of electronic typewriters, all typewritten characters had the same width, unlike the variable width of characters in printing type. Consequently a poem which lined up perfectly on the typewritten page according to Laughlin's metric would lose its shape when set in type by a printer, and the reader would never recognize

Laughlin's prosodic accomplishment. For another, has any formal device anywhere in literature ever been so inflexible, so difficult? These are objections that have been raised by many. But I want to argue strenuously against them, against the idea that the technical and structural elements of poetry are artificial or somehow external to poetic purpose. On the contrary they are *intrinsic* to the poem. Even a metric as arbitrary as Laughlin's when considered schematically, i.e. abstractly, like the lettered rhyming pattern of a sonnet, becomes necessary and inevitable when embodied in the concrete poem; without it the poem could not exist. All poets in all times, writing in all languages and traditions, even poets of our time who write in free forms (since their freedom rapidly becomes conventional), have used such components of form, not as impediments—why in the world would they want to do that?—not even as compositional aids, but as the very source from which expressive language, via the imagination, derives.

Laughlin would deny the charge of artificiality categorically. In the poem "Technical Notes" he begins:

> Catullus is my master and I mix
> a little acid and a bit of honey
> in his bowl   love
> is my subject...

and he continues:

> I prefer

> to build with plain brown bricks
> of common talk American talk then
> set 1 Roman stone

> among them for a key I know Ca-
> tullus knew a poem is like a blow
> an impact strik-

> ing where you least expect this I
> believe and yet with me a poem
> is finally just
> a natural thing.

Which was the title of his first book, *Some Natural Things* (1945). Yet this poem, though containing an uncharacteristic short line in each stanza, is written in Laughlin's typewriter metric and is a remarkably succinct explanation—and illustration—of what he has aimed for. It isn't easy. Most natural things aren't.

At any rate Laughlin, who was trained in the classics and was at the same time steadfastly attached to *avant-garde* writing, has held to his own way of writing for many years, nearly sixty altogether. A life-time. And what a marvel this new collected edition is! As he pro-gressed Laughlin began to allow a three-space deviation from the first line in some of his poems, occasionally more than that. And he did poems in other styles too, long-line poems and prose poems. His type-writer prosody was never a *must*. Yet he has stuck with it for by far the larger part of his work, and has enlivened and varied it in many ways: by using decidedly colloquial diction interlaced with occasional ele-gant phrasings, by running many different syntactical and rhetorical arrangements across his strict line structures, by adopting into his own style words and idioms, especially those taken from classical models, that would be called poeticisms by most other contemporary writers, by infusing his poems with very original observations and with strong comic, ironic, and erotic feeling as well as with intimations of politi-cal, social, and cultural criticism. Which brings us to the substance of his poems.

If Williams was the primary influence on Laughlin's metric, Ezra Pound was his most congenial tutor in matters of cultural affinity. Laughlin has told how Dudley Fitts at Choate loaned him books and gave him guidance, with the result that Laughlin became a lifelong reader of the classics. "Catullus started with Fitts," he has said. At the same time Fitts put Laughlin onto important contemporary poets, including E.E. Cummings, whose poems were full of typewritten effects that possibly influenced the young student and whose erotic mode without doubt did influence the attitudinal feasibilities of Laughlin's mature work. At Harvard Laughlin continued his studies, then took a year off to enter the "Ezuversity," that is, he lived in Rapallo and saw Pound daily, talked with him (or mostly listened), took Pound's advice about what to read and how to read it. He became acquainted with modern European languages. What an extraordinary educational boost for a young man! Politics was another matter, however. Laughlin has at times professed an interest in Social Credit, as have many others who understand monetary issues—for my part socialized credit, if cooperatively administered, seems a fine remedy for our crisis in banking today and the general economic iniquity—but Laughlin never caught Pound's ranting style of argument. Even in 1936, Laughlin has said, he detected signs of Pound's disabling paranoia and obsessive behavior.

What Laughlin got from Pound, I think, was something of the grand spirit of the older poet's vision of a multicultural, polylingual, fundamentally agrarian, craftsmanly, and austerely mercantile civilization, held together by history, by the secular order of justice, and by the spiritual order of the natural world. Beyond this he got a sense of the pleasure, the constructive gratification, to be found in playing with language. No other American poet I know has come as close as Laughlin to using language as Pound did in the *Cantos*. Yet the styles of the two poets are completely different, almost at odds with one another. Pound went at language in grim seriousness, he learned smatterings of Chinese, Egyptian, and other faraway languages; he relied tenaciously on tags from Greek and Latin as mementos of consolidated meaning, what he called glyphs; he interspersed his poems with passages in modern European languages, including not just French, Italian, and German, but Portuguese, Slavic bits, and of course La langue d'oc, or more properly Lo lenga d'òc, as linguists refer to it today. (In Pound's time and earlier the language was called, inaccurately, Provençal.) Laughlin's practice, in contrast to Pound's, has been lighter, more comic and ironic, and in fact, though the forcefulness of Pound's language-joining cannot be denied, Laughlin has integrated different languages more closely than Pound did. Here is part of one my favorites, "In Another Country":

Giacomino!

    she called vieni qua splashing her
    arms in the clear green water vieni
    subito and so I followed her swim-
    ming around a point of rock to the

    next cove vieni qua non hai paura
    and she slipped like an eel beneath

the surface down through the sunken
entrance to a hidden grotto where

the light was soft and green on fine-
grained sand é bello no? here we can
be together by ourselves nobody else
has ever been here with me it's my se-

cret place here kiss me here I found
it when I was a little girl now touch
me here é strano questa luce com' un
altro mondo so strange this light am

I all green? it's like another world
does that feel good? don't be afraid
siamo incantati we're enchanted in
another world O Giacomino Giacomino

sai tu amore come lui è bello? Com' è
carino sai quanto tu mi dai piacere?
sal come lei ti vuol' bene? lie still
non andare via just lie still lie still.

How poignantly, excitingly this evokes the sense of a love affair in a
foreign country! And part of the effect comes from the interfusion of
languages, which is no impediment to most readers. I've never studied
Italian, but I can take in the Italian passages in this poem easily, even
the ones not translated in the poem itself, and if I am unable to pro-
nounce them correctly I can still say them in a way that is pleasing to
me. Has any poet other than Laughlin done this as well? The closest is
Hemingway in some of his stories, or Joyce in part of his monumental
fictions, but I think Laughlin does it better, more completely, and less
laboriously—that is, more naturally.

Then there are the comic poems in ski-German, a language half-
Austrian and half-American, all mixed together, which Laughlin
picked up during his many skiing expeditions in the Alps. (He was a
fine skier and wrote articles for ski magazines.) Funny, ironic, touching
poems. No one has a better understanding of the American in Europe,

the sense of mingled inferiority, arrogance, confusion, relish, and time-sorrow that all of us feel over there.

But his French poems are the most varied and numerous of Laughlin's experiments with other languages, and are among my favorites of all his work. Some are in correct French, touching or ironic love poems, others are in Americanized French, some play with French argot and double entendre. Myself, I hear most of them as decidedly Americanized, perhaps because I've heard Laughlin speak French and that's the way he speaks it; I can understand him easily though I have trouble with native Francophones. People who don't know French at all will no doubt find these poems difficult and I suspect some who know French well may find them ill-advised or even offensive. But Laughlin wasn't writing for either group; rather his aim originally was for the thousands of us who know enough French to understand, say, two-thirds of *Paris Soir*. Now for this collected edition he has made for the first time American translations—trots really—in the hope that these will assist readers whose French is less than mediocre or doesn't exist at all.

But the important, the imperative thing to understand about these poems is that he wrote them to say what can't be said otherwise. I don't mean ideas or images; these may be conveyed in any adequate language. I mean feelings, the unparaphrasable minutiae of feelings. In poetic theory recently languages have been held to be codes intrinsically identifiable with particular classes and cultures. Then how is a poet to get outside the codes, beyond arbitrariness, free from the social and political stereotypes? One way is by working on the edges of the codes, at the point where codes intersect. This is what Laughlin has done. In his French poems he gives us nuances of feeling and attitude, chiefly comic and ironic and almost always erotic, that aren't accessible in any other language. The result is poetry lighter and generally more ingratiating than Pound's, for instance, poetry I like very much indeed.

In effect Laughlin has created his own code. It is French of a kind, but upon it he has imposed his own rhythm, syntax, and intonation. Readers in France might say it is flatter than real French. But Laughlin, knowing his own precise cultural location, would answer, okay, but it's also more *natural*. Of course it has references outward to thousands of cultural antecedents, all languages do, but it remains self-bonded and infrangible. And incidentally what it registers are not simply nuances of feeling but touches of intonational and prosodic finesse unavailable anywhere else. Many of these poems seem to me remarkably beautiful. Try this one.

LA LANGUE ENFANTINE

Quand elle dort et s'éveille
pour un instant (comme si elle

était troublée par un rêve) elle
parle dans une langue enfantine

une langue très douce et presque
imperceptible qui est difficile

à comprendre   parfois c'est un
discours amoureux racontant des

choses qu'elle hésite à dire en
plein jour   j'attends avec im-

patience cette langue enfantine
et ses petites histoires tendres.

Easy enough to read if you have any French at all, but here is Laughlin's translation.

THE INFANTILE LANGUAGE

When she's asleep and wakes for a moment
as if she were troubled by a dream
she speaks in an infantile language
a language that's soft
and almost inaudible, difficult to understand
sometimes it's an amorous story
telling things she'd be reluctant to say by day
I wait with impatience for this infantile speech
with its tender little tales.

It's clear right off that Laughlin is unable to translate his poem any better than anyone else would. *Douce* means much more than soft, if only because it's the word one uses to a French child who's being too loud-mouthed; "Douce, douce, chéri." And of course he has had to abandon the couplets and the metrical scheme. But would a gifted French translator be able to put it into French either? I'm not a linguist, but for me the straightforward Americanized syntax takes it out of French almost entirely. And this cultural doubleness is what gives the original poem its edge. For isn't it clear in Laughlin's French that the poem is, however light, a poem of amorous jealousy, that these "petites histoires tendres" are much more than "tender little tales"? The sexuality of the poem is what Laughlin's Americanized French conveys but the translation does not. And I suspect that a translation into full literary French would have to be, not necessarily more explicit, but more heavily couched in innuendo to capture his same quality.

Here is another I particularly like.

LA LUCIOLE

Je te vois voltigeante dans la
nuit et je te poursuis pour t'at-

traper tu es presqu'insaisissable
mais à la fin je te tiens mais

quand j'ouvre la main tu n'es
pas là tu m'as échappé de nou-

veau qu'est-ce que tu chasses
c'est clair que ce n'est pas

moi je plains la vélocité de
tes alternances affectives

mais je ne sais pas si je veux
te faire changer car si tu é-

tais toujours prévisible serais
tu rasante comme les autres?

And the translation:

THE FIREFLY

I see you flashing in the night and try to catch you
But it's almost impossible to seize you
When I open my hand you're not there, you've escaped me again
What are you hunting for?
It's clear that it's not me
I begrudge the speed of your changes of affection
But I don't think I'd want to change you
If you were always predictable
Might you not become as boring as the others?

Here the big difference between the original poem and the translation hinges on *rasante* in the last line. The translation lays all onus of disaffection on the "firefly," but *rasante* means something like "sating" or "surfeiting," not just "boring," which when you think about it lays equal onus on the one who is, or might be, sated, the one who is doing the chasing. Still, this is a difference between pure French and pure English. The spirit or dharma of the poem comes from the intersection of codes, the language neither French nor English. Would any French poem begin with the two straight declarative statements of Laughlin's poem? Immediately the tone of gentle but edgy sexual jealousy makes itself heard. When I first saw this poem in manuscript three or four years ago, I read it with perfect understanding—all except the title. After I had read the text I had to go to my Larousse to find out what *luciole* means. I had guessed it must be something like "firefly," but the topic of the poem is so plainly a young foxy French woman teasing the speaker, who is unmistakably American, that the simile becomes extraneous. And notice the elegance of "tu es presqu'insaisissable / mais à la fin je te tiens . . ." This is very good lyric writing indeed.

Is it that Laughlin's Americanized French sounds a little archaic too? These poems remind me more of something from Auvergne in the old language, descended perhaps through the *Roman de la Rose*, parts of Villon, and Du Bellay, than of anything in contemporary French. I think Laughlin would not be displeased by this.

And of course Laughlin's poems are unpunctuated because medieval manuscripts were unpunctuated too.

Most of Laughlin's French poems are love poems, and so are most of his others. The point has been made that we are deficient in love poems. It's true. You can go through hundreds of books and magazines of serious writing from the past ten or fifteen years and you'll find very few. Why? I don't know, though I'm sure the answer would comprise many complicated factors. But after teaching graduate workshops for ten years I do believe the young people's failure to write poems to their boyfriends and girlfriends is part of the general demoralization caused by the inanity of our popular culture today and the outrage of our political and economic culture. Because young people don't write about much of anything else either, and that's a fact. They have no overriding passion, beyond perhaps an anger too diffuse to be expressed. I'm not surprised that the best love poetry by young people I've read lately has been by black, Latino, native American, Asian, and lesbian and gay poets. Well, Laughlin is of the old school. His love poems are not angry, not beset by any problems that weren't problems for Catullus, Propertius, and Arnaut as well. The freshness of Laughlin's poems, the part that is not old-school, comes, first, from their settings in our own time, the hotels of London and Paris, the restaurants of New York and San Francisco, etc., the undifferentiated inevitable contemporaneity of our own minds; second, from their diction, which is our own natural spoken language minus the jargon; and third, from their authenticity. Without going into Laughlin's personal life, one can say that his love poems are authentic. They were written to or about particular women. Were these women loved in the way of eros or in the way of agape? It is a question people ask. But to my mind, though the terms are classical the distinction between them is decidedly post-classical, not to say churchly and finical. Laughlin's poems, in which you find sexiness but not much sex, are written in the lovely integrated paganism that Christianity comes round to at last in pursuing its own loving ends, and are conceived with this whole evolution in mind.

TO LOVE IS TO HOLD DEAR

to hold the hand if it is
given   or to hold only a

finger if the hand is clo-
sed   to hold all that is

dear be it near or far be
it seen or heard   and if

it be in the unseen that
too is ever close & dear.

Such stunning lyricism within the rigorous metric of counted em
picas. One could do a prosodic analysis of this poem that would go on
and on and would be rewarding down to the last trembling of the oscil-
lograph.

I SAW HER FIRST

on the red-on-black amphora
in the museum at Delphi and

knew at once she was Helio-
dora the girl in Meleager's

poem with her hair in a fil-
let and her tiny feet and her

breasts like white roses then
thirty years later we were to-

gether in a faded room in that
small hotel in the rue de la

Harpe she spoke French of
course and at first she was

shy but then she was tenderly
passionate yes it was Helio-

dora will she ever come back
to me might she even come to

stay I make my prayer to the
gods that Heliodora return.

Many of Laughlin's love poems use classical names and references—never in pedantry but rather for the resonances, the almost tactile warmheartedness, of human eroticism from the beginning. And I can't resist quoting another, which is more than a love poem; it is a compressed philosophy of morals and esthetics.

CARITAS PERFECTA

absolute love was defined by
the Scholastics and Pascal was

not bad on the subject either
but for me it's a personal &

concrete matter that has to
do with you & the way you are

with me which is all of it &
as absolute as anything can be.

You must turn, however, to the poems themselves as they fold against one another in the leaves of this book. Many of them, the love poems and others, may seem rather alike at first, yet each is written with a subtly different focus, a perceivably special gleam of feeling. They support one another, making together a context stronger than the mere linearity of a series. One must gather them into one's reverie collectively, like the tiles of a mosaic.

James Laughlin was born in 1914 in Pittsburgh into the family which had a founding interest in the Jones & Laughlin Steel Corporation. But he left Pittsburgh at an early age—in effect when he went to Choate School in Connecticut at the age of fourteen—and later divested himself of whatever holdings he had in the steel business and, one gathers, of much—but not all; he has always held the family name in good esteem—of the familial and class loyalties he had as a boy. Many of his poems about his childhood are so ironic that they almost, though never quite, break through into asserted bitterness. In "Easter in Pittsburgh," for instance, he refers to "the strike," when he and his brother were sent "out to the farm with mother" for a week for their own protection, and though I'm not sure which strike this was—from the time of the great Homestead strike against Carnegie in 1892 until well into the 1930s strikes by steelworkers in Pittsburgh were common—the attitude of the poet toward his family's involvement in the oppression of the workers is unmistakable. And many other poems, a great many, reflect a similar cast of mind.

Laughlin was not a child of the 1960s, however. His rebellion consisted of becoming a businessman on his own, as in the development of the ski resort at Alta, Utah, which has been a huge success. His rebellion consisted of becoming a writer, a friend of writers—Gertrude Stein, for instance, for whom he worked as chauffeur and general aide in the summer of 1934—and the publisher of many writers whose works his family and their associates would have found shocking, enigmatic, and probably despicable. It consisted of an invariable and mostly serene independence, which led him, for instance, into competitive skiing at an early age and a bad crash and back injury on the Sherburne Trail on lower Mount Washington (yet he continued skiing enthusiastically and many, many years later taught me the rudiments of cross-country skiing in the Litchfield Hills of Connecticut); into a desire to travel in India and Burma in the early 1950s and to study the literary and spiritual traditions of those countries, an interest which shows up in many poems; and into a desire for romantic, practically chivalrous, adventures in practically every corner of the world. An exotic then? A playboy? A prodigy? Yes, something of all these; but a hardworking, ordinary guy as well. At New Directions he has done everything: published, edited, designed, and produced, written ad copy and blurbage, peddled books to the stores, and answered his own phone. Until recently he calculated the royalties himself, and he still sends out handwritten royalty checks against his personal bank account. At his home in Connecticut, where he lives in virtual retirement, he receives and reads copies of outgoing mail and manuscripts from the New York office.

I wonder how many people would be surprised to learn that New Directions, which has published Stein, Pound, Williams, Henry Miller, Rexroth, Patchen, Oppen, the surrealists and lettrists and language poets, has also published Conrad Aiken, Yvor Winters, Mark Van Doren, John Crowe Ransom, and Robert Penn Warren. In connection with his proprietorship of New Directions, Laughlin once wrote:

". . . for better or worse, there has been no editorial pattern beyond the publisher's inclinations, his personal response to the manuscripts which came his way." Thus an additional confirmation of independence.

Incidentally, some years back when I wrote that Laughlin had hurt himself when skiing down Mount Washington as fast as he could, he corrected me. "It was the Sherburne Trail near the bottom of the mountain," he said. In other words Laughlin is a literalist, factualist, and precisionist—you see it if you look at the details in his poems—and it's worth remembering that when he was younger he was a close literary and personal friend of Marianne Moore. Was she an influence too? Her insistence on unsentimental accuracy can be found in his writing, and maybe her complex syllabic verse reinforced Laughlin's typewriter metric as well.

Beyond his friendships with the great originators of modernism, Laughlin has been close to many writers of his own generation, people like Delmore Schwartz, Thomas Merton, Kenneth Rexroth, Edward Dahlberg, Kenneth Patchen, Tennessee Williams, Dylan Thomas, Lawrence Ferlinghetti, Denise Levertov, and dozens of others. Yet in his own work he has never, I mean never, shown the least tendency to imitate any of these writers, and this is impressive. What is also impressive is that with a few important exceptions—Schwartz, Ferlinghetti, Levertov—none of these writers has shown much regard for Laughlin's own poetry nor any notion of helping to promote it. Perhaps they thought he must be powerful enough to promote it himself. Or perhaps—just perhaps—writers are such monsters of ego that they can't take an interest in any writing unlike their own, especially a publisher's. Fact: a publisher's or editor's role is to be on the receiving end of a constant one-way stream of authorial self-aggrandizement. It gets pretty tiresome.

But Laughlin did not promote himself. His first four or five books were small, were published obscurely, and distributed primarily to friends. Much of his writing was filed away in typescript. Though he won awards and distinctions as a publisher, both in this country and abroad, few people knew his poetry and he remained in the literary background. (The only prize he has won for his poems, a good one but a foreign one, is the French Prix Malrieu, which was given in 1987 to a book of translations from his poetry by Alain Bosquet.) Then his *Selected Poems*, a book much smaller than the present *Collected Poems* but

618

still comparatively sizable, was published in 1986 by City Lights in San Francisco, and more readers, including a few critics and reviewers, became acquainted with his work. At the same time, or a little earlier, Laughlin had begun publishing essays about his experiences with Stein, Pound, H.D., Djuna Barnes, Williams, and other early modernists, and about his understanding of their lives and works, from which it was clear that he was extremely knowledgeable and critically sensitive. His years of editing had given him more insight into and sympathy for different kinds of creative aptitude and disposition than he—or probably anyone—could have gotten in school. As a consequence he was invited to various universities to lecture. He was an adjunct professor for two years at Brown University, for instance, where he did courses on Pound and Williams; he traveled to other universities for conferences and seminars. He became, in other words, a more conspicuous figure on the general literary scene than he had been before as a publisher and editor. And now this hefty new collection of his own poems in all their variety and brilliance will certainly bring much more attention to his work and verify his place among the best American poets of his time.

In a letter to me Laughlin once wrote: "What my poems are about is the juxtaposition of contemporary life with ancient cultures." He was trying to do what writers always try to do: boil it all down to the nub. This is how writers save their lives and consciences, by doing their damnedest to be *objective* about the long, long, devilishly hard work into which they have put their hearts and souls and minds. And no doubt Laughlin's letter does in a way offer an approach to his intentions. The destruction of cultures, the loss of values and meanings, is for him simply awful. The continuity of human imaginative goodness, from Lao-tse and Li Po and the masters of the Hindu classics to Homer, Catullus, Dante, Villon, and so on down to the few splendid writers of our own time, is for him indispensable and is what all of us, in our extreme predicament, can truly rely on. In his small poems, which are not so small, this idea is what he has fortified and nurtured; his poems are a work of salvage. On the other hand the statement in his letter is reductive, obviously. His poems are also about language, about sex, love, injustice, the poignancy of existence, about a thousand other things, as every reader of this book will discover.

Even this does not go far enough, however. For no poet can say what his or her poems are about, because no poet can *see* what his or her poems are about. Isn't it so? James Laughlin's poems are about James Laughlin. No felicity of attitude nor fervor of intention nor incisiveness of topic or belief can add one atom to the enduring resources of human culture. Without Laughlin's unique joining of knowledge and feeling in his own mind—and I say *unique* advisedly—without his independent sensibility, his poems would be no more than the products of any good workshop in the schools. But how far they are from anything of the kind! It is plain as the nose on anyone's face that these poems are exceptional. Nothing else like them exists. I have not mentioned, in the interest of decent brevity, his translations, his poems in what he calls "dog-Latin," his picture poems (done with scissors, rubber cement, and a Canon copier), his long-line elegies and other discourses, his parodies, or the really wonderful poems by his friend Hiram Handspring, an obstreperous comic doppelgänger who can say things that wouldn't fit into poems written in propria persona. And then, finally, those poems near the end of the book about the death of his son Robert, few in number but among the most compelling of their kind I've ever read—see if it isn't so. All these add variety and liveliness to this collection; all add to the representation of Laughlin's sensibility.

And this—what we sometimes call "voice" or "personality" or "spiritual propensity" or even "genius," but which is rather the whole individual human indescribability—is what makes James Laughlin's poems a distinct and fascinating part of the literature of this century and, in the manner of classical impersonality—for who was Catullus but a name?—of all the centuries before.

—HAYDEN CARRUTH

I TAKE A CERTAIN PRIDE

in the fact that in my verses
it is not extremely difficult
to tell what I'm trying to say.

from **A SMALL BOOK OF POEMS**

THE LITTLE DOG LAUGHS

Credo ut intellegam
this little lead dog
silver paint Airedale

MADE IN JAPAN costs
only ten cents at the
5&10 but her life goes

past shall I wrap it
to nightschool and a
future all her own

credo ut intellegam?
the little yellow men
and women love their

emperor (costs only ten
cents) they all would
die for him they all

would   some nights her
feet hurt so after ten
hours on them   chiliasm

isn't Chile but when He
cometh when He cometh
(sang in school) and oh

when will they see why
the pen is quicker than
the shovel? yes, never!

623

let them all die for him
let her feet hurt because
credent ne intellegant

&

this little dog laughs
to see such a mess and
the cat has more lives

than you or I want!

from **SELECTED POEMS**

MY GRANDDAUGHTER

Daphne (age 2) can't say
her "f's"   she shows me the

pictures of "girasses" in
her book & when she brushes

her teeth she asks if she
can have a "dental sauce."

more STOLEN POEMS

A MOMENT ON EARTH

She was quite mad (paranoid
or schizoid or both) but out

of her head (with its lovely
Etruscan profile) would come

(without any sense of or-
ganization) small groups of

words which were the stuff
of an extraterrestrial poetry

of course she herself didn't
know it was poetry (or care)

but often I wrote down her
words and tried (with no suc-

cess) to arrange them into a
formal poem   she killed her-

self one rainy night in Sara-
gosa by hurling herself in

front of a bus   this was I
knew to be expected   that

she would disappear from my life
and her mysterious un-

intelligible verses with her.

LONGLINE POEMS

DYLAN

One of us had to make the official identification of Dylan's body at
    the Medical Examiner's Morgue
Brinnin and I tossed a coin and I lost
It was a crummy building in the hospital complex on First Avenue
    and the basement, smelling of formaldehyde, was a confusion of
    trolleys with rubber sheets covering bodies
A little old man in a rubber apron was in charge
He put on his glasses to read the name I had written on a slip of
    paper and looked around, trying to remember
He lifted one sheet. "Is this him?" It wasn't
Two or three more who weren't "Old Messy" of the pubs of Soho and
    Chelsea
Finally we found him and he looked awful, all bloated
"Insult to the brain" was what it said on the autopsy report, too
    much booze for too many years
The old man sent me to a window to confirm the identification
    where there was a little girl about five feet high, struggling with
    the forms, using a pencil stub
She got me to write "Dylan" for her on the form because she had
    never heard of such a name and couldn't spell it
"What was his profession?" she asked
I told her he was a poet; she looked perplexed
"What's a poet?" she asked
I told her a poet was a person who wrote poems
She put that down, and that's what it says on the form:
Dylan Thomas—a poet (he wrote poems).

1953

YOUR EARLY LIFE

For Variety

What were you like when you were a little girl, down there in
  Montevideo,
where your brother drowned in the River Plata, or did he really
  drown, you say they never found his body, a catastrophic trauma
  for the family, especially you other children?
But you've never shown me a picture and I can't visualize you then or
  hear you speaking Spanish,
or was it mostly French because of Mam'selle Claude who came from
  Tours, where the most perfect French is spoken, who made you
  copy out pages and pages of irregular verbs and made fun of your
  little drawings of animals and birds,
what has become of them, didn't you save any of them, I'd like to see
  them.
And what did the great poet Supervielle say when you met him in
  your grandmother's salon,
surely he must have taken such a pretty little girl on his knee and
  told her some enchanting story, perhaps about the *voleurs d'en-
  fants*, though he would not have frightened you.
Why can't you remember how you got that little scar on your
  shoulder?
What children's illnesses did you have—measles, chicken pox,
  whooping cough, fevers indigenous to the region?
Apart from your brother's drowning, what was the worst thing that
  happened to you when you were little, and what was the best?
Did you wear ribbons in your hair or a barrette, did you have a charm
  bracelet, did you have a little gold cross on a chain?
Were you allowed to keep bunnies in a hutch in the garden?
  Somehow I don't think you had a dog, it would have messed up
  the flower beds that old Ernesto, whom you children called Erizo
  (the hedgehog) was so proud of.
Did you believe the things the sisters told you that year you were at
  the convent when Mam'selle Claude had gone back to Tours to
  help with her mother's dying?

628

Did parrots ever come to the garden, did you pick up their feathers
and save them? I don't think there could have been monkeys in
the city, and I hope there weren't snakes. Probably there were
toads and snails. Did Mam'selle Claude tell you not to touch
toads because they would give you warts?

Why have you never mentioned excursions into the country, don't
they have picnics down there?

But of course you would not have gone to the beach after what
happened to your brother.

The miniature of your mother in your locket is very beautiful, which
does not surprise me as you are so beautiful.

There is no picture of your father, but I imagine him as rather severe,
with a full beard, very dignified as befitted a successful merchant
who ran for alcalde of the city, even though he lost.

Why do I see you in an outfit of lacy, beribboned pantaloons, am I
just remembering a painting by Renoir or did you really wear
them?

Was there a time when you were a tomboy, climbing the biggest
trees in the garden?

Who were your closest girlfriends, certainly you would not have been
allowed to have any boyfriends, or to go in the streets without
Mam'selle Claude or a servant.

There are some other questions I would like to ask you but they
might seem indelicate.

But I do have to see you and hear you speaking, I must know as
much as possible about what you were like as a little girl.

from **FUNNY PAPERS BY HIRAM HANDSPRING**

L'ABÉCÉDÉRIEN DE LA LUBRICITÉ*

Si tu le permets, je veux prendre ton *arrière-train* pour rejoindre
    Henri Miller à Dijon
Je veux déguster ton *artiche* comme les feuilles d'un artichaut sauce
    hollandaise
Stupéfait de luxure, je prendrai ta *baba* au rhum Jamaica
Dans le costume de Monsieur Hulot je descendrai de ma cabine à
    roues pour me plonger dans ton *baigneur*
Je suis l'avocat de ton *bavard*, je te défendrai bien, tu n'iras pas au
    cachot
Quant aux *brioches*, je préfère les croissants, mais s'il s'agit des tiennes,
    elles me conviennent
Quand j'étais le plus petit à table on voulait toujours me donner le
    croupion du dindon; maintenant que je suis star de cinema j'ai de
    plus grandes exigences
Mon enfance était vraiment dure; ma mère faisait fumer mon *dargif* à
    coups de sa brosse à cheveux; je ne te veux pas comme maman
Derechef je dis, je suis grand lecteur mais pas hypocrite; je suis
    pingre deton *derche*
C'est vrai que la police tient mon dossier à jour, mais je ne suis pas
    dangereux; puisque tu ne portes que des pantalons de ski je ne
    pense pas que tu aies un slip à *dossière*
Je dois admettre que je ne sais pas grand'chose des *entremichons* mais
    les lignes de ton corps sortent d'un dessin du Tintoret
C'est dans le *Faubourg* St. Germain que souvent je te vois avec ton amie
    Oriane de Guermantes; tu portes aussi des pantoufles rouges
Qui était le *Père Fouettard?* Je pourrais écrire sa biographie de toutes
    pièces mais ça me prendrait du temps. J'espére que ça n'a rien à
    faire avec les fouets; je ne vais jamais te faire de mal
Ne t'inquiète pas de ton *gagne-pain*: je m'en chargerai afin que tu
    n'aies jamais besoin de te défendre comme ces pauvres filles dans
    l'histoire de Momo et Madame Rosa

* Translation in Notes.

Une *miche,* ça sonne comme une niche, qui est jolie, mais aussi
comme une mouche, qui ne l'est pas. Alors je préfère la précé-
dente. Quant aux niches, j'aime à la folie la niche de gauche de
Bérénice quand elle essaie de la mettre dans son verre à vin.

On ne peut rien faire avec les *mouilles* qui ne soit pas, à mon avis,
assez crasseux et dégueulasse, par exemple se torcher

Est-ce imbécile de dire qu'une paire de *noix* est belle? chacun à son
goût; il y a des gens qui aiment les mordre, je le sais

Oui, je suis con comme un *panier* mais ce n'est pas toi qui m'as rendu
idiot

On dit en anglais qu'on est "hoist with one's own *pétard*"; ça arrive
quand on se met en colère pour un rien

Le *pétoulet* est une rara avis qui habite les jungles lointaines de
l'Amazonie et jouit d'un lien symbiotique avec des fourmis; il n'y
en a pas en France sauf dans les livres pornographiques

Quelqu'un a dit que je suis paysan parce que je bouffe à six heures du
soir mais je n'ai jamais de ma vie mangé de *petrousquin*

Comme tu sais, en latin petra veut dire une pierre, mais *pétrus* n'a
assurément rien à faire avec Saint Pierre; l'Eglise de Rome n'est
pas fondée sur l'enculement

C'est sans doute un problème pour le philosophe des Ecoles (ou pour
le bon docteur Lacan?): est-ce que le *pont arrière* est plus attirant
que le Pont d'Avignon? Mais c'est le pons asinorum qui m'attire
le plus

Ah non, il y a des bêtises que font les enfants, comme manger le
popotin, qu'on doit oublier; ce n'est pas leur faute, ils ont tant de
curiosité, et pourquoi pas, le corps est aussi inexplicable que la vie

Je saute *postère*; toujours la même chose; c'est merdique. Il m'arrive un
soupçon honteux: la posterité de Charlemagne aime mieux le cul
que le con. Peau de zob, ma défonceuse!

J'ai toujours eu une manque de *pot* avec les fentes, je suis trop mono-
mane, je leur donne des complexes; mais un jour 'y aura une qui
verra combien je suis sympa

Tu penses que *prose* veut dire La Rochefoucauld? Polope, ma pisseuse,
c'est encore cette histoire d'où sort la merde; mais si c'est de la
prose, qu'est-ce que la poésie? Raconte-moi ça!

Ça continue avec *prosinard,* même chose; j'en ai assez, je vais chercher
une michette pour me divertir

Et voilà *tafanard*; c'est la même chanson. Ils sont loquaces ces culards, ces shnoques. Ils me font chniquer

Au moins *troussequin* est un mot de quelque substance. Ça vient de trousser, c'est à dire de posséder une femme. C'est pas trop tôt! Elle allait s'endormir

La *turbine à chocolat*, c'est certainement graphique, ou comme disent les matelots "suivre le chemin de crotte"

"Hello, I'm Marilyn Monroe," j'étais la princesse des *valseurs*, je savais tortiller mes fesses en marchant; toutes les reines des vaches m'ont imitée

Je vais mieux dans la vase, c'est quand j'ai de la chance avec les nanas, quand j'ai du *vase* et je fais zizi-panpan et m'amuse bien.

RANDOM POEMS

ADMONITION

To tie a girl up with string
as if she were a package for

future delivery is no longer
an acceptable procedure   times

have changed and certain at-
titudes must be reconsidered.

CATULLUS V

Let us live, my Lesbia, and let us love each other,
caring nothing for what jealous old men may say
      about us.
Suns set and then they rise again,
but when our sun sets, that brief light, there will
      be only a perpetual night of slumber.
Give me a thousand kisses, and a hundred more,
another thousand and a second hundred,
then another thousand and another hundred.
And when we have kissed many thousand times
we will lose count but go on kissing
so that no one with the evil eye
can hurt us or stop our endless lovemaking.

DEATHFEAR

get out of here   get
out of my godown out

of my neat storehouse
where like a squirrel

for winter I've piled
all my methings   yes

they're mine   I found
them   I brought them

I stored them   so get out
of here you hear   it's

not time yet for you
to come   it isn't time.

DE CONTEMPTU MUNDI

wrote Bernard of Cluny (al-
most 3000 lines of it with

rhymes both vertical & hori-
zontal)   he sure was right and
[
it hasn't gotten any better
hic breve vivitur hic breve

plangitur hic breve fletur
and yet and yet when on your

loveliness I gaze and hear
your lovely laughter dulce

ridentem maybe it's not as
bad as Bernard said it was.

FLAVIUS TO POSTUMIA

O in her bower let me lie,
My soul there to restore;
If she deny me I would die
And worship her no more.

In Heaven other angels are,
Less beautiful than she,
But having in their hearts, methinks,
A greater charity.

Oft in my youth I was too proud
And did a fair one spurn,
But now I pay a double price
As for her love I burn.

O Eros, hear my plaintive cry
And let me in her bower lie.

I AM THE METOPOSCOPER

I can look at your forehead
and tell what you are really

like   I learned this skill out
of old books and with a great

deal of trial-&-error prac-
tice   some people think they

can do it without sufficient
training but they make ter-

rible mistakes   they marry the
wrong wife and it comes apart

or they take as a business
partner someone I could have

told them was a real crook
I am the forehead watcher.

IF A POET

can't get the girl
he wants with his

words he'd better
get out of the po-

etry business and
go work in Wall St

and try to buy her.

FOLK WISDOM

holds that cat dander
is a specific for de-

spair (though Webster
gives anger as a second

meaning for dander) when
a poet receives another

rejection slip from the
Atlantic but what if the

poet is allergically aluri-
ophobic should he try

selling real estate the
price of houses is rising.

IF YOU ARE ONLY FLIRTING

tell me before you hurt me I'm
only a shepherd from the hills

I don't know city ways & when
you touch my hand or crinkle

your eyes at me I think that
means that you like me & yet

& yet you do it so sweetly
perhaps it's worth the risk

I fear you are a danger but
you've utterly enchanted me.

I LIKE TO THINK OF YOU

out on the town having
a good time with your

young friends gyrating
your pretty butt to the

aboriginal beat of the
bongo and if when he

brings you home you give
a kiss to the young Picas-

so who took you danc-
ing is that the end of

the world   I doubt it.

IS THERE A DANGER

of turning a girl into an ikon
through excessive admiration

of her corporeal loveliness
can eyes greedy for beauty

calcify like those of the
Medusa   can fingers that

love to touch her harden
the soft flesh   can the

tongue as it kisses leave a
marmoreal coating   beware

O beware   today she is your
living delight   tomorrow she

could be only a monument.

I WANT TO BE ECHOPRACTIC

and copy you as much as I
can with due allowance for

the difference in sex since
you are graceful & delicate

and I am gross & clumsy
I'd like to mirror your

movements your body language
and echo your speech   can I

acquire that little touch of
accent which makes every-

thing you say sound differ-
ent and charming   can I dup-

licate the way you drop your
voice a tone when you begin

a sentence that is teasing
and funny   there are a hun-

dred little signifiers that make
you what I love so much

I study them I watch for them
and I want to be echopractic

I'D LIKE TO BE PUTTY

in your hands you must
shape me into the per-

son you can really love
I have no mirror to see

myself (it's only you I
see) so with your gentle

fingers you must mold me
as you'd like to have me be.

IT WAS THE FIRST TIME

we had made love and I asked
her what she would like me to

do what would give her pleas-
ure   but she wouldn't tell me

she said I must find out for
myself   it would be better so.

THE LAST CARESS

For Variety

When we were sitting side by
side on the banquette in the

restaurant and you told me in
such a distant little voice

that you thought you had fal-
len in love with someone else

you took my hand and pressed
it against your thigh   it was

certainly a gesture of agape
of caritas not one of coquet-

ry and it helped if only some-
what to diminish my despair.

THE LONG-DISTANCE RUNNER

He came out of the womb running
and he's running still from one

part of nowhere to another   show
him a wall and he'll try to hur-

dle it   doesn't he know that on
the other side there's nothing

different   but off in the distance
there's always a mirage (he sees

in it what he wants to see) he must
go faster and faster until he trips

and smashes his head on a stone

M & K

Murine and Kleenex were lovers
And gosh they sure could love,
But was there a little problem,
Who should push and who should shove?

But is that the way they do it?
(I'm such an innocent lad.)
To me it's all a mystery,
And my mother said it was BAD.

MAXIMA DONA FERENS

Quas ad Lucinam tot epistoles
poeta mittet catapultae non

sunt sed simulacra Lucinae tabu-
larum imperiles quot insignes

cordium coniunctorum sperat.

MOON & SUN

May I upon thy beauty gaze,
All liquefaction gone,
And apprehend in full amaze
The beauty of the sun?

Nay, 'tis the moon which is thy mark
For thou art Luna's peer;
Thine absence were the seat of dark
Were not thy moonrise near.

'Twixt sun & moon the battle's joined
Thy beauty to possess,
And many a pretty phrase is coined
Its radiance to assess.

May the globes of light requite my plea;
Then shall I feed my eyes on thee,
Now and in perpetuity.

OBSESSION

is a word with unfortunate con-
notations but I readily confess

that I'm obsessed with you   ob-
sidere is the Latin root and for

Terence that meant "to sit down
near" and indeed I would like to

sit as near you as possible   and
for Caesar it meant "besiege"

but my intentions are the oppo-
site of hostile   with Plautus it

sometimes meant "haunt" and you
do haunt me especially in my

dreams   but let us choose Cicero
for whom it could mean "watch

over"   yes I want to watch over
you with tenderness and care.

THE POWER OF POESY

I did not really realize how much
poetry affected our lives until we
had to block off the back door to

the office because Gregory Corso
would come roaring in through it
unannounced to borrow five dollars

or explain about love & life &
death & poetry or ask to borrow
my desk chair for the electric

chair in his new film and now
every time I wish to visit the
gent's room I have to walk all

the way around by the switchboard
through the reception room yes
the power of poesy is very great.

SHE SAID IN APOLOGY

they aren't very big are
they but I told her let

us not be concerned with
minute particulars it is

the inner light I cherish.

PAINTINGS IN THE MUSEUMS OF
MUNICH AND VIENNA

SHAMEFUL BEHAVIOR

Cranach's *Lot and His Daughter*
is such a shameful picture I

won't attempt to describe it
they both deserved to burn &

drinking at the same time!

SIC TRANSIT CORPUS MUNDI

In Geertgen van Haarlem's
Destiny of Earthly Remains

we see that there has al-
ways been a parking prob-

lem in the cemetery   a new-
comer is being lowered in-

to his grave while below
a man is shoveling old

bones into a bonfire.

THE IMPORTANCE OF READING

In Jan de Beer's *Martyrdom of
the Apostle Matthew* the holy

man is still reading his book
as the axe comes down on his

neck (he is a veritable Har-
old Bloom) richly dressed

officials watch the event
with complete indifference.

"LAY DOWN HIS SWEET HEAD"

In Brueghel's *The Search
for a Lodging* Mary is

warming the baby's bot-
tom at a brazier and a

little dog has curled
itself up in the cradle.

THE GOLDEN AGE

In Cranach's *Golden Age* plants
and flowers extend their leaves

and blossoms to cover the pu-
denda of the naked couples who

are disporting themselves in a
ring around the apple tree   near

them 2 baby lions & 4 deer
are having a good time too.

THE BEAUTY OF ART

The Beauty of Art is eternal
but female pulchritude has

diminished since I came here
first in 1933   the girls now

have large feet like small
boats and they look as if

they had been sucking lemons.

A PROBLEM OF STRUCTURE & LANGUAGE

In Brueghel's *Tower of Babel*
everybody is busy building

but we know it will all fall
down because they don't know

what they are talking about
& no text understands itself.

SANCTITY

In Holbein's *Martyrdom of*
St. Sebastian the archers

(who look so bored) have
pierced the saint with

many arrows but there is
no blood   this shows us

he was indeed most holy.

WHEN THINGS WERE BETTER

In Cranach's *Paradise* we see
Eve being pulled out of Adam's

stomach by a bearded old man in
a red robe (a neat trick if you

can do it) and many other edi-
fying events are also to be

seen in this beautiful picture.

MOMENTS ON EARTH

SHE IS SO PRACTICAL

and like a boy scout is prepared
the only person I know who saves

catalogs (you never know when
you'll need something or some-

thing will come in handy)   she
has them well organized in plas-

tic sacks from the Korean deli
one for tools one for electrical

gadgets one for linen & pillows
one for adornments & fragrances

one for expansion of her knowl-
edge in various areas (which is

already considerable) one for
household remedies one for

items for the kitchen   oh I a-
dore my collector of catalogs

she is providential   often she
sends me little gifts things

that I never realized I needed
until they arrive in the mail.

NOWADAYS

in the films they fall into bed
like apples dropping off a tree

I guess I'm square but I prefer
the reruns of old pictures where

more is left to the imagination
Miss Hepburn (Audrey that is) only

looks at Mr Grant in a certain
way and you know that's the real

thing love that will last forever.

THE BOX

On the day it was delivered
to the house he saw that the

black metal box was much small-
er than he had expected   it would

fit on the shelf between the Odes
and Satires of Horace   he never

tried to open it of course   each
morning when he came to his study

he checked to make sure that the
box was safe on the shelf   (but

who would want to take it)   then
one day the box looked different

it hadn't been moved but it seemed
bigger   its growth continued from

day to day almost imperceptibly it
grew each night   soon he had to

move it to fit between Burckhardt
and Spengler on the shelf   then

the books near the box began to
change color to become much more

black   when the box would no long-
er fit on one shelf he had to saw

part of the bookcase away   then
the whole room began to turn black

as if the wood had been charred
finally the morning came when the

box was bigger than the room   his
desk was inside the box and there

was no longer a window to let in
light   he himself was inside the

black box a prisoner of blackness.

THE ATMAN

It is taught that the soul
is carried away on the last

breath of the body (animula
vagula blandula wrote the

Emperor Hadrian)   it is waft-
ed aloft on the dying breath

to the place beyond ulti-
mate distance   the place no

man may know or imagine
there to reside invisible

for endless time borne away
into the blessed nothingness.

REAL BONES

I'm glad you're not plump
like the girls of Renoir

with their rumps like pump-
kins   I prefer the slim wom-

en of Modigliani   when I hold
you I can feel the bones of

your spine & your hips   real
bones real girl real sub-

stance that is there for
my fingers to fasten to.

BUILDING 520, BELLEVUE

Building 520 at Bellevue is a temple

It is a shrine to Thanatos, the personification of death, marble and
glass and aluminum with a long inscription on the wall of the
atrium in somewhat cockeyed Latin

Which tells us that this is a joyous place, a hortulus memoriarum, a
garden of fond memories, quis risum non excludet, where laugh-
ter is not banished

There is soft Muzak, Schubert's "Ave Maria" and "Humoresque"
while I was there

The dignified male receptionist in a slightly Renaissance uniform
directed me respectfully to the office of Miss Bland

Miss Bland is loveliness itself, wearing a dress of cheerful, sunny silk

She has been trained, I think, in ballet as well as psychology; she
speaks softly in an accent of either Bryn Mawr or Radcliffe

The drapes of her office match the color of her frock

A most courteous young lady who writes rapidly in a nice script, the
very model of a modern civil servant

"Ah yes," she says, glancing at her computerized list, "you are visit-
ing Number 29, who came to us yesterday morning."

A few more particulars, and then, almost apologetically, "Is there
anything you can tell me, this is for our statistical records, any-
thing about Number 29's last moments, that is the method of
his decease?"

I told her what little I cared to tell her. "Ah yes," she said with a
small sigh, "a kitchen knife," and she wrote that down

Then she pressed a button on her intercom, "May we have Number
29?" She said, "If you'll just take a seat for a moment."

It became a longer and longer moment, then I heard her, quite angry,
on her intercom, "Damn it, Harry, what are you doing with
Number 29 down there?"

She led me through her office to another room, where a sign on the
door said "Viewing Room," a small room where one wall was a
plate-glass window, the whole room bathed in a soft glow from
hidden lights

Here the Muzak was different, it was I think a Richard Rodgers'
   arrangement of "Jesu Joy of Man's Desiring," but very soft
There were comfortable chairs for those who might need them "Shall
   we?" asked Miss Bland, and when I nodded she pressed a button
   beside the window
Number 29 rose slowly from below as if unseen arms were raising
   him on an open palanquin, very slowly he came up from below
He was entirely covered, except for his face and some of his hair in a
   kind of cape, its material of an off-white color, which was like a
   vestment
He resembled one of Manzu's sculptures of a cardinal stretched out
   on his bier
And he had now the long, thin face of his ancestors because there was
   no blood left in him
I spoke silently, to that silent form, saying "I pray you will have a
   good crossing."
And perhaps I only imagined that he answered, "Thanks Dad, thanks
   for coming. I'll miss you. Thanks for everything."
Miss Bland said, very gently, "Is that he?" I told her that was he
When I signed the form she took me out into the light of day.

SORROW

   .

       has its wonders too which
       teach the heart new lines

       what is a son gone a son
       whom life destroyed   a son

       is a little sack in which we
       poured part of ourselves

       some of our breath some of
       our blood and when the son

has taken himself away the
sack is empty and will hold

nothing else again   before
God this is a strange won-

der   a line we never read be-
fore nor ever wished to read

the sorrow of this wonder
will remain   the wonder of

this sorrow will remain.

THE BAVARIAN GENTIAN

For Gritli Haensli

You picked a gentian
that day we spent in

the alpine meadow above
Mittenwald and with a

kiss pressed it into
the pages of the book

from which I was read-
ing you the poems of

Lawrence   later it fell
from the book but left

a brownish stain where
it had been placed with

love   a mark & a memory.

CAN I CATCH UP WITH THE FUTURE?

It's out there ahead of me
I'm sure it's there   some-

times I can almost touch it
as if it were not a mirage

but something tangible like
the pencil I'm holding   the

future is bound to happen
as surely as the past has

happened   but will I be
in it   will I still be alive

and where will you be   that's
what really matters   will we

be together   that's why I'm
running to catch the future.

THE DEATH WALKERS

Both of them were walking toward
their separate deaths   their con-

versations (if you could call their
talking that) were distinct mono-

logues   each of them had to tell
his story but they didn't really

listen to the other's tale   as
they drew nearer to their deaths

the isolation was intensified
he began to grow deaf and had

to ask what? what? when he heard
the sound of her voice coming

toward him   he had to put him-
self in touch with a jolt   he

had to force himself to join
her when they should have

been walking hand in hand.

A CURIOUS ROMANCE

He would write a message to her
with his finger in the dust on

some table top in the old family
house (deserted since the grand-

parents had died) and when she
came there (perhaps years later)

she would answer him (they were
cousins who had known each other

only in childhood) this exchange
went on for a long time until her

death   the caretaker understood
and did not obliterate their de-

clarations   the words can still
be deciphered by a visitor who

opens the curtains to the light.

THE DARK MUTINOUS SHANNON WAVES

I have heard them as I lie
sleepless at night & later

seen them in dreams   who
led me here   who left me

here alone   whose voice is
now silent   whose form is

hidden   will anyone return
to speak with me bringing

a message   or is it time
for me to set out in the

falling snow on my journey
into the region where dwell

the vast hosts of the dead?

THE DEEP POOL

I want you to plunge into my life
as if you were diving into a deep

pool in the sea   let nothing be
hidden from you   hold your breath

and swim underwater to explore
every crevice in the rock and

the coral   make your way through
the undersea vegetation question-

ing the strange creatures which
you may encounter   let the fish

gossip with you about me   ques-
tion the giant squid and the

poisonous stingray   they can
tell you much about me (some of

which you may not like to hear)
let nothing be hidden   you must

know me as I was before you came.

FOR THE FIRST TIME

he sat down with his arms
on the table and his head

bent down onto his arms
it was a position in which

he might be found by some-
one who had noticed his ab-

sence at work and come to
look for him in the house

he had been thinking about
positions for several weeks

he wanted one that would
look natural as if he had

just fallen asleep (on his
bed perhaps or in an arm-

chair or even lying on the
floor) but this was the

first time he had actually
assumed a position mod-

eling it as if he were sitting
for the brush of an artist.

THE HOLY RIVERS

The veins on the back of my hand (now that I'm old) stand out like
rivers on a map. The two largest veins are the Brahmaputra and the
Ganges which converge near Howrah and flow into the Bay of
Bengal. The Brahmaputra rises in Tibet and carries down to the
plains the Tantric wisdom of the Buddhist lamas. The goddess Ganga
sprang from the feet of Vishnu high in the Himalayas and became
the flowing hair of Shiva Nataraja as he danced the world into
existence. One early morning at Benares I saw ten thousand pilgrims
drinking the filthy water of the Ganges to purge themselves of sin
and watched the burning of the dead on the ghats along the river's
edge. All this is imagined in the veins of my hand. I ask you to take
it in yours and trace the holy rivers with your finger.

I CANNOT COMMAND YOU

to obey me in my dreams
my power is insufficient

and such favors cannot
be bought   I could dangle

the baubles of a princess
and you would only smile

and avert your eyes   some-
times your figure in the

dream is taken by a shadow
a shadow that could be that

of anyone (or no one)   the
shadow is mute   once I or-

dered a slave to beat the
shadow   no master the slave

replied such an act would
bring retribution upon us

both   the shaman agreed
she is without evil and

protected by her innocence
she is inviolate   you are

a powerful king but you
will never compel her to

do your will in your dreams.

IN EGYPT'S LAND

There were two who imagined
each other   it was all good

and satisfying for both of
them each dreaming his dream

until he became frightened
it wouldn't last and tried

to turn her into reality
that was a fatal mistake.

FLOATING

but not with joy
somewhere between

water and sky be-
tween past and fu-

ture floating be-
tween the light and

darkness between
the known and the

unknown powerless
to direct any move-

ment only able to
wait & keep floating.

SHE ASKS ME

if I really believe in the gods
I tell her I do but explain that

the gods are drunk a lot of the
time at their nonstop parties

up there on Olympus   we must be
mindful that it is more or less

an accident if for a few brief
moments they pay attention to

663

their job of looking after us
down here below   don't count on

the gods and don't waste money
on expensive sacrifices   if they

respond to our prayers it is
usually just a whim or because

we are pawns in a row with some
other god or they are irritated

by a bad throw in their tedious
games with the dice   the gods

are endlessly bored   it is a
very dull profession and the

weather never changes   yet the
gods can at times be useful to

poets as furniture to fill an
empty space or two in a poem.

LAYERS

that don't peel like an onion
not tightly joined   perhaps

more like those little Russian
wooden dolls where six identi-

cal shapes fit perfectly in-
side each other   now add time

and you have it   the layer of
childhood   the layer of ado-

lescence   the layer of blos-
soming (whatever form that

takes) and so on to the layer
the Hindus call the ashram age

when we live in the forest
or go through the villages

with our begging bowls   and
yet however hard we try to

find the great nothingness
to escape the layers they

are always there unforget-
ably wrapped around us de-

termining what we will be.

MY INSTRUCTIONS

MAKE IT SIMPLE

make it so simple a child
of six can understand the

words (if not the sense)
then take out all the words

that aren't doing anything
useful   so Ezra instructed me

665

breaking the point of his
pencil as he stabbed at

the offending words   and
Bill told me also to make

it simple   as simple as
something you might see

walking down Ridge Road
to the drugstore   whatever

you see with your own eyes
can be real   but make what

you saw as plain as you can.

WITH A COLD FLAME

boil it down said Ken-
neth   try to reduce it

to a skeleton or to a
tiny crystal   but a

crystal reflecting light
let there be few edges

in its shape no more than
those in a grain of sand

boil it down but boil
it with a cold flame.

MERRY MADNESS HALL

Here we are in Merry Madness Hall
where all the fools are dancing

the language poets are licking
each others' ears   the maha-

rishis are doing obscene katha-
kali   the fake geniuses are mix-

ing crack and booze   the decon-
structionists will only waltz

backwards   the Soho painters are
dripping their silly messes on

the carpets   what makes a whole
generation go barmy   who knows

but it's happened before   you can
find all of them in Hieronymus

Bosch's *Garden of Earthly Delights.*

NOW STRIKE THE GOLDEN LYRE AGAIN

that I once more thy dulcet voice
may hear intoning sounds my heart

can hardly bear so soft so sweet
they are   but yet I know one day

this music must cease for me and
then the air itself will grieve.

READING THE OBITUARY PAGE IN
THE TIMES

He was a messy sort of person
who never quite finished any-

thing he started   there was a
garden of girls who had found

him unsatisfactory for one rea-
son or another   with men friends

he was the master of the short
conversation   after ten minutes

there was really nothing more to
say   the truth was that he dis-

liked himself extremely   he had
to press his brains against his

skull to understand anything
more difficult than the news-

paper   all his life he never
understood what made a car

run   computers were out
of the question   in old age he

became foolish about money try-
ing to make more go out than

came in   this annoyed the bank
and worried the children   he

didn't kill himself but he
constructed his death as if

he were drawing diagrams
for a newly born Euclid.

REMEMBRANCE

It was too good to be changed
what we had there in Austria

that summer when we were young
(I liked it best when you wore

your dirndl and put your hair
in a long braid)   now two quite

different people will be meeting
again for the first time in many

years   different people meeting
shyly and tentatively   studying

each other with curiosity   do
you remember we'll each say   do

you remember when we swam in
the lake near Sankt Wolfgang

do you remember our walks in
the Belvedere Gardens   memo-

ries are secure   let there be
no interference from the pre-

sent and so no disappointment.

A SLEEPLESS NIGHT

and I find myself remembering
Delmore's torments of insomnia

and his frightening death in
that shabby hotel after he had

driven away all his friends
with his violent accusations

dear Delmore sober or drunk
the funniest man I ever knew

I reach for my pad and try to
force out of a sullen head a

line or two that might get
through to you (wherever you

are) but nothing will come
that could make you laugh

then the whole ceiling of my
darkened room becomes an enor-

mous TV screen where you
are lying in an open coffin

your face puffed up with under-
taker's wax your hair slicked

down your eyes glued shut your
lips smeared over with rouge.

THE SACKS

Coming down the village lane
I overtook an old man carrying

two sacks one over each shoul-
der   I could tell how heavy

they were by the way he stag-
gered as he walked   let me

help you I said give me one
of the sacks   thank you he

answered but I must carry
them both myself one of mine

and one hers   but what's in
them I asked   if you don't

know what is in them there's
no point in my telling you

when I lost sight of him his
knees were buckling from the

weight but both sacks were
still slung over his back.

THE SCRIBE

For Cynthia Zarin

She is listening and writing
as he is telling her his life

her eyes are on her notebook
as she writes   the movement

of her pen makes a soft scur-
rying sound   telling and lis-

tening and writing his life
races along on her page but

is it a true telling we are
hearing (a life has crevices

where error collects)   now and
then her pen stops moving and

her eyes rise from the page
as she questions him about

his life with a grave and
doubting glance   is what he

is telling her true or is it
only Mara   is it illusion a

life that never happened.

OUT IN THE PASTURE

the sheep have formed
a nibbling ring around

the old horse   all they
do is munch grass but

it's like a conversation.

&

two newborn lamb twins
have lain down near the

mother ewe   they're tired
from sucking because she

keeps pulling away from
them as if she were bored

with them   three white
stones against the green

field   one big one and
two small ones like those

stones in the Kyoto garden.

SNOW IN MAY

When I looked out the win-
dow I thought it had snowed

in the night because the
blossoms of the shadblow

made such a whiteness and
my true love told me (hop-

ing I guess to entertain me)
that she can count 34 lovers

and I replied that her tally
doesn't make me jealous though

I am nearly twice her age
and can barely recall half

that number (and most only
fleeting shadows) for she

who is last is the best the
most passionate and the most

tender the only one I want
to remember when it is time

to make the dark journey.

TEMPORARY POEMS

Sam'l Johnson in his famous
dictionary (1755) defined

Grub Street as the name of
a street in London "much in-

habited by writers of small
histories and temporary poems"

even small histories are too
much for me but I think I

can grub out a few temporary
poems which like the blossoms

of the columbine may last a-
bout three days   to hope for

a longer life for them would
only be another example of

"the vanity of human hopes."

THE STRANGER IN THE HOUSE

There was a stranger in the
house   he had been there a

long time but never became
a part of the family   for

years (try as he would) he
could not make himself one

of them   they shared the
same blood but were never

of the same mind   whatever
the stranger said it wasn't

the right thing to please
them   he lived in a little

forgotten room in the at-
tic   no one ever visited

him there except a young
girl who appeared to him

in his dreams but she was
always gone when he awoke.

THE TRAGEDY OF TIME

is that when we
were children

and first sus-
pected its exist-

ence it seemed
to us to be end-

less but years
later when we had

to confront an
ending we came to

understand that
time does not

really exist and
isn't something

from which we
can take comfort.

THE PRISONER'S SONG

No I'm not in Sing Sing
this prison is inside my-

self   its bars are my
bones my skin is its

wall   who but I was the
judge who passed sen-

tence upon me   memory
was the chief witness

against me   after such
testimony I could only

admit my guilt   and now
memory is my jailor   I

have no hope of pardon
nor any hope of escape.

TWO CHILDREN

play children's games   one
is a boy and one is a girl

so they play games like I'll
be the doctor and you be the

nurse or they make a house
out of chairs from the kitch-

en and old sheets   but they
aren't too old for the sand

box   that sometimes ends in
tears when they get tired

of castles and start throw-
ing sand at each other   but

mostly they get on pretty
well there are no other

children their age on the
block for them to play with

but in the house nextdoor
there is a very old woman

who watches them play
and takes delight in their

games   she savors their in-
nocence   it helps her for-

get for a while things she
doesn't want to remember.

YOUR EYES

In those days when we were
first together you used to

keep your eyes tight closed
while we were making love

I called you my sleeping
beauty and you said you

could see me clearer see
inside me when your eyes

were closed   but I was jeal-
ous imagining they were

shut because you wanted to
watch him (the other one)

at those moments (feel my
touch but see him)   then

I made the forbidden voyage
over the black water (the

voyage forbidden to Brah-
mins) and now that I have

returned unscathed your eyes
are wide open when we embrace

they are as open as the bronze
eyes of Sita in the temple at

Patna   they pierce me with love.

WHAT MATTERS

There's an old drunk
who sleeps on the side-

walk near my office   he
covers himself with news-

papers from the trashcans
if it rains   his eyes are

too bad to read so he
doesn't know about the

hostages   and if he did
he wouldn't give a damn

he doesn't seem to mind
being homeless   all he

cares about is how soon a
passerby will give him

enough change for his pint.

THE WELCOME

Before sleep comes I put down
my book and lie on the bed

eyes closed remembering friends
who have already gone where I

too must soon go   in this peace-
ful darkness I see their faces

clearly just as they were before
age came upon them   there's

George with the sardonic lip-
twist in his smile and Robert

cocking his head a bit to the
side as he speaks   and there's

dreamy Jack who seems to be
looking at something in the

distance   these and a dozen
more come crowding to greet me

they stretch out their hands
to welcome me just as Proclus

and Simonides bid welcome
to Meleager as he stepped

ashore there in my book.

TWO PARABLES FROM *THE OCEAN OF STORY*

STORY OF THE SNAKE WHO TOLD HIS SECRET TO A WOMAN

A snake who was afraid of the birdgod Garuda
Took the form of a man and hid himself in the house of a courtesan.
This courtesan was very adept in the ways of giving pleasure;
She usually received a gift of five hundred elephants.
With the magic power of *nagas* the snake was able to give her five
    hundred elephants every night.
The courtesan cajoled him to tell her who he was and how he
  could
        obtain so many elephants.
Mad with love for her, the snake confessed that he was really a *naga*
    turned human
Who was hiding for fear of Garuda.
"Don't tell anyone my secret," he warned her;
But she told everything to her procuress.

In the form of a man Garuda had been searching the world for the
    snake.
By chance he came to the house of the courtesan and approached the
    procuress.
"I'd like to be entertained here for the night; I'll pay of course."
"Let me tell you," she replied, "We have a snake living here,
A very rich snake who gives five hundred elephants; can you match
    that?"
Guessing it must be the snake he wanted Garuda entered the
    courtesan's house.
There he found the snake sunning on the roof.
He changed back into his birdlike form, swooped down, killed the
    snake and ate him.

STORY OF THE FOOL AND THE CAKES

A traveler bought eight cakes for a *pana*
He ate six of them without feeling satisfied
But the seventh cake satisfied his hunger
"I have been cheated," he cried
"Why didn't I eat the last cake first
The one that relieved my hunger?
Why did I waste my money on those other cakes
That I could have saved for another day?
Thus he complained that his hunger was only gradually satisfied
The villagers laughed at him for his ignorance.

CRUCIFIXION IN THE DESERT

There are bones inside
the pain   a voice is ex-

plaining what happened
then another voice pre-

dicts what will happen
the bones try to move

but the pain becomes too
sharp   the bones can only

hang inside the pain   now
the voices are talking

about the blood   don't lis-
ten it won't help   the pain

goes on and does not stop
it will never stop never.

AVE ATQUE VALE

My father

I sat on the edge of the bed
and held his hand   it was dry

and cold   I squeezed the hand
but of course there was no re-

sponse   they had dressed him
in one of his Scottish tweed

suits with the deer's-horn
buttons on the side pockets

and put on the Princeton
(orange and black) tie   I

had come to say goodbye   I
was crying but suddenly my

sadness changed to resent-
ment even to anger almost

to hatred   why are you de-
serting me   how dare you

leave me   in my rage I
pulled up his shoulders

and shook him as hard as
I could   I raised him

further and banged his head
against the pillow   I want-

ed to make him open his eyes
how can you abandon me   you

the one who loved me most.

EXPERIENCE OF BLOOD

I never knew there was so much blood
in a man until my son killed himself

he did it with a kitchen knife stab-
bing himself all over and cutting his

wrists   then he got into the bathtub
and died there in the water   that's

where we found him   but could he have
changed his mind for a moment   the floor

was a carpet of blood & blood was spat-
tered on the walls the basin was cov-

ered with blood   did he stand there
looking at himself in the mirror still

wondering who he really was and then
went on with it   I had to wipe away the

blood   it took me four hours to do it
but I couldn't have asked anyone else

because after all it was my blood too.

THE EMPTY ROOM

My wife Ann

As he passes the open door
he can see there is no long-

er anyone in the room   no one
is lying in the bed and no

one is attending the recum-
bent figure   the water glass

with its bent drinking straw
is gone from the bedside ta-

ble   there are no flowers
in the vase none of her fa-

vorite red and blue anemo-
nes   the window shades have

been raised because the
room need no longer be

kept darkened   now sun-
light is flooding the

room   in its neatness
and emptiness it is for

him a scene of terror
what can he do with

what is left of his life?

A SECRET LANGUAGE

(1994)

A SECRET LANGUAGE

I wish I could talk to your body
less cautiously I mean in a

language as forthright as its
beauty deserves of course

when we make love there is the
communication of touch fingers

on flesh lips on innermost
flesh but surely there must be

a kind of speech body in body
that is even deeper than such

surface touching a language
I haven't yet learned or haven't

learned well enough hard as
I've tried will I ever master

that secret language for you?

DOES LOVE LOVE ITSELF

the most sometimes I've suspected
that may be true a new person comes

into my life (and I into hers) we
are together as much as possible

discovering who we are and what we
can be to each other   no day but has

its little adventure of the feelings
but then as we become more habitual

the thought may occur what is it
that is really taking place   am I

in love only with her or am I
like the insatiable Don in Mozart's

opera infatuated with the idea of
being in love again of being

attached to someone new is the god
Eros self-regardant that busybody

of the myths did he like Narcissus
become his own mirror   does love

love itself the most?

THE COUNTRY ROAD

(1995)

THE DEPARTURE

They say I have to go away soon
On the long trip to nowhere.
Put things in order, they say.
But I've always been disorderly
So why start that now?
Not much time, they say.
What to do with it?
Not much different, I think,
Than what I've been doing.
My best friends have always been
The ones in books.
Read a few pages here, a few there.
No complaints, few regrets,
Thanks to everybody.

THE REVENANT

Others might call what I'm doing
Remembering but that's only the
Starting point. It's raining and
I'm lying on the living room sofa
Listening to some Mozart as I
Go over on the screen in my mind
Some of the things we did when
You were still alive. I see you
So clearly, it's almost as if you
Had just walked in and sat down
Near me. But then the real part
Begins. Yes, I repeat, the real
Part, our life together after
You had died. At first after

Your going I thought that every-
Thing was over. There were many
Empty months, long stretches of
Time when I didn't know what to
Do or where to go. And then, it
Was a miracle, something out of
Another world, you began to make
Your returns. The first time you
Came back (I marked it in my
Diary) was on the third of June
Two years ago. I couldn't touch
You of course though you looked
So real I put out my hand to
Try. You laughed and said, "Get
Up, you lazy man. It's a lovely
Day and we're going to take
A walk up to Old Man McMullen's
Pond; we can skinny-dip there
If there's no one around." And
So it was, the first of many
Times we've been out together.
Of course when people pass
Us they don't see you, they
Greet me as if I were alone.
That doesn't upset me since
I know you're there for real.
I never know ahead which days
You'll be coming but that's
All right. I know you'll come
Again when you can. I work at
Home in my old house at the
Edge of the forest. I'm more
Or less of a hermit and only
Go to the village for food
And the mail about twice a
Week. I think you're very
Generous with your time. I've
Stopped keeping track of the
Days we've had together. I

Don't venture to ask about
Your nights or where you go
When you leave me. We don't
Talk about things like that.
At first our jaunts were only
Here in the neighborhood.
Then you began suggesting
Places further away, some
Quite far away. Last March
It was the Arizona desert
When the wildflowers were
In bloom. I was frightened
About that trip; I had to
Go by plane; what if you
Couldn't get there or find
Me? But you didn't cause me
Worry, you were there at the
Tucson airport when I left
The plane. I had brought
Sleeping bags to camp out
On the floor of the desert
As I like to do every spring
If I can; the cooing of the
Desert doves is a sweet sound
Never to be forgotten. I had
Hopes you would stay with me
But you didn't. Half an hour
After the sun had set you
Promised you would be back
In the morning and dissolved
Into the darkness. One moment
You were there and the next
You weren't. I became more
Confident, I knew now I could
Rely on you. Our trips grew
Long and adventurous. In July
It was the little glacier inn
Above Zermatt and in August
The Due Torre in Verona. But

That was a mistake; we had
Stayed there once when you
Were alive and to be there
Without you was unbearable.

Are we getting too bold, are
We risking the happiness we
Have? For next year we're
Talking about India. When
You were alive we often
Dreamed of going to India.
I had been there but you
Never had. There would be
Days in Kashmir and the
Foothills of the Himalayas.
Jaipur and Benares, where
At dawn thousands bathe to
Wash away their sins. Puri
For the Jagannath festival.
The Caves of Ajanta with the
Buddhist saints smiling their
Eternal smiles. Konarak and
Khajuraho, where the stone
Lovers are forever embracing.
In the south the temples of
Chidambaram and Mahabalipuram.
Yes, we'll be going to India,
The land of all wonders and
Of fabulous transformations.
Sita, the wife of Rama, can
Become Ayonija or Lakshmi.
Siva is Nataraja and Rudra
And Mahadevi and many others.
Will we, in India, be also
Transformed? Will it even be
Granted to us that I may
Touch you and perhaps make
Love to you again?

IS MEMORY

Something we have
Or something we've lost?
How much remains of what
Happened when it first took place?
I imagine that I see you clearly,
Every detail of our first embrace,
That I still hear each word you spoke,
And the tones of your voice
As you spoke them. Yet how much
Of what comes back may be illusion,
Born of longing for what
Might later have been?

THERE'S NEVER A NEVER

in love what once was
lovely can always return

when the storm clears or
the wind drives the clouds

away don't be hasty don't
lock the door of your heart

there's never a never in love.

WHO IS SHE? WHO WAS SHE?

After forty years, perhaps more,
She has reappeared in my life
Of dreams, the beautiful woman
Dressed all in white, with long
Hair and a constant but enigmatic
Smile. The curious thing was her
Silence. She was mute. Though we
Were lovers, she never spoke a
Word to me. She was as quiet as
The night-shrouded grove of
Redwoods in which we used to
Meet. She was passionate but
Without a voice. Never a word,
But always smiling. I remember
Many things about her. She had
Soft and knowledgeable hands
When she caressed me. After an
Hour or so she would disappear.
One moment we would be enlaced
And the next she would be gone.
I would search for her among
The trees but she was not there.

Now that she has returned after
So many years, as real, as vivid
As ever, I hope that she'll enter
My world again, that she'll
Speak to me and tell me her
Name, tell me her story. I'd
Like to be able to summon her
When I have need of her love.

HERE IS MY HAND

take it in yours and open the
fingers to uncover the palm

study the lines of my hand
what do you see in them   are

they veins of a leaf recording
some plan in nature that is be-

yond our understanding   or are
they a map (roads crossing and

roads diverging) which tells
how our fates converged how

we were drawn to each other in
love how there were times when

we lost our way but then re-
joined to be always together.

ANIMA MEA

After we had made love
a girl with big eyes and
warm breath started to
talk about my soul   hush
I said hush and beware
if I have a soul it's
only a box of vanities
tied with frightened
pieces of string.

LITTLE SCRAPS OF LOVE

Your letters, infrequent
But so sweet, so wandering
In what they relate, are
Little scraps of love.
What would I do without them?
They're food when I'm feeling
Hungry for you, so far away.
Please pick up your pencil
As often as you can, even if
It's only for a postcard.
And don't forget the childish
Pictures of us holding hands.

THE SEARCH

She writes that she cannot
Find me in her dreams. She
Has been searching for me
Night after night but with
No success. "Why are you
Hiding from me?" she asks,
"Did I do something to
Offend you, to hurt you?
I think you must have
Misunderstood what was
Meant as a sign of love."

"Look further, look deeper,"
I write her. "The world of
Dreams is vast. It has many
Passageways that lead to

Corners no one has ever
Visited. Don't abandon the
Search too easily. Don't
Give up. I have encountered
You in *my* dreams, beautiful
As you always were, your
Voice the same, unchanged.

"Yet what difference does
It make where we meet, in
Your dreams or in mine?
Does it matter if we are
Insubstantial? We still
Can speak the words we
Know, the words of love."

THE PRANKSTER

Who can foretell the pranks of that mischievous boy Eros? Who can
    guess at his whims?
Who knows where and when he will direct one of his joy-
    or pain-bearing arrows?

I have known sweet Nephrosyne for ten years,
The friend of my wife Portulaca,
The loyal wife of Ephrastus, my companion in arms,
The model of matronly virtues.
I thought of her as my sister, I confided in her and sought her coun-
    sel in matters of the heart,
I admired her beauty as I would that of a painting of Apelles.

And then, without warning, without any solicitation on my part
That dangerous boy launched one of his arrows;
True it flew to lodge in my heart, where it is embedded
And I cannot tear it loose even if I would.

Nephrosyne is no longer my placid sister, she is the object of my
    calorous desires.
When she approaches I tremble with longing.
My eyes are riveted on her beauty, on the grace of her movements.
That boy's arrow has wounded me deeply.
Will it also bring me bliss?

THE COUNTRY ROAD

In the painting that hangs in our dining room
A country road, a dirt road, is winding up the slope of a mountain
    ridge;
It begins in pastureland and goes up through scattered trees to dense
    woodland.
It is a scene in western Pennsylvania near the farm where we went in
    summer
To get away from the heat of the city.

I say that the road "is winding," not "winds,"
Because, for me, the painting sometimes seems to be still in progress,
Though the dear lady who did it has been dead more than fifteen years.
Some days, if I'm alone as I pass through the room,
I may notice some very small alteration in the composition
As if the artist were still working on it.
A tree may have slightly changed its position in the landscape,
Or the farmhouse and barns in the middle distance;
A patch of color in the pasture or the cornfield of the foreground may
    appear different;
The contour of the mountain ridge against the sky has been moving.
Even in the direction that the road is taking, its curves are never
    precisely the same.
It's always a sun-filled scene, but the quality of the light may vary.
As my eyes walk that familiar road, where I walked so often as a child,
I see things I hadn't detected before,
Little things of no great importance, but I'm aware of them.

A FLORILEGIUM

THE PURPLE CLEMATIS

Each day the purple clematis climbs further up the wire beside
    the kitchen door
Green fingers twine around the strands of wire
And soon there is another blossom with a yellow star at its center
Whom are you chasing, I ask the flower
Are you racing the horses of the sun?
     Do you imagine that Phaëthon, son of Helios, has time to
     fall in love with you?
Surely you've heard that he is condemned to die every evening
How like a man, she answers, what do I care about the drivers
    of chariots?
I'm only looking for a small crack in this wall
Where I may conceal myself from that ruffian, the north wind
    Boreas
Who only too soon will be here with his cruel winter.

THE WILD GERANIUM

How like a flower does Chloe gently bend her head
At the approach of wind or rain
Then comes the sun and quickly she's herself again
Not arrogant but confident of her beauty.

ANTHEA

Anthea greenly creeps the ground
Her tiny flower hardly to be seen against the rocks
But country people know of her healing power
Zeus promised it for her in recompense
When he forced her mother, the sweet nymph Cleomine.

IN THE MEADOW

the sheep in their feeding
have scattered from each

other and I see that they
have formed (white dots

against the green) the pat-
tern of the constellation

Canis Major which in the
night sky surrounds Sirius

the Dog Star   Sirius the
dog of Orion the hunter

who was loved by Eos the
goddess of the dawn and

she had him stung to death
by scorpions because he

didn't requite her love.

BITTERSWEET

is the plant of jealousy,
Celastrus scandens, a woody vine
with small greenish flowers
succeeded by yellow capsules
which burst open when ripe
revealing its scarlet seeds.

Taste the seed and it is first
sweet but then turns very bitter.

Nature ordains that bittersweet
fasten itself upon other plants
and even trees; its hungry tendrils
twine voraciously around each twig
and branch to consume them.

Beware the bittersweet, dear girl.
Perhaps it may first give you
a sweet taste of vengeance,
but later it will embitter you,
rob you of joy, give you great pain.

Ἔρος δηὖτέ μ' ὁ λυσιμέλης δόνει,
γλυκύπικρον ἀμάχανον ὄρπετον —Sappho

Eros once again limb-loosener whirls me
sweetbitter, impossible to fight off, creature stealing up
(I.P, fr. 130)

CLOUDS OVER THE SUN

Sometimes when I can't fall asleep
I lie in bed trying to understand
What happened. I remember us so
Happy together, so many happy little
Things we shared that were quite
Apart from the glorious lovemaking.
And then . . . and then . . . The picture
Mists over, the details of the picture
Become unclear. There was never a
Quarrel, not even a disagreement.
There was certainly no intrusion

Of another person. I can't describe
What happened. It was as if clouds
Moved slowly across the sun but then
Didn't move on. It became a season
Of clouds as sometimes it is in the
Alps. No rain, no storm, just dark
Days, and nights when we were side
By side but some sort of screen
Was between us. I go over and over
It in my mind, trying to remember
Some conclusive incident. Did I,
Unconsciously, implant some fear in
You, fear of something that I
Couldn't recognize as part of me?
Something that made you feel pain
But I couldn't feel it? Did I come
Down with some hidden illness, some
Sort of genetic curse? Three years
Of loneliness. How can I hasten
The movement of the clouds across
The sun?

"WHEN I WAS A BOY WITH NEVER A CRACK IN MY HEART"

I roamed all roads, hungering to find out
What they meant when they spoke of love.
I was holding my heart in my hand,
Offering it to anyone who would take it.

She who was the first was older than I.
She knew men and their ways.
She had suffered from some who threw her away after
    their amusement.
Now she was seeking an innocent
Whom she could shape to her pleasing.

I will not condemn her;
She taught me so much that I had to learn one way or
    another.
But I soon began to fear her, beautiful and passionate as
    she was.
I knew she would alter me in ways I didn't want to accept.
It was only a matter of time till she would incise a crack in
    my heart,
A crack that would not quickly heal.
So I went on my way;
I took to the road again looking for another less demanding.

THEY ARE SUSPENDED

as if from the branch
of a giant oak   their

bodies whirl in the
wind   they are alive

but cannot reach out
to touch each other

they love each other
dearly but for some

reason it's impos-
sible for them to

come together   they
can't embrace   is it

a gallows from which
they are suspended?

WHY?

In an old letter found
in a drawer she mentions,
almost casually, marks on
her wrists, she writes that
"they can now hardly be seen."
Who? When? Why? that superb
girl, what agony was she
passing through?

THE RAIN ON THE ROOF

Tonight the small talk of the rain
Is speaking to us again.
It began as a storm,
Then quieted down into a steady patter.
It's a reassuring sound that tells us
Everything is going to be all right;
We'll wake up to good weather.

Each of us can hear in the rain-talk
Whatever voice we most want to hear;
Our mother's or that
Of a never to be forgotten lover.

When you turn over and wake
We listen together.
When you drift back to sleep
I lie watching you.
I listen to your breathing
And the rain-talk tells me
That our time together
Will always be happy.

CATULLUS XXXII

Ipsitilla, my sweet, dear girl,
Little furnace, send word at once,
Please, that I may spend the
Afternoon with you. And if I may,
Be sure no other cocks are let
Into your henhouse. And don't
You go walking the streets;
Stay home and have ready for me
Nine of your nicest continuous
Fucks. (And don't forget the
Wine.) May I come as soon as
Possible? I've had my lunch
But I'm hot for it and my
Prick is trying to poke holes
In my shirt and the blanket.

WHY DOES LOVE HAPPEN?

It's not so simple
As the biological imperative
To propagate, though
There's that of course.
But it's also the way you look
At me, your face alight with joy,
And the way your voice sounds
In the dark. What makes *my* love
Come to you? Once I asked
But you wouldn't answer. It was
Your secret. Keep it so.

THE LOST SONG

This song that I have made to tell of you,
"Made out of a mouthful of air,"
Who but I will ever sing it,
Who will know who made it,
Or for whom it was made?

THREE KINDS OF PEOPLE

There are I—people
And we—people
And them—people.
My son Robert, the one who killed himself
When he was twenty-two,
Was an I—person
From the time he was fired from first grade
For upsetting the other children,
And at the next school
The boys locked him in a sports locker
Because he was so objectionable
And he was there for six hours.
I'm an I—person too,
But less obnoxious than poor Robert,
Saved because I've had loving we—people around me,
Three wives and a peerless daughter.
My son Henry is a them—person to the core.
He doesn't have to work at it,
It's natural to him, as if it were in his blood,
To see what other people need for their well-being
And put that ahead of his own comfort and desires.

THE WOMAN IN THE PAINTING

For Vanessa

Cries to the artist who has just finished
Her portrait: talk about me, write about me,
Give a lecture. I want everyone to know
How important I am, how important it is
That you've painted me the way you have.
They must recognize the forms in my body,
The interplay of colors and shapes.
If you must you can even bring in
Mondrian's theosophy and Sacred Geometry.
I'm not content to be silent on
The museum wall, let me speak
As well as be beautiful.

THE TROPHY WIVES

Are at each other again.
Belinda had been sending out her dinner invitations,
Inscribed in calligraphy by her secretary
And delivered by the chauffeur in the Rolls,
        accompanied by a rose.
Pulcheria is now sending hers garlanded by a rare
        orchid.
Belinda has adopted a fashionable hospital
For which a splendid charity ball will be held at
        The Waldorf.
Pulcheria is more intellectual;
She has taken a literary academy under her bountiful
        wing
At which she will reign over a conference of
        international scholars

Who will dispute the ever vexing problem of whether poetry
   Should be made of truth or beauty.

And what do the husbands think of this competition of the
   graces?
They have gone back to their offices to make more and more
   and more money.
They are delighted that their pretty little women have
Found ways to amuse themselves so harmlessly.
They chuckle to each other about it.

A DIFFICULT LIFE

My mother referred to it
as "the unpleasant side

of marriage" when she
was thirteen a crazy man jump-

ed out of the bushes along
Woodland Road and exposed

himself   a profound love
of Jesus carried her through

a long life which was dif-
ficult to bear   I tried to

love her as much as I could
but I'm afraid I didn't add

much consolation to it   I
threw the novel of her fa-

vorite author Lloyd C. Doug-
las out the window of the

train telling her it was
junk   she was past tears.

IN THE SECRET GARDEN

Melchior Dinsdale was Euphemia's favorite poet, bar none.
From the day when Miss Applegate had first pointed out his
work in the *Pegasus Junior High Anthology* Euphemia had
thrilled, throughout her being, to the poet's intimations of
sensuality and expression of unbridled passion. She trembled
as she read his sonnets. Many of them she memorized.
Sleepless, she would lie abed reciting the chants of sacred
(and profane) love, imagining that they might have been
written to her. If only she could share her admiration, and
her longing, with the venerable poet himself. Surely he
would not be totally unresponsive to her deep feeling.

How great then was Euphemia's excitement when she
received word from her aunt, Lady Parfait of Bladderstone
Hall, that the Laureate would soon be visiting at the Hall,
and that Euphemia might be one of the party if she so
desired.

How will this story end? Will Euphemia find happiness?
Or will she be defiled, her heart broken, as has happened to
others before, by the licentious old poet?

MR. HERE & NOW

I love words, I eat words,
But I don't chase them
Like the poet Carruth,
Who when he was young
Studied a page of the
Big Webster every morning.
I like to find a new word
By serendipity, a word
That has been waiting for me
In some book, and if it
Pleases me when I've looked
It up, it becomes part
Of me like one of the pimples
On my skin which I like to
Scratch for the fun of it
The way some children do.

Today's new word was
Haecceity (2 "c"s in the
Middle), hardly a melopoeic
Word. It's quite hard to
Pronounce. But it has much
Substance because it means
Thisness (and by later usage
Here and now.) It comes from
The Latin pronoun *haec*,
Which means this. Just remember
Hic, haec, hoc from school.
What's more substantial than
A *this*; it's closer to us
Than a *that*. If you have a
This you have something you
Can grab hold of, that won't
Slip away from you, that may

Persist as long as you're
Around in the here and now.

I found the word in a book
By a very learned Irishman
Of letters who is reputed to be
A bibulator of prowess. To show
His education he had put the
Word in Latin as *haecceitas*.
I knew at once that this strange
Word would be part of my permanent
Verbal paraphernalia, not to
Toss it about indiscriminately,
Not to use it to show off,
But to hold it in store for
The pleasure of a word-pal
With whom I correspond, who
Will know that I'm praising
His rare *thisness* and thanking
Him for being my Mr. Here & Now.

A LOVED BOOK

Has lain on a side table
In the living room for years,
Now seldom read, though Mary
Dusts it once a week. It's
Aubrey's *Brief Lives*. John Aubrey
Of Wiltshire and Trinity College
(1626–97). He knew everybody who
Mattered and etched them tersely
In immortal thumbnails; got down
"The significant scraps" about

Them. It was Auden who told me
About Aubrey, that summer we were
Teaching at Beloit. "He'll tell
You more about a person in a
Sentence than most writers
In a page." Dear, crinkly-faced
Auden. Evenings he would sit
At the college's out-of-tune
Piano banging out *Carmen*,
Singing the words in a hideous,
Raucous voice. Aubrey and Auden,
Two great, good men gone down.
And what will I leave? Typing.
A lot of foolish typed pages.

HOW DID LAURA TREAT PETRARCH?

The contemporary records are somewhat vague.
They speak of her beauty and her devotion.
The poems to her have romantic imagery,
But they don't get down to the nitty-gritty.
Did she mend his socks? Did she put up
With his tantrums? Did she make copies
Of his poems? Rub balm on his sore neck?
These are important questions for today's poets
As they set about to choose a life's companion.

THE MERCY IN IT

An old man gone weak in the legs,
Who once danced the hours away,
Must now be content with his books
And what the poets say.

Let him sit in his chair in the sun
And watch how his flowers are growing,
There muse on the past
And on truths that are still worth knowing.

Let him walk with his cane by the lake,
Where the water so slowly moves,
Hearing talk in the clouds
That tells of his heart's old loves.

PERMANET MEMORIA

Age has done its dreaded work.
We are no longer what we were
When we met by the Aegean shore
And discovered we loved one another.
Now our hair is white and our limbs
Are weak, our skin is wrinkled,
There is no desire to be satisfied.
But there is still memory.
Let us give thanks to the kind god
Who provides the consolation of memory.
We can enflesh ourselves in memory.

GRANDFATHER

Sits on a chair at the
Kitchen table shelling
Peas into a bowl. He
Looks contented, even
Happy, smiling as he
Works. If you ask him
A question he probably
Won't answer. He has
No idea what my name is,
Or even, I guess, that
I'm his grandson. He's
93 but he has to be kept
Busy or he'll start to
Root around in closets
All over the house. What
Does he think is lost?
No matter, he has been
Asked to shell peas.
He's happy doing it. And
We'll have peas for lunch.

IT'S DIFFICULT

For him to walk very far now
Even with his cane. His steps
Waver as if they can't decide
Which way to go. What he likes
Best is to lie in the sun on
The long chair meditating. If
The sun is bright he tips his
Hat over his eyes. He lets his

Mind wander. He doesn't want
To think about what is going
On in the world, the killing,
The endless killing. He knows
It has always been so from
Time immemorial and nothing
Can be done about it. Century
After century it will go on;
It's the nature of the beast.
He lies in the sun with his
Eyes closed rereading in his
Mind all the books he has
Most loved. Scene by scene
and character by character
He relives them. This morning
It was that idiotic French girl
Who desperately wanted what she
Could never hope to have and
Ended up eating arsenic. This
Afternoon it may be fables in
Ovid: Persephone raped off
To the underworld and her
Mother wandering over half
The earth in search of her;
Theseus and abandoned Ariadne;
Orpheus and limping Eurydice,
Two ladies who didn't have
The best of it. Or that love-
Silly Russian woman who gave
Up her son for a rotten man
And threw herself on the tracks
In front of a locomotive. It's
His consolation that there
Are more books he loves to
Think about than there are
Days he's likely to need them.
Good or bad, foolish or brave,
As they may be, the book people

Are his true friends. They are
There in his mind to help him
Get through his difficult days.

A TOAST TO THE FORGOTTEN POETS

Everyone reads Simonides
and Alcaeus but who re-

members Diarchus of Cor-
inth   Horace and Catullus

will be singing as long as
time lasts but what of the

sweet-tongued Stereus who
drowned himself in the Tiber

the poets of the Pléiade
have statues in every pro-

vincial town square   Henri
Ladoule hasn't even an alley

named for him in his native
village in Picardy Shake-

speare has been translated
into every language but the

Bantus know nothing of George
Jarvis author of *Dialogues*

with Satan   O brothers in
obscurity I drink to you

my companions yes I shall
join you soon in oblivion.

SOME AMATORY EPIGRAMS FROM *THE GREEK ANTHOLOGY*

Melissa pulled one reddish hair
From her braid and tied my hands
With it. I was her prisoner. I
Told her never to let me go.
                    Paulus Silentiarius (V, 230)

Sometimes secret love affairs
Yield more honey than those
Which are open.
                    Paulus Silentiarius (V, 219)

She kissed me one evening with
Wet lips; her mouth smelt sweet
As nectar. I'm drunk with her
Kiss. I have drunk love in
Abundance.
                    Anonymous (V, 305)

Melissa's beauty is the gift of
The god Eros; Aphrodite charmed
Her bed; the Graces gave her grace.
                    Meleager (V, 196)

In my heart Eros himself created
Sweet-voiced Melissa, the soul
Of my soul.

Meleager (V, 154)

Might it not be that someday in
Legend soft-gliding Melissa will
Surpass the Graces themselves?

Meleager (V, 148)

I swear, I swear it by Eros, I
Would rather hear her whisper in
My ear than listen to Apollo
Playing his lyre.

Meleager (V, 141)

I held her close, we were breast
To breast, hers supporting mine,
Her lips joined with mine. As for
The rest, the little bedlamp was the
Only witness; I am silent.

Marcus Argentarius (V, 128)

Her kiss is like the lime that
Catches birds. Her eyes are fire
And when she looks at me I also burn.
If she touches me she has me caught fast.

Meleager (V, 96)

I wish I were a rose, a pink rose,
For you to pick and press against
your snowy breasts.

Anonymous (V, 84)

Beauty without charm is only pleasing.
It's nothing to remember. It's like
Fishing with bait but no hook.
>> *Capito* (V, 67)

We fell in love, we kissed, you gave
Yourself to me, we had much pleasure.
But who am I, and who are you? How
did it happen that we came together?
Only the Kyprian goddess knows.
>> *Anonymous* (V, 51)

Gray are her lovely eyes, her cheeks
Of crystal. Could you not call her
Sweet mouth a rose? Her neck is of
Marble, her breasts smooth as marble.
Her small feet? They are more charming
Than those of silver-footed Thetis.
>> *Rufinus* (V, 48)

For so long, my darling, I prayed to
Have you with me at night, touching
And caressing. And now your love has
Brought me that happiness. You are
Beside me, naked. But why do I become
Drowsy? I owe you this felicity forever.
>> *Rufinus* (V, 47)

Beware a girl who is too ready.
But also one who hangs back too
Long. One is too quick, the other
Too slow. Look for one who is
Neither too plump nor too thin.

Too little flesh is as bad as too
Much. Never run to excesses.

Rufinus (V, 42 & 37)

Whether you have colored your hair
Dark or have it its natural shade,
It frames your dear face in beauty.
The god Eros loves your hair and
Will still be twining his fingers
In it when it is gray.

Anonymous (V, 26)s

Shall we take a shower together,
Soaping ourselves and rubbing each
Other, flesh to flesh; then put on
Our robes and sip a good wine? The
season of such joys is short; then
Comes old age and finally death.

Rufinus (V, 12)

Make the bedlamp tipsy with oil;
It's the silent confidant of things
We seldom dare to speak of. Then
Let it go out. There are times when
The god Eros wants no living witness.
Close the door tight. Then let the
Bed, the lovers' friend, teach us
The rest of Aphrodite's secrets.

Philodemus (V, 4)

APOKATASTASIS

The notion that after death all things recur in eternal
simultaneity—Unamuno makes a great case for it.

I wandered up there above the clouds,
Or was it down on the far shore of Lethe?
I wasn't lonely because everyone
Who'd ever lived whom I wanted to know
Was there, still alive but aethereal:
Sappho and Propertius, Rochester, even
Bertran de Born, all there and talking
Happily together, no fights now, poets
Of many tongues, complete simultaneity,
Like the new tricks they're going to do
With television. A cacophony, you ask,
Deafening, so much wisdom sounding
Together? No, it wasn't that at all.
It was like happy bees humming
In the meadows near Olympia, or like
The music of the spheres, but a music
Without trumpets or tympani, a gentle
Susurration that rose through the moon's
Light and past the orbit of the sun
To a distant galaxy where creatures
Not like us were listening for it.

RUBBING DRY STICKS

Eros has broken his bow,
He has had to send it to the shop
For repairs, but he's still
Starting conflagrations of the heart
By rubbing dry sticks together.

Who here in the village
Would have dreamed it possible
That those two could have become
What the gossip columnist of the
Goshen Star calls an "item"?
Lump-faced Louella who's retired
From teaching social sciences
In the grade school; she received
A medal from the State Department
Of Education for forty years
Of devoted service. And bibulous Bob
Who never kept a job for more
Than a year but everybody loves him.
Now he lives on welfare. Eros smiles
Io Hymen . . . Hymenaeus Io!
It's a happy sight to see the two
Antique lovers strolling hand in hand
Along the village street, not to
The bar, love has put Bob on the
Wagon, but to the pizza parlor.
Io Hymen . . . Hymenaeus Io!
Their wedding has been announced.
Our beloved First Selectman will
Preside at the ceremony in the
Town Hall. Everyone in the village
Will come to wish them well.
Io Hymen ... Hymenaeus Io!
Will Eros be hiding in the back
Of the room scanning the faces
For his next triumph?

Catullus LXI

HER HAIR

For several years I've been casting
Covert amorous glances at Berenike.
Ones her husband won't notice but
I hope she does. Though she never
Gives any sign of recognizing my
Ardor. Berenike has the most
Enticing hair I've ever seen on
Any woman. She is much in my
Fantasies and performs superbly
In them. But I fear that if once
She welcomed me to her bed that
Might be the end of my obsession.
What if she puts her flowing
Tresses in curlers at night? It
Would do for two or three times, of
Course, so as not to hurt her
Feelings, but then it would be
Over. Better things as they are.

PENELOPE VENIT ABIT HELENE

It was raining during her lunch
hour and to keep dry she went
into one of those shabby little
theatres near Times Square.
In the next seat was a well-
dressed benevolent looking
gentleman perhaps in his sixties.
Because he resembled her father
back in Des Moines she did not

feel frightened when he took
her hand and drew it to his
waist. Such a nice old man.

(After Martial, Ep I.62)

THE WOOD NYMPH

For Erica

Sometimes when I am working
In the forest clearing brush from
The hemlocks, a wood nymph approaches
Walking her two small dogs.
Soft-footed and undulant she glides
Through the trees, a figure of grace,
A nymph of surpassing beauty.
Sometimes in her passage she'll stop
To greet me. *Xaire*, she says, *xaire
Broté*; greetings to you, mortal man.
Clear-voiced, she speaks as if
She were singing. She tells of
The spirits that inhabit the marshes.
She is the guardian of those who
Live in bogs and wetlands.
She never identifies herself
But I think she may be Melissa
of Kalymnos, the child of Athena
By a mortal named Euclidon; she
Was renowned for her singing.

L'ENGLOUTI

How deep is the pit? Is it bottomless?
I thought I had touched bottom. I felt
I had drowned when Hermione, a girl
Whose wit was her wealth, let herself
Be seduced by the gold of the vulgar
Herondas. But worse was to follow.
Next it was Euterpe, wildly passionate
Euterpe, who destroyed me with her discovery
That she prefers girls to men. My friends
Commiserate but I'm past consolation:
Englouti is the French word for my
Condition. I'm afraid to return to the city.
What further disaster may await me there?

HER HEART

For Anne Carson

is a volcano in eruption
many fearless men have perished there
Menippus of Macedonia, Sardonicus of Tyre,
Cyaxeres the Mede, Kartikeya, lord of the Hindu Kush,
their valor aroused admiration
but their fates were sealed
from the moment they laid eyes on her.
It was like the game called "the vizier's choice"
at the court of Aurangzeb.
They were dazzled by her beauty
and lost all power of judgment.
After their pleasure, they slipped
into her fiery crater
and were consumed.

SHE DOES NOT WRITE

Though she must know her silence
Is a painful burden for me to bear
(*Un fardeau grave*, as the French would say).
When we said goodbye at the station
There were little tears on her cheeks
(*Des larmes de tendresse*).
But that was ten days ago
And she has not written
(*Aucun petit mot pour me dire*
Quelle pensait à moi).
Is she already forgetting
What passed between us?

A ROOM IN DARKNESS

Night is a room darkened for lovers.
The sun is gone, and our daytime concerns
and distractions with it.
Now in the darkness we are close together
As lovers are meant to be.
Whether we sleep or wake
Nothing intrudes between us.
We are soothed and protected
By the darkness of our room.

BELIEVE ME

There can be shadows in the dark
Not many can see them
But a lover can see them
As he waits for the beloved to join him
And a lover can hear even the fall of a naked foot
As the beloved approaches
He can hear the soft breathing
That is rising in expectation
As he stretches out his hand in the darkness
To welcome her to the place of love.

THE IMMANENCE OF YOUR BODY

It's nearly three years since we've been together,
Since we made love.
The circumstances of life have kept us apart.
But tonight as I sit here in half-darkness,
Listening to the *Four Last Songs*,
Remembering things about you,
I'm convinced of the immanence, the indwelling,
Of your body in mine.
You're a part of me again.
I feel your every touch.
I can feel the warm pressure of the flow
Of your bloodstream against mine.
I pray that my body is equally
Immanent in yours,
That we have not heard our last song.

LA VITA NUOVA

Thanks to my Virtual-Reality headset
I can now embrace her back at the same
time as her front.
Love expands; it was never like this
in the days of Catullus.

EROS RIDENS

When they make love it's hard
For her to keep serious about
What they're doing. She can be
Passionate for a few minutes
As they pleasure each other
But then she'll begin to laugh.
It strikes her how comical are
The movements of bodies. "You
Are like a lizard." She'll say,
"A squirmy lizard." And she'll
Laugh that delicious laugh. Yet
The more she mocks their play,
The more he loves her; the more
She makes them both so happy.

THE WRONG MAGIC

When you went away
My youth went with you
Everything happy from childhood on
Had come together in you

Why couldn't I hold you?
I tried so hard to work a magic on you
But I wasn't sorcerer enough
It wasn't, I guess, the kind of
magic that spoke to you
Or perhaps it wasn't magic at all
Just my illusion of magic.

THE CHANGE

when it came was nothing sudden
it was so gradual they didn't

notice it was coming and when
it began they weren't aware it

was happening   it wasn't some-
thing they talked about at all

it began with such little things
like the way she kissed and how

long a kiss would last and what
her tongue would no longer do

(until there were no more kisses)
then where she wanted him to touch

her and what she wanted to touch
such gradual little differences

such an undeliberate alternance
in her tactile affection   it was

as if nothing was changing with
intention   sometimes there would

be a little change of tone when
they were talking   she lost in-

terest in some of her prettiest
dresses replacing them with ones

that were less colorful and more
severe   it was all so tentative

as if she were groping   then one
day they realized (both at the

same time) it was something they
could speak of could bring into

the light but there was no bit-
terness no recriminations   they

knew they would always be to-
gether   the best of it would

always be the same   that was
assured but each would be free

to act without asking as the
change would require of them.

DO THEY MAKE LOVE?

Don't pick at it, my nurse says,
It won't get well if you pick at it.

I've never seen him but I think
I know what he looks like.

I know it itches but if you don't
Leave it alone it will get worse.

I can't guess what he says to her
But I hear what his voice sounds like.

Remember what happened to Albert,
His leg got infected from scratching.

I don't dare imagine that he touches
Her, or that she touches him.

Albert had to go to the hospital,
They nearly had to amputate his leg.

If he touches her I want him to die.

BY THE IRISH SEA

These tired old waters
that today so softly

caress the shingle are
full of history for me

Saint Patrick bringing
the cross to the pagan

Gaels   the wretched Span-
iards of the Armada drown-

ing as their ships broke
up in the great storm

and my own people sailing
from Scotland to Ireland

to find a new home in the
Pale in the troubled time

of Bonnie Prince Charlie
but the message the sea

gives me now is a happy
one that soon I'll be

flying over these waters
back to you my true and

bonnie lass back to you.

THE RISING MIST AT ARD NA SIDHE

When I awake at dawn, at the *alba*,
A soft mist is rising from Loch Caragh.
Tá ceo bog eirí ón loch.
It fingers up from the garden through the trees.
It is reaching for Macgillicuddy's Reeks,
The mountains that stand up from the lake.

The scene could be a Japanese scroll painting
Of Lake Biwa and the hills beyond Kyoto.
But this is not Japan, it is Ireland.
I've not been sleeping on a tatami
With the little wooden pillow block under my neck.
Ketsin is not beside me in the room with walls made of paper.

They wrote me with great respect that Ketsin had died;
That was some forty years ago, she had died in childbirth.
(But this is not Japan, it is Killorglin.)
The slight form of Ketsin is not near for me to touch.
Her frightened smile and her almost inaudible voice no longer
    compose a person.
She will not have twined flowers into my western shoelaces.
She will not bring me my wake-up tea.
She will not ask the morning question:
"Are you awake now, my lord?"

LOST

Some of my friends have all
The luck when it comes to
Dreams. They have such a variety
Of wonderful, exciting dreams:
Dreams about sexy mysterious
Girls; dreams about stupendous
Meals in Parisian restaurants:
Mystical dreams that can be
Interpreted in interesting ways.
I have only one dream that is
Always the same. I'm lost in
A huge foreign city where I've
Never been. I'm afraid I'm
Going to miss an important
Appointment if I can't find

My way. Someone very important
But I can't remember his name.
There are people in the streets
But they don't speak English.
I get frightened. I begin to
Run from street to street. I
Run faster and faster till I
Wake up. Where is that city?

ATTRACTED BY THE LIGHT

For Vanessa

This warm evening, a very small bug
Has flown through the open window,
Landed on my head and is exploring
My hair. It tickles, but like a Jain
I'll not try to kill it. One of God's
Creatures. And am I not lucky
That at 79 I still have enough hair
To seem attractive to the bug?
You to whom I'm sending these lines,
Do you still think of me, far away
There in London as you are?
For me you are still the light.

DE CONTEMPTU MORTIS

What is consciousness that it
Leaves us when most we need it
To save what little we have

Managed to construct? Will the
Pale torch of loving soon be
Sputtering out for me? The
Children joke at table whether
Grandfather should be buried
Or burned. What difference
Could it make? Does their humor
Mask any affection that will
Last when life takes them by
Their little necks and shakes
Them as it can, rich or poor?
Tell me a happy fable that
Off in a distant galaxy some
Creature with three eyes is
Watching over me? That can't
Be so, believe me, it's not so;
Walk up or down, turn right
Or left, it isn't so. We came,
We breathed a bit of air, we go.

A TROUBLING CASE OF AGNOSIA

Some mornings, thank heavens
Not every day, when he gets up
And goes into the bathroom to shave
He's troubled to find that the face
In the mirror isn't his own.
Who is this stranger who has come
In the night? The intruder is
Definitely not himself, though
There may be points of resemblance,
His ears, say, or his color of hair.
Who is he? Has he ever seen anyone
Who looked like him before? not

That he can remember. Occasionally
There will be a reappearance
Of the uninvited visitor. He has
Begun to assign names to these
Repeaters: Long-nosed Jack,
Fat-faced Harold, who looks a bit
Like his own Uncle Harold, Willy
The Turnip. He's glad to see them
Come back, if someone has to be
There in the mirror. They reassure
Him that he's not entirely crazy.
But they are disconcerting.
Fortunately they don't follow
Him down to breakfast or out into
The street. They are only the
Mirror people. In a way he's
Getting rather fond of them,
Would miss them if they moved
To the house of someone else.

IMPRISONED

For Gertrude

It has been a long sentence for you
In the prison of my gloom
Where I sit scribbling verses
In my untidy room.

I could read to you from old books,
But what would that avail?
You're of the merry world,
I of my lonely cell.

Do you ever suspect how much I love you,
For that is what is true,
As I scribble my quare rhymes,
Rhymes that I make for you.

A WINTER'S NIGHT

The outside, where the snow
Is softly and soundlessly
Falling (there is no wind
Tonight) has brought its quiet
Into the house that was noisy
All day with TV voices,
The telephone ringing,
And the happy shouts of children
Romping from room to room.
Now, except for me, sleep
Has taken over the house.
I bring the silence of the dark
Outside into it. I wrap that
Around my cares. Soon I too
Will be sleeping.

THE LONGEST YEAR

Began with snowstorms, one after another.
In March a frantic night of wind took down
The huge sugar maple that showed a hundred
Rings when it was cut up for firewood.
Spring was dubious and too short, a hot
Summer too long. A child drowned in Tobey
Pond, it was horrible. Only in October
Were there a few perfect days with the leaves
Ablaze. Again before its time, baleful winter
Set in. Cars skidded on the icy roads.
At Christmas a false thaw deceived us
For a week before a deadly ice storm had
The branches of the trees cracking like
Rifle shots as they broke off all night.
It was a battlefield in the woodlot
Next morning. I didn't count the days
Of that malevolent year, I only wished
Never to see such another . . . until,
Blessed miracle, it was true spring,
The lilacs blooming, the daffodils
Nodding, and you, Persephone, came up
From the world below to seek me out.

WAITING FOR TARTUFFE

They all told him that happiness
Was just around the next corner
Or beyond the bend of the river.
It didn't matter that his face
Was a discolored, lopsided pumpkin;
His happiness was out there waiting

For him, his own proprietary bliss.
All he had to do was keep his nose
Clean as Jefferson specifies in the
Declaration. But as the boring
Years rolled by he came to realize
They had all been lying to him,
They were all liars. There was no
Kind of happiness, great or small,
With his name stamped on it. Such
A thing simply did not exist. It
Dawned on him. that the name
Inscribed on his birth certificate
Was not the one his parents had
Told him; it was a man named Tartuffe.

THE INVISIBLE PERSON

Life kept rolling her over
like a piece of driftwood

in the surf of an angry sea
she was intelligent and beau-

tiful and well-off she made
friends easily yet she wasn't

able to put the pieces to-
gether into any recognizable

shape   she wasn't sure who
she wanted to be   so she

ended up being no one in par-
ticular   she made herself al-

most invisible she was the
person you loved so much who

really wasn't there at all.

AS LONG

as you don't fall in love with him
you won't be harmed
he'll be kind to you
he'll amuse you with jokes & stories

he'll feed you delicious dinners
he'll send fragrant blooms
he'll buy you baubles
but if you begin to have feelings
more tender than he deserves
run, run, run, for the nearest exit.

THE EXOGAMIST

Her thin right arm
the skin so white
and smooth (port-
manteau passions?)
soft startled eyes
glaukopis Kupris
eyes of the Kyprian
bread on the point
of a knife no exit
but enticing danger.

CANSO

She's the wife of a man who lives
In the village, a decent enough sort
Of fellow. I see her rarely, we might
Meet in the street once a month.
But sometimes in the night I wake
From sleep and discover her near me.
I feel that her beauty is infusing me,
It's taking possession of me.
Without touching her I'm being joined
To her. (It's not a sexual fantasy;
There's no tumescence.) But there is
An enlacement. Not always but usually,
This bonding seems to be taking place
In the past. I see a small river
Winding through a green valley.
I see low hills. I see a towered castle
On one of the hills. In the cedared
Garden of that castle I see my lady
Seated on silken cushions. She is wearing
A peaked head-dress and a richly brocaded
Gown. Which *canso* should I sing to her,
One that tells of sad longing, or one
That tells of joy?

SO ALBERTINE

wasn't a girl but a handsome
young taxi driver and after

his mum croaked he gave her
fine furniture to the male

bordello   all that superb
writing came out of shall

we say a certain untidiness
but who am I to be censori-

ous   *le raplapat se réplique*
diversement et le jin-jin se

jete comme nous le voulons.

HOMAGE TO FELLINI

Found Lines in 8 1/2

Do you study what is printed
On chewing gum wrappers before
You throw them away? If you did
Perhaps you would have some
Knowledge to understand what
Life is about. Or if only every
Other word you write were the truth
Your time on the spinning ball
Would not have been totally wasted.
If I could answer your questions
I would, believe me, but since
I can't answer them, let there be
Dedication to silence. When will
The script be ready? When can we
Finally start shooting? Or is
There no film to be made?

THE HITCHHIKER

Good Friday Spell

The innocent fool
Made wise by pity
Came through our
Village, but nobody,
Not even the children,
Recognized who he was.
He did no harm, he smiled
But spoke to no one
And no one spoke to him.
Perhaps he was with us
For only ten minutes,
But we were blessed.

THE LEAST YOU COULD DO

he told her, would be to forget
your pride of ownership for an hour
and let her come to sit by my bed
for that fraction of time.
What could we say in an hour
that would hurt you, or would take
anything away from what you've had?
What looks could we exchange
that would harm you in any way?
It's more than ten years
since we were lovers; in ten years
we haven't seen each other.
Is it so strange that we want
to meet again for the last time,
to look at each other, to listen to

each other's voices, ever
so gently to touch hands?
It's the least you could do.

THE LOTOPHAGOI

Take care   you may be drifting
toward a distant shore from

which there is no return   no
not death but a land like

that of the *lotophagoi* (the
lotos eaters)   Odysseus found

them on the African coast
they were gentle happy peo-

ple who had tasted of the
fruit of the lotos which

made them forget who they
were and lose all desire

to return to their homes
or be themselves again.

TWO FABLES FROM *THE OCEAN OF STORY*

Adapted from the Tawney-Penzer translation of Somadeva's *Katha Sarit Sagara* (Sanskrit, 3rd century A.D.)

STORY OF THE CHANDALA GIRL WHO WANTED TO MARRY A PRINCE

In the city of Chidambaram there was a very pretty
Girl who was determined to marry a prince,
Even though she was a Chandala, the lowest of all the castes.
One day she saw the son of the king who was making a tour of
    inspection of the city.
She followed his entourage hoping her beauty would catch   his
    eye.
At that moment a holy hermit came by.
The prince got down from his elephant and prostrated   him-
    self before the *sadhu*.
This showed the girl that a holy man was greater than a prince.
    She followed the *sadhu*.
Soon they reached a temple of Siva, where the holy man knelt
    and worshiped.
The girl made obeisance to the *lingam* and even dared to   kiss
    it.
Then a mongrel dog ran into the temple, sniffed
Around and did as dogs do right on the *lingam*.
Was the dog superior to Siva? How could she wed a dog?
The dog ran into the street and she followed it
To the house of a young Chandala man she knew who was a
    carter.
The dog leapt up to greet the young man and licked his face.
That settled it, the girl was reconciled to her caste,
And her mother sent for the matchmaker.

There was an astrologer who would stop at nothing to
    make money.
He left his home province thinking he could do better
    elsewhere.
There he went about advertising his skill and learning.
He had with him his son who was nine years old.
He embraced his son in the town square and shed tears
    over him.
When the people questioned him the wicked man told
    them:
"I know all that is past, and the present,
And what will come in the future.
I can foresee that my child will die in seven days.
That is why I am weeping."
His words aroused the wonder and sympathy of the
    people.
On the seventh day the astrologer killed
The boy while he was still sleeping.
When the people saw that the prophecy had come true,
They believed in his mastery of the art of prediction.
They honored him with rich gifts.
He acquired much wealth and returned to his own
    province.

HAIKU

Now when I open my electric
Shaver to clean it a fine
Gray sand falls in the bowl.

THE OLD MEN

From way back, from when
I first came to live here
In Norfolk, I remember seeing
The old men of the village
Trudging down through the
Main street to the post office,
Or the grocery, or the pharmacy,
To get their mail or do an
Errand for the wife. Old men
Who walked slowly, some of them
With canes, they were retired
And had no place to go in any
Hurry. They would gather by twos
And threes to chew the fat
Even if there was nothing
To talk about except the weather.

Now I have a cane myself and walk
Pretty slowly, especially
If the street is icy, as it was
This morning. Young Jack Thompkins,
Mel's boy, spotted me
On the ice with my cane and
Came over to ask if he could
Help me up the steps of the
Post office. I felt a bit
Foolish but accepted his offer.
He took my arm and we made it
In good shape.

IN THE NURSERY

I'm nearly 80 but my wife and
The servants look after me as
If I were a child of about 4.
I've forgotten how to read so
They read aloud to me, stories
About Babar the elephant and
Other animals that I like.
I eat what they put before me
But yesterday I spat out on
The table something I didn't
Like. Toys are borrowed for me
To play with from a neighbor's
Children. I like best a little
Yellow car that will run across
The floor if I wind it up. They
Took me to get my hair cut; the
Barber gave me a lollipop to
Keep me quiet from wiggling.
Today they gave me a pad and
Crayons to draw with. I've
Drawn all the animals I know;
A dog with five legs by mistake
Made them laugh. It's hard for
Me to remember. I know my name
Is Jack, they call me that, but
What's the rest of it? One
Day I heard them talking about
Me and the doctor who comes
To see me now and then. They
Said he said I should be
Myself again in a few more
Weeks, just keep him quiet
And be patient with him.

THE WANDERING WORDS

This morning at breakfast, when I meant to say,
"Where's the marmalade?" my voice said instead,
"Where's the drawbridge?" and later
At the post office, when I handed my package slip
To Betty, the clerk, I asked her please to
Bring my strawberries. "Where would you get
Strawberries in December," she asked as she
Brought me my package of books. You see about
Six weeks before I'd had what the neurologist
Called a TIA, a little stroke. "Nothing
To worry about," he said. "It's normal
At your age. Take an aspirin a day and
It will go away." But it hasn't. Some wires
Must be crossed in the computer in my brain.
At first when the words began to wander
I was frightened. Was I going crazy?
Then I was annoyed. It was an embarrassment
With strangers to have to try to explain.
But now I think the wanderers are funny.
I wait with anticipation to hear what
Curious malapropism will pop out next.
I jot them down on a card I keep in my
Shirt pocket to see if there is a pattern.
I'm going to rearrange them into a poem,
A poem that may turn out to be
A surrealist masterpiece as good as
André Breton's "Soluble Fish"
Or his "Communicating Vases."

BENIGNUS QUAM DOCTUS

The wise old neurologist at Mass General,
The one whom other specialists look up to
Because he knows all there is to know
About strokes, has taken away what strangely
I had come to consider a valuable asset,
That is my belief that I had had a stroke
Myself. And why did I imagine that such
An accident was an advantage? In the
Weeks after the supposed event I had
Learned to live with the fear of it.
I had come to believe that it settled
The problems of the debility of old age
And even the greater one of how death
Would come and the probable time
Of death's coming. The stroke became
A kind of assurance and comfort.

This kind and learned old man
Questioned me for nearly an hour
About my symptoms and medical history.
He had me walk up and down the corridor
To see how straight I walked, how much
My gait wavered. Then he gave me
The news that I hadn't had a stroke
After all. There were no indications
Of a cerebral accident. I thanked him.
"But Doctor," I asked, "if there was
No stroke why is my head so constantly
Dizzy, and why has memory deserted me?"
"I'm not a psychiatrist,' he told me.
"But the condition you describe is
Often associated with a state of
Anxiety." I thanked him again and
Left the hospital, my head spinning
As usual.

Pride, covetousness, lust, anger,
Gluttony, envy and sloth. Anxiety
Is not in the list of sins. What
Have I done, or what was done to
Me in a comfortable life to be
Rewarded with anxiety? Could it
Be the unforgivable sins of the
Fathers, sins from which there
Is no escape?

MY HEAD'S TRIP

I was sitting here typing
At the kitchen table. Nothing
Special about that, it was just
Another sonnet. But suddenly
My neck began to wobble, at
First gently then more and
More violently. There was
No pain, just this strange
Motion. All at once the top
Of my spine gave way and
My head fell to the floor.
It bounced twice then rolled
Slowly down the hall toward
The living room. No pain.
No blood came out of my head
But it left a track of white
Powder, like flour or salt.
I was afraid to follow it to
Find out what it was going
To do next. I'm even more
Afraid to lift my hands
From the typewriter to find

Out what is now on top of
My spine where my head used
To be. What if there is
Nothing there at all?

THE DAY I WAS DEAD

The three hours I was
in the morgue when
they thought I was
dead but I wasn't
were the worst part
of my whole life
they had me tied
to a stretcher in
a box in the wall
and they couldn't
hear me hollering
I was getting so
cold I was near
to frozen dead
the way they found
out I was alive was
when they came to
do the autopsy
I think there's
been some mistake
one doctor said to
the other you're
damn right there's
been some mistake
I told them get me
some fucking brandy
before I turn into
a block of ice.

HEART ISLAND &
OTHER EPIGRAMS

(1995)

THE HAPPY POETS

What's happiness?
It's to lie side
By side in bed
Helping each other
Improve our poems.

THE TWO OF THEM

One kept his stomach full.
The other nourished his imagination.
It was a perfect arrangement
Until some confusion arose
As to which one should do which.

IN SCANDINAVIA

at country dances the
girls tuck the boys'

handkerchiefs in their
armpits and give them

back to be sniffed.

YOU'RE TROUBLE

aren't you asked the pretty
lady with whom I'd been con-

versing at the dinner party
I was trouble I told her when

I was young lots of trouble
but now I'm old and harmless.

THE OLD MAN'S LAMENT

He says that when the posthos
don't work no more it's like

the pain an amputee feels in
the foot that's been cut off.

THE VOYEUR

Pull up your skirt
just an inch or two

above your knees
sit quietly where

I may watch you
from across the

room   I am old and
impotent but such

small pleasures can
still give me delight.

IN THE HIGHSTREET OF TRALEE

Run girl, run!
Under your blue blouse
The birdie paps are flying.

God made you thus
To pleasure us
Against our dying.

PASSPORT SIZE WILL DO

I beg you to send me your picture
For my album of imaginary conquests
You will be in excellent company
I am not (even in my imagination)
Promiscuous and invite only the best.

AT THE POST OFFICE

It makes his day when
by happy chance he en-

counters her on his morn-
ing visit to the post office

it's as if a rose had
opened to greet him.

I SUPPOSE

the rhetoricians might call this
a variety of the pathetic fallacy

but when we talk on the telephone
I imagine I hear cunt in your voice

the soft slish of honey on silk as
Henry Miller used to describe it.

DEATH LURCHES TOWARD ME

but the gods do have
some pity   in these

last months the verses
seem a bit less paltry

not quite so garrulous
touches of truth in them.

A VISIT TO PARIS

Why not, asked my French
friend, have your red

ribbon of the Légion
sewed to your pyjamas?

THE MUSIC OF IDEAS

(1995)

CARRAIG PHADRAIG

In Tullaherin where the dainty toadsfoot blossoms on
    old stone walls,
Where swallows soar up from the tall hedgerows,
We thought we were lost and stopped to ask an old
    man
The way to get to Carraig Phadraig.
"This lane will take ye there," he said, "but it is fierce
    contrary.
Better ye go round by Callan."

Yes, in any language life can be fierce contrary.
Co naidre an Botlar Leat:
May the road rise with you.

IN MACROON

In Macroon was an old gray woman
Thin as a wind gone by.
A dab colleen was scoffing her,
Scoffing that she could fly.

"Give her a punt and she'll fly for you,
Take up her broom and fly."
I said to that chit, "You're dab now
But your sad time will come by and by."

THE EMIGRATION

And the land, meaning the ancestral potato patch,
The value thereof, as sold, to be divided in equal parts among the
    three of them, the two brothers and the sister,
Given before me, Michael O'Dougherty, Justice of Peace,
Here in my house in Portaferry, County of Down, this
    16th day of September, 1824,
Devidetus pariter in tres partibus,
Which is bad Latin but this was Ireland,
Signed by Alexander and James, their hands and seals, and an X for
    the sister, Eliza.

Everything sold except for a few portables, the money put into
    household crockery,
By steamer from Cork to Baltimore, thence by wagon across
    Pennsylvania, selling the crockery to the farmers,
All gone by the time they reached Pittsburgh, the money enough to
    buy a small house and a store, a going concern.
The rest is history, well, a kind of history.
It was the Civil War that established the fortune—by that time there
    was a small iron foundry—
Making rails for the Northern armies.

But there was no trace of them when we found the spot where the
    place might have been,
No trace of it at all, the farms and fields all gone, even the stone
    walls and hedgerows gone,
To make way for condominia built by a Belfast developer,
Mostly for sale to Germans for their holidays;
Such a pleasant view over Strangford Lough, an arm of the Irish Sea,
Which the Danes called *Strangfjord* when they raided there back God
    knows when.
Fat Germans hiking around in short pants and Tyrolean hats.
All the family records, if there were any, apparently destroyed when
    the parish church burned up in 1878.

THE PETITION

They will say that you were never born,
That your beauty was never seen in any place or time.
They will say that we never loved.
Can I silence fools with a little rhyme?

THE ENIGMA

Can two lovers ever name
The great secret
They want to tell each other?
They speak, they look, they touch
But the term eludes them.
No poet ever told it to them,
No singer sang it: the aleph,
The irrefutable mandala.

THE SELFISH ONE

She keeps her beauty for herself,
Eyes, lips, fair cheeks, dear breasts,
She keeps all of them for herself.
She will not share them, or any part of them
With a lover, no matter how ardent he may be,
No matter how he prays for her favor.

Is she not afraid, this self-regardant girl,
That some god will look down

And taking note of her greed,
Rape her away from among mortals
To work upon her brutal passion
That will destroy her cherished loveliness?

THE MUSIC OF IDEAS

Reverberates in the poet's ear.
At times it thunders. Pound rhymed
Ideas in the *Cantos*, a complexity
Of tones that elicits astonishment.
We smaller poets must be content
With lesser harmonies. Our little
Minds are incapable of the great
Organ fugues. Better to be silent?

OLD MEN

Old men fall in love
With young girls readily.
They have dear memories they'd like
To relive while still they can.
Be kind to them, maidens.
The day may come when
You'll understand what it is
To need to recapture
The raptures of the past.

LONGING & GUILT

It's past midnight but he
Can't sleep. He thrashes
In bed, probing his memory
For answers that may never
Come. He longs for her; he would
Like to be encompassing her
With his love. But she is
Far away, perhaps never to
Be regained. How much of
The distance that is now
Between them came about
Because he never learned
To love her in the way she
Needed to be loved? Guilt
And longing together are a
Terrifying torment. It's
No wonder he can't sleep.

THE NAP

Now you're awake but sleepy; then you've dozed off.
In a few minutes you come to a bit stiff,
Annoyed to be awake again, resentful that your sleep was so short.
Such catnaps have no dreams; nothing happens in them.
They are a lapse in activity, an interruption of thinking.
Sometimes there is puzzlement: where have you been, what were you
    doing
When you fell asleep? What's to be done now?
The first thought (if it can be called a thought;
It's more an animal instinct) is to slump back on the chair where
    you've been reclining

And resist reentry into waking life.
Close your eyes again, resume the sojourn in nowhere.
Let time stop moving, let life wait a little longer.
Wait a bit before you get up to do things.
Stop time till then.

THE MOVEMENTS

To reason, or to make my mind
Proceed logically through the steps
Of an equation, are things I have
Never mastered (or particularly
Wanted to master). What attracts
Me is the sideways broad jump,
The hop and skip through what
Pound called "the phalanx of
Particulars." I invent by
Association (or sometimes by
Dissociation as Gertrude Stein
Did). And Nabokov told me that
What came next in the story should
Never be what the reader expected.
What I do, I guess, is a kind of
Painting: the juggling of forms
And colors. I try to keep many
Balls in the air at one time.

HER POEMS

If I were still a child
These perfect little poems
That pierce like needles
Would set me to sobbing
In one she says
        "Place two people
        completely at ease
        with each other
        in this picture

        She cannot imagine such a scene
        for herself, now."

And in another
        "A man wakes
        brings his coffee
        to the sagging porch
        the day glistens

        She thinks
        I had this once
        She thinks
        I will never have it again."

No, I'm not crying, I'm not a child
I'm angry because I know
Who caused some of this needless sadness.

From "Long Before This," by Deborah Pease

THE EFFORT TO LIVE

A beautiful girl, and intelligent.
She had a pleasant husband who was not demanding
And a job that wasn't too boring.
But she gave the impression that
It was a great effort for her to live.
Letters weren't answered, bills weren't paid.
Often there wasn't anything in the fridge,
She forgot things, the dog wasn't walked.
The apartment was often dusty.
She would sit in front of the TV
But not turn it on, she'd stare at nothing.
She seldom answered the telephone.
Making conversation at a party was hard for her.
She'd start to say something, then stop.
She'd been to a shrink, but he said she wasn't
        depressed, didn't need pills.
She told her husband everything was all right.
It was just an effort for her to live.
Was there some heaven of which she was thinking
        where she'd rather be?

HIS PROBLEM

Was an excessive interest
In the life of language.
There was no place for the
Emotions in his existence.
He was passionately absorbed
In words, as much with words
Themselves as with what they
Were saying. More and more,

The words built a wall around him,
Shutting him off from those
He should have loved and
Those who wanted to love him.

HARRY

When I was four my nurse
Gave me a boy-doll named Harry.
He was not a baby-doll
He was a boy. He became
My best friend. He slept
Beside me in bed. I took him
Around with me. I rode him
On my tricycle. He sat on the
Table when I was eating.
The kids teased me about him,
But I didn't care. He was my pal.

When I was eight my mother
Snatched Harry and gave him
To the Salvation Army. I never
Saw him again. I don't know who
Got him. There has been a hole
In my heart ever since.

DE NADA

I ran into her quite by accident.
It was near the public library
in New York. Obviously, she was
Lost. She had put her leather
Briefcase down on the sidewalk
And was searching in a small red
Address book. Tall. Blondish but
Quiet looking. Wearing a neat
Silk business suit, blue with
White trim, the sort of thing
She could have ordered out of a
Talbot's catalogue. Lightweight
For that warm summer day. She
Looked up from her little book.
"Do you know where . . . ?" "Let
Me help you find it," I said in
The same breath with her question.
It was an instant attraction. You
Know how these things happen. Or
Do you, they happen so rarely?
I was in no hurry. There was a
Nice bar nearby. She had a date,
Perhaps looking for a job. But the
Way she smiled I could tell she
Would have accepted an innocent
Invitation. But I left her at
The entrance of the building she
Was looking for. "Thanks ever
So much," she said, a gentle
Accent from a good school, "I
Was really lost." "De nada," I
Said, which is "Don't mention it"
In Spanish. Why did that phrase
Come to me, in Spanish, it's
Years since I've been in Spain.

I picked up her briefcase from
The sidewalk and handed it to
Her. She entered her building.
I turned and walked up Fifth
Toward the club. That was two
Summers ago. I still see her
Clear. Blondish. Shoulder-length
Hair. The trim little blue silk
Suit that probably she got from
The Talbot's catalogue. De nada.

IN THE BANK

At the counter a girl customer
Is talking to the teller about
The hair spray she uses. She has
Been given her money but goes on
Talking about hair spray. She
Seems quite unaware that I'm
Waiting in line. It's annoying.
She isn't pretty, no fun to
Watch and a raspy voice. I shift
From foot to foot. Well, I guess
My life can wait a bit for hers
While she settles the important
Business of hair sprays. I learn
Now that there's another brand
Of hair spray she has seen in a
TV commercial that may be better
Than the one she is using. That's
Quite possible. Her long brown
Hair is stringy and it has no
Shine to it, I notice that another
Teller down the counter is no

Longer busy and I move down to
Her. For some reason, though I've
Never seen her before, I tell her
That her hair is lovely today.
She asks me with a straight face
Whether I'd like tens or twenties.

OF THE SNAPSHOT

That you sent me, protesting
That the angle from which it was
Taken concealed your breasts,
Never fear, my darling, I remember
Your lovely breasts so well,
So tangibly, the look of them,
The feel of them, that even if the
Photograph had been taken from
Behind your back I could see them
As if they were before me, as real
As if I were about to hold them
And fondle and kiss them.

SHE MUST CARRY THE WEIGHT
OF HER BEAUTY

Wherever she goes. "Oh," her envious friends
Say, "she's gorgeous, I wish I could look
Like her." Little do they realize that
Such beauty is a burden that gives her
No rest. Every detail of her apparel,

Whatever she chooses to wear, must live up
To her body's perfection. She wears herself
Out selecting garments and accessories
In the boutiques. But that's only
A small part of it. Men stare at her
With unconcealed wantonness and women
With jealousy. She is whispered about
By both sexes. Untrue stories are
Invented about her. Any slight change
In her appearance is discussed.
Sometimes when she looks at herself
In her mirror she mutters, "Damn you,
Damn you; mother was plain, why can't
I resemble her?" Her beauty is an
Onerous burden, but she must bear it.

THE MISTRESS OF IMPROBABILITY

You imagine you can purify me
With your sweet smile and your
Gentle affection. You suggest
We can be good friends, not lovers.
Oh yes, I do love you in that way;
I'm grateful for your tender concern.
But is it possible, given my nature
And my amorous history, to erase
So many years in which love meant
Passion, meant assault, meant conquest?
Yeats wrote: "You think it horrible
That lust and rage should dance
Attendance upon my old age."
You scoff at Yeats as a frustrated
Old man, but I'm deep shrouded in his
Bitterness. There can be no tranquil

Old age for me, no resignation from
Fervors and fevers. No calm for me
As long as we cross paths, as long as
I must observe your sinuous undulations
As you walk; or as long as I see the
Flash of the improbable in your eyes.
Yes, that's the word for you, the
Improbable, the unexpected. You never
Do or say what the others do. That,
Beyond your corporeality, is your
Attraction. You're the mistress of
Improbability. You're an endless
Series of surprises which you can't
Suppress or I resist.

HERE & THERE

For Maria Britneva St. Just

Beloved friend, you are no longer here.
They telephoned last week to say that
Without my permission, without any
Warning, you had bought a one-way ticket
For an extended journey. You are no
Longer where I had expected always to be
Able to find you. Suddenly you are
There, but where is there? Does anyone
Know where there is? Has anyone ever
Been to there and returned to inform
Us? The books on this subject are
Unintelligible. The maps to there
Are illegible. It's obvious that
There has been an inexplicable error,
An error that makes no sense for
Either one of us. Here and there

Have somehow become interchangeable.
Everyone knows that there is not here
And that here is not there, but in our case
They have become one and the same place.

Yes, I declare that as far as I'm
Concerned you are still here as you
Have been for so long. I fax you that
Urgent message. Please fax me your
Confirmation that I am still there
With you, wherever there may be.

ON DEATH ROW

In the State Prison of Texas
There is a prisoner named Graham
Who may (or may not) have done a murder
Twelve years ago. All this time
He has been waiting to learn his fate,
While one judge or another pondered to decide
Whether he should be injected with death.
I try to put myself inside him,
To imagine what he does with his time,
How he endures the waiting
There on death row in the State of Texas.
Here is a curious thing
(But I'm a very curious person).
As I envisage him in his cell
On death row in the State of Texas
He is lying on his bunk, reading his bible;
It's hot and he has no shirt on.
As I watch, another person passes through the bars
But without their being unlocked by the guard.

She seems to float through the bars
Like some kind of liquid. She sits
Down beside him to comfort him,
There on death row in the State
Of Texas. To my amazement I discern
It is you who are the visitor, you,
White and beautiful, he black and
Forlorn. I hear your familiar voice,
The soft voice that I love, telling
Him that whatever the final judgment
May be, all will be well for him

There on death row in the State of Texas.

VIGILIA SANCTORUM

It is told that John Baskerville,
The great English printer of the
Early eighteenth century, slept
Every night in his own coffin.
This was, of course, common among
Certain heautontimorumenic monks
Of the Middle Ages, and among the
Fourth-century Desert Fathers.
Proud pharaohs, wishing to assure
Regal service in the next life,
Often sepulchrated their favorite
Slaves in small wooden boats in
The tombs, alive and ready to
Work. I don't go so far. Our
Wintry climate here in New
England isn't suitable for
Coffin-sleeping; But winter
Or summer, I never fail to

Lustrate Thanatos daily, with
Diet Coke if goat's milk is
Not available. The brother of
Thanatos is sleepy Hypnos,
Who seldom wakes up to eat
Or drink. What would be to
His taste? Pomegranate nectar?
The juice of antipodal kiwis?
I worry about Hypnos. But they,
They say that he seizes only
Those who are dreaming. I try
To keep from falling asleep.

THE LITTLE VISION

It's late and I'm lying abed
Slowly falling asleep. Now I
Can feel my eyelids beginning
To press down over my eyes,
Which are about to close . . .
Then there is an interruption.
My not quite sleeping mind has
Summoned a little vision of you
The way we were the last time
We were together. The vision
Awakens me with a start. I'm
With you again. The vision is
There for several moments
Then sleepiness returns. My
Eyes do close. I drift away
To wherever it is we go when
We are asleep.

MOMENTS IN SPACE

No exact moment is recorded for
When I left time and entered
Space; nothing precise that I
Could put down in my diary. The
Journalists were vague about it,
Using condolent euphemisms that
Weren't believed (there had been
So many cries of "wolf"). The lady
Judge at the probate court was
Annoyed. "I *must* have a date,"
She said. It was gradual, not
What I'd anticipated. It reminded
Me of dirty water running out
Of a bathtub with a little swirl
And sucking sound when it was
All empty. Of course everyone
In the village knew something
Was happening. I would meet them
In the pharmacy or at the post
Office and not remember the
Names of people I'd known for
Fifty years. I think they'll
Miss me; I gave them a lot of
Laughs, the village eccentric.

It's too soon to give much of
A report on space. I'm just
Beginning to get my bearings.
No asteroids or astronauts in
Their capsules so far. No trees
Or grass but beautiful cloud
Formations. It's a relief not
To have to bother with eating.
Few people around and none
I'd met in books. (I'd like

To see Godot again.) But space
Is endless, it stretches out
To nowhere. I may be a million
Light-years away in space.

THE ENGINES OF DESIRE

On the sixth day of creation
God saw that he was behind schedule,
He was not going to get finished
With the job on time. He consulted
His engineers and they concluded
That there would have to be some
Duplication of moving parts.
Specifically, there would not
Be time to fashion separate and
Discrete mechanisms for evacuation
And reproduction. He sent his men
Back to their drawing boards and
These functions were combined.
This decision, this poor planning,
Has led over the centuries to infinite
Amounts of dubious art and literature
Only to be described as execrable.

So God created man in his own image . . . male and female
he created them . . . and God said to them, Be fruitful and
multiply.

PHANTOMS

(1995)

ALONG THE MEADOW STREAM

The fluffy grasses on the edges
Of the stream hide my drifting line
And fly from the trout. Over the years
A deal of dreaming has drowned
In the limpid water. "Your mooning
Makes no knowledge," my grandfather
Used to tell me. "Let the fish be.
Get back to your books, lazy boy."
His voice has gone two lives away;
It stirs the water no longer along
The banks of the meadow stream.

MOTET: *AVE VERUM CORPUS*

My mother could not wait to go
To Jesus. Her poor, sad life
(Though she was money-rich)
Was made for that, to go to
Waiting Jesus.

Jesus loved her, that she knew,
There was no doubt about it,
Up there above, somewhere among
The twinkling stars, there was
A place of no more tears where
He was waiting for her, blood-
Stained palms and side, he
Was waiting.

SWEET CHILDHOOD

Why can't we pretend that
We're children who are
Playing with each other;
Not really understanding
What we're doing, but it's fun
It feels good and there is
An urgent curiosity to study
Each other's parts. Sweet childhood,
Happy time of innocence, come back
For us, bring back an hour
When everything was gentle and new.

THAT AFTERNOON

when we were walking in the sunbright woods
and you were laughing so deliciously,
"dulce ridentem" said Horace of his girl Lalage
when suddenly I did what I'd been longing to do,
pulling you to me and touching for an instant
your sweet little breast, an impulse of courage,
and of course you sprang away,
but you did not reproach me, you put your arm
around my shoulders, as if to say
you were pleased by my avowal . . .

but the god was jealous of my happiness;
you haven't come to walk with me again.

MANY LOVES

She changes the way
she does her hair for
each new admirer   if
she is to have many
loves she wants to be
a different person
for each one of them.

JACK JIGGER

They call me Jack Jigger because
I'm entirely made of little pieces
Taken from other people (some are
Alive, some dead). If there were
An autopsy the coroner would have
A hard time identifying which bits
I was born with, which were really
Mine. I can hear him saying to his
Assistant: "There's a lot of foreign
Stuff in here, things I never ran
Across before." When I walk fast
I hear a kind of rubbing inside,
Like bits of paper rustling. That's
How it is, pieces of paper moving
Against each other. The doctor has
Tried every kind of coagulant.
But no use. He's given up on me.

OPHELIA

She wanders in the meadow
Picking posies; she wanders
Among the willows singing
Sad little songs that have meaning
Only for her. She falls (or walks)
Into the stream, but she doesn't
Struggle in the water because
She imagines she's flying
Up into the clouds, high up
Where there are no more troubles.

THE TRANSIENTS

She told me there had only
been three great loves in her life
but there were quite a few
transients, as she called them.
Don't misunderstand me, she said,
I've never been wild,
but you know how it is,
when you're young and going out
quite a bit, exploring life,
when a man gets insistent,
a nice enough man you like a little,
it's just too tiring to say no
because it means making a scene.

THE DAZE OF LOVE

Comes sometimes from
the blaze of light
when an asteroid
passes us too near.

There is also
the softer radiance
when we are separated
and sink into sleep
thinking of each other.

DIE BEGEGNUNG

It was in a dark forest
Where one night I was lost
Donner und Blitz
    Erfüllung und Verlust
        Schmerzen und Wonne
            Gelächter und Tränen
I encountered a hooded figure
Who was my other self
He gave me his hand and fair words
And followed me back to this city
Where he has never left my side
    Sorge und Freude
        Einsicht und Zweifel
My other self, my constant companion.

THE NEW YOUNG DOCTOR

at the clinic is fresh
out of medical school
and hospital internship.
He's up to date on all
the new cures he reads
about in the journals.
Some of the old fogies
here in the village
won't go to him, but
I think he's great. At
my last check-up he
told me I'd probably
live to he a hundred
because I have such a
good pulse in my feet.

NOW AND THEN

He falls asleep a lot,
Only catnaps but it's rude
And embarrassing when there's company.
He's sitting in his stuffed chair,
More or less attentive to the conversation,
Then suddenly he drops off.
"Where have you been, Gramps?"
His granddaughter asks him.
"Just on a trip," he tells her.
"Now and then I like
To take a little trip."

THE CALENDAR OF FAME

"Farewell, farewell, my beloved hands,"
Said Rachmaninoff on his deathbed:
And Joseph Hofmann, the great pianist,
Invented the windshield wiper
From watching his metronome.
Genius that I am, all that I can do
Is hit wrong keys on my typewriter.

THE SECRET ROOM

People forget (if they ever knew it)
That they hear their own voices
Not through their ears
But in their own throats
Is their an image as well
For every breath of sound?

Yes, there's an image
But it seldom can be seen.
It moves too rapidly
And does not linger,
It escapes the eye.

Yet nothing, sound or sight
Is entirely lost—every sensation
Every face or voice
Is stored in the hidden room.
At the back of the brain
Only the keeper of dreams
Has the key to that hidden room.

THAT VERY FAMOUS POET

His rhymes splatter on the page
Like raindrops in a storm. It's
As easy as that. They require
No guiding intelligence. (Pound
said of Petrarch that he had an
Assistant to put in the adjectives;
It didn't matter where they came
In the line.)

It's a bit more complicated for him
When it comes to whole stanzas.
But he has the answer for that too.
There's a sink in his study. He
just turns on the faucet and lets
It run till it slows to a drip.

To be sure he has to type the poems
Out or run them through his word
Processor. That can be difficult
When all he has to work with is
Squishy liquid, but he has some
Little pink sponges to soak up
The wet. No sweat. It's easy.

COPROPHILUS

a poet whose talent is
as small as his minus-

cule mentula has been
slandering me in the

taverns alleging that
my verses are stolen

from those of my friend
Catullus   he misses the

mark I simply ridicule
the opinions of a man

(if he is a man) who
can only ejaculate if

he has dined on his
own foul excrement.

SO LITTLE TIME

St. John Perse

We have so little time
To be born to the instant,
And it is the instant,
What happens in the instant,
That decides what matters
In the poem or in love.
Wait for the instant, and
When it comes seize it.
It may never come again.

WHERE IS THE COUNTRY

We were always searching for,
That happy country we read about
In books when we were young?
Once we thought we'd found it,
And for a time we visited there,
But then we knew we'd been deceived;
It was not the dreamed-of country.
Or had we just deceived ourselves?
In making the choice of each other
Had we destroyed the happy land?

UNTIL THE SPRING BREAKS

(1995)

THE KITCHEN CLOCK

How can we make it run backwards,
That taciturn white circle with
Its torpid black hands? We only
Touch the hands when standard
Time comes to shorten our daylight
Saving to lengthen our days. That
Clock is lazy; I'd like to throw
Eggs at it. But I don't want it
To go forward faster, as if it
Were drawn by death. Let it run
Gently backwards, pausing to
Greet happy times again: the
Day when the schoolboy wrote
His first poem; the day when
The first jonquil bloomed in
His little garden; the day when
His father tossed him into the
Lake without water wings to
Prove to him he could swim.
En arrière, ruckwärts and *in
Dietro*; those are your orders,
Lazy clock, until the spring
Breaks and it doesn't matter
What you do anymore.

PETRARCH & LAURA

What if by chance (and I grant
it is remote) after my death

I were to become Petrarch and
you by the maggoty scholars

were discovered as my Laura
what would the judgment of

time be on our relationship
what would they write about

me as a lover and what would
they say about you   would they

show me as inconstant grasp-
ing for random affections

would they show you as timid
unable to bear the strains I

imposed on you   history has
many twistings & turnings

the fame we long for may
never be granted   who knows

but might it not be well for
you dear Laura to reconsider

some of your denials   it
was not thus in Avignon.

THE HUMOR OF THE COMPUTER

This is a very remarkable machine, it will

do almost anything it is asked to do,

but sometimes it does what *it* wants to do,

which can be rather confusing.

Let us be grateful for the antics

of the curious mind of the machine

and its humorous little inanities.

THE LOST FRAGMENTS

(1997)

THOSE TO COME

Will those who come after us
remember who we were except for
three or four generations of
family? Will there be a child
who amuses herself by going
through cartons of old letters
in the attic? Will she draw
crayon pictures of the people
she reads about, showing what
she imagines we were like?

I'd be a fool to hope that any
of my verses would remain in
print. I must value them by
the amusement I have in composing
them. Just that, nothing more.

But what happened to make me
grow old so soon? When I was
young I never thought of old
age, of what it would be like.
And why can I recall only part
of some scene I'd like to relive
now? Where have the lost fragments
gone? As I lie wakeful in bed
what I see is a long corridor
of closed doors.

THE LOVE POEMS OF
JAMES LAUGHLIN

(1997)

LOVE BEARING GIFTS

The poet hurls so many letters at
Lucina, he is like a catapult. But
her images are so incomparable
he hopes it means that there
will be a conjunction of hearts!

THE EVENING STAR

You came as a thought when I was
past such thinking. You came as a
song when I was finished singing.
You came when the sun had just begun
its setting. You were my evening star.

THE LIGHTHOUSE

You are my lighthouse. Ceaselessly
your rotations beam over the sea
and land. Birds are guided by them
and so are travelers lost in the
moors. You are my compass and light.

CLASSIC LOVE POEMS

THE BIRD OF ENDLESS TIME

Your fingers touch me like a bird's wing,
like the feathers of the bird that returns
every hundred years to brush against a peak
in the Himalayas until the rock's been
worn away and the kalpas are ended.

A CLASSIC QUESTION

"Ingenium nobis ipsa puella facit."
Propertius wrote that it's the girl
who makes the poems. But is the obverse
true? Will poems make a girl? I'm
really not so certain about that.

From Sextus Propertius.

THE COMING OF SPRING

The Spring season is approaching,
who will help me meeting with my dearest?
How shall I describe the beauty of the dearest,
Who is immersed in all beauties,
That color all the pictures of the universe . . .

*Kabir (1440–1518), abridged, translation by Ezra Pound
from the English of Kali Mohan Ghose.*

THE CRANE

Go away, crane! Leave the garden!
You have not told my love,
the prince of the seashore,
the torment that I suffer.
Go away, crane! Leave the garden!

From the Tamil of Shilappadikaram, *Third Century A.D.,
translation by Alain Daniélou.*

THE GROWTH OF LOVE

I see Love grow resplendent in her eyes
with such great power and such noble thought
as hold therein all gracious ecstasies,
from them there moves a soul so subtly wrought
that all compared thereto are set at naught.

From Guido Cavalcanti (1255–1300), translation by Ezra Pound.

HER LOVELINESS

There where this lady's loveliness appeareth,
is heard a voice which goes before her ways
and seems to sing her name with such sweet praise
that my mouth fears to speak that name she beareth,
and my heart trembles for the grace she weareth.

From Guido Cavalcanti (1255–1300), translation by Ezra Pound.

THE HONEYBEE

You do everything, Melissa, just the
way your namesake the honeybee does.
When you're kissing me honey drips
from your lips, but when you ask
for money you have a sharp sting.

From Marcus Argentarius.

THE LOCUST

Locust, beguiler of my loves and persuader of sleep,
mimic of nature's lyre, play for me a tune with your
talking wings to deliver me from the pains of care
and of love. In the morning I'll give you a fresh
green leek and drops of dew sprayed from my mouth

Meleager of Gadara (flourished 60 B.C.).

THE LOVERS

Radha looked on the god Krishna who desired only her,
who long had wanted dalliance with her. His face
was possessed with desire. It showed his passion
through tremblings of glancing eyes. It was like
a lotus pond with a pair of wagtails at play.

From the Hindu Gita-Govinda *(12th Century), translation by Keyt.*

THE LOVER'S COMPLAINT

I swear I do not ask too much:
O make that thoughtless girl
who yesterday made me
her spoils of war either love me
or let me share her bed to prove I love her.

From Ovid's Ars Amatoria, *Horace Gregory translation.*

REMEMBRANCE OF HER

No man can ever pass a day in boredom who has
    remembrance of her,
for she is the beginning and birth of all joy: and he who
    would praise her
no matter how well he speaks of her, he lies!

*From the troubadour Peire Vidal (1175–1205), translation from
Provençal by Paul Blackburn.*

THE VISIT OF EROS

Philodemus remembers how we first made the bedlamp
tipsy with oil, then let it go out. We knew there
are times when Eros wants no witness.
We had the bed, the lover's friend, to teach us Aphrodite's
secrets, the things of which we seldom dare to speak.

THE SECRET ROOM

(1997)

LOOKING INWARD

IN OLD AGE

The pace of time changes
And is strangely bifurcated.
Day to day it races along,
Too fast for enjoyment.
The sled is careening down the hill
Toward the big oak where it will crash.
But at night, as I lie sleepless,
Time seems hardly to move.
Each scene that passes through my head
Is almost stationary,
Often lingering longer than I can bear.

BACK THEN

It was so comfortable, so
prideful a house of bone
and blood to live in, but
now, fifty years later it's
a sack of bulging guts.
Afraid now to look in the
mirror when he's taking a
shower, loose skin hanging
all over him and more mottled
brown spots on it every day.

Hair with a natural wave
rippling back from his brow,
nearly all gone now with a
big bald spot on the top.

Nights in bordellos, parading
up and down in front of them
without a stitch on, twanging
the whangus like a drumstick
to make them twitter and laugh.

Back then it was beat them
all down the ski run, play
five sets or thirty-six
holes, but now it's don't
stand if you can sit, and
don't forget your cane.

Did he think then how good
he had it and reckon what
it would be now? And where,
he wonders, is the wisdom of
age they talk about so much?

THE ACCUMULATION

I'm looking down on them, my
children and my grandchildren,
as they struggle to get rid
of all the mess I've left
accumulated in the house. "My
god," they sigh, "couldn't
he have gotten rid of some
of these books and magazines
while he was still around to
know who would want them?"
Did he ever throw away a book
that was sent to him by some
struggling writer? The people

from the Salvation Army came
to look at them. They threw up
their hands in astonishment.
They estimated there were
fifteen hundred linear feet
of shelving full of books.
It would take ten truckloads
to cart them away and then
there would be the problem
of disposing of them. They
said the EPA had strict laws
for disposing of paper without
smoking up the atmosphere.
Where I was I couldn't give
any advice. And if I could
communicate what would I say?
I would just have to plead
I suffered from bibliomania.
A long life of bibliomania
and now no way to make
up for it.

THE HEALER

Ben Wiesel was my shrink,
a man to keep in my mind
forever. When I'd come into
his office each month for my
session he would take a
quick look at me, he could
read how I was from the way
I looked, and then he would
ask to see the poems that
I'd written since my last

visit. He'd go over them
very deliberately looking
for signs and symbols. He
read my condition from the
poems. We would only talk
about them when he came on
something that troubled him.
Then his questions would be
piercing but put with a
delicious humor and inter-
spersed with wonderful
anecdotes. He would cock
his head to one side as he
told his stories. He didn't
use any psychotropic jargon.
He didn't give me orders. He
just drew me into a mind
that was wise from twenty
years of practical teaching.
I'd leave his office walking
on air, cheerful as a butterfly.

When I came to Ben I was a
mess, in a fair way to ruining
my life. Ben put me back on
track. He's been dead now three
years, but he's still with me.
When I write a poem that I
think he would like, I mark
it "for Ben" at the side of
the page.

I'M WALKING VERY SLOWLY TODAY

Outside and even in the house,
It's such a beautiful winter day.
I want to make it last.
It snowed in the night, there is no wind,
And the snow is clinging to every branch
Of the trees. Hundreds of tiny white branches
Reaching, but for what? Don't they know
They'll be melted and gone in a few hours?
Even now the sun has come out
With an almost violent brightness.
The snow on the trees is turning
To particles of glistening ice.
Such a shining, a cold radiance.
In a few hours the trees will be bare again,
With the snow under them roughened
Where the ice buds fell into it.

I've been walking as slowly as possible,
Outside as I go to the barn to feed the sheep
And inside as I hunt for the books
I need for something I'm writing.
The brilliance of light pours in
Through the windows. I move very slowly.
I don't want this snow-light to end.
I'd like to stretch it out endlessly.
I'm eighty and I want more such days,
But I know I'm not likely to be given them.

HOW MAY I PERSUADE HER

To take up a few naughty ways?
She is fair as the Kyprian, the
Gray-eyed, silver-footed goddess
Of love, Aphrodite, but she, my
Passion, is so timid, so chaste.
She smiles like the divinity
And pretends that she likes me.
She flirts like Horace's darling
Lalage, but if I move near to
Touch her, if it's only to brush
The sweet little breasts under
Her tunic, she cowers as if I
Were the Minotaur. When she
Moves her delicious body it's
The graceful glide of Terpsi-
Chore, but if I pursue her
She stiffens her beauty. The
More I admire her the more
Her reticence makes me tremble
With frustration. I plead with
Her that I'm not lustful Apollo
Pursuing Daphne in the woodland.
She laughs at the comparison
And tosses her pretty curls.
I tell her that Aphrodite, who
Sprang from the foam of the sea,
Played love-games with Ares,
The god of warlike frenzy, though
She was married to Hephaestus,
And suffered nothing but a little
Talk at the parties on Olympus.

She becomes serious and suggests
She is not the lady in question.
How may I persuade her to take
Up just a few naughty ways?

THE FUTURE

Is the future all around us,
but we are unaware of its
intentions, ignorant of the
claims it may enforce upon
us? Was Ovid aware that he
would be exiled to a dull
town on the Black Sea?
Could Charles expect that
he would have his head
chopped off? Lincoln no
doubt feared that he would
be assassinated, but when
and how?

Speculations of this kind
tell us nothing about our
own destinies. There is no
higher power to tell us
what is going to happen.

The ancients put their
questions to oracles,
such as the one of Zeus
at Dodona and that of
Apollo at Delphi. At
Epidaurus, Asclepius
interpreted dreams. But
most of the responses of
the oracles had double
meanings.

And what of the three
fateful spinsters Clotho,
Lachesis and Atropos? Don't
bother to petition them.

They're only interested in
their spinning wheels. They
don't know or care about us.
The future will be whatever
happens.

THE GIRL IN THE MIST

One early morning in April
When I was out for a before-
Breakfast walk there was motion
At the edge of the wood and
A woman's figure came walking
Toward me through the mist.
I was so startled that anyone
Should be out at that hour
I hardly registered on who
She might be or what she
Looked like. As I stood there
She kept moving slowly toward
Me, one arm extended. She did
Not speak or look at me directly.
In a few moments she was gone,
Lost in the mist. On other
Mornings I watched for her
But she never returned.

THE MALEVOLENT SKY

The sky was always too close
over them. With the sun by day
and the stars by night it pressed
them down into the earth. It pressed
them tighter together than they
could bear. Once they had been
tender lovers, but the remorseless
sky destroyed them. The sky turned
them into walking corpses, into
shades of their former selves.

AN ELEGY OF MIMNERMUS

How much joy is left in life
Without the blessing of foam-
Born Aphrodite? Let me die now
That I can no longer have love
Secrets and the gifts of desire
And the pleasures of soft beds.
These were the blossomings of
Youth, giving happiness both
To young men and their lovers.
But age brings aches and bad
Smells to the man who has
Grown old. It makes evil
Flourish in his body and
Mind. It wears down the heart.
For him the warmth of sunlight
Is diminished. Children fear
Him and women despise him.
Cruel is the treatment with
Which the gods punish old age.

GODSPLAY

Sisupala

Sisupala was of royal blood but he had three
Eyes and four arms. His parents found this
A very frightening omen; they thought they
Had better get rid of him, expose him in the
Forest to be devoured by tigers, but as they
Left the city, a voice called to them from
The sky: "Don't be frightened. Keep the child.
The one who will kill him one day has already
Been born. Till then he will be your favorite,
Rich in fortune and fame." The mother felt better
And called out to the voice: "Who is it who will
Kill my son?" "You'll know him," the voice
Answered, "by this sign. If the boy is on the
Knees of the killer, his third eye will disappear
And two of his arms will fall off."

The king and queen set off on their travels
With many servants, and taking Sisupala, that
Was the baby's name. They visited all of the
Neighboring monarchs in their palaces. At each
Place they asked the host to take the baby on
His knees . . . but nothing happened. Not long
After their return home they were visited by
The divine prince Krishna, who was still small,
And his older brother, Balarama. They began to
Play with little Sisupala. As soon as Krishna
Had taken him upon his knees the baby's third
Eye fell away from his face and two of his
Arms vanished. The god would be the one to
Kill her son. "Promise me, O divine one,"
The mother prayed, "that if ever my son
Offends you, you will pardon him." "Even
If he offends me a hundred times, I will
Forgive him," Prince Krishna replied.

But the fate which had been predicted had
Eventually to be carried out. Many years
Later the great king Yudhishthera organized
A magnificent ceremony of sacrifice in honor
Of his coronation. All the lesser kings and
Warriors were invited to Yudhishthera's palace
For the occasion. Prince Krishna was present
And the sacrifices were dedicated to him.
But the arrogant Sisupala had the temerity
To challenge this choice. "Neither by his
Achievements nor by his lineage," he said, "is
This lord entitled to such an honor." He put
His case so cleverly that many of the guests
Agreed with him. Would they block the rites
Of sacrifice? That might lead to misfortune
For the whole kingdom.

King Yudhishthera did all he could to calm
Down Sisupala, but without success. The great
King then turned for advice to Brahma, his
Grandfather. The old man smiled and said:
"Krishna will settle the argument. What
Can a dog do against a lion? This king
Seems a lion until the real lion wakes.
All we can do is await the outcome." Sisupala
Was enraged to be compared to a dog. He threw
Insults at Brahma, but the venerable one
Remained cool. He called for silence and
Recounted the story of Sisupala and the
Predictions that were made when he was a baby.
Sisupala lost his head in his anger. He drew
His sword and threatened Brahma, hurling
Insults at him. The old man kept his dignity.
"I'm not afraid," he declared, "for we have
With us the supreme one we most venerate.
If any of you want a quick death, let him
Do battle with the dark-skinned god who
Carries in his hands the disk and the mace.

When this rash man dies he will find
Himself in the belly of the blue god."

Hearing what was said, Krishna looked
With compassion on the angry king.
But Sisupala continued his impious
Raving. Krishna told him, "The cup of
Your wickedness is now full to the brim."
As he said this the divine weapon, the
Flaming disks, rose over Krishna's head.
The cloud of fire encircled the helmet
Of Sisupala. He was split in two from
His head to his feet. The soul of the
Sinner caught fire and entered into
The body of Krishna. By the compassion
Of the god, Sisupala became one with
Him. Thus was the prophecy fulfilled.

THE GREEN HAIR

My hair is turning from gray
to green. The villagers pretend
not to notice it except for a
few of the kids. The pharmacist
gave me a bottle of something
he said would recolor my hair
but it didn't work. It just
made it more green, and greasy
too. My wife has knitted a
little ski hat to cover it up,
but I have to shave extra hard
to get the green off from my
chin. I went to the Cymotrical
Institute in Hartford. They

said my condition would require
drastic treatment. They proposed
that all my old hair be pulled
out and they would implant new
hair on my scalp. They quoted
a price of five thousand dollars
for doing that. The hell with
them. I grew resigned to having
green hair. Then a friend suggested
consultation with his shrink.
The shrink, a very experienced
man, thought my trouble must be
psychosomatic. He had never
seen anything like it. After
several sessions of Freudian
therapy he reached a conclusion.
"You appear to be in good shape
physically but it's clear that
that your head wants to cease
living. Your hair is going green
because it wants to match the
green of the grass where you
are going soon. You have,
let me put it scientifically,
'graveyard hair.'" He charged
me five hundred dollars for
that wisdom. The hell with him.

THE FEATHERED CLEFT

Why did you have to guard it
So fanatically, as if its penetration
Would bring you unbearable shame?
If you had been more generous

Both of our lives
Might have been so happy,
Two different people.

DE IUVENTUTE

When I was a young man
chasing girls I was so
hot to get into them I
never had time to learn
to savor the pleasures
of it. Fuss and rush
was all it was. And on
to the next.

Now that I'm old and
girls will have none
of me I must try to
imagine what it would
have been like with
each of them if I
had taken some pains
to learn to please them.

THE COUNTRY OF HOPE

I live in a small country of hope.
Those who want to make a success
in life choose larger, more dynamic
countries. But such places frighten

me. I haven't been to New York
in two years. Here in my rural,
hopeful, domain I can relax with no
pressure to do anything important.
Here nobody bothers me or creates
problems. I'm the village eccentric.
I have no job and I do rather odd
things if I feel like doing them.
The villagers all smile at me
in the street. I think they're
eager to see what odd thing
I'll do next. I'm a fixture.
They point me out to visitors
from other towns.

But I was speaking of hope,
my country of hope. What is it
that I'm hoping for? That
changes from day to day,
as if my hoping had something
to do with the weather. But
I can have strong hopes even
on rainy days. I should perhaps
explain that I have enough
to live on from my Social Security
checks. No problem there.
I usually lie in bed until
my hope for the day comes to me.
My hopings are pretty punctual.
They usually arrive by eight o'clock.
Then I get up to shave and make
breakfast. I don't loll in bed.
In good weather I go for a walk
in the woods. A walk is conducive
to good hoping. The exercise
helps to firm up the hope,
to fix it in place, you might say.
Then I get down to work, reading

the dictionary to acquaint myself
with new words. I'm up
to the "R"s now. Reverist, reversement,
reversionary, revertal, revestry.
I skip all the scientific words;
they're no use to me.

Today's hope is a strong one:
that there will be a letter from
you at the post office. Are you
all right? It's been a long time.

DOORS

(A divertimento from *Byways*)

I often find myself thinking about doors.
Open doors and closed doors. In our house
The back door is usually left open so that
Rupert, our dog, can get in or out
Without barking, or Allen, the hired man,
Can come in for a glass of water on a hot
Day, or when the UPS man comes in his
Truck with a package. But the front door
Is almost always locked. Uninvited
Visitors must ring the bell. This gives
Us time to peek out a window to see who
They are and whether we want to see them.
At night both doors are locked though
There has been no crime in our village
Within my memory, but you never know,
The way things are in this country now.

The house doors are really not very
Interesting. What's more important are

My *internal* doors: the door to my
Heart and the little trapdoor in the
Back of my brain in which poems
Come through.

My heart-door is like a revolving
Door, the kind you find at banks or
Big hotels. That door has been
Revolving steadily for nearly
Sixty years. It opened first when
Verna, the little girl who lived
Next door, pulled me into the woods
To let me play with her nipples.

Since then my heart-door has been
Almost constantly revolving. This
May sound unfeeling but I can no
Longer recall all the pretty ones,
And some not so pretty, who have
Set that door to swinging, around
And around.

Because there's usually a surviving
Scrap of paper with a poem, or part
Of a poem on it, I find it easier
To keep track of the movements of
The secret brain-door in my head.
It doesn't revolve. It's like a
Trapdoor that works up and down.
It's not very large, a mouse could
Barely get through it.

The first time it opened was when
I was about thirteen, my first year
At boarding school. The door opened
And out came a rhymed sailor's chantey,
A subject I'd copied from John Masefield,
Who was then poet laureate in England.

With pride I took it to my teacher,
Mr. Briggs. He read it quickly and
Tore it up. "Young man," he said,
"This isn't poetry, it's just verse."
The door in my brain snapped shut.

Since then the brain-door must
Have opened a hundred times.
Mr. Briggs is long dead but I can
Still see his eyes glaring at me
And hear his barked rebuke. Open
And shut, open and shut. Time
After time it's only verse. That
Little door is my guillotine.

THE CHASM

What was it that came
between us? It was like a
hidden chasm.

We grew up in adjacent houses
in a big city. We were about the
same age and played together
every day. We rode each other's
bicycles. We shared a birthday
party each year. We didn't talk
about it, we didn't need to, but
we knew that when we grew up we
would get married.

Our excessive attachment worried
both sets of parents. They decided
we must be pried apart. When I was

thirteen I was sent to a boarding
school in Switzerland. The students
were of twenty-two nationalities,
including Prince Metternich and
the Shah of Persia, who was a
stinker. Every Saturday night his
guards took him to a whorehouse
in Geneva. His father wanted to
make a man of him. One day some
German boys tried to hang a Belgian
from a tree in the park, but he
was rescued before he died. I
had few friends but something
made me different than I had
been. I did nothing bad but
when I got home my grandfather
deplored the fact that I had
"been exposed to so much
medical knowledge."

When I came home you were much
taller, but we went to dancing
school together. That fall you
were sent to a fancy boarding
school in Virginia where riding
horses was the big deal. Your
father bought you your own
horse and you took care of it.
It was wartime and in your
school the girls had marching
drill, using sticks for guns.
You were so good at this that
they made you a captain. Next
year you were voted "head of
school" by your classmates.
You won most of the prizes
for being the best in your
lessons.

We remained friends but there
was a parting of the ways. We
were beginning to be grownups.
I went to Harvard and you went
to Mount Holyoke. You never
invited me to come to any of
your college proms. In freshman
year at Harvard I had my first
brush with "medical knowledge."

After college we didn't see
much of each other because
I was working in New York.
You were such a pretty girl,
I wasn't surprised when you
soon married a young business
man from a prominent family
in Baltimore. I received an
invitation to the wedding
but decided not to go. I
didn't want to watch you be
married to someone else. I
still felt that you belonged
to me. And sometimes I still
feel about you that way. But
there's this chasm that has
opened between us.

I LISTEN FOR

any little sound
even a tiny noise

that would break
the silence the

ting of a finger-
nail on a glass

the click of a
heel on the floor

even the rustle
of your dress

against your knee
any one of these

would convince me
you still exist

THE CHANTING BELL

The sound we hear is the bell
Of a buoy at the mouth of the
Harbor. Have you ever wondered
What its message for us is?
These days there are no ships
To warn in that channel. What
Is the rocking bell relentlessly
Telling us? Surely it is talk
Of death, but listen a while,
Let the sound sink in, could
It not also be an eerie love-
Song, reminding us that love
Even though it was transitory,
Abides with us into eventide.

THE COLD LAKE

That day when we went up
To Sanct Wolfgang, high
In the little mountains
Above Salzburg, the water
Was so cold we could only
Stay in it swimming about
Ten minutes. Though the
Sun was shining we came
Out shivering, our teeth
Chattering. We ran to the
Little dressing box we had
Rented. It was so tiny we
Had to stand up to make
Love to get warm.

THE EMPTY SPACE

The wise old shaman told me
that the space between our

lives and our illusions can
be a desert littered with

the dried-up bones of dead
rodents or for some of us

it may be a sargasso sea
of rotting algae don't ex-

pect that the life the
child imagines as he plays

his infantile games is the
one the gods will mete out

to him, there is an empty
space between what we think

we could be and what we are
so spake the all-knowing one

THE GODS

are diseased. It's pandemic. All
that mead they've been drinking
night and day up there on Olympus.
It has sickened their bodies to
the point of putrefaction, and
turned their minds into cesspools.
They've forgotten their responsi-
bilities for us earthlings. Our
fates no longer mean anything to them.
Tell me Euparchus, my learned friend,
were they any better in chaos, when
the first of them were formed out
of the void of nothingness? I think
you once told me that when their
sickness became notable, clever
Hermes, the messenger, came down to
fetch up the great physician Hippo-
crates, hoping that he could diag-
nose and cure the divine ones.

Hippocrates examined a number of
them, male and female. He was
appalled at what he discovered.

In his Medical Aphorisms he set
down the following illnesses:
lientery, anasarca, stangury
various suppurations, phrenitis,
putrid eructations, erysipelas,
dysuria, pustules of scabies,
quartan fever, empyema, ileus,
bloody flux, sphacelus, and
other diseases which he had
never encountered before.
Euparchus, I asked, with all
these terrible plagues why are
all the gods not dead?

The gods are immortal, Euparchus
answered, how can they die when
they are immortal. Unless the
world ends they will go on tor-
menting us forever.

Is there nothing we can do to
protect ourselves from their
vindictive malice?

All I can suggest, and probably
it will do no good, is to ignore
the gods. Let's give up on the
costly sacrifices to beseech
a mercy that no longer exists.
I shall lustrate myself for
them no more.

That evening after Euparchus
had gone something began to
itch at the back of my bad
memory. Hadn't I once seen
a denigration of the gods in
the kollemata of Tantalus

of Sidon in the Palatine
Library at Heidelberg? My
memory is unreliable, but
hadn't Tantalus written
something like this?
αἳ δὲ ψυχαὶ αὐτῶν μήχαναι εἰσὶ
ἀλλήοις ἐπὶ ταῖς διαφθειρίαις ἡδοναῖς
"Their souls were only instruments
of each others' dissolute pleasures."

THE LADYBUG

A ladybug has been walking
round and around the rim of

my milk glass   she's smart,
she doesn't try to get down

into the milk where she'd
drown   she waits till I take

a drink of the milk, then
goes to the place where my

lips have left a little smear
and imbibes that   if humans

could be that intelligent.

AUTO-DA-FÉ

The irrevocable decision has
come down from the fathers
of the Holy Inquisition that
I am to burn. I'll be a fire
for the faithful to make them
even more faithful. The time
of the actual combustion will
be at the pleasure of the civil
authorities. No doubt they'll
do it on a holiday to amuse
a large crowd. I try not to
feel anger at these people
or even at the friars. I try
to believe that I'm being
punished for my own faults,
that I'm not a victim.

While waiting I'm confined
in a dungeon of the castillo
which is mostly populated
by criminals. They make a
good deal of noise but it
isn't too bad otherwise
except that my cell has no
window. But I have a pallet
to sleep on and a bucket for
excretion. The food is slop
but no worse than what they
gave us in the army when we
were fighting the Moors in
the South. Nico, the jailer
who has no shoes and the
most crossed eyes I've ever
seen is a very decent sort.
He's sorry for me. He says

he prays for me, not that
that will do any good. Now
and then he comes into
my cell to chat with me
and give me the news of
what's happening outside.
He's from Andalusia and
has some pretty good jokes.

They've given me a Bible
but the light is too bad
to read it, even if I
wanted to. Mostly I lie
on my pallet and think
about what I may have
done to get into this fix.
The decisions of the
Inquisition are never
published and my trial,
if you can call it that,
was all in Latin, which
I hardly understand,
except for some parts
of the Mass. But I
thought I heard that the
word *saevitia* (cruelty)
was spoken several times
in the friars' discourse.
Cruelty! What had I done
in my life that was so
cruel that I should die
for it in the cruelest
way to die, at the stake?
Once in the army I had
broken the nose of an
idiot corporal, but we
made up after the fight.
On the whole I'm mild-

tempered and have always
been a "do unto others"
sort of person. Where
was my cruelty?

I was puzzled until an
answer, at least a
possible answer, came to
me in a bad dream, a
nightmare that I had
every so often, always
the same, that I called
the dream of the turtle.

I'm a little boy about
eight. I'm playing in the
garden of my great
uncle's house in Córdoba.
There is motion in the
ageratum and out crawls
a little turtle. It is
only about eight inches
long. It moves very
slowly, each of its four
little feet in a separate
rhythm. When it sees me
the turtle stops moving,
pulling its head and legs
under its shell for fear
of me. The shell is so
beautiful, green and brown,
shiny, with a pattern of
black markings. A lovely
little creature. I dare to
pick it up. It doesn't try
to bite me. It's not a
snapper. Full of curiosity,

the way a child is, I try
to pull its body out of
its shell. But I can't
budge it. Then I become
angry with the little
beast. I must see what's
inside it. I go to the
toolhouse and fetch a
chisel and hammer.
Obsessively I attack
the turtle's hard shell,
breaking holes in it.
There is no blood but
there is a gray liquid
about the inner parts.
Something keeps pulsing
which must be the heart.
The head, still retracted,
seems to be attached to
the stomach.

In a frenzy which I've
never understood I
destroy the poor turtle
into a pile of sticky bits.
Then my uncle comes out
of the house and sees
what I've been doing. He
strikes me and puts me over
his knee for a hard
spanking. He sends me to
my room and tells me
there will be no supper
for me that evening. I
must reckon on what I've
done to one of God's
creatures. I have utterly

shamed myself, the most
cruel thing he has ever
seen anyone do.

The dream of the turtle.
Saevitia intolerabilis,
an offense against God.

ROSALINDA, THE DREAMER

This beautiful girl, aged 26,
was distraught; she feared
she was losing her sanity
because she couldn't tell
whether her eyes were open
or closed when she was dreaming.
Was what she was in her dreams
reality or illusion? She was
having nervous palpitations.

She came to my office because
I'm a specialist in neuro-
ophthalmology. Examination
revealed no optical disease. At
hazard, because I had never
encountered such a case,
I suggested that she glue
pennies to her upper lids
before going to bed.

A few weeks later she was back
in my office, reporting complete
recovery. "Gosh, doc," she said,

"You're a wonder. Now I always
know where I am and who I am."
Such a lovely girl; we're engaged
to be married next month.

THE UNEXPECTED VISITOR

Today, in my very own house,
there was a woman making herself
at home whom I swear I never
saw before. I'm not one to
forget a pretty face, but this
one was totally new to me.
Blonde curls in a style that
used to be the thing about
1970. No raving beauty but
nice looking, an air of
refinement. She was dressed
in slacks and a red silk
blouse. I spotted her as I
was coming downstairs to the
front hall. I could see from
there that she was stretched
out on the living room sofa,
smoking a cigarette and
reading a book.

Who could she be? I went out
to the kitchen to see if
Sandy, the maid, knew who
she was. "A lady, Mr. L. I
haven't let anyone in all
day." "Take a look please,
Sandy, to see if you recognize

her. She might be a friend of
my wife's whom you would know."
Sandy was gone several minutes.
"I don't get it, Mr. L. There's
nobody in that end of the
house. I checked all the rooms,
even the bathrooms."

I ran back to the living room.
The woman was still there on
the sofa. Was she a spook? Why
couldn't Sandy see her?
Suddenly she spoke, a
rather mellifluous voice.
"Well, here you are. I hope
you're glad to see me. Have I
aged so much you aren't
able to recognize me?"
"I don't mean to be rude but
I'm positive we've never
met." "Perhaps not in the
flesh, but I know I'm the
girl about whom you wrote
your beautiful poems 'Touching'
and 'The Enlacement.' I know
them by heart." She began
to recite "Touching" but I
stopped her. "You must know,
I'm sure," she said, "that poets
write imaginary poems, ones
to an imaginary lady like
some of the ones that the
Troubadours wrote." "I don't
believe you. Those are my
poems and you can't take
them from me. " I told
her I was very flattered

that she admired my poems
but why had she come to
call on me?

We were silent for a moment.
Then she asked if I ever
wrote poems to men. She
said that the old Greek
poets wrote poems both to
women lovers and to boys,
that she had heard that
in ancient Greek there
was a special adjective
for "boy-loving" poems.

"I want you to write for
me," she said, "one of your
most passionate poems to a
remarkable young man to
whom I'm attracted. You
can do it, please write
it for me. I'm so stupid
with words. Promise me
you'll write it. I'll be
back to see you in three
weeks. I hope you can have
it ready by then."

At that, she rose from the
sofa, threw me a kiss with
her finger and disappeared.
She was gone without trace.
What am I going to write
for her, for the young man
with whom she is in love?

POETS ON STILTS

Writing on stilts is in vogue
these days. The taller the stilts
the easier to be in fashion.
Very few poets now want to walk
with their feet on the ground,
they might get their shoes wet.

These poets buy their stilts
at some beanery. Stilts from a
creative writing course are
especially prized. Such stilts
are the tallest.

Stilts can give a superior view
of almost anything the poet
wants to write about. Altitude
makes the poet feel important
and it gets him into the club.

But a word of warning to
stiltwalkers. The higher they
fall from their stilts, the
bigger the smash when they
hit the pavement.

THE TRUTH TELLER

As I was walking along the sidewalk
Of 14th Street I encountered a mad-
Woman who, without pause, was talking
To herself in a loud voice, making

Wild gestures as she went along. I
Turned around to follow her, thinking
She might have a message for me, some-
Thing I ought to know about. Perhaps
She was in her fifties, a dumpy
Little person, her hair all in
Unkempt tangles. She was wearing
A bright red dress which must have
Been given her by the Salvation
Army. Her high sneakers were filthy.

Although I got close to her, she
Was hard to understand. At times
Her voice rose to a shout. Was it
Yiddish, Polish, Italian she was
Speaking? None of those that I
Could recognize. Was she echolalic?
Probably she had been let out of
A mental hospital as harmless.
Then I got it: she was cursing
God in very rough language. "You've
Made a fucking mess out of this
Fucking world. No place for us
Poor people to live, nothing to
Eat unless we beg for it. Only
The fucking rich people have
Anything and they don't give a
Shit about us. And the fucking
Police rousting us out of the
Good begging streets, fucking
Bastards the lot of them."

That was the message, and it
It was the truth, a true message.
When we stopped for the lights
At Eighth Avenue I reached for
My wallet and gave her all the
Bills I had. She didn't thank

Me, didn't even look at me. She
Just stuffed the money into the
Neck of her dress and ran across
The avenue, still shouting and
Swearing. "Fucking world you've
Made, all shit, fucking shit."

SWAPPING MINDS

For Vanessa

Melissa and I were sitting
by the little lake in Green
Park in London playing
"swapping minds." It's an
old game that came down from
the lowlands. It was a fine
day so we had brought a
little picnic. Melissa
makes wonderful pâté, as
good as anything from Fortnum
& Mason. Yummy. And we had
a half bottle of Chardonnay
between us.

Here is how the game of
"swapping minds" goes. It's
not a child's game, it's
very intellectual, or should
I say psychological. Just
imagine Melissa and I are
talking. She says something
to me, "James why are you
always so arrogant?" But,
obviously that's not what
she is thinking. To answer

her I must try to imagine
what she *was* thinking when
she asked that. I must swap
minds with her.
I ventured the following:
"Melissa, you have the most
lovely white skin in England,
you must be careful not to
get sunburned."

Melissa: "James, why do you
pretend you are Scots when
you're really of Irish descent?"

James: "Melissa, are you
remembering the handsome
Russian boy you met in the
Hermitage on your trip to
Russia and he took you to have
an ice cream with him?"

Melissa: "James, did the
other boys at school tease
you because you were so bad
at games?"

James: "Do you really love
me or are you just flirting?"

Melissa: "I'm sorry, James,
but the response is in your
mind, not in mine."

That was the end of the
"swapping game" for that
day, and such a happy day
it was, there in Green Park,
watching the ducks on the
pond.

THE SECRETS

The secrets of your body
are difficult to unlock
and difficult to solve.
I see you moving about
the house or walking in
the garden; your movements
are ordinary. But when I
watch you closely sometimes
I sense that certain gestures
of your body, quite apart
from what you may be saying,
are eluding my understanding.
These are rare qualities
of your physical being.

How may I define what I
observe? My feelings as I
watch you are so tenuous,
so vague. Should I even be
concerned about these strange
perceptions? Is my mind
afloat in wanderings? How
could your body's secrets
harm me? It's not as if you
had a contagious disease.

Perhaps it's I who have a
disease: a longing for
complete knowledge and
possession. Probably that's
what makes me so curious
about the secrets of your body.

THE ROAD OF DREAMS

For years I didn't pay much
attention to the things I
saw in dreams. Of course as a
child I was terrified by
nightmares, that kidnappers
were coming to get me. But
in grownup life I usually
found the happenings in my
dreams comical. I'd wake up
laughing. When later I read
some of the dreams of Freud's
patients they seemed too pat.
I wondered if the old man had
concocted them to prove his
diagnoses.

But now since old age has
engulfed me I'm having a
different kind of dream,
one that seems to be trying
to give me messages. One
persistent dream is recurrent.
I call it the road dream
because I'm always walking
on a road, one that I can't
recognize or identify where
it is. But it is serial. I
seem to be making progress
in my travel on this
road. The scenery along
the road changes from night
to night.

This dream has become like
a journey. I'm going somewhere

but I can't guess where. There
are no milestones and no signs.
Where does the road lead?
What is my destination?

A NIGHT OF RAGAS

Those all-night concerts in India
that began at dusk and went on till
nearly dawn. In the open, the audience
squatting on the ground. A platform
for the performers. The singer, usually
suggesting the melody and a soft
tabla, played with the hands, giving
the rhythm. The songs were the love
ragas of Krishna and Radha. The god
and the cow-herding girl he loved:

> Let the earth of my body be mixed
> with the earth my beloved walks on.
> Let the fire of my body be the brightness
> in the mirror that reflects his face.
> Let the water of my body join the waters
> of the lotus pool he bathes in.

Till I learned that the scale of Vedic
music is different than ours, sometimes I
thought a woman's voice was flat; it was
dropping eighth tones, but when I got
used to the scheme of it, the singing
became very compelling. It moved me
deeply. I can hear it still and see
the scene, the audience silent in its
appreciation of the artistry. The

shadows over the crowd lit up by
flaming lamps on the sides of the
square and over the performers'
platform.

MY MIND

is drifting down the river
like a dead leaf that is
caught in the current. Now
and then it gets stuck in
an eddy. It swirls around,
but doesn't sink and goes
on down the stream. *We* know
that the river leads to the sea,
but this is not the kind
of knowledge that a floating
leaf possesses. It has no
idea of a destination, or
when it will be so wet it
will disintegrate and join
the soil of the bank.

Little leaf, shall I think
of you as Psyche or as the
mother of the muses,
Mnemosyne? In my muddled
life these were in conflict.
Often it was hard to tell
them apart. Two voices
speaking in concert.

Now that worldly memory
is leaving me, let me hymn

my thanks to both of them,
for the lifelong pleasures
they have given me.

THE LOVE PUDDLE

is not deep but it's
usually muddy. If you

stray into it you won't
drown but you may come

out of it looking like
a tramp and with your

feelings more dishevel-
led than your trousers.

You may feel guilty or
feel betrayed or even

disgusted, you'll wonder
why you walked through

the love puddle instead
of going around it. But

you know you'll do it
again—that's for sure.

LOVE IS THE WORD

Love is the word he hopes
that she will utter at
dusk as they have been sitting
on the bank of the river,
watching the dark fall and
quietly talking, but not
about themselves.

Love is the word he would
so much like to hear.

Gently, he takes her hand
but there is no response
to the pressure of his
fingers. While there is
light enough, they watch
the eddies in the water.

Love is the word he would
so much like to hear.

What should he say to
make her speak it? They
have been keeping company
for several months, but
they are both so shy. He
has no experience with
wooing other girls. She
never talks about such
things. He has no inkling
of whether she has had a
lover.

Love is the word he would
so much like to hear.

When it's full dark they
can no longer see the eddies
in the water but they hear
the various sounds that the
river makes as it follows
its course to the sea.
Then there is a brightening
in the air over the forest
across the stream and a moon,
a nearly full moon, appears.
He wants to linger but she
looks at her wristwatch and
says: "My goodness, it's
after nine, I must go home."
She rises abruptly and starts
walking to where they have
left the car on the highway.
He tries to take her arm to
guide her through the trees,
but she says: "Don't worry
about me, I know the way, I
can see it in the moonlight."

*Love is the word he would so
much have liked to hear.*

THE LANGUAGE OF MY MIND

I've been trying to read
the language of my mind.
I'd like to be able to
write the kind of poem
that Gary writes, but
it's hard to do, hard

to get his concrete
simplicity and his
intonation.

I study the language
that's in my mind but
it gets confused because
words start turning into
pictures. My eye is so
visual.

So many mountains and
rivers. Kanchenjunga
at Darjeeling. The
Ganges at Benares. One
after another my page
fills up with scenes
and people.

Ezra on the beach at
the Lido. The big
glacier above Zermatt.
Sri Nalanda expounding
Vedanta at Trivandrum.

I cover my eyes to blot
out the kaleidoscope of
scenes. That's better.
The words begin to come
back. Now I recite the
mantra *om mani padme
hum*. That's not my
language but I'll try
to make it mine. I'll
say it's the jewel
at the heart of the lotus.

LUCINDA

It's not hard to write love
poems to Lucinda because we've
never met, I've never set eyes
on her. She answers my letters
in a pretty girlish hand, but
when I request a photo it never
comes. I tell her I don't care
if she has three Picasso eyes,
I know how perfect her soul is
from other evidence.

It all began when she sent me
her stories to publish at New
Directions: exquisite, subtle,
sensitive stories that bowled
me over. A girl who could write
such stories could only be the
one I'd been dreaming of ever
since I became a publisher.

I actually know more about
her than you might suspect.
For me she is Catullus' Lesbia
and Tibullus' Delia, she's
Herrick's Julia, Rochester's
Phillis. Four yummy girls
anthologized into one. What
more could any publisher desire?

THE LOGODAEDALIST

I am Bosco, the logodaedalist.
It's my job to repair broken-down words,
To make old, sick words sound new,
And make some of them seem like two words
    instead of just one.
Gertrude Stein worked at this trade
But she wasn't always too good at it.
I think she didn't always understand
That no matter how sick a word was
It still had to mean something,
Almost anything would do but something.
In the end she gave up trying.
But I'm only eighty and I intend to keep trying.
I'm Bosco, the obsessed logodaedalist.
As long as there are any loose words around
I'll try to make them hop, skip and jump for you,
And maybe make them say something
You didn't know they meant.

THE LONG MOMENT

For Elizabeth Lund

It was October and the woods
where they walked that afternoon
were ablaze with red and orange
color. Down at the lake there
was a heron standing motionless
on one leg. What was he doing
here so late in the year?

When they got back to the house
she made tea and they sat for
an hour talking about the poets
they loved. She was so pretty
and so bright. And she had a
sense of humor.

When it came time for her to
drive back to Boston, he went
out to open her car door for
her. But he didn't close the
door at once. There was some-
thing he would have said to
her if he dared.

She didn't start her car right
away. Did she have something
to say to him, too, but didn't
know how to put it?

There was a long silent moment
between them as they looked at
each other. But it became an
almost ludicrous moment. Then
they shook hands very formally,
and she drove away.

THE LONGEST JOURNEY

As a young man, full of eagerness,
I set out to conquer my little
sphere. If it were only a finger's
width, it would be mine, all mine.
And I walked, as the old poet said,

"multas per gentes et multa per aequora"
in pursuit of the voices that called me.
And some were where I expected
to find them and some were not.
And as I drew near to them many
faded away and were no longer audible.
Now, in old age I think back to those
I loved rather than to anything
I took from anyone for my enrichment,
for I know now that "the beauty is in
the walking; we are destroyed
by destinations."

THE BLACK HOLES

that the astronomers have
discovered are up in the
astral galaxies. They are
immeasurably distant, far
away beyond calculation.
But I know of one that is
very near at hand. It's
called anima (the soul)
and it's inside my body,
linked to my heart and my
brain by a cord of electrons.
Its blackness and depth,
which I'll never be able
to penetrate, are the locus
of doubt, of the ultimate
unanswerable questions:
who am I and what are all
of us doing on this earth?

AKHMATOVA'S MUSE

She comes to the poet only
Late at night, when the
Poet is sleepless, waiting
For her visit. Life is so
Uncertain. Is the muse a
Living person or a shade?
It's impossible to discern
In the darkness if she is
Old or young. Well, what
Matters it when without the
Muse there would be no song.

Now the muse has come at
Last; it's nearly dawn.
But tonight she stares at
The poet as if she doesn't
Know her. It's frightening.
The poet must put her to
The test. She asks the muse
Whether it was she who
Guided Dante on his journey
Through Hell. The muse is
Silent for a moment as if
She can't remember. At last,
Very quietly, she answers,
"Yes it was I who led him
Through the circles of Hell."

THE ALEATORY TURTLE

who lives in my flower
garden never seems to
know where he wants to go.
He zigzags through the
plants with no obvious
destination. Now and then
he'll retract his head
under his carapace as if he
wanted to get his bearings,
but soon his head will pop
out and he'll be on his
way again, plodding along ever
so slowly, one leg after
another. Does he take
note of me? Is he afraid
of me? From the deliberation
of his movements I can't
tell. I like him, he does
no harm. He's not one of
those snappers that are
over in the marsh. I enjoy
watching him and like to
work in the garden when
he's there. I've often
wanted to follow him to
see where he goes and find
out what he eats. But he's
so slow it would take hours
to pursue him. I have an
affinity with my turtle.
Like him I'm a slow mover
now that I'm old. There's
something between us but
I can't define what it is.
He is my friend the turtle.

Am I to him a friend?
Does he know what a man
is? Am I his man? I hope so.
You can't have enough
good friends.

AN AMOROUS DIALOGUE

The first time I saw her I trembled
At her beauty. But the second time
There was mockery, even hostility
In her tone. On our next meeting,
To defend myself I used lines from
Martial, one of his nasty bits:
Os et labra tibi lingit, catellus;
Non miror, merdas si libet esse
Cani (which means: your little dog
Licks your face and lips: I'm not
Surprised, I knew dogs like to eat
Shit). To my surprise she understood
What I had said and replied from
The same poet: ventris onus misero,
Nec te pudet, excipis auro (aren't
You ashamed to deposit your load
In a golden bowl, you show-off?).
"You are a crude vain pig," she
Told me, "but at least you have
Something between your ears."

After that we met now and then
In various romantic locations
Along the banks of the Isar in
Munich. There were little word
Swords from both sides. But

When we'd exhausted each others'
Shafts there were no amorous
Sequels to our conversations.
She demurred at being kissed
And even refused to hold hands
As we strolled through the
English Gardens. It was back
To the beginning. I trembled
At her beauty and she called
Me "Schweinlichkins." I'd like
To know what has become of her.
Whom is she tormenting now?

THE APSARASES

I think someone is watching
Me. Someone is following me,
I'm sure, but is not visible.
How do I know I'm being
Followed? There are little
Sounds of someone walking
Behind me, sounds as soft
As the flutter of a bird's
Wings, but when I turn around
There is no one there. And
Sometimes if I wake up in
The night I sense there is
Someone in the darkness. One
Day I walked on the beach
And there were strange marks
On the sand but they weren't
Like footprints. I suppose
I should be frightened but
I'm not.

In the puranas of Hindu
Mythology we may read of
The apsarases, sacred nymphs,
Who can make themselves
Invisible, and who can fly
Great distances, even over
The oceans. One of their
Roles is to protect and
Guide persons whom the gods
Have chosen to find dhamma-
Pada, the true way, the
Path to virtue and wisdom.

THE ACROBATIC DANCERS

For Anne Scoville

The two dancers, one a woman
and the other a man, who are performing
on the stage of a theatre, are,
to tell the truth about them,
lost. They are completely lost.
This, of course is not known
to the audience, which gives
them thunderous applause as
they take their bows.

But they are lost in the world
and to each other. As they sit
on the bench backstage, getting
their breath after the exertion
of dancing, she asks him, "Who
are you anyway, I don't know you."

"I think my name is Hippias," he
answers, "but I'm not quite sure.
For that matter, who are you?
Have I seen you before?"

"Probably not," she says, "I'm
from Ionia. There they called
me Nerissa after my mother."
When they had changed in
their dressing rooms they met
again at the stage door of
the theatre.
There were more questions.
"Where are we supposed to go
now?" "I don't know. My
control is Terpsichore, but she
hasn't sent me any word
of instruction." "I'm in
the same boat. My man is
Apollo but he's always
out chasing maenads in the
woods or getting drunk up
on Olympus. Not a word from
him all week."

"Well Hippias," Nerissa
says, "the gods are idiotic,
but we'll have to eat till
we hear from them. Isn't
that a McDonald's down the
street? Let's go there and
hope for the best."

Note: The poet despairs of answering the dancers' questions.
He hopes that his friend the sculptress can do better using
visual methods.

ALL THE CLOCKS

in the house have stopped running.
They've quit moving their hands
at different times. It's very confusing.
The kitchen clock stopped at 6:35.
The grandfather clock, that has to be
wound with a key, gave up at 10:15,
and the key won't turn in it now.
The alarm clock by my bed is mute
at 4:30. How did I manage when I was
a child and couldn't tell time?
I went by light and dark. And whether
I was hungry. That will have to
do me till the clocks end
their strike. Or will the strike
spread to other houses? I must
call up the neighbors to see
whether their clocks have given
up too and what they are doing
about it. This situation is a
nuisance but, honestly, I don't
really blame the clocks. Can you
imagine what it's been like for
them? Minutes, hours, days, weeks,
months, years plodding around
the same circular treadmills,
being taken for granted, no thanks
to them from anybody. This could
stop the world. If we get out of
this somehow and history goes
on, will historians write about
the revolution of the clocks?

SATURN

Many among the ancients believed
that Saturn was the bringer of
old age and death. But be of
good comfort. The true mythology
sets forth that as a god he was
benevolent, the founder of
agriculture at Rome, where his
reign was called the age of
gold. His *saturnalia* celebrated
the growing of crops and was
a period of general festivity.

EPIGRAMS AND COMIC VERSES

CARROTS

Little girls in France, even
in the best families, are told
that if they eat their carrots
they'll grow up with pink thighs.

BETTER THAN POTIONS

Our village love counselor
tells her lovelorn young

clients that kittens cannot
be caught but if you stay

where you are and do some-
thing interesting the kit-

ten will soon come to you.

THIRTY-NINE PENTASTICHS

THE TENDER LETTER

C'était à Paris. She was Jeanine, young, pretty and
bright. Une jeune fille bien élevée. They often had
me to Sunday dinner. I thought we were just friends.
Then the note to my hotel: "Je voudrais être ta
maîtresse" In three months she was dead of cancer.

I TRAVEL YOUR BODY

I travel your body, like the world,
your belly is a plaza full of sun,
your breasts two churches where blood
performs its own, parallel rites,
my glances cover you like ivy . . .

"I travel your body . . . .": Octavio Paz, from Sunstone *(abridged),*
translation by Eliot Weinberger.

THE LIVING BRANCH

If I existed as a tree
I would not be a conifer, cone-bearing
My nature would be deciduous, a long
Process of leaves, falling, falling
From the living branch.

Deborah Pease, the first stanza from a poem in The Feathered Wind.

ALL GOOD THINGS PASS

The girl at the order desk of the University
Press from whom I used to buy my Loeb Library
classics is now a telephone hitched to a
computer. She would wrap her long legs around
my neck and I imagined she was Tara of Cos.

THE SNAKE GAME

Henry looked like a shoeclerk but was a spell-
binder. He persuaded a friend to let him put a
garter snake into her vulva. Exciting at first
but then the snake wouldn't be pulled out. He
had to take her to the hospital emergency room.

Henry Miller.

THE IMMEASURABLE BOUNDARIES

Heraclitus wrote that we would not discover
the boundaries of the soul even if we traveled
all the world's roads. At eighty I've traversed
a good many of them, but now I've stopped walking.
The boundaries of the soul are immeasurable.

PENELOPE TO ULYSSES

Penelope to the tardy Ulysses:
do not answer these lines, but come, for
Troy is dead and the daughters of Greece
Rejoice. But all of Troy and Priam himself
are not worth the price I've paid for victory.

Ovid, from the Heroides, *translated by Howard Isbell.*

THE FIRST TIME

It was the first time we had made love.
I asked her what she would like me to do
to give her pleasure. But she wouldn't
tell me. She said I must find out for
myself. It would be better so.

THE ANGLO-SAXON CHRONICLE

This year long dragons swam in fire
across the sky in Northumbria.
This was the year of the great gale.
And this year died Harthacanute:
Everything he did was unworthy of a king.

Guy Davenport, translator.

TANKA

In the *Dhammapada* it is written
that the body is a strong fortress
made up of bones, plastered with
flesh and blood, wherein lurk
pride, deceit, decay and death.

From the Dhammapada *(1st Century B.C.).*

THE LONG FEET PEOPLE

Pliny relates in his *Natural History* that
in Iluria there's a race with feet a *pes*
long, turned backwards, with 16 toes. On
hot days they lie on their backs, using
their feet to shade themselves from the heat.

TWO FOR ONE

The painter Schiele knew he was two people,
and that he needed separate girls. When he
saw the Harms sisters in the street he hung
nude pictures of himself in his window. Edith
Harms married him. Adele became his model.

WORD SALAD

Neurologists call the babbling
of the patients in dementia "word
salad." Looking at recent verses
I realize that they are mostly
good examples of "word salad."

THE FANTASIST

Ronald Firbank the decadent novelist liked
to play out his fantasies. When Lady Cunard
invited him to lunch at the London Ritz he
studied the menu with care and ordered *one*
pea, which he sent back because it was cold.

THE PISSING OF THE TOADS

Concerning the venomous urine of toads, conceptions
are entertained which require consideration. That a
Toad pisseth, and this way diffuseth its venome,
is generally received, not only with us but also
in other parts, as the learned Scaliger observed.

From Thomas Browne's Pseudodoxia Epidemica, Enquiries into
Certain Vulgar Errors *(1646)*

THE GOOD LIFE

Nabokov remembers that when he was young,
early in July his grandfather's carriage
and a team of horses would be loaded on a
railroad flatcar for the trip across Europe
to Biarritz in France for the annual holiday.

THE SEASHELL

Someone brought me a seashell.
Singing inside is a sea from a map.
My heart fills up with water
and little tiny fish, silvery, shadowy.
Someone brought me a seashell.

Federico García Lorca, translated by Alan S. Trueblood.

THE SMILE OF THE DESERT

In the desert I felt a thrill of pleasure—such as only
the captive delivered from his dungeon can experience.
The sunbeams warmed me into renewed life and vigour, the
air of the desert was a perfume, and the homely face of
Nature was as a smile of a dear old friend.

Sir Richard Burton, a passage from the Personal Narrative of a Pilgrimage
to Al-Madinah & Meccah *(1885).*

SALAD DRESSING AND AN ARTICHOKE

It was please it was please carriage cup in an ice-
cream, in an ice cream it was too bended bended with
scissors and all this time. A whole is inside a part, a
part does go away, a whole is red leaf. No choice was
where there was and a second and a second.

Gertrude Stein, from Tender Buttons *(1914).*

THE SWEET SINGER

Sappho led a band of lovely girls
on Lesbos, and she sang to them
sweet singing: "Desire has shaken
my mind as wind in the mountain
forest roars through the trees."

THE WRITER AT WORK

On opening night of his play *Under Milk Wood*,
Dylan Thomas is backstage lying on his tummy
writing new lines for the cast: "Organ Morgan
at his bedroom window playing chords on the
sill for the fishwife gulls in Donkey Street."

THE GOD OF THE SUN AND FIRE

Glory to Agni, the high priest of the sacrifice.
We approach you, Agni, with reverential homage in
our thoughts, daily, both morning and evening.
You the radiant, the protector of sacrifices,
the constant illuminator, be as a father to us.

Excerpt from the First Mandala of the Rig Veda *(circa 1500 B.C.), abridged.*

THE MAGIC FLUTE

That summer in Munich we were Papageno and Papagena.
We walked along the Isar and in the Englische Garten
and went to a different opera almost every night. But
it was Mozart who set us dreaming and made us fall
in love. Beautiful days and now happy memories.

THE RAVAGED VIRGIN

Aphrodisia in Anatolia is famed in mythic
history because it is recorded in Hesiod's
Theogony that there Zeus raped the nymph
Cleonia. He did it by disguising himself
as a water buffalo. She said it hurt a lot.

886

ODD GOINGS ON IN PHILADELPHIA

The painter Eakins was an odd duck. For him art
depended on the nude figure. But using nude
models wasn't enough. He wanted his girl students
to know the "joints and machinery" of the body.
He had himself photographed with them in the buff.

THE MAN OF TAO

The nonaction of the wise man is not inaction.
It is not studied. It is not shaken by anything.
The sage is quiet because he is not moved,
Not because he wills to be quiet.
Still water is like glass.

A fragment from Thomas Merton's version of The Way of Chuang Tzu *(1965).*

AN UNUSUAL GIRL

In Lucerne beautiful Birgita liked to circle
the Matterhorn in her Piper Cub. Evenings you
might find her with friends in her bathtub
enjoying live fish in an intimate way while
the phonograph played Schubert's *Trout Quintet.*

THE HETAERA

Ani Leasca, a Greek cocotte who worked Zurich,
could have modelled for Apelles. I never fingered
her expensive flesh, but when she wasn't engaged,
she liked to play pool in the Dolder, regaling
me with the kinks of the richest men in Europe.

THE RIGHT GIRL

Rufinus advised Thelon to beware a girl who seems
too eager. Or one who hangs back too long. One is
too quick, the other too slow. Look for one neither
too plump nor too thin. Too little flesh is as bad
as too much. Best, he said, never to run to excesses.

THE RESCUE

From New Orleans Tenn wrote me a wonderfully
comical letter. He was being relentlessly
pursued by a pretty girl. She was cramping
his style; would I get her off his back? A
very sexy girl; she soon had me on *my* back.

THE SCULPTOR

Brancusi didn't have much to say but he
cooked a great Romanian stew and liked
after eating to swing upside down by his
knees on a monkey's trapeze while his
phonograph blared out Ravel's *Bolero*.

GOOD PHILOSOPHY

When I give you an apple, if you love me
from your heart, exchange it for your
maidenhead. But if your feelings are what
I hope they are not, please take the apple
and reflect on how short-lived is beauty.

Plato (4th century B.C.).

AN EXQUISITE LIFE

Robert Montesquiou, the exquisite model
for Proust's Charlus, kept pet bats in
silver cages, and for his famous receptions
had each room of his dwelling sprayed
with a different suggestive perfume.

THE INVITATION TO MAKE LOVE

Show her drawings of animals making love, then
of humans. The sight of erotic creatures such
as geese will make her curious. Write amorous
messages to her on palm leaves. Tell her your
dreams about her. Tickle her toes with your finger.

Excerpts from the Sanskrit of Vatsyayana's Kama Sutra
(circa 5th century A.D.), translated by Alain Daniélou.

POEMS NEW AND SELECTED

(1998)

FOREWORD

Many of the writings in this book should be called verse rather than poetry. Poetry is an exalted, almost mystical writing in its nature. Poetry works with devices such as metaphor and verbal decoration. This writer seldom aspires to such high levels of expression. His writings are most often the statement of facts as he has discerned them. Many are reports on perceived feelings, his own and those of others; or a placing with imagination; or recollections from reading of matters with which classical writers were concerned. There is a minimum of decoration.

The writer's intention is summarized in the passage of one of his verses which states:

SOME PEOPLE THINK

that poetry should be a-
dorned or complicated. I'm

not so sure. I think I'll
take the simple statement

in plain speech compress-
ed to brevity. I think that

will do all I want to do.

The Greek origin of the term epigram is a scratching on stone. The most pleasing of these verses aspire to live up to that definition. Many fail, but a few succeed.

JAMES LAUGHLIN

INTRODUCTION

James Laughlin's poetry comes mainly in two sizes, short-line poems and long-line poems, and the table of contents here insists on that division. He began by writing in short lines and, of course, he has frequently returned to that form. These poems seem to me to belong at the center of his achievement. Their hold on the exact phrase, intonation, or cadence also makes possible, when he comes to write long-line poems, a flowing distinctiveness and clarity, where many another poet might sound merely diffuse. There is no Whitmanian afflatus: what we hear is the tone of the speaking voice modulated as between friends, the diction nicely adjusted to conveying the matter in hand without overemphasis.

The first poem I ever read by Laughlin happened to be of the short-line variety. Its title was "Above the City." I found it quoted whole by Marianne Moore in an essay called "Humility, Concentration, and Gusto" in her *Predilections*, which I acquired in 1956. At first the poem puzzled me, but rapidly puzzlement turned to delight. There seemed to be two patterns at work, the visual and the oral, each refusing to become reconciled with the other without negotiation and without the reader's active cooperation:

> You know our office on the 18th
> floor of the Salmon Tower looks
> right out on the
>
> Empire State & it just happened
> we were there finishing up some
> late invoices on
>
> a new book that Saturday morning
> when a bomber roared through the
> mist and crashed
>
> flames poured from the windows
> into the drifting clouds & sirens
> screamed down in
>
> the streets below. . . .

And so it goes unstoppably on, until guided into its coda by three deft but unobtrusive internal rhymes—"realized," "surprised," "eyes"—one in each of the three concluding stanzas. One sees why Marianne Moore was taken by this poem, she whose visual arrangement of her verse so delighted in antagonizing eye and voice. She even went as far as to reorder the last two stanzas and wrote to Laughlin, "Can you condone it?" "I could indeed," the poet gallantly responded when he reprinted "Above the City." Yet one is relieved that he also retained the poem in its original form where the last stanza violates the line count of those preceding, but has more verbal muscularity than Miss Moore's—despite its extra line, which is empowered, in Doctor Johnson's phrase, with "more weight than bulk." Indeed, fundamentally the relation of eye to ear in Laughlin stands far nearer to William Carlos Williams than to Miss Moore. The latter is more interested in arranging her words as if they were patternings on some kind of sampler, elegantly displayed, but not invariably aiming for that precarious unity where the seen and the heard both challenge and reinforce each other, until it is the ear that becomes the final arbiter and measure. In Laughlin one sees the closeness to Williams' playing off the two elements against each other, of (as he says) "poem against metric." Williams unfortunately has a weakness for terminology that sometimes renders ambiguous what he is saying. In "poem against metric" here "metric" seems to gesture toward the way words lie visually on the page and not to the countable recurrence of a beat. This he also sees as a partnership between the oral or "verbal invention" and visual layout. "The poem is here, but the metric is *here*," as Williams writes to one correspondent, "and they go along side by side—the verbal invention and the purely metrical invention—go along arm in arm, looking for a place where they can embrace."

In first reading "Above the City," I liked all the brisk work the eye was called on to do, and I enjoyed that first real shock, the enjambment or stanzaic leap to the famous skyscraper that appears in stanza two. At the same time you heard the speaking voice pulling against stanzaic layout. I could not have known then—long before the publication of Hugh Witemeyer's edition of the correspondence of the two poets—that Laughlin and Williams had been discussing the matter with each other in the late thirties. "Damn the bastards," wrote Williams, "for saying that you can't mix auditory and visual standards in poetry. . . .

What they . . . do not know, is that an auditory quality, a NEW auditory quality, underlines and determines the visual quality which they object to." Laughlin himself had been speaking about the "tension . . . between the strictly artificial visual pattern and the strictly natural spoken rhythms," in opposition to his Harvard associates, who disputed this aspect of his poetry.

The earliest of Laughlin's books that I have in my possession bears the date of 1945. It was poems from this collection, *Some Natural Things*, which opened *The Collected Poems* of 1994. Between these two dates you might imagine a good deal of fame as a poet would have come his way. Yet look into any of the anthologies—into, say, the benchmark *Norton Anthology of Modern Poetry*—and you can be sure of not finding Laughlin there. The same is true of literary histories—*The Columbia History of American Poetry*, for example: silence. As a famous publisher, you might think he would be regarded as a phenomenon, a publisher who writes excellent verse. One of the blurbs on the 1994 *Collected Poems* says, "Here is America's great popular poet, if only the bastards read poetry." Perhaps one day, when people tire of all those phoney novels, he will be. But not yet.

Over thirty years ago, I asked Henry Rago, the last of the great editors of *Poetry (Chicago)*, why one could trace so few notices of Laughlin's books. "Because," said Rago, "he never avails himself of the system of promotion—he even refrains from sending out review copies." So perhaps Laughlin's own modesty is partly to blame? Clearly he had dubious feelings about being his own publisher and apologizes to and for himself in "The Publisher to the Poet":

> *Right hand blush never*
> *for left handed brother*
>
> *action and thought are*
> *children of one mother*

Laughlin's career as a writer began with Latin and Greek at Choate school. Catullus has always been one of his touchstones. In the notes to *The Collected Poems* (called typically "Not-Notes") he tells us of the next step: "After a boring freshman year at Harvard I took off for Europe and enrolled in Pound's Ezuversity at Rapallo. He was, by all odds, my greatest professor. . . . And my education continued for thirty years after I became his publisher." "Ezra," a recent poem of some length (and an earlier version of "Some Memories of E.P."), charts this formative relationship:

> You said I was
> Such a terrible poet, I'd better
> Do something useful and become
> A publisher, a profession which
> You inferred required no talent
> And only limited intelligence.

One of the suggestions made by Pound for this publishing venture was the work of his friend—and soon to become Laughlin's friend—William Carlos Williams. Williams was just the man Laughlin needed to know and read. More, perhaps, even than Pound, it is the stylistic influence of Williams—with a dash of Cummings in the punctuation or lack of it—that enabled Laughlin to develop his own style. Its form—before he went in for longer lines as the imaginary poet Hiram Handspring—was dictated by the typewriter: "The rule is that in a couplet any second line has to be within two typewriter spaces of the line preceding it." The result is a breaking up of those curious things words and sentences and a pleasurable dislocation between what one sees and the cadence of what one reads—you are not meant to pause at the end of every line, as in the verse of Robert Creeley any more than in Marianne Moore's syllabics:

> You know that comical
> puppy has grown up in-
>
> to a marvelous hunting
> dog he's in the woods
>
> all day and brings out
> rabbits by the dozen
>
> but the funny thing is
> he never hurts them he

doesn't even bite them
just carries them home

in his mouth & leaves
them on the porch for

us poor little things
at first they're much

too scared to move but
in a little while they

shake themselves & hop
away to the woods again

It is out of such domestic incidents and the pleasures and pains of love and of family life that Laughlin creates many of his best poems. He has, of late, written of the suicide of his son Robert and the death of his wife Ann. These are unusually harrowing incidents for Laughlin (he writes about them with never a false note), yet it is often the inevitable painful collisions of family relationships, our violations of one another, that give substance to his poems. Laughlin insists that he writes "light verse," but it is not of the Odgen Nash kind. The lightness betokens a sensitivity in handling deceptively simple, but tricky subjects. The head in "Step on His Head" is only a bobbing shadow jumped on by his children, but the incident is fraught with pain to come:

now I duck my head so they'll
miss when they jump & they screech

with delight and I moan oh you're
hurting you're hurting me stop and
they jump all the harder. . .

The crucial poem of Williams for Laughlin in helping him towards his characteristic style was the former's "The Catholic Bells" with its own dislocations:

        . . . ring for the lame

        young man in black with
        gaunt cheeks and wearing a
        Derby hat, who is hurrying
        to 11 o'clock Mass (the

        grapes still hanging to
        the vines along the nearby
        Concordia Halle like broken
        teeth in the head of an

        old man). . . .

It was after reading this that Laughlin wrote "Easter in Pittsburgh,"
his longest poem to date, and one in which the subject matter of the
family—the uncle who preaches and drinks, the sacked maid and gov-
erness, the strike in Pittsburgh and tear gas at the steel mill—all comes
into focus and availability. Lowell in *Life Studies* seems to have learned
something from Laughlin's poem and also from his "The Swarming
Bees" (on Uncle Willy, another drinking relation). Lowell, writing
about William Carlos Williams and also paying tribute to "The
Catholic Bells," says of Laughlin at Harvard: "our only strong and
avant-garde man was James Laughlin . . . . He knew the great, and he
himself wrote deliberately flat descriptive and anecdotal poems. We
were sarcastic about them, but they made us feel secretly that we didn't
know what was up in poetry." Williams' two poems on his own par-
ents, "Adam" and "Eve" of 1936, appeared to have given food for
thought to both Lowell and Laughlin.

     It was in "Easter in Pittsburgh" that Laughlin most energetically
carried forward the dramatic qualities that Williams had discovered in
the cadences of the natural speaking voice when he had written "The
Catholic Bells." This was an historic moment. It seemed to Williams
that Laughlin had taken what he himself had done and extended its
possibilities. The realization and mark of understanding between the
older poet and the younger show significantly in a letter Williams
wrote to Laughlin in 1939: "The Easter in Pittsburgh is a milestone.
That's a noteworthy poem, a revolutionary poem in more ways than

one. I'm thinking of the form of it. . . . It gains dignity at your hands, it reveals the possibilities in the form, possibilities for the long sought dramatic unit of speech, of composition that can go anywhere it wants to." Williams then confesses, "The one thing that has disturbed me at times is that my studies and labors in the form of verse have not shown a quality susceptible of further development. I've had a few imitators but no one, till now, who seemed to be able to take what I've done and step it up to the next level."

The marks of Laughlin's poetry are its humanity and its variety of both themes and idiom. Besides the poems in English, there are those in "(American) French," at least one in ski-slopes German, and those that use Italian. The most beautiful of these last form a sequence which recounts a love affair between the young poet and an Italian girl, "In Another Country":

> she called vieni qua splashing her
> arms in the clear green water vieni
> subito and so I followed her swim-
> ming around a point of rock to the
>
> next cove vieni qua non hai paura
> and she slipped like an eel beneath
> the surface down through the sunken
> entrance to a hidden grotto where
>
> the light was soft and green on fine-
> grained sand è bello no? . . .

A number of the poems have this "light that never was on sea or land" ("è strano questa luce com' un / altro mondo"), but the majority take place in the world of common experience, as effortlessly unstrained as Williams' poem on the plums in the icebox.

One values these poems for their use of a wide and unexpected subject matter—the small boy, for instance, who fashions cardboard hatchets, bloodstains their blades with red crayon, and lays them affectionately on his father's work desk. "Anything," as Williams stated, "is good material for poetry. Anything. I've said it time and time again." Laughlin evidently agrees with this contention. Yet there is more to the end result than the sheer randomness of merely "some natural things" (the title of one of his books). In describing his way of writing ("Technical Notes"), Laughlin explains that he prefers, as against using poetic diction,

> to build with plain brown bricks
> of common talk American talk then
> set 1 Roman stone
>
> among them for a key

This keystone and sense of cumulative architecture in these carefully assembled structures represent the conversion of everyday matter into the matter of art. "With me a poem," says Laughlin,

> is finally just
> a natural thing

And yet, as Guy Davenport has put it, in "a neat oblong of phrases, squared away on the page, each line [is] a little event in itself." These events impress us for the shapeliness of their appearance, their having been "squared" into inevitability and also possessing a keystone. What we listen to is the natural speech with which Laughlin begins now brought to an aesthetic focus by the heard measure of the poems. These are the products of many decades in which "the shaping spirit of the imagination" combines its forces with those of nature.

CHARLES TOMLINSON

BOOK I NEW POEMS

PATTERNS

I'm past eighty now and as I sit down
at the typewriter to slip a fresh
sheet of paper under the roller
I see again that the raised veins
of old age make a pattern on
the back of my left hand.
What kind of pattern is it?

It's nothing recognizable in nature,
it's not the leaf from a tree;
nothing like that. It must be
a message, and I know what the message
is; that, to put it in a poetic way,
there will soon be a knocking
at the door.

But for the interim what does
the writing in the pattern say?
Is it the inscription on the stone
that is the lintel of the temple
of the oracle at Delphi? Does it
spell out the prophecy of Tiresias
that Odysseus will live to return
to Ithaca and the arms of Penelope?
Is it the scrawl that Ariadne
made on the beach of Naxos when
she was waiting for Theseus to return?

THE ILLUSION

Looking through my new book of poems
that has just come from the bindery
I see that many lines of black type are
printed on white paper.
So what? This is nothing exceptional.
Many thousands of versifiers have written
before me, and as many more will follow me
if the world lasts.
So what? Here today and gone tomorrow.
The illusion of poetry.

THE SPY

I'm convinced from a few words
she let drop that while she lay
beside me in bed, I asleep
and she awake, she began to spy
on my dreams. I must find out
what she was after.

Was she trying to find out
if I still loved her? I do,
very much. Is some jealousy
at work? Did I talk to Jennifer
too much at the party? (Jennifer
can be very amusing.)

Does she suspect that as much
as I show my love for her
I'm really some kind of monster
that doesn't belong in the human race?

How should I trap the beautiful
intruder? Should I perhaps
pretend to talk in my sleep
and make up something that
would dispel her anxiety
and put her mind at rest?

THE BURGLAR

There was a man here in the village
who chased girls to steal from them.
He didn't want money or anything
material. It was their personalities
he was after. He wanted their minds
and how their minds worked. Some
social gesture or mannerism that
he could make his own. Body language,
a tone of voice. The way they laughed.
How they used their eyes. The walls
of his mind came to be a gallery
of his thefts. He didn't harm the
girls but in his way he possessed
them. Few of them were aware of
what was happening when he moved
on to another prey. They attached
other reasons to his abandoning
them. How did it end? I don't
know, he moved away to another
town. His collection must be
vast by now, a huge mosaic.

SON IO L'AMORE

That's what she whispered to me
as we were walking beside the sea
near the abandoned Greek temple
of Paestum. I am love she told me
in an accent I could hardly understand.
A peasant girl who was tending a few sheep
in the meadow below the temple.
Not a beautiful girl but there was
such a radiance in her face.
Son io l'amore. She left her sheep
to graze and we walked along
the beach together in the summer warmth.
I didn't try to make love to her,
that would have been a desecration.
For a few moments she became a handmaiden
of the temple. Son io l'amore.
I never saw her again; I had to drive
to Salerno to meet friends.
That was half a century ago.
But now and then she enters my memory
and I hear her speaking in the accent
I can hardly understand. Son io l'amore.

VOICES IN THE NIGHT

Lately as I've been drifting
off into sleep I've been
hearing voices in the darkness
of my bedroom, voices that
I can't identify. One voice
is that of a woman (her

laugh is that of a woman)
and the other is a man's,
deeper in tone. Some nights
only one speaks. But often
they both talked, carrying
on a conversation. At first
I couldn't understand them,
but soon I got the hang of
their lingo. It was English
but a very formal English.
Their syntax wasn't modern;
it was old-fashioned, perhaps
the way people talked at the
turn of the century.

In their conversations they
often talked about another
person, a man who seemed to
have led an adventurous life
and who had been attracted
to women. The female
voice was very critical of
the way he had exploited
women. Apparently he had
been married three times
and had a series of love
affairs. The male voice
condoned his promiscuity,
even praised it. "A real
man," he said. One night
they got into an argument
about this fellow. "If
you'd only known him, how
awful he was, what an
egotist, how selfish." I
thought I caught a little
catch in her voice when
she said that. The male
voice just laughed.

Ordinarily I fell asleep
while the voices were
talking. But the other
night some things they
were saying startled me
awake. Talking about *him*
they said that he had lived
in Connecticut and that he
had published a book of
erotic verse. "Highbrow stuff,"
the male voice said, "full of
steamy classical allusions."

Could they be talking about me?
I was made certain of that
when the female voice recited
part of a poem, and it was one
of my poems:
> "He tried to make her
> understand that her
> body was part of his,
> which was what gave
> her her beauty and charm."

I stopped listening for their
voices. Now I turn up my bedside
radio to blot them out. I know
enough about myself already
without their help.

THE BREAD-KNIFE

Hugh MacDiarmid the voice
of the Scots revival wrote

in "The Kind of Poetry I
Want" that he dreamed "of

poems like the bread-knife
which cuts three slices at

once"   this puzzled me un-
til I read his biography

and realized that the knife
must be his hero Vladimir

Ilyich Lenin slicing thru
the sinews of capitalism

and he added "ah Lenin poli-
tics is child's play to what
this kind of poetry must be."

IN THE DARK WOOD

I'm dreaming, and as dusk falls
I see the figure of a tall man
coming toward me in the dark woods.
I recognize the figure as my father.
He looks to be in his late thirties,
about the time I was born. Yes,
my father, but he isn't wearing

his usual clothes, either his
dark suit for church or his
golfing outfit, a windbreaker
and knickers.

What he is wearing is very strange.
It's white and like a Roman toga,
reaching down to his ankles.
But he is barefoot. He's walking
very slowly, putting one foot
forward, a pause, and then
the other. When he comes around
a big oak I see why he's going
so slowly. Behind him, lying on
her belly, a woman is clutching
his legs. Each time he takes
a step she pulls herself
along the ground to follow him.
She is not wearing Roman dress
but a fashionable modern
evening gown. She has on
silk stockings and high-heeled
red slippers. She is wearing
a string of pearls. She looks
about twentyfive, as she would
have been when I was born.
A beautiful woman, as she is
in the full-length portrait
of my mother by Penrhyn
Stanlaws that hung at one
end of the dining room in
the house on Woodland Road.

I am so startled by this
apparition that I can't
speak to them. And if I could
what would I have to say to them?
Would I have asked him why

her frigidity mattered so
much to him that he took up
with other, and inferior,
women? Would I have asked
her why she didn't understand
that the others were merely
transient diversions?

I said nothing, and they
did not appear to see or
recognize me. It was an
agony for me to watch them,
slowly and painfully, abandon
me in that frighteningly
dark wood.

THE STRANGER

"They're only loaned to us,"
my grandmother told me, "and
before you know it there's
a person there." A person you
never knew before. In some
ways he's like you (perhaps
in the color of hair) but a
new person whom you have to
learn to love. But it's not
the kind of love which produced
the stranger. You have to
begin to learn about the
love the stranger needs and
wants. And you must learn
that often the stranger
will hurt you in ways you

at first can't understand.
You must accept the stranger
as he is because you made
him come to be.

ILLNESS

is a kind of prison in which the doctor
is the warden and the nurses are the guards.
There are no bars on the windows. It's not a
gloomy place; flowers make it bright and
cheerful. No court jury sets the length of
the sentences. That decision rests with
the warden, who prides himself on his
humanity. There are rules in his mind
which often seem arbitrary or confusing
to the prisoners. They can never tell
how long their incarceration will last.
It can be only a few days or it can be
a month or two. And there are some
prisoners who are never released at all;
dangerous cases. It is whispered on the
wards that they end up in the morgue.
I'm hoping that my stay will be short.
Though my cell is the most comfortable
I've ever had it's hard to bear or understand
Why I'm in it.

IN THE GOD'S DREAMS

Am I a character in the dreams
of the god Hermes the messenger?
Certainly many of my dreams
have nothing to do with the
common life around me. There
are never any automobiles or
airplanes in them. These
dreams belong to an age in
the distant past, to a time
perhaps when nothing was
written down, to the
time of memory.

I chose Hermes not out of
vanity but because from what
I've read about him he had a
pretty good time, was not
just a drunkard on Olympus.
In his traipsings delivering
divine messages he must have
met some pretty girls who
gave him pleasure. We know
that he invented the lyre
for the benefit of poets,
and Lucian relates in his
Dialogues of the Dead that
he was the god of sleep
and dreams.

My dreams are not frightening,
they are not nightmares. But
their irrationality puzzles
me. What is Hermes trying to
tell me? Is he playing a game
with me? Last Monday night

I dreamt about a school for
young children who had heads
but no bodies. Last night it
was a cow that was galloping
in our meadow like a horse.
Another night, and this one
was a bit scary, I swam across
the lake with my head under
water, I didn't have to breathe air.

What is the message of these
dreams? Into what kind of world
is Hermes leading me? It's not
the world described daily in the
New York Times. A world of
shadows? A kind of levitation?

How can I pray to Hermes to lay
off these senseless fantasies,
tell him that I want *real* dreams
such as my shrink can explicate.

I've looked up lustration in
the dictionary. Its definition
is not encouraging: "a prefatory
ceremony, performed as a preliminary
to entering a holy place." That's
too impersonal. I want a man-to-man
talk with Hermes, telling him to
stop infesting my nights with
his nonsense.

HER LIFE

is the lives of the birds. She
watches them by the hour from
her kitchen window as they peck for
the food she has put out for them
in the feeder. The food they like
best comes in 25-lb. sacks, too
heavy for her to lift, she has to
have UPS bring it. She keeps the
grains in a garbage can, scooping them
out with a ladle as she needs it.

Many kinds of birds come to her
feeder. Sparrows, mourning doves,
chickadees, blue jays that frighten
the smaller birds; thrushes, blue-
birds that have their own house
perched on the fence rail; humming-
birds, juncos, rose-breasted
grosbeaks, finches, and some that
she can't identify in her bird
guide. She is sad when winter comes
and some of her friends take off
for the south.

The birds are her comfort; they
help her to go on with her life,
which has been hard to bear. Her
beloved husband died three years
before from cancer, a hard death.
And now her son has married a
vulgar woman who thinks only
of money. But she has her dear
birds. They comfort her. They
come every day and never let
her down.

THE WEIGHT GUESSER

One summer when he was college
age he had a job as a weight
guesser in a traveling carnival.
If he could guess a person's
weight within ten pounds he
would win ten dollars. But if
he was off by ten pounds
he had to fork over a ten-spot.
He got pretty good at the guessing
and made money over the summer.

But later in life when he
was interested in a girl
and wanted to make out with her
he found that the system didn't
work very well. The girl he
wanted was more concerned in his
valuation of her charm and beauty
than being weighed.

I CANNOT SEPARATE HER

from the beautiful body.
She has charm and a very
gay spirit; in every way
she's attractive. Intelligent
and she reads good books.
But it's the faultless body
that forces me to make a fool
of myself, pursuing a virtuous
girl I could never possess.

THE VISITOR

When I closed my eyes I could see
the head of a girl in half-light.
But was it you? She had your
aristocratic arch of the neck
and your pretty curls, but where
were your laugh and your sparkle?
And your glance toward me wasn't
particularly affectionate.

I ran through the catalog of
past loves but this girl was
not there. She must have been you.
But the frown? How had I
displeased you? Please tell me,
but then visions can't talk.

The telephone rang: I opened
my eyes to go answer it. Drat!
It was the broker who wants me
to buy Bell Atlantic stock.
I went back to the sofa to close
my eyes again. But you were
gone, perhaps never to reappear.

THE FIXATION

"A woman's breasts bear the paradoxical burden of being aesthetic organs."

His English governess could undress
or dress without removing her outer
garment. The child asked her why she did
that but she wouldn't offer an explanation.
He learned something important when little

917

Yerma, the girl nextdoor, led him into
the bushes to show him her nipples.

He didn't learn much more until he
and his brother were on the night
train from Pittsburgh to New York.
In those days there were Pullman
sleeping cars in which the porters
made lower and upper berths,
separated by heavy green curtains.
He was in an upper berth, his
brother was across the aisle.

When he was settled in his berth
and had changed into his pajamas
he noted that light was coming
from the adjacent lower berth.
The porter hadn't closed the
curtains tightly. He looked
down through the gap and saw
a lady who was naked, no nightgown
or anything on. She was leaning
against her pillows playing with
her . . . he didn't know what to
call them then. They were soft
and beautiful and hung down as far
as her tummy. At the end of them
were little pink circles with
buttons that stood up when
she touched them.

When he heard the porter walking
down the aisle he pulled back his
head and stopped looking. He never
told his brother what he had seen,
but as he grew up the sight of the
lady never left his memory. It was
his secret that he carried into
adulthood and even into old age.

HER MEMORY BANK

It has no entrance. For years
I walked past the building
But could never find how to get in.
As I go past the windows
I can see clerks piling up
Stacks of money, but there is
No way to get at it, the money
I need so badly.

I enquire about the memory bank,
But none of my friends has ever
Heard of it. They think I'm crazy
Or hallucinating. They tap
A finger to their heads when
I ask about the memory bank.

They say there is no such bank,
But I know better. I have some
Wonderful memories from your
Memory bank and I want more.

LOVE SONG

As we lived together
it dawned on me from

little things she said
or did there had been

lovers before me, but
it didn't matter. For

me she was always fresh
as a daisy and has so

remained in my heart
all the years we have

been parted, fresh as a
daisy through the years.

THE MAN WHO FOLLOWED ME

Often last year I was down in the
village, walking let's say from
the pharmacy to the post office
or the grocery, when I noticed
that a young man, a stranger,
seemed to be following me. I'd
never seen him before in the
village, where everyone usually
knows everyone else. Our village
is a small one. When I approached
this fellow, who was wearing a
leather jacket over a T-shirt,
he didn't stop to talk to me
but took off through the bushes
on the slope below the town hall.
I asked about him there and at
the post office, but nobody had
seen him or knew anything about him.

This fellow didn't show up every
day but he would appear two or
three times a week, though never
on Sundays. He got on my nerves.

Finally I'd had enough and ran
back to accost him. I asked who
he was and what he wanted with me.
He raised a hand, almost a menacing
gesture, and replied in a voice
that was like a groan. "Don't you
recognize me? You've known me
most of your life." And then he
was off into the bushes. It was
eerie and it was frightening.
What kind of a supernatural
trap was I getting into?

The apparitions continued intermittently.
I was almost beginning to accept them,
without fear. Then there was a news
story in the *Winsted Citizen* about
the body of a young man, who could
not be identified, which had been
found drowned in Mad River which
runs with great force through Winsted.

I couldn't resist visiting the coroner's
office. One glance at the corpse under
the rubber sheet and I knew it was
my pursuer, though his face was contorted
in agony. They said he would be buried
in a pauper's grave. I certainly didn't
want him. But I still wonder whether
he was a part of me, a part that
I didn't want to remember.

THE REPRISE

I'm very old now
and my strength is failing
but I want to make love with you
before I die. It couldn't be
the wild love-making of youth
I'm beyond that now.
But let it be quiet love,
touching and kissing,
the pressing together
of our naked bodies.
I want to kiss you all over
in every part of your
beautiful body, every
lovely inch of it.
And please touch me
the way you used to do.
I want to make love with you
before I die.

DESDEMONA'S HANDKERCHIEF

caused a mass of mischief
that ended in her death.
Beware my beloved lady
let not jealousy poison
our happiness. I am as weak,
as prone to fantasy
as any lover. Don't put me
to the test. Lock up your
handkerchiefs where no
malicious meddler
can find them.

DIANA'S SELF MIGHT TO THESE WOODS RESORT

It all happened (if it happened at all)
many centuries ago, but when I saw you
in your untouched purity, I knew that
the old myth was true, that you, Diana,
were wandering innocently in the woods
until the amorous god pursued you and
irrevocably altered your being.

LOVE DOES NOT MAKE A DISPLAY OF ITSELF

But when you finally think you've met Miss Right
it's hard to keep the lid on.
You try not to let your friends know
what has happened, in case something goes wrong.
Was it a mistake to take her to Paris for a week
before we got married? Something strange
happened in the restaurant on the Eiffel Tower.
We were sitting at a table with a view;
we were looking down at the meandering Seine
and the Champs de Mars with Napoleon's tomb.
She seemed to be enjoying herself
but suddenly she stopped smiling and talking
and her eyes went glazed. It was as if
I was a stranger who had offended her.
I had the feeling that she didn't know who I was.
When this mood went on for two days
I flew her back to New York, where her mother
took over. Her mother made her go to a shrink
but the pills and therapy didn't do any good.
I brought flowers for her every day,
anemones, her favorite flower,

but she never spoke to me or seemed
to recognize me. Her father got me alone
to tell me that we weren't suited for each other.
I guess the shrink told him that.
He said he was breaking off our engagement
and that I was not to try to see her again.
Love does not make a display of itself.
Was that what, in my happiness, I had done
without knowing it? I was so crazy about her
I guess I didn't realize the effect on her.

LOST BRAINS

He felt as if his brains
were jumping out of his head.
It had begun when he saw her
flirting with another man
at a party. The man was a
nobody who liked to pick up
girls. She swore that no one
else meant anything to her.
But when it happened again,
this time in a crowded bar,
his head started spinning
and he knew that his brain
was going to jump out through
his ears. Without her he would
become a nobody too.

NUNC DIMITTIS

Little time now
and so much hasn't
been put down as I
should have done it.
But does it matter?
It's all been written
so well by my betters,
and what they wrote
has been my joy.

"HARRY"

The Death of Harry Levin

This whole sad business of a friend's dying.
What box does that go in among the storage spaces in
    my head?
Filed not alphabetically, not chronologically, scattered
    boxes piled where they dropped when there was a
    death, no markings on them.

Harry. My grief, and perhaps his relief that there's no
    more pain to be gotten through. His face on the
    obituary page of the *Times* is serene and confident.
What later happens to him, the superb stylist and
    paragon of scholars, will be to his credit.
So I still see him in the small neat house where over
    the years
I've most often come to talk with him,
The best advisor an unschooled young publisher could
    have.
He will be sitting composed and erect at his
    workdesk.

Unlike my desk at home, his desk has no books or
    papers piled up on it.
He gives the sense that anything he might want to refer
    to is in his head.
The students whisper about his photographic memory.
They boast of it to students in other courses as if it were
    their own.
I myself never took a course with him;
Nevertheless, when he had the time
He was ready to advise me about
Books I should publish at New Directions.

FATA MORGANA

Like the weather, her visits were
uncertain. Often I would wait for
weeks, fearing I had lost her.
Then, toward midnight, there would
be a scratching at my door. She
never knocked, she would scratch
like a cat with her long nails, and
I awakened myself for pleasure,
for the generosity with which
she dispensed her charms.

She spoke a little English but
she would never tell me about
herself, whence she came or
what her history had been.
To this day I know only the
mysterious radiance of her
being, how when I held her
in my arms she could unleash
an unbridled passion.

She would never stay with me
for long. Then, with a kiss
she would be off. Where was
she going when she left me?
Was there another lover, or
lovers, waiting for her visit?
Nor did she ever tell me her
name. So, to myself, I call
her Fata Morgana, the best
loved of King Arthur's
damsels

FUNERALS

in our village are short and to the point.
While the mourners are finding their seats
Etta Andrews plays "Now the Day Is Over."
No one is ashamed to wipe his or her eyes.
Then the Reverend stands up and reads
the Lord's Prayer with the mourners
speaking it with him. Then there is a hymn,
usually "Rock of Ages" or one chosen by
the wife of the deceased. The deceased,
I might say, is never present, except for
an urn prepared by Mr. Torrant, who is
always squinting. Next there are remarks
by the Reverend. He is a kind man and
can be relied upon to say something nice
about the life of the departed, no matter
how much he may have been scorned or even
disliked.

The Reverend's eulogies are so much the
same, with appropriate readings from scripture,

that I gave up listening to them years ago.
Instead, unheard, I eulogize myself,
the real picture of how I've been in
the village. I admit that I was self-satisfied
and arrogant. I didn't go to much pains
to provide diversions for my wife. When
the children and grandchildren came for visits
I lectured them and pointed out their faults.
I made appropriate contributions to the
local charities but without much enthusiasm.
I snubbed people who bored me and avoided
parties. I was considerate to the people
who worked in the post office. I complained
a great deal about my ailments. When I'm
asked how I'm doing, I reply that I'm
not getting any younger. This inveterate
response has become a bore in the village.

After the Reverend's eulogy is over
there is another hymn, and the benediction.
As they leave everyone, except me, presses
the flesh of the bereaved with appropriate
utterances. But I get away as quickly as
I can. If they don't bore me I like
almost all the people in the village.
But as they go, I tick them off. I've
been to at least fifty funerals. When
will mine be?

A COMMONPLACE BOOK OF PENTASTICHS

(1998)

Commonplace books have been an engaging adjunct of literary performance for hundreds of years. Everyone knows this, and most of us, one way or another, have kept commonplace books of our own, notebooks in which we copy out fragments from our reading, anything that seems especially trenchant or felicitous. Often we add our own commentaries. Some such books are famous, of course, those assembled by William Byrd and Thomas Jefferson and W. H. Auden, for instance; but hundreds and hundreds have been published. Some scholars think the original commonplace books were kept by medieval philosophers and natural scientists for purposes of research and in preparing arguments; but this is fanciful. The idea is universal.

Who is surprised, consequently, to learn that James Laughlin, one of the most finely educated and widely acquainted editors and publishers of our time, has kept a commonplace book? He's a natural for it.

A more particular question is why has he cast his jottings into pentastichs, five-line verses. The reason must be deep in his unconscious memory. Probably he himself doesn't know. But Laughlin is a poet as well as an editor, a poet of acknowledged standing, and if we look at his poems of the past sixty years or so we find that he prefers, on one hand, a language of natural, nearly conversational plainness and, on the other, metrical forms that are arbitrary and artificial in the extreme. Not that he uses conventional rhyme and meter; he never does. But he likes to invent for himself tight prosodic restraints within which to arrange his phrasings. Isn't this the poetic impulse in general, or part of it? One way or another all poets do the same. At any rate it's hard to think of authentic exceptions. The pentastich is merely the most recent of Laughlin's inventions.

Of course you can find plenty of precedents. Five-line stanzas abound in any anthology. One thinks of Tennyson's "Tears, Idle Tears" or Poe's "To Helen," or perhaps Charles Olson's "fivers" in his *Maximus*. Or one remembers the *quintil* in French, the *lira* in Spanish. But for Laughlin the pentastich is not a stanza, it is a complete poem. Our commonest pentastich, in this sense, is undoubtedly the limerick, but five-line epigrams can be found from Empedocles to J. V. Cunningham. The Japanese *tanka*, a highly developed literary form, has influenced many Western poets, notably Adelaide Crapsey, whose "cinquains" in an unrhymed syllabic pattern of her own invention have a subtlety of movement that is wholly admirable. But to my mind these precedents have impinged on Laughlin's pentastichs scarcely at all. As the reader of this book (or any of his others) will find, Laughlin raids the classics, ancient and modern, with rapacious facility in search of what makes the substance of poetry, the substance of human thought and feeling, but in verbal usage he has not imitated anyone.

Laughlin has chosen his cited passages from an extraordinary range of sources, yet he himself is very much a presence among them. Some passages from foreign literatures he has translated himself, others he has taken from translations already existing, whichever is handiest; he has put them all into pentastichs and he hasn't refrained from excerpting or making necessary minor alterations, though I have seen the whole work in progress and I can verify that he has done no mischief. Then at the end he has placed a number of pentastichs derived from his own earlier poems—revisitings, so to speak. What a conglomeration! The wise, trivial, funny, poignant, even the foolish: a fine jumble. In effect it is an attestation to human existence in all its thoughtfulness and hunger, its fear and love and sexuality. For the reader it is a survey of literature that will never be found in a classroom—praise whatever gods may be—but indubitably will be found in loving and longstanding proximity on many a bedside table.

HAYDEN CARRUTH

A GREAT EMPEROR

Akbar, the greatest of the Mogul emperors, who
united the fiefdoms of India as far south as
the Godavari, was also a man of intellect. He
maintained at his court sages of all religions
and had the *Mahabharata* translated into Persian.

TRYING TO PLEASE

Berenice cried when she couldn't fit her breast
into the Emperor's wine glass. She wanted to
have him think of her as a Grecian charmer. Her
brother, Agrippa, consoled her with the thought
we can't always make our bodies do what we want.

THE APPLICANT

First, are you our sort of person?
Do you wear a glass eye, false teeth
Or a crutch, a brace or a hook,
Rubber breasts or a rubber crotch,
Stitches to show something's missing?

Sylvia Plath, from Ariel

ENJOY THE PASSING HOUR

There's no use asking, Leuconoe, what end the gods
have set for us, or consulting the Chaldean astrologers.
Better to enjoy what comes, whether Jove gives more
winters or this is the last. Cut short your hopes.
Reap the harvest of today, don't trust the morrow's.

Horace (abridged).

THE TALKING TRUCK

In our town there's a young man who drives
a snappy red pickup. He has its sound
system wired so that when he passes you
on the road it will sing out a cheerful
"Have a good day!' Greater love hath no truck.

IF I DIE

What will you do, God, if Death takes me?
I am your jug (if someone breaks me?)
I am your drink (if curdling cakes me?)
I am your trim, your trade—it makes me
think: with me goes your meaning too.

Rainer Maria Rilke Possibility of Being. *Trans. J.B. Leishman.*

AN EVENING'S ENTERTAINMENT

For a Hollywood party in honor of Henry
Miller the hostess rented a starlet to keep
him amused. Things went well till the girl
rushed from the bedroom screaming: "All
the old bastard wants to do is bite my toes."

TRIPARTITE

My twin brother, Brendan, wears gloves that
Don't match. He says it's because he is
Two persons. He became three when he detached
His memory and sent it to live in Iowa. Too
Many things he doesn't want to think of again.

Brendan Gill.

LOGODAEDALY

In the tradition of medieval logodaedalists,
Perec wrote a 284-page book with no "e's" in it,
like this: "It's all in vain, his subconscious
starts buzzing around in him again, buzzing around
and within him, choking and suffocating him."

George Perec, A Void. *Trans. Gilbert Adair.*

AN ESKIMO SONG

I will walk with leg muscles which are
strong as the sinews of the shins of the
little caribou calf, strong as the shins
of the hare. I won't go towards the dark,
I'll walk only towards the light of day.

From the Anerca Collection.

THE EXILES

banished for their opinions to remote
parts of Russia are a little feared and by no
means confounded with ordinary mortals.
Dangerous people have that kind of attraction
which notorious Don Juans have for women.

Alexander Herzen, a passage from Childhood, Youth and Exile.
Trans. J. D. Duff.

THE MIME

Herondas was a mime who performed in wine
shops. I looked forward to his *Whorehouse
Manager*, but felt let down. It was about
a legal trial for rape. Nothing about a
brothel and Greek girls' hot tricks.

AN EXISTENCE OF EXILE

It was an existence of exile from the world.
He never saw a human face or figure, nor even
an animal; there were no familiar objects
along the way, there was no ground below, nor
sky above, yet the space was full of things.

Paul Bowles, from The Sheltering Sky.

TEMPUS LOQUENDI

To every thing there is a season, and a time to every
purpose under the heaven; a time to be born, and a
time to die . . . a time to weep and a time to laugh . . .
a time to mourn and a time to dance . . . a time to
keep silence, and a time to speak. . . .

From Koheleth, the Book of Ecclesiastes *(abridged).*

ONE LOST

When she saw how shamelessly I proclaimed
my lack of courage, she ceased to find me worthy
of pity. She considered me despicable. She left me
at once. It was too much. At the gate of the
hospital that evening she did not kiss me.

Louis-Ferdinand Céline, from Journey to the End of the Night.
Trans. H. P. Marks.

TIME IS THE MERCY OF ETERNITY

What can you say in a poem?
Past forty, you've said it all. . . .
The holiness of the real
is always there, accessible
in total immanence. . . .

Kenneth Rexroth, from the Collected Shorter Poems.

THE EMPEROR MAKES A POEM

"And now the moon had set. The Emperor thought
of the girl's mother and wondered, making a poem
of the thought, with what feelings she had watched
the sinking of the autumn moon; 'for even the Men
Above the Clouds were weeping when it sank.'"

From Lady Murasaki's The Tale of Genji. *Trans. Arthur Waley.*

TIME IN INDIA

The old man at the temple told me that Sita
was his grandmother. Sita, the wife of the
hero Rama, who cut off the nine heads of
Ravanna, the demon king of Ceylon. How long
ago was that? There is no time in India.

Cf. The Ramayana.

THE AFTERLIFE

This afterlife from earlier
lives—it's not what we sighed
for! (Survival it may be.)
Tell me, mirror, what I know: "Oh,
your karma isn't what *you* decide."

M. L. Rosenthal, from Offstage Music.

TELLING TALES

Herodotus was the "father of history," but now and then
a grain of salt is recommended. Sometimes he treated
hearsay as fact. For example, the Danube does not rise
in the Pyrenees and the sun's course is not affected
by wind. Plutarch wrote a treatise on his "malignity."

EVERY DAY EXCEPT SUNDAY:
A TRIPLE PENTASTICH

the old ones visit the Supermarket.
It gives them something to do after
they've watched the soap operas on
TV, after they're dusted the house
and started something for dinner.

Very few of them have cars but the
Supermarket sends a bus around to

pick them up and take them home.
They haven't the money to buy much,
many of them live on relief, but

the bus is good advertising. The
clerks know most of them by their
first names. "How you doing today,
Margaret?" "Have a good day, Helen."
"You too, Joe." It's their antiphony.

THY TREASURE

The flatterer will quit thee in Adversity. But
the Fool will never forsake thee. If thou hid'st
thy Treasure upon Earth, how can'st thou expect
to find it in Heaven? Give not thy Tongue too
great a Liberty, lest it take thee Prizoner.

Edinburgh, 1713.

THE REVELATION

   There you will reveal
to me the things my soul desired,
   and in a flash, O love,
   there you will restore
what but a day ago you gave to me.

St. John of the Cross, Spiritual Canticle. *Trans. Willis Barnstone.*

940

ARLI

She had a dog named Arli whom she had
taught to think and typewrite on a special
machine with huge keys that Arli could press
with his nose. Arli's messages were right on,
you could ask him questions about the dead.

THE AFFIRMATION

Sophia Antonova wished me good-bye
as if she had not heard a word of my
impious hope, but she turned for an instant
and declared in a firm voice—
"Peter Ivanovich is an inspired man."

Joseph Conrad, concluding passage from Under Western Eyes.

FAIR WOMEN

Fair women I saw passing where she passed;
and none among them women, to my vision;
but were like nothing save her shadow cast.
I praise her in no cause save verity's,
none other dispraise, if ye comprehend me.

Guido Cavalcanti (1255–1300). Trans. Ezra Pound.

A CEREMONY

If he has to micturate at night, Bill likes
to go outside into the darkness to do it.
As he pees he looks up at the stars and
listens for the hooting of owls. He says it
makes him feel truly a part of nature.

I FEEL DRUNK ALL THE TIME

Jesus it's beautiful! Great
mother of big apples, it's a
pretty world. You're a bastard Mr. Death
and I wish you didn't have
no look-in here.

Kenneth Patchen, Collected Poems.

A VISIT TO HARLEM

When I was young we'd go up to Harlem to the
Lynx, where if you put a five dollar bill on
the edge of the table, a lovely young girl
would daintily lift her skirt and pick it
up with her snatch without using her hands.

DIFFICULTY IN HENRY JAMES

Henry James had from the middle of his writing
life to its end an increasing reputation for
being difficult beyond reason: obscure in style,
tenuous in theme, and subtle to the point of
exasperation in both detail and point of view.

R. P. Blackmur, from Studies in Henry James, *ed. Veronica Makowsky.*

THIS FOREIGN LANGUAGE

You come into the world not speaking it. . . . It's
their language and they've spoken it . . .
and you haven't spoken anything . . . you've been
involved in looking and feeling. . . . And they keep
speaking their own foreign language.

David Antin, from "Real Estate" in the book Tuning.

THE VIPER

For years I was under the spell of that woman.
She used to appear in my office completely naked
and perform contortions that defy imagination,
simply to draw my poor soul into her orbit
and above all to wring from me my last penny.

Nicanor Parra, Antipoems. *Trans. W. S. Merwin.*

VIENNA

"Vienna," said the doctor, "the bed into
which the common people climb, docile
with toil, and out of which the nobility
fling themselves ferocious with dignity,
I can still remember all of it today."

Djuna Barnes, from Nightwood.

THE DOUBLE HEADS

Upon one body
Double heads opposing chop-
Stick beaks in order,
Peck peck pecking off to death,
One bird: both heads and body.

Japanese linked verse, c. 1500. Author unknown.
Trans. Edwin Brock.

THE FULFILLMENT

No man can utterly fulfill
what's in his heart but when he does
it seems but a little thing. When
he is satisfied his love is perfect
his heart proves the defect.

Aimeric de Belenoi (1217–42). Trans. from Langue d'Oc, Paul Blackburn.

FIDELIO: EZRA POUND

Ezra and Olga and I were staying at the Goldene Rose
in Salzburg. We went to hear Toscanini conducting
Fidelio in the Festspielhaus. Ezra never liked Beethoven.
After ten minutes he rose up and shouted: "What can you
expect, the man had syphilis?" Toscanini didn't miss a beat.

THE FRENCH

The French are such an orderly race.
They tell how the grande horizontale
Liane de Pougy offered her lovers
only the upper part of her body, the
lower being reserved for her husband.

HARD TIMES

The unquiet and feverish state of mind in which
Dickens finished *Hard Times* was more than the aftermath
of intense effort. . . . Significant was the mingling
of his feelings about his private life with his realization
of how much was wrong with England and the world.

Edgar Johnson, from Charles Dickens: His Tragedy and Triumph *(abridged).*

THE BHARATA

As the body cherishes the food it eats, as
an ambitious servant seeking promotion
serves willingly a master of noble birth,
so all poets serve and cherish Bharata,
as it was in the making of this magnificent epic.

Bharata: *a prince descended from the Pandavas, rivals of the Kauravas;
from the* Mahabharata. *Trans. P. Lal.*

FLAUBERT'S HANDBOOK OF CLICHÉS

Extirpate: Verb only applied to hearsay and corns.
Free Trade: Cause of all business troubles.
Frog: Female of the toad.
Gaming: Wax indignant at this fatal passion.
Genius: No point admiring . . . it's a neurosis.

From The Dictionary of Accepted Ideas. *Trans. Jacques Barzun.*

VEDANTA

The primary elements of Vedanta are Vidya, the
absolute, and Maya, the illusory. In Vedanta
there is no evil as such, only the unreal
appearance of evil or ignorance such as a barren
woman, a horned hare, or water in a mirage.

THE CANTICLE OF THE CREATURES

Be praised, O Lord, for Sister Moon and
the stars; Thou hast formed them in the
heavens, clear, precious and beautiful.
Be praised, O Lord, for Sister Water, the
which is so useful, humble and precious.

St. Francis of Assisi, fragment. Trans. Eleanor L. Turnbull.

A HEALTH PROBLEM

I saw on TV that millions of men suffer from
toenail fungus. That's awful, but my sickness
is worse. I suffer from corrosion of the soul.
I no longer go to church and I read subversive
books about Krishna and Buddha. No pill for that.

PAOLO AND FRANCESCA

We read of Lancelot, by love constrained;
Alone, suspecting nothing, at our leisure.
Sometimes at what we read our glances joined,
Looking from the book each to the other's eyes.
And then the color in our faces drained . . .

Dante, Inferno, *fifth canto. Trans. Robert Pinsky.*

FREEDOM FROM REBIRTH

He whose mind is unsteady and whose heart
is impure, never reacheth the goal, but is born
again and again. But he whose mind is steady
and whose heart is pure, reacheth the goal,
and having reached it is born no more.

From the Katha Upanishad *(c. 900 B.C.). Trans. Swami Prabhavanada.*

VIGILS

It is repose in light, neither fever nor languor, on
a bed or on a meadow. . . . It is the friend neither violent
nor weak. . . . It is the beloved neither tormenting nor
tormented. . . . Air and the world not sought. Life. . . .
Was it really this? And the dream grew cold.

Arthur Rimbaud, from The Illuminations. *Trans. Louise Varèse.*

A WOMAN OF THE SANKHINI TYPE

She is of medium build, her foot is long and covered
with prominent blood vessels. She has a yoni which
is ever moist with love fluid that has the smell
of salt. Her temper is violent in spasm when she
thrusts her nails into the flesh of her partner.

From the Sanskrit Kokkokam.

948

A WINTRY CHRISTMAS

It's winter, so cold, and three feet of
snow. I think of Villon's lines about
the hungry wolves. "Sur le Noël, morte
saison, lorsque les loups vivent de vent."
Wolves have nothing to eat but the wind.

INSCRIPTIO FONTIS

Stay here thy way, O voyager,
    for terrible now is the heat;
Thy tired feet can go no farther now,
Balm here for weariness is in
    sweet reclining.

Andrea Navagero. (16th-century Latin). Trans. Ezra Pound.

GOD IN POLITICS

"You may believe you're descended from monkeys.
I don't believe it. I think you're a creature
of God. I believe that God created heaven and
earth. I think you have a right to insist that
Godless evolution not be taught to your children."

Patrick J. Buchanan. Excerpt from a campaign speech.

THE WAY OF RENUNCIATION

A selfless man who has renounced
the fruit of his action attains peace.
But the man who is not selfless
and who is led by desire is attached
to the fruit and therefore is bound.

From the Bhagavad-Gita. Trans. Swami Nikhilananda.

KANKHA-REVATA

A campfire at midnight
eats at the circle of darkness
subduing the shadows
for all who pass.
Ever so are the Tathagata's words.

Tathagata: one who incarnates enlightenment.
Written in Pali script on palm leaves (c. 90 B.C.).
Trans. Andrew Schelling and Anne Waldman.

THE HAIR SHIRT

Eleanor of Aquitaine, a spirited girl who
wrote troubadour cansos, married at fifteen
the king who slept in a hair shirt and became
Saint Louis. "I thought I had married a
man, but found I had married a monk."

THE COURTSHIP OF
THOMAS MORE'S DAUGHTERS:
A DOUBLE PENTASTICH

In his *Utopia* Thomas More prescribed that couples
should see each other stark-naked before marriage.
When Sir William Roper askt for the hand of a More
daughter he was led to a chamber where both girls were
abed. More whippt the sheete off, exposing the modest

maidens on their backs, with their smocks raised to the arme-
pitts. But at once they turned on their bellies;
Quoth Roper: "I have seen both sides," and he slappt
one daughter on the buttock. "Thou art mine," he ex-
claimed. And in this was all the trouble of the wooeing.

Adapted from Aubrey's Brief Lives.

WHAT'S NEW?

Last year the Serbs took 200 Muslims out into
the woods and shot them. What's new? A thousand
years ago when the Indian Muslims overran Java
they lopped off the heads of a hundred Buddhist
monks who were praying at the temple of Borobudur.

THE LINGUIST

The poet Edouard Roditi mastered a dozen
languages. He got high-paying jobs for
simultaneous translations at international
conferences. His pride was a Portuguese-
Turkish performance, done without a slip.

A HAPPY ENDING

After a difficult life with many
disappointments the poet Larus,
at ninety, drifted away into
the land of Otherwhere. He couldn't
remember anything, even who he was.

THE JOY OF YOUR CHARM

The charm of how you are gives me such joy
that my desire pleasures me every day.
Now totally and in full you mistress me,
how overmastered I am, I can scarce say.
Before I saw you I determined to love you.

Guilhem Cabestanh (1190–1212). Trans. Paul Blackburn.

HUNGER

The hunger of the rich man
knows no end,
the man & the woman, both insatiable,
reduce the world's flesh to a sauce
& smear it over their wrists and thighs. . . .

Jerome Rothenberg, from New Selected Poems.

HIS HAND: TWO LINES FROM LEAR, ACT V

Now that he's old and foolish,
his hand smells of mortality.
Wash it as he may, he can't regain
the scent of the time when lovely
hands longed to touch and caress it.

THE WRONG BUTTON

Fine people. Aristocrats running the family business.
I was so honored when they put me on their board.
Then disaster. A careless girl pushed the wrong
computer button. All the sales records erased.
Everything gone. The end of a great company.

953

THE WISE MAN

Crusty Diogenes was homeless, he lived in
a tub with stray dogs. But his wit ruled
Athens. He pointed out that philosophy can
often turn a young man from the love of a
beautiful body to love for a beautiful mind.

A TRIP THROUGH AFRICA

Ages ago an archeologist, Albert, alias Arthur,
ably attended an archaic African armchair
affair at Antibes, attracting attention as an
archeologist and atheist. . . . Albert advocated
assisting African ants. All are astounded.

Walter Abish, from Alphabetical Africa, *a novel in which each chapter
contains only words beginning with the successive letters of the alphabet.
The form originated in the Middle Ages.*

WANDERER'S NIGHT-SONG

You who look down from the heavens to comfort
our pain and sorrows and my doubly wretched
heart, bring me refreshment, I'm weary with
the struggle—why this rapture and unrest?
Let your peace descend upon me and remain.

Adapted from Goethe.

OF ZENO THE PHILOSOPHER

Neither winter's cold, nor endless rain,
Nor blazing sun can overpower him.
Terrible illness does not move him.
Night and day, intending, he pursues
His discipline to the utmost.

Diogenes Laertius, Lives and Opinions of Eminent Philosophers
(c. 200–250 A.D.). Trans. Barry Magid.

THE SECRET LINE IN LOVING

There is a sacred, secret line in loving
which attraction and even passion cannot cross—
even if lips draw near in awful silence
and love tears at the heart.
Friendship is weak and useless here. . . .

Anna Akhmatova. Trans. Jane Kenyon.

THE YOUNG PRIEST

She had a friend, a young priest,
who would sit by her bed for
hours, just watching her nude
body. He never spoke or touched
her. A new form of prayer?

LANGUAGE

I resist philosophy, systems.
But I've always admired Unamuno,
whose name means
"one world"
but in no known language.

Frederick Smock.

THE YOUNG DEER

The under leaves of the lespedeza
When dew is gathering
Must be cold:
On the autumn moor
The young deer are crying.

Lady Sagami (10th-century Japan). Trans. Arthur Waley.

WANT

I do not want to be a
Mammologist
I would like a lot
Of rupees and go and
Use them in a store

Anne Waldman.

FLAUBERT'S EARLIER LIVES

My present self is the consequence of all my vanished
selves. I was boatman on the Nile . . . a procurer in
Rome . . . I died during the Crusades from eating
too many grapes on the beach in Syria . . . I was pirate
and monk...perhaps Emperor of the East, who knows?

From a letter to George Sand, 29 September 1866. Trans. Francis Steegmuller.

WOMEN

There is no fury like a woman searching
for a new lover. When we see a woman meekly
chewing the cud beside her second husband,
it is hard to imagine how brutally, pettily
and implacably she has got rid of the first.

Cyril Connolly, The Unquiet Grave.

ON WEALTH

What may be achieved by a man who has gained
great wealth is like watching a fight between
elephants having climbed to the top of a hill.
Let riches be gathered; it is the steel that cuts
through the pride of foes; nothing is sharper.

From the medieval Tamil of Tiruvalluver's Tirukkural.
Trans. A.N.K. Aiyangar.

THE HEALER

Hippocrates of Cos, the great physician,
left us the message that health is the
greatest of all possible human blessings,
and that we should learn how by our own
thought to derive benefit from illnesses.

IN THE AUVERGNE

A shepherdess is waiting for her lover by
a big oak. But he doesn't come. "Have I
been deserted? I thought he loved me, and
I love him so much." The evening star
rises; she is still alone, and weeping.

A folksong.

HER BEAUTY

Criseyde was this lady's name aright;
As to my dame, in al Troyes citee
Nas noon so fair, for passing every wight
So aungellyk was hir natyf beautee
That lyk a thing immortal semed she. . . .

Chaucer, from Troilus and Criseyde.

VOLTAIRE AND CHRISTIANITY

Voltaire's *Republican Ideas* called the Christian
priesthood an outrage against the Gospels.
The *Catechism of the Normal Man* made plain
that "Detest your enemy like yourself" was
the great maxim of Christianity.

Wayne Andrews, from Voltaire.

ON AWAKENING

When you awake, say to yourself—Today
I shall encounter meddling, ingratitude,
violence, cunning, jealousy, self-seeking,
all of them the results of men not
knowing what is good and what's evil.

Marcus Aurelius Antoninus, from To Himself

SWEARING

Do not swear by the heavens, because
they are the throne of God. Do not
swear by the earth, as it is his
footstool. Do not swear at all; let your
yes be your yes, and your no your no.

From the Logia of Yeshua. *Trans. Guy Davenport.*

HUMAN SOCIETY

I experienced sometimes that the most
sweet and tender, the most innocent and
encouraging society may be found in any
natural object, even for the poor misanthrope
and most melancholy man.

Thoreau, from Walden.

THE TRUTH

Truth and right are my bases.
I hate frauds and hypocrites.
And if I vacillate sufficiently
avoiding them
my rancor sinks, and I find all is well.

Peire Cardenal (1225–72). Trans. Paul Blackburn.

AFTER DEATH

The First Bardo. From the moment of death
and for sometimes four days afterwards,
the Knower, in the case of the person deceased,
is in a very deep sleep or trance, unaware
that it has been separated from the human body.

The Tibetan Book of the Dead. *Trans. W. Y. Evans-Wentz.*
Bardo: state between death and rebirth.

THE GOOD LIFE

Dr. Pangloss told Candide: "All events are linked
together in the best of worlds; if you had not been
driven out of a castle by hard kicks upon your hinder
parts for daring to make love to Cunegund, you
would not be here now eating citrons and pistachio nuts."

Voltaire, the conclusion of Candide *(abridged).*

AFTER THE FLOOD

As soon as the idea of the flood had abated,
a hare paused in the clover and bell-flowers
and prayed to the rainbow through the spider's
web. What jewels gleamed in hiding . . .
What flowers gazed all about them.

Arthur Rimbaud, from the Illuminations. *Trans. Helen Rootham.*

THE TWO GODDESSES:
DEMETER AND PERSEPHONE

Nothing about the Eleusinian Mysteries
was so striking as the initiates' awe
of Demeter's gift, the grain and their hope
of life after death. The ear of grain
is the most perfect epoptic mystery.

Carl Kerenyi, from Eleusis. *Trans. Ralph Manheim.*

STORIES

The Seller of Stories lowered his arm and
held out a hand to me as if he were offering
me something. I give you tonight's moon, he
said, and I give you whatever story you feel
like hearing. I know you want to hear a story.

Antonio Tabucchi, from Requiem. *Trans. Margaret Jull Costa.*

THE ANCIENT OCEAN

Ancient ocean, crystal-waved, you resemble those
bluish marks on the battered backs of cabin boys;
you are a vast bruise inflicted upon the body
of earth; I love this comparison. You recall
the crude origin of man. I salute you, ocean!

From Lautréamont's Maldoror. *Trans. Guy Wernham.*

THE IDOLS OF JAPAN

In the island of Zipangu their idols are fashioned
in a variety of shapes, some having the heads
of oxen, some of swine, of dogs, and other
animals. . . . The ceremonies practiced before their
gods are too wicked and diabolical to be related.

From The Travels of Marco Polo. *Trans. Manuel Komroff.*

962

IN HAC SPE VIVO

The apogee in the career of the great
philosopher Wittgenstein was when he
phoned Bertie Russell to tell him he
had discovered a cure for the common
cold. But no, alas, he hadn't found it.

*"In this hope I live," motto on Pericles' shield, Shakespeare's play,
Act II, Scene II.*

IN HIDING

The room seems to be empty. Covers heaped
on the bed, pillows on the floor. Where
can you be? Then mewing, like a cat's, comes
from under the bed, I pull you out by a
leg. Please don't play this game again.

THE RUSSIAN GIRL

The little Russian girl who kept Tenn cheerful
when he was rehearsing a play, usually got her
way, as when I picked her up at the Ritz to
go to dinner and she asked the concierge which
was the most expensive restaurant in the area.

EPIPHANY, ANNE CARSON

Holding the gifts on their knees they rode carefully
over the steppes and tableland and across long
frozen afternoons dusted with diamonds.
Nothing so precious had ever been known.
Treasure bursts at the tip of the heart.

THE STORY OF HAPPINESS

Happiness, unknown woman,
There's a childhood picture
Of the two of us,
Your hands are covering my eyes,
All but your arms are cut off.

Charles Simic, from Walking the Black Cat.

BETROTHAL IN ASSAM

Among the Nagas of Assam unmarried girls sleep
in the granary door where bachelors wearing cowry
shells as medals of prowess come to visit them.
When a girl gets pregnant they line up the men
and she can choose the one she'd like to marry.

District Commissioner Mills, anecdotal.

PROCUREMENT

They met at M.I.T. Her family was Swiss.
They were in arms procurement. They had a
villa on the lake near Geneva. A brawny girl.
She took his virginity as if she were picking
an edelweiss. But he was given a job in the firm.

THE BELOVED CLOWN

The well-born but impoverished Boston poet
Jack Wheelwright was beloved in society for
his eccentricities. One night, on entering
a ballroom, he got under a rug and crawled
the length of it to offer a lily to the hostess.

THE MERRY LIFE

I return to my cask. Up, lads, and to the
wine! Gulp it down, mes enfants, in brimming
cups. Or if you don't like it, leave it alone. . . .
I'm not one of those tiresome Germans who
make their comrades drink by brute force.

François Rabelais, from Gargantua and Pantagruel. *Trans. J. M. Cohen.*

THE GREAT MOTHER

Not all those who pass
In front of the Great Mother's chair
Get past with only a stare.
Some she looks at their hands
To see what sort of savages they were.

Gary Snyder.

THE BLINDFOLDED LOVERS

In Magritte's painting, *Les Amants*, the lovers
have cloths over their heads while they're
kissing. That can't be much fun. But maybe
the fun is for each to kiss an ideal lover they've
never encountered and are only imagining.

THE BORN POET

Stesichoros of Sicily had no choice
but to become a poet. One day as
he lay in his cradle a nightingale
flew down and lit on his lips. The
little baby began to sing at once.

THE KING-SWAN

In a great lake there lived a king-swan named
Passion, He spent his days in pastimes. One day
death visited him in the form of an owl. "Where do
you come from?" asked the swan. "I came because
I heard of your great virtues," replied the owl.

From the Panchatantra *(Kashmir, 200 B.C.). Trans. A.W. Ryder.*

OF KNOWLEDGE

We should make the knowledge of others our
own. Too often we resemble the man who
needing fire goes to his neighbor's to get it
but having found it he stays to warm
himself, forgetting his family at home.

Michel de Montaigne. Trans. George B. Ives.

THE CONQUEROR

Alexander the Great was a severe disciplinarian.
If on the march to India a soldier broke the rules
he would be bound and small stones would
be stuffed down his throat till he suffocated.
It's odd that no one can find Alexander's tomb.

A LULLABY

Golden slumbers kiss your eyes,
Smiles awake you when you rise,
Sleep, pretty wantons, do not cry,
And I will sing a lullaby:
Rock them, rock them, lullaby.

Thomas Dekker. First stanza.

LADIES FIGHTING

In Yorkshire late happen'd a desperate fight
'Tween a *Jacobite* lady and a *Williamite*,
'Twas fought with such courage no man could do more,
Nor the like was ne're known 'tween two women before;
For each met in the field with her sword by her side. . . .

The Pepys Ballads *(1690), ed. Hyder Rollings (abridged).*

IN VINO VERITAS

As he excelled in that licentious merriment which
wine incites, Rochester's friends encouraged him
in excess and he willingly indulged it. He was
for five years together continually drunk, so much
inflamed as not to be master of himself.

The Life and Death of John, Earl of Rochester, *Bishop Gilbert Burnet, D.D.*

THE CAREER GIRL

Theodora was the greatest empress of Byzantium,
the daughter of a bearkeeper at the Constantinople
zoo. She was so good a courtesan that she was
married by the Emperor Justinian. He made her
joint ruler, but she was smarter and was the boss.

Lambros J. Lambros, anecdotal.

LO KHOR (YEAR WHEEL)

In the center is a magic square; the numbers add
up to 15 in any direction.

492

357

816

The numbers
in the square are used to determine the most
appropriate day to undertake a project.

From the Tibetan Astrological Calendar.

LINES

In the *Dhammapada* it is written
that the body is a strong fortress
made up of bones plastered with
flesh and blood, wherein lurk
pride, deceit, decay and death.

TOUT EN ORDRE

At Versailles only the Queen may have pompons
on her coach-covers; fastened with nails, and of
any color she pleases. Duchesses have
blue covers. Wives of eldest sons of dukes
have red covers. Widows have black velvet.

From Historical Memoirs, Le Duc de Saint-Simon *(1788).*
Trans. Lucy Morton.'

LA POÉSIE

At my Swiss school Maître Jacquet was fierce when
he was coaching hockey but tender teaching us
French poetry. I could recite reams of Sully
Prudhomme: "Des yeux sans nombre ont vu l'aurore;
maintenant ils dorment au fond des tombeaux."

CABESTAN

"It is Cabestan's heart in the dish."
"No other taste shall change this."

The betrayed husband has killed
the lady's lover and served up his
heart for dinner. When she realizes
the monstrosity she throws herself
from the window of the castle.

See Ezra Pound, Canto IV.

970

WITTGENSTEIN'S LADDER

My propositions are elucidatory in this way:
he who understands me finally recognizes
them as senseless, when he has climbed out
through them, on them, over them. (He must
throw away the ladder after climbing it.)

From the Tractatus. *Ed. Marjorie Perloff.*

WHO I AM

I hereby declare myself world-wide, oviparous,
giraffe, haggard sinophobic, and hemi-
spherical. I quench my thirst in the
wellsprings of the atmosphere that laughs
concentrically and farts with my uncertainty.

Max Jacob from "The Cock and the Pearl," Le Cornet à Dés.
Trans. Bill Zavatsky.

LE TEMPS PERDU

All that elegant refinement of sensibility,
but when Proust's beloved mother died
he gave her furniture to a male brothel,
and the scholars have discovered that Albertine
was a handsome but uneducated taxi driver.

CONTENTMENT

Père Ubu: by my green candle, shitter, certainly
I'm content. I'm a captain of dragoons, I'm King
Wenceslas' confidential officer. I've been decorated
with the Order of the Red Eagle of Poland. I'm
ex-King of Aragon, what more do you want?

Alfred Jarry, Ubu Roi. *Trans. Barbara Wright.*

A LOVER'S OATH

Khiron swore to Ionis that no one, woman or
man, would ever be dearer to him. But we
know lovers' oaths don't penetrate to
celestial ears. Now he's mad for a pretty
boy, and poor Ionis has a broken heart.

Callimachus of Cyrene, b. 310 B.C.

JOYCE'S WORDS

Joyce maims words. Why? Because meanings
have been dulled, then lost, then perverted
by their connotations, until their effect on
the mind is no longer what it was when they
were fresh, but grows rotten as *poi.*

William Carlos Williams, from a symposium on Joyce and Finnegans Wake.

THE LONG SLEEP

Let us live, Lesbia, and let us love,
caring nothing what people say about us.
Suns set and rise again, but when our sun
sets, that brief light, there will be
only a night of perpetual slumber.

Catullus V (abridged).

LIFE STORY

After you've been to bed together for the first time,
without the advantage of any prior acquaintance,
the other party very often says to you,
Tell me about yourself, I want to know all about you,
what's your story? And maybe they really do. . . .

Tennessee Williams (abridged).

THE CONVERSATION:
A DOUBLE PENTASTICH

It always begins about three hours after
dark when most humans are asleep. Then
the barking of the four dogs on the farms
nearby commences. The voice of each dog
is readily distinguishable by its tone.

They never all speak at once. One will
begin and the others answer in turn. It's
a kind of music and it's a conversation.
But what do they talk about, what are
they telling each other? I wish I knew.

THE LABYRINTH OF LINES

As the years pass, he fills the empty
space with images of mountains, islands,
houses and people. Just before he dies,
he discovers that the patient labyrinth
of lines traces the image of his own face.

Jorge Luis Borges, "The Creator." *Trans. Alastair Reid.*

THE GODDESS OF TORMENT

To thee clepe I, thou goddesse of torment,
Thou cruel Furie, sorwing ever in peyne;
Help me, that am the sorwful instrument
That helpeth lovers, as I can, to pleyne,
For wel sit it, the sothe for to seyne. . . .

Chaucer, Troilus and Criseyde.

THE CADENCE OF THE WORLD

I noticed a lightness that moved me. It probably
was how things were, myself included, all of us
transparent in the cadence of the world. A coming
and going, urging and denying, and in between,
untouchable, the way of existence.

Gottfried Benn, Primal Vision. *Trans. E. B. Ashton.*

THE LIFE OF CHIVALRY

So then it was that she and Sir Gawaine
went out of the castle and supped in a
pavilion, and there was made a bed and
Sir Gawaine and Lady Ettard went
there to bed together for two nights.

Sir Thomas Malory, from Le Morte d'Arthur.

EASTER MONDAY

An enormous chocolate egg surrounds the day,
Its pieces cheap and gritty to the teeth; we look out
Through cellophane, company with the yellow cotton chicks.
Outside it rains; we see the splashes covering the sky,
Hear it swish on an Indian file of motor cars which climbs
        the hill.

Edwin Brock, from Invisibility Is the Art of Survival *(1972).*

THE MANYOSHU

She wrote to the poet that she
loved the embrace of his words.
He stopped adoring the moon
and covered many pages with
more of them for her pleasure.

The Manyoshu (760 A.D.) is the classic collection of early Japanese verse.

DINNER WITH TRIMALCHIO

The course that followed was spaced around a circular tray
where over the twelve signs of the Zodiac the chef had put
the most appropriate food: a pair of testicles and kidneys
over Gemini . . . virgin sowbelly on Virgo . . . over Scorpio
a crawfish . . . a lobster on Capricorn . . . on Aquarius a goose . . .

From The Satyricon of Petronius Arbiter. *Trans. William Arrowsmith.*

CLEOMENES ON DEATH

Doest thou thinke it a glorie for thee
to seek death, which is the easiest
matter, and the presentest unto any man;
and yet, wretche that thou art, thou fliest it
more cowardly & shamefully than battell.

Plutarch, chapter on Agis and Cleomenes in the Lives of Noble Grecians
and Romans. *Trans. Sir Thomas North.*

AT THE SKY'S EDGE

Love among the mountains: eternity that patience
of the earth simplifies our human sounds: one
arctic-thin cry from deep antiquity until now:
rest, weary traveler, a wounded ear's already
laid your dignity bare, one arctic-thin cry.

Bei Dao. Trans. David Hinton.

DE CORPORE HOMINUM

When Pound translated De Gourmont's
Physique de l'Amour did he really
believe the Frenchman's theory that sperm
rising to the brain produces creativity
or did he just assume it was a joke?

MORTALITY

Preparing to die, the French poet Alain
Bosquet wrote: "No more me tomorrow;
my lines will be flabby as a fried egg
and void of meaning; no more me tomorrow;
the world won't even notice my absence."

DESIRES AND DEATH

A man acteth according to the desires to which
he clingeth. After death he goeth to the next
world bearing in his mind the subtle impressions
of his deeds; and after reaping the harvest of
his deeds, he returneth to the world of action.

From the Brihadaranyaka Upanishad. Trans. W. Y. Evans-Wentz.

DESIDERIUS ERASMUS

His name was Gerard Gerard, which he translated into
Desiderius Erasmus: he loved not Fish, though borne
in a Fish-towne. He was begot (as they say) behind
dores. He was a tender Chitt, and his mother would not
entrust him at board, but tooke a house for him. . . .

From Brief Lives, *John Aubrey (1626–97).*

MESSALINA

That Messalina, leaving the arms of her
twenty-five, or more, lovers—is, and I'm
translating literally: *still ardent*, the words
become a bit coarse in French, even
among men, and the Latin is self-explanatory.

Alfred Jarry, The Supermale. *Trans. Barbara Wright & Ralph Gladstone.*

SONG FOR SILKWORMS

Every province and kingdom under heaven, no city has
avoided shield and sword. Why can't the weapons be
cast into ploughshares, and every inch of abandoned
field tilled by oxen? Don't condemn heroes to weep
like heavy rains, leave man to grain, women to silk. . . .

Tu Fu (abridged). Trans. David Hinton.

THE MARVELOUS ASS

The tale spread far and wide. My exploits
soon made my master an illustrious personage.
"There goes the man," folks said, "who dines
with an ass, a dancing ass that understands
human speech and can answer with signs."

Apuleius, from The Golden Ass. *Trans. Jack Lindsay.*

THE GRASP OF LOVE

I thought there could be
No more love left anywhere.
Whence then is come this love,
That has caught me now
And holds me in its grasp?

Princess Hirokawa (8th century). Trans. Donald Keene.

DIE VERWIRRUNG

All those eggheads going crazy trying to figure
out what makes things tick. Don't they know
that "Unser Philosophie ist eine Berichtigung des
Sprachgebrauch"? A smart fellow named Otto
Kretschmer told me that in a Vienna bierstube.

DE PERENNITATE

When Montesquiou was posing for his
portrait by Whistler, one day he got restless
and moved his eyes away from the artist,
who suggested: "If you will look at me for
an instant longer, you will look forever."

MAN PINES TO LIVE

Man pines to live but cannot endure the days
of his life. The learned covet the customs of
the savages. They envy the panther. The poet
wants to be an animal. "Submit, my heart. Sleep
the sleep of the brute," said Baudelaire.

Edward Dahlberg, from The Sorrows of Priapus.

THE CEASELESS RAIN

It rains gently and unceasingly, it rains
listlessly but with infinite patience, as
it has always rained upon this earth, which
is the same color as the sky—somewhere between
soft green and soft ashengray. . . .

Camilo José Cela, from Mazurka for Two Dead Men.
Trans. Patricia Haugaard.

NERO POISONS BRITANNICUS

He demanded a poison that should be most quick
and made a trial thereof in a kid and then in
a pig. When the pig died he commanded it be
given to Britannicus as he sat at supper with
him, who no sooner tasted it than he fell dead. . . .

From Lives of the Twelve Caesars, *Suetonius. Trans. Philemon Holland.*

DE SENECTUTE: MARY BAKER EDDY

Mary Baker Eddy wrote that man
is neither old nor young. He is
a spiritual idea that never dies.
I no longer fear the first knock.
Let the door open wide, I'm ready.

THE DECLINE AND FALL OF THE
ROMAN EMPIRE

When Edward Gibbon presented a volume
of his *Decline and Fall* to George III
(who was the crazy king) the monarch
said, "Another damn thick book, always
scribble, scribble, eh, Mr. Gibbon."

NOT MY LONELINESS, BUT OURS

The most of men are all too much myself,
my shed externals, as feces, hair, skin,
discarded clothes, useless to me and dead.
From oneness, what should we say we hadn't said
before together? Nothing to say to them. . . .

William Bronk, from The World, the Worldless *(1964). Abridged.*

NOT WAVING BUT DROWNING

Nobody heard him, the dead man,
But still he lay moaning:
I was much farther out than you thought
And not waving but drowning.
Poor chap, he always loved larking. . . .

Stevie Smith, from Collected Poems. *Abridged.*

CARRIAGES

If the carriages of Kings and Princes bore
like moderation in peace, as they afford
in Tempests of Warre, surely the estates
of Kingdomes and the affayres of this world
would longer flourish and be better governed.

Sallust, The Conspiracy of Catiline. *Trans. Thomas Heywood.*

A DIFFICULT COURTSHIP

Genji thought long about her. Though she had
with so strange and inexplicable a resolution
steeled her heart against him to the end,
each time he had remembered that she had gone
forever it filled him with depression.

Lady Murasaki, The Tale of Genji. *Trans. Arthur Waley.*

THE NOVELIST, MAUDE HUTCHINS

M. H. had imagination, but when she was planning
a new novel she scribbled phrases and plot twists
on 3x5 cards which she'd store in a jade vase.
Ready to write, she'd dump the cards on the
floor, get down on her knees and arrange a book.

ON HER PRETTINESS

What the eye of the beholder sees
has *existenz*. Was it not Ignatius
of Freiburg who proved in 1166
that the waterfall only exists
because we can see it or hear it?

DESIRE FOR THE IMPOSSIBLE

Caligula: Now listen! I'm not mad; in fact I've
never felt so lucid. What happened to me is
quite simple; I suddenly felt a desire for
the impossible. That's all. Things as they
are, in my opinion, are far from satisfactory.

Albert Camus, Caligula. *Trans. unidentified.*

THE OMNISCIENT AUTODIDACT

Kenneth Rexroth knew everything and would
tell you about it. He had a photographic
memory. After lunch he would lie in his
bathtub for two hours doing some light
reading, such as a history of Chinese science.

CONSCIENCE AT YALE

L's wealth made him feel guilty. Once a week
a poor boy came to his college room to help
him with his beetle collection. When rumors
spread of what L had given the maid at term's
end, the woman was fired by the house master.

DOVE STA MEMORIA

In memory's locus taketh he his state
formed there in manner as a mist of light
upon a dusk that is come from Mars and stays.
Love is created, hath a sensate name,
his modus takes from soul, from heart his will.

Guido Cavalcanti (1255–1300). Trans. Ezra Pound.

PUBLIC RELATIONS

Martial urged his friend Faustinus
to work faster on his book and to be
seen in the right company. What
you do *now* will count. Glory comes
late to the ashes of the great dead.

IN LOVE WITH YOU

In love with you
I have lost all sense of
Hiding from men's eyes.
If in exchange for meeting you
Is death so great a price to pay?

Ariwara no Narihiro (c. 860). Trans. Donald Keene.

THE OLD MAN'S SOLUTION

He was losing his memory so he had
a surgeon insert his mind in her head
to remember things. She was good on
names and dates, but most remarkably
she'd recall things that never happened.

THE BIRTH OF AN EMPEROR

Claudius was born at Lyons, in the year when
Julius Antonius and Fabius Africanus were
consuls, upon the Kalends of August, that
very day on which an altar there was dedicated
to Augustus. Tiberius Claudius Drusus was his name.

Suetonius, The Lives of the Twelve Caesars. *Trans. Philemon Holland.*

THE ABYSS

Pascal's abyss went with him, yawned in the air.
—Alas! All is abyss! Desire, act, dream,
Word—I have felt the wind of terror stream
Many a time across my upright hair,
Above, below, around me, shores descending. . . .

Baudelaire, Flowers of Evil. *Trans. Jackson Mathews.*

THE OTHER SHORE OF THE SEA

It is time, love, to break off the somber rose,
shut up the stars and bury the ash in the earth;
and, in the rising of the light, wake with
those awaking, or go in the dream, reaching the
other shore of the sea which has no other shore.

Pablo Neruda, from a tape. Trans. Alastair Reid.

PREMULA'S PROBLEM

Quintius, her mentor, tries to make
love to her. She rather likes him
because his learning enlarges her head.
But he, poor old man, cannot enlarge
himself in bed. It's quite a problem.

After Catullus.

THE PERSIAN WOMAN

The fair one comes forth muffled and wrapped; the beast,
her dromedary, kneels; she mounts, turning her
latticed head toward us; I hear a tiny giggle; she
whispers to a slave girl nearby; the auditor also
laughs; they draw the little curtains; the camels start. . . .

Sir Richard Francis Burton, Personal Narrative of a Pilgrimage to
Al-Madinah and Meccah. *Ed. Edward Rice.*

PROVIDENCE, FORTUNE & FATE

Whilst a man confideth in Providence, he should not
slacken his exertions; for without labor he is
unable to obtain the oil from the seed. Fortune
attendeth that lion amongst men who exerteth himself.
They are meek who declare fate the sole cause.

From the Sanskrit, Vishnu-Sarma's Hitopadela *(c. 1002 A.D.).*

REMEMBRANCE OF HER

No man can ever pass a day in boredom
    who has remembrance of her,
for she is the beginning and birth of all joy:
    and he who would praise her
no matter how well he speaks of her, he lies!

Peire Vidal (1175–1205). Trans. Paul Blackburn.

THE SOLDIER POET

Archilochos was the second great Greek poet,
next after Homer. His name means First Sergeant;
he was a mercenary. Satire and toasty lyrics
were his forte. Menander called him a "thistle
with graceful leaves." Wasps infest his tomb.

THE SMART MAN

That old know-it-all Cicero said that
the wicked flourish like a green bay
tree, and that an old love pinches like
a crab. A smart man but nobody liked him
much and Augustus had him executed.

RENAISSANCE POLITICS

Since the Pope will soon die, the Bishop of Gurk
has been dispatched to Rome to help us behind the
papal throne. This matter will require a notable
sum of money. We hope that your bank will be able
to advance us a loan of up to three hundred ducats.

From "Hapsburgs and Fuggers" in The Portable Renaissance Reader.
Eds. Ross & McLaughlin.

THE SHADOWY FIGURE

Behind the moving screen of years there
is, unseen by passers-by, a shadowy
figure. Even among his friends few know
that he exists. But the figure knows who
he is and is reconciled to being a shadow.

ON SPELLS

"Begging priests and soothsayers will go to
the wealthy and convince them that if you want
to harm an enemy, at very little expense,
they will persuade the gods through charms
and binding spells to do your bidding."

Plato. Trans. W. B. Fleischman.

ARTAUD ON VAN GOGH

He is a painter because he recollected nature as if he
had re-perspired it and made it sweat, made it spurt
forth in luminous beams onto his canvas, in monumental
clusters of colors . . . the fearful pressure of apostrophes,
stripes, commas, bars . . . ocular clashes taken from life. . . .

Antonin Artaud, abridged. Trans. Mary Beach.

TO SURYA

His bright rays bear him up aloft, the god who
knoweth all that lives. The constellations pass
away, like thieves, together with their beams,
before the all-beholding sun. Swift and beautiful
art thou, O Surya, maker of the light.

*A hymn from the Rig-Veda (1200 B.C. or earlier). Ed. from Sanskrit by Nicol
Macnicol. Abridged.*

SIR WALTER RALEIGH: A DOUBLE PENTASTICH

Raleigh loved a wench well; and one time getting
up one of the Mayds of Honour against a tree in a
Wood who seemed at first boarding to be something
fearful of her Honour, she cryed, "Sweet Sir
Walter, will you undoe me?" At last as the danger

and the pleasure at the same time grew higher,
she cried in extasey, "Sisser Swatter Sisser
Swatter." She proved with child, and I doubt not
but this Hero took care of them both, as also
that the Product was more than an ordinary mortal.

A STATEMENT FOR EL GRECO AND
WILLIAM CARLOS WILLIAMS

Toledo shines out like no other city.
And Poe has risen
With his variable ways, and his jaw set at an angle.
Toledo, with no name carved to it saying: here lies . . .
Toledo, with the face of no man at the window.

Kay Boyle, from A Glad Day *(1938).*

SLAVES OF THE GODS

Lucian of Samosata was not taken in by
the gods. "Why do men make sacrifices
to the gods? They are fellow slaves with
men. With the gods the thing goes on to
infinity. And your slavery will be eternal."

See Lucian's Zeus Catechised.

THOSE WONDERFUL PEOPLE

Well all right if that's the
way it is that's how it is and
I'll just have to put you
back in my special box that's
labeled "wonderful people."

TOUCHING

I'd like to touch you in beautiful
places, places that no one else
has ever found, places we found
together when we were in Otherwhere,
such beautiful hidden places.

A SOLUTION

If a poet can't get the girl
he wants with his words he'd
better get out of the poetry
business and go to work on Wall
Street and try to buy her.

SUGARING TIME

It's sugaring time and the buckets are hanging
from the maples. I can hear the plip-plip of
the drops falling into them. An old man
rounds the bend. He's staggering drunk from
the water he's been stealing from the buckets.

SPRING COMES AGAIN

The spaces in time seem to be narrowing.
Days rush along as if they were running a
race. But the marching order of daffodils,
hyacinths, and white clouds of shadblow
are as military as when I was a child.

A MOMENT OF VANITY

A moment of happy vanity came to me in Urbino,
the seat of the one-eyed condottiero, Duke "Feddy,"
who gathered so many artists and scholars at his
court. I was dickering for a book and the seller
told me, "Lei se defende bene in Italiano."

"You defend yourself well in Italian."

IN MEMORY OF ROBERT FITZGERALD

O best of friends it's years since you crossed
the Lethe but still you often visit me in happy
memories: how you cocked your head when you were
talking, how you helped me with my Greek, and
our battles as Achilles and Hektor on the links.

YOUR LOVE

Your love reminds me of the
sense of humor of one of those
funny plumbers who like to switch
the handles on the hot and cold
faucets in hotel wash basins.

THE LIFE OF WORDS

When he was young he read many books,
he devoured them. Later he tried to be a
writer. But he discovered that words
have a life of their own, often not
saying what he wanted them to say.

LIVING IN THREE WORLDS

I live in three worlds, the one around
me and the one in my thoughts where you
live and the one in my old books where
I can read what you and I did when we
were once together in another life.

AN ADMONITION

To tie a girl up with string as if she
were a package for future delivery is
no longer an acceptable procedure.
Times have changed and certain atti-
tudes must now be reconsidered.

ARS GRATIA ARTIS

In the next chair of the barber shop the
director of the world's greatest museum
with its $28 million Rembrandt was catching
hell from the barber for having ruined the
line of his sideburns with an electric razor.

THE HEALER

Ben Wiesel, my beloved shrink, who rescued me from
the Slough of Despond, knew the right way to treat
a mad poet. Each session he would ask to see
my new poems. He commented on them with care
and I never had to utter a single word.

THE FIRST NIGHT

we spent together was like
school. Each was trying to
teach the other what we
liked or did not like. Love
was becoming a real thing.

ELUSIVE TIME

In love it may be dangerous to reckon on
time or count on it. Time's here and then
it's gone. I'm not thinking of death but
of the slippage, the unpredictable loss of
days on which we counted for happiness.

THE DISCOVERY

When will he discover that he's a joke, that the
smiles that greet him in the post office are really
hidden laughter, suppressed by politeness, that
when he leaves they laugh about him and his
pretensions to being an important poet and big brain.

THE DANCE OF THE SKIN

Over your flesh the skin dances.
But don't try to talk about the
dancing of the skin. Better to
say nothing at all. Just lie still
and feel it move. Just lie still.

ARS POETICA

Some think poetry should be
adorned or complicated. But I'll
take the simple statement in
plain speech. I think that
will do all that I want to do.

AN APOLOGY

She said, in apology, they aren't
very big, are they? But I told her:
let us not be concerned with the
minute particulars, it is only
your inner light that I cherish.

I DON'T KNOW WHERE SHE IS
WANDERING TONIGHT

Someone saw her in Ectaban and another in
Samarkand. The world is full of seductions
for a beautiful girl. I'll send word by
carrier pigeon that there will always be
lodging for her in my ever faithful heart.

A PROPOSAL

I want to breathe you in, not the
sweet odor of your skin but your
breath. As close as that, the two
of us breathing as one, one body,
one person, and one soul.

THE STARGAZER

A lovely girl, but after we'd had a few dates she
let me know, quite kindly, that I wasn't intelligent
enough to attract her. How right she was! Today she
is eminent in the field of astro-ethnography. She
plots the movement by the stars of primitive peoples.

THE SCAR

You have burned yourself deep
into me. I know now that you
don't love me enough but the
burn scar is inside me and
I think it will never heal.

THE TRIBUTE

You know how a cat will bring a
mouse it has caught and lay it at
your feet. So I bring you new
poems as my tribute to your
beauty and promise of my love.

THE TOAST

Past midnight. I'm in bed
sipping the glass of juice
and vodka that helps me sleep.
Each sip is a toast to one of
the girls I loved in the past.

THE WISDOM OF THE OWL

Your error said the owl was dehumani-
zation. It wasn't a girl you wanted
but a love object, and for what you
were willing to give you couldn't
expect one that would turn you alive.

EDITOR'S NOTE

The present, hefty volume consists of all the poems in James Laughlin's books and pamphlets that were published or prepared in his lifetime, together with his poetry contributions to the anthologies that he edited (*New Directions in Prose & Poetry*, nos. 1–55, 1936–91; *A Wreath of Christmas Poems*, 1942; *Spearhead*, 1947; *A New Directions Reader*, 1964) and the posthumous *The Way It Wasn't: From the Files of James Laughlin* (2006). It is also the companion volume to his verse memoir, *Byways* (2005). Taken together, the two books represent virtually the entire body of his work as a poet. Omitted from *Byways* are the fragmented, often incomprehensible, unfinished segments of his long autobiographical poem. Not included in the *Collected Poems* are those poems that were published in magazines but which he chose not to include in his books, as well as those that he wished not to publish at all. Their number in not considerable, and given JL's astonishing prolificness in the last years of his life, their inclusion would hardly affect his standing as a poet. As it is, *The Collected Poems of James Laughlin, 1935–1997*, holds between its covers some 1,250 poems.

As with *Byways*, JL left no instructions for organizing his *Collected Poems*. It seemed obvious to group the poems by their original book publication, arranged chronologically, and this, in fact, is the approach I took, with the following exceptions. The contributions JL made to his anthologies (and also to *The Way It Wasn't*), but not included in his poetry books, comprise two sections of "Uncollected Poems" (1935–1948 and 1984–1997), while the illustrated "Picture Poems" and "(American) French Poems" are, for the sake of cohesion, drawn from a number of his collections. For the rest, it would have been good to have been able to present the poems in each of JL's books in the exact order and sequence in which they originally appeared. However, from his very first publications to his last, he recycled a great number of his poems; some appeared a half dozen times or more in various collections, occasionally under new titles or slightly changed ones, and now and then he even used the same title for more than one poem. And then there are the earlier poems that he recast into the five-line form of his later "pentastichs." Except in the case of these last (which are essentially new poems, because of the complete reworking of the line-breaks), it was important that none of the poems be repeated in the present volume. But it was equally important that readers as well as literary historians be able to reconstruct the contents of JL's books as they were first arranged; for this, they need only to turn to page 1007, "Appendix: Tables of Contents of James Laughlin's Books and Pamphlets."

The *Collected Poems* owes a great deal to the late John A. Harrison, whose "A Selective List of Published Writing, 1932–2002, By and About James Laughlin" prepared the ground for all subsequent study of JL's work. However, not all of the poetry publications listed in Harrison's bibliography have their own titled sections in the present volume. This is because he listed broadsides (which are not books as such), chapbooks, and special editions that in some cases contain only a single poem, but whose contents were afterward included by JL in his full collections, whether large or small and whether in trade or limited editions (the line between these latter two being very fine when it comes to JL's books). Then, too, some of the limited editions include poems that JL published nowhere else. All the omitted publications are mentioned in the Notes. In the end, the criteria for establishing the book-titled sections of the *Collected Poems* were these: the publications should consist of two or more poems collected in book form for the first time, be at least sixteen pages in length, and be bound, whether sewn or glued, as any normal book would.

Turning to the Notes, they are minimally interpretive and are essentially intended as a guide to readers making their way through a book unavoidably as complex as this one. JL's own feelings ran alternately hot and cold about the usefulness of notes, both for his poems and those of his ND authors. When he did employ them for his own work, they could be seen, on the one extreme hand, as erudite, intricate, and long, and on the other, elementary as dictionary entries and perhaps even unnecessary. Nevertheless, he wrote them all intentionally and with care, and they surely belong here with his poems in so comprehensive a volume. Included in the Notes, in addition to JL's own annotations, are: for each book-titled section, his acknowledgments, his dedication, if any, and other words of note in the front matter; the colophon page, if any; the reprint history, if there is one, for each of the poems, and any substantive text revisions; translations of his

(American) French poems as well as foreign words and phrases whose meaning isn't clear from the text, these often in brackets; allusions and cross-references to *Byways* and other poems in the *Collected Poems*, sometimes with relevant bibliographical data. In JL's own cross-references, the page numbers have been changed to reflect the present volume. No attempt has been made to mirror the visual style of JL's original notes, which varied from book to book according to the designer's specifications, but something of the original look has been preserved in the book dedications and epigraphs and in the colophon pages.

Finally, in the poems and in JL's own notes, I took it upon myself to make silent spelling corrections, fix obvious typos, and repair occasional errors in his otherwise excellent Latin and Greek. This book is his, and these are things he surely would have wanted me to do.

PETER GLASSGOLD

APPENDIX

THE FOURTH ECLOGUE OF VIRGIL (1939)

The Fourth Eclogue of Virgil

SOME NATURAL THINGS (1945)

The Poet to the Reader. The Publisher to the Poet. On the Gift of a Sapphire to My Wife. The Mountain Afterglow. The Hairs of My Grandfather's Head. The Mountain. Easter in Pittsburgh. The Visitor. The Cat & Dog at Love's Door. Go West Young Man. A Letter to Hitler. Fragment [". . . come out of the"]. In the Snow. Paper & String. Old Dr God. The Hunting Dog. Fragments from America I Love You. When Does the Play Begin? The Avalanche. I See in the Paper That You're Engaged. Confidential Report. The Return of Love. War Poems. What the Pencil Writes. Crystal Palace Market. The Last Poem to Be Written.

REPORT ON A VISIT TO GERMANY (AMERICAN ZONE) 1948 (1948)

In the Train. In Darmstadt. How Does It Look? Why Not? Song of the GIs & the MGs. Logistics. Hard to Translate. Stuttgart: In a Nightclub (Illegal). O Frères Humains.

A SMALL BOOK OF POEMS (1948)

Above the City. Hard & Soft. The Summons. No Comparison. The Judges of the Secret Court. The Voices. Patent Pending. Now Love Speaks. The Man in the Subway. That Other World. Getting Paid. The Sinking Stone. Down We Go. The Swarming Bees. Amo Amas Amat. Busy Day. Highway 66. The Generations. This One Rhymes. Technical Notes.

THE WILD ANEMONE & OTHER POEMS (1957)

The Wild Anemone. The Empty Day. How Fortunate. Fragment ["Well here's to"]. Another Fragment. A Modest Proposal. A Bad

Night on Third Avenue. On the Fire. Step on His Head. It's Warm Under Your Thumb. Financial Review. In the Museum at Teheran. A Bit Different. Metropolitan Bard. Well All Right. Rome: In the Café. The Prisoner. The Trout. To a Certain Publisher. Your Love. Complaint & Prescription. A Piteous Sight. You Worry Me. Cynthia in California. That Old Dog in the Road. Martha Graham. Prognosis. Near Zermatt: The Drahtseilbahn.

SELECTED POEMS (1959)

The Mountain Afterglow. The Hairs of My Grandfather's Head. Easter in Pittsburgh. Old Dr God. Fragments from America I Love You. When Does the Play Begin? Confidential Report. What the Pencil Writes. Above the City. The Summons. The Cave. Angles of Vision. Patent Pending. Down We Go. The Swarming Bees. Song of the GIs & the MGs. A Modest Proposal. Step on His Head. Financial Review. A Bit Different. The Trout. Prognosis. He Lives in a Box.

THE PIG/POEMS (1970)

The Pig. The Ship. You Were Asleep. Figlio Mio. Ars Gratia Artis. Those Old Gods. Your Error. What the Animals Did. Song. Spring in the Subways. That Lamb. Saxo Cere. Pleasure *Now*. The Full Life. America I Love You. I Follow My Beard [1937].

IN ANOTHER COUNTRY: POEMS 1935–1975 (1978)

Foreword [Robert Fitzgerald].
The Mountain Afterglow. The Mountain. Go West Young Man. Fragment [". . . come out of the"]. In the Snow. When Does the Play Begin? Crystal Palace Market. What the Pencil Writes. The Last Poem to Be Written. Hard & Soft. The Summons. That Other World. The Man in the Subway. Getting Paid. Highway 66. The Generations. This One Rhymes. Technical Notes. In Darmstadt. O Frères Humains. The Difference. Upstate New York. Fragment from America I Love You. The Cave. The Ship. Figlio Mio. Song. Saxo Cere. The Full Life. The Wild Anemone. The Empty Day. How Fortunate. A Modest Proposal. Step on His Head. In the Museum at Teheran. The Trout. Cynthia in California. Prognosis. Near Zermatt: The Drahtseilbahn. You Were Asleep. The Kind-. It Does Me Good. The Woodpecker. A Long Night of Dreaming. In Another Country.

Dropkick Me Jesus. The Kenners' Cat. James My Namesake. I Have Heard. Junk Mail. So Much Depends. Some of Us Come to Live. Some People Think. What Are You Smiling About. You and Me. The Delia Sequence [To Kalon. My Soul Revolved. Across the Wide Water Lay Japan. We Sit by the Lake. You Are My Disease. You Have Burned. If in the Night I Wake. That Click. It Was All. You Came as a Thought. I Have Drifted.]. A Failure of Communication in the Animal Kingdom. The Child. Dans les Traces d'Ezra Pound, or Monsieur Roquette's Pants. The Care and Feeding of a Poet. The Casual Kiss. Cordelia. Being Much Too Tall. Can You Tell. Herodotus Reports. Into Each Life. Is It Written. Love Is Cumulative. The Junk Collector. Is What We Eat. My Old Gray Sweater. The *Non*-World. Persephone Wears Bluejeans. A Small Group. Why. Social Note. The Goddess. Alba. The French. Here I Am. The House of Light. The Hitchhiker. To Smile or Not to Smile. You Know How a Cat. Why Won't You Ignite. Will We Ever Go to the Lighthouse? The Old Comedian.

STOLEN POEMS. Why Shouldn't I. I Love the Way. Among the Roses. Antiphilus. And Will That Magic World. Cultural Note. Ἐνθάδε τὴν ἱερὴν κεφαλὴν κατὰ γαῖα καλύπτει, ἀνδρῶν ἡρώων κοσμήτορα, θεῖον Ὅμηρον. Felix. Saeta. Having Failed. The End of It All. I Am Aware. I Hate Love. In Hac Spe Vivo. J'ayme Donc Je Suis Je Souffre Mais Je Vis. Love Is a School. Berenice. To Be Sure. Occidit Brevis Lux. No My Dear. Nothing That's Lovely Can My Love Escape. El Camino de Amor. Ravings of the Depraved Monk Benno of St. Gall Who Went Mad from Carnal Longings in His Cell and Forgot How to Write Good Latin. Timor Amoris Conturbat Me. ὁ πατήρ. Two Letters on Samos [Posidippus to Philaenis. Philaenis to Posidippus.]. She Seemed to Know. Two Fragments from Pausanias [I Am Not Pittheus. At Methana.]. We Met in a Dream. What Is It Makes One Girl. With My Third Eye. At Eleusis. You Invited Me. How Shall I Find My Way. You Are My Future. Da Mi Basia Mille. Three Skirmishes in the Endless Battle [The Psychomachia. The Tauro-machia. The Hypnoerotomachia.]. Tuesdays at 87 Rue de Rome. A Lady Asks Me. A Cento from Ajar's *La Vie Devant Soi*. Dream Not of Other Worlds. I Want to Breathe. As in Music / A Reprise / Across Time [Paris, 1675. San Francisco, 1945.]. Je Est un Autre. Les Amants. Write on My Tomb.

(AMERICAN) FRENCH POEMS. The Importance of Dictionaries. La Luciole. J'ignore Où Elle Vague Ce Soir. Pour Bien Aimer. Elle N'est Plus Noctambule. Dois-je Reprendre. La Gomme à Effacer. La Fleur Bleue. Je Suis un Cerf-volant Saugrenu. Le Mordu de la Moto. Orphée. Les Vieillards. La Voix Qui Chante dans Mon Coeur. Elle Dit Que Je Mets des Gants. Elle A la Tête Qui Danse. Deux Fantaisistes. L'Hermine. **LONG-LINE POEMS.** The Bible Lady. The Deconstructed Man. "He Did It to Please His Mother." Tamara. O Hermes Trismegistus. Skiing without Skis. A Leave-taking. Tennessee.
FUNNY PAPERS BY HIRAM HANDSPRING. Girls as Windmills. My Muse. At Our House. The Cardiac Autoscope. The Bubble Bed. I Belong. The Lament of Professor Turbojet. Highlights of the Goliad Parade. Take Off Your Socks!! The Parodist. Preguntas sin Respuestas. Ein Kitzbuehler Tag (1947) [German]. Ein Kitzbuehler Tag (1947) [English].
Notes.

TABELLAE (1986)

I Saw Her First. My Watch. Caritas Perfecta. Who Is the Child. The Mirror Girl. You've Set the Words. Why Do You Never Enter My Dreams. I Feel at Home. I Live in Three Worlds. Eros as Archaeologist. Qui Nunquam Amavit. Le Jardin des Délices. Under His Microscope. La Langue Enfantine. The Dance of the Skin. A Suggestion. Arachne. The Prisoner of Childhood. Eyes Are the Guides of Love. After Rochester. Σοί με λάτριν γλυκύδωρος Ἔρως παρέδωκε, Ἡλιοδώρα. Two Spoons. What Is the Need. Apsaras. Le Voyage Innomé. Τό Σῶμα. Touching. Last Words. Properate Tempus. The Unsatisfactory Dream.

THE OWL OF MINERVA (1987)

Advice to Aurelius. The Owl of Minerva. The Fate of Actaeon. For Me All Time All History Is NOW. She's Not Exactly Like You. Il Pastor Fido. The Party on Olympus. After the Hugging Is Over I'll Still Treasure You My Dear. The Songbird. Some Memories of E.P. (Drafts & Fragments) [Rapallo (1934). Austria (1936).]. The Beautiful Muttering. Above the City. The Family Portrait. The People Boxes. The Fisherwoman. The Secretary's Story. A Failure of Communication in the Animal Kingdom. The Believer. Waiting for the Light. The Maze. Not Perfect Like You. lines after cummings. Eyes Are the

Guides of Love. O Best of All Nights, Return and Return Again. Can Language Be Taught with the Fingertips? Like the Octopus. The Hour Glass. Her Sweet Deceit. Haiku (slightly overlength) ["Winter has come"]. Confessio Amantis. That Night in Milan. Her Line Will Be Busy. The Mysterious Disappearance. The Word Machine. Can There Be a Female Bodhisattva? καὶ ποθήω καὶ μάομαι κὰτ ἔμον στάλαχμον. A Night at the Opera. The Large Opera Singer. An Anti-Love Poem. Holes. A Job Description. After Martial. Two Onanists. Terror. Report from the Missing Persons Bureau. Premula's Problem. One of the Great Lines. Kulchur. Ipse Dixit. I Know How Every Poet. The Gift. Gracious Living. Cincinnatus in Utah. Eating & Dying. L'Arrivée du Printemps. Tu Sais, Je Crois. La Voix Qui Chante dans Mon Coeur. La Baptême de Celui Qui Noye. Le Blessé. C'est à Mourir de Rire. La Débine de Mon Coeur. Je Ne Suis Pas Veinard. Je Suis le Comédien. Les Mots Secrets. Le Poète Englouti. Je Suis Raplaplat.

ΚΟΛΛΉΜΑΤΑ (1988)

The Questions. The Interdiction. ἡ μοῖρα αὐτῆς. Our Bicycles. The Unknown City. The Happy Poets. The Problem Struck Me. An Anginal Equivalent. The Limper. So Slender. A Graceful Exit. The Escape. Die Heimat. Now Love Speaks. A Translation. Elusive Time. L'Avertissement. It Can Happen. The Maker of Dreams. The Bird of Endless Time. The Kiss ["In the films when the couples kiss"]. By the Numbers. The Atman of Sleep. In Half Darkness. My Delights. I Love to See You. Her Reply. The Beautiful One. Love's Altar. The Unanswerable Question. The Importance of Silence. The Hand Trick. To Love Is to Hold Dear. Rhyme. Our Meetings. Still Pond No More Moving. When I'm Missing You. Eyes Closed. The Enlacement. The Smallest Blessing. The Gifts. The Revenants. The Poem Seen as a Shell Game. The Sorrows of Smindyrides. A Shard of History. Enigma Variations. Somewhere in France. A Parable. A Parenthesis. The Inn at Kirchstetten. Mon Secret. The Drawing Lesson. A Book About Nothing. Instructions. The Inviolable Maiden. In the Ballet. A Second Person. The Sense of It.

THE BIRD OF ENDLESS TIME (1989)

I. The Happy Poets. The Maker of Dreams. The Interdiction. In the Ballet. The Bird of Endless Time. The Kiss ["In the films when the couples kiss"]. Somewhere in France. Blood. Instructions. Mon Secret.

THE MAN IN THE WALL (1993)

Last Words of Charles Willson Peale. An Apotropaic Decision. Kenneth Rexroth. The Oracles. The Bonding. The Intruder. Our Domain. A Problem of Semantics. Ten Dollars Reward. The Scar. Heart Island. The Prisoner. It's Spring. Making a Love Poem. The Sensualist of Pain. The Self-tormentors. The Thinking Machine. The Vagrant. Contra Deconstructionem. The English Governess. Two Scenes from the Literary Scene & A Letter. The Aesculapians. What Is Hoped For. Are You Still Alone. The Flemish Double Portrait. The Imaginary Diary. The Afterthought. La Tristesse. The Rodent. An Attestation. The Biographer. Agatha. A Certain Impermeable Person. The Chips Are Flying. The Time Stealer. That Voice. The Story of Rhodope. Catullus xlviii. Cicero Wrote. Blue Booties & Pink Booties. Clutches. A Door That Opens. Before I Die. Charles Bernstein. The Moths. To Get to Sleep. The Moving Cloud. The Old Indian. The Kiss ["What did Klimt mean by"]. Bless You, Mr. President. The Dialogue. At the End. The Calves. The Third Life. The Master of Stupidity. Murderer. To Mistress Kate Gill. The Punishment. Odi et Amo. The Darkened Room. A Parable from *The Ocean of Story*. Don't Try to Explain. The Transformation. The Mathematics of Chaos. Ibykus. Panem et Circenses. The Actress. The Sultan's Justice. An Amorous Enjoinder. Expectations. Una Ricordanza Tenera. Der Rosenkavalier.

THE COLLECTED POEMS OF JAMES LAUGHLIN (1994)

Acknowledgments.

Collaborators.

A Note on the Notes.

Introduction [Hayden Carruth].

The Person. Technical Notes. I Take a Certain Pride.

from **SOME NATURAL THINGS.** On the Gift of a Sapphire to My Wife Ann. Easter in Pittsburgh. The Mountain Afterglow. The Visitor. The Mountain. Go West Young Man. The Frightened Bird. A Letter to Hitler. In the Snow. Old Dr God. The Hunting Dog. Fragments from America I Love You. When Does the Play Begin? The Avalanche. The Return of Love. Confidential Report. What the Pencil Writes. Crystal Palace Market. The Last Poem to Be Written.

from **A SMALL BOOK OF POEMS.** The Summons. Above the City. Amo Amas Amat. No Comparison. The Judges of the Secret Court. The Voices. Patent Pending. The Little Dog Laughs. The Full Life.

Now Love Speaks. That Other World. Getting Paid. The Sinking Stone. Down We Go. The Swarming Bees. Busy Day. The Generations. This One Rhymes.

from **REPORT ON A VISIT TO GERMANY** (American Zone) (1948). In the Train. In Darmstadt. How Does It Look? Why Not? Song of the GIs & the MGs. Logistics. Hard to Translate. Stuttgart: In a Nightclub (Illegal). O Frères Humains.

from **THE WILD ANEMONE.** The Wild Anemone. How Fortunate. A Modest Proposal. A Bad Night on Third Avenue. Step on His Head. It's Warm Under Your Thumb. In the Museum at Teheran. A Bit Different. Metropolitan Bard. Rome: In the Café. Well All Right. The Trout. Highway 66. Your Love. A Piteous Sight. Cynthia in California. Martha Graham. Prognosis. Near Zermatt: The Drahtseilbahn. He Lives in a Box.

from **IN ANOTHER COUNTRY.** Upstate New York. The Ship. Figlio Mio. Song. Saxo Cere. You Were Asleep. The Kind-. It Does Me Good. In Another Country.

from **STOLEN & CONTAMINATED POEMS.** Why Shouldn't I. I Float Between the Spheres. Like Him I Need the Past. Ἐνθάδε τὴν ἱερὴν κεφαλὴν κατὰ γαῖα καλύπτει, ἀνδρῶν ἡρώων κοσμήτορα, θεῖον Ὅμηρον. We Met in a Dream. Among the Roses. You Invited Me. Nothing That's Lovely Can My Love Escape. Cultural Note. What Is It Makes One Girl. Two Letters on Samos [Posidippus to Philaenis. Philaenis to Posidippus.]. In Hac Spe Vivo. I Hate Love. No My Dear. This Is the Morte Saison. Write on My Tomb. You Came as a Thought. Not-Notes.

from **SELECTED POEMS.** Some Memories of E.P. (Drafts & Fragments) [Rapallo (1934). Austria (1936).]. Some of Us Come to Live. The Beautiful Muttering. Knowledge. What the Animals Did. Your Error. Two Ships. When You Danced. Junk Mail. I Like You. Dropkick Me Jesus. The Kenners' Cat. James My Namesake. My Granddaughter. I Have Heard. So Much Depends. What Are You Smiling About. Some People Think. The Delia Sequence [To Kalon. My Soul Revolved. Across the Wide Water Lay Japan. We Sit by the Lake. You Are My Disease. You Have Burned. If in the Night I Wake. That Click. It Was All. You Came as a Thought. I Have Drifted.]. A Failure of Communication in the Animal Kingdom. The Child. The Care and Feeding of a Poet. Cordelia. Herodotus Reports. Is It

Windmills. My Muse. At Our House. The Cardiac Autoscope. The Bubble Bed. The Lament of Professor Turbojet. Preguntas sin Respuestas. Ein Kitzbuehler Tag (1947) [German]. Ein Kitzbuehler Tag (1947) [English]. Take Off Your Socks!! L'Abécédérien de Lubricité.

from THE OWL OF MINERVA. Advice to Aurelius. The Owl of Minerva. The Fate of Actaeon. Il Pastor Fido. The Party on Olympus. The Songbird. The Family Portrait. The People Boxes. The Fisherwoman. The Secretary's Story. The Believer. Waiting for the Light. The Maze. Eyes Are the Guides of Love. Like the Octopus. The Hour Glass. Her Sweet Deceit. lines after cummings. Tanka ["Winter has come"]. Confessio Amantis. The Mysterious Disappearance. Can There Be a Female Bodhisattva? An Anti-Love Poem. A Night at the Opera. The Large Opera Singer. Holes. A Job Description. After Martial. Terror. Premula's Problem. Ipse Dixit. Cincinnatus in Utah. I Know How Every Poet.

from THE BIRD OF ENDLESS TIME. The Happy Poets. The Maker of Dreams. The Interdiction. Still Pond No More Moving. In the Ballet. The Bird of Endless Time. Kissing ["In the films when the couples kiss"]. Somewhere in France. The Revenants. The Smallest Blessing. The Cold. The Enlacement. The Hand Trick. Rhyme. The Unanswerable Question. The Importance of Silence. The Escape. Die Heimat. Ein Kleines Herzlied. A Little Heartsong. An Anginal Equivalent. Elusive Time. In Half Darkness. It Can Happen. By the Numbers. The Problem Struck Me. The Beautiful One. The Drawing Lesson. Our Meetings. I Love to See You. Her Reply. Our Bicycles. The Waiters' Ballet. A Parable. A Translation. The Blue Footprints. A Sweet Kiss. At the Boule d'Or. Danger / Road Under Repair. Ever So. Mei Axis Mundi. The First Night. Floating Free. It's Indelicate. The Long Night. Her Letters. In the Salzkammergut. It's March. Poets. The Unenlightened Face. The Sorrows of Smindyrides. At Benares. The Endless Mirrors. The Limper. The Atman of Sleep. A Graceful Exit. Then and Now. Hope Springs. My Ambition. Maledictus in Plebe Sit. God Bless America! He Dreamed His Death. Digging Down to China. A Shard of History.

from THE PICTURE POEMS. Apsarases. The Doppelgaengers. The Reclining Position. La Langue Enfantine. The Infantile Language. The Family Council of the Yakovlevs. Multos per Annos et Multas per Noctes Umfricus Invictus Dabat Voluptatem Virginibus Vicinitatis

sed Nunc sub Hibiscum Diuturnum Somnem Quiescat cum Mentula Erecta. καὶ ποθήω καὶ μάομαι κὰτ ἔμον στάλαχμον. Carmina Gemina. Les Amants. The Inner Life of the Septic Tank. The Blowpipe Game. The Kiss ["What did Klimt mean by"]. Market Discounts Love. The French. Asmodeus. L'arrivée du Printemps. The Coming of Spring. To My Lady in a Distant Land That She Forget Me Not. The Munich Courier. Ingenium Nobis Ipsa Puella Facit. Encounter at the Casino, Aix-les-Bains. Ten Dollars Reward. Making a Love Poem. The Nereid. **RANDOM POEMS.** After Rochester (or somebody). Admonition. An Apotropaic Decision. Ars Gratia Artis. Arachne. Catullus V [English]. Catullus V [Latin]. Deathfear. The Dance of the Skin. De Contemptu Mundi. Σοί με λάτριν γλυκύδωρος Ἔρως παρέδωκε, Ἡλιοδώρα. Eros as Archaeologist. Flavius to Postumia. I Am the Metoposcoper. If a Poet. Folk Wisdom. If You Are Only Flirting. I Live in Three Worlds. I Like to Think of You. Into Each Life. I Saw Her First. Is There a Danger. I Want to Be Echopractic. I'd Like to Be Putty. It Was the First Time. The Last Caress. Last Words. The Long-distance Runner. What Is the Need. M&K. Love's Altar. Maxima Dona Ferens. The Mirror Girl. Moon & Sun. Obsession. The Power of Poesy. The Prisoner of Childhood. Properate Tempus. The Questions. Qui Nunquam Amavit. Τό Σῶμα. She Said in Apology. So Slender. Touching. A Suggestion. Two Spoons. Under His Microscope. The Unsatisfactory Dream. Who Is the Child. Why Do You Never Enter My Dreams. Paintings in the Museums of Munich and Vienna [Shameful Behavior. Sic Transit Corpus Mundi. The Importance of Reading. "Lay Down His Sweet Head." The Golden Age. The Beauty of Art. A Problem of Structure & Language. Sanctity. When Things Were Better.].
MOMENTS ON EARTH. You've Set the Words. La Tristesse. She Is So Practical. The Jealous Gods. Nowadays. The Box. The Atman. Real Bones. Before I Die. Building 520, Bellevue. When I'm Missing You. Sorrow. The Bavarian Gentian. Can I Catch Up with the Future? The Death Walkers. A Curious Romance. The Dark Mutinous Shannon Waves. The Deep Pool. For the First Time. The Holy Rivers. I Cannot Command You. In Egypt's Land. Floating. She Asks Me. Layers. My Instructions [Make It Simple. With a Cold Flame.]. Merry Madness Hall. Now Strike the Golden Lyre Again. Lines to Be Put into Latin. Reading the Obituary Page in *The Times*. The Poem Factory. The Rodent. Remembrance. A Sleepless Night. The Sacks. The Scribe. Out

in the Pasture. Snow in May. Temporary Poems. The Stranger in the House. The Tragedy of Time. The Prisoner's Song. Two Children. The Vagrant. Your Eyes. The Poem Seen as a Shell Game. The Mathematics of Chaos. What Matters. The Welcome. Two Parables from *The Ocean of Story* [Story of the Snake Who Told His Secret to a Woman. Story of the Fool and the Cakes.]. Crucifixion in the Desert. The Creatures of Prometheus. The Moths. The Shameful Profession. The Lost Secrets. Bless You, Mr. President.

☥ Ave Atque Vale. Experience of Blood. The Empty Room.

A SECRET LANGUAGE (1994)

A Secret Language. Silentium Aureatum Est. For a Clever Young Person. Does Love Love Itself. A Certain Impermeable Person. The Imaginary Diary. Don't Try to Explain. The Lost Secrets. Apsaras. In the Museum at Teheran. The First Night. Lines to Be Put into Latin.

THE COUNTRY ROAD (1995)

The Departure. The Revenant. Is Memory. There's Never a Never. Who Is She? Who Was She? Here Is My Hand. Anima Mea. Little Scraps of Love. The Search. The Prankster. The Country Road. A Florilegium [The Purple Clematis. The Wild Geranium. Anthea.]. In the Meadow. Bittersweet. Clouds Over the Sun. "When I Was a Boy with Never a Crack in My Heart." They Are Suspended. Why? The Rain on the Roof. Catullus XXXII. Why Does Love Happen? The Lost Song. Three Kinds of People. The Woman in the Painting. The Trophy Wives. A Difficult Life. In the Secret Garden. Mr. Here & Now. A Loved Book. How Did Laura Treat Petrarch? Les Consolations. The Mercy in It. Permanet Memoria. Grandfather. It's Difficult. A Toast to the Forgotten Poets. Some Amatory Epigrams from *The Greek Anthology*. Apokatastasis. Rubbing Dry Sticks. Her Hair. Penelope Venit Abit Helene. The Wood Nymph. Does Love Love Itself. L'Englouti. Her Heart. She Does Not Write. A Room in Darkness. Believe Me. A Secret Language. The Immanence of Your Body. La Vita Nuova. Eros Ridens. The Wrong Magic. The Change. Do They Make Love? By the Irish Sea. The Rising Mist at Ard Na Sidhe. Lost. Attracted by the Light. De Contemptu Mortis. A Troubling Case of Agnosia. Imprisoned. A Winter's Night. The Longest Year. Waiting for Tartuffe. The Invisible Person. As Long. The Exogamist. Canso. So

Albertine. Homage to Fellini. The Hitchhiker. The Least You Could Do. The Lotophagoi. Two Fables from *The Ocean of Story* [Story of the Chandala Girl Who Wanted to Marry a Prince. Story of the Astrologer Who Killed His Son.]. Haiku ["Now when I open my electric"]. The Old Men. In the Nursery. The Wandering Words. Benignus Quam Doctus. My Head's Trip. The Day I Was Dead.

BYWAYS. Prologue—the Norfolk Santa Claus—Dawn. Ezra (Pound). My Aunt. The Wrong Bed—Moira. The Desert in Bloom. Are We Too Old to Make Love? The Ancestors. Tom Merton.

THE EMPTY SPACE: TWELVE POEMS (1995)

The Cold Lake. Die Begegnung. Dans l'Attente. Waiting. The Empty Space. Here & There. I Listen For. The Chanting Bell. Back Then. Intransigence. Better Than Potions. At the Post Office.

HEART ISLAND & OTHER EPIGRAMS (1995)

Heart Island. For the Finders Within. Your Love. A Suggestion. Some People Think. Touching. Catullus XLVIII. I Live in Three Worlds. The First Night. The Happy Poets. Haiku (slightly overlength) ["Winter has come"]. The Two of Them. Dropkick Me Jesus. The Gift. The French. In Scandinavia. Skiing in Tahiti. You're Trouble. Admonition. Well All Right. Mei Axis Mundi. Write on My Tomb. The Old Man's Lament. Dans l'Attente. What Are You Smiling About. The Voyeur. In the Highstreet of Tralee. Die Heimat. Passport Size Will Do. At the Post Office. Lines to Be Put into Latin. Kulchur. I Suppose. The Kiss ["In the films when the couples kiss"]. Elusive Time. La Vita Nuova. Death Lurches Toward Me. At the End. A Visit to Paris. Les Consolations. The Consolations. The Importance of Silence. There's Never a Never. Haiku ["Now when I open my electric"].

THE MUSIC OF IDEAS (1995)

Carraig Phradraig. In Macroon. The Mercy in It. The Emigration. The Petition. The Enigma. The Selfish One. The Music of Ideas. Old Men. Longing & Guilt. The Nap. The Movements. Her Poems. The Effort to Live. His Problem. Harry. De Nada. In the Bank. Of the Snapshot. She Must Carry the Weight of Her Beauty. The Mistress of Improbability. Here & There. On Death Row. Vigilia Sanctorum. The Little Vision. Moments in Space. The Engines of Desire.

PHANTOMS (1995)

Along the Meadow Stream. Harry. Motet: *Ave Verum Corpus*. Sweet Childhood. That Afternoon. Many Loves. The Selfish One. She Does Not Write. Jack Jigger. Ophelia. Anima Mea. The Transients. The Petition. Believe Me. The Daze of Love. The Enigma. Old Men. A Winter's Night. Die Begegnung. The New Young Doctor. Now and Then. The Calendar of Fame. The Secret Room. That Very Famous Poet. Coprophilus. Homage to Fellini. So Little Time. The Music of Ideas. Where Is the Country. His Problem.

THE SECRET WORDS (1995)

In Another Country. Song. An Apotropaic Decision. Silentium Aureatum Est. Like Him I Need the Past. The Inscription. The Bible Says. Losing Body Heat. Long and Languorous. You've Set the Words. The New Book. Mei Axis Mundi. Ever So. Lines to Be Put into Latin. Catullus XLVIII. Odi et Amo. Technical Notes. The Bonding. Ἐνθάδε τὴν ἱερὴν κεφαλὴν κατὰ γαῖα καλύπτει, ἀνδρῶν ἡρώων κοσμήτορα, θεῖον Ὅμηρον. La Tristesse. Knowledge. A Translation. The Firefly. La Luciole. She Walks No Longer in the Night. Elle N'est Plus Noctambule. My Secret. Mon Secret. Orpheus. Orphée. The Nameless Voyage. Le Voyage Innomé. She Says That I Put on Gloves. Elle Dit Que Je Mets des Gants. The Blue Flower. La Fleur Bleue. The Eraser. La Gomme à Effacer. The King's Bowman. Le Hoqueton. I Don't Know Where She Is Wandering Tonight. J'ignore Où Elle Vague Ce Soir. The Garden of Delights. Le Jardin des Délices. I'm Fed Up with My Life. Je Suis Raplaplat. The Secret Words. Les Mots Secrets. The Ermine. L'Hermine. I Am a Preposterous Beetle. Je Suis un Cerf-volant Saugrenu. I'm Not Lucky with Girls. Je Ne Suis Pas Veinard. The Oracles. Now Strike the Golden Lyre Again. The Afterthought. The Story of Rhodope. Are You Still Alone. At the End. The Bird of Endless Time. Una Ricordanza Tenera. Der Rosenkavalier. The Dark Mutinous Shannon Waves. Our Meetings. The Printer to the Poet [D. von R. Drenner].

UNTIL THE SPRING BREAKS (1995)

The Kitchen Clock. The Prisoner. The Poem Factory. Petrarch & Laura. The Humor of the Computer. The Punishment.

Tahiti. The Gods. The Ladybug. Auto-da-Fé. Rosalinda, the Dreamer. The Unexpected Visitor. Poets on Stilts. The Truth Teller. Swapping Minds. The Secrets. The Road of Dreams. A Night of Ragas. Motet: *Ave Verum Corpus*. My Mind. That Afternoon. Coprophilus. The Secret Room. That Very Famous Poet. My Shoelaces (*From* Byways). The Love Puddle. Moments in Space. Love Is the Word. The Language of My Mind. Lucinda. The Logodaedalist. The Long Moment. The Longest Journey. Longing & Guilt. The Black Holes. Akhmatova's Muse. The Aleatory Turtle. An Amorous Dialogue. The Apsarases. The Acrobatic Dancers. All the Clocks. Along the Meadow Stream. His Problem. Where Is the Country. Now and Then. The New Young Doctor. A Winter's Night. The Daze of Love. The Transients. Ophelia. Jack Jigger. Many Loves. The Bird of Endless Time. Sweet Childhood. Saturn.

EPIGRAMS AND COMIC VERSES. Some People Think. In the Highstreet of Tralee. The Voyeur. Passport Size Will Do. At the Post Office. Heart Island. For the Finders Within. Carrots. The Happy Poets. The Two of Them. The Gift. In Scandinavia. You're Trouble. The Old Man's Lament. Dans l'Attente. Waiting. I Suppose. Elusive Time. Death Lurches Toward Me. Better Than Potions. A Visit to Paris.

THIRTY-NINE PENTASTICHS.

A Note on the Form.

The Tender Letter. I Travel Your Body. The Living Branch. All Good Things Pass. The Snake Game. The Locust. The Immeasurable Boundaries. The Honey Bee. Penelope to Ulysses. The Lover's Complaint. The First Time. The Anglo-Saxon Chronicle. Tanka ["In the *Dhammapada* it is written"]. The Long Feet People. Two for One. Word Salad. The Fantasist. The Pissing of the Toads. The Good Life ["Nabokov remembers that when he was young"]. The Seashell. The Smile of the Desert. Salad Dressing and an Artichoke. The Sweet Singer. The Lovers. The Writer at Work. The God of the Sun and Fire. The Magic Flute. The Ravaged Virgin. Odd Goings On in Philadelphia. The Man of Tao. An Unusual Girl. The Hetaera. The Right Girl. The Rescue. The Sculptor. Good Philosophy. An Exquisite Life. The Crane. The Invitation to Make Love.

From BYWAYS. The Rubble Railroad. In Trivandrum.

From **BYWAYS**. An Honest Heart . . . A Knowing Head. The Wrong Bed—Moira. The Desert in Bloom. In Trivandrum.

A COMMONPLACE BOOK OF PENTASTICHS (1998)

Introduction [Hayden Carruth].

A Great Emperor. Exquisite Life. Trying to Please. The God of the Sun and Fire. The Applicant. Enjoy the Passing Hour. Two for One. The Talking Truck. If I Die. An Evening's Entertainment. Tripartite. Logodaedaly. An Eskimo Song. The Lovers. The Exiles. I Travel Your Body. The Mime. An Existence of Exile. Tempus Loquendi. One Lost. Time Is the Mercy of Eternity. The Emperor Makes a Poem. Time in India. The Afterlife. Telling Tales. Every Day Except Sunday: A Triple Pentastich. Thy Treasure. The Revelation. Arli. The Fantasist. An Unusual Girl. The Affirmation. Fair Women. A Ceremony. I Feel Drunk All the Time. A Visit to Harlem. Difficulty in Henry James. This Foreign Language. The First Time. The Viper. Vienna. The Double Heads. The Fulfillment. Fidelio: Ezra Pound. The French. The Visit of Eros. Hard Times. The Bharata. Flaubert's Handbook of Clichés. Vedanta. The Canticle of the Creatures. A Health Problem. Paolo and Francesca. Freedom from Rebirth. Vigils. A Woman of the Sankhini Type. The Immeasurable Boundaries. Good Philosophy. A Wintry Christmas. Inscriptio Fontis. God in Politics. The Way of Renunciation. Kankha-Revata. The Hetaera. The Writer at Work. The Hair Shirt. The Courtship of Thomas More's Daughters: A Double Pentastich. What's New? The Linguist. A Happy Ending. The Joy of Your Charm. Hunger. His Hand: Two Lines from Lear, Act V. The Wrong Button. Singing Her Name. The Wise Man. A Trip Through Africa. The Happy Poets. Wanderer's Night-song. Of Zeno the Philosopher. The Seashell. The Secret Line in Loving. The Young Priest. Language. The Honeybee. The Young Deer. Want. Flaubert's Earlier Lives. Women. On Wealth. The Healer. In the Auvergne. Her Beauty. Voltaire and Christianity. On Awakening. Swearing. Human Society. The Truth. After Death. The Good Life ["Dr. Pangloss told Candide . . . "]. After the Flood. The Good Life ["Nabokov remembers that when he was young"]. The Two Goddesses: Demeter and Persephone. Stories. The Ancient Ocean. The Idols of Japan. In Hac Spe Vivo. The Anglo-Saxon Chronicle. In Hiding. The Russian Girl. Epiphany, Anne Carson. The Story of Happiness. Betrothal in Assam. The Invitation to Make Love. Procurement. The

Beloved Clown. The Merry Life. The Great Mother. The Blindfolded
Lovers. The Born Poet. The King-Swan. Of Knowledge. The Lover's
Complaint. The Conqueror. A Lullaby. Ladies Fighting. The Crane. The
Locust. In Vino Veritas. The Career Girl. The Living Branch. Lo Khor
(Year Wheel). Lines. The Long Feet People. Tout en Ordre. La Poésie.
Cabestan. Wittgenstein's Ladder. Who I Am. Le Temps Perdu.
Contentment. A Lover's Oath. Joyce's Words. The Long Sleep. Life Story.
The Conversation: A Double Pentastich. The Labyrinth of Lines. The
Goddess of Torment. The Cadence of the World. The Life of Chivalry.
The Growth of Love. Easter Monday. A Classic Question. The
Manyoshu. Dinner with Trimalchio. Cleomenes on Death. At the Sky's
Edge. De Corpore Hominum. Mortality. Desires and Death. The Man of
Tao. Desiderius Erasmus. Messalina. Song for Silkworms. The Marvelous
Ass. The Grasp of Love. Die Verwirrung. De Perennitate. Man Pines to
Live. The Ceaseless Rain. Nero Poisons Britannicus. De Senectute: Mary
Baker Eddy. The Decline and Fall of the Roman Empire. Not My
Loneliness, But Ours. Not Waving But Drowning. Carriages. A
Difficult Courtship. The Novelist, Maude Hutchins. On Her Prettiness.
Penelope to Ulysses. The Coming of Spring. Desire for the Impossible.
Odd Goings On in Philadelphia. The Omniscient Autodidact.
Conscience at Yale. Dove Sta Memoria. The Pissing of the Toads. Public
Relations. In Love with You. The Old Man's Solution. The Birth of an
Emperor. The Abyss. The Other Shore of the Sea. Premula's Problem.
The Persian Woman. Providence, Fortune & Fate. Remembrance of Her.
The Ravaged Virgin. The Soldier Poet. The Snake Game. The Smart
Man. Renaissance Politics. Salad Dressing and an Artichoke. The Sweet
Singer. The Shadowy Figure. The Smile of the Desert. The Sculptor. On
Spells. Artaud on Van Gogh. To Surya. Sir Walter Raleigh: A Double
Pentastich. A Statement for El Greco and William Carlos Williams.
Slaves of the Gods. Those Wonderful People. Touching. The Tender
Letter. A Solution. Sugaring Time. The Rescue. Spring Comes Again.
The Magic Flute. A Moment of Vanity. In Memory of Robert Fitzgerald.
Your Love. The Life of Words. Living in Three Worlds. An Admonition.
Ars Gratia Artis. The Healer. The First Night. Elusive Time. The
Evening Star. The Discovery. The Dance of the Skin. The Bird of Endless
Time. Ars Poetica. All Good Things Pass. An Apology. I Don't Know
Where She Is Wandering Tonight. A Proposal. The Stargazer. The Scar.
The Tribute. The Toast. The Wisdom of the Owl.

NOTES

Abbreviations for some frequently cited titles. The full contents of all JL's poetry publications listed below—both books and chapbooks—are included in the Appendix (p. 1007), even those that do not have separate sections in the present volume.

A   *Angelica: Fragment from an Autobiography.* New York: The Grenfell Press, 1992.

B   *Byways: A Memoir.* Edited by Peter Glassgold. New York: New Directions, 2005.

BET   *The Bird of Endless Time.* Port Townsend, WA: Copper Canyon Press, 1989.

CBP   *A Commonplace Book of Pentastichs.* Edited by Hayden Carruth. New York: New Directions, 1998.

CP1994 *The Collected Poems of James Laughlin.* Wakefield, RI, and London: Moyer Bell, 1994.

CR   *The Country Road.* Cambridge, MA: Zoland Books, 1995.

ES   *The Empty Space: Twelve Poems.* Ellsworth, ME: Backwoods Broadsides Chaplet Series, 1995. [See Appendix]

HI   *Heart Island & Other Epigrams.* Isla Vista, CA: Turkey Press, 1995.

HL   *The House of Light.* With woodcuts by Vanessa Jackson. New York: The Grenfell Press, 1986.

IAC   *In Another Country: Poems 1935–1975.* Selected by Robert Fitzgerald. San Francisco: City Lights Books, 1978.

K   Κολλήματα. Lunenburg, VT: The Stinehour Press, 1988.

LF   *The Lost Fragments.* Dublin: The Daedalus Press, 1997.

LPJL   *The Love Poems of James Laughlin.* New York: New Directions, 1997.

MI   *The Music of Ideas.* Waldron Island, WA: Brooding Heron Pres, 1995.

MW   *The Man in the Wall.* New York: New Directions, 1993.

ND   *New Directions in Prose & Poetry.* Anthology series edited by James Laughlin et al., nos. 1–55. Norfolk, CT, and New York: New Directions, 1936–1991.

OM   *The Owl of Minerva*. Port Townsend, WA: Copper Canyon Press, 1987.

PH   *Phantoms*. With photographs by Virginia Schendler. New York: Aperture, 1995.

PAW   *Pound as Wuz: Essays and Lectures on Ezra Pound*. St. Paul, MN: Graywolf Press, 1987.

PNS   *Poems New and Selected*. New York: New Directions, 1998.

PP   *The Pig/Poems*. Mount Horeb, WI: The Perishable Press Limited, 1970.

RVG   *Report on a Visit to Germany (American Zone) 1948*. Lausanne: Henri Held, and Norfolk, CT: New Directions, 1948.

S   *Spearhead: 10 Years' Experimental Writing in America*. Anthology. New York: New Directions, 1947.

SBP   *A Small Book of Poems*. Milan: Giovanni Scheiwiller, and Norfolk, CT: New Directions, 1948.

SCP   *Stolen & Contaminated Poems*. Isla Vista, CA: Turkey Press, 1985.

SL   *A Secret Language*. With woodcuts by Vanessa Jackson. London: Cast Iron Press, 1994.

SNT   *Some Natural Things*. Norfolk, CT: New Directions, 1945.

SP1959 *Selected Poems*. Norfolk, CT: New Directions, 1959. Published simultaneously, with the title *Confidential Report and Other Poems*, in London by Gaberbocchus Press.

SP1986 *Selected Poems, 1935–1985*. San Francisco: City Lights Books, 1986.

SR   *The Secret Room*. New York: New Directions, 1997.

SW   *The Secret Words: Poems*. Coffeyville, KS: The Zauberberg Press, 1995. [See Appendix]

T   *Tabellae*. New York: The Grenfell Press, 1986.

TWIW *The Way It Wasn't: From the Files of James Laughlin*. Edited by Barbara Epler and Daniel Javitch. New York: New Directions, 2006.

USB   *Until the Spring Breaks*. Louisville, KY: White Fields Press, 1995.

WA   *The Wild Anemone & Other Poems*. New York: New Directions, 1957.

UNCOLLECTED POEMS AND TRANSLATIONS (1935–1948)

A Birthday Fugue. *ND1* (1936).

The Glacier and Love's Ignorant Tongue. *ND1* (1936); reprinted in *ND50* (1986)—the fiftieth anniversary edition—with this headnote by JL:

> Needless to say, the poem which follows has never been reprinted. But it does speak for my obsession with skiing, and particularly ski mountaineering, part of my life which has annoyed many New Directions authors when I was not in the office to attend personally to their books.
>
> Most American skiers think that skiing is riding up a ski lift and skiing down a slope packed by a Thiokol snow-groomer. How many thousand feet can you do a day? For me, that is not skiing. Skiing is going off into the high peaks of our West or the European Alps with a pack on your back and seal skins attached to the bottom of the skis to make them grip. You spend the nights in little huts and climb peaks where the views seem limitless. When you ski down it's in fresh, untracked snow. With each turn you send up a cloud of snow-spray. It feels like a sensual rhythmic dance.
>
> I was never able to persuade Pound that there should be a few lines of skiing in the *Cantos*. God knows everything else is there, including troutfly-tying. The only reply I ever got related to my pleas was in a letter of 1947:
>
> > "Are you doing ANYTHING? Of course if you spend ³/4s of your time slidin' down ice cream cones on tin tray…"
>
> Actually, skiing on glaciers is not very exciting because they are almost all very flat. Only high up, under the ice-falls below a peak, is it interesting. Up there are the crevasses, where the surface of the glacier has been fractured by pressure. To ski such slopes you must go roped to a guide who will haul you out if you break a snowbridge. That never happened to me.
>
> The most famous glacier skiing is in the Haute Route between Zermatt in Switzerland and Chamonix in France. Five days of it down several connecting glaciers, spending the night in huts. Wonderful vistas of peaks and unbroken snow. And there is the Fox Glacier on the South Island of New Zealand. It runs from the west flank of Mount Cook down to the Tasman Sea. As you descend, the landscape around the glacier changes from arctic to flowering spring. But it's a long climb back up.

On Your Left St. Patrick's Cathedral and On Your Right Rockefeller City. *ND2* (1937).

Warning! *ND2* (1937).

What My Head Did to Me. *ND2* (1937).

Poor Man's Love Song. *ND3* (1938).

Made in the Old Way. *ND3* (1938).

The Rose That Tastes of Love. *ND3* (1938).

This Rolling Stone. *ND3* (1938).

Oh Mr. Tchelitchew How Could You Be So Mean. *ND3* (1938).

Love Like the Wind. *ND3* (1938).

That Big Lie. *ND3* (1938).

Speech Before Departure. Pseudonym, Tasilo Ribischka *ND4* (1939).

A Letter to Dostoyevsky. *ND4* (1939).

Which Words to Use. *ND4* (1939).

It Doesn't Make Sense Does It? *ND4* (1939).

Epithalamium. *ND4* (1939).

The Fourth Eclogue of Virgil. Translation. Norfolk, CT: New Directions, 1939. Reprinted in *A Wreath of Christmas Poems*, edited by James Laughlin and Albert M. Hayes (Norfolk, CT: New Directions, and New York: Blue Ox Press, 1942; revised, 2nd edition, New York: New Directions, 1972), with the following headnote:

> Surely Virgil's "prophetic" Eclogue must be the oldest of all Christmas poems for it was written about 40 B.C. Actually the poet sang of the coming Golden Age to honor the birth of the son of Pollio, an important Roman politician of the day. But the people of the Middle Ages became convinced that Virgil had had a revelation and was really announcing the birth of the King of Kings. It was the Emperor Constantine himself who first publicized the idea. Later the allegory was developed by the learned scholar Servius and by many others after him. Thus Virgil came to be almost a saint in the minds of Christian writers, and Dante chose him for his guide on the path

of salvation in the *Divine Comedy*. This translation is by J. Laughlin.

Excerpted for a 3rd edition called *Christmas Poems*, New York: New DIrections, 2008, with headnote given as an afternote ending, "This translationis by James Laughlin."

Song in Time of Drought. *ND5* (1940). Translation, from *Le Grand Jeu* (1928) by Benjamin Péret.

My Final Agonies. *ND5* (1940). Translation, from *Le Grand Jeu* (1928) by Benjamin Péret.

Round of the Sidewalks. *ND5* (1940). Translation, from *De Derrière les Fagots* (1934) by Benjamin Péret.

And So On and So Forth. *ND5* (1940). Translation, from *De Derrière les Fagots* (1934) by Benjamin Péret.

Georgia. *ND5* (1940). Translation, from *Georgia* (1926) by Phillipe Soupault.

Poem with an Extra Line. *ND6* (1941).

How Sad. *ND6* (1941).

Soldiers' Poetry Department. ND9 (1946). Three poems: "our joes"; "glossing's gloss"; and "et iterum venturus" (title: from the Credo of the traditional Latin Mass, *Et iterum venturus est cum gloria*, "And he shall come with glory").

Psychomachia in Juke Time. Pseudonym, Tasilo Ribischka.

Liberty. *ND9* (1946). Translation, from *Poésie et Vérité* (1942) by Paul Eluard.

Notice. *ND9* (1946). Translation, from *Au Rendez-vous Allemand* (1942) by Paul Eluard.

JL note:
On the housewalls in the streets of Paris the Germans spread "Notices," threats, lists of hostages, which frightened some people and made everyone ashamed.

Courage. *ND9* (1946). Translation, from *Au Rendez-vous Allemand* (1942) by Paul Eluard.

Dawn Dissolves the Monsters. *ND9* (1946). Translation, from *Au Rendez-vous Allemand* (1942) by Paul Eluard.

Killing. *ND9* (1946). Translation, from from *Au Rendez-vous Allemand* (1942) by Paul Eluard.

To Her of Whom They Are Dreaming. *ND9* (1946). Translation, from *Au Rendez-vous Allemand* (1942) by Paul Eluard.

An Old Schoolbook. *ND10* (1948).
The unusual typewriter setting of the original is simulated here

SOME NATURAL THINGS (1945)

Acknowledgments (copyright page):
Some of these poems were first published in *Poetry, The Nation, The Partisan Review, The New English Weekly, The Harvard Advocate, Twice A Year* and *Circle.*

Epigraph:
"Nihil in intellectu quod non prius in sensu" [Latin: "Nothing in the mind not first in the senses"—John Locke]

Quoted often by JL as an analogue of William Carlos Williams' "No ideas but in things." See "Dream Not of Other Worlds," p. 330, and "The Thinking Machine," p. 556, and notes.

Colophon:
This edition was printed by Carroll Coleman at his Prairie Press in Muscatine, Iowa in May 1945, the types used being Bulmer, set by hand, and the paper Ansbach.

The Poet to the Reader. On the book jacket, front flap. No reprint.

The Publisher to the Poet. In the front matter, facing the title page. No reprint.

The Gift of a Sapphire to My Wife. Published in *S*; reprinted in *CP1994* with the title, "On a Gift of a Sapphire to My Wife Ann."

Mountain Afterglow. Published in *S*; reprinted in *SP1959, IAC, SP1986, CP1994, PNS.*

JL note:
The Wasatch Mountains at Alta, Utah. [*CP1994, PNS*]

The Hairs of My Grandfather's Head. Published in *ND1* (1936); reprinted in *SP1959, SP1986.*

The Mountain. Reprinted in *IAC, CP1994.*

> JL note:
> Kanchenjunga—one of the most spectacular peaks of the Himalayas, forty-five miles north of Darjeeling and 28,146 feet in elevation. I saw it in 1954 when working for The Ford Foundation in India. [*CP1994*]

Easter in Pittsburgh. Published in *ND5* (1940); reprinted in *S, SP1959, SP1986, CP1994, PNS.*

The Visitor. Published in *S*; reprinted in *SP1986, CP1994.*

The Cat & Dog at Love's Door. Published in *ND1* (1936). No reprint.
> In *ND1*, arranged in quatrains instead of couplets.

Go West Young Man. Published in *ND3* (1938); reprinted in *IAC, SP1986, CP1994.*

A Letter to Hitler. Published in *ND4* (1939); reprinted in *S, SP1986, CP1994.*

Fragment. Published in *ND6* (1941); reprinted in *IAC.*

In the Snow. Published in *ND3* (1938); reprinted in *IAC, CP1994.*
> In *ND1*, arranged in quatrains instead of couplets.

Paper & String. Published in *ND4* (1939); reprinted in *S.*

Old Dr God. Published in *ND5* (1940); reprinted in *S, SP1959, SP1986, CP1994.*

The Hunting Dog. Published in *ND4* (1939); reprinted in *CP1994.*

Fragments from America I Love You. A serial poem in untitled parts. "There was a little black"; published in *ND4* (1939); reprinted in *SP1959, IAC, CP1994.* "The first thing he said"; published in *ND4*; reprinted in *SP1959, CP1994.* "He was talking so fast"; published in *ND4*; reprinted *CP1994.* For later additions, see pp. 109, 110, 145, and notes.

JL note to "The first thing he said":
Dillinger—John Dillinger, notorious American bank robber and murderer, gunned down by the FBI in 1934. [*CP1994*]

When Does the Play Begin? Published in *ND5* (1940); reprinted in *S*, *SP1959*, *IAC*, *SP1986*, *CP1994*.

The Avalanche. Reprinted in *CP1994*.

I See in the Paper That You're Engaged. Published in *ND4* (1939). No reprint.

Confidential Report. Published in *ND6* (1941); reprinted in *SP1959*, *CP1994*.

In *ND6*, title: "Confidential Reports."

JL note:
White House—Franklin D. Roosevelt. [*CP1994*]

The Return of Love. Reprinted in *CP1994*.

War Poems. No reprint.

What the Pencil Writes. Published in *ND6* (1941); reprinted in *SP1959*, *IAC*, *SP1986*, *CP1994*, *PNS*.

Crystal Palace Market. Published in *ND6* (1941); reprinted in *IAC*, *SP1986*, *CP1994*.

The Last Poem to Be Written. Published in *S*; reprinted in *IAC*, *SP1986*, *CP1994*, *LPJL*, *PNS*.

JL notes, opening couplet:
"When, when & whenever..."—"Quandocumquigitur [*sic*] nostros mors claudet ocellos." Pound's version of Propertius III, 5." [*SP1986*]
Propertius, in the "Nox mihi candida." [Latin: "For me bright night."] [*CP1994, PNS*]
The first two lines are from Pound's Propertius. [*LPJL*]

In this poem involving the *Elegiae* of Propertius, JL follows the numbering and organization of Lucianus Mueller (Leipzig: Teubner, 1892), whose recensions often differ in this respect from other editions of Propertius. In Mueller, III.5.1

and III.7.1 correspond to 2.13.17 and 2.15.1 in G. P. Goold's Loeb Classical Library edition (Cambridge, MA: Harvard, 1990). Cf. Pound, "Homage to Sextus Propertius," VI, 1 and VII, 1. See also "No My Dear," p. 185, and note.

Last line. **Donna del mio cuor.** Italian: "Lady of my heart."

REPORT ON A VISIT TO GERMANY (AMERICAN ZONE) 1948

(1948)

Colophon:
TWO HUNDRED COPIES OF THIS REPORT WERE PRINTED FOR NEW DIRECTIONS BY HENRI HELD AT LAUSANNE ON GUARRO [PAPER] IN GARAMOND TYPES THIS IS COPY NUMBER—

In the Train. Reprinted in *CP1994.*

In Darmstadt. Reprinted in *IAC, CP1994.* Cf. "In Frankfurt" in *B*, pp. 230–31.

How Does It Look? Reprinted in *CP1994.* Cf. "How Did They Look?" in *B*, p. 231.

Why Not? Reprinted, *CP1994.*

Song of the GIs & the MGs. Reprinted in *SP1959, SP1986, CP1994.* Cf. "Song of the GI's and the MG's" in *B*, pp. 234–35.
In *SP1959* and *SP1986*, arranged in tercets with a concluding quatrain. *SP1986* adds a subtitle: "*Germany, 1947.*"

JL note:
MG—The American Military Government after World War II. [*CP1994*]

Logistics. Reprinted in *CP1994.*

Hard to Translate. Cf. *B*, pp. 236–37.

Stuttgart: In a Nightclub (Illegal). Reprinted in *CP1994*, with an additional stanza:

> A queer (with fine eyes) tells
> me that when he was fifteen &
> out on boy scout camping trips

the gang would all masturbate
into a frying pan and eat the
stuff friend it tasted good he
claimed now I ask you is that
authentic German Kinsey or has
he just got hunger and sex fer-
menting together in his starved
head? They were very fine eyes.

O Frères Humains. Reprinted in *IAC, CP1994*. Cf. *B*, p. 241.

JL note:
The title is from Villon's *L'Épitaphe*: "Frères humains, qui après nous vivez /
N'ayez les coeurs contre nous endurcis…" (Human brothers who live after us
/ let not your hearts be hardened against us…) [*CP1994*]

A SMALL BOOK OF POEMS (1948)

Acknowledgments (copyright page):
Some of these poems first appeared in *The Ark, Contemporary Poetry, The
Quarterly Review, Now, The Briarcliff Quarterly, Epoch* & *New Directions*.

Dedication:

For Bill Williams
any way you look at him—writer
or man—in his time: none better

Colophon:
Five hundred copies of this book were printed in Milan in June 1948 at the
Officine Grafiche "Esperia": fifty copies on special paper, in the series "all' In-
segna del Pesce d'Oro," numbered I to L, for the friends of the publisher, Gio-
vanni Scheiwiller; and four hundred fifty copies for New Directions, New
York, for sale in the United States.
This is copy number:—

Above the City. Published in *ND9* (1946); reprinted in *SP1959, OM, CP1994,
PNS*.

JL note:
For a reading of younger poets at The Grolier Club in New York in 1948
Marianne Moore rewrote the last two stanzas of this poem as follows:

none of us had been surprised be-
cause we'd always known that those
two Paragons of

progress sooner or later would demonstrate
before our eyes their true
     relationship

In her letter Miss Moore asked: "Can you condone it?" I could indeed." [*OM, CP1994*]

In *ND50* (1986), JL elaborates:
I find nothing in the correspondence which indicates that M.M. tinkered with Pound's poems when she was at *The Dial*, as she did with some of Hart Crane's, to his extreme annoyance. They say she was an incorrigible editorial fixer—always the perfectionist—and I can vouch for her ability. At one point I had sent her a copy of a poem I had written about an airplane crashing into the top of the Empire State Building, an event I witnessed from my office window. Some months later Miss Moore was on the phone. "Mr. Laughlin, I do hope you won't be *too* angry with me. The other evening I was doing a reading, and I wanted to read one of *your* poems. But I felt that 'Above the City' could be slightly improved in small ways. I hope I was not presumptuous." No, I was not angry, not in the least. I didn't actually see the revision till many years later, when Pat Willis showed it to me in the Moore collection at the Rosenbach Museum in Philadelphia. Miss Moore had *remade* the poem—and it's now certainly one of my best.

Hard & Soft. Reprinted in *IAC*.

The Summons. Reprinted in *SP1959, IAC, SP1986, CP1994, PNS*.

No Comparison. Reprinted in *CP1994*.

The Judges of the Secret Court. Reprinted in *CP1994*.

JL notes:
In the poem "The Judges of the Secret Court," the reference is to Kafka's novel *Amerika*. [Copyright page, *SBP*]
    Karl Rossman—a young immigrant, is the protagonist of Kafka's novel *Amerika*. Kafka fantasizes about a "Great Nature Theatre of Oklahoma," which is the goal of Karl's Candide-like journey. [*CP1994*]

Patent Pending. Reprinted in *SP1959, SP1986, CP1994*; republished separately by Gaberbocchus Press, London, in 1958, and again in 1993 by Turkey Press, Isla Vista, CA.
    the parables of Jesus / on their fingernails. Changed to "a saying of Gautama / on each fingernail" in *SP1959, SP1986*, and in the Turkey Press pamphlet; to "some sayings of Gautama / on the fingernails" in the Gaberbocchus broadside. *CP1994* returns to the original version.

Now Love Speaks. Reprinted in K, *CP1994.*

The Man in the Subway. Reprinted in *IAC.*

That Other World. Reprinted in *IAC, CP1994.*

Getting Paid. Reprinted in *IAC, SP1986, CP1994.*

The Sinking Stone. Reprinted in *SP1986, CP1994, LPJL, PNS.*

Dedication, "For Maria," added in *CP1994, LPJL, PNS.*

Down We Go. Reprinted in *SP1959, CP1994.*

The Swarming Bees. Reprinted in *SP1959, SP1986, CP1994.*

JL notes:
Heber J. Grant—President of the Church of the Latter-Day Saints in the 1930s. [*SP1986*]

The poem is set in Salt Lake City. Heber J. Grant was President of the Mormon Church of the Latter-Day Saints in the 1930s. [*CP1994*]

Amo Amas Amat. Reprinted in *CP1994.*

Title. Latin, based on the singular conjugation, present tense: "I love, you love, he (she, it) loves."

Busy Day. Reprinted in *CP1994.*

Highway 66. Reprinted in *IAC, CP1994.*

The Generations. Reprinted in *IAC, SP1986, CP1994.*

See *B*, pp. 64–83, for JL's memories of his parents' marriage.

This One Rhymes. Reprinted in *IAC, CP1994.*

Technical Notes. Reprinted in *IAC, SP1986, CP1994, SW, PNS.*

JL note:
Catullus—Gaius Valerius Catullus (84–54 B.C.), greatest of all the Roman lyric poets.

Milton—John Milton (1608–74), *Paradise Lost* and *Paradise Regained.* He wrote a highly Latinate English. [*CP1994*]

THE WILD ANEMONE & OTHER POEMS (1957)

Acknowledgments (copyright page):
Some of these poems first appeared in *Poetry* (Chicago), *Partisan Review, Semi-Colon, New Directions, Das Lot.*

Colophon:
STAMPERIA VALDONEGA VERONA

The Wild Anemone. Reprinted in *IAC, SP1986, CP1994.*

Dedication, "For Ann," added in *CP1994.*

The Empty Day. Reprinted in *IAC.*

How Fortunate. Reprinted in *IAC, CP1994.*

Fragment (From "America I Love You"). Reprinted in *SP1959* as an untitled part in the serial poem "Fragments from America I Love You." For other "fragments," see pp. 64–67, "Another Fragment," p. 110, "America I Love You (a fragment)," p. 145, and notes, as well as the note that follows immediately below.

Another Fragment. Reprinted in *SP1959* as an untitled part in the serial poem "Fragments from America I Love You" (see previous note); reprinted in *SP1986* as a separate, titled poem, "Self-control."

A Modest Proposal. Reprinted in *SP1959, IAC, CP1994.*

A Bad Night on Third Avenue. Reprinted in *CP1994.*

JL note:
Cynthia—the girlfriend of the Roman poet Propertius. [*CP1994*]

See "Cynthia in California," p. 124, and note.

On the Fire. No reprint.

Step on His Head. Reprinted in *SP1959, IAC, SP1986, CP1994, PNS.*

It's Warm Under Your Thumb. Reprinted in *SP1986, CP1994.*

Dedication, "For Maria," added in *CP1994.*

JL note:
The reference is to Henry James's novel *The Golden Bowl*.
The Maluva creeper figures in the Buddhist *Dhammapada*. [*CP1994*]

Financial Review. Reprinted in *SP1959*.

In the Museum at Teheran. Reprinted in *IAC, CP1994, SL, PNS.*

JL note:
Teheran—the capital city of Iran.
Azerbaijan—a region in southest Russia that was under Persian and
Mongol rule in ancient times. [*CP1994*]

A Bit Different. Reprinted in *SP1959, CP1994.*

Metropolitan Bard. Reprinted in *CP1994.*

Well All Right. Reprinted in *SP1986, CP1994, HI,* and in a revised version
in *CBP* with the title "Those Wonderful People" (see p. 992).

Rome: In the Café. Reprinted in *SP1986, CP1994, PNS.*

The Prisoner. Reprinted in *SP1986* and *CP1994* where, as "The Frightened
Bird," it is incorrectly included among the poems in *SNT*.

The Trout. Published in *ND16* (1957); reprinted in *SP1959, A New Directions
Reader,* edited by Hayden Carruth and J. Laughlin (New York: New Directions,
1964), *IAC, SP1986, CP1994, PNS.*

Dedication, "for George Revay," added in *CP1994.*

JL notes:
"Qu'est-ce j'ai fait…"—"What in Heaven's name have I done to have a daugh-
ter who is such garbage?" [*SP1986, CP1994*]
    The scene is Geneva in the 1940's. [*CP1994*]

To a Certain Publisher. No reprint.

Your Love. Reprinted in *SP1986, CP1994, HI,* and in a revised version in *CBP*
(see p. 995).

Complaint & Perscription. Published in *ND16* (1957); no reprint.

A Piteous Sight. Reprinted in *CP1994*.

You Worry Me. Published in *ND4* (1939); no reprint.

Cynthia in California. Reprinted in *IAC, CP1994*.

> JL note:
> Propertius's girlfriend Cynthia often gave him a hard time. [*CP1994*]
>
> See "A Bad Night on Third Avenue," p. 111, and note.

That Old Dog on the Road. No reprint.

Martha Graham. Published in *ND16* (1957); reprinted in *SP1986, CP1994, PNS*.

Prognosis. Reprinted in *SP1959, IAC, SP1986, CP1994, PNS*.

> JL note:
> Lao-tze—legendary Chinese philosopher of the 6th century B.C., author of the
> Tao-te-ching, the central text of Taoism. [*CP1994*]

Near Zermatt: The Drahtseilbahn. Reprinted in *IAC, SP1986, CP1994, PNS*.

> Dedication, "For Maria," added in *CP1994, PNS*.

> JL note:
> A *Drahtseilbahn* is a motor-driven cable to which Swiss peasants attach loads
> they wish to take up to their chalets high on the mountainsides. [*CP1994*]

SELECTED POEMS (1959)

> Acknowledgments (copyright page):
> Some of these poems first appeared in *Horizon, The Nation, The Partisan Review,
> Poetry,* and *The Quarterly Review.*

The Cave. Reprinted in *IAC, SP1986, PNS*.

Angles of Vision. No reprint.

He Lives in a Box. Reprinted in *SP1986, CP1994*.

THE PIG / POEMS (1970)

Acknowledgments (copyright page):
Some of these poems first appeared in *Agenda, The Nation, New Directions 1938, Pittsburgh Festival Overture, Stony Brook,* and *Unicorn Press Broadsides.*

Dedication:
FOR D.F. 1903–1968

Colophon:
there are 183 copies of THE PIG handset & printed in palatino and smaragd on shadwell handmade 48 copies on beige the rest on white. the binding is by elizabeth kner in chicago this spring of 1970

The Pig. No reprint.

The Ship. Reprinted in *IAC, SP1986, CP1994.*

You Were Asleep. Reprinted in *IAC, SP1986, CP1994, LPJL.*

Dedication, "For Ann," added in *CP1994, LPJL.*

Figlio Mio. Reprinted in *IAC, CP1994.*

Ars Gratia Artis. Reprinted in *CP1994* and in a revised version in *CBP.* Title. Latin: "Art for Art's Sake."

Those Old Gods. No reprint.

Your Error. Reprinted in *SP1986.*

What the Animals Did. Reprinted in *SP1986, CP1994.*

JL note:
Plus ça change...: these verses about big business raids and mergers were written fifteen years ago. [*SP1986*]

Song. Reprinted in *IAC, SP1986, CP1994, SW, PNS.*

Spring in the Subways. No reprint.

That Lamb. No reprint.

Saxo Cere. Reprinted in *IAC, SP1986, CP1994.*

JL notes:

"Saxo Cere / comminuit / brum"—the famous tmesis of Ennius. The stone splits the two parts of the brain. [*SP1986*]

The quote is from the Roman poet Ennius, famous for his use of tmesis. In English the line might be: [with a] stone [the] cere [he] smashed bellum. [*CP1994*]

Pleasure <u>NOW</u>. No reprint.

The Full Life. Reprinted in *IAC, CP1994*.

America I Love (a fragment). Reprinted in *CP1994*, where it is included in *SNT*, the last among the "Fragments from America I Love You." For other untitled sections of this serial poem, see pp. 64–67, p. 109, 110, and notes.

I Follow My Beard. Published in *ND3* (1938); no reprint.

IN ANOTHER COUNTRY: POEMS 1935–1975 (1978)

Acknowledgments (copyright page):

Some of these poems first appeared in *Agenda, Ambit, Harper's, Mother Jones, The Nation, New Directions in Prose & Poetry, New Dimensions, Out of the War Shadow, Pittsburgh Festival Overture, Poetry, Poetry Australia, Stony Brook, Unicorn Broadsides* and *Yes! Press Broadsides*.

The Difference. No reprint.

Upstate New York. Reprinted in *SP1986, CP1994*.

The Kind-. Reprinted in *SP1986, CP1994*.

It Does Me Good. Published in *ND30* (1975); reprinted bilingually in *ND46* (1983) with its Old English translation by Peter Glassgold, *HL, SP1986, PNS*.

The Woodpecker. No reprint.

A Long Night of Dreaming. Reprinted in *SP1986*.

In Another Country. Reprinted in *SP1986, CP1994, SW, PNS*.

JL note:

Tesoro—treasure.

Credere—Believe! Obey! Fight! The Fascist slogan.

Com' allora al ponte—as it as then at the bridge.

Ma se tu vuoi—but if you'd like to, this evening after the promenade at the corner near the newsstand when the clocks strike nine.

Vieni qua—come here…vieni subito—come quickly.

Vieni qua—come here, don't be afraid.

È bello no?—it's beautiful isn't it?

Sai tu amore—do you know darling how beautiful he is? how sweet he is? and how much you please me? do you know how much she loves you?

Etruria—the country of the Etruscans south of Rome. [CP1994]

UNCOLLECTED POEMS (1984–1997)

Are Our Neuroses. Published in *ND48* (1984).

Can I Batter My Way. Published in *ND48* (1984).

The Needle Is Stuck. Published in *ND48* (1984).

My Favorite Newspaper. Published in *TWIW.*

Some Voices from Canto 74. Published in *PAW.*
  Ego scriptor. Latin: "I the writer."
  OU TIS. Greek, transliterated: "No one; no man."
  Quis loquitur. Latin: "Who is speaking?"
  Jedermann. German: "Everyone."
  sic locutus est. Latin: "so he said."

The Inventors. Published in *ND54* (1990).

Haecceity. Published in *TWIW.*
  Cf. "Mr. Here & Now," p. 716.

STOLEN & CONTAMINATED POEMS (1985)

Acknowledgments (copyright page):

Some of these poems were first published in *Ambit* (London), *Iowa Review,* *New Directions in Prose & Poetry, The Paris Review,* and *Carcanet Review* (Manchester), "You Came as a Thought" and "No My Dear" were first published in *Poetry*.

Many thanks to Robert Fitzgerald and W. H. Ferry for their editorial assistance.

Dedication:

for E.P.
wherever he 'zat

Καὶ σέο, Ἔσρ' ὦναξ, σοφίης ἴδμεν βέλος ὀξύ,
ἀλλ' οὐ τιτρῶσκον, †ὦν γλυκὺ †κρῆμα.

We know, revered Ezra, the deadly arrows of your wisdom,
But they do not wound us, they are a healing balm.

(*The Greek Anthology* VII, 132)

The anonymous Greek epigram is addressed to the philosopher Protagoras. The Greek for "they are a healing balm" is conjectural.

"Author's Note":
Stolen and contaminated poems require additional commentary. A section of jottings and recollections follows the poems. JL [See below]

Colophon (hardbound edition):
This edition of *Stolen & Contaminated Poems* is limited to 200 copies on Frankfurt Cream 40 copies on Turkey Press handmade paper and was printed from Dante type by Sandra Liddell Reese
This is number—

Colophon (paperbook edition):
This edition was photo-offset for the author from the letterpress edition set in Dante type and printed at Turkey Press by Sandra Liddell Reese

The notes for this book—and for this section in *CP1994*—are grouped together at the end as "Not-Notes." (With some omissions and minor punctuation changes, many of them are included as well in the endnotes to *SP1986*. Only significant differences are given here. The text on the verso of the part title to these "Stolen Poems" reads: "The sources of the thefts will be found in notes at the back of the book.") JL introduces his "Not-Notes":

Notes would be too pretentious, as if the reader were not educated. Jottings rather, recollections of how poems got written—the way a poet talks between poems in a reading. And some commentary, mostly recollections, about sources. Eliot told me, years later, that he regretted having loaded *The Waste Land* with notes. And Pound always said: "Let 'em dig it out for themselves." These two instructed me in stealing from earlier poets, and contaminating the product. Or let's call it: "echoes across time, as in music."

My learned son-in-law has explained to me that there are Latin rhetorical terms, going back to the Renaissance, which define what I do. My outright thievery would be *imitatio*, as when Jonson uses Martial. *Contaminatio*, the mixing of sources, the interlingual collage technique which Pound loved, was a term "first coined by the 19th-century German philologue Friedrich Leo to define Plautus' combination of material from more than one model or source. But long before that such fragmenting and mixing of prior texts was already an old imitative practice when Poliziano resorted to it in the *quattrocento*." Pound's juxtapositions are part of his ideogrammatic method, which doubtless began when he saw in Fenollosa's notebooks how in Chinese poetry the meaning-characters are placed against each other without connectives.

I used to imagine that I was writing macaronics; when I researched the genre I found that I was kidding myself. Teofilo Folengo (1491–1544), who is called the father of the macaronic, did not, I think realize its potential. In his *Phantasie Macaronicae* he mixed real Latin words with words Latinized from the vernacular. In the purest kind of macaronic the first line would be Latin, the second would be Italian but would carry on the "story" of the first, then Latin again, doing the same to the end. Much as I like puzzles that is too hard for me. Try it. So I content myself with *imitatio* and *contaminatio*. The fun and the challenge of the macaronic have persisted through history. Drummond of Hawthornden was good at it and there were many other afficionados all over Europe. A fascinating little book, if you can find it, is *Macaronic Poetry* collected by James Appleton Morgan, New York, Hurd and Houghton, 1872. Morgan, who writes as if he were a gentleman amateur, must have spent decades hunting in libraries to find so many examples of bizarre poetic forms. He quotes Hallam as saying in *Literature of the Middle Ages*, "The writing of Macaronic Poetry is a folly with which every nation has been inoculated in its turn." Well, I'm glad I was inoculated. It may be a folly, but it has given me a lot of pleasure.

It is debatable that dropping Latin and Greek from the school curriculum has advantaged the student who wants to learn to write well. I have only a smidgin of Latin and less Greek, but I do know where some of the best sounds and figures in my head come from—and I dare say that Messers Davenport, Kenner and J. Williams (though they are in no way complicit in this statement) would attest to that.

Why Shouldn't I. Reprinted in *SP1986, CP1994.*

JL "not-note":
I am a magpie and don't feel guilty about stealing poems. There is a long history of borrowing. Catullus got his "Ille me par esse deo videtur" ["He seems

to me like a god," Catullus LI] from Sappho's "Phainetai moi keinos isos theoisin." Virgil borrowed from Homer and Apollonius of Rhodes. Terence got some fine plots from Menander, and Shakespeare used Holinshed and various Italians. Dante draws on troubadour stories. And, in our day, Eliot and Pound are full of lifts. Isn't it part of what is meant by the "tradition"?

If I take so much from Pound it is because so much of what is in my head he put there. After a boring Freshman year at Harvard I took off for Europe and enrolled in Pound's Ezuversity at Rapallo. He was, by all odds, my greatest professor, lending me his books to read and explaining what was good about them. And my education continued for thirty years after I became his publisher. His letters were full of instruction.

Like Him I Need the Past. Reprinted in *CP1994, SW.*

JL "not-note":
"Him," of course, is Pound. Who else? E.P. was much more interested in Sigismundo Malatesta than in Federigo da Montelfeltro of Urbino, but I have always been fascinated by Feddy's half hacked-off nose, as we see it in all the portraits (the one by Piero della Francesco is the most famous but there are 46 others, if you include the medals, in Sangiorgi's *Iconografia*). Who whupped him? I've scanned the contemporary chroniclers, and they don't say. A sore subject. [Cf. *B,* pp. 108–9]

One of life's great satisfactions befell me in Urbino. I was gassing with the lady in the *tabaccheria* about Feddy, and she said: "Ma Lei difende bene in Italiano."—"You defend yourself well in Italian." [Cf. *B,* p. 109]

"Mistah Kurtz—he dead," from Conrad's *Heart of Darkness*, was the epigraph Eliot chose for "The Hollow Men."

John Baskerville was certainly the greatest English 18th-century printer-publisher. Variants of the type he designed are still in use. I have some of his superb editions of the classics. He arranged to be buried in an upright position. The lion story is apocryphal.

The young English king is Henry Plantagenet (about whom Shakespeare also has things to say) whom the troubadour warrior Bertrand de Born defeated at Hautefort. When we were shooting Lawrence Pikethly's documentary on Pound, I stood on the battlements of the castle and watched it all happen again as Yves Roquette of Bézier, the Occitan reciter, read from the poems of En Bertrans. [See "Dans les Traces d'Ezra Pound," p. 294, and note, and *B,* note to "The Ancestors," p. 289]

Prester John—a legendary priest and king who ruled over a vast, wealthy empire in either Asia or Africa. [Added in *CP994*]

El Cid (died 1099)—a Spanish soldier whose exploits were romanticized in many literary works. He fought against the Moors but the Spanish king banished him. He then served the Muslim ruler of Saragosa, fighting against Moors and Christians alike. [Added in *CP1994*]

Genji—Prince Genji, hero of Lady Murasaki Shikubu's epic novel of 11th-century Japan *The Tale of Genji*. [Added in *CP1994*]

Je Est un Autre. Reprinted in *SP1986* (with endnote).

JL "not-note" (omissions in *SP1986* in brackets):
My first experience of publishing Rimbaud was traumatic. Delmore Schwartz had done what seemed to me a fine English version of the *Saison en enfer*. I didn't bother to check it against the original as I was sure he knew more French than I did. But he didn't, and there was a scandal. Later I asked Louise Varèse to do both the *Saison* and the *Illuminations*. These are still in print. [Not in *SP1986*]

"Je est un autre"—from Rimbaud's letter to his friend Izambard of May 13, 1871. Rimbaud wrote "Je est" instead of the normal "Je suis" ("I is" instead of "I am"), meaning, I think, that he wanted to be two people.

"'Either was the other's mine"—from "The Phoenix & The Turtle," attributed to Shakespeare. [I like to read passages from "The Phoenix & The Turtle" at wedding dinners. But I've been rebuked for being highbrow. Maybe so, but it's a great poem, whoever wrote it.]

Of course, Rimbaud is making two out of one, while Shakespeare is making one out of two, but this is the computer age, and each of these operations is in the binary system [—or must there be a zero?].

How now, young Flavius, whence come these depraved fancies?

Oh no, Sir, I mean yes Sir, they come from the learned Dr. Kenner.

Pox on the fellow, he's a Ranter and a scroundrel. He's another Socrates.

Yes Sir, I mean no Sir, he's a very kind gentleman, Sir, and he's kind to cats. He has a capacious heart, Sir.

[The betting is that H.K., formerly famous for *The Pound Era*, the best lit/hist/crit book of the century, will be the first to figure out how a computer can be made to think like an android. For H.K.'s ἀλουροφιλία ("love of cats") see my earlier poem "The Kenners' Cat / on whom I sat" (see p. 280).]

Ἐνθάδε τὴν ἱερὴν κεφαλὴν κατὰ γαῖα καλύπτει, ἀνδρῶν ἡρώων κοσμήτορα, θεῖον Ὅμηρον. Reprinted in *SP1986* (with endnote), *CP1994, SW.*

JL "not-note":
Pound was right, I think, when he said that Greek is the finest language for poetry. What other one gives us such beautiful, and such varied sounds in every word? The title lines are from Anonymous in *The Greek Anthology*, Book VII, Number 3.

"Now the earth covers that sacred man, the divine Homer,
Who marshalled the heroes."

"And Ole Ez said…"—the lines are from Pound's "Cantico el Sole."

> "The thought of what America would be like
>   If the Classics had a wide circulation
>   Troubles my sleep . . . "

When he first published the poem in *Instigations* in 1920 it was appended to an essay against censorship. But neglect of the classics was always one of his concerns.

Professor F is Robert Fitzgerald, a man of infinite kindness, who straightens out my Latin and Greek and Italian.

JL endnote:
The title is from *The Greek Anthology*, VII, 3: "Now the earth covers that sacred man, the divine Homer, who marshalled the heroes."

Lines 2–5 are from Pound's "Cantico del Sole."

Professor F is Robert Fitzgerald, who told me the story.

I Float Between the Spheres. Reprinted in *CP1994*.

JL "not-note":
When Tom Merton went off in 1968 on his trip to Asia, he told me that if anything happened to him, he wanted me to edit and publish the journal he would be keeping. The pages reached me soon after is death, but it took me two years to get his *Asian Journal* ready for the printer. Tom had written the journal late of nights, often very hurriedly; it was a typical Merton first draft, which he would have reworked if he had lived. He had copied passages from source books on Buddhist Tibetan and Hindu philosophy, but had not often indicated his sources so that I could check the texts. To identify them, I had to write to many of the friends he had made in Asia who had loaned him books. Then followed a self-taught and erratic course in Oriental thought and religion so that I could correct his transcriptions and do the notes and glossary. I even acquired a Sanskrit dictionary. A little knowledge is indeed a dangerous thing, but now I have terms such a *dzogchen* and *sunyata* floating happily around in my head. In a way they keep me in touch with Tom, one of the best friends I ever had.

"*Dzogchen*: Tibetan, 'great perfection.' . . . It is considered by Nying-mapa lamas to be the highest esoteric system. . . . *Dzogchen* may be defined as the simplest and most beneficial way to rediscover instantly for oneself the transcendental awareness that is within . . . it leads to the All-inclusive Enlightenment through the total transformation of all forms of bondage including one's physical body into the perfectly illuminating form." (Letter to J. L. from L.P. Lhalungpa, a friend T.M. made in Delhi.)

Sunyata: Sanskrit, "emptiness, the void." A basic concept in certain schools of Buddhism . . . "Enlightenment of the nature of essencelessness . . . to be combined with *karuna* (universal compassion) to form *bodhicitta* (enlightened-mindedness)." (S. B. Dasgupta). . . . The Dalai Lama has called *sunyata* "the knowledge of the ultimate reality of all objects, material and phenomenal."

We Met in a Dream. Reprinted in *SP1986* (with endnote), *CP1994, PNS.*

JL "not-note" (omission in *SP1986* in brackets):
[I hate people who want to tell me their dreams. But this dream was so compelling, with its shocks of recognition, and the strange meetings of characters—though both were poets—that I couldn't resist telling it. I knew it was Leopardi because there is a portrait of him in my edition. And I even remember how he looked from my stamp-collecting days as a boy. And Williams, of course, I had known for forty years. Leopardi spoke in English. Well, he could read it. Discourse in dreams can sometimes be very lucid, but with me it fades almost instantly on waking. I had only the sense after I awoke that very profound matters had been discussed.]

"ermo colle…" the first lines of Leopardi's "L'Infinito" are: "Sempre caro mi fu quest'ermo colle, / E questa siepe, che da tante parte / Dell'ultimo orizonte il guardo esclude." "Always dear to me was this lonely hill / and this hedgerow which hides so much / of the distant horizon from my sight."

Leopardi's *Operette Morali* were prose pieces as rich as prose-poetry in which he set forth his personal philosophy, often in dialogues with the great dead (Plotinus, Copernicus) which imitated the style of Lucian. He called them "the true harvest of my life."

"of love and desire…" from William Carlos Williams's poem "Perpetuum Mobile: The City.""…"a man who became a city" says the author's note to *Paterson.* Williams would have known Leopardi's "L'Infinito" through his friend Kenneth Rexroth's translation of it.

"nothingness" see Thomas Merton & D. T. Suzuki, *Wisdom in Emptiness*; the Zen concept descends, of course, from Madhyamika *sunyata.*

"naufragar" (from the Latin, *navis frangere*—break up of the ship?). The last line of "L'Infinito," surely one of the finest lines in Italian poetry, is: "E il naufragar m'è dolce in questo mare." "And it is sweet for me to sink in that sea" (of infinity).

"great falls" Williams's Great Falls of the Passaic River; the theme of "death by water" in *Paterson.*

"beyond all earthly love"—the message of Dante's *Paradiso.* The final line is: "L'Amor che move il sole e l'altre stelle." "That love which moves the sun and the other stars."

Among the Roses. Reprinted in *SP1986* (with endnote), *CP1994.*

Stat rosa pristina nomine / nomina nuda tenemus. Latin: "The ancient rose persists through its name, mere names are what we have."

JL "not-note":
My war with the Structuralists and their progeny began late, when I was teach-
ing a seminar on Pound & Williams at Brown. Elio Vittorini, the Italian novelist
whom I had published much earlier, told me that I should read Barthes, but I
never got around to it. So at Brown the students from the Semiotics Department
were pelting me with mysterious terms I couldn't understand—bad words like
asymptotic and hermeneutic and spatiality. I must say they were very patient
with me. They loaned me books to read, and I tried, oh I tried. But no light
gleamed. Their signifiers and their signifieds were all semioclasm to me. I'll
stick with Wilson and Trilling and Harry Levin, thank you. And toss, as here,
my puny pebbles at the new barbarians.

   I found "stat rosa pristina... ." in John Updike's *New Yorker* review of
Eco's *The Name of the Rose*, and a learned friend of my daughter's helped me
trace it to the medieval monk Bernard of Cluny's *De Contemptu Mundi* ["On
Contempt of the World"], a pious work lamenting the depravity of the
world—some 3,000 lines of Church Latin ingeniously constructed with in-
ternal as well as end rhymes. "Hic breve viv*itur*, hic breve plang*itur*, hic breve
fle*tur* [Here for a short time one lives, here for a short time one mourns, here
for a short time one weeps]," etc. But posterity has not been denied Bernard;
one of his lines reappears in "Jerusalem the Golden."

   "unless the scent of a rose" is from the end of Book V of Williams's *Pa-
terson*, but the rose, as symbol for Floss, appears also in a number of the short
poems.

   I wish I could claim the youthful vigor of the sixth stanza but I had this
story from a more adventuous classmate at Choate.

JL endnote:
"Stat rose pristina..."—essentially, "it's the name which makes the thing."
From Umberto Eco's *The Name of the Rose*, and he apparently found it in a
lugubrious long poem by the medieval monk Bernard of Cluny, *De Contemptu
Mundi*.

   "unless the scent of a rose" is from the end of Book V of Williams's *Pa-
terson*. The rose is a symbol for his wife, Floss.

See below, "De Contemptu Mundi," p. 634, and note.

You Invited Me. Reprinted in *SP1986* (with endnote), *CP1994*.

Dedication, "for Margot," added in *CP1994*.

JL "not-note":
She was so beautiful and sang so beautifully. I already knew Pound's transla-
tion of the Charles d'Orléans rondeau, so it was the immediate combination.
Had E.P. been reading Burns? He rendered "la gracieuse bonne et belle" as
"she is so fair and bonny."

"In quella parte dove sta memoria"—from Guido Cavalcanti's "Donna Mi Pregha," which Pound translated several times, the last and best version turning up as Canto XXXVI.

"Cannot be reft from him" is distorted from Canto LXXXI. [Included in *SP1986* endnote, below]

JL endnote (*SP1986*):
"Dieu qu'il la fait bon regarder"—from Charles d'Orléans (1391–1465).

"In quella parte dove sta memoria"—from Guido Cavalcanti (*c.* 1250–1300), the "Donna Mi Pregha" canzone.

JL "not-note" addition, *CP1994*:
Pound's translation of the Charles d'Orléans poem:

DIEU! QU'IL LA FAIT

From the French of Charles d'Orléans (1391–1465)

God! That mad'st her well regard her,
How she is so fair and bonny;
For the great charms that are upon her
Ready are all folks to reward her.
Who could part him from her borders
When spells are always renewed on her?
God! That mad'st her well regard her,
How she is so fair and bonny.
From here to there to the sea's border,
Dame no damsel there's not any
Hath of perfect charms so many.
Thoughts of her are of dreams order:
God! That mad'st her well regard her.

In JL's poem, lines 4–5 and 30–31, 10–12, 19–22, 34–35 correspond to the following lines in Pound's translation, above: 1–2, 3–4, 5–6.

Nothing That's Lovely Can My Love Escape. Reprinted in *SP1986* (with endnote), *CP1994, PNS*.

JL "not-note" (omission in *SP1986* in brackets):
[Bob Hutchins was the greatest man/mind I ever knew. I met him when I was publishing some of his first wife Maude's delightful novels. When Bob was chosen to be assistant director of the Ford Foundation, he called me from Pasadena and asked if I would care to help him spend some money on cultural good deeds, an invitation I could hardly refuse. International Cultural Publications and the polylingual magazine *Perspectives/ Perspektiven/Profils/Prospetti*

followed, but that is another story. One of Bob's best gifts to me was to send me out to India to help set up the Indian Southern Languages Book Trust. For some reason, I had imagined I would not like India, but I never liked any place better. It was another world, as far spiritually from Presbyterian Pittsburgh where I had grown up as it was on the globe. A glorious ancient culture, as rich as any around the Mediter-ranean, with which I fell deeply, and permanently, in love.]

The poem is stolen from various books about the Hindu gods. For the Krishna stories see Nivedita & Coomaraswamy: *Myths of the Hindus and Buddhists*. I brought home from India a little bronze figure of Baby Krishna playing with his butter ball and a Telugu glass painting of Krishna on his lotus leaf guarded by a cobra. Krishna's favorite among the *gopis* who herded the kine was Radha. The love duets of Krishna and Radha are the basis of Bengali poetry. See *In Praise of Krishna*, translated by E. C. Dimock, Jr. & Denise Levertov.

To Be Sure. Reprinted in *SP1986* (with endnote), *PNS*.

JL "not-note":
"poluphloisboio thalasses" was one of Pound's favorite tags from Homer. He loved the onomatopoeia of it. In book I, line 34 of the *Iliad* we find: "be d' akeon para thina poluphloisboio thalasses"—"silently he made his way to the shore of the loud-roaring sea." In Pound, the tag first appears in *Personae* in Part VI, "Stele," of "Moeurs Contemporaines":

> "After years of continence
>   he hurled himself into a sea of six women.
> Now quenched as the brand of Meleager,
>   he lies by the poluphloisboious sea-coast."

So I have a license, I guess, to apply the phrase to love troubles. Such a tag, the sound of it, resides in my head until the "moment of application" arrives.

JL endnote:
"o poluphloisboio thalasses"—"the loud-roaring sea." One of Pound's favorite tags from Homer (*Iliad*, I, 34). See "Stele" (*Personae*, page 181 [p. 179, revised edition, 1981]) and in the *Cantos*.

You Have Replaced. No reprint.

JL "not-note":
Es ist der Geist der sich den Körper baut, said Schiller. It is the mind which forms the body. It is the light within. Always and everywhere the same.

In Hindu mythology Parvati, who is sometimes called Bhavani, was one of the wives of the god Shiva. She was the daughter of the god who personifies the Himalayas, and was also considered an embodiment of the Divine Mother Goddess Kali, or, more abstractly, Shakti, the female creative power. Bronzes of her opulent femininity can be seen in major museums.

Felix. Reprinted in *SP1986* (with endnote).

JL "not-note" (omission in *SP1986* in brackets):
[After I had studied with Pound at Rapallo he advised me to return home and finish up at Harvard. (Not that "Haaavud" was any better than any of the other U.S. "beaneries" which he despised, but he thought, and so correctly, that if I got a diploma, my family would help me to become a publisher.) At Harvard I majored in Latin and Italian, writing my honors paper on Lucretius and Dante. Lucretius and his Epicurean atoms were heavy going, but Dante was a delight.]

"Felix qui potuit cordis cognoscere causas"—"Happy is he who can understand the reasons of the heart"—is a pun on Virgil's tribute to Lucretius (*Georgics* II, 490): "Felix qui potuit rerum cognoscere causas"—"Happy this man who understood the causes of things (in nature)." The poem flows out of the pun.

Cultural Note. Reprinted in *SP1986* (with endnote), *CP1994*.

O bella mia patria. Italian: "O my beautiful homeland."

JL "not-note":
For the basis of this unlikely story see H. V. Morton, *A Traveller in Italy*, New York, 1964, pages 304–5. Morton repeats the libel that the sarcophagus in the abandoned monastery near the Portoni della Bra is really a beautified horse-trough, but I *know* that

". . . here lies Juliet, and her beauty makes
This vault a feasting presence full of light."

An inscription on the tablet marking the spurious home of the Capulets in Verona reads:

"Tanto piansero i cuori gentili
E i poeti cantarano."

"[This was the house of the Capulets, whence spring Juliet,] for whom so many gentle hearts have wept, and poets have sung." [Added in *CP1994*. *SP1986* simply gives the original Italian, beginning with *per cui* ("for whom"), but without translation.]

What Is It Makes One Girl. Reprinted in *HL, SP1986* (with endnote), *CP1994, PNS.*

JL "not-note":

How far can one go with contamination? Some distance with a source such as Kenner to work from. I find him applying Pound's ideogrammatic method to literary history and criticism. Elements of collage are there for the taking. One could do hundreds of constructions such as this from *The Pound Era*. The tags for this poem are from pages 451–52.

"Omne quod manifestur..."—*Ephesisans*, V, 13. All that is manifest is light.

"Risplende in sè..."—From Guido Cavalcanti's "Donna Mi Pregha" canzone. The lady has asked the poet to tell her "Of an affect that comes often and is fell ... Love by name." In part of his reponse he explains how Love, in "Spreading its rays...is its own effect unendingly ..." (Pound's translation).

"The light descending . . ." Pound's explication, in his Confucian "Terminology," of the Chinese character: "The light descending (from the sun, moon and stars). To be watched as component in ideogram indicating spirits, rites, ceremonies."

"Lux enim per se..." Bishop Robert Grosseteste (*c.* 1170–1253). For light by its nature pours forth itself into every region."

The last three lines are my rescription from William Carlos Williams's "Asphodel, That Greeny Flower," pages 181–82 in *Pictures from Breughel*.

JL refers here to Pound's translation of Cavalcanti's "Donna Mi Pregha" in *Ezra Pound: Translations*, page 133 (New York: New Directions, 1954), not the version in his *Cantos*.

Pound's Confucian "Terminology" can be found in his *Confucius* (New York: New Directions, 1969).

JL endnote (*SP1986*), which substitutes the following short paragraph for the longer opening in the preceding "not-note:"

The greater part of this poem is stolen from Hugh Kenner's *The Pound Era*, pages 451–52.

In Hac Spe Vivo. Reprinted in *SP1986* (with endnote), *CP1994, PNS.*

JL "not-note" (omissions in *SP1986* in brackets):

[Let no one say there are no good programs on the tube, or at least on PBS stations. I am now enjoying *Brideshead* for the fourth time, and the British production of the Shakespeare plays have been a delight. Watching the plays, I began jotting down on a pad lines or images which particularly pleased me. Later I tried putting them together in *cento* style to see if I could make a poem of them. The game was to have as few made-up connectives as possible. In this *cento* from *Pericles* there are only nine words which are not found from the bard.]

["In hac spe vivo" is the motto on Pericles' shield at the tournament in Act II, Scene II. "In this hope I live."]

The patchwork *cento*, a work composed with passages from an earlier author, has an ancient lineage. In the *Princeton Encyclopedia*, R. J. Getty tells us that the earliest known example is by one Trygaeus who made his own poem with the lines from the *Iliad* and the *Odyssey*. Virgil was much "centoed," as in the *Centum nuptialis* of Ausonius. In Italy there was a *Petrarcha spirituale* (1536) and in England a *Cicero princeps* (1608). See J. O. Delepierre, *Tableau de le littérature de centon chez les anciens et chez les modernes* (1874–75) and R. Lamacchia, "Dall'arte allusiva al centone," *Atene e Roma*, n.s. 3 (1958).

[A variant of the procedure is to contaminate with the introduction of another author. When I watched *Coriolanus*, Delmore Schwartz's verse play *Coriolanus and His Mother*, which I published in 1938, was much in my mind. Delmore must have taken his title from the lines of the First Citizen in I, I: "though soft-conscienced men can be content to say it was for his country, he did it to please his mother. . . ." But in working out his thesis and plot Delmore made liberal injections from the doctrines of Freud. The title of my Coriolanus poem is "'He Did It to Please His Mother,'" but I do not give it here because it goes beyond strict contamination to my comments on Delmore's tragic life.]

For JL's poem "'He Did It to Please His Mother,'" see p. 336, and note.
JL endnote (*SP1986*) opens with the following paragraph:
All of the phrases, except the connectives, are, with some modification, from *Pericles*.

Two Letters on Samos. Reprinted in *SP1986* (with endnote), *CP1994*.

JL "not-note":
Dudley Fitts started me reading *The Greek Anthology* at Choate in 1931, and I've been reading it ever since, in his translations which I later published at New Directions, and in many others. Considering that it must have been done a good seventy years ago, that of W. R. Paton in the Loeb Library still sounds very fresh, and the notes are excellent. Except for the sweep of the epic poets, I find that everything about every aspect of life is in the Anthology—name a human situation and it's there—all as beautifully handled, with as keen psychological understanding, as could ever be. This, surely, is the book for that desert island.

This poem is not a paraphrase but a recombination of themes and characters from the Anthology. Posidippus and Philaenis, Procne and Polucron are all there, but saying and doing other things. I merely pulled the puppet strings to make them say what was on my mind in a contemporary situation.

JL endnote (*SP1986*):
The names of the characters are from *The Greek Anthology*, but the story is contemporary.

En Provence. No reprint.

JL "not-note":
Was love in the castles of Provence really as exalted, as spiritual, as the chron-
iclers in their *vidas* would have us believe? Je m'en doute. And Pound's pun-
ning on *alba*—both the dawn and the time when lovers had to get back to
the right beds—may confirm this interpretation. (But the scholars would like
to confuse me with their theories about the Courts of Love and the Albigensian
Heresy.)

"Trobar"—Provençal, "to make verses for singing"; hence, "troubadour."

"Trobar clus"—enclosed, hermetic composition in which the troubadour
put hidden meanings in his song.

"Trobar ric"—rich, dense composition in which the troubadour loaded
much figuration into his poem.

NB: these verses are done in "trobar leu"—easy composition.

A Cento from Gary / Ajar's *La Vie Devant Soi*. Reprinted in *SP1986* (with
endnote).

Editor's translation:

> Am I a bad penny?
> Was I born wrong?
> It seems to me that all I do is muck up.
> I'm just a comma in the great book of life.
> I'd like to live in clover, but I live by word-of-mouth.
> I lie like a quack to bring good cheer.
> I think life isn't a snap for everyone, especially not for me.
> When I cry, I bawl like a calf.
> Does one have to kiss someone's ass to be happy?
> Life often gives me goose flesh.
> Sometimes I'm fed up with what's going on in the world.
> Will I fizzle out?
> I'd give my eyes for a new life.
> I am a bad penny.

In *SP1986*, lines 5–6 of the French read, "J'ai peur que je ne suis...." etc.,
that is "I'm afraid I'm not. . . . "

JL "not-note":
I came late to Romain Gary. He was just a name to me until my friend Sabine
put me on to him. I owe her much for that alone. Apparently the professors
in this country do not consider him an important writer; the Yale Library
computer tells me that there has been only one doctoral dissertation about
him, and most of the English translations of his books are out of print. But
what an inspired master of comic writing he is. In the tradition, I think, of
Céline and Henry Miller.

Gary would surely have known Miller because, when he was Consul General of France in Los Angeles, Gary used to come to Big Sur to swim and meditate on the beach of the great rocks. Chapter I of his autobiographical novel *La Promesse de l'Aube {Promise at Dawn}* begins: "C'est fini. La plage de Big Sur est vide et je demeurre couché, à l'endroit où je suis tombé." ["It's over. The beach at Big Sur is empty and I remain lying on the sand, right where I've fallen."] The beach at Big Sur was for Gary, as it is for me, one of the "sacred places," as Pound called them. Gary has not yet received his due in this country as an important writer, but what a satisfying writer he is. "Ut doceat, ut moveat, ut dilectet," [Latin: "That it teach, that it move, that it delight"] wrote Pound of literature in Canto LXXXIX, quoting from Rodolphus Agricola. Gary delights me, and often moves me, and sometimes he teaches me, especially when he is hallucinating in some of the Ajar books about the "other self."

The other self, the double, the doppelgaenger—that is what fascinates me most about the strange story of Romain Gary and pseudonymous Ajar. As Émile Ajar he wrote four books (are they really novels? *Pseudo* is at times a prose poem) in great secrecy, having the scripts sent to a Paris publisher by a friend in Rio de Janeiro. When he finally confessed in *Vie et Mort d'Émile Ajar* [*Life and Death of Émile Ajar*], Gary explained that he became Ajar because "Je n'aimais plus le gueule qu'on m'avait donné." "I didn't like the mug they had given me." Or was it the mug he had given himself? Gary's suicide farewell note was brief and, characteristically, a bit offhand. Let me try some of it in my colloquial.

> "This has nothing to do with Jean Seberg. The lovers of broken hearts will have to look elsewhere... .It's only depression if that is something I've had since I've come of age, that helped me to write what and how I write and how I've written. . . . I've said everything I had to say... (Je me suis enfin totalement exprimé)."

But has he told us everything? I suspect that he may have made the decision he did because he never found the *other self* who could make him happy.

I too have an obsessive need to be someone else, to have a credible-to-myself double. The comic poet Hiram Handspring is a fool. Professor J. Roger Dane (Joyce told me my name meant "Danish Pirate" in Gaelic) is a learned idiot. Also he is a fraud. He is a professor of dental surgery, not of literature. The records of the University of Saskatoon have revealed this fact. But recently a new double has been birthing in my head. A French one, no name as yet assigned. He has written some thirty poems in a totally American kind of French which bears no resemblance to the *langue de Tours* [i.e., the "pure" language]. Because he writes in a language that does not exist this poet makes me feel like someone else. And because it is an unknown language he (I) can get away with romantic lines that would be ludicrous in English. That gives

1060

a sentimental pleasure. "Trahit sua quem-que voluptas," wrote Virgil. ["Every-one is drawn by his own taste."]

There are, of course, scientific explanations for these phenomena. Meyers, three volumes of him, is the authority on psychiatric studies of "doubling." As for writing in a language which I had not used since 1929 when I was in school at Le Rosey in Switzerland, there is a term for that, too. My shrink explained to me when I went to him in considerable agitation, fearing that I might be starting over the edge. "Oh yes," the reassuring man explained, "we call that cerebro-pseudo-regression. It's rare but not dangerous. Take half a Valium if it bothers you." He went on to say that sometimes the brain gets overstuffed and shuts down certain synapses for relief. My French had been suppressed. "Have you hit your head recently?" he asked. I recalled that diving at the lake one day I had gone too deep and struck my head on the bottom. "That could be it," he said, "that little bump opened the synapses. Don't worry about it." Eager for fame, I asked if he would write me up for one of the journals. "It's not that uncommon," he said, "really nothing new." I was crestfallen. There is nothing *new* about me. There is nothing new under the sun. But perhaps I have found another self.

JL writes in greater detail about Gary/Ajar in an Afterword to *The Life Before Us,* Ralph Manheim's translation of the novel *La Vie Devant Soi,* which ND issued in 1986. For JL's Hiram Handspring poems, see "Funny Papers by Hiram Handspring," pp. 341–356, and pp. 630–32." His "(American) French Poems" can be found on pp. 215–66. See Introduction, p. xiv, for more on JL's "dou-bles."

JL endnote (*SP1986*):
Romain Gary, after becoming one of the most famous writers in France, an-nounced: "J'étais fatigué de la gueule qu'on m'avait donné" ("I was tired of the mug which [the critics] had given me") and, in the greatest secrecy, wrote four novels under the name of Émile Ajar. The true authorship was not rec-ognized until after his death, when his "Ajar confession" was published by his son.

I Hate Love. Reprinted in *HL, SP1986* (with endnote), *CP1994, PNS.*

JL "not-note":
Another pastiche and pseudo-macaronic from *The Greek Anthology.* But these are real poets, who actually said, more or less, what I represent them as saying. And had as little comfort as I from saying it.

"echthairo ton erota"—from Alcaeus, Book V, Number 10 in the Loeb edition.

"hoplismai pros erota"—from Rufinus, Book V, Number 93.

"hiere kai luchne"—from Meleager, Book V, Number 8. [Greek text reads, "Nux hiere..."; that is, "Holy night."]

JL endnote (*SP1986*):
From *The Greek Anthology*, V, 8, 10, 93.

Flown Away. No reprint.

Il pleure dans mon coeur / mon coeur qui est mis à / nu. French: "There's weeping in my heart / my heart which is stripped / bare."

JL "not-note":
It was through the poet Charles Henri Ford that I became infatuated with Baudelaire, this at the time when I was mangling his translations for *The Mirror of Baudelaire* in ND's "Poets of the Year Series." About 1945 I ran into Baudelaire in the New York subway and wrote a deadpan poem about this hallucination. Over the years, ND published six other books by or about Baudelaire, including the one by Sartre.

"Il pleure dans mon coeur"—from Verlaine, *Romances sans Paroles.*

Mon coeur mis à nu [*My Heart Stripped Bare*] is Baudelaire's autobiographical notebook, wherein he says: "I have felt in my soul two conflicting emotions, the horror of life and the ecstasy of life."

The annetta is the very rare little blue butterfly, *Lycaeides melissa annetta* (Edwards & Nabokov), which Vladimir Nabokov found on an anthill in Albion Basin the summer when he and his family were staying at the Alta Lodge in Utah, at the time when I was playing at being an innkeeper.

For JL's poem about meeting Baudelaire, see "The Man on the Subway," p. 92.

No My Dear. Reprinted in *SP1986* (with endnote), *PAW, CP1994.*

sunt apud infer- / nos tot milia formosarum. Latin: "there are in hell so many thousands of beautiful women."

despicit et magnos recta / puella deos. Latin: "a proper girl despises even the mighty gods."

JL "not-note":
Pound's *Homage to Sextus Propertius*, which Yeats called the finest example of free verse of the period, is not a translation, but a rescription in which E.P., in his persona of the Roman poet, wrote what he thought Propertius might have written if S.P. had "Rip Van Winkled and come to and wrote a poem in Yanqui." (postcard of 1935 to J.L.) Pound did not follow Propertius's sequence but made a collage of passages which he particularly liked. The Latinists were horrified, but the technique probably foreshadowed the ideogrammatic method which would determine the structure of so many of the *Cantos*.

The first, seventh, eighth and last lines are mine, but otherwise the poem is Pound's, his versions following the Latin phrases which inspired them. Following the numbering of Mueller's edition (Leipzig, 1892) from which Pound worked, the first quotation, Part IX, [section] 2 in Pound, is from Propertius III, 26, [3], and the second is Pound, XII, [line 28], Propertius II, 32, [46].

JL endnote (*SP1986*):
"sunt apud infernos . . . "—Propertius, III, 26
"despicit et magnos . . . "—Propertius, II, 32
Pound's rescriptions (the *Homage to Sextus Propertius* was *not* intended to be a translation) follow the Latin lines. The passages will be found on pages 223 and 228 of *Personae* [pages 218–19 and 223, revised edition, 1981].

Cf. Propertius, II.28.49 and II.34.46 in G. P. Goold's Loeb Classical Library edition (Cambridge, MA: Harvard, 1990). See also "The Last Poem to Be Written," p. 75, and note.

In *PAW*, the poem appears with the following headnote: "Auctor Ignotus, 1983" (Latin: "Author Unknown").

This Is the Morte Saison. Reprinted in *CP1994*.
que les loups se / vivent de vent. French: "when the wolves live on the wind."

JL "not-note":
Villon stood high in the Pound canon, and E.P. wrote one of his two operas, *Le Testament*, to passages from Villon. There is hardly a good poet who has not tried his hand at translating Villon. My tribute takes off from the second stanza of the *Petit Testament*:

> En ce temps que j'ay dit devant,
> Sur le nouvel, morte saison,
> Que les loups se vivent de vent
> Et qu'on se tient en sa maison,
> Pour le frimas, près du tison,
> Me prinst le vouloir de brisier
> La très amoureuse prison
> Qui me souloit bien débriser.

> In that said year then, to repeat,
>> Near Christmas, those dead winter days,
> When wolves find only wind to eat,
>> And each man in his lodgings stays,
>> Cheating the cold before the blaze
> I felt the wish to break at last

From love's close prison, in whose ways
My heart had broken in time past.
            —*Tr. by H. B. McCaskie*

The spelling in texts of Villon varies greatly, and the more familiar reading is "noël" for "nouvel." Surely the figure of the hungry wolves living off the winter wind is as good as they come.

Some time later, there was a special connection with Villon for me when I was doing the notes for Merton's posthumously published poem *The Geography of Lograire* and discovered that for his title he not only had the Logos in mind but also Villon's real name, which was François des Loges.

H. B. McCaskie's translation is added in *CP1994*.

Write on My Tomb. Reprinted in *SP1986* (with endnote), *CP1994*, *PNS* (as epigraph). The poem also appears on the back cover of the special paperbook edition of *LPJL* that was distributed at the memorial service held for JL on January 9, 1998, at the American Academy of Arts and Letters in New York City.

JL "not-note" (omission in *SP1986* in brackets):
Ταῦτ' ἔχω ὅσσ' ἔμαθον καὶ ἐφρόντισα, καὶ μετὰ Μουσῶν
σέμν' ἐδάην· τὰ δὲ πολλὰ καὶ ὅλβια τῦφος ἔμαρψεν.
    [Taken] very freely from Crates of Thebes, *The Greek Anthology*, Book VII, 326.

Translation of Crates' epigram: "However much I possess of important things, these I studied and thought and learned from the Muses; of my many riches vanity took hold."

PICTURE POEMS (1986–1994)

Most of the poems in this section are grouped together in *CP1994* as "The Picture Poems." In the present volume, two are added that were first collected in *SP1986* ("The Ravings of the Depraved Monk…" and "Les Amants") and four others from *MW* ("The Flight of the Nethrobods," "Ten Dollars Reward," "Making a Love Poem," and "The Kiss"). However, "The Man in the Wall" (p. 511), which is accompanied by a photograph by Virginia Schendler, remains as the title poem for the section *MW*.

Part title illustration, as in *CP1994*.

Ravings of the Depraved Monk . . . Published in *SP1986* (with endnote); reprinted in *CP1994* without the illustration.

Editor's translation:

> Concerning the penetration of the opening of the vulva
> in the course of time many words have been written
> and in Martial and Catullus we read
> the successes and rejections of big
> dicks but all flesh is as grass
> we know sorrow after sex.

JL endnote (*SP1986*):
The Latin, such as it is, is not suitable for the family audience. [In *CP1994*, appended to the "Editor's Note" that follows the poem.]

Les Amants. Published in *SP1986*; reprinted in *CP1994*.
Title. French: "The Lovers."

The Flight of the Nethrobods. Published in *MW*; no reprint.

Ten Dollars Reward. Published in *MW*; reprinted in *CP1994*.

Making a Love Poem. Published in *MW*; reprinted in *CP1994, PNS*.

The Doppelgaengers. Published in *CP1994*; no reprint.
Cf. "Two for One," p. 882.

The Reclining Position. Published in *CP1994*; no reprint.
Per nebulas surgit lux. Latin: "Light rises through the clouds."

La Langue Enfantine / The Infantile Language. Published in *T*; reprinted in *CP1994*. In *T*, the poem appears in French only and without the illustration.

The Family Council of the Yakovlevs. Published in *CP1994*; no reprint.
Je suis au bout de mon latin. French: "I'm at my wit's end" (literally, "at the end of my Latin").

Multos per Annos... Published in *CP1994*; no reprint.

καὶ ποθήω καὶ μάομαι κὰτ ἔμον στάλαχμον. Published in *OM*; reprinted in *CP1994*. The poem in *OM* omits the translation of the title and appears without the illustration.

JL note (*OM*):
(Sappho: *I yearn—I burn*)

Carmina Gemina. Published in *CP1994*; no reprint.
Title. Latin: "Twin Songs."

The Inner Life of the Septic Tank. Published in *CP1994*; no reprint.

The Blowpipe Game. Published in *CP1994*; no reprint.

Market Discounts Love. Published in *CP1994*; no reprint.

The French. Published in *SP1986*; reprinted in *CP1994, HI.* The poem appears in *SP1986* without the illustration. A new version is included in *CBP*; see p. 945.

Asmodeus. Published in *SP1986*; no reprint.

L'Arrivée du Printemps / The Coming of Spring. Published in *OM*; reprinted in *CP1994, PNS.* In *OM* and *PNS*, the poem appears only in French and without the illustration.

To My Lady in a Distant Land That She Forget Me Not. Published in *CP1994*; no reprint.

The Munich Courier. Published in *CP1994*; no reprint.

Ingenium Nobis Ipsa Puella Facit. Published in *CP1994*; no reprint. A new version of this poem, titled "A Classic Question," is included in *LPJL*; see p. 814.
Title. Latin: "My girl herself makes the inspiration."

Encounter at the Casin, Aix-les-Bains. Published in *CP1994*; no reprint.

The Nereid. Published in *CP1994*; no reprint.

(AMERICAN) FRENCH POEMS (1986–1997)

The poems in this section are taken from several of JL's later books and grouped together in the manner of *SP1986* and *CP1994*. The lone poem in English, "The Importance of Dictionaries," stands as an introduction to the rest. Of JL's many French poems, only four are not included among these "(American) French Poems": "A Cento from Gary / Ajar's *La Vie Devant Soi* (see p. 183), because it is drawn directly from the words of another author; "La Langue Enfantine" and ""L'Arrivée du Printemps," which can found in the "Picture Poems" (see pp. 199 and 209) ; and "L'Abécédérien du Lubricité," which is ascribed to JL's verse-writing double, Hiram Handspring (see p. 630). For JL's comments on his newer anonymous (American) French-writing double, see in his note to the Gary/Ajar cento, p. 1061.

The Importance of Dictionaries. Published in *SP1986;* reprinted in *CP1994.*

Dictionnaire du / français argotique et populaire. *Dictionary of Slang and Vulgar French*, published by Larousse in several editions and edited by François Caradec.

> JL note:
> Mallarmé—Stéphane Mallarmé (1842–98), the French poet.
>   Degas—Edgar Degas (1834–1917), the French Impressionist painter.
> [*CP1994*]

Orphée / Orpheus. French, published in *HL;* reprinted in *SP1986, CP1994, SW.* English translation, published in *CP1994;* reprinted in *SW.*

La Gomme à Effacer / The Eraser. French, published in *HL;* reprinted in *SP1986* (with endnote), *CP1994, SW, PNS.* English translation, published in *CP1994;* reprinted in *SW, PNS.*

le Tes- / tament. Changed to "la / Bible" in *CP1994, SW, PNS.*

> JL endnote (*SP1986*):
> Gomme à effacer—an eraser.
>   The first two lines are from Émile Ajar's [Romain Gary's] *La Vie Devant Soi.*

Je Suis un Cerf-volant Saugrenu / I Am a Preposterous Beetle. French, published in *HL;* reprinted in *SP1986, CP1994, SW.* English translation, published in *CP1994, SW.*

La Luciole / The Firefly. French, published in *HL;* reprinted in *SP1986, CP1994, SW, PNS.* English translation, published in *CP1994, SW, PNS.*

J'Ayme Donc Je Suis Je Souffre Mais Je Vis / I Love Therefore I Am I Suffer But I'm Alive. French, published in *SP1986* (with endnote), where it is included among a section of "Stolen Poems"; reprinted in *CP1994.* English translation, published in *CP1994;* no reprint.

JL endnote (*SP1986*):
"J'ayme donc je suis"—the motto which Pound had on his stationery when he was confined in St. Elizabeths Hospital. Apparently not Old French but from "amo ergo sum" in Canto LXXX, and before that, of course, from Descartes: "Cogito ergo sum [Latin: 'I think therefore I am']."

JL note:
[Repeat of preceding *SP1986*]
        Hercules—in Greek and Roman mythology the hero of great strength and mighty deeds.
        Prometheus—in Greek mythology the Titan who fashioned man out of clay and brought down fire for him from the gods. [*CP1994*]

J'Ignore Où Elle Vague Ce Soir / I Don't Know Where She Is Wandering Tonight. French, published in *SP1986;* reprinted in *CP1994, SW, PNS.* English translation, published *CP1994;* reprinted in *SW, PNS,* and in a revised version in *CBP.*

Pour Bien Aimer. Published in *SP1986;* no reprint.
        Editor's translation:

              TO LOVE WELL

              it isn't indispensable
              to windmill or

              ride a rocking horse as we
              have told our friends in the

              Indies of course for the young
              these practices are amusing

              but when you reach a
              certain age you realize that

              what is worth the effort are
              only spiritual athletics.

Elle N'est Plus Noctambule / She Walks No Longer in the Night. French, published in *SP1986;* reprinted in *CP1994, SW, PNS.* English translation, published in *CP1994, SW, PNS.*

        Prester John. In the French, changed to "Prêtre Jean" in *CP1994, SW, PNS.*

JL note:
Prester John—legendary Christian priest and king who ruled over a vast, wealthy empire in either Asia or Africa. [*CP1994, PNS*]

Dois-je Reprendre. Published in *SP1986*; no reprint.
Editor's translation:

> MUST I GET BACK
>
> my will to live for
> ten years I
>
> let myself drift along
> followed the path of
>
> uncertainty and then one
> day a miracle came
>
> to help me that wasn't
> like so many others
>
> a mirage must I now
> get back my will to live?

La Fleur Bleue / The Blue Flower. French, published in *SP1986* (with end-note); reprinted in *CP1994, SW*. English translation, published in *CP1994*; reprinted in *SW*.

JL endnote (*SP1986*):
Les Fleurs Bleues—roman de [novel by] Raymond Queneau.

JL note:
Suggested by Raymond Queneau's novel *Les Fleurs Bleues*. [CP 1994]

Le Mordu de la Moto. Published in *SP1986*; no reprint.
Editor's translation:

> THE MOTORCYCLE FREAK
>
> I'm coming back to this thing
> I don't care about this stupid
>
> minotaur if he's mortal he'll
> put his foot in it

and you'll regret it
me I can wait

the gods are my pals
they invite me to eat

with them on Olympus every
Saturday night they have

a bout for this
here minotaur guy

that amuses them I don't worry
myself it's not the end

of everything I'll make love
before rejoining the earth.

Les Vieillards. Published in *SP1986*; no reprint.
  Editor's translation:

  OLD MEN

  are smitten so easily
  they don't realize

  the effect their foolishness
  has on the well-

  brought-up young people they
  see in the fields

  a beautiful young flower and they
  rush to pick it

  without thinking of the grief
  their ardor can give

  old age is sometimes
  sad except for each dream

  being always the most beautiful
  the most intoxicating

  recalling the salad days.

La Voix Qui Chante dans Mon Coeur. Published in *SP1986*; reprinted in *OM*.
Editor's translation:

THE VOICE SINGING IN MY HEART

I'm smitten by a voice
but it isn't that of a

Maria Callas a clear voice but
A soft sweet liquid voice that flows

like a brook imagine
a voice that's both that

of a little girl slightly hesitant
and of a goddess who is ordering my

life but when she pays me a visit
in my dreams the voice

I hear is that of Rhodope
the wood nymph who knew

how to talk with the birds
the trees and even the flowers.

Elle A la Tête Qui Danse. Published in *SP1986;* no reprint.
Editor's translation:

SHE HAS A MIND THAT DANCES

and that's why I adore her
if I tell her something

she tosses my words in the air
like a juggler and returns them to me

so changed so beautiful that I
hardly recognize them and she

takes my ideas and breaks them up
in such a way they're new

and fresh thanks to her the
exchange turns sparkling and that

she is so beautiful is a most pleasant
something extra.

Elle Dit Que Je Mets des Gants / She Says That I Put on Gloves. French, published in *SP1986;* reprinted in *CP1994, SW.* English translation, published in *CP1994;* reprinted in *SW.*

L'Hermine / The Ermine. French, published in *SP1986;* reprinted in *CP1994, SW.* English translation, published in *CP1994;* reprinted in *SW.*

JL note:
Some passages are in Parisian argot. [*CP1994*]

Le Jardin des Délices / The Garden of Delights. French, published in *T;* reprinted in *A, CP1994, SW.* English translation published in *A;* reprinted in *CP1994, SW.*

JL's earliest translation in *A* (a short novel) is substantially different in form from the version in the present volume, which is how the poem appears in *CP1994* and *SW.* That first translation reads:

> Sometimes I don't see you too clearly
> You are charming and beautiful, you speak
>   like two angels talking at once
> I suspect a mystery, I sense that there is a corner
>   of your nature where no one may enter
> What are you hiding in that corner of your soul?
> Will you let me visit there one day? Is it
>   a secret garden?
> I make my supplication to the gods that it is
>   the garden of my delights
> The garden I have been seeking for so long.

Le Voyage Innomé / The Nameless Voyage. French, published in *T;* reprinted in *CP1994* and *SW.* English translation, published in A, *CP1994, SW.*

un / jour. "one / day"; in *A,* "une / nuit" that is, "one / night"—which is how the English reads as well in *CP1994* and *SW.* Again, as with the preceding poem in the present collection, JL's English translation in *A* is substantially different in form from the version in *CP1994* and *SW,* and also in some wording, as well as having another title:

THE NAMELESS JOURNEY

Where does she go when she closes her eyes
    when we are making love?
She is there at my side and she is not there
If I touch her she trembles but says nothing
One night I asked her where she was traveling
This time, she smiled and answered
Don't be worried, I'll never go far from you
The country which I visit is the land
Of the poems you have written for me.

Deux Fantaisistes. Published in *SP1886;* no reprint.
    Editor's translation:

TWO DREAMERS

each was in love
only seeing in the other

what she wanted to see
both creating for themselves

the illusion of loving in the other
an imaginary creation but

one day alas they found
themselves in front of the mirror

of reality and they
recognized each other

as they truly were.

Tu Sais, Je Crois. Published in *OM;* no reprint.
    Editor's translation:

YOU KNOW, I BELIEVE

that you set me afire
from the moment I saw you

and heard you
speak a remarkable

thing happened to me
how to explain this

isn't easy it's necessary
perhaps to look for

an oneiric metonomy I
thought I had some

tiny fishes
frolicking in my blood.

Le Baptême de Celui Qui Noye. Published in *OM;* no reprint.
  Editor's translation:

THE BAPTISM OF ONE WHO IS DROWNING

In the baptism of certain
creeds there is a total

immersion and so it was for
me a year ago I didn't

know you and then it happened
the revelation that transformed

my life since then I swim
in your being and as the

poet has written "sweet
is my shipwreck in this sea."

Regarding the final couplet, see JL's "not-note" for "We Met in a Dream,"
p. 1052.

Le Blessé. Published in *OM;* no reprint.
  Editor's translation:

THE INJURED MAN

I want to bare my wounds
to everyone I have to show

how she has consumed me it was
a horrible massacre they say

it was my fault that I
tried to swallow her that

may be I don't deny it but
she is so succulent I

can't control myself.

C'est à Mourir de Rire. Published in *OM;* no reprint.
Editor's translation:

IT'S TO DIE LAUGHING

that I pursue you I who
am a worn-out scamp with

nothing much upstairs
and you are such a pretty piece with

such a brain but we read
how Sigismundo was

crazy about the fair Ixotta and
also perhaps poisoned

his wife to have her
(I wouldn't do anything as

stupid as that) and Goethe
73 years old that summer

in Marienbad felt his
dick harden and ran downstairs

to his study when
he heard the song

of the streetwalker in the lane
oh if I must perish it's from

the cool and delicious poison
of your laughing that I wish to die.

La Débine de Mon Coeur. Published in *OM;* no reprint.
    Editor's translation:

> MY HEART'S MISERY
>
> It's my forte to run away
> one day I'm whole and the
>
> next nothing if you smile I'm
> in the clouds but when you withdraw
>
> it's a plunge into the pit
> it's a bumpy car but it's
>
> not funny it's no longer an amusing
> children's game I
>
> run away because you no longer love me
> enough but even this praiseworthy
>
> act doesn't serve to soften you.

Je Ne Suis Pas Veinard / I'm Not Lucky with Girls. French, published in *OM;* reprinted in *CP1994; SW*. English translation, published in *CP1994, SW*.

Les Mots Secrets / The Secret Words. French, published in *OM;* reprinted in *CP1994, SW*. English translation, published in *CP1994, SW*.

Je Suis le Comédien. Published in *OM;* no reprint.
    Editor's translation:

> I AM THE COMEDIAN
>
> of love I'm called Snagarelle
> the imaginary cuckold and I
>
> try to make people laugh I wish
> to give you pleasure but I want
>
> you to laugh at the same time we see
> when looked at from afar what

lovers do is a little odd
don't you find it seems

to me that the system isn't
modern isn't practical

no details but you understand
what I mean and it's for that

that I try to make people laugh.

Le Poète Englouti. Published in *OM;* no reprint.
Editor's translation:

THE SPELLBOUND POET

He mutters his lines
in a stupor he is drunk

as a lord with the sound of words
the words don't matter he chases

after all of them in any language
even if he doesn't understand them

(he feels deprived because he
cannot make ring the

Devanagari and Pali letters)
around him you hear a

buzzing it is the words
that swarm like bees

in his head come I beg you
to the poet's aid

let him hear your sweet
voice and your laughter instead of

this endless torrent of words.

Je Suis Raplaplat / I'm Fed Up with My Life. French, published in *OM;* reprinted in *CP1994, SW*. English translation, published in *CP1994;* reprinted in *SW*.

> JL note:
> Much of the poem is in argot.
>> j'en ai assiz de la gueule que l'on m'a faite—quotation from the suicide note of the French novelist Romain Gary, one of the most successful of his day. [*CP1994*]

For Romain Gary, see "A Cento for Gary/Ajar's La Vie Devant Soi," p. 183, and note.

L'Avertissement / Caution. French, published in *K;* reprinted in *BET, A*. English translation, published in *A,* untitled; no reprint. The title, "Caution," added in the present volume by the editor.

Les Consolations / The Consolations. French, published in *CR;* reprinted in *HI, PNS*. English translation, published in *CR* (untitled)*;* reprinted in *HI, SR* (without the French), *PNS*.
> **treasures.** Changed to "delights" in *HI, SR, PNS*.

Mes Souffrances. Published in *BET;* no reprint.
> Editor's translation:

> MY SUFFERINGS

> I suffer because I am
> ugly and she's so beautiful I

> am nearly blind and she
> sees everything so clearly I walk

> on all fours and she flies
> like a swallow I bite my

> tongue when I speak but
> she sings like the nightingale

> my sufferings are unbearable
> but when she throws me

> a smile I forget them all.

Mon Secret / My Secret. French, published in *K;* reprinted in *BET, CP1994, SW, PNS.* English translation, published in *CP1994;* reprinted in *SW, PNS.*

Le Hoqueton / The King's Bowman. French, published *BET;* reprinted in *CP1994, SW.* English translation, published in *CP1994, SW.*

Les Patineurs / The Skaters. French, published in *BET;* reprinted in *CP1994.* English translation, published in *CP1994.*

Les Chimères de Sainte-Hélène / The Chimeras of Saint Helena. French, published in *BET;* reprinted in *CP1994.* English translation, published in *CP1994;* no reprint.

> JL notes:
> (Collage from AUBRY: *Sainte-Hélène;* ROSEBURY: *Napoleon, the Last Phase;* FORSYTH: *History of the Captivity of Napoleon at St Helena;* BRICE: *Les Espoirs de Napoléon à Sainte-Hélène;* BERTRAND: *Cahiers de Sainte-Hélène;* FIRMIN-DIDOT: *La Captivité de Sainte Hélène;* THOMPSON: *Napoleon Bonaparte.*) [*BET*]
> The poem deals with the last weeks of Napoleon's illness when he was exiled on the island of Saint Helena. [*CP1994*]

Dans l'Attente / Waiting. French, published in *HI* and also included in the broadside *ES* (see Appendix); reprinted in *SR.* English translation, published in *SR;* no reprint.

> In *ES,* an English translation, credited to Sylvester Pollet, reads:
> > With patience I await
> > The day when you will find
> > It was always me
> > You had in mind.

L'Hyperesthésie / Hyperaesthesia. French, published in *SR;* no reprint. English translation, published in *SR;* no reprint.

> JL note:
> After Mallarmé. [*SR*]

Sais-tu / Do You Know. French, published in *SR;* no reprint. English translation, published in *SR;* no reprint.

THE HOUSE OF LIGHT (1986)

Acknowledgments (copyright page):
Some of these poems first appeared in *Ambit* (London), *Carcanet Review* (Manchester), *Harbor Review, Paris Review,* and *Poetry Australia,* and in *In Another Country* (City Lights Books) and *Stolen & Contaminated Poems* (Turkey Press). Eight of the woodcuts first appeared in *Ambit*.

The book includes twelve abstract woodcuts by Vanessa Jackson, one of which also appears on the front cover.

Colophon:
200 copies printed by hand at The Grenfell Press,
January-February 1986. The text paper is *Rives,*
The cover paper is *Dieu Donne*. The binding
is by Claudia Cohen. The type, set by
Michael Bixler, is Monotype *Poliphilus*.
All copies are signed by the
author and the artist.

Will We Ever Go the Lighthouse? Reprinted in *SP19896, CP1994, PNS.*

Alba. Reprinted in *SP1986, CP1994, PNS.*

JL endnote [*SP1986*]:
The *Alba* was a favorite form among the troubadour poets. "Alba" means "dawn" in Provençal, and it usually tells of the parting of lovers at dawn, or as Pound told me, "time for them to get back to their own beds."

In the note above, read "as Pound put it" in JL note, *CP1994.*

The House of Light. Reprinted in *SP1986, CP1994, PNS.*

SELECTED POEMS, 1935–1985 (1986)

Acknowledgments (copyright page):
Some of these poems first appeared in *Stolen & Contaminated Poems*, The Turkey Press, Santa Barbara, and in the following magazines: *Agenda* (London), *Almanaco del Specchio* (Milan), *Ambit* (London), *Antigonish Review, Carcanet Review* (Manchester), *Conjunctions, Exquisite Corpse, Frank, Harbors Review, Harper's, Horizon* (London), *Iowa Review, The Nation, New Directions in Prose & Poetry, Oink!, Open Spaces, Osiris,*

Paideuma, Ploughshares, Poetry, Poetry Australia, Stony Brook, and *Translation.*

"The Deconstructed Man" ("Multas per gentes") was first published by The Windhover Press, Iowa City.

The notes for SP1986 are grouped together at the the back of the book. JL introduces them:

> The point of the notes is to show how we are a part of a long poetic tradition. Old lines have echoes that can still enrich our own. The tradition exposed here is eclectic and eccentric—little wonder, since it is based so much in the Pound canon and mystique. Pound was a charismatic teacher but he never insisted that anti-Semitism and fascism be included in the package. I hope that the tradition which attracts me will also interest some others.

The Person. Published in *ND39* (1979); reprinted in *CP1994.*

The Philosopher. No reprint.

That Summer in Spain. No reprint.
> See "When You Danced," p. 279.

All Those Tales. No reprint.

Two Ships. No reprint.

How Can You Escape. No reprint.

When You Danced. Reprinted in *CP1994.*
> See "That Summer in Spain," p. 276.

I Like You. Reprinted in *CP1994.*

Dropkick Me Jesus. Reprinted in *HI.*

The Kenners' Cat. Reprinted in *CP1994.*

> JL endnote (*SP1986*):
> Jasper—vide Pound: Canto LIII, page 265: "In marble tower of Lou Tai doors were of jasper . . . "

> JL note:
> Hugh Kenner—greatest of the Pound scholars. *The Pound Era.*
> > Jasper—vide Pound: *Canto LIII*: "In marble tower of Lou Tai doors were of jasper..."

Bucky Fuller—Buckminster Fuller (1895–1983), American architect and engineer who developed the Dymaxion principle.

Genghis Khan—(1167–1227), Mongol conqueror who overran much of Asia and Europe.

Attila—(406–53), King of the Huns, whose invasions terrorized Europe.

Arjuna—in Hindu mythology, the friend of the god Krishna in the great battle between the Pandavas and the Kurus in the *Mahabharata* epic. Their dialogue on war in the *Baghavad-Gita* section of the poem sets forth one of the central doctrines of Hindu philosophy.

Hannibal—(247–182 B.C.), the Carthaginian general who attacked Rome in the Second Punic War. He crossed the Alps with elephants.

El Bertrans—the troubadour warrior Betrand de Born. [*CP1994*]

For more on Hugh Kenner and his cat, see in JL's "not-note" for "Je Est un Autre," p. 1050.

James My Namesake. Reprinted in *CP1994.*

   gradus ad Par- / nassum. Latin: "step to Parnassus."

JL note.:
"Gradus ad Parnassum—a Latin dictionary of prosody."

I Have Heard. Reprinted in *CP1994.*

JL note:
Post mortem meam—after my death. [*CP1994*]

Junk Mail. Reprinted in *CP1994.*

So Much Depends. Reprinted in *CP1994, PNS.* Previously included, along with "Some of Us Come to Live," in JL's two-poem booklet *Lines for Ezra Pound and William Carlos Williams,* a limited edition published by The Grenfell Press (New York, 1983). Introducing that publication, JL writes:

Pound and Williams met in 1902 when they were students at the University of Pennsylania. Pound was doing graduate work in Romance Languages, and Williams was in Medical School. Their close friendship continued until Williams's death in 1963. In those sixty years each bcame a great poet and each "made it new" in his own way.

JL note:
William Carlos Williams's last book of poems, published posthumously in 1962, *Pictures from Brueghel,* contained a sequence of short poems inspired by paintings of the Flemish genre painter Pieter Brueghel (1525–69). See *Collected Poems,* Volume 2, pages 385 to 394. [*CP1994*]

Some of Us Come to Live. Reprinted in *CP1994, PNS*. Previously published in *Lines for Ezra Pound and William Carlos Williams* (see preceding note).

Some People Think. Reprinted in *CP1994, HI, SR, PNS*. Previously published separately as a limited edition in 1984 by James L. Weil, New Rochelle, NY.

What Are You Smiling About. Reprinted in *CP1994, HI*.

You and Me. No reprint.

The Delia Sequence. Reprinted in *CP1994*.

   To Kalón.

   JL endnote (*SP1986*):
   "pulchra et docta"—"beautiful and learned."
         "the lady Maeut"—the legends say that Maeut (Maent) was the great love of the troubadour Bertrand de Born. When she rejected him, he wrote "Domna puois de me no-us chal [Lady, because you care nothing for me]," in which he described the good features of other ladies and attributed them to Maeut.

   JL repeats the preceding endnote as a footnote in *CP1994*, and adds the following:

   To Kalon (*The Beautiful*)
      . . .
            cansos—troubadour songs.
            trobar clus—the "closed style," complex and highly ornamented, of one of the school of troubadour poets.
            Holst—Gustav Holst (1874–1934), English composer whose masterpiece was the orchestral suite *The Planets*.

   You Came As a Thought. In *CP1994*, the poem appears twice, in the *SCP* section and in "The Delia Sequence" as here. A different version, with the title "The Evening Star," in included in *LPSL* and reprinted in CBP. See p. 87. In *SCP* itself, the poem has the following "not-note," which is repeated for the most part in *CP1994* (omissions in brackets):
         This is the last poem, the coda, in the "Delia Sequence," [which was] written [a good] many years ago. [The preceding ones are a bit too mushy to preserve. Much longing doth not (necessarily) a good poem make. Delia was the Roman poet Tibullus's girlfriend.]

Flebis et arsuro positum, Delia, lecto,
       tristibus et lacrimis oscula mixta dabis.
flebis: non tua sunt duro praecordia ferro
       vincta, nec in tenero stat tibi corde silex.
                    * * *
interea, dum fata sinunt, iungamus amores:
       iam veniet tenebris Mors adoperta caput;
iam subrepet iners aetas, nec amare decebit,
       dicere nec cano blanditias capite.

                                        —Tibullus, I,I

Those last four lines illustrate one of the conventions of the Elegaic Poets:
that before fate closes us off we should make the most of love. Thus in the *nox
mihi candida*, which is surely one of the great erotic poems in any language.
Pound renders Propertius's

       dum nos fata sinunt, oculos satiemus amore
              nox tibi longa venit, nec reditura dies.
                    * * *
While our fates twine together, sate we our eyes with love;
For long night comes upon you
                     and a day when no day returns.

Propertius and Tibullus were close contemporaries in the 1st century
B.C. Probably they knew each other. The "dum fata sinunt" appears in both
poems. Or was this a common expression around Rome?
    Is Delia the same girl who turns up in Herrick in a later incarnation?
Cynthia gave Propertius a hard time, and Delia seems to have been rough on
Tibullus now and then. My Delia always gladdened me but she never quite
got the message of how lovable I am. And as Cicero said, "an old love pinches
like a crab."

In *CP1994,* JL adds his translation of the passages from Tibullus in his
"not-note":

       You'll weep for me, Delia
       When I'm stretched on the bed for burning.
       You'll give me kisses mixed with bitter tears.
       Yes, you'll weep; your heart is not cased in metal,
       Your heart is not unyielding stone.
       . . .
       Meantime, while the fates permit it
       Let us be one in love.
       Soon death will come,

His head hooded in shadows.
Soon old age will be upon us,
When it will no longer be seemly
To talk love talk, when our hair is white.

For more on Pound and Propertius, see JL's notes on "The Last Poem to Be Written" and "No My Dear," pp. 1036–37 and 1062–63.

I Have Drifted.
Dedication, "For Carolina," added in *CP1994*.

JL note:
Ariadne—in Greek mythology the royal maiden whom the hero Theseus abandoned on the island of Naxos.

A Failure of Communication in the Animal Kingdom. Reprinted *OM, CP1994*.

The Child. Reprinted in *CP1994*.

Dans les Traces d'Ezra Pound, or Monsieur Roquette's Pants. No reprint.
Title. French, "In the Footprints of Ezra Pound..."

JL endnote (*SP1986*):
Monsieur Roquette—working with Lawrence Pitkethly's film crew on the Pound documentary I heard that great Occitan reciter Yves Roquette declaim from the battlements of Hautefort castle, Bertrand de Born's stronghold in the Dordogne, Bertrand's "War Song" which Pound translated so brilliantly.
　　Old Possum—Pound's nickname for T. S. Eliot was "Old Possum," and Eliot called Pound "Brer Rabbit." A record of the walking trip which the Pounds and Eliot made through troubadour country in 1912 will be found in Philip Grover's *Ezra Pound: The London Years*.
　　Arnaut de Marvoil—see Pound's poem "Marvoil" in *Personae*. The pun in Pound's "Alfonso the half-bald" escaped me until Florian Eidenbenz, our Swiss soundman, pointed it out. Such indecencies could not be printed in London in 1908.

The Care and Feeding of a Poet. Reprinted in *CP1994*.

The Casual Kiss. No reprint.

Cordelia. Published in *ND48* (1984); reprinted in *CP1994*.

JL note:
Cordelia—the virtuous daughter of King Lear in Shakespeare's play.
    Goneril & Regan—Cordelia's wicked sisters.
    The last three couplets of the poem are phrases from the play. [*CP1994*]

Being Much Too Tall. No reprint.
    la donna / così mobile. Italian: "the woman so changeable."

Can You Tell. No reprint.

Herodotus Reports. Reprinted in *CP1994*.

    JL note:
    Forellen—trout. Schubert's "Trout" Quintet.
        Henry—Henry Miller. [*CP1994*]

    See also JL's *Random Essays* (Mt. Kisco, NY: Moyer Bell, 1989), pp. 53–54.

Into Each Life. Reprinted in *CP1994, PNS*.

    Dedication, "For Annie Dillard," added for *CP1994*.

    JL endnote (*SP1986*):
    "ces dames galantes"—the reference is to the Seigneur de Brantôme's *Vies des Dames Galantes* (*The Lives of Fair & Gallant Ladies*). Brantôme was a 16th-century courtier, soldier, author, and memoirist.

    JL note:
    ces dames galantes—ladies of fashion.
        En Bertrans—the troubadour Bertrand de Born whose castle was Hauteford.
        the poet saw her—the story goes that Dante met his beloved Beatrice only once when she was crossing a bridge over the Arno in Florence. [*CP1994*]

It Is Written. Published in *ND48* (1984); reprinted in *CP1994*.

Love Is Cumulative. Reprinted in *CP1994*.

The Junk Collector. Reprinted in *CP1994, PNS*.

Is What We Eat. Reprinted in *PNS*.

My Old Gray Sweater. Reprinted in *CP1994, PNS*.

JL notes:
Gary Snyder—the poet and environmentalist. [*CP1994*]
    Gary: the poet and environmentalist Gary Snyder. [*PNS*]

The *Non*-World. Reprinted in *CP1994.*

JL note:
Herodotus—(*c.* 484–*c.* 425 B.C.), the Greek who has been called "the father of history." I suspect that he was gullible about some of the stories he heard from travelers to distant regions.
    Sappho—the Lesbian poet who lived in the 7th century B.C. Her work survives only in fragments quoted by grammarians.
    Ovid—Publius Ovidius Naso (43 B.C.–18 A.D.), one of the greatest of the Roman poets, author of the *Metamorphoses*, the source for many classic myths.
    Ariosto—Ludovico Ariosto (1474–1533), Italian epic-romantic poet, author of *Orlando Furioso*, an influence on Shakespeare.
    Rochester—John Wilmot, Earl of Rochester (1647–80), bawdy-satiric poet and notorious rake.
    Villon—François Villon (1431–63), greatest of the Medieval poets, vagabond and rogue, very modern in tone. [*CP1994*]

Persephone Wears Bluejeans. Reprinted in *CP1994.*

JL note:
Persephone—in Greek mythology the daughter of Zeus and Demeter, the goddess of crops. She was carried off by Hades who made her the queen of the lower world. After a long search her grieving mother found her and arranged for her to spend part of the year up on earth. Her annual return symbolized spring and fertility. [*CP1994*]

A Small Group. Reprinted in *CP1994.*

Why. Reprinted in *CP1994, PNS.*

JL endnote (*SP1986*):
Suggested by the line in Gérard de Nerval's "El Desdichado" ["The Wretch"]: "Le prince d'Aquitaine à la tour abolie" ["The prince of Aquitaine at the ruined tower."]

JL note:
Nerval—Gérard de Nerval (1808–55). French romantic writer. The poem is "El Desdichado." It tells of "Le Prince d'Aquitaine à la tour abolie." The line appealed to T. S. Eliot and is quoted on the last page of *The Waste Land.* [*CP1994, PNS*]

Social Note. Reprinted in *CP1994*.

The Goddess. Reprinted in *CP1994, PNS*.

Here I Am. Reprinted in *CP1994*.

> JL endnote (*SP1986*); repeated in *CP1994* (omissions here in brackets):
> Mount Sumeru—symbolically, the center of the Cosmos in the mandalas of
> Tibetan Buddhism.
> > Taishan—the sacred "Great Mountain" of China. [In *The Pisan Cantos*
> > Pound gave its name to one of the Carrara mountains which he could see from
> > the Disciplinary Training Center at Pisa.]

The Hitchhiker. Reprinted in *CP1994*.

To Smile or Not to Smile. Reprinted in *CP1994*.

You Know How a Cat. Reprinted in *CP1994*.

Why Won't You Ignite. Reprinted in *CP1994*.

The Old Comedian. Reprinted in *CP1994, PNS*.

I Love the Way. Reprinted in *CP1994*.

> JL endnote (*SP1986*):
> "nun d' hote moi gumne glukerois meleesi peplesai"—"and now you are close
> to me naked with your lovely limbs." From Rufinus, in *The Greek Anthology*,
> V, 47.

> JL note:
> The poem is by Rufinus in *The Greek Anthology*, V, 47. The line reads literally:
> "now you are close to me with your sweet limbs." [*CP1994*]

Antiphilus. Reprinted in *CP1994*.

And Will That Magic World. Reprinted in *CP1994*.

> JL endnote (*SP1986*):
> "Y ha de morir" is from Machado.

> JL note:
> > ¿Y ha de morir contigo el mundo mago
> > donde guarda el recuerdo

los hálitos más puros de la vida
la blanca sombra del amor primero...
                —Antonio Machado

And is the magic world to die with you,
the world where memory keeps
life's purest breaths—
white shadows of first love...
                —Tr. by Alan Trueblood [*CP1994*]

Saeta. Reprinted in *CP1994*.

   JL endnote:
   Feria de la Semana Santa in Seville.

   JL note:
   Saeta—a song sung in religious ceremonies in Spain, here referring to the fes-
   tival of Holy Week in Seville. [*CP1994*}

Having Failed. Reprinted in *CP1994*, *PNS*.

The End of It All. Reprinted in *CP1994*.
   carpe diem. Latin: "seize the day."
   casi demasiado tarde. Spanish: "almost far too late."

   JL endnote (*SP1986*); repeated in *CP1994* (addition in brackets):
   The "ecologist" is the Chilean poet Nicanor Parra [author of the famous "anti-
   poems"].

I Am Aware. Reprinted in *CP1994*.

   JL note:
   The Greek characters are fictitious.
        Marathon—(490 B.C.) the historic victory of the Athenians in the Persian
   Wars. [*CP1994*]

Love Is a School. Reprinted in *CP1994*.

   JL endnote (*SP1986*):
   "Love is a school..."—"Night Letters, IV," in Thomas Merton's *18 Poems* (1986).

   JL note:
   "Love is a school," from "Night Letters, IV" in Thomas Merton's *18 Poems*,
   the love poems to "M." [*CP1994*}

Berenice. Reprinted in *CP1994*.

JL endnote (*SP1986*):

Racine's *Berenice*, recalled by a contemporary instance.

JL note:

Berenice—the heroine of one of Racine's most enigmatic dramas, based on the life of a Jewess from Palestine (born A.D. 28) who became the mistress of the Roman emperor Titus. It is reputed that she had an incestuous relationship with her brother Agrippa. [*CP1994*]

Cf. "Trying to Please," p. 933.

Occidit Brevis Lux. Reprinted in *CP1994*.

JL endnote (*SP1986*):
From Catullus V.

JL note:

Occidit brevis lux—the brief light sinks.

Nox est perpetua dormienda—night is an endless sleeping—from Catullus V. [*CP1994*]

El Camino de Amor. Reprinted in *CP1994*.

JL endnote (*SP19986*); repeated in *CP1994* (addition in brackets):
[El Camino de Amor—The Road of Love.]

"Ni las noches…"—"Neither the nights of love that we did not have, nor your sobbing beside the window…" (Neruda)

"No es lo mismo…"—"It is not the same to be alone and to be without you." (Enrique Lihn)

"Caminante…"—"Traveler, there is no road, the road is made when we walk on it." (Machado)

Timor Amoris Conturbat Me. Reprinted in *CP1994*.

JL endnote (*SP1986*); repeated in *CP1994*.

"Timor Amoris Conturbat Me"—"The Fear of Love Disquiets Me." A pun on "timor mortis [of death] conturbat me," the refrain of William Dunbar's "Lament for the Makers."

"puella nam mi…"—Catullus XXXVII, 11–12. "My girl who has left me, though she was loved as she will never be loved again."

"nunc iam illa…"—Catullus VIII, 10–11. "Don't chase after her, or be miserable, but with your mind set be firm and endure."

'Ο Πατήρ. Reprinted in *CP1994*.

> JL endnote (*SP1986*):
> Ho Pater—"the father,"

> JL note:
> 'Ο Πατήρ—The Father.
>> Polycrates and Anthea are fictitious characters.
>> The *Philoctetes* is a tragedy by Sophocles. Philoctetes, on the way to the siege of Troy, is bitten in the foot by a serpent. His pain is so severe that he has to be left on the island of Lemnos, where the play takes place. [*CP1994*]

She Seemed to Know. Reprinted in *CP1994*.

> JL endnote (*SP19896*); repeated in *CP1994*.
> Drawn from Hardy, *Tess of the D'Urbervilles*, at the end: ". . . the President of the Immortals . . . had ended his sport with Tess."
>> ". . . in a gleam of Cos / in a slither of dyed stuff"—Pound's rescription of Propertius 1,2,2: "et tenues Coa veste movere sinus."

Two Fragments from Pausanias. Reprinted in *CP1994*.

> JL endnote (*SP1986*); repeated in *CP1994*:
> Pausanias—the Greek traveler and geographer of the 2nd century A.D.
>> Pittheus—in Greek legend, the king of Troezen, said to be the wisest man in the world.

With My Third Eye. Reprinted in *CP1994, PNS*.

> JL endnote (*SP1986*); repeated in *CP1994*:
> Stolen from various books on Tibetan and Tantric Buddhism. "Om mani padme hum" is the best known of the Tibetan Buddhist mantras. The novice aspiring to *dzogchen*, the "great perfection," prostrates himself 100,000 times while chanting the mantra, which means, literally, "the jewel at the heart of the lotus," but has many symbolic ramifications. The concept of the (mystical) Third Eye appears to have begun as magic in the Swat Valley of India and was probably brought to Tibet in the 8th century A.D. by Padma Sambhava, the "great guru," who sold it to the hardy but superstitious mountaineers. An ashram is an Indian hermitage. "Ashram time" is the fourth and last stage of the Brahmanical scheme of life, when the householder leaves his family and becomes a hermit (vanaprastha) or homeless mendicant (sannyasi).

At Eleusis. Reprinted in *CP1994*.

> JL endnote (*SP1986*):
> *dromena & epopte*. My thanks to Kay Davis for her treatment of the Eleusinian

Mysteries in *Fugue and Fresco: Structures in Pound's Cantos*. Actually Pound had told me about the mysteries in 1935, though his account was confused with the theory he had appended to his translation of De Gourmont's *Physique de l'Amour* about creativity coming from sperm, which rose to the brain. Is the whole idea one of his leg-pulls?

The version of the poem in *CP1994* is longer and accompanied by a new JL note:

AT ELEUSIS

—For John Nims

I was living underground
I was wandering in dark-

ness and confusion. I was
unable to slake my thirst

for understanding then you
appeared among the mystae

in the ritual procession
of the initiated I think

Persephone had sent you to
find me you took my hand

and with your touch I ex-
perienced dromena the thing

done then I attained the
epopteia the state of see-

ing what the eye cannot see
you placed the crown on my

head and I came above ground
to a life of which you are

the force and the center.

Eleusis—the town of Eleusis in Attica owed its fame to a great shrine of Demeter (and her daughter Persephone, the goddess of spring renewed) where the Eleusinian mysteries were performed. There is a splendid book by Carl

Kerenyi: *Eleusis*, Princeton University Press, 1967, which explains the rituals and their significance. I first heard about the mysteries from Pound; they are a recurrent theme in the *Cantos* and an element in his composite religion.

mystae. Latin: "priests" (of the mysteries).

How Shall I Find My Way. Published in *ND48* (984); no reprint.

JL endnote (*SP1986*):
"forfended place"—from *King Lear*.

You Are My Future. Reprinted in *CP1994*.

JL endnote (*SP1986*); reprinted in *CP1994* (omission in brackets; addition in curly brackets; editor's translation in double brackets).
"the descent beckons…"—from William Carlos Williams, "The Descent."
["facilis descensus…"—a corruption of Virgil's "facilis descensus Averno [[into hell]]," here "the descent into senility is easy."]
{Primavera—Botticelli's masterpiece of the female figure symbolizing spring.}

Da Mi Basia Mille. Reprinted in *CP1994*.

JL endnote (*SP1986*):
"Da Mi Basia Mille"—from Catullus V.

JL note:
Da Mi Basia Mille—Give Me a Thousand Kisses. From Catullus V
Eros—the little Greek god of love, usually represented as a winged archer who shoots his arrows at gods and men.
Saint Sebastian—3rd-century Christian martyr, a lad beloved by the Emperor Diocletian who had him killed with arrows for embracing Christianity.
[*CP1994*]

Three Skirmishes in the Endless Battle. Reprinted in *CP1994*.

JL endnote (*SP1986*); repeated in *CP1994* (additions in brackets; editor's comments in double brackets):
Psychomachia—the conflict of the soul with the body. A conventional subject for Christian-Latin poetry of the Middle Ages.
[Berggasse—Freud lived in the Berggasse in Vienna.]
[Prudentius—4th-century Christian Latin poet, famous for his rhymed hymns.]
[Pudicitia—chastity.]

[Sodomita Libido—perverse lust.]

Tauromachia—a bullfight.

Hypnerotomachia—the battle between sleep and love. One of Aldus's most beautiful editions was the *Hypnerotomachia Poliphili* [[*The Dream-love Battle of Poliphilo*]] (1499), "a bizarre and curious mixture of pedantry and sensualism by a Dominican monk named Francesco Colonna, who wrote in Italian weirdly mixed with Latin, Greek, and even Hebrew" (D. C. McMurtrie: *The Book*).

"post coetum venit somnus"—after love comes sleep.

"illa meos somno…"—Propertius, II,15,7–8 [[Loeb Classical Library]]. And Pound's rescription of the lines on page 220 of *Personae* [[pages 215–16, revised edition, 1981]].

Tuesdays at 87 Rue de Rome. Reprinted in *CP1994*.
cher Maître. French" "dear Master."

JL endnote [*SP1986*]:
Stolen from Hugh Kenner, *A Colder Eye*, pages 144–45.

Schuldorff, in *Die Morphologie des Verbrechertumsgeisteshaltung* [*The Morphology of the Criminal Mind*], cites the case of Steinbrenner, who stole only for the sexual satisfaction of confessing his crime to his victim. We see this also in certain films in which the mastermind criminal plots a perfect crime but leaves some clue for the detective because he *wishes* to be caught.

It is impossible to translate Mallarmé.

JL endnote:
Tuesdays—87 Rue de Rome in Paris was the house number of the great Symbolist poet Stéphane Mallarmé; it was here that his famous "Tuesday evenings" for his writer and artist friends were held.

Tout au monde—everything in the world exists to become a book.

L'encrier—Mallarmé is the most difficult of all poets; this line appears to say: the inkwell, crystal-like consciousness, with its drop of shadowy liquid related to something being present…

Epstein's Rock Drill—the London sculptor Sir Jacob Epstein (1880–1959) was famous for his sculpture of a man drilling rock with a jackhammer. Pound and Wyndham Lewis greatly admired this very abstract piece.

The Seven Tailors—the names of church bells in a Dorothy Sayers mystery. [*CP1994*}

"The Seven Tailors" is a reference to the seven church bells in Dorothy Sayers' mystery *The Nine Tailors*.

A Lady Asks Me. Reprinted in *CP1994*, *PNS*.

Dedication changed to "For Sophie Hawkes" in *CP1994* and *PNS*.

dompna de cortes dig e-l dous ris. Provençal: "I speak of the courtly lady's sweet smile." The phrase is JL's.

sirventes. Provençal: troubadour songs usually of an invective nature.

JL endnote [*SP1986*]; repeated in *CP1994* and in *PNS* (with some omissions, here in brackets):

> "A Lady Asks Me"—the opening line of Guido Cavalcanti's "Donna Mi Pregha" canzone.
>
> Marcabru—one of the 12th-century troubadours.
>
> "non amet neguna…"—from "Dirai Vos Senes Duptansa" ["I Will Tell You without Staggering"] of Marcabru, the last line.
>
> Bernhart de Ventadorn—another 12th-century troubadour.
>
> "mais val mos mals…" from "Non Es Meravelha S'eu Chan" ["It's No Marvel If My Song's the Best"] of Bernhart de Ventadorn, the fourth stanza. [I find it impossible to approximate the sounds of the short, stabbing Provençal words because the English words which take the meaning are too long.]
>
> ["I have heard someone walking…"—parody of Eliot's tone in *Four Quartets*.]
>
> "tant ai mo cor…"—from "Tant Ai Mo Cor Ple de Joya" of Bernhart de Ventadorn, the first stanza.
>
> ["An old book of fair language…"—a parody of Chaucer.]

For more on Cavalcanti's "Donna Mi Pregha," see notes to "You Invited Me" (pp. 1053–54) and "What Is It Makes One Girl" (pp. 1056–57).

Dream Not of Other Worlds. Reprinted in *CP1994*.

JL endnote (*SP1986*):

> From *Paradise Lost*, Book VIII, Raphael's advice to Adam:
>
> > "Heav'n is for thee too high
> > To know what passes there, be lowly wise;
> > Think only what concerns thee and thy being;
> > Dream not of other worlds…"
>
> "nihil in intellectu . . . " Probably from one of the Scholastics, which William Carlos Williams may have known for his "no ideas but in things."

JL note (*CP1994*) repeats the first endnote entry in *SP1986* and has the following as the second:

> No idea but in things—William Carlos Williams's version of the apothegm of the Scholastics: Nothing in the mind which wasn't first in the senses.

For more on "Nihil in intellectu…," see in notes to the epigraph for *Some Natural Things*, p. 1034.

I Want to Breathe. Reprinted in *CP1994, LPJL.*

JL endnote (*SP1986*):
The Greeks believed that the pneuma (air/breath) was a spirit superior to both body and soul, and the Stoics held that it was an ethereal fiery stuff, a cosmic principle.

As in Music / A Repose / Across Time. Reprinted in *CP1994.*

JL note:
Madame de Lafayette's great novel *The Princess of Clèves.*
  Rexroth—Kenneth Rexroth, the San Francsco poet. [*CP1994*]

The Bible Lady. Reprinted in *CP1994.*

The Deconstructed Man. Reprinted in *CP1994, PNS.* Previously published as a limited edition in 1985 by The Windhover Press, Iowa City, IA.
  paideuma. Greek: Greek: "instruction."
  Tom's Wendy. Changed to "Tom's Margie" in *CP1994.*
  paradiso terrestre. Latin: "earthly paradise."
  The entire final stanza, beginning with, "Lie quiet Ezra," is omitted in *CP1994.*

JL endnote (*SP1986*); repeated with omissions (in brackets) in *CP1994* and with an addition (in curly brackets) in *PNS.* Editor's translations in double brackets.
  "Multas per gentes…"—Catullus, CI, the elegy for his brother. "By strangers' coasts and waters, many days at sea" (Robert Fitzgerald's version). The next line was composed by Fitzgerald in our golfcart in Carolina, on request for how Catullus would deal with airplane travel [["and also many aerial journeys"]].
  Polumetis—the Homeric epithet for Odysseus, the man of many counsels.
  Troorak—a beach town near Sydney, Australia.
  Rapallo—a seaside town near Genova where Pound lived for many years.
  "J'ai rêvé dans la grotte…"—Gerard de Nerval: "El Desdichado" [["The Wretch"]]. "I was dreaming in the grotto where the mermaids swim."
  "I have lingered…"—Eliot: "Prufrock." The lines inspired by Nerval.
  "Voi che sapete…"—Cherubino's aria in Mozart's *The Marriage of Figaro.* [["You know what a thing love is… / I feel an affection full of desire / now a delight, now a torment"]]
  in ogne parte…"—"in every place where memory leads me." Suggested by the lines in Cavalcanti's "Donna Mi Priegha": "In quelle parte dove sta memoria."

"A ristorar le pene..."—Zerlina's duet in Mozart's *Don Giovanni*. [["To share the pains of an innocent love"]]

Ma in Ispagna..."—Leporello's patter song in *Don Giovanni*. [["But in Spain there are already one thousand and three"]]

"risplende ognun sa luce..."—"each one gives forth her light which will never die."

Restif—Restif de la Bretonne, the 18th-century novelist and libertine, who was called "the Rousseau of the gutter" and "the Voltaire of the chambermaids."

"sola et magna (mater)"—"the one and great mother."

"Gertrude's Mother"—Gertrude Stein and Virgil Thompson did an opera together, *The Mother of Us All*.

"the Virgin & the Whore"—one of Williams's themes in *Paterson*.

"ma basta per oggi..."—"enough for today's catalog of girls."

"posh P & O boats"—the Pacific and Orient Line steamers which travelers from England took in the old days. "Posh" stood for "port-side-out-starboard-side-home." Because of the terrible heat in the Red Sea it was desirable to get a cabin on the north side of the ship, away from the sun.

"C'est moi dans la poubelle"—"I'm the one in the trashcan." In the 1960s, after he had become depressed, Pound was in Paris and Beckett took him to a performance of *Endgame*.

"there in the bolge..."—Dante tells the story of Bertand de Born in *Inferno*, XXVIII, 118ff.

"E'l capo tronco..."—"Certainly I saw, and to this hour I seem to see, a trunk going headless, even as went the others of that dismal throng, and it held the severed head by the hair, swinging in his hand like a lantern, which looking upon us, said, 'Ah me!'" (Pound's translation, *The Spirit of Romance*, page 45)

"bos chavaliers fo..."—"He was a good knight and a good fighter, a good poet and wise and well-spoken." From the *vida* (legendary life) of Bertrand de Born.

[San Michele—Pound is buried in the island cemetery of San Michele in the lagoon near Venice.]

[Dioce—(Deioces in Herodotus) the 7th-century B.C. king of the Medes who revolted against the Assyrians and built the fabulous city of Ecbatana, whose battlements, Herodotus says, "are planted with silver and gold." In Canto LXXIV this becomes: "To build the city of Dioce whose terraces are the colour of stars."]

[Wagadu—a mythical city in Africa, which Pound learned about from the German anthropologist Leo Frobenius. See Douglas Fox, *African Genesis*.]

{"in paradisum..."—"may the angels lead you into paradise."}

"He Did It to Please His Mother." Reprinted in *CP1994*.

JL endnote (*SP1986*); repeated in *CP1994* (addition in brackets):
Some of the lines are from Shakespeare's *Coriolanus*.

Delmore Schwartz's play [*Coriolanus and His Mother, The Dream of One Performance*] was in his first book, *In Dreams Begin Responsibilities* (1938).

Berggasse—Freud lived in the Berggasse in Vienna.

For more on Delmore Schwartz's play, see JL's note for "In Hac Spe Vivo," p. 1057.

Tamara. No reprint.

O Hermes Trismegistus. Reprinted in *CP1994*.
    Columbia. Changed to "Yale" in *CP1994*.
    our wells. Changed to "our water" in *CP1994*.

JL endnote (*SP1986*); repeated except for the first entry in *CP1994* (added here in brackets):
Hermes Trismegistus—Hermes, the thrice greatest, author of the *Hermetic Books* of occult wisdom. Medieval alchemists loved him.

[Hermes Trismegistus—the Greek god Hermes in his roll as inspirer of secret books of metaphysics and occult wisdom, known as the "hermetic books" of neo-Platonism and alchemy.]

Thoth—the Egyptian god who was possessed of all secret wisdom.

Spatiality, asymptotic, hermeneutic—terms drawn from Structuralism and Semiotics.

Skiing without Skis. Reprinted in *CP1994*.

JL note:
Parsenn—a famous ski-racing course at Davos in the Grisons section of Switzerland.

schwendi—a hamlet of peasant chalets and farms on the mountainside. [*CP1994*]

A Leave-taking. Reprinted in *CP1994, PNS*.

Tennessee. Reprinted in *CP1994*.

JL note:
Lincoln Kirstein—man of letters and patron of the New York City Ballet.

Hart Crane—(1899–1932) American poet, author of *The Bridge*.

Laurette Taylor—American actress whose portrayal of the mother, Amanda Wingfield, in Williams's *The Glass Menagerie* was a sensation in 1945. [*CP1994*]

Girls as Windmills. Reprinted in *CP1994*.

> JL note:
> Leporello—the comic manservant of Don Giovanni in Mozart's opera.
> Sancho Panza—the servant in Cervantes' *Don Quixote*. [*CP1994*]

My Muse. Reprinted in *CP1994*.

> JL note:
> de mortuis…a pun on the Latin "de mortuis nihil nisi bonum"—of the dead say nothing but good, which becomes, "of the dead-in-the-head & art say nothing but good."
> Gregory Corso—the poet, author of *The Happy Birthday of Death, Elegiac Feelings American*, etc.
> Helicon—the mountain of the Muses in Greek mythology.
> Philemon & Baucis—in Greek mythology, a poor old couple who entertained Zeus and Hermes hospitably, when they visited the earth in disguise and were repulsed by the rich. For this, Philemon and Baucis were saved from a deluge that overwhelmed the land where they lived, and their dwelling was transformed into a temple, of which they were made the priest and priestess. They were also granted their request to die at the same time, and were changed into trees, whose boughs intertwined. [*CP1994*]

At Our House. Reprinted in *CP1994*.

The Cardiac Autoscope. Reprinted in *CP1994*.
The final line, "[ADVERTISEMENT]," is omitted in *CP1994*.

The Bubble Bed. Reprinted in *CP1994*.

> JL note:
> Nausicaä—In the *Odyssey*, the daughter of the Phaeacian king Alcinous. The shipwrecked Odysseus approaches her as she is playing ball with her maidens on the shore after washing the palace linen. She receives him kindly and leads him to her father. . . . See also the Nausicaä section of Joyce's *Ulysses*.
> Lotophagoi—In the *Odyssey*, a fabulous people who eat the fruit of the lotus, whose property is to make those who eat it forget their home and wish to remain forever in Lotus-land.
> Poluphloisboio thalasses—Pound's tag from Homer for the recurrent sound of the surf ["the much-roaring sea"].
> William Burroughs—contemporary American experimental novelist, author of *Naked Lunch*. [*CP1994*]

I Belong. No reprint.

The Lament of Professor Turbojet. Reprinted in *CP1994*.

Highlights of the Goliad Parade. No reprint.

Take Off Your Socks! Reprinted in *CP1994*.

JL note:
Bertrand—the troubadour-warrior Bertrand de Born…Hautefort in the Dordogne was his castle.

    Richard—Richard Coeur de Lion. He was killed fighting the French in 1199 at the Château de Chalus in the Dordogne by an arrow from a crossbow, then a newly invented weapon.

    Tu es atroce—You're impossible, you have no refinement. [*CP1994*]

The Parodist. No reprint.
Verfremdungseffekt. German: "alienation effect," making the familiar strange.

Preguntas sin Respuestas. Reprinted in *CP1994*.
Title. Spanish: "Questions without Answers."

JL note:
Nicanor Parra—Chilean poet, author of *Antipoems* and *Emergency Poems*.

    Muchachos: boys; Niñas, girls.

    Teargas—Parra teaches at the university of in Santiago. I attended his class. There was a student riot and the dictator sent troops. A teargas bomb was hurled through the window and we took shelter in the men's room.

    Shopless barber—in Talca there was a barber who had no shop. He wore a placard "Shopless Barber" and cut hair in the park.

    Great landowners—we had lunch at their club. [*CP1994*]

Ein Kitzbuehler Tag (1947). Both the German and JL's English translation reprinted in *CP1994*.
Title. "A Day in the Kitzbuehl Range."
Die Niederlandische Koenig'n—The Queen of Holland. Changed in *CP1994* to "Die Niederlandische Prinzessn"—"The Princess Royal of Holland."

JL footnote for the German (*SP1986*); repeated in *CP1994*:
NB: Ski German, which is devoid of grammar, is what I picked up from ski teachers and mountain guides when I was in Austria in my youth.

JL footnote for the English (*SP1986*); repeated in *CP1994* (addition in brackets):
[Princess Royal of Holland—]This actually happened.

TABELLAE (1986)

Published anonymously, i.e., with no author or acknowledgments given.
Title. Latin: "Writing Tablets."

Epigraph:

> *Ego tam doctae nobis periere tabellae,*
> *Scripta pariter tot periere bona!*

> *aut dixit: "Venies hodie, cessabimus una:*
> *hospitum tota paravit Amor,"*

> So my learned writing tablets are lost
> and much good writing with them.

> [and once she had written on them:]
> "You will come today and we will rest together:
> Love has prepared a welcome for you all night long."

> *"ingenium nobis ipsa puella facit."*

> "My genius is no more than a girl!"

> *"dum nos fata sinunt, oculos satiemus amore:*
> *nox tibi longa venit, nec reditura dies."*

> "While our fates twine together, sate we our eyes with love;
> For a long night comes upon you
>   and a day when no day returns."

> —Propertius
> Translation by Ezra Pound

Colophon:

> 100 copies printed at The Grenfell Press,
> New York, fall 1986. The typeface is
> Bembo, cast by Michael Bixler;
> The paper is J. Whatman 1949,
> and the bindings are by
> Claudia Cohen.

I Saw Her First. Reprinted in *CP1994*.

>   JL note:
>   Delphi—the site of the famous Delphic Oracle in the shrine of Apollo on the
>   slope of Mount Parnassus in Greece.
>
>   Meleager—Meleager of Gadara, the lyric poet who flourished around 60
>   B.C. [*CP1994*]

My Watch. No reprint.

Caritas Perfecta. No reprint.
>   Title. Latin: "Absolute Love."

Who Is the Child. Reprinted in *CP1994*.

The Mirror Girl. Reprinted in *CP1994*.
>   In *CP1994*, the second and third stanzas read: "ing in love all his life / he
>   had pursued love but // never found it quite as / he wished it to be what"....

You've Set the Words. Reprinted in *CP1994, SW*.

Why Do You Never Enter My Dreams. Reprinted in *CP1994, LPJL*.

>   JL note:
>   Falernian—a Roman wine. [*CP1994*]

I Feel at Home. No reprint.

I Live in Three Worlds. Reprinted in *CP1994, HI,* and in a revised version
in *CBP* with the title "Living in Three Worlds."

Eros as Archaeologist. Reprinted in *CP1994, PNS*.

Qui Nunquam Amavit. Reprinted in *CP1994*.

>   JL note:
>   Qui Numquam Amavit...from the 4th-century *Pervigilium Veneris* (*The Vigil
>   of Venus*). Cras amet qui numquam amavit—tomorrow he will love who never
>   has loved before.
>
>   Philemon and Baucis—in Greek mythology, a poor old couple who en-
>   tertained the gods Zeus and Hermes when they visited the earth in disguise.
>   They were granted their request to die at the same time, and were changed
>   into poplars, whose boughs intertwined.

Tristan—the lover of Isolde in Arthurian legend and Wagner's opera.

Abelard—Peter Abelard (1079–1142), French philosopher, who secretly married his pupil, Heloïse, and was emasculated by her uncle.

Sir John—Sir John Falstaff, the comic character in Shakespeare's historical play. [*CP1994*]

Under His Microscope. Reprinted in *CP1994*.

The Dance of the Skin. Reprinted in *A, CP1994, LPJL*, and in a revised version in *CBP*.

A Suggestion. Reprinted in *CP1994, HI, LPJL*.

Arachne. Reprinted in *CP1994, LPJL*.

The Prisoner of Childhood. Reprinted in *CP994*.

Eyes Are the Guides of Love. Reprinted in *OM, CP1994, PNS*.

JL note:
Propertius—the Roman poet Sextus Propertius (50 B.C.–16 B.C.).
oculi sunt—as Englished in the title.
dulce ridentem—from the last line of Horace's "Integer Vitae" ["Blameless in Life"] Ode, I, 22.
dulce ridentem Lalage amabo, dulce loquentem: I'll love my sweetly laughing, sweetly talking Lalage. [*CP1994*]

After Rochester. Reprinted in *CP1994*.
Title. In *CP1994*, changed to "After Rochester (or somebody)."

Σοί με λάτριν γλυκύδωρος Έρως παρέδωκε, Ήλιοδώρα
Reprinted in *CP1994*.

JL note:
The quotation is from Rufinus in *The Greek Anthology* (V, 22) but I have changed the ugly name Boöpis to Heliodora.

Two Spoons. Reprinted in *CP1994, LPJL*.

What Is the Need. Reprinted in *A, CP1994*.

Τό Σῶμα. Reprinted in *CP1994*.

JL note:

Τό Σῶμα—the body. [*CP1994*]

Touching. Reprinted in *A, CP1994, HI, LPJL,* and in a revised version in *CPB.*

Last Words. Reprinted in *CP1994.*
"**Rosebud.**" In *CP1994,* changed to "Bluebell" (*sic*).
and my last. In *CP1994,* changed to "and if my last."
"**Strawberry.**" In *CP1994,* changed to ""Sugarplum."

JL note:

Mehr Licht—more light.

 Gertrude—Gertrude Stein. The full quote is: "What is the answer," and when her companion was silent, "In that case, what is the question?" [*CP1994*]

Properate Tempus. Reprinted in *CP1994.*

JL note:

Properate—hasten time! [*CP1994*]

The Unsatisfactory Dream. Reprinted in *CP1994.*

THE OWL OF MINERVA (1987)

Acknowledgments (copyright page):
SOME OF THESE POEMS FIRST APPEARED IN *Ambit* (LONDON), *Antaeus, Antigonish Review, Chelsea, Cold Water Business, Conjunctions, Exquisite Corpse, Interim, Iowa Review, Light Year, Nota Bene* (PARIS), *Paris Review, Ploughshares, San Jose Studies, Scripsi* (MELBOURNE), and *Tabellae* (GRENFELL PRESS).

 THE TYPE IN THIS BOOK IS FOURNIER, SET BY WALKER & SWENSON, BOOK TYPOGRAPHERS. BOOK DESIGN BY TREE SWENSON.

Epigraph:
 et iam Luna negat totiens descendere caelo,
 nigraque funestum concinit omen avis.

PROPERTIUS II, xxviii, lines 37–38

[JL's translation, added in *CP1994*: "And now the moon refuses to come down from / the sky and the black bird sings an omen of doom."]

Dedication:

For HAYDEN CARRUTH

Advice to Aurelius. Reprinted in *CP1994*.

The Owl of Minerva. Reprinted in *CP1994*.

JL note:

"When philosophy paints in gray, then has a shape of life grown old; the Owl of Minerva spreads its wings only with the falling of the dusk."

—Hegel: *Grundlinien der Philosophie des Rechts*
[*Foundations of the Philosophy of Right*]

& George-Bill-Fred was no doubt recalling that Mephistopheles said to the bewildered student:

*"Grau, teurer Freund, ist all Theorie,
Und gruen des Lebens goldner Baum."*

*"My friend, all theory is gray,
and the golden tree of life is green."*
Faust—the Studierzimmer [study] scene [*OM*]

JL repeats the note in *CP1994*, changing "& George-Bill-Fred" to "Hegel," and adding after "the bewildered student": "in Goethe's *Faust*." He also appends the following:

Quinquatrus—in Roman religion, originally a festival of Mars at which the sacred shields were purified. Later the same day was regarded as the birthday of Minerva.

Hegel—G.W.F. Hegel (1770–1831), German philosopher.

"the owl for all its [*sic*] feathers"—from Keats's "St Agnes Eve" in *Lamia*.

Etruria—the center of Etruscan civilization in Italy.

The Fate of Actaeon. Reprinted in *CP1994*.

JL note:

Actaeon—in Greek mythology, Actaeon by accident while hunting came upon the naked Diana (Artemis), goddess of hunting and wild life as she was bathing in the woods surrounded by her attendant nymphs. She changed him into a stag in which form he was pursued and killed by his own hounds. Ovid tells the story in the *Metamorphoses*.

hic dea silvarum…—here the goddess of the wood when she was tired from hunting loved to bathe her maiden limbs in the crystal water.

circumfusauque Dianam…—then the nymphs thronged around her, trying to hide her body with their own. [*CP1994*]

For Me All History Is *NOW*. No reprint.

She's Not Exactly Like You. Reprinted in *PNS*.

    que / valha vos qu'ai perduda. Provençal: "I've lost [a lady] of your worth."

    Domna puois de me / no-us chal. Provençal: "Lady, since you no longer love me."

    See "Our Meetings," p. 444, and note.

Il Pastor Fido. Reprinted in *CP1994, PNS*.

    liceo. Italian: "lyceum."

The Party on Olympus. Reprinted in *CP1994*.

    JL note:

Olympus—the mountain in Thessaly which was the home of the gods.

    psychomachia—the symbolic conflict between soul and body. A conventional subject for Christian-Latin poetry in the Middle Ages. See p. 384.

    Hermes—the crafty god of luck and wealth, inventor of the lyre, messenger of the gods and conductor of souls of the dead to Hades (the Roman Mercury).

    the Cyprian—epithet for Aphrodite, goddess of love, who was born in Cyprus (the Roman Venus). [*CP1994*]

After the Hugging Is Over I'll Still Cherish You My Dear. No reprint.

    JL note:

Metamorphoses, VIII, 632–25, 711–13, 717–18. [*OM*]

JL paraphrases only portions of Ovid's Latin. Arthur Golding's classic Elizabethan translation of these lines reads:

> Howbeet twoo honest auncient folke, (of whom shee *Baucis* hight
> And he *Philemon*) in that Cote theyr fayth in youth had plight:
> And in that Cote had spent theyr age. And for they paciently
> Did beare their simply povertie, they made it light thereby
>   ...
>
>   And bycause
> Our yeeres in concord wee have spent, I pray when death neere drawes
> Let bothe of us toogither leave our lives: that neyther I
> Behold my wyves deceace, nor shee see myne when I do dye.
>   ...
>
>   *Philemon* old and poore
> Saw *Baucis* floorish grene with leaves, and *Baucis* saw likewyse
> *Philemon* braunching out in boughes and twigs before hir eyes.

The Songbird. Reprinted in *CP1994, PNS.*

JL note:
Parsifal—Wagner's opera based on one of the Arthurian legends.

Wozzeck—opera based on a play by Buechner, by Alban Berg; one of the masterpieces of 20th-century music.

Kindertotenlieder—song cycle by Gustav Mahler (Songs of Dead Children). [*CP1994, PNS*]

Some Memories of E.P. (Drafts & Fragments). Reprinted in *CP1994, PNS.*

JL note (*CP1994*); repeated only in part in *PNS* (the entries for "ut doceat...," "salite," "Princess Maria," and "Schwungeld"; omissions in brackets):
ut doceat...—let it teach, move, and delight. [Before Agricola, the phrase was first used by Quintilian.]

i mercanti di cannoni—title of an Italian book on arms manufacturers.

the Mysteries—the Greek Eleusinian mysteries. See the poem "At Eleusis" for explanation, p. 324.

salite—paths.

micci...—kitty, kitty, kitty, come here; here's something to eat.

"Albuggero"—Pound's derisive name for the Albergo (hotel) Rapallo where he ate most of his meals.

Gaudier—the French sculptor Henri Gaudier-Brzeska (1891–1915), one of the founders of Vorticism. Pound wrote a book on his work after he was killed in World War I.

Kung—Chinese name for Confucius.

Deer Bull—William Carlos Williams. The two poets used comic names in their letters to each other. Their lifelong friendship began when they were students at the University of Pennsylvania.

And one year...—These lines parody the Cantos in which Pound recounted the campaign of the Italian Renaissance warrior dukes.

Princess Maria—Pound's daughter, Mary. She was raised in her childhood by a peasant family, the Markers, at Gais in the Italian Tyrol. She later married Prince Boris de Rachewiltz.

the Lady—Olga Rudge, mother of Mary de Rachewiltz.

Schwungeld—stamp scrip. [Its use was part of the economic theories of an obscure German named Silvio Gesell in whom Pound was interested.] At one time stamp scrip was issued by the town of Woergel [in Austria] but the Vienna central bank suppressed it. [For an account of Pound's economic theories see the chapter "Pound's Economics" in my book *Pound as Wuz.*]

the man—Beethoven.

Cf. *B*, pp. 83–87, 100–05, 128–29, and *PAW*, pp. 2–12.

The Beautiful Muttering. Reprinted in *CP1994, PNS.*
poluphloisboio thalasses. Greek: "the much-roaring sea."
sic scriptum est. Latin: "as it was written."

JL note:
the blind singer—Homer who was said to be blind.
    Chidambaram—Hindu temple in South India.
    Ramayama—Sanskrit epic of 3rd century B.C. [*CP1994*]

The Family Portrait. Reprinted in *CP1994.*

The People Boxes. Reprinted in *CP1994.*

The Fisherwoman. Reprinted in *CP1994.*

JL note:
diktuon theraon—[Greek:] "casting the net in eager pursuit." [*OM*]

The Secretary's Story. Reprinted in *CP1994.*

The Believer. Reprinted in *CP1994.*

Waiting for the Light. Reprinted in *CP1994.*

The Maze. Reprinted in *CP1994.*

Not Perfect Like You. No reprint.

lines after cummings. Reprinted in *CP1994.*

O Best of All Nights, Return and Return Again.

JL note; repeated in *CP1994.*
(After the *Pervigilium Veneris* & Propertius's "Nox mihi candida.") [Latin: *The Vigil of Venus*; "For me bright night"] [*OM*]

Can Language Be Taught with the Fingertips? Reprinted in *CP1994.*
a bad time. In *CP1994*, "a hard time."

JL note:
Paestum—a Greek temple, dedicated to Poseidon, the god of the sea. It was built about 600 B.C. on the southwest coast of Italy near Salerno. It is fairly well preserved and a great sight.
    Lesbia—the girl to whom many of Catullus's greatest poems were written.
    the "pedicabos"—Catullus's homosexual poems. [*CP1994*]

Like the Octopus. Reprinted in *CP1994, PNS.*

The Hour Glass. Reprinted in *CP1994.*

Her Sweet Deceit. Reprinted in *CP1994.*
Dedication, "For Vanessa," added in *CP1994.*

Haiku (slightly overlength). Reprinted in *CP1994* as "Tanka," and in *HI.*

Confessio Amantis. Reprinted in *CP1994.*

> JL note:
> Confessio Amantis—the lover's confession.
>> Concitatio—excitement of old age.
>> Rapallo—see the poem "In Another Country" on page 155.
>> Her tunic—a line from Part VII of Pound's "Homage to Sextus
> Propertius."
>> Her long—a parody from Rochester, or is it Herrick?
>> Sometime—a line from Eliot's *Four Quartets.*
>> And yes—the last line from Joyce's *Ulysses*; Molly Bloom is speaking.
> [*CP1994*]

That Night in Milan. No reprint.

Her Line Will Be Busy. No reprint.

The Mysterious Disappearance. Reprinted in *CP1994.*

The Word Machine. No reprint.

Can There Be a Female Bodhisattva? Reprinted in *CP1994.*

> JL note:
> Bodhisattva—in Mahayana Buddhism, one who having attainted enlighten-
> ment (bodhi) is on his way to Buddhahood but postpones his goal to keep a
> vow to help all life attain salvation. [*CP1994*]

A Night at the Opera. Reprinted in *CP1994.*

> JL note:
> (An arrangement of the English captions from a TV production
> of Donizetti's *Anna Bolena* with Joan Sutherland. Metteurs-en-scène
> [French: "directors"]: Jill Levine & Vanessa Jackson. [*CP1994*]

The Large Opera Singer. Reprinted in *CP1994*.

An Anti-Love Poem. Reprinted in *CP1994*.
agua mineral sin gas. Spanish: "uncarbonated mineral water."

Holes. Reprinted in *CP1994*.

JL note:
Vedantists—scholars of Vedanta, in Sanskrit, literally, end of the *Vedas*, i.e., the *Upanishads* and the commentaries on them, from which was derived a form of mystical ontology.
Walter Abish—American novelist, author of *How German Is It*. [*CP1994*]

A Job Description. Reprinted in *CP1994*.

JL note (*OM*); repeated in *CP1994* (translations in brackets added by the editor, JL addition in double brackets):
Laforgue: *Moralités Légenaires: Salomé* [*Moral Tales: Salome*].
The Princes of the North wait upon the Tetrarch in his palace: "Ils s'entretenaient parmi les grands: le grand Mandarin, le Grand Maître des Bibliothèques, l'Arbitre des Elégances, le Conservateur des Symboles, le Répétiteur des Gynécées et Sélections, le Pope des Neiges et l'Administra-teur de la Mort, entre deux rangs de scribes maigres et rapides, la calme au côté, l'encrier au coeur.... Alors, précédés de l'Ordonnateur-des-milles riens, le Tétrarque et son entourage se mirent en devoir de faire à leurs Hôtes les honneurs du palais, du titanique palais funèbre veiné de blême."
["They were conversing with the court officials: the Great Mandarin, the Lord Master of the Libraries, the Arbiter of Elegance, the Keeper of Symbols, the Tutor of Selection and of the Gynaeceum, the Pope of the Snow Cult, and the Administrator of Death, between two lines of thin, swift scribes, who had their quills hanging at their sides and their inkwells slung over their hearts....After the collation, preceded by the Ordainer-of-the-Thousand-Odds-and-Ends, the Tetrarch and his attendants took it upon themselves to show the Palace, the titanic, funereal, white-veined Palace, to their guests."—Tr. by William Jay Smith]
Pound: *Instigations: Our Tetrachal Precieuse (A Divigation)*
"...chief mandarins in clump, the librarian of the palace (Conde de las Navas), the Arbiter Elegantium, the Curator major of Symbols, the Examiner of the High Schools, the Supernumerary priest of the Snow Cult, the Administrator of Death, and the Chief Attendant Collector of Death Duties....
"Under impulsion of the Arranger of Inanities the pomaded princes next began their inspections of the buildings."

[[Jules Laforgue—(1860–87), one of the first French poets to write in free verse. His work influenced Pound, T. S. Eliot, and Joyce. The *Moral Tales* parody figures of literature and legend such as Hamlet, Lohengrin, and Salome. Pound's commentary extends Laforgue's wit.]]

After Martial. Reprinted in *CP1994*.

JL note:
Martial—Marcus Valerius Martialis (A.D. 40–104), Roman poet renowned for his satiric wit. Model for the modern epigram.
    The poem refers to Robert Bly. {*CP1994*]

Two Onanists. No reprint.

Terror. Reprinted in *CP1994*.

Report from the Missing Persons Bureau. No reprint.

Premula's Problem. Reprinted in *CP1994* and in a revised version in *CBP*.

One of the Great Lines. No reprint.

Kulchur. Reprinted in *HI*.

Ipse Dixit. Reprinted in *CP1994*.
    Title. Latin: "He himself said it."

JL note:
Source: a broadcoast on National Public Radio. [*CP1994*]

I Know How Every Poet. Reprinted in *CP1994*.

JL note:
Horace—Quintus Horatius Flaccus (B.C. 65–8), Roman poet, the most famous of his period, who wrote odes, satires, epodes, and epistles. [*CP1994*]

The Gift. Reprinted in *HI, SR, PNS*.

Gracious Living. Reprinted in *CP1994*.

Cincinnatus in Utah. Reprinted in *CP1994*.

Eating & Dying. No reprint.

    confit d'oie. French: "potted goose."

    camarero. Spanish: "waiter."

    tachino. Italian: "turkey."

    Hasenpfeffer. German: "rabbit stew."

    Forellen. German: "trout."

    Rehrucken mit Preiselbeeren. German: "saddle of venison with cranberries."

ΚΟΛΛΉΜΑΤΑ (1988)

Epigraph (copyright page):

κολλήματα
The glued sheets of papyrus
made into rolls on which Greek poets
inscribed their poems

Colophon:

ONE HUNDRED AND FIFTY COPIES
OF THIS BOOK HAVE BEEN PRINTED
AT THE STINEHOUR PRESS
LUNENBERG, VERMONT
SPRING 1988

The Questions. Reprinted in *CP1994*.

The Interdiction. Reprinted in *BET, CP1994*.

ἡ μοῖρα αὐτῆς. Reprinted in *CP1994* with the title "The Jealous Gods."

    Title. Greek: "her fate."

Our Bicycles. Reprinted in *BET, CP1994, PNS*.

The Unknown City. No reprint.

The Happy Poets. Reprinted in *BET, CP1994, LPJL, PNS*.

    In LPJL, only the first five lines appear—JL's translation of Propertius—and without stanza breaks.

The Problem Struck Me. Reprinted in *BET, CP1994*.

An Anginal Equivalent. Reprinted in *BET, CP1994, PNS.*

> JL note:
> Martial—Marcus Valerius Martialis (A.D. 40–104), born in Spain, he made a career in Rome. Renowned for his epigrams and satirical verse, especially those spiced with gross obscenity. [*CP1994*]

The Limper. Reprinted in *BET, CP1994.*

> In *CP1994*, JL's translation follows the lines by Rilke:
> > "Were you not always distracted by expec-
> > tation, as though all this were announcing
> > someone to love?"
>
> JL note:
> Rilke—Rainer Maria Rilke (1875–1926), the greatest lyric poet of modern Germany. One of his masterpieces is the *Duineser Elegien* [*Duino Elegies*]. [*CP1994*]

So Slender. Reprinted in *A, CP1994.*
the rope did stand. In *CP1994*, "did" is italicized.

> JL note:
> Ladakh—the region in northern India that lies between Kashmir and Tibet in the foothills of the Himalayas.
> Benares—the most holy of the Hindu pilgrimage sites where the pilgrims bathe in the Ganges. [*CP1994*]

A Graceful Exit. Reprinted in *BET, CP1994.*

> JL note:
> The four women's names are those of heroines in Henry James novels. [*CP1994*]

The Escape. Reprinted in *BET, CP1994.*

Die Heimat. Reprinted in *BET, CP1994, HI.*

> JL note:
> Die Heimat—[German:] native land. [*CP1994*]

A Translation. Reprinted in *BET, A, CP1994, SW, LPJL, PNS.*

Elusive Time. Reprinted in *BET, CP1994, HI, SR, PNS*, and in a revised version in *CBP.*

It Can Happen. Reprinted in *BET, CP1994.*

> JL note:
> amor lux est—[Latin] love is light.
> > c'etait un coup foudre—[French] it was a bolt from the blue [said Ariane...
>].
> > ganz wie ein blitz—[German] [completely] like lightning. [*CP1994*]

The Maker of Dreams. Reprinted in *BET, CP1994.*

The Bird of Endless Time. Reprinted in *BET, CP1994, SW, SR, PNS,* and in a revised version in *LPJL, CBP.*

> JL note (*BET*); repeated in full in *CP1994, SR, PNS,* and shortened in *LPJL, CPB.*
> Kalpa: in Hinduism, an eon, a vast period of time that encompasses the creation and dissolution of a universe.
>
> Kalpa: in Hinduism an eon.

The Kiss. Reprinted in *BET, CP1994, HI.*

> JL note:
> Zephyrus—in Greek mythology, the personification of the West Wind; the father of Achilles' horses, Xanthus and Balius. [*CP1994*]

By the Numbers. Reprinted in *BET, CP1994.*

> JL note:
> Rexroth—Kenneth Rexroth (1905–82), American man of letters who wrote poems about the California Sierras.
> > Gödel's Proof—Kurt Gödel (1906–78), Czech-American mathematician and logician. He proved that various branches of mathematics are based in part on propositions that are not provable within mathematics itself.
> > Sikkim—a mountainous region in northeast India. Buddhism is the state religion, though most of the inhabitants are Hindus. [*CP1994*]

The Atman of Sleep. Reprinted in *CP1994, LPJL.*

> JL note (*CP1994*); repeated in *LPJL* (omission in brackets):
> Atman—Sanskrit: breath, [self,] soul.

In Half Darkness. Reprinted in *BET, CP1994, LPJL, PNS.*

My Delights. No reprint.

I Love to See You. Reprinted in *BET, CP1994.*

Her Reply. Reprinted in *BET, CP1994.*

The Beautiful One. Reprinted in *BET, CP1994.*

Dedication, "For Charles Simic," added in *CP1994.*

Love's Altar. Reprinted in *A, CP1994, LPJL.*

The Unanswerable Question. Reprinted in *BET, CP1994, LPJL, PNS.*

JL note (*K*); repeated in *BET, PNS:*
The last two lines echo the language of Pound's Cavalcanti translations.

The Importance of Silence. Reprinted in *BET, CP1994, HI, LPJL.*

The Hand Trick. Reprinted in *BET, CP1994.*

To Love Is to Hold Dear. No reprint.

Rhyme. Reprinted in *BET, CP1994, LPJL.*

Our Meetings. Reprinted in *BET, CP1994, SW, PNS.*

JL note (*K*); repeated in *BET, CP1994* (additions in brackets), *PNS.*
The translation from the Bengali of Radha's hymn to Krishna is from Levertov
& Dimock: *In Praise of Krishna.*

The duet in German is from Act 1, Scene 5 of Wagner's libretto for *Tristan und Isolde.*

> Passionate longing-song
> Swelling and blooming
> Languishing love
> glow of high bliss
> deep in the heart
> jubilant desire...

Bertrand de Born's compleynte when Maheut de Montagnac has given him gate follows the text of Roubaud's anthology, *Les Troubadours.*

> Lady, since you no longer care for me
> and have sent me away for no good reason
> I don't know where to look for love

because never will there be such rich joy for me
or ever found again in your likeness
Since there cannot be a lady the equal
of the one I've lost
I never want to have a lover again.

[Krishna—one of the most important gods in the Hindu pantheon, the eighth avatar (earthly incarnation) of the god Vishnu. Legend has it that he was born on a lotus leaf and grew up near Vrindaban in Bengal as a cowherd. He fell in love with Radha, most beautiful of the *gopis* (cowherd girls), a subject much celebrated in Indian art and poetry.]

[Bertrand de Born—the Provençal troubadour.]

See "She's Not Exactly Like You," p. 382, and note.

Still Pond No More Moving. Reprinted in *BET, CP1994.*

When I'm Missing You. Reprinted in *CP1994.*

JL note:
Mélisande—in Debussy's opera *Pelléas et Mélisande* she sings the aria "Mes longs cheveux descendent" as she lets her long hair down from the castle tower to Pelléas who is waiting in the garden below. [*CP1994*]

Eyes Closed. No reprint.

The Enlacement. Reprinted in *BET, CP1994, LPJL, PNS.*

The Smallest Blessing. Reprinted in *BET, CP1994.*

The Gifts. No reprint.

The Revenants. Reprinted in *BET, CP1994, PNS.*

JL note (*K*); repeated in *BET, CP1994* (additions in brackets), *PNS.*
[Paolo & Francesca—young lovers in Dante's *Inferno.*]
" . . . Nessun maggior dolore
Che ricordarsi del tempo felice
Ne le miseria . . . "
[No greater grief is there to remember
a happy time in a time of misery.]
—Dante: *Inferno*, 121–23

The Poems Seen as a Shell Game. Reprinted in *CP1994.*

The Sorrow of Smindyrides. Reprinted in *BET, CP1994*.

A Shard of History. Reprinted in *BET, CP1994*.

> JL note:
> the false Dmitri—a complicated bit of 16th-century Russian history in the
> days of Ivan the Terrible and Boris Godunov. When a czarevich was murdered
> four "false Dmitris" appeared to battle for the throne. [*CP1994*]

Enigma Variations. No reprint.

Somewhere in France. Reprinted in *BET, CP1994*.

> JL note:
> Stendhal—pseudonym of Marie Henri Beyle (1783–1842), France's greatest
> novelist of his time. *The Red and the Black; The Charterhouse of Parma.* [*CP1994*]

A Parable. Reprinted in *BET*.

Parenthesis. Reprinted in *BET*.

The Inn at Kirchstetten. Reprinted in *BET, CP1994, PNS*.

> **Dichtungen.** German: "Poems."
> **How can I thank B for her ear, her mind, her affection?** Changed to
> ". . . thank you B, for your ear, your mind, your affection?" in *BET, CP1994,
> PNS*.
> **little crimes so she.** Changed to "little crimes so you" in *BET, CP1994,
> PNS*.
> **The sound of the rain on the window. . . .** Etc. Entire paragraph omitted
> in *PNS*.
> **She was disgusted . . . her. . . .** Changed to "You . . . you. . . . " in *BET,
> CP1994, PNS*.
> **Sometimes she would say.** Changed to "Sometimes you would say" in
> *BET, CP1994, PNS*.

> JL note:
> Georg Trakl—(1887–1914) Austrian poet, one of the best writing in German
> of his time; a difficult life, he was tormented by alcohol, drugs, and a passion
> for his little sister, and killed himself in the end. [*CP1994*]

The Drawing Lesson. Reprinted in *BET, CP1994*.
Dedication, "For Vanessa," added in *CP1994*.

A Book About Nothing. Reprinted in *BET*.

> JL note (*K*); repeated in *BET*; editor's translation in brackets.
> These verses take off from bits of Flaubert's correspondence. On 16 January 1852 he wrote to his impossible girlfriend Louise Colet: "Ce qui semble beau, ce que je voudrais faire, c'est un livre sur rien, un livre sans attache extérieure..." ["What I think is good, what I would like to do, is a book about nothing, a book without a link to anything beyond itself..."] and on 8 February 1852 he told her that he didn't want there to be a single authorial comment. To his great friend George Sand he wrote on 5 December 1866: "Je trouve même qu'un romancier *n'a pas le droit d'exprimer son opinion* sur quoi ce soit. Est-ce que le bon Dieu l'a jamais, son opinion?" ["I also think that a novelist *doesn't have the right to express his opinion* about anything. Did the good Lord ever say, 'in my opinion'?"]

Instructions. Reprinted in *BET*
om mani padme hum. Sanskrit: "hail to the jewel in the lotus."

The Inviolable Maiden. Reprinted in *BET, CP1994*.
As JL hints in the "Editor's Note," the Greek phrases are strange and largely incomprehensible.

> JL note, appended to the "Editor's Note" in *CP1994*:
> The poem parodies the stories and style of Sir Thomas Malory's 15th-century classic, the *Morte Darthur*, our basic source for the Arthurian legends. Morgen le Fay, a sorceress, was the treacherous sister of King Arthur.

In the Ballet. Reprinted in *BET, CP1994*.

A Second Person. No reprint.

The Sense of It. No reprint.

THE BIRD OF ENDLESS TIME (1989)

> Acknowledgments (copyright page):
> Some of these poems first appeared in *The American Voice, Antaeus, Chelsea, Conjunctions, Exquisite Corpse, Interim, Kentucky Poetry Review, New American Writing, New York Quarterly, Paris Review, Poetry, The Quarterly, Scripsi, Sud, Third Rail, West Coast Review, The Yale Review,* and in the book *Kollemata* (Stinehour Press).

> Dedication:
> FOR EDOUARD RODITI

Epigraph:

"The meanings in language are not original,
any more than the sounds;
They accrue from all the generations of human use."
—ROBERT DUNCAN

A "Biographical Note" precedes the colophon page at the back of the book:
Born October 30, 1914, in Pittsburgh, James Laughlin began publishing po-
etry, and short stories, while in his teens, and as a twenty-two-year-old soph-
omore at Harvard University, he founded New Directions in 1936. Over the
past fifty years, he has served as the publisher of Ezra Pound, H.D., William
Carlos Williams, Henry Miller, Kenneth Rexroth, Denise Levertov, Gary Sny-
der, and many others. As a champion of literature in translation, New Direc-
tions has published Boris Pasternak, Vladimir Nabokov, Pablo Neruda,
Octavio Paz, and other writers from all over the world.

Laughlin's *Selected Poems* was published by City Lights Books in 1986,
and Copper Canyon Press published new poems, *The Owl of Minerva*, in 1987.
He has been awarded honorary degrees from Colgate University, Hamilton
College, Duquesne University, Cornell (Iowa), Yale University, and Brown
University. He has received the American Academy and Institute Award for
Distinguished Service to the Arts, the Annual PEN Publisher Citation, the
National Arts Club Medal of Honor for Literature, and in 1988 was awarded
the Prix Jean Malrieu for the French translation of his poems.

Laughlin presently divides his time between his home in Connecticut
and the New Directions offices in New York City.

Colophon:

The type in this book is Fournier.
Composition is by The Typeworks, in Vancouver.
Book design by Tree Swenson.
Book manufactured by McNaughton & Gunn.

Blood. No reprint.

The Cold. Reprinted in *CP1994*.

The Golden Years. No reprint.

The Waiters' Ballet. Reprinted in *CP1994*.

JL note:
Grand Véfours—a famous restaurant in Paris; the décor goes back to the 18th
century.

mudras—the symbolical hand gestures in Indian Bharat Natyam danc-
ing. [*CP1994*]

After Hardy. No reprint.

Am I Not Lucky. No reprint.

At the Boule d'Or. Reprinted in *CP1994, PNS.*

Ein Kleines Herzlied / A Little Heartsong. German, reprinted in *CP1994,* together with JL's English version.

The Blue Footprints. Reprinted in *CP1994.*

Danger / Road Under Repair. Reprinted in *CP1994.*

An Invitation. No reprint.

Ever So. Reprinted in *CP1994, SW.*

Mei Axis Mundi. Reprinted in *CP1994, HI, SW.*

> JL note:
> Mei Axis Mundi—{Latin:] the axis of my world.
>> Sumeru—Mount Sumeru; symbolically, the center of the Cosmos in the mandalas of Tibetan Buddhism.
>> Taishan—the sacred peak of China. [*CP1994*]

The Ritual. No reprint.
> **venerandam.** Latin: "to be revered."
> **choros nympharum.** Mixed Greek and Latin: "chorus of nymphs."
> **Hymni Deorum.** Latin: "Hymns of the Gods."
> Cf. Ezra Pound, *Personae*, "Ur"-Canto III, final stanza.

A Sweet Kiss. Reprinted in *CP1994.*

Such Grace. No reprint.

The First Night. Reprinted in *CP1994, SL, HI,* and in a new version in *CBP.*

Floating Free. Reprinted in *CP1994.*

Prolepsis. No reprint.

The Offering. No reprint.

It's Indelicate. Reprinted in *CP1994*.

Her Letters. Reprinted in *CP1994, PNS*.
    chaleur. French: "warmth."

    JL note (*BET*); reprinted in *CP1994* (with JL's translation), *PNS*:
Elle n'en continuait pas moins à lui écrire des lettres amoureuses, en vertu de
cette idée qu'une femme doit toujours écrire à son amant.

    Mais, en écrivant, elle percevait un autre homme, un fântome fait de ses
plus ardent souvenirs…
                    —Emma's letters to Léon, *Madame Bovary*

    She still continued to write him love letters by virtue of her idea that a
woman should always be writing to her lover.
    But in writing she perceived a different man, a phantom constructed
from her most ardent memories.

The Long Night. Reprinted in *CP1994*.

    JL note:
Madame de Maintenon—(1635–1719), mistress and then second wife of Louis
XIV, the Sun King. [*CP1994*]

In the Salzkammergut. Reprinted in *CP1994*.

    JL note:
"Koos"—J.J. Van der Leeuw, the Dutch philosopher and theosophist, author
of *The Fire of Creation* and *Gods in Exile*. In H.D.'s *Tribute to Freud*, "Koos" Van
der Leeuw is the man whom H.D. often met coming down the stairway at
Berggasse 19 from Freud's office. His wealth came from his family's plantation
in Sumatra. He was killed when he tried to fly solo from Vienna to Capetown
and crashed in the Atlas.
    Salzkammergut—the region of mountain lakes above Salzburg. [*CP1994*]

    Cf. *B*, pages 116–21.

It's March. Reprinted in *CP1994, PNS*.

    JL note:
Brueghel—Pieter Brueghel (1525–69), the Flemish genre painter. [*CP1994*]

Poets. Reprinted in *CP1994*.

The Unenlightened Face. Reprinted in *CP1994*.

> JL note:
> In Buddhist doctrine "attachment" to the material things in life is the principal impediment to spiritual development. [*CP1994*]

Thumbs Up! No reprint.

At Benares. Reprinted in *CP1994*.

> JL note:
> Benares—one of the most holy places of Hindu India, where thousands come to purify themselves in the filthy water of the river Ganges. [*CP1994*]

The Endless Mirrors. Reprinted in *CP1994*.

Thirteen Ways of Looking at a Lovebird. No reprint.

Then and Now. Reprinted in *CP1994, PNS*.

Hope Springs. Reprinted in *CP1994*.

The Big Clock. No reprint.

God Bless America! Reprinted in *CP1994*.

My Ambition. Reprinted in *CP1994*.
   Euro- / païsche Literatur und La- / teinisches Mittelalter. German: "European Literature and the Latin Middle Ages."

> JL note:
> Edward Dahlberg—(1900–77), American writer, author of *Because I Was Flesh, The Sorrows of Priapus,* etc., unquestionably the most cantankerous writer New Directions has ever published. [*CP1994*]

A Kind of Knowledge. No reprint.

Maledicti in Plebe Sint. Reprinted in a shorter version in *CP1994*, omitting the last three stanzas and with the title changed to "Maledictus in Plebe Sit."
   Title. Latin: "Curses Be on the People."
   sic pallescet lux. Latin: "thus the light shall fade."

JL note:

Maledictus in Plebe Sit—a curse on the people (St. Ambrose).

deconstruction—let the term stand for all the bughouse critical theories from Semiotics to Lacanism which have poisoned English departments for fifteen years. [*CP1994*]

He Dreamed His Death. Reprinted in *CP1994*.

Digging Down to China. Reprinted in *CP1994*.

Hic Jacet. Reprinted in *PNS*.

Title and first line. Latin, translated at the end of the poem: "…here lie ashes / dust and nothingness…."

THE MAN IN THE WALL (1993)

Acknowledgments (copyright page):

Some of these poems first appeared in *Agni, Ambit* (London), *Chelsea, Compost, Conjunctions, Exquisite Corpse, Grand Street, Interim, Kentucky Poetry Review, Light, New American Writing, New Directions in Prose & Poetry 55, The New York Quarterly, Open Eye, Osiris, Paris Review, Parnassus, Pearl* (Denmark), *Poetry, Scripsi* (Australia), *The Three-penny Review, West Coast Line.* "La Tristesse" originally appeared in *The New Yorker*.

The poems in this book were written after the assembling of the *Collected Poems* of 1992.—JL

Despite JL's note concerning the contents of *MW*, a number of the poems do in fact appear in his *Collected Poems*, eventually published in 1994.

Dedication:

FOR GERTRUDE

Frontispiece (facing the title poem):

Photograph by Virginia Schendler

The Man in the Wall. Published in *ND55* (1991); no reprint.

Little Bits of Paper: An Ars Poetica. No reprint.

The New Book. Reprinted in *SW*.

For the Finders Within. Reprinted in *HI, PNS*.

Lines to Be Put into Latin. Reprinted in *CP1994, HI, SL, SW, SR*.

The Figure in the Stone. No reprint.

The Shameful Profession. Reprinted in *CP1994, PNS*.

The Poem Factory. Reprinted in *CP1994, USB*.

The Ewige Weibchen & the Mermaids. No reprint.
Title. "Ewige Weibchen." German: "Eternal Wife."

My Own Name. No reprint.

The Lost Secrets. Reprinted in *CP1994, SL*.

JL note:
Sanskrit—"knowledge" from "I know," held to have been born of the breath of God.
Vedic—from the *Vedas*, early primary scriptures of Hinduism. [*CP1994*]

Grumpus at 78. No reprint.

Knowledge. Reprinted in *CP1994, SW*.

JL note:
Spengler—Oswald Spengler (1880–1936), German historian and philosopher, author of *The Decline of the West*. [*CP1994*]

It Is So Easy. No reprint.

Jack. No reprint.

In My Imagination. Reprinted in *LPJL*.

The Inscription. Reprinted in *SW*.

JL note (*MW*):
(written at the moment of half-consciousness when the dream moves toward thought)

The Creatures of Prometheus. Reprinted in *CP1994*.

JL notes:
The Gulf War. "The Creatures of Prometheus" is the title of a ballet by Beethoven. (*MW*)

The title is that of a ballet by Beethoven.

Prometheus—in Greek mythology he stole fire frôm heaven and brought it down to mankind. In the poem he stands for modern military technology. [*CP1994*]

It Won't Be Long Now. No reprint.

The Flight of Icarus. No reprint.

For more on JL's doppelganger Hiram Handspring, JL's "not-note" for "A Cento from Gary / Ajar's *La Vie Devant Soi*," p. 1059, as well as "Funny Papers by Hiram Handspring," pp. 341–56 and 630–32.

Losing Body Heat. Reprinted in *SW, PNS*.

The Church Ladies. No reprint.

How to Talk About Sex. No reprint.

Hiram Handspring. JL's doppelganger. See above, the note for "The Flight of Icarus," p. 528.

"L'argent n'a pas d'odeur." No reprint.

Title. French: "Money doesn't smell."

JL note (*MW*):
(I first saw *L'Orage* when I was visiting Anne de Biéville at his family's crumbling château in Brittany. To restore the south wing the masterpiece had to be sold to the Margrave of Hesse-Felderstein. The painting can now be seen (Wednesday afternoons only) at Schloss Heldensgluck near Ulm.)

Acid Rain. Reprinted in *LPJL*.

The Bible Says. Reprinted in *SW, LPJL*.

Five Years Ago: Five Lives Ago. No reprint.

The Love-candy Teaser. No reprint.

Time Running Backwards. Reprinted in *PNS*.

The Enchanted Birchtree. No reprint.

For a Clever Young Person. Reprinted in *SL*.

The Respectful Clutch. No reprint.

> jeunes filles bien-élevées. French: "well brought-up young girls."

What the Old Bedouin Told Me. Reprinted in *PNS*.

> JL note (*MW*); repeated in *PNS*:
> In Arabic there is no exact equivalent for our word "history." A Bedouin might
> say, "in my long ago."

Skiing in Tahiti. Reprinted in *HI, SR*.

My Cousin Alexander. No reprint.

The Stranger. Reprinted in *PNS*.

Silentium Aureatum Est. Reprinted in *SL, SW, PNS*.
> Title. Latin: "Silence Is Golden."

An Interrogation. No reprint.

> JL note (*MW*):
> The four words are those sometimes used by doctors in the test for memory
> loss in old people. They are repeated four times in the midst of other talk;
> then the patient is asked what he can remember.

Long and Languorous. Reprinted in *SW, LPJL, PNS*.

The Last Words of Charles Wilson Peale. No reprint.

An Apotropaic Decision. Reprinted in *CP1994, SW*.

Kenneth Rexroth. No reprint. Previously published separately in 1992 as *Electric Rexroth, No. 1* by Tetsuya Taguchi, Kobe, Japan.

The Oracles. Reprinted in *SW*.

The Bonding. Reprinted in *SW*.

The Intruder. No reprint.

Our Dominion. No reprint.

A Problem of Semantics. No reprint.

The Scar. No reprint.

Heart Island. Reprinted in *HI, SR, PNS*.

The Prisoner. Reprinted in *USB*.

It's Spring. No reprint.

> JL note:
> "cyclicals": those suffering from bi-polar illness.

The Sensualist of Pain. No reprint.

The Self-tormentors. No reprint.

The Thinking Machine. Reprinted in *PNS*.
　　Williams's ni- / hil in intellectu quod / non prius in sensu.... See the epigraph for *SNT*, p. 1034, and "Dream Not of Other Worlds," p. 330, and note.

The Vagrant. Reprinted in *CP1994*.

Contra Deconstructionem. No reprint.
　　Title. Latin: "Against Deconstruction."

The English Governess. No reprint.

Two Scenes from the Literary Scene & A Letter. No reprint.

The Aesculapians. No reprint.

What Is Hoped For. No reprint.

Are You Still Alone. Reprinted in *SW*.

The Flemish Double Portrait. Reprinted in *PNS*, with the last stanza omitted.

The Imaginary Diary. Reprinted in *SL*.

The Afterthought. Reprinted in *SW, PNS*.

La Tristesse. Reprinted in *CP1994, SW, PNS*.

> JL note:
> La Tristesse—sorrow.
>> Army prison camp—in 1945 Ezra Pound was detained in the U.S. Army Disciplinary Training Center near Pisa; it was here that some of his finest work, *The Pisan Cantos*, was written.
>> *Tard, très tard*—late, very late in life I came to know you, Sadness.
>> *Les larmes*—I was drowned by the tears I had created.
>> Ovid—(43 B.C.—18 A.D.), one of the greatest of the Latin poets. The *Tristia*, one of his masterpieces, was written when he was exiled to Pontus on the Black Sea for having offended the Emperor Augustus. [*CP1994*]

The Rodent. Reprinted in *CP1994*.

An Attestation. Reprinted in *PNS*.

The Biographer. No reprint.

Agatha. Reprinted in *PNS*.

A Certain Impermeable Person. Reprinted in *SL, PNS*.

> Dedication. Omitted in *SL*.

The Chips Are Flying. No reprint.

> JL note (*MW*):
> Fortran, Cobol, Linda—computer languages.

The Time Stealer. Reprinted in *PNS*.

That Voice. No reprint.
> Cf. "In Trivandrum," *B*, page 255.

The Story of Rhodope. Reprinted in *SW, PNS*.

Catullus xlviii. Reprinted in *HI, SW*.

Cicero Wrote. No reprint.

Blue Booties & Pink Booties. No reprint.

Clutches. Reprinted in *PNS*.

A Door That Opens. No reprint.

Before I Die. Reprinted in *CP1994, PNS*.

> Dedication. Changed in *CP1994* to "In memory of Jeanine Lambert" and in *PNS* to "For Jeanine Lambert."
> Cf. "The Tender Letter," p. 879.

Charles Bernstein. No reprint.

The Moths. Reprinted in *CP1994, PNS*.

To Get to Sleep. No reprint.

The Moving Cloud. No reprint.

The Old Indian. No reprint.

Bless You, Mr. President. Reprinted in *CP1994*.

The Dialogue. No reprint.

At the End. Reprinted in *HI, SW*.

> JL note (*MW*):
> At Benares, on the bank of the Ganges, the bodies of the dead are consumed on pyres of sandalwood.

The Calves. Reprinted in *PNS*.

The Third Life. No reprint.

The Master of Stupidity. No reprint.

> JL note (*MW*):
> (Written in 1991)

Murderer. No reprint.

To Mistress Kate Gill. No reprint.

The Punishment. Reprinted in *USB*.

JL note (*MW*):
For the veracity of this story see page 11 of *The Oxford Companion to Classical Literature*.

Odi et Amo. Reprinted in *SW*.

JL note (*MW*):
Catullus lxxxv

> Odi et amo. Quare id faciam, fortasse requiris.
>   nescio, sed fieri sentio et excrucior.

> I hate and love. Why? You may ask but
> It beats me. I feel it done and ache.
> —Ezra Pound

The Darkened Room. No reprint.

Don't Try to Explain. Reprinted in *SL*.

The Transformation. No reprint.

The Mechanics of Chaos. Reprinted in *CP1994*.

JL note:
Puranic shastras—some of the early Sanskrit scriptures of Hinduism.
Shiva Nataraja—the God Shiva is often represented as Nataraja, the king of dancing. One central legend of Hinduism is that as Nataraja he exemplified the creative principal by "dancing" the creation of the cosmos. In the iconography of this legend his flowing hair stands for the waters of the sacred river Ganges.
Babel—the biblical Tower of Babel with its confusion of many languages.
Cronos—in Greek cosmogenic mythology the creator of the human race.
[*CP1994*]

Ibykus. No reprint.

JL note (*MW*):
The story of the cave is in Book IV of *The Aeneid*.
Ibykus was a native of the Aeolio-Dorian colony of Rhegium in Magna Graecia in the 6th century B.C. He was a lyrical poet who spent part of his life at the court of Polycrates of Samos. In legend, Ibykus was killed by rob-

bers. A flock of cranes was passing overhead and Ibykus called out, "Those cranes will avenge me." One of the robbers, later seeing a flock of cranes, said to his companion, "There go the avengers of Ibykus." This was heard and the murderers were brought to justice. The story is retold in a poem by Schiller.
—*The Oxford Companion to Classical Literature*

Panem et Circenses. No reprint.
Title. Latin: "Bread and Circuses."

The Actress. No reprint.

The Sultan's Justice. Reprinted in *PNS*.

An Amorous Rejoinder. No reprint.

Expectations. No reprint.
JL note (*MW*):
"word the world" / Emerson

Una Ricordanza Tenera. Reprinted in *SW*.
Title. Italian: "A Tender Memory."

Der Rosenkavalier. Reprinted in *SW*.
eier und speck. German: "eggs and bacon."

THE COLLECTED POEMS OF JAMES LAUGHLIN (1994)

Dedication:
for Ann and Gertrude

Acknowledgments (front matter p. ix, following Contents):
The larger part of the poems in this volume are drawn from earlier books, to whose publishers I acknowledge my great debt: *In Another Country* and *Selected Poems 1935–1985*, City Lights Books (Lawrence Ferlinghetti); *Stolen & Contaminated Poems*, Turkey Press (Harry & Sandra Reese); *The Owl of Minerva* and *The Bird of Endless Time*, Copper Canyon Press (Tree Swenson & Sam Hamill); *Angelica, The House of Light*, and *Tabellae*, Grenfell Press (Leslie Miller); *Kollemata*, Stinehour Press; *The Pig*, Perishable Press (Walter Hamady).

Some of these poems first appeared in: *Agenda* (London), *Agni, Akzente* (Munich), *Almanacco dello Specchio* (Milan), *Ambit* (London), *American Poetry, The American Voice, Antaeus, The Antigonish Review* (Nova Scotia), *Approach, Il*

Caffè (Rome), *Caravel* (Mallorca), *Chelsea, City Lights Review, Compass, Conjunctions, Edge* (Tokyo), *Exquisite Corpse, Fantasy, Frank* (Paris), *Grand Street, The Harbor Review, Horizon* (London), *L'Humidité* (Paris), *in'hui* (Paris), *Interim, Iowa Review, Kentucky Poetry Review, Line, Light, Das Lot* (Berlin), *The Nation, New American Writing, New York Quarterly, Nota Bene* (Paris), *Oink, The New Yorker, Open Places, Osiris, Paideuma, Paris Review, El Pez y la Serpiente* (Managua), *Pearl, Ploughshares, Poesia* (Rome), *Poetry, Poetry Australia* (Sydney), *Puckerbrush Review, The Quarterly, San Jose Studies, Scarlet, Scripsi* (Melbourne), *Semi-Colon, Smoke, Steaua* (Bucharest), *Stony Brook, Sud* (Marseille), *Talisman, Ulaznica* (Belgrade), "*Seep*" (Karachi), *Threepenny Review, West Coast Review, The Yale Review*. René Magritte's *Les Amants* is reproduced on page 417, courtesy of the Richard Zeisler Collection, New York.

The poem *Les Amants*, on p. 417 in *CP1994* appears on p. 190 in the present volume.

JL note ("Collaborators," p. xi):

For many years a whimsical doppelgänger known as Hiram Handspring has operated a small poetry factory turning out comic and scurrilous poems written in long-line free verse. He is also reponsible for most of the "picture poems" in this volume, which were executed on a Canon PC-20 Copier. Handspring's name and, in fact, the creation of his identity has been variously attributed to Robert M. Hutchins, one-time director of the Ford Foundation, to the publicist W. H. "Ping" Ferry, and to Professor J. Roger Dane of the University of Saskatoon, Canada.

The poems written in "American French" go back to the year 1929, which was spent in the Swiss School Le Rosey at Rolle on Lake Geneva. Interest in French was revived about 1982 when I met an aristocratic Frenchwoman, Cristine (her nickname was "Variety"), a filmmaker, who was the editor for Lawrence Pitkethly's "Voices and Visions" film of Ezra Pound for which I was adviser. We conversed entirely in French and the sound of the language brought back what I had learned of it in school. I began to write poems in "American French," American because the style of the poems is not classic or often correct French. Many of the words are suggested by English cognates; the metric is not French but is American speech-rhythm cadence. With the aid of the Larousse *Dictionnaire argotique* I amused myself doing a few poems in the Parisian argot. I'm grateful to Barbara Wright, Edouard Roditi, and Variety for corrections in the *soi-disant* French.

Over the years, the poet and critic Hayden Carruth has been my poetry guru. His comments have been invaluable.

JL note ("A Note on Notes," p. xiii):

Much of what these poems do is juxtapose or confront elements of contemporary life with elements from a number of ancient cultures. But with the expansion of many fields of learning, and the exclusion of Latin and Greek from the curriculum, learning is far more specialized these days. This is especially true of the classics. So I have added a number of notes throughtout the book, intended to enlighten and explain references in the poems which may not be obvious to the reader.

> The meanings in language are not original
> any more than the sounds;
> They accrue from all the generations of human use.

> —Robert Duncan

For more on Hiram Handspring, see JL's "not-note" for "A Cento from Gary/Ajar's *Le Vie Devant Soi*," p. 1059, "Funny Papers by Hiram Handspring," pp. 341–56, and pp. 630–32.

JL's "(American) French Poems" are found on pp. 215–66.

I Take a Certain Pride. No reprint.

The Little Dog Laughs. Published in *ND1* (1936) and reprinted only in *CP1994*, where it is mistakenly grouped among poems from *SBP*.

> JL note:
> Credo—I believe that I may understand. (St. Anselm)
> chiliasm—the doctrine of Christ's expected return to reign on earth for 1,000 years.
> credent—they believe so they need not understand. [*CP1994*]

My Granddaughter. No reprint and not previously published; in *CP1994*, incorrectly considered to be from *SP1986*.

A Moment on Earth. No reprint.

Dylan. Reprinted in *PNS*.

Your Early Life. No reprint.

> JL note:
> Montevideo—the capital of Uruguay is on the river Plata.
> Supervielle—Jules Supervielle (1884–1960), one of the most important modern French poets, was born in Montevideo. New Directions published a *Selected Writings* in 1967.
> voleurs—Supervielle's most famous novel was *The Stealer of Children*.
> alcalde—mayor. [*CP1994*]

L'Abécédérien de la Lubricité. Published in *ND51* (1987); no reprint. Editor's translation:

THE ABECEDARIAN OF LUBRICITY

With your permission, I want to ride your *caboose* to rejoin
    Henry Miller in Dijon
I wish to savor your *ass* like the leaves of an artichoke
    with hollandaise sauce
Overwhelmed with lust, I'll grab your *baba*-with-Jamaican rum
Dressed like Monsieur Hulot I'll come downstairs from my
    torture chamber to plunge into your *butt*
I am the counsel for your *rear*, I'll defend you, you won't
    go to the clink
As for *buns*, I prefer croissants, but as concerns yours, they
    suit me fine
When I was very little they'd always give me the *pope's nose* at dinner; now
    that I'm a movie star I have more extravagant needs
My childhood was really tough; my mother warmed my *ass* with strokes of
    her hairbrush; I don't want you to be like mama
Once again I say, I'm a great reader but not hypocritical; I'm a tightwad
    with your *tush*
It's true that the police keep my dossier up-to-date, but I'm not dangerous;
    since you wear only ski pants I don't think you have *split* panties
I have to admit that I don't know much about *hairy asses* but the lines of
    your body are from a drawing by Tintoretto
It's in the *Faubourg* [backside] St. Germain that I often see you with your
    friend Oriane de Guermantes; you too wearing red slippers
Who was *Père Fouttard* [the bogeyman; bum]? I could write his complete
    biography but that would take time. I'm hopeful that his has nothing
    to do with whips; I'm never going to hurt you
Don't worry about *peddling your ass*; I'll make sure that you never have to
    get by like the poor girls in the story of Momo and Madame Rosa
A *miche* [keister], that sounds like niche, which is neat, but also like a fly,
    which isn't. I prefer the first. As for niches [tits], I'm crazy about
    Berenice's left breast when she tries to fit it into her wineglass
You can't do anything with *assholes* that would be filthy or disgusting
    enough, for example, wipe them
Isn't it idiotic to say that a pair of *cheeks* is beautiful? each to his own taste;
    there are people who love to bite them, I know
Yes, I'm a *stupid ass* but it's not you who made me a fool
They say in English, "hoist with his own *pétard*" [bomb; fart]; this happens
    when you get angry over nothing

The *pétoulet* [poop chute] is a rare bird that lives in the far-off jungles of the
Amazon and enjoys a symbiotic bond with ants; there are none in
France except in pornographic books

Someone said I'm a peasant because I eat at six in the evening but I never
in my life munched *bumkin*

As you know, in Latin petra means pierre [rock], but *pétrus* [butt] certainly
has nothing to do with Saint Peter; the Church of Rome isn't founded
on buggery

It's no doubt a problem for the academic philosopher (or for the good Doc-
tor Lacan?): is the *rear end* [lit., rear bridge] more attractive than the
Pont d'Avignon? But it's the bridge of fools [Latin: lit., bridge of
asses] that attracts me most

No, there are silly things that children do, like nibbling a *bottom*, that one
must forget; it's not their fault, they are so curious, and why not, the
body is as inexplicable as life

I hump the *posterior*; always the same thing; it's shitty. I get a little
ashamed: the posterity of Charlemagne loves ass better than pussy.
Skin of my dick, my whammer!

I've always had a need for *quim* [lit., ass with slits], I'm really monomania-
cal, I give them complexes; but one day there will be one who sees
how sympatico I am

You think that *prose* means La Rochefoucauld? Not at all, my pisser, it's
still the story of where the shit comes out; but if it's the asshole, what
is poetry? Tell me that!

That continues with *prosinard* [asshole], same thing; I've had enough of it,
I'm going to look for a whore to enjoy myself

And there's *tail*; it's the same song. They are talkative, these prats, these
dopes. They make me sick

At least *troussequin* [heinie] is a word with some substance. It comes from
trousser, that is to say, to roger a woman. It's not too soon! She was
about to fall asleep

The *chocolate engine*, that's pretty graphic, or as sailors say, "follow the track
of scats"

"Hello, I'm Marilyn Monroe," I was the princess of *fannies* [lit., waltzers], I
knew how to wiggle my ass while walking; all the queens would imi-
tate me

Dirty stuff suits me best, that's when I have luck with girls, when I have
some *ass* and am fucking and really enjoying myself.

JL headnote:
This poem is written in Parisian argot and is untranslatable, which is just as
well as it is pornographic. Its publication caused a scandal for the magazine in
Amiens which printed it. In each segment the word or phrase printed in italics
is a slang term for an erotic part of the body, to which Professor Handspring,

who researched scatology in the most depraved quarters of Paris, has appended a definition or commentary expressed in argot. [*CP1994*]

For Handspring, see JL's "not-note" for "A Cento from Gary/Ajar's *Le Vie Devant Soi,*" p. 1059, "Funny Papers by Hiram Handspring," pp. 341–56, and JL's note on "Collaborators," p. 1132.

JL notes:

N. d. E.: L'auteur a tenu à ce que soit respectée la manière dont il s'exprime en français et dont il use de l'orthographie français. [The author is anxious that the manner in which he expresses himself in French and the French spelling he uses be respected.] [*ND51*]

Sources: François Caradec, *Dictionnaire de français argotique et populaire* [*Dictionary of Slang and Vulgar French*] (Paris, Larousse, 1977); and a few phrases from Émile Ajar (pseud. Romain Gary), *La Vie Devant Soi.*

Method: Free association and punning of sounds & sense, some of it interlingual; punning between normal and argotic meanings of words, as in the last verse between "vase"—"rain" and "vase"—"the anus." Some parodic echoes of Flaubert's *Dictionnaire des Idées Reçues* [*Dictionary of Accepted Ideas*].

Purpose: A comic commentary on anal eroticism and "le culte des fesses" ["ass worship"] in France. [*ND51*, *CP1994*]

Admonition. Reprinted in *HI* and in a revised version in *CBP*, with the title "An Admonition."

Catullus V. No reprint.

In *CP1994*, JL's translation is followed by the original Latin:

V

Vivamus, mea Lesbia, atque amemus,
rumoresque senum severiorum
omnes unius aestimemus assis.
soles occidere et redire possunt:
nobis cum semel occidit brevis lux,
nox est perpetua una dormienda.
da mi basia mille, deinde centum,
dein mille altera, dein secunda centum,
deinde usque altera mille, deinde centum
dein, sum milia multa fecerimus,
conturbabimus illa, ne sciamus,
aut nequis malus invidere possit,
cum tantum sciat esse basiorum.

Deathfear. No reprint.

> JL note:
> godown—in India a storeroom. [*CP1994*]

De Contemptu Mundi. No reprint.

> JL note:
> De Contemptu Mundi—on contempt for the world.
> Bernard of Cluny—an Englishman who became a Cluniac monk and, around 1150, composed a 3000-line poem in Latin hexameters, "On Contempt for the World," which had both vertical and horizontal rhymes.
> hic breve—here briefly we live, here briefly we bewail our lot, here briefly we weep. [*CP1994*]

> See notes for "Among the Roses," pp. 1052–53.

Flavius to Postumia. No reprint.

I Am the Metoposcoper. No reprint.

> JL note:
> Metoposcopy—the art of discovering character from the markings of the forehead. μέτωπον—forehead; οχοπός—the watcher. See Girolamo Cardano: *Metoposcopia*, Paris, 1658. "Cardano should be counted as one of the forerunners of Lombroso's psychiatric criminal types." [*CP1994*]

If a Poet. No reprint.

Folk Wisdom. No reprint.

If You Are Only Flirting. No reprint.

I Like to Think. No reprint.

Is There a Danger. No reprint.

> JL note:
> Medusa—in Greek mythology one of the Gorgons who with their gaze could turn a person into stone. Medusa was mortal, beloved by the sea-god Poseidon, who got her with child. She was slain by the hero Perseus. From her blood came the winged horse Pegasus, a symbol of poetry. [*CP1994*]

I Want to Be Echopractic. No reprint.

I'd Like to Be Putty. Reprinted in *LPJL*.

It Was the First Time. Reprinted in *LPJL* and in revised a version in *SR* and *CBP* with the title "The First Time."

The Last Caress. No reprint.

> JL note:
> agape—from Greek, a love feast among primitive Christians. It ended with the "holy kiss."
> > caritas—from Latin, loving others for the sake of God. [*CP1994*]

The Long-distance Runner. No reprint.

M&K. No reprint.

> JL note:
> after rereading Richard Aldington's *The Love of Myrrhine and Konallis*. [*CP1994*]

Maxima Dona Ferens. No reprint.

> JL note:
> > Maxima Dona Ferens—bearing great gifts.
>
> > Paraphrase of the Latin:
> > The poet hurls so many letters at Lucina he is
> > like a catapult. But his images of her are so incomparable he
> > hopes it means that will be a conjuction of hearts.
>
> The verse is not quantative, such as any schoolboy at Eton or Winchester would be able to produce; the words are simply imposed on an American free-verse cadence. [*CP1994*]

Moon & Sun. No reprint.

> liquefaction—an echo from Herrick's great line in "Upon Julia's Clothes." Robert Herrick (1591–1674).
>
> > When as in silks my Julia goes,
> > Then, then (me thinks) how sweetly flowes
> > That liquefaction of her clothes.
> >
> > Next, when I cast mine eyes and see
> > That brave Vibration each way free;
> > O how that glittering taketh me! [*CP1994*]

Obsession. No reprint.

JL note:
The citations are from Cassell's *Latin Dictionary*.

Terence—(185–159 B.C.), one of the two great Roman comic dramatists. The other was Plautus (254–184 B.C.). Both had considerable influence on English playwrights.

Caesar—Julius Caesar (100–44 B.C.), Roman general and dictator. If you didn't suffer through his *Gallic Wars* in school you will certainly have seen Shakespeare's play about him.

Cicero—(106–43 B.C.), orator, rhetorician, philosopher, politician. A character in Shakespeare's *Julius Caesar*. A stuffed shirt but he had immense influence on writers for many centuries. [*CP1994*]

The Power of Poesy. No reprint.

Corso—Gregory Corso, contemporary American poet, author of *The Happy Birthday of Death, Long Live Man,* etc. His bohemian antics are legendary. [*CP1994*]

She Said in Apology. No reprint.

The Paintings in the Museums of Munich and Vienna. No reprint.

SIC TRANSIT CORPUS MUNDI. Latin: "so passes away the flesh of the world."

MOMENTS ON EARTH. In *CP1994*, this section has the following epigraph and dedication:

> Amor e 'l cor gentil sono una cosa,
>> Sì come il saggio in suo dittare pone,
>> E così esser l'un sanza l'altro osa
>> Com'alma razional sanza ragione.
>> Falli natura quand'è amorosa,
>> Amor per sire e 'l cor per sua magione,
>> Dentro le quai dormendo si riposa
>> Tal volta poca e tal lunga stagione.
> Bieltate appare in saggia donna pui,
>> Che piace a gli occhi sì, che dentro al core
>> Nasce un disio de la cosa piacente;
>> E tanto dura talora in costui,
>> Che fa svegliar lo spirito d'Amore.
>> E simil face in donna omo valente.
>>> —Dante: *La Vita Nuova*, XX

—For Angelica

Love is but one thing with the gentle heart,
    As in the saying of the sage we find.
    Thus one from other cannot apart,
    More than the reason from reasoning mind.
When nature amorous becomes, she makes
    Love then her Lord, the heart his dwelling-place,
    Within which, sleeping, his repose he takes,
    Sometimes for brief, sometimes for longer space.
Beauty doth then in modest dame appear
    Which pleaseth so the eyes, that in the heart
    A longing for the pleasing thing hath birth;
And now and then so long it lasteth there,
    It makes Love's spirit wide awake to start:
    The like in lady doth a man of worth.
                    —Translated by Charles Eliot Norton

She Is So Practical. No reprint.

Nowadays. No reprint.

The Box. No reprint.

The Atman. No reprint.

> JL note:
> Atman—Sanskrit: breath, self, soul.
>   Animula—from the famous poem of the Roman Emperor Hadrian: "charming little wandering soul." [*CP1994*]

Real Bones. No reprint.

> JL note:
> Renoir—Pierre Auguste Renoir (1841–1919), he liked his models plump.
>   Modigliani—Amedeo(1884–1920), he liked them skinny. [*CP1994*]

Building 520, Bellevue. Reprinted in *PNS*.

Sorrow. No reprint.

The Bavarian Gentian. Published in *ND54* (1990) as "The Blue Gentian"; no reprint.

> Dedication added in *CP1994*.

In *ND54*, the second and third stanzas read:

> the alpine meadow a-
> bove Pontresina & with
>
> a kiss pressed it into
> the pages of the book

JL note:
"Bavarian Gentians" is one of the most beautiful poems of D. H. Lawrence.
[*CP1994*]

Can I Catch Up with the Future? No reprint.

The Death Walkers. Published in *ND54* (1990); no reprint.

A Curious Romance. No reprint.

The Dark Mutinous Shannon Waves. Reprint in *SW*.

JL note:
The last three lines are from the ending of Joyce's story "The Dead." [*CP1994*]

The Deep Pool. Published in *ND54* (1990). No reprint.

For the First Time. No reprint.

The Holy Rivers. Published in *ND54* (1990). No reprint.

I Cannot Command You. No reprint.

In Egypt's Land. No reprint.

Floating. No reprint.

She Asks Me. No reprint.

Layers. No reprint.

JL note:
ashram—Sanskrit, a hermitage. The third in the Brahmanical four stages of
life: the student, the householder, the hermit, the homeless mendicant.
[*CP1994*]

My Instructions. Published in *ND54* (1990); no reprint.

> JL note:
> Pound / Williams / Rexroth [*ND54, CP1994*]

Merry Madness Hall. No reprint.

> JL note:
> maharishis—followers of the Hindu guru.
>   kathakali—folk-dance dramas of South India; the plots are based on stories from the legendary *Ramayana*.
>   Bosch—the great painting *The Garden of Earthly Delights* by the Flemish painter Hieronymus Bosch (1450–1516) is in the Prado in Madrid. [*CP1994*]

Now Strike the Golden Lyres Again. Reprinted in *SW*.

> JL note:
> (The title is from Dryden's "Alexander's Feast" in the *Ode in Honour of St. Cecilia's Day*.) [*CP1994*]

Reading the Obituary Page in *The Times*. No reprint.

> JL note:
> Euclid—the 4th-century Greek mathematician whose deductive system founded geometry. [*CP1994*]

Remembrance. Reprinted in *LPJL*.

> JL note:
> Sankt Wolfgang—a lake in the Salzkammergut region above Salzburg.
>   Belvedere—the gardens of the Belvedere Palace in Vienna. [*CP1994*]

A Sleepless Night. No reprint.

> JL note:
> Delmore—Delmore Schwartz (1913–66), American man of letters. Some of his books were published by New Directions. [*CP1994*]

The Sacks. No reprint.

The Scribe. No reprint.

> JL note:
> Mara—Sanskrit, the personification of evil, an enemy of the Buddha who tried to tempt him from the path of enlightenment.

Cynthia Zarin wrote the profile of JL which appeared in *The New Yorker*, March 23, 1992. [*CP1994*]

Out in the Pasture. No reprint.

Snow in May. No reprint.

Temporary Poems.

JL note:
Johnson: *The Rambler*, 1751. [*CP1994*]

The Stranger in the House. No reprint.

The Tragedy of Time. No reprint.

The Prisoner's Song. No reprint.

Two Children. No reprint.

Your Eyes. No reprint.

JL note:
black water—high-caste Brahmins in India are forbidden to cross the ocean.
Sita—wife of Rama in the 3rd-century Sanskrit epic the *Ramayana*.
Patna—a city in Bihar on the Ganges in northeast India. [*CP1994*]

What Matters. No reprint.

The Welcome. No reprint.

JL note:
Proclus—a character in *The Greek Anthology*.
Simonides—a great Greek lyric poet (556–468 B.C.).
Meleager—Meleager of Gadara, a poet renowned for his elegaics on love and death (*circa* 60 B.C.).
stepped ashore—the spirits in Elysium are welcoming a newcomer as he crosses the river Styx. [*CP1994*]

Two Parables from *The Ocean of Story*. No reprint.
The first section, "Story of the Snake Who Told His Secret to a Woman," was first collected separately in *MW* with the title, "A Parable from *The Ocean of Story*.

JL note (the first entry also appears in *MW*):
Adapted from the Tawney-Penzer translation of Somadeva's *Katha Sarit Sagara* (Sanskrit, 3rd century A.D.).

Garuda—in Hindu legend the "carrier" of the god Vishnu. Today the name of the Indonesian national airline is Garuda.

nagas—in Hindu mythology the nagas were a fabulous race of snakes who could take on human form.

"The Fool and the Cakes" is adapted from *Avadanas* 66 of the *Panchatantra*. [*CP1994*]

Crucifixion in the Desert. No reprint.

JL note:
The Gulf War. [*CP1994*]

Ave Atque Vale. Reprinted in *PNS*.
Title. Latin: "Hail and Farewell."

Experience of Blood. Reprinted in *PNS*.

The Empty Room. Reprinted in *PNS*.

A SECRET LANGUAGE (1994)

Acknowledgments (copyright page):
Some of these poems were first published by New Directions, Copper Canyon Press, Moyer Bell, Grenfell Press, *Ambit* and *The New York Quarterly*.

The book includes six woodcuts by Vanessa Jackson.

Colophon:

THIS book was designed,
printed and published
in a limited edition
of 200 copies by
Penelope Hughes-Stanton
at the Cast Iron Press,
1 Morocco Street,
London SE1 3HB.
The type, Monotype
Baskerville, was cast by
Brian Hubbard.
The paper is

mould-made Somerset.
The book was bound by
the Fine Bindery.

A Secret Language. Reprinted in *CR, LPJL, PNS.*

In *CR* and *LPJL*, the poem is arranged without couplets, with added
punctuation and first lines capitalized:

> I wish I could talk to your body
> Less cautiously; I mean in a
> Language as forthright as its
> Beauty deserves. Of course,
> When we make love there is the
> Communication of touch, fingers
> On Flesh, lips on innermost
> Flesh, but surely there must be
> A kind of speech, body in body,
> That is even deeper than such
> Surface touching, a language
> I haven't yet learned, or haven't
> Learned well enough, hard as
> I've tried. Will I ever master
> That secret language for you?

Does Love Love Itself. Reprinted in *CR.*

In *CR*, the poem is arranged without couplets, with added punctuation
and first lines capitalized:

> DOES LOVE LOVE ITSELF
>
> The most? Sometimes I've suspected
> That may be true. A new person comes
> Into my life (and I into hers). We
> Are together as much as possible,
> Discovering who we are and what we
> Can be to each other. No day but has
> Its little adventure of the feelings.
> But then as we become more habitual,
> The thought may occur: what is it
> That is really taking place? Am I
> In love only with her, or am I,
> Like the insatiable Don in Mozart's
> Opera, infatuated with the idea of

Being in love again, of being
Attached to someone new? Is the god
Eros itself self-regardant? That busybody
Of the myths, did he, like Narcissus,
Become his own mirror? Does love
Love itself the most?

JL note:
Narcissus: in Greek mythology, a beautiful youth who fell in love with his own image in a forest pool. He died of his vanity. The story is in Ovid's *Metamorphoses*. [CR]

THE COUNTRY ROAD (1995)

Acknowledgments:
Some of these poems first appeared in *Agenda* (London), *Agni, Ambit* (London), *American Verse, Boulevard, Chelsea, Conjunctions, Exquisite Corpse, Grand Street, Harvard Magazine, Harvard Review, Hudson Review, Interim, Iowa Review, Loyalhanna Review, The New Yorker, Parnassus, Sulfur, Threepenny Review, Vuelta* (Mexico City), and *The Yale Review.*

Book design by Tree Swenson.
Cover painting, *The Country Road*, is by Marjorie Phillips.

Dedication:

for

LEILA & DANIEL

The Departure. Reprinted in *PNS*.

The Revenant. No reprint.

JL note:
Revenant: one who returns after death. [CR]

Is Memory. Reprinted in *PNS*.

There's Never a Never. Reprinted in *HI, LPJL*.

Who Is She? Who Was She? No reprint.

Here Is My Hand. No reprint.

Anima Mea. Reprinted in *PH, LF, LPJL, PNS*.

> JL note:
> Anima Mea: my soul. [*CR, PNS*]

Little Scraps of Love. Reprinted in *LPJL*.

The Search. Reprinted in *PNS*.

The Prankster. No reprint.

> JL note:
> Eros: in mythology the boy god whose arrows kindled love.
> Apelles: A Greek of the 4th century B.C., considered the greatest painter of antiquity.
>   The other Greek names are fictitious. [*CR*]

The Country Road. Reprinted in *PNS*.

> JL note:
> Oil painting of *The Country Road* was done by Marjorie Phillips in Western
> Pennsylvania about 1940. [*CR*]

A Florilegium. Reprinted in *PNS*.

> JL note:
> Florilegium: a collection of flowers.
>   Phaëthon: in Greek mythology the son of Helios, the sun, who met his
>   death trying to drive his father's chariot of horses across the sky.
>   Anthea: my name for my muse. [*CR, PNS*]

In the Meadow. No reprint.

Bittersweet. No reprint.

Clouds Over the Sun. No reprint.

"When I Was a Boy with Never a Crack in My Heart." Reprinted in
PNS.

> JL note:
> "When I was a boy...": from Yeats, "The Meditation of the Old Fisherman"
> [*CR*]
>   Title: from Yeats, "The Meditation of the Old Fisherman." [*PNS*]

For another use by JL of the Yeats poem, see *B*, pp. 292–93.

They Are Suspended. No reprint.

Why? No reprint.

The Rain on the Roof. No reprint.

> JL note:
> "small talk of the rain": Thom Gunn. [CR]

Catullus XXXII. No reprint.

> JL note:
> If the elegant Latin euphemisms are converted to U.S. colloquial, this is what the poem says. [CR]

Why Does Love Happen? Reprinted in *LPJL*.
my **love.** Changed to *"your* love" in *LPJL*.

The Lost Song. Reprinted in *LF, LPJL*.

> JL note:
> "Made out of a mouthful of air": Yeats, "He Thinks of Those Who Have Spoken Evil of His Beloved." [CR]
> > The quoted second line is from William Butler Yeats. [*LPJL*]

Three Kinds of People. No reprint.

The Woman in the Painting. No reprint.

The Trophy Wives. No reprint.

> JL note:
> "Conspicuous waste," as Thorstein Veblen described it.
> > Thorstein Veblen: American economist and social critic (1857–1929).
> He pioneered in studying the role of technicians in modern society. [CR]

A Difficult Life. No reprint.

In the Secret Garden. No reprint.

Mr. Here & Now. No reprint.
Cf. Haecceity." p. 167.

A Loved Book. No reprint.

How Did Laura Treat Petrarch? Reprinted in *PNS*.

JL note (omission in *PNS* in brackets):
Petrarch: Francesco Petrarca (1304–74), the great Italian poet and humanist of the Renaissance. His sonnets immortalized the anonymous "Madonna Laura," his lifelong inspiration, who may have been the wife of a Provençal nobleman.
["La bella giovanetta, ch'ora è donna....The beautiful girl that was my lady...."] [*CR, PNS*]

The Mercy in It. Reprinted in *MI, PNS*

JL note:
Parody of Yeats. [*CR, PNS*]

Permanet Memoria. Reprinted in *PNS*.

JL note:
Permanet Memoria: the survival of memory. [*CR, PNS*]

Grandfather. No reprint.

It's Difficult. No reprint.

JL note:
Idiotic French girl: Flaubert's Madame Bovary.
The Greek girls are all in Ovid's *Metamorphoses*.
love-silly Russian woman: Tolstoy's Anna Karenina. [*CR*]

A Toast to the Forgotten Poets. No reprint.

JL note:
Simonides and Alcaeus were famous Greek poets; Horace and Catullus were Roman.
The Pléiade: a group of neoclassical French poets in the 16th century; Ronsard and du Bellay were the most famous.
Diarchus, Stereus, Ladoule, and Jarvis are all fictitious. [*CR*]

Some Amatory Epigrams from *The Greek Anthology*. Reprinted in *PNS*.

JL note:
the Kyprian: Aphrodite was born on Cyprus.
Thetis: in Greek mythology one of the Nereids (sea nymphs), the mother of Achilles. [*CR, PNS*]

These translations were originally intended as a "classical correlative" to the "Melissa" section of JL's verse memoir, *Byways*. See *B*, pp. 316–19.

The Apokatastasis. No reprint.

Title. Greek: "return, restoration."

JL note:

Unamuno: Miguel de Unamuno (1864–1936), Spanish existential philosopher.
Sappho et al.: poets of different times and cultures.
Olympia: a plain in Greece that was an important religious center during antiquity. [CR]

Rubbing Dry Sticks. No reprint.

JL note:

Hymen: in Greek mythology Hymen, son of Apollo and Urania, is the god of marriage. "Hymenaeus Io" is the refrain in Catullus's epithalamium for the wedding of his friend Mallius. [CR]

Her Hair. No reprint.

JL note:

Berenike: in a poem by Callimachus she is the wife of Ptolemy III, the king of Egypt. It's a long story, but her comely tresses end up as a constellation in the night sky. See Catullus LXVI, the "Coma Berenices" ("The Lock of Berenike"), Pope's *Rape of the Lock*, and Racine's play *Bérénice*, in which she has become the lover of the Roman Emperor Titus. [CR]

Penelope Venit Abit Helene. Reprinted in *PNS*.

JL note:

Update of a famous poem by Martial. A noble Roman lady goes to the baths at Baiae, which were notorious for loose morals. She enters the place as virtuous as Penelope, the wife of Ulysses, but leaves it a slut like Helen of Troy. [CP, PNS]

The Wood Nymph. Reprinted in *PNS*.

JL note:

Melissa and Euclidon: fictitious characters. [CR, PNS]

L'Englouti. No reprint.

JL note:

L'Englouti: the drowned man.
The Greek characters are fictitious. [CR, PNS]

Her Heart. Reprinted in *PNS*.

> JL note:
> Menippus et al.: fictitious characters.
> > Aurangzeb: 17th-century Mogul emperor of India. A tough nut; he gained the throne by defeating his three brothers and imprisoning his father, Shah Jahan. [*CR, PNS*]

She Does Not Write. Reprinted in *PH*.

> JL note:
> Un fardeau grave; a heavy burden.
> > Des larmes de tendresse: tears of tenderness.
> > Aucun petit mot....: not even a word to tell me she's thinking of me.
> [*CR*]

A Room in Darkness. Reprinted in *LPJL*.

> JL note:
> The first line comes from William Carlos Williams, "Complaint." [*CR, LPJL*]

Believe Me. No reprint.

The Immanence of Your Body. No reprint.

> JL note:
> *Four Last Songs*: by Richard Straus, Schwartzkopf singing them. [*CR*]

La Vita Nova. Reprinted in *HI*.
Title. Italian: "The New Life."

Eros Ridens. No reprint.

> JL note:
> Eros Ridens: the love god is laughing. [*CR*]

The Wrong Magic. No reprint.

The Change. No reprint.

Do They Make Love? No reprint.

By the Irish Sea. Reprinted in *LF*.

> JL note:
> The Pale: in the 14th century the English, who controlled the land around

Dublin, built a great wooden fence, many miles long, to protect themselves from the wild Irish, whence the saying "beyond the pale."

Bonnie Prince Charlie: Charles Stuart, Scots "Pretender" to the throne of England (1720–88). [CR]

The Rising Mist at Ard Na Sidhe. Reprinted in *LF, PNS*.

JL note:
alba: Provençal, the dawn.
Tá ceo bog....: repeats the title in Irish. [CR]

Lost. Reprinted in *PNS*.

Attracted by the Light. Reprinted in *LPJL*.

JL note:
Jain: member of an Indian sect, a branch of Hinduism, which arose in the 6th century. Jains believe that no living thing should be killed, not even a worm or a bug. [CR]

De Contemptu Mortis. Reprinted in *PNS*.

JL note:
De Contemptu Mortis: in contempt of death. [CR, PNS]

A Troubling Case of Agnosia. No reprint.

JL note:
Agnosia: in psychopathology, loss of the ability to recognize familiar persons or objects. [CR]

Imprisoned. Reprinted in *PNS*.

JL note:
quare: Irish dialect, queer. [CR, PNS]

A Winter's Night. Reprinted in *PH, LF, SR*.

The Longest Year. No reprint.

JL note:
Persephone: in Greek mythology, the goddess of fertility. She was kidnapped by Pluto, god of the underworld, but won the right to return to earth for eight months each year. Her return symbolizes the coming of spring. She is celebrated in the cult of the Eleusinian mysteries. [CR]

Waiting for Tartuffe. No reprint.

> JL note:
> Tartuffe: the pious hypocrite—scoundrel, swindler, liar, lecher—in Molière's play. [CR]

The Invisible Person. Reprinted in *PNS.*

As Long. No reprint.

The Exogamist. No reprint.
  glaukopis Kupris. Greek: "gleaming-eyed Cyprian (Aphrodite)."

> JL note:
> Exogamy: marriage outside of a specific tribe. [CR]

Canso. No reprint.

> JL note:
> Canso: Provençal, a troubadour love song. [CR]

So Albertine. No reprint.

> JL note:
> Albertine: the girl Proust loved so much was really a male taxi driver.
> le replapat….: Paris argot; put modestly it says: boredom copies itself in various ways and our heads lead us where we will. [CR]

Homage to Federico Fellini. Reprinted in *PH, LF.*

> JL note:
> Fellini: Federico Fellini (1920–93), the great Italian film director whose scripts ask so many tantalizing questions. [CR]

The Hitchhiker. No reprint.

> JL note:
> In Wagner's Good Friday opera about the Knights of the Holy Grail, a main theme is the revelation that the stranger, Parsifal, is the predicted "innocent fool" who will heal the wounds of Amfortas, the leader of the knights. [CR]

The Least You Could Do. No reprint.

The Lotophagoi. No reprint.

JL note:

Nine days I drifted on the teeming sea / before dangerous high winds. Upon the tenth / we came to the coastline of the Lotos Eaters, / who live upon the flower. We landed there / to take on water. All ships' companies / mustered alongside for the midday meal. / Then I sent out two picked men and a runner / to learn what race of men that land sustained. / They fell in, soon enough, with Lotos Eaters, who showed no will to do us harm, only / offering the sweet Lotos to our friends— / but those who ate the honeyed plant, the Lotos, / never cared to report, nor to return: / they longed to stay forever, browsing on / that native bloom, forgetful of their homeland.

Odyssey, Book IX, 83–97
Tr. Robert Fitzgerald
[CR]

Two Fables from *The Ocean of Story*. Reprinted in *PNS*.

JL note:

sadhu: Sanskrit, ascetic or hermit.

lingam: Sanskrit, the phallic column in shrines under which Siva (Shiva) the destroyer-creator god of Hinduism is usually worshiped. [CR, PNS]

Haiku. Reprinted in *HI*.

In *HI*, a fourth line is added:

At eighty the sands of time.

The Old Men. No reprint.

In the Nursery. No reprint.

The Wandering Words. No reprint.

JL note:

André Breton: the leader of the French Surrealist movement (1896–1966). [CR]

Benignus Quam Doctus. No reprint.

JL note:

Benignus Quam Doctus: as kind as he is learned. [CR]

My Head's Trip. No reprint.

The Day I Was Dead. No reprint.

The book includes twenty-three wood engravings by M. L. Breton.

Dedication:

This book, in which random images and
apothegms indulge themselves in a game
of free associations, is dedicated to

Terry Halliday

Colophon:

HEART ISLAND was printed on Nideggen and Kitakata
papers. The type is Walbaum, cast by Michael Bixler.
The wood engravings, reproduced here from polymer
plates, were made by M. L. Breton whose work appears
in the 1863 edition of *Dictionnaire Infernal* published
by Jacques Collin de Plancy. De Plancy was a compiler
of works about medieval literature, occult sciences and
mythology. Originally published in 1818, it was revised
and reprinted several times. All design, printing and
binding by Sandra and Harry Reese. The edition is
226 copies of which 200 are signed and numbered.
This is author presentation copy letter—

The Happy Poets. Reprinted in *SR, PNS*.

The Two of Them. Reprinted in *SR, PNS*.

In Scandivania. Reprinted in *SR, PNS*.

You're Trouble. Reprinted in *SR, PNS*.

The Old Man's Lament. Reprinted in *SR, PNS*.

The Voyeur. Reprinted in *SR*.

In the High Street of Tralee. Reprinted in *SR*.

Passport Size Will Do. Reprinted in *SR*.

At the Post Office. Reprinted in *SR, PNS*.

I Suppose. Reprinted in *SR, PNS.*

Death Lurches Toward Me. Reprinted in *SR.*

A Visit to Paris. Reprinted in *SR.*

THE MUSIC OF IDEAS (1995)

Dedication:

for Vanessa & John

Colophon:

Three hundred copies of *The Music of Ideas* were
printed on a 1920 C&P treadle-operated letterpress.
Of these, 26 copies, lettered A-Z, & signed by the
author, printer, & binder, were printed on Rives
Lightweight & bound by hand into cloth & paper
over boards. The remainder of the edition was
printed on Mohawk letterpress, & bound by hand
into full cloth over boards. The type is Caslon 337,
set by Jim Rimmer of Pie Tree Press & Typefoundry.

This project was completed during the fall &
winter months, as construction began on the
publisher's much needed bindery addition &
they celebrated their 12th year on the island.

The publisher, Brooding Heron Press, is located on Waldron Island, WA.

Carraig Phadraig. No reprint.

JL note:

Carraig Phadraig: Cormac's Chapel in the great fortress-abbey on the mound
called St. Patrick's Rock in County Tipperary was built about 1130 by Cormac
McCarthy, King of Desmond and Bishop of Chasel, for the monks to sing the
praise of God and the Anglo-Norman men-at-arms to keep down the heathen.
[*MI*]

In Macroon. No reprint.

JL note:

punt: an Irish pound.
    dab: silly. [*MI*]

The Emigration. Reprinted in *LF*.

    Devidetus pariter in tres partibus. Latin: "Let it be divided equally into three parts."

    Cf. *B*, "The Ancestors," page 9.

The Petition. Reprinted in *PH, LF*.

The Enigma. Reprinted in *PH, LF*.

The Selfish One. Reprinted in *PH*.

The Music of Ideas. Reprinted in *PH*.

Old Men. Reprinted in *PH, LF*.

Longing & Guilt. Reprinted in *SR*.

    Dedication, "For Vanessa," added in *SR*.

The Nap. No reprint.

The Movements. No reprint.

Her Poems. No reprint.

The Effort to Live. No reprint.

His Problem. Reprinted in *PH, SR*.

Harry. Reprinted in *PH*.

De Nada. No reprint.

In the Bank. No reprint.

Of the Snapshot. No reprint.

She Must Carry the Weight of Her Beauty. No reprint.

The Mistress of Improbability. No reprint.

Here & There. First published in the broadside *ES* (see Appendix); reprinted in *MI, SR*.

    In *SR*, the dedication reads: "In Memory of Maria Britnieva St. Just."

On Death Row. No reprint.

Vigilia Sanctorum. No reprint.
　　Title. Latin: "The Vigil of the Saints."
　　JL note:
　　The Heautontimorumenos: The Self-tormentor, a play by Menander, later rewritten
　　by Terence. [*MI*]

The Little Vision. No reprint.

Moments in Space. Reprinted in *SP, PNS*.

The Engines of Desire. Reprinted in *SR*.

PHANTOMS (1995)

　　The book includes twenty-seven color photographs by Virginia
Schendler.
　　Prefatory note (front matter page i):

> Any aesthetic connections the
> reader may find between
> the photographs and the poems in
> this book are incidental.
>
> The pictures do not illustrate
> the poems, and the poems do not
> comment on the pictures.
>
> It is simply that two friends
> who admire one another's work decided
> to make a book together.

Along the Meadow Stream. Reprinted in *LF, SR*.

Motet: *Ave Verum Corpus.* Reprinted in *SR*.
　　Title. Latin: "Hail the True Body."

Sweet Childhood. Reprinted in *LPJL, SR*.

1158

That Afternoon. Reprinted in *LF, SR*.
> *dulce ridentem.* Latin: "laughing sweetly."

Many Loves. Reprinted in *LF, SR, PNS*.

Jack Jigger. Reprinted in *LF, SR*.

Ophelia. Reprinted in *LF, SR*.

The Transients. Reprinted in *LF, SR*.

The Daze of Love. Reprinted in *LPJL, SR*.

Die Begegnung. First published in the boadside *ES* (see Appendix);
reprinted in *PH, SR, PNS*.
> Title. German: "The Encounter."

> **Donner und Blitz / Erfüllung und Verlust / Schmerzen und Wonne
> / Gelächter und Tränen.** German: "Thunder and lightning / Fulfillment
> and loss / Griefs and delights / Laughter and tears."
> **Sorge und Freude / Einsicht und Zweifel.** German: "Sorrow and joy /
> Insight and doubt."

The New Young Doctor. Reprinted in *LF, SR*.

Now and Then. Reprinted in *LF, SR*.

The Calendar of Fame. Reprinted in *LF, SR, PNS*.

The Secret Room. Reprinted in *SR, PNS*.

That Very Famous Poet. Reprinted in *LF, SR*.
> Title. In *LF*, changed to "The Very Famous Poet."

Coprophilus. Reprinted in *SR*.
> Title. Latin: "The Shit-lover."
> **mentula.** Latin: "penis."

So Little Time. No reprint.

Where Is the Country. Reprinted in *SR*.

UNTIL THE SPRING BREAKS (1995)

Colophon:

Limited edition
of
150 copies

The Kitchen Clock. No reprint.

En arrière, ruckwärts, in / Dietro. French, German, Italian: "backward."

Petrarch and Laura. No reprint.

The Humor of the Computer. No reprint.

THE LOST FRAGMENTS (1997)

Colophon:

THE LOST FRAGMENTS
by
James Laughlin

is issued in a paperback edition
of 250 copies

Dedalus Editions 12

Those to Come. Reprinted in *SR, PNS*.

THE LOVE POEMS OF JAMES LAUGHLIN (1997)

Dedication:
For Gertrude

Colophon:

Printed in Giovanni Mardersteig's
Dante types by Heritage Printers.

Design by Jonathan Greene.

Love Bearing Gifts. No reprint.

The Evening Star. Reprinted in *CBP*. Cf. "You Came as a Thought," p. 292.

The Lighthouse. No reprint.

The Bird of Endless Time. Reprinted in *CBP*.

> JL note:
> kalpas: in Hinduism an aeon.

Cf. the longer version of this poem, p. 434.

A Classic Question. Reprinted in *CBP*.
Cf. another version of this poem, titled "Ingenium Nobis Ipsa Puella Facit," among "Picture Poems," p. 212.

The Coming of Spring. Reprinted in *CBP*.
In *CBP*, JL's postscript reads:
> Kabir (1440–1518), abridged. Trans. Ezra Pound, adapted from an English version by Kali Mohan Ghose.

The Crane. Reprinted in *SR, PNS, CBP*.
In the reprints, JL's postscripts differ slightly from *LPJL*:
> Lines from the Tamil of the *Shilappadikaram* (3rd century A.D.), translated by Alain Daniélou. [*SR, PNS*]
>> From the Tamil *Shilappadikaram* (300 A.D.). Trans. Alain Daniélou. [*CBP*]

The Growth of Love. Reprinted in *CBP*.

> In *CBP*, JL's postscript reads:
> Guido Cavalcanti, trans. Ezra Pound.

Her Loveliness. Reprinted in *CBP* as "Singing Her Name."

The Honeybee. Reprinted in *SR, PNS, CBP*.
In *SR* and *PNS*, the poem is titled "The Honey Bee," and JL's postscript reads:
> Marcus Argentarius (1st century A.D.).

> In *CBP*, JL's postscript reads:
> Marcus Argentarius (fl. 1st century A.D.).

The Locust. Reprinted in *SR, PNS, CBP.*

In *SR* and *PNS,* JL's postscript reads:
Meleager of Gadara, fl. 60 B.C. (condensed).

In *CBP,* the postscript abbreviates "flourished" to "fl."

The Lovers. Reprinted in *SR, CBP.*

In the reprints, JL's postscripts differ from *LPJL:*
An excerpt from the Sanskrit of Jayadeva's *Gita-Govindi* (12th century A.D.),
the love songs of Krishna and Radha, translated by George Keyt. [*SR*]
    From the Sanskrit of Jayadeva's *Gita-Govindi* (12th century). Trans.
George Keyt. [*CBP*]

The Lover's Complaint. Reprinted in *SR, CBP.*

In the reprints, the first lines reads, "I swear I do not ask too much of
heaven:"; JL's postscripts differ from *LPJL:*
Ovid, a passage from the *Ars Amatoria* [*The Art of Love*], translation by Horace
Gregory. [*SR*]
    Ovid, from the *Ars Amatoria.* Trans. Horace Gregory. [*CBP*]

Remembrance of Her. Reprinted in a revised version in *CBP.*

The Visit of Eros. Reprinted in *CBP.*
In *CBP,* the third and fourth lines read: "are times when Eros wants no
witness. We had the / bed, the lover's friend," etc.

THE SECRET ROOM (1997)

Acknowledgments (copyright page):
SOME OF THESE POEMS FIRST APPEARED IN *Agenda* (London), *Agni, Ambit* (London), *Doubletake, Exquisite Corpse, Grand Street, Harvard Review, Interim Iowa Review, Paris Review, Parnassus, Partisan Review, Poetry, The Threepenny Review*; in the following volumes by James Laughlin: *The Bird of Endless Time* (Copper Canyon Press, Port Townsend, WA), *The Country Road* (Zoland Books, Cambridge, MA), *The Empty Space* (Backwoods Broadsides, Ellsworth, ME), *Heart Island* (Turkey Press, Isla Vista, CA), *The Man in the Wall* (New Directions, New York, NY), *The Music of Ideas* (Brooding Heron Press, Waldron Island, WA), *Phantoms* (Aperture Books, New York, NY); and in *Contemporary Authors Series*, vol. 22 (Gale Research, Detroit, MI).

Dedication:

for
PAUL & HENRY
AND THEIR FAMILIES

In Old Age. Reprinted in *PNS*.

Back Then. First published in the broadside *ES*; reprinted in *SR*.

The Accumulation. No reprint.

The Healer. No reprint.
    Cf. the much shorter poem on the same subject in *CBP*, p. 958.

I'm Walking Very Slowly Today. Reprinted in *PNS*.

How May I Persuade Her. No reprint.

The Future. No reprint.

The Girl in the Mist. No reprint.

The Malevolent Sky. No reprint.

An Elegy of Mimnermus. Reprinted in *PNS*.

    JL note:
    An imitation. [*SR, PNS*]

Godsplay. No reprint.

    JL note:
    Transcribed from a French translation of the Sanskrit. [*SR*]

The Green Hair. No reprint.

The Feathered Cleft. No reprint.

De Iuventute. No reprint.
    Title. Latin: "On Youth."

The Country of Hope. No reprint.

    JL note:
    Title from Anne Carson, "The Anthropology of Water." [*SR*]

Doors. No reprint.

Despite its subtitle, this poem is not included in *B*, not because of its subject matter but its loose metric, in which it differs considerably from JL's other verse memoirs.

The Chasm. No reprint.

I Listen For. First published in the broadside *ES* (see Appendix); no reprint.

The Chanting Bell. First published in the broadside *ES* (see Appendix); no reprint.

The Cold Lake. First published in the broadside *ES* (see Appendix); no reprint.

The Empty Space. First published in the broadside *ES* (see Appendix); no reprint.

The Gods. No reprint.

> JL note:
> Hippocrates, *The Aphorisms*, Books V, VI & VII. [SR]

The last four lines of the poem are not from Hippocrates but are JL's words preceded by Guy Davenport's translation of them into Greek. See *Guy Davenport & James Laughlin: Selected Letters*, edited by W. C. Bamberger (New York & London: W. W. Norton, 2007), page 191.

The Ladybug. No reprint.

Auto-da-Fé. No reprint.
  Saevitia intolerabilis. Latin: "unbearable cruelty."

Rosalinda, the Dreamer. No reprint.

The Unexpected Visitor. No reprint.
  For JL's poems "Touching" and "The Enlacement," see pp. 373 and 447.

Poets on Stilts. Reprinted in *PNS*.

The Truth Teller. No reprint.

Swapping Minds. Reprinted in *PNS*.

The Secrets. Reprinted in *PNS*.

The Road of Dreams. No reprint.

A Night of Ragas. Reprinted in *PNS*.

> JL note:
> "Let the earth of my body....": Denise Levertov's translation in *In Praise of Krishna*. [*SR, PNS*]

My Mind. No reprint.

The Love Puddle. No reprint.

Love Is the Word. No reprint.

The Language of the Mind. No reprint.

Lucinda. No reprint.

The Logodaedalist. No reprint.

The Long Moment. No reprint.

The Longest Journey. No reprint.

> JL note:
> *"multas per gentes et multa per aequora"* [Latin: *"through many peoples and over many seas"*]: Catullus CI.
> > "the beauty is in the walking....": attributed to Gwyn Thomas. [*SR*]

The Black Holes. No reprint.

Akhmatova's Muse. No reprint.

The Aleatory Turtle. No reprint.

An Amorous Dialogue. No reprint.
   "Schweinlichkins." German: "Little Piggy."

> JL note:
> Martial: 1, xxxiii and 1, xxxvii. [*SR*]

The Apsarases. Reprinted in *PNS*.

All the Clocks. Reprinted in *PNS*.

The Acrobatic Dancers. No reprint.

Saturn. No reprint.

Carrots. No reprint.

Better Than Potions. First published in the broadside *ES*; reprinted in *SR*.

THIRTY-NINE PENTASTICHS. In *SR*, JL introduces this section as follows:

A Note on Form

A "pentastich" refers simply to a poem of five lines, without regard to metrics. The word is Greek derived, from *pentastichos*, though few examples survive from ancient times. In *The Greek Anthology*, there are some anonymous five-line epigrams, as well as one each by Empedocles, Palladas, Palladius, and (perhaps) the Emperor Constantine. Some other, later examples of five-line poems can be found in French, Italian, Spanish, and Chinese poetry. In English, the best-known five-liner is, of course, the popular limerick, though Tennyson and Poe used rhyming forms of fine-line continous stanzas. The most developed pentastich is the classic Japanese *tanka*, in lines of 5, 7, 5, 7, 7 syllables. The *tanka* influenced the American poet Adelaide Crapsey (1878–1914), whose posthumously published "cinquains" won her praise from the anthologist Louis Untermeyer as an "unconscious imagist." Charles Olson's "fivers" in *The Maximus Poems*, in the sequences "Some Good News," "Stiffening in the Master Founders' Wills," and "Captain Christopher Levett (of York)," are in open form. The present "Thirty-nine Pentastichs" is a selection of recent short-line compositions in natural voice cadence, many of them jottings and paraphrases of commonplace book notations.

This note is repeated, somewhat abbreviated, in *PNS*. See p. 1172.

The Tender Letter. Reprinted in *PNS*, *CBP*.

C'était à Paris....Une jeune fille bien élevée...."Je voudrais être ta maîtresse.'" French: "It was in Paris....A well brought-up young girl....'I would like to be your mistress.'"
Cf. "Before I Die," p. 580.

I Travel Your Body. Reprinted in *PNS*, *CBP*.
In *CBP*, JL's postscript reads:
Octavio Paz, *Sunstone* (abridged). Trans. Eliot Weinberger.

The Living Branch. Reprinted in *PNS, CBP.*

> In *CBP,* JL's postscript reads:
> Deborah Pease, *The Feathered Wind.*

All Good Things Pass. Reprinted in *PNS, CBP.*

The Snake Game. Reprinted in *PNS, CBP.*

The Immeasurable Boundaries. Reprinted in *PNS, CBP.*

Penelope to Ulysses. Reprinted in *PNS, CBP.*

> In *CBP,* JL's postscript reads:
> Ovid, *Heroides.* Trans. Howard Isbell.

The First Time. Reprinted in *CBP.*
> Cf. the longer version of this poem in *CP1994,* p. 640.

The Anglo-Saxon Chronicle. Reprinted in *CBP.*

> In *CBP,* JL's postscript reads:
> Adapted by Guy Davenport.

Tanka. Reprinted in *PNS.*

The Long Feet People. Reprinted in *PNS, CBP.*
> **pes.** Latin: a Roman "foot," measuring approximately 11.66 inches.

Two for One. Reprinted in *PNS, CBP.*

Word Salad. Reprinted in *PNS.*

The Fantasist. Reprinted in *PNS.*

The Pissing of the Toads. Reprinted in *PNS, CBP.*

> In *CBP,* JL's postscript reads:
> Thomas Browne, *Pseudodoxia Epidemica, Enquiries into Certain Vulgar Errors*
> *(1646).*

The Good Life. Reprinted in *CBP.*

The Seashell. Reprinted in *CBP*.

> JL's postscript in *CBP* reads:
> García Lorca. Trans. Alan S. Trueblood.

The Smile of the Desert. Reprinted in *CBP*.

> In *CBP*, JL's postscript reads:
> Sir Richard Burton, *Personal Narrative of a Pilgrimage to Al-Madinah & Meccah.*

Salad Dressing and an Artichoke. Reprinted in *CBP*.

The Sweet Singer. Reprinted in *CBP*.

The Writer at Work. Reprinted in *PNS, CBP*.

The God of Sun and Fire. Reprinted in *PNS, CBP*.

The Magic Flute. Reprinted in *PNS, CBP*.
> Cf. *B*, "Are We Too Old to Make Love?" p. 26.

The Ravaged Virgin. Reprinted in *CBP*.

Odd Goings On in Philadelphia. Reprinted in *CBP*.

The Man of Tao. Reprinted in *CBP*.

An Unusual Girl. Reprinted in *PNS, CBP*.

The Hetaera. Reprinted in *PNS, CBP*.

The Right Girl. Reprinted in *PNS*.

The Rescue. Reprinted in *PNS, CBP*.

The Sculptor. Reprinted in *PNS, CBP*.

Good Philosophy. Reprinted in *PNS, CBP*.

An Exquisite Life. Reprinted in *PNS, CBP*.

The Invitation to Make Love. Reprinted in *PNS, CBP*.

> In *CBP*, JL's postscript reads:
> From the Sanskrit, Vatsyayana's *Kama Sutra*. Trans. Alain Daniélou.

Acknowledgments (copyright page):

The poems "I Cannot Separate Her" and "Lost Brains" originally appeared in *The New Yorker*, "Nunc Dimittis" in *DoubleTake*, "Funerals" and "Illness" in *Grand Street*, and "An Honest Heart...A Knowing Head" in *Agni*.

The epigraph on page vii, "Write on My Tomb," was originally published in James Laughlin's *Stolen & Contaminated Poems* (1985).

Most of the poems in this volume were selected from the following books by James Laughlin: *Some Natural Things* (1945), *A Small Book of Poems* (1948), *The Wild Anemone* (1957), *In Another Country* (1978), *Stolen & Contaminated Poems* (1985), *Selected Poems, 1935–1985* (1986), *The Owl of Minerva* (1987), *The Bird of Endless Time* (1989), *The Man in the Wall* (1993), *The Collected Poems of James Laughlin* (1994), *Heart Island & Other Epigrams* (1995), *The Country Road* (1995), and *The Secret Room*. For details, see below, p. 1162.

The epigraph, "Write on My Tomb," appears on p. 186 in the present volume.

Dedication:

For

GERTRUDE

"A Note on Publication" appears at the very end of the *PNS*, listing the poems in the collection according to the books by JL from which they were taken, at times incorrectly. In the editor's notes, such errors have been fixed. Some of these poems are assigned to different books of his, published earlier than the ones listed below, but as limited editions, while others are included in the section "American (French) Poems" or are found in JL's verse memoir, *Byways* (2005).

James Laughlin chose the poems for the present volume in the months before his death in November 1997. The poems selected from his earlier books were originally published in the following collections:

Some Natural Things (1945): "The Cave," "Easter in Pittsburgh," "The Last Poem to Be Written," "Mountain Afterglow," "Technical Notes," "What the Pencil Writes."

A Small Book of Poems (1948): "Above the City," "The Sinking Stone," "The Summons."

The Wild Anemone (1957): "In the Museum at Teheran," "Martha Graham," "Near Zermatt: The Drahtseilbahn," "Prognosis," "Rome: In the Café," "Step on His Head," "The Trout," "The Wild Anemone."

In Another Country (1978): "In Another Country," "It Does Me Good," "A Long Night of Dreaming," "Song."

Stolen & Contaminated Poems (1985): "I Hate Love," "In Hac Spe Vivo," "Nothing That's Lovely Can My Love Escape," "To Be Sure," "We Met in a Dream," "What Is It Makes One Girl."

Selected Poems, 1935–1985 (1986): "Alba," "The Deconstructed Man," "Elle N'est Pas Noctambule," "The Goddess," "La Gomme à Effacer," "Having Failed," "The House of Light," "Is What We Eat," "J'ignore Où Elle Vague Ce Soir," "The Junk Collector," "A Lady Asks Me," "A Leave-taking," "La Luciole," "My Old Gray Sweater," "The Old Comedian," "Some of Us Come to Live," "Some People Think," "So Much Depends," "Why," "Will We Never Go to the Lighthouse?"

The Owl of Minerva (1987): "L'Arrivée du Printemps," "Eyes Are the Guides of Love," "Like the Octopus," "Il Pastor Fido," "Some Memoirs of E.P. (Drafts & Fragments)," "She's Not Exactly Like You," "The Songbird."

The Bird of Endless Time (1989): "An Anginal Equivalent," "At the Boule d'Or," "The Bird of Endless Time," "The Enlacement," "The Happy Poets ['It's my delight to recite']," "Her Letters," "Hic Jacet," "In Half Darkness," "It's March," "Our Bicycles," "Our Meetings," "A Parable," "The Revenants," "Then and Now," "A Translation," "The Unanswerable Question."

The Man in the Wall (1993): "The Afterthought," "Agatha," "An Attestation," "Before I Die," "The Calves," "A Certain Impermeable Person," "Clutches," "The Flemish Double Portrait," "Long and Languorous," "Making a Love Poem," "The Man in the Wall," "The Shameful Profession," "Silentium Aureatum Est," "The Story of Rhodope," "The Stranger ['There was a knock on the door']," "The Sultan's Justice," "The Thinking Machine," "Time Running Backwards," "The Time Stealer," "La Tristesse," "What the Old Bedouin Said."

The Collected Poems of James Laughlin (1994): "Ave Atque Vale," "The Beautiful Muttering," "Building 520, Bellevue," "Dylan," "The Empty Room," "The Eraser," "Eros as Archeologist," "Experience of Blood," "The Firefly," "I Don't Know Where She Is Wandering Tonight," "The Inn at Kirchstetten," "Into Each Life," "Mon Secret," "The Moths," "My Secret," "O Best of All Nights, Return and Return Again," "With My Third Eye."

Heart Island & Other Epigrams (1995): "At the Post Office," "Les Consolations," "The Consolations," "Elusive Time," "The Gift," "The Happy Poets ['What's happiness?']," "Heart Island," "In Scandinavia," "The Old Man's Lament," "The Two of Them."

The Country Road (1995): "Anima Mea," "The Country Road," "De Contemptu Mortis," "The Departure," "The Desert in Bloom," "Do They Make Love?," "A Florilegium," "Her Heart," "How Did Laura Treat Petrarch?," "Imprisoned," "The Invisible Room," "Is Memory," "The Mercy in It," "Penelope Venit Abit Helen," "Permanet Memoria," "The Rising Mist at Ard Na Sidhe," "The Search," "A Secret Language," "Some Amatory Epigrams from *The Greek Anthology*," "Two Fables from *The Ocean of Story*," "When I Was a Boy with Never a Crack in My Heart," "The Wood Nymph," "The Wrong Bed—Moira."

The Secret Room (1997): "All Good Things Pass," "All the Clocks," "The Apsarases," "Die Begegnung," "The Calendar of Fame," "The Crane," "The Darkened Room," "An Elegy of Mimnermus," "An Exquisite Life," "The Fantasist," "The God of the Sun and Fire," "Good Philosophy," "The Hetaera," "The Honey Bee," "The Immeasurable Boundaries," "The Invitation to Make Love," "I Travel Your Body," "I'm Walking Very Slowly Today," "In Old Age," "In Trivandrum," "The Living Branch," "The Locust," "The Long Feet People," "The Magic Flute," "Many Loves," "Moments in Space," "A Night of Ragas," "Penelope to Ulysses," "The Pissing of the Toads," "Poets on Stilts," "The Rescue," "The Right Girl," "The Sculptor," "The Secret Room," "The Secrets," "The Snake Game," "Swapping Minds," "Tanka," "The Tender Letter," "Two for One," "An Unusual Girl," "Word Salad," "The Writer at Work," "You're Trouble."

BOOK I—NEW POEMS

None of the poems in this section were reprinted in *CBP*, JL's last book to be compiled before his death.

The Bread-knife.

"The Kind of Poetry I Want." MacDiarmid's actual words regarding Lenin are: "Ah, Lenin, politics is child's play / To what this must be."

In the Dark Wood.

JL note:
"The Dark Wood": From Dante's *"selva oscura"* in the first strophe of his *Inferno*. [*PNS*]

The Fixation.

JL note:
"A woman's breasts....": Natalie Angier, from a review in *The New York Times* of Marilyn Yalom's book, *A History of the Breast*. [*PNS*]

Diana's Self Might to These Woods Resort.

JL note:
Title: a line from Purcell's opera, *Dido and Aeneas*. [*PNS*]

Love Does Not Make a Display of Itself.

JL note:
Title: a line from the Episcopal marriage service. [*PNS*]

Lost Brains.

JL note:

"He felt . . . his head": The line is from the British film *Dance with a Stranger*.
[*PNS*]

Nunc Dimittis.

Title. Latin, the opening words of the Canticle of Simeon, Luke 2: 29–
32, traditionally included at Catholic and Anglican evening prayers; *Nunc
dimittis servum tuum, Domine,* "Lord, now lettest thou thy servant depart."

BOOK VII—PENTASTICHS

A Note on Form

A "pentastich" refers simply to a poem of five lines, without regard to metrics.
The word is Greek derived, from *pentastichos*, though few examples survive
from ancient times. In *The Greek Anthology*, there are some anonymous five-
line epigrams, as well as one each by Empedocles, Palladas, Palladius, and
(perhaps) the Emperor Constantine. Some other, later examples of five-line
poems can be found in French, Italian, Spanish, and Chinese poetry. In Eng-
lish, the best-known five-liner is, of course, the popular limerick, though Ten-
nyson and Poe used rhyming forms of fine-line continous stanzas. The most
developed pentastich is the classic Japanese *tanka*, which influenced the Amer-
ican poet Adelaide Crapsey (1878–1914), whose unrhymed "cinquains" won
her praise from the anthologist Louis Untermeyer as an "unconscious imagist."
Charles Olson's "fivers" in *The Maximus Poems* are in open form. The present
selection of "Pentastichs" is of short-line compositions in natural voice ca-
dence, many of them marginal jottings and paraphrases of commonplace book
notations.

A COMMONPLACE BOOK OF PENTASTICHS (1998)

Acknowledgments (copyright page):

Some of the poems in this volume were included in James Laughlin's *The Secret
Room* (1997). "The Ancient Ocean" and "On Awakening" were first published in
DoubleTake.

THANKS ARE MADE TO THE FOLLOWING FOR THEIR TEXTS OR TRANSLATIONS:
*Walter Abish, Gilbert Adair, David Antin, Willis Barnstone, Jacques Barzun, Mary
Beach, Bei Dao, Edwin Brock, William Bronk, Camilo José Cela, Margaret Jull Costa,
Guy Davenport, Brendan Gill, David Hinton, Patricia Hougaard, Howard Isbell,
Edgar Johnson, Donald Keene, Jane Kenyon, George Keyt, P. Lal, Lambros J. Lambros,
J. B. Leishman, Jack Lindsay, Barry Magid, W. S. Merwin, Octavio Paz, Deborah
Pease, Marjorie Perloff, Robert Pinsky, Edward Rice, Alastair Reid, Jerome Rothenberg,
Charles Simic, Andrew Schelling, Frederick Smock, Gary Snyder, Antonio Tabucchi,*

Alan S. Trueblood, Eleanor Trumbull, Anne Waldman, Eliot Weinberger, Barbara Wright, Bill Zavatsky.

Colophon:

This is the last book of his own that James Laughlin helped to prepare during his lifetime. The manuscript had been completed and sent to the typesetter before his final illness and death in November 1997. He saw and approved everything in it except this colophon.

None of the poems in *CBP* were reprinted in JL's two other posthumous books, *Byways* (2005) and *The Way It Wasn't* (2006). However, a number of them appeared, in different form, in his earlier poetry collections; those included in the present section of this volume are noted here.

Trying to Please. In another version, previously published in *SP1986* as "Berenice" (see p. 319); reprinted in *CP1994*.

Tempus Loquendi.
Title. Latin: "A Time to Speak," Eccl. 3:7.

Fidelio: Ezra Pound.
Cf. "Some Memories of E.P. (Drafts & Fragments)," p. 387, and note.

The French. In another version, included in "Picture Poems" in the present volume, p. 207; published in *SP1986*; reprinted in *CP1994, HI*.

A Wintry Christmas.
"Sur le Noël . . . de vent." French: "At Christmas, the dead season, when the wolves live on the wind."
Cf. "This Is the Morte Saison," p. 186, and note.

Inscriptio Fontis.
Title. Latin: "Inscription for a Fountain."

The Blindfolded Lovers.
Cf. "Les Amants," p. 190.

In Vino Veritas.
Title. Latin: "In Wine, Truth."

Tout en Ordre.
Title. French: "Everything in Order."

La Poésie.
Title. French: "Poetry."
"Des yeux . . . des tombeaux." French: "Countless eyes have seen the dawn; now they lie deep in the grave."

Le Temps Perdu.
Title. French: "Lost Time."

De Corpore Hominum.
Title. Latin: "On the Human Body."

Die Verwirrung.
Title. German: "The Muddle."
"Unser Philosophie…Sprachgebrauch"? German: "Our philosophy is a correction of linguistic usage"? Cf. *B*, p. 58.
bierstube. German: "beerhall."

De Perrenitate.
Title. Latin: "On Perpetuity."

De Senectute: Mary Baker Eddy.
Title. Latin: "On Old Age…"

The Omniscient Autodidact.
Cf. "Kenneth Rexroth," p. 545; "The Old Bear: Kenneth Rexroth," *B*, p. 215.

Dove Sta Memoria.
Title. Italian: "Where Memory Liveth" (as in Ezra Pound's translation of Cavalcanti). See note to "You Invited Me," pp. 1053–54.

Premula's Problem. In another version, previously published in *OM* (see p. 411); reprinted in *CP1994*.

Remembrance of Her. In another version, previously published in *LPJL* (see p. 817).

Those Wonderful People. In another version, previously published in *WA* as "Well All Right" (see p. 117); reprinted in *SP1986, CP1994, HI*.

Your Love. In another version, previously published in *WA* (see p. 121); reprinted in *SP1986, CP1994, HI*.

Living in Three Worlds. In another version, previously published in *T* as "I Live in Three Worlds" (see p. 364); reprinted in *CP1994, HI*.

An Admonition. In another version, previously published in *CP1994* as "Admonition" (see p. 633); reprinted in *HI*.

Ars Gratia Artis. In another version, previously published in *PP* (see p. 139); reprinted in *CP1994*.

The Healer. In another, much longer version, previously published in *SR* (see p. 823).

The First Night. In another version, previously published in *BET* (see p. 483); reprinted in *CP1994, SL, HI*.

Elusive Time. In another version, previously published in *K* (see p. 432); reprinted *BET, CP1994, HI, SR, PNS*.

The Dance of the Skin. In another version, previously published in *T* (see p. 367); reprinted in *A, CP1994, LPJL*.

I Don't Know Where She Is Wandering Tonight. In another version, included in "French (American) Poems" in the present volume, p. 224; first published *CP1994*; reprinted in *SW, PNS*.

ACKNOWLEDGMENTS

The Collected Poems of James Laughlin 1935–1997 is the companion volume to *Byways: A Memoir* (2005), and as with that earlier book, many people played a part in bringing it into being. Once again, I am especially grateful to the Trustees of the New Directions Ownership Trust (Daniel Javitch, chair, Peggy L. Fox, Donald S. Lamm, and Griselda Ohannessian), which holds the copyrights to James Laughlin's work.

Walter Hamady (The Perishable Press Limited), Leslie Miller (The Grenfell Press), and Harry and Sandra L. Reese (Turkey Press), publishers of small-press editions of JL's works, helped in the painstaking task of gathering copies of those published books and pamphlets of his that I didn't already own. Anne Marie Candido (University of Arkansas) and Rosmarie Waldrop (Brown University) pointed to the whereabouts of some of his more obscure books; Martin Bax and Kate Pemberton (*Ambit*), Tony Crawford (Hale Library, Kansas State University), David Hamilton (*The Iowa Review*), Craig Miner (Wichita State University), and Bradford Morrow (*Conjunctions*) gave additionally crucial advice. Rebecca Newth Harrison (University of Arkansas), Marjorie Perloff, and Eliot Weinberger sent me material from their personal collections. But the greatest number of publications were generously supplied by various libraries and their librarians: Leslie A. Morris and Peter Accardo, the Houghton Library, Harvard University; Rosemary Cullen, the John Hay Library, Brown University; Breon Mitchell, the Lilly Library, University of Indiana; and the staffs of the Vassar College Libraries and the Department of Special Collections, University of Kansas Libraries. Ian Mac-Niven, JL's biographer, once more magnanimously shared his latest research, while Elizabeth Christenfeld, Peter Constantine, Burton Pike, and Richard Sieburth offered their linguistic expertise. To all of the aforementioned, I give much appreciative thanks, and as always to my wife, Suzanne Thibodeau, for her welcome and perceptive editorial comments. And so, too, to my longtime friends and former colleagues at New Directions, Laurie Callahan, Barbara Epler, Thomas Keith, Sylvia Frezzolini Severance, Anna Della Subin and, above all, my editor, Peggy L. Fox.

PETER GLASSGOLD

INDEX OF TITLES

INDEX OF FIRST LINES

Love you that so long a, 71

L's wealth made him feel guilty.
Once a week, 985

Lucian of Samosata was not taken in
by, 992

M

Madame de Lafayette, in her
salon..., 331

make it so simple a child, 665

Make the bedlamp tipsy with oil,
726

Mallarmé told Degas that poems,
217

Man pines to live but cannot endure
the days, 980

Many among the ancients believed,
877

Martial urged his friend Faustinus,
985

Mary Baker Eddy wrote that man,
981

May I upon thy beauty gaze, 643

Melchior Dinsdale was Euphemia's
favorite poet..., 715

Melissa and I were sitting, 856

Melissa pulled one reddish hair, 723

Melissa's beauty is the gift of, 723

Methought an angel from the air,
369

M. H. had imagination, but when
she was planning, 983

Might it not be that someday in,
724

M. Mallarmé has put a curse on me,
327

more lovely than all others, 180

Most of them begin with a few
words, 512

Mother when does the, 67

Multas per gentes et multa per
aequora vectus, 333

Murine and Kleenex were lovers, 642

Muses, 20

must fall occasionally a new, 299

My brother being the eldest had,
423

my dear wife asked me this morn-
ing, 285

My father was an expert automo-
bilist, 578

My friend Klaus a German goes, 82

My friend the ecologist tells, 316

My hair is turning from gray, 832

My head can lend no succour, 181

My mother could not wait to go, 791

My mother referred to it, 714

My muse keeps irregular hours, 341

My old friend has departed..., 339

My present self is the consequence
of all my vanished, 957

My propositions are elucidatory in
this way, 971

My rich old scotch, 49

My soul is frying, 111

My twin brother, Brendan, wears
gloves that, 935

N

Nabokov remembers that when he
was young, 884

Neither winter's cold, nor endless
rain, 955

Ne me confondez pas avec ce fripon,
260

Neurologists call the babbling, 883

Night is a room darkened for lovers,
732

Nightly I await you, 365

Ni las noches de amor que no, 320

Nine hundred thousand prisoners of
war, 40

1985, 469

1953, 469

Nobody heard him, the dead man,
982

No exact moment is recorded for, 786

No I'm not in Sing Sing, 677

People forget (if they ever knew it),
797
Pére Ubu: by my green candle, shit-
ter, certainly, 972
Philodemus remembers how we...,
817
play children's games   one, 678
Pliny relates in his *Natural History*
that, 882
Poets are invited to submit
poems..., 204
Preparing to die, the French poet
Alain, 977
Principles of Geometry, 42
probably in a battered trunk, 454
Procne your charming servant has,
181
Propertius wrote that it, 212
Pull up your skirt, 762

Q

Quand elle dort et s'éveille, 199
Quas ad Lucinam tot epistoles, 642
Qu'aurait été ma vie si tu, 255
que je ne lui parle pas franche-, 235
que je te poursuis moi qui, 244
quelqu'un l'a vue à Ectaban, 224
Que toujours tu habites ma maison
de rêves?, 266
que tu m'as bien allumé, 242
Quintius, her mentor, tries, 411
Quintius her mentor tries to make,
987
qui potuit cordis cognoscere, 178

R

Radha looked on the god Krishna
..., 816
Raleigh loved a wench well; and one
time getting, 991
Really said the leopard, 11
reminds me of the sense, 121
Reverberates in the poet's ear, 772
Right hand blush never, 47

Rilke writes of the expectation, 428
Robert Montesquiou, the exquisite
model, 889
Roblinus is our leading literary, 409
Ronald Firbank the decadent novel-
ist liked, 883
roots for acorns which, 137
Rufinus advised Thelon to beware a
girl who seems, 888
Run girl, run!, 763

S

said Pound (out of Homer), 522
said Propertius oculi sunt, 369
said Rimbaud & nothing in po-,
172
Said the Governor of Louisiana, 413
said the owl was dehu-, 140
Sam'l Johnson in his famous, 675
s'amourachent trop facile-, 231
Sappho led a band of lovely girls, 885
Saw a girl in a food, 75
says Alcaeus echthairo ton, 184
searches the ruins of my youth, 365
Sed pia Baucis anus parilique aetate
Philemon, 385
seemed to be making fun of, 314
s'en vont traînant leurs chevilles,
261
se sont éprendues chacune, 242
Shall I be punished more severely,
380
Shall we take a shower together,
726
She bites off chunks of time, 572
She changes the way, 793
She comes at eleven every morning,
117
She comes to the poet only, 870
She doesn't come anymore to visit
me in my dreams, 226
She fell in love with the face, 497
She had a dog named Arli whom
she had, 941